W9-AMM-273

THE ENCYCLOPEDIA OF
NEGRO LEAGUE BASEBALL

THE ENCYCLOPEDIA OF
NEGRO LEAGUE BASEBALL

THOM LOVERRO

Foreword by Wilmer Fields,
President, Negro League Baseball Players Association
Pitcher, Homestead Grays (1939–1950)

☑® Facts On File, Inc.

The Encyclopedia of Negro League Baseball

Copyright © 2003 by Thom Loverro

Facts On File, Inc.
132 West 31st Street
New York NY 10001

Library of Congress Cataloging-in-Publication Data

Loverro, Thom.
    The encyclopedia of Negro league baseball / Thom Loverro ; foreword by Wilmer Fields.
        p. cm.
Includes bibliographical references and index.
    ISBN 0-8160-4430-9
    1. Negro leagues—Encyclopedias. 2. Baseball—United States—Encyclopedias. 3. African American baseball players—Encyclopedias. I. Title.
    GV875.AIL68 2005
    796.357´64´08996073—dc21   2003001075

Fact On File books are available at special discounts when purchased in bulk quantities for businesses, associations, institutions, or sales promotions. Please call our Special Sales Department in New York at (212) 967-8800 or (800) 322-8755.

You can find Facts On File on the World Wide Web at
http://www.factsonfile.com

Text design by Joan M. Toro
Cover design by Cathy Rincon

Printed in the United States of America

VB Hermitage 10 9 8 7 6 5 4 3 2 1

This book is printed on acid-free paper.

There is no work that I can do without my family being the driving force behind it; so everything I do is dedicated to my wife, Elizabeth, and my two sons, Rocco and Nick. But this book is also dedicated to all those black ballplayers who were forced to create their own version of the national pastime, and did so with style and greatness and did not let the hatred that kept them away from major league baseball take away their love for the game itself.

Contents

Foreword

There has been a lot written about the days of Negro League baseball, and a lot of stories that have been told, some of them true, some of them not true. But there is one thing that is important to remember about the game we played—we loved it. That's why we played. It certainly wasn't for the money. It was for the love of baseball and the way we played it.

Much has been made of the way generations of great black ballplayers were denied a chance to play major league baseball because of discrimination. But that door swung both ways. Generations of baseball fans were denied a chance to see some of the greatest players ever to play the game. They missed seeing Josh Gibson hit, or Cool Papa Bell run, or so many other men who could have played side by side with players like Stan Musial and Joe DiMaggio and held their own and then some.

Those fans got robbed because we played a different type of baseball. It was competitive. You didn't see many 10-1 games. If you were pitching, you were usually out there for all nine innings, and that meant the games were usually close, maybe 2-1 or 4-2, or something like that. I was relieved only once in my whole career pitching in Negro League baseball.

Sometimes we outdrew the major league teams. When we would play in Washington at Griffith Stadium on a Sunday or a holiday, we would sometimes get 20,000 fans, when the major league team would be drawing only about 7,000. When Satchel Paige and the Kansas City Monarchs would come to town, we could get a crowd of about 30,000. But they were mostly black fans and not that many white fans. They missed something great, and they were great times.

They were hard times, too. We would travel 400 miles to play one good game, and sometimes we would play three games a day. We would be on the road for weeks at a time, and we would have just one road uniform and one holiday uniform. It was inconvenient, but we were having fun, too, and it didn't really bother us because we loved the game. We watched out for one another, sharing things, the good and the bad times.

As president of the Negro League Baseball Players Association, we still watch out for one another, more than 50 years since we played ball together. The association sends money to Negro League players who need it during the holidays. We help players get health benefits through Major League Baseball. We help set up autograph shows for players to earn some money. We have reunion dinners and get together and talk about old times, and we still have a good time together.

The Association also tries to represent the history of Negro League baseball. We put programs on for church groups. We have been part of programs at the Smithsonian. We go into schools and talk to kids. They always ask us about the segregation of the game and how tough it was to play. It was tough, but they were good times, and I think we just overlooked the difficulties.

What we won't overlook, though, and what we never want overlooked is the contribution that we made to America's national pastime. We were a big part of the game, and we don't want people to forget that. Books like this one and others that have been written in the past will help remind people that when they look back on the history of the great game of baseball, it was black and white.

Wilmer Fields
President, Negro League Baseball Players Association
Pitcher, Homestead Grays (1939–1950)

Acknowledgments

It would have been impossible to put this book together without the help of the library staff at the National Baseball Hall of Fame in Cooperstown, N.Y. They were very helpful in my search for information on Negro League players and courteous in my numerous trips there. I would also like to thank the Negro League Baseball Players Association, an organization of former Negro League ballplayers that has done outstanding work to help former ballplayers and to also proudly represent the great contributions that black ballplayers made to the game of baseball, even though they were banned from playing in the major leagues. I would also like to thank my agent, Jake Elwell, and my editor at Facts On File, James Chambers, for the patience and diligence to see this massive project through. And finally I would like to thank all the writers and researchers who have paved the way along this very difficult road to find the story of Negro League baseball: people like Robert Peterson, James Holway, Mark Ribowsky, Larry Lester, Dick Clark, Todd Bolton, and many others, including the Society for American Baseball Research, who have been the pioneers in researching this important part of our history.

Introduction

The great ballplayers and characters of Negro League baseball remain among the few sports legends who are largely unknown, which seems to make curiosity about them only grow. At a time when baseball fans can watch Barry Bonds or Sammy Sosa every night on their satellite dish, these Negro League ballplayers and the events and places in their history are legends we have never seen. There is very little footage of these players and their games, so they have taken on mythic proportions.

But Negro League baseball was in fact real, and so is the tremendous interest in the history of the game. Some of the greatest stars named to baseball's All-Century Team, such as Hank Aaron and Willie Mays, got their start in Negro League baseball, and other great ballplayers, such as Roy Campanella, Don Newcombe, and Satchel Paige, all were first Negro League stars.

In this information age, there is a tremendous thirst for history and a strong attraction for the stories of past places and personalities, when some of the greatest talents in the history of baseball were barred from the major league game. The chronicles of Negro League baseball are an important part not just of sports of the 20th century, but of the history of society as well.

It is a history that dates back to the days before the Civil War. Ironically, military teams that played baseball during the war were integrated. However, when the war ended, the start of segregated Negro League baseball began with the first Negro League championship on record in 1867, when the Brooklyn Uniques beat the Philadelphia Excelsiors 37-24.

Despite sporadic attempts by black ballplayers to play organized major and minor league baseball—Fleet Walker, acknowledged by some to be the first black to break baseball's color line, signed to play with Toledo of the American Association in 1878—the sport continued to evolve into a segregated business. It was a rough road for those who tried to organize barnstorming Negro teams into a league. After the International League banned the hiring of black players in 1887, the League of Colored Base Ball Clubs was formed, but it didn't last one season.

When Rube Foster, a legendary black pitcher, manager, and owner, organized the Negro National League in 1920—one year after the Chicago White Sox World Series betting scandal rocked major league baseball—a sustained and successful effort at organized Negro League baseball finally took hold. Foster passed away in 1930, but he had in place the foundation for Negro League baseball that would continue, as the game began its golden age that same year, when Josh Gibson caught in his first Negro League game.

The 1930s saw the arrival of such stars as Gibson, Paige, Cool Papa Bell, and other great ballplayers, organized this time by Pittsburgh racketeer Gus Greenlee, who started a rival Negro League, and their legends grew among both black and white fans alike, particularly because of the popularity of exhibition games between black and white all-star teams.

As in major league baseball, World War II cut deeply into the rosters of Negro League baseball. Unlike major league baseball, however, the Negro Leagues would never recover, mainly because the time had finally come for baseball to take the step and integrate the game, with the arrival of Negro League star Jackie Robinson with the Brooklyn Dodgers in 1947. Others would follow, and Negro League teams began to disappear, with only barnstorming exhibition teams devoid of the great talent of the past still playing by the mid-1950s.

The collapse of the color barrier was hailed as one of the greatest moments not only in baseball in the 20th century, but in the development of American society. Yet progress didn't come without a price. The camaraderie and pleasure of playing in the Negro Leagues was replaced with prejudice, which still ran deep within the major leagues. Black players languished in minor league systems as major league teams enforced a quota system to limit the number of black players on their rosters. In addition to the racism they had experienced off the field, in the hotels and restaurants that had refused to serve them, they were now feeling it from their new white teammates, some of whom made it clear they didn't want to be on the same team with black players.

It was never easy—when they were excluded and when they were included. Black players could be barred from the major leagues, but they couldn't be kept from playing the game. Every time they took the field in a Negro League game, these players showed a nation how good and joyful the game could be and reminded a nation that it hadn't even reached first base when it came to one of its bedrock values—all men are created equal.

Entries A to Z

Aaron, Henry (Hank)

b. 1934

Henry Aaron is the greatest home run hitter in the history of major league baseball, and he got his start in Negro League baseball during the fading days of the game. Born in Mobile, Alabama, Aaron played for a local Negro team called the MOBILE BLACK BEARS when he was 17 years old. The manager of the Bears, ED SCOTT, was a former Negro League ballplayer with the NORFOLK STARS, where his manager had been BUNNY DOWNS, who was now the business manager of the INDIANAPOLIS CLOWNS. The Clowns, who emphasized showmanship as much as baseball, played in the NEGRO AMERICAN LEAGUE. Downs had Scott doing some scouting for the Clowns, and Scott arranged for the Clowns to come to Mobile to play the Bears in 1951 as part of a barnstorming tour. They played at Mitchell Field, and Aaron, who was playing shortstop at the time, had an impressive game, with two doubles and a home run. Aaron wrote in his biography with Lonnie Wheeler, *If I Had a Hammer*, that "after the game, Bunny Downs came up and asked me how I'd like to play shortstop for the Clowns. Well, I knew Mama wouldn't go for that one. I had to go back to school in the fall and try to stay there. But anyway, Mr. Downs came home and talked to Mama and said that when school was out next year he'd send for me. I figured I'd never hear from him again." But Aaron did hear from the Clowns, and in the spring of 1952 they

signed Aaron to a $200-a-month contract. When he first arrived, Aaron said he was given a hard time by the veteran players: "The Clowns didn't think too much of rookies," Aaron wrote. "They had a lot of veterans on the team, and they had won the Negro League championship the last couple of years without any 150-pound teenagers. I was just a nuisance to most of them, a raggedy kid who was in the way. They made fun of my worn-out shoes, and they asked me if I got my glove from the Salvation Army." Aaron had also come to the Clowns with an unorthodox hitting style, batting cross-handed, but his manager in Indianapolis, "BUSTER" HAYWOOD, changed his style to the more conventional grip that would go on to be the greatest home run swing in the history of baseball. At one point, Aaron was leading the league in hitting, reportedly batting over .460, and it has been widely reported that Aaron was the league batting champion in 1952. But Aaron wrote he didn't believe he was the league batting champion, and believed his average that year was well below .460. He wound up being the Clowns' top attraction: "They had posters made up with my picture on them," Aaron wrote. "I even had top billing over King Tut and Spec Bebop, the guys who made the Clowns clowns." Negro Leaguer OTHA BAILEY, who played against Aaron, said he was the best hitter he had ever seen: "Willie Mays was good, too, but his bat wasn't nothing like Hank Aaron's," Bailey said in a 1997 interview with *Sports Collectors Digest*. "I ain't seen

Before Hank Aaron made major league history by hitting 755 career home runs, he got his start in Negro League baseball, first with a local black team in his hometown of Mobile, Alabama, with the Mobile Black Bears when he was 17 years old and then with the Indianapolis Clowns in 1952. Aaron reportedly led the league in hitting with a .460 average. (NATIONAL BASEBALL HALL OF FAME LIBRARY, COOPERSTOWN, N.Y.)

none like him. Willie, his wrists wasn't as good as Hank Aaron's. Hank Aaron had good wrists. We were throwing him curveballs that got by him and he'd wrist the ball out of the ballpark."

In his book, Aaron also talked about the discrimination the Clowns would run into on their barnstorming tours. One time, after playing at Griffith Stadium in Washington, they had breakfast in a restaurant in the city: "I can still envision sitting with the Clowns in a restaurant behind Griffith Stadium and hearing them break all the plates in the kitchen after we were finished eating. What a horrible sound. Even as a kid, the irony of it hit me: Here we were in the capital in the land of freedom and equality, and they had to destroy the plates that had touched the forks that had been in the mouths of black men. If dogs had eaten off those plates, they'd have washed them."

He would soon be moving on to the major leagues. Aaron was sought after by a number of teams. Former Negro League great WILLIAM "JUDY" JOHNSON, who was scouting then for the Philadelphia Athletics, tried to sign Aaron. Also, the New York Giants were after Aaron as well, which could have brought Aaron and WILLIE MAYS together in the same Giants outfield. But Dewey Griggs would eventually sign him to a contract for the Milwaukee Braves, who paid Clowns' owner Syd Pollock $10,000 for Aaron's contract.

In 1952, he was assigned to the Eau Claire, Wisconsin, farm team for the Braves, where he won Rookie of the Year honors. The following season he moved up to the Jacksonville team in the South Atlantic ("Sally") League, the first black player in the league. He batted .362 with 22 home runs and 125 RBIs in 137 games, was named the league's Most Valuable Player, and was promoted to the Braves in 1954, where he began his historic major league career—23 years with Milwaukee and then Atlanta when the franchise moved after the 1965 season, finishing up his final two seasons back in Milwaukee with the Brewers. Aaron rewrote the record book. He holds more major league batting records than any other player in the game's history—among them career bests in RBIs, 2,297; extra base hits, 1,477; and most total bases, 6,856. He would also finish third on the all-time hit list, with 3,771, and tied for second in runs, with 2,174—with Babe Ruth. But it is Aaron's career home run record—755—that is considered his greatest accomplishment, and he was tied to that record with Ruth in the sense that his march toward Ruth's once seemingly unbreakable 714 career home runs mark was also Aaron's greatest burden. As Aaron grew closer to Ruth's record, he received volumes of hate mail, much of it racist. But Aaron showed grace and courage under pressure, and on April 8, 1974, Aaron slammed an Al Downing pitch into the Braves' bullpen at Atlanta Fulton County Stadium, breaking Ruth's record.

This former Negro League player retired in 1975 and would go on to work in the Braves' front office, first as a vice president and director of player development and currently as a senior vice president and assistant to the president. He is considered one of the premier figures in baseball history.

Abernathy, James

James Abernathy was an outfielder for the KANSAS CITY MONARCHS from 1945 to 1947.

Abernathy, Robert W.

Robert Abernathy played the outfield for the INDIANAPOLIS CLOWNS and the Boston Blues in 1946 and 1947.

Abreau, Eufemio

Eufemio Abreau was a catcher, first baseman, and outfielder for various editions of the CUBAN STARS baseball squads from 1919 to 1934.

Acme Colored Giants

White businessman Harry Curtis started the Acme Colored Giants in 1898 in Celeron, New York, an apple-farming area in the southwestern part of the state. The team played in the Iron and Oil League—a league of white teams—and Curtis declared that "we will have the strongest colored team in America," but after winning just eight of 49 games, Curtis disbanded the team and came up with a new version of the team, this one with white players and without the word *Colored*.

Active Club of Philadelphia

The Active Club of Philadelphia were a team of black players in the 1880s in Philadelphia.

Adams, Ben

Ben Adams pitched for the Memphis Red Sox in 1953.

Adams, Emery (Ace)

Emery Adams pitched from 1932 to 1946 for the Baltimore Elite Giants, New York Black Yankees, and Memphis Red Sox.

Adams, Malachi

Malachi Adams was an umpire in the League of Colored Baseball Players in 1887, working Lord Baltimore games in Baltimore.

Adkins, Clarence

Clarence Adkins played the outfield for the Memphis Red Sox in 1931.

Agnew, Clyde

Clyde Agnew was a pitcher for the Baltimore Elite Giants in the early 1950s.

Akers, Charley

Charley Akers played a shortstop for the Hilldale baseball club in 1924.

Akron Black Tyrites

The Akron Black Tyrites were a team out of Akron, Ohio, that played in the NEGRO NATIONAL LEAGUE in 1933.

Albany Bachelors

The Albany Bachelors, out of Albany, New York, were one of a group of black teams that began play in the North after the Civil War.

Albany Giants

The Albany Giants were a team out of Albany, New York, that played in the NEGRO NATIONAL LEAGUE in 1926.

Albertson, Johnny

Johnny Albertson played shortstop for the New York Black Yankees and Brooklyn Royal Giants from 1936 to 1939.

Albright, Thomas

Thomas Albright pitched for the New York Cubans in 1936.

Albritton, Alexander

Alexander Albritton was a pitcher for the Wilmington Potomacs, Washington Potomacs, Baltimore Black Sox, Atlantic City Bacharach Giants, and the Hilldale club from 1921 to 1925.

Alexander, Calvin

Calvin Alexander pitched for the New Orleans Crescent Stars in 1922.

Alexander, Freyl John

John Alexander served as president of the Homestead Grays in the early 1910s.

Alexander, Grover Cleveland (Buck)

Buck Alexander pitched from 1923 to 1926 for the Indianapolis ABC's, Cleveland Elites, Chicago Giants, and Detroit Stars.

Alexander, Hub

Hub Alexander was a catcher for the Chicago Giants in 1913.

Alexander, Joseph

Joseph Alexander was a catcher for the Kansas City Monarchs in 1950.

Alexander, Spencer

Spencer Alexander played the outfield for the Newark Eagles in 1940 and 1941.

Alexander, Ted (Red)

Ted Alexander was a pitcher for the New York Black Yankees, Indianapolis ABC's, Birmingham Black Barons, Homestead Grays, Chicago American Giants, Cleveland Bears, and Kansas City Monarchs from 1938 to 1949.

Alfonso, Angel

Angel Alfonso was a shortstop, second baseman, and third baseman for the Cuban Stars in the NEGRO NATIONAL LEAGUE and the Cuban Stars in the EASTERN COLORED LEAGUE from 1924 to 1930.

Algona Brownies

The Brownies were an interracial team based in Algona, Iowa, in the early 1900s. It consisted of former players from the Unions of Chicago and the Columbia Giants. In 1903, the team was transformed from a team of blacks and whites to all black.

All-American Black Tourists

The Tourists were a team of black players organized by Negro Leaguer Bud Fowler in 1899. They played while wearing full-dress suits and formal outfits.

All Cubans

The All Cubans were one of the many versions of black baseball teams that used the Cuban identity as a promotional gimmick, although, despite claims, many of the players were not Cuban. The All Cubans toured the United States playing black baseball teams in the early 1900s.

Allen, Clifford (Crooks)

Clifford Allen pitched for the Homestead Grays, Memphis Red Sox, Philadelphia Stars, Hilldale, Baltimore Black Sox, and the Atlantic City Bacharach Giants from 1932 to 1938.

Allen, Dave

Dave Allen was a catcher and infielder for the Trenton Cuban Giants and Pittsburgh Keystones in 1887.

Allen, Homer

Homer Allen pitched in the early 1930s for the Monroe Monarchs.

Allen, Hosea (Buster)

Hosea Allen pitched for the Jacksonville Red Caps, Cincinnati Clowns, Indianapolis Clowns, and the Memphis Red Sox from 1942 to 1947.

Allen, Newt (Colt)

b. 1901, d. 1988

Newt Allen played second base, shortstop, and the outfield for a series of black baseball teams from 1920 to 1948—the ALL NATIONS team, Kansas City Tigers, Kansas City Monarchs, St. Louis Stars, Detroit Stars, Homestead Grays, and Cincinnati Clowns. At 5-foot-7 and 169 pounds, Allen teamed up with shortstop Dobie Moore to make one of the best double-play combinations in the history of Negro League baseball and was one of the leaders of the Monarchs team that won 10 league championships. According to records, Allen's best year was 1929, when he batted .330 with 24 doubles and 23 stolen bases. He reportedly batted .351 the following season.

In an interview with the *Kansas City Star*, Allen said he grew up in Kansas City, and as a young boy worked for the Monarchs at the park at 20th and Prospect Streets: "I pulled the canvas and filled the water jug and things like that," he said. As a hometown boy, Allen became one of the favorites of Monarch fans, who loved his dazzling field play. In documents filed at the National Baseball Hall of Fame, Allen said his greatest achievement in baseball "was when I made an unassisted triple play." Allen, who was a switch hitter, also played with such Negro League great infielders as Willie Wells and Jesse Williams.

In an interview on file at the Hall of Fame, conducted by author John Holway, Allen talked about his batting skills: "I was a pretty good bunter if I have to say so, a pretty good hit-and-run man," he said. "As I stayed in baseball, I learned how to hit the way the ball was pitched." Allen also talked about the rough-and-tumble play of the Negro Leagues: "I was a rough ballplayer, but we were all friends," he said. "You have a certain feeling toward a fellow that's nice and never had any nasty words against you. A lot of times I had a nasty feeling within myself, not against a ballplayer. I was pretty bad playing ball, yes, run over a man, throw at him. I did a lot of wrong things. But I got results out of it, because they were leery of what I was going to do, and I'd get by with it. . . . We used every trick in the book to win a ball game. All kinds of good tricks and nasty ones."

He learned enough to become a successful manager, and managed the Monarchs to five Negro American League pennants. When he was 41, Allen played in his final Negro World Series in 1942, as his Monarchs swept the Homestead Grays in four games. In the Holway interview, Allen reflected on some of the rivalries they had, particularly with Rube Foster's Chicago American Giants: "There would be quite a few arguments and sometimes a lot of fist throwing," he said. "We had three or four great fights there in Chicago. . . . We did a lot of throwing at one another, running over one another, jumping at each other. Some guy would get temperamental enough to swing at someone, and the ballplayers and spectators would mix it up. It took all the 35th Street police to stop it. They'd throw out the first three or four that started the ruckus and keep on playing. Then when Chicago came here, 17,000 to 18,000 people would come out to see who was going to start a fight. The owners were all making money." Allen also played winter baseball in Cuba and toured the Far East with other black ballplayers in the 1930s.

Allen, Todd

Todd Allen was an infielder and manager for the Chicago American Giants, Lincoln Giants, Bowser's ABC's, Louisville White Sox, and Indianapolis ABC's from 1911 to 1925.

Allen, Toussaint (Tom)

Toussaint Allen was a first baseman for the Wilmington Potomacs, Havana Red Sox, and Newark Stars from 1914 to 1926.

All Nations team

The All Nations team consisted of white, black, Chinese, and Cuban players, as well as players of other nationalities and women. Started by J. L. Wilkinson in 1912, with a four-year run that ended in 1916 (although it was briefly revived in 1919, after World War I ended), the All Nations club was a traveling baseball and music show, often bringing a dance band on the road with them. Reports are that they brought a wrestling show with them as well, and sometimes their own bleachers. The All Nations team played some of the best Negro teams in the country, such as the Leland Giants in Chicago and the Indianapolis ABC's. According to reports, the All Nations team beat the ABC's twice in 1916, and the ABC's were presumed to be the best Negro baseball team in the country that year. Negro League pitching great Jose Mendez managed the team for a period, and fellow Cuban baseball star slugger Cristobal Torrienti also played for All Nations. John Donaldson, the standout left-hander, pitched for All Nations, as did Bill Drake.

Almagro, Jorge

Jorge Almagro was an outfielder for the Pittsburgh Crawfords in 1945.

Almeida, Rafael

Cuban-born Rafael Almeida got his start in baseball in America with black teams, playing third base and the outfield for the Havana Cuban Stars and All Cubans from 1904 to 1907. He was one of several light-skinned Cuban players who were signed by the Cincinnati Reds in 1911 and managed to play major league baseball for three seasons, batting .270 in 95 games. A 1914 story in the newspaper *Sporting Life* described how much the Reds missed Almeida after he was released after the 1913 season: "Several of the Cincinnati players wish that the club had kept Rafael Almeida," the article stated. "The quiet, amiable Portuguese-Cuban was a soothing, not a disturbing, influence, and how he could play that ball when called upon in a pinch. He could play the outfield, too. It was one of the great errors of 1913 when Almeida was sent away, and he'd be extremely useful now."

Almentero, Juan

Juan Almentero pitched for the New York Cuban Stars in 1916.

Alonso, Rogelio

Rogelio Alonso pitched for the Cuban Stars from 1927 to 1930.

Alsop, Clifford

Clifford Alsop pitched for the Kansas City Monarchs from 1920 to 1922.

Alston, Thomas
b. 1931, d. 1993

Thomas Alston played first base for the Greensboro, North Carolina, Red Wings—the town where he was born—in 1948. He was signed by the St. Louis Cardinals and played four major league seasons for the Cardinals—1954, when he appeared in 66 games and batted .246 with four home runs and 34 RBIs; 1955, when he played in 13 games and batted .125; 1956, when he played in just three games, going hitless in two plate appearances; and 1957, playing in nine games, with 17 at bats and five hits, for a .294 average.

Altman, George Lee
b. 1933

George Altman was one of the last black ballplayers to have started in Negro League baseball. Born in Goldsboro, North Carolina, the 6-foot-4, 200-pound Altman played outfield for the Kansas City Monarchs in 1955, batting .263. He signed with the Chicago Cubs and played in their minor league system until 1959 when he was brought up by the Cubs. He stayed in the major leagues for nine seasons with Chicago, Cincinnati, and the New York Mets, batting .269 with 101 home runs and

403 RBIs in 991 games. After being sent to Class AAA Tacoma by the Cubs, Altman went to play in Japan until 1975, where he hit 205 home runs and drove in 656 runs.

Alvarez, Raul
Raul Alvarez pitched for a variety of versions of the Cuban Stars from 1924 to 1933.

Amaro, Dionisio (Dave)
Dionisio Amaro pitched for the Indianapolis Clowns from 1953 to 1955.

American Negro League
The American Negro League was formed in 1929 by owners from the failed Eastern Colored League. The league included a number of teams from that defunct league—the New York Cuban Stars, Baltimore Black Sox, Atlantic City Bacharach Giants, Harrisburg Giants, and Hilldale Field Club, plus a new team, the Homestead Grays. The league lasted just one year, with the Black Sox winning the league championship.

Ammon Field
Ammon Field was located at Bedford and Wylie Avenues in Pittsburgh, Pennsylvania, and is where the Pittsburgh Crawford Giants played in the early 1930s.

Amoros, Edmundo (Sandy)
b. 1930, d. 1992
Sandy Amoros was best known for his spectacular play for the Brooklyn Dodgers to help beat the New York Yankees in the 1955 World Series. Earlier he played first base and the outfield for one year of Negro League baseball, for the New York Cubans in 1950, before breaking into major league baseball. Born in Matanzas, Cuba, Amoros was called up to the Dodgers in 1952 and played with the club until 1960. Coming over from the L.A. Dodgers, he finished his career with Detroit in 1960, having a career batting average of .255 in 517 games. He became a World Series legend in the seventh and deciding game of the 1955 series: He was brought in the game in the seventh inning to replace Junior Gilliam in left field, after Gilliam was moved to second base to replace Don Zimmer, who was pinch hit for in the sixth inning. With nobody out and two men on base, Yogi Berra hit a high fly ball to left that nearly went foul into the stands at Yankee Stadium. Amoros, who had been playing in left center, made a long run for the ball and a remarkable catch, then turned and threw to first base to nail Gil McDougald for a double play.

Anchor Giants
The Anchor Giants were a black baseball team managed by Henry Sellars that played in the 1900s in the Philadelphia area.

Anderson, Andy
d. 1987
Andy Anderson played the outfield for the Chicago American Giants in 1951.

Anderson, Elijah
Elijah Anderson was an umpire in the League of Colored Baseball Players in 1887, working Louisville Fall Citys' games.

Anderson, Lewis
Lewis Anderson was a catcher for the Chicago American Giants and Baltimore Black Sox from 1930 to 1933.

Anderson, Ralph
Ralph Anderson played the outfield for the Homestead Grays and Indianapolis ABC's in the early 1930s.

Anderson, Robert James
Robert James Anderson was an infielder for the Chicago American Giants, Philadelphia Giants, Gilkerson's Union Giants, and Peters' Union Giants from 1915 to 1925.

Anderson, Theodore (Bubbles)
Theodore Anderson was a second baseman and catcher for the Wilmington Potomacs, Washington Potomacs, Kansas City Monarchs, Birmingham Black Barons, and Indianapolis ABC's from 1922 to 1925.

Anderson, William
William Anderson was an outfielder for the Nashville Elite Giants and Birmingham Black Barons from 1927 to 1931.

Anderson, William (Bill)
William Anderson was a pitcher for the Philadelphia Stars, Homestead Grays, New York Cubans, and Brooklyn Royal Giants from 1940 to 1947.

Andrews, Herman
Herman Andrews was an outfielder, pitcher, first baseman, and manager for the Washington Black Senators,

Birmingham Black Barons, Chicago American Giants, Memphis Red Sox, Jacksonville Red Caps, Indianapolis ABC's, Cleveland Bears, Detroit Wolves, Philadelphia Stars, Homestead Grays, New York Cubans, Columbus Blue Birds, and Pittsburgh Crawfords from 1930 to 1943. In 1937, Andrews was one of a group of Negro League players recruited by Dominican Republic dictator Rafael Trujillo to play for his Los Draganos teams in the political baseball war in that country.

Anthony, Lavance (Pete)

Lavance Anderson was a catcher for the Houston Eagles and New York Cubans in the early 1950s.

Anthony, Thad

Thad Anthony was a catcher for the Baltimore Elite Giants in 1950.

Arango, Luis

Luis Arango was a first baseman and third baseman for the Cuban Stars and New York Cubans from 1925 to 1939.

Arctic Park

Arctic Park was a field on Long Island, New York, that was the home of the Acmes of Long Island, a black team that played in the late 1800s.

Arenas, Hipolito

Hipolito Arenas was an outfielder and third baseman for the Atlanta Black Crackers in 1932.

Arencibia, Edward

Edward Arencibia pitched for the New York Cubans in 1948.

Arguelles, Martinano

Martinano Arguelles pitched for the New York Cubans in 1950.

Argyle Hotel

The Argyle Hotel was located in Babylon, New York, and sponsored what is believed to be the first professional black baseball team in 1885. One of the waiters, Frank P. Thompson, had formed a black baseball team called the Keystone Athletics in Philadelphia, and the hotel hired the team to entertain the guests and also work as waiters. They later joined up with the Manhattans of Washington and the Orions of Philadelphia and were called the New York Cuban Giants, the first in a long line of black teams that would use that name and variations of it. It is believed they tried to pass themselves off as Cuban. Some players included George Williams, Shep Trusty, Abe Harrison from the Orions; Ben Holmes, George Parego, and Ben Boyd from the Athletics; and Clarence Williams and Arthur Thomas from the Manhattans. Another member of the team was Sol White, an early Negro League baseball player, manager, and historian. The 350-room hotel opened in 1882 and closed in 1897.

Ariosa, Homero

Homero Ariosa was an outfielder for the New York Cubans from 1947 to 1950, batting .338 in his final season with the Cubans. He was signed by the Brooklyn Dodgers and spent parts of seven seasons with the Dodgers and Detroit Tigers organizations. Ariosa continued playing baseball in the Mexican League for many years, playing 27 games in 1968 and getting into one game as a pinch hitter in 1972.

Armour, Alfred (Buddy)

Alfred Armour was an outfielder and shortstop for the Chicago American Giants, Homestead Grays, St. Louis Stars, Cleveland Buckeyes, New Orleans Stars, and the Indianapolis ABC's from 1936 to 1950. Records show his best Negro League seasons were 1939, when he batted 474 with St. Louis in an unknown number of at bats; 1940 with New Orleans and St. Louis, when he hit .389 in 19 at bats; and Cleveland in 1944, when batted .325 in 157 at bats.

Armstead, James

James Armstead was a pitcher and outfielder for the Baltimore Elite Giants, St. Louis Stars, Indianapolis ABC's, and the Philadelphia Stars from 1938 to 1949.

Armstrong, Louis
b. 1901, d. 1971

Louis Armstrong, the great New Orleans jazz musician, known as "Satchmo," owned a semipro Negro baseball team called the New Orleans Smart Nine in the 1930s.

Arnold, Paul

Paul Arnold was an outfielder for the Newark Dodgers in 1934 and 1935.

Arthur, Robert

Robert Arthur pitched for the Pittsburgh Crawfords in 1946.

Ascanio, Carlos (Earthquake)
b. 1916, d. 1998

Carlos Ascanio was a first baseman for the New York Black Yankees in 1946.

Ash, Rudolph

Rudolph Ash was an outfielder and pitcher for the Chicago American Giants, Hilldale baseball club, and Newark Stars from 1920 to 1926.

Ashby, Earl
b. 1921

Earl Ashby was a catcher for the Cleveland Buckeyes, Birmingham Black Barons, Homestead Grays, and Newark Eagles from 1945 to 1948. He was born in Havana, Cuba, and records show that Ashby batted .286 in 1945 with Cleveland and .254 in 1947 with Homestead.

Ashville Blues

The Ashville Blues were a team out of Ashville, North Carolina, that played in the Negro Southern League in 1945.

Askew, Jesse

Jesse Askew was a shortstop for the St. Louis Stars in 1936.

Atkins, Abe

Abe Atkins was a third baseman and shortstop for the Toledo Tigers in 1923.

Atkins, Joe
b. 1922

Joe Atkins was a third baseman for the Pittsburgh Crawfords, Cleveland Buckeyes, and Newark Eagles from 1946 to 1948. He was born in Pittsburgh, Pennsylvania, and records show that he batted .335 for Cleveland in 1947. The 6-foot-1, 190-pound Atkins played minor league baseball until 1954.

Atkins, Stacy

Stacy Atkins was a pitcher for the Chicago American Giants in 1950.

Atlanta Black Crackers

The Atlanta Black Crackers were one of the original teams in the Negro Southern League, playing there from 1920 to 1936. In 1937, they played in the NEGRO AMERICAN LEAGUE and played the Memphis Red Sox in the league championship series. However, after Memphis took a three game to two lead over Atlanta, the series was canceled because of financial and scheduling disputes, and the Black Crackers left the league after that season. The franchise moved to Indianapolis briefly but then returned to Atlanta and reentered the Negro American League in 1938. They won the second-half title of the split season, but the championship series, again against Memphis, the first-half champions, was canceled after just two games. The name Crackers came from the Atlanta Crackers, the white team that played in the Southern Association. Both teams played at Ponce de Leon Park in Atlanta. Some of the players who were on the Black Crackers roster included second baseman Gabby Kemp, who also managed the 1938 squad, shortstop Pee Wee Butts, first baseman Red Moore, and pitchers Bo Mitchell and Bullet Dixon.

Atlantic City Bacharach Giants

The Atlantic City Bacharach Giants were a black baseball team based in Atlantic City, New Jersey, formed when the Jacksonville (Florida) Duval Giants moved to Atlantic City in 1916. Two city aldermen, Henry Tucker and Thomas Jackson, owned the team and named it after the mayor of Atlantic City, Harry Bacharach. Napoleon Cummings, who played for the Bacharach Giants, talked about the move from Jacksonville in the book, *Only the Ball Was White*, by Robert Peterson: "We had this club—the Duval Giants—down in Jacksonville. It was pretty informal and we didn't make much—we just got peanuts. But we were working on other jobs, too. I had this job in a grocery store, but I wanted to be a ballplayer. In 1916 Tom Jackson and Henry Tucker—they were a couple of politicians around here in Atlantic City—brought us up here. They happened to see us down in Florida and brought us up here on behalf of the mayor. They got the name, the Bacharach Giants, from the mayor here, but he didn't put any money into the club. . . . Jackson and Tucker got money from somewhere and helped us along, but we made our own way." Cummings also told about challenge of playing against white teams up north: "We all had guts because we had a lot of experience down in Florida," he said. "We all worked downtown in Jacksonville, and we had a lot of experience during the Jack Johnson and Jeffries fight—there were thousands of whites in our part of town—and we had guts when we came up here. Of course, we had no chance to play baseball with whites down there, but we worked downtown with a whole lot of white fellas. And when we came up here and started playing ball with white boys, they were more scared of us than we were scared of them. Because we had such a hell of a ball club. We had a powerful ball club. There were other colored clubs here then, but we broke them up. We were so strong, and everybody wanted to play the Bacharachs. We played so many ball clubs, and beat everybody, that people came all the way from Philadelphia to see who the Bacharachs were." However, the team folded in 1918 and was purchased by John Connors, who moved it to New York. In the move, Connors made Barron Wilkins, a Harlem gangster and nightclub owner, a co-owner of the team, now the New York Bacharach Giants. The team folded again in 1923 and was revived back in Atlantic City by Tucker and Jackson and became part of the EASTERN COLORED LEAGUE. The Bacharach Giants won back-to-back Eastern Colored League Championships in 1926 and 1927 under player-manager Dick Lundy. Both years they lost to the Chicago American Giants, champions of the NEGRO NATIONAL LEAGUE, in the Negro League World Series. In 1928, the Bacharach Giants were purchased by Isaac Nutter, a black owner and also the newly selected president of the Eastern Colored League. Two years later, the team folded again, then was resurrected yet again in a few years, although it was never again the force it had been in black baseball.

Some of the players for the Bacharach Giants, in addition to Lundy, one of the premier shortstops in black baseball history, included third baseman Oliver Marcelle, center fielder Chaney White, shortstop John Henry Lloyd, and pitchers Rats Henderson, "Cannonball" Dick Redding, Jesse "Mountain" Hubbard, and Jesse "Nip" Winters. One of the places the Bacharach Giants played was a former Greyhound race track on South Carolina Avenue in Atlantic City.

Atlantic City Johnson Stars

The Atlantic City Johnson Stars were a black baseball team that played in Atlantic City in the 1930s and 1940s. Negro League great John Henry Lloyd played for the Stars well past his prime playing days, finally retiring at the age of 58.

Auburn Park

Auburn Park was a baseball field in Chicago at the corner of Wentworth and 79th that served in the early 1900s as the home of several Negro baseball teams owned by Frank Leland, including the Unions of Chicago, later changed to the Chicago Union Giants, and still later the Leland Giants.

Augustine, Leon

Leon Augustine was an umpire in the NEGRO NATIONAL LEAGUE in the 1920s.

Austin, Frank Samuel
b. 1922, d. 1960

Frank Austin was a shortstop and outfielder for the Philadelphia Stars from 1944 to 1948. Austin, who was born in Panama, signed a minor league contract with the New York Yankees at the end of the decade. Records show he batted .362 over 689 Negro League games, and 268 in several years of minor league baseball with the Newark Bears and Portland Braves. His best minor league season was with Portland in 1951, when he batted .293 with 70 RBIs in 167 games. He retired after the 1956 season.

Austin, Tank

Tank Austin was a pitcher for the Birmingham Black Barons, Atlanta Black Crackers, and Nashville Elite Giants from 1930 to 1932.

Awkward, Russell

Russell Awkward was an outfielder for the Cuban Stars and Newark Eagles in 1940 and 1941.

Bacharach, Harry

Harry Bacharach was the mayor of Atlantic City who helped bring the Jacksonville (Florida) Duval Giants to Atlantic City in 1916 and for whom the team was named.

Bacharach Park

Bacharach Park was a greyhound racetrack in Atlantic City that was converted to a baseball field where the Atlantic City Bacharach Giants played.

Bailey, Otha William

Otha Bailey was a 5-foot-6, 150-pound catcher who played for the Houston Eagles, Birmingham Black Barons, Cleveland Buckeyes, and New Orleans Eagles from 1950 to 1955. In a 1997 interview with *Sports Collectors Digest,* Bailey said he had a chance to try out for the Brooklyn Dodgers but missed out because, of all things, he stayed in bed too long: "I was in Miami during the winter months and when they came to spring training [in 1951], Roy Campanella, he asked me to come to the Dodgers camp, but I overslept," Bailey said. "I woke up and it was too late. They were gone. I saw them a couple of weeks later in Miami. Campy asked me what happened, and I told him. . . . I figure I might have missed a little chance there." Bailey wasn't very big,

but he had a strong arm, and runners were afraid to take bases on him: "We had some guys who could run like a rabbit," he said. "I'd get some of them out. I'd get more of them out than they'd steal. If one would get one, I'd be hoping he'd run. One time I played for about three weeks and I didn't have to throw nobody out because nobody ran."

Bailey, Percy (Bill)

Percy Bailey was a pitcher for the Baltimore Black Sox, Nashville Elite Giants, Detroit Stars, Cole's American Giants, and New York Black Yankees from 1927 to 1934.

Baird, Thomas Y.

Tom Baird was a white businessman and owner of a Kansas City poolroom who became partners with J. L. Wilkinson in the Kansas City Monarchs in 1930 when Wilkinson began using lights for night games—the first professional baseball team to use lights. One of Baird's contributions to the Monarchs was a barnstorming deal one summer with the House of David that included signing female Olympic athlete Mildred "Babe" Didrikson to play for the House of David. When the Brooklyn Dodgers signed Jackie Robinson away from the Monarchs in 1945, Baird threatened to sue Dodgers general manager Branch Rickey. Baird backed off his threat after receiving severe criticism in the black press. Before Wilkinson died in 1948, he sold his half of the Monarchs to Baird. In 1955, Baird sold the team to a black businessman named Ted Rasberry. Baird was then hired by the Kansas City Athletics as a scout.

Baker, Edgar
Edgar Baker was a pitcher for the Memphis Red Sox in 1945.

Baker, Eugene
b. 1925, d. 1999
Gene Baker was a shortstop with the Kansas City Monarchs from 1948 to 1950. He batted .293 in his first season in 69 games, followed by a .236 average in 1949 in 88 games with the Monarchs. Born in Davenport, Iowa, Baker was signed by the Chicago Cubs in 1950 and spent several years in the minor leagues before being called up to the Cubs in 1953. Baker's tenure in the minors was a source of controversy. According to the Jules Tygiel book *Jackie Robinson and His Legacy*, Baker "was the best fielding shortstop [in the Pacific Coast League], if not the minor leagues. Yet during his first three seasons Baker received minimal attention from the Cubs' hierarchy. In the spring of 1953, Baker seemed ready to take over at shortstop for the Cubs, but the club used him sparingly in exhibitions before returning him to their minor league team in Los Angeles. Baker's demotion drew cries of outrage and charges of discrimination. [Sportswriter] Sam Lacy called the situation 'the prize stinkeroo of the 1953 spring training season' and 'one of the scurviest deals in baseball.' Baker, by virtue of his absence became 'the most controversial figure in Chicago baseball circles.'" Baker, who batted .284 with 20 home runs, 99 RBIs, and 20 stolen bases, wound up being called up in September, but he was not the first black player for the Cubs. Earlier that season, while Baker was injured, they brought a shortstop named Ernie Banks up to the major league team. Baker would be moved to second base in 1954. In eight major league seasons with the Cubs and Pittsburgh—including being part of the Pirates' 1960 World Series championship team—Baker batted .265 with 39 home runs and 227 RBIs in 630 games.

Baker, Henry
Henry Baker was an outfielder for the Indianapolis ABC's from 1925 to 1932.

Baker, Lamar
Lamar Baker was a pitcher for the New York Black Yankees in 1950.

Baker, Norman
Norman Baker was a pitcher for the Newark Eagles in 1937.

Baker, Rufus
Rufus Baker was an infielder and outfielder for the New York Black Yankees from 1944 to 1947.

Baker, Sammy
Sammy Baker was a pitcher for the Chicago American Giants in 1950.

Baker, Tom
Tom Baker was a pitcher for the Baltimore Elite Giants in 1940.

Baker, Welton B.
Welton Baker was the business manager for the Atlanta Black Crackers in 1937 and 1938.

Baker Field
Baker Field was the 18,000-seat home of the Philadelphia Phillies from 1887 to 1938 (also known as Baker Bowl and Philadelphia Park) and also hosted some Philadelphia Giants Negro League games shortly after the turn of the century, among other Negro League games that would be played there—including the 1921 showdown between the Chicago American Giants and the Hilldales (Hilldale Field Club).

Baldwin, Robert
Robert Baldwin played shortstop for the Cleveland Elites, Cleveland Tate Stars, Indianapolis ABC's and Detroit Stars from 1923 to 1926.

Ball, George Walter (Georgia Rabbit)
George Ball was a pitcher and outfielder who played for the Chicago Union Giants, Algona Brownies, Leland Giants, Philadelphia Giants, Cuban X Giants, St. Louis Giants, Chicago American Giants, Lincoln Stars, Lincoln Giants, and Mohawk Giants from 1902 to 1923. In his book, *History of Colored Baseball*, former Negro League player and historian Sol White said Ball "was one of many colored pitchers who would no doubt land in the big league."

Ball, Walter
Walter Ball was a pitcher for the Philadelphia Giants, Leland Giants, Chicago Giants, Chicago American Giants, St. Louis Giants, Mohawk Giants, Brooklyn Royal Giants, and Chicago Union Giants from 1903 to 1923.

Ballestro, Miguel
Miguel Ballestro was a shortstop for the New York Cubans in 1948.

Baltimore Atlantics
The Baltimore Atlantics were a black baseball team in Baltimore in the 1880s.

Baltimore Black Sox
The Baltimore Black Sox were a black baseball club that played in Baltimore from 1916 to 1934. They were an independent team until 1923 when, under the ownership of two white owners, George Rossiter and Charles Spedden, they joined the EASTERN COLORED LEAGUE until the league folded in 1928. In 1929, they won the AMERICAN NEGRO LEAGUE pennant, the only year the league was in existence. That championship team featured an all-star defense with Jud "Boojum" Wilson at first, player-manager Frank Warfield at second, Dick Lundy at shortstop, and Oliver Marcelle at third. Other players on the team included outfielder Rap Dixon and pitchers Jesse Hubbard, Holsey "Scrip" Lee, Pud Flourney, and Laymon Yokeley. Satchel Paige pitched for the Black Sox briefly in 1931. The team was unaffiliated in 1930 and 1931. In 1930, the Black Sox played the New York Lincoln Giants in a doubleheader at Yankee Stadium—the first black teams to play in the ballpark. The Black Sox joined the East-West League in 1932, but that league also lasted just one year. They played their final two seasons in the NEGRO NATIONAL LEAGUE. Among the Baltimore ballparks they played in were Maryland Park and Westport Park.

Baltimore Elite Giants
The Baltimore Elite Giants, owned by a black numbers operator named Tom Wilson, began in 1921 in Nashville, Tennessee. They joined the Negro National League in 1930, and in 1931 they moved briefly to Cleveland and then back to Nashville. In 1935, the team moved to Columbus, Ohio, where they were known as the Columbus Elite Giants. The following season the franchise moved to Washington and then on to Baltimore in 1938, where they played until the franchise folded in 1950. The Baltimore Elite Giants played in the NEGRO NATIONAL LEAGUE from 1938 to 1948. In the team's final two seasons, 1949 and 1950, they played in the NEGRO AMERICAN LEAGUE. In 1939, they defeated the Homestead Grays, winners of the regular season pennant, for the playoff championship of the Negro National League and won the Negro American League title in 1949. Among the franchise's players were Hall of Famers pitcher Leon Day and catcher Roy Campanella, Negro League greats Wild Bill Wright, Henry Kimbro, and Bill Hoskins, and future major league players pitcher Joe Black and second baseman Junior Gilliam. Tom Wilson sold the team in 1946 to black businessman Richard Powell.

Baltimore Grays
The Baltimore Grays were a black baseball team that played in Baltimore in the 1940s.

Baltimore Stars
The Baltimore Stars were a black baseball team that played in Baltimore in the 1930s.

Bankes, James
James Bankes was a pitcher and outfielder for the Baltimore Elite Giants and Memphis Red Sox from 1950 to 1952.

Bankhead, Daniel (Dan)
b. 1920, d. 1976
Dan Bankhead was a pitcher for the Chicago American Giants, Birmingham Black Barons, and Memphis Red Sox from 1940 to 1947. Born in Empire, Alabama, Bankhead was an impressive Negro League hurler, and when George Sisler and Branch Rickey came to see Bankhead pitch for Memphis in 1947, he struck out 11. He was then signed by the Dodgers for a reported $15,000 and came up the same year as Jackie Robinson. He pitched three seasons for the Dodgers, in 1947, 1950, and 1951, posting a career record of 9-5 in 62 career appearances. The 6-foot-2, 190-pound Bankhead went on to pitch in Mexico until retiring after the 1966 season. He was the brother of fellow Negro League player Sam Bankhead and had three other brothers who played organized ball as well—Fred, Garnett, and Joseph.

Bankhead, Fred
Frank Bankhead, one of the Bankhead brothers, was a pitcher for the Birmingham Black Barons and the Memphis Red Sox from 1937 to 1948.

Bankhead, Garnett

d. 1991

Garnett Bankhead, one of the Bankhead brothers, was a pitcher for the Homestead Grays in 1948.

Bankhead, Joseph

Joseph Bankhead was a pitcher for the Birmingham Black Barons in 1948.

Bankhead, Sam

b. 1905, d. 1976

Sam Bankhead was an infielder, outfielder, and pitcher for the Pittsburgh Crawfords, Homestead Grays, Birmingham Black Barons, and Nashville Elite Giants from 1931 to 1947. He scored the winning run for the Crawfords in the seventh and deciding game against the New York Cubans in the 1935 Negro League World Series. Born in Empire, Alabama, Bankhead was a 14-time All Star who batted .285 over his career. He was one of a series of Crawford players, led by Satchel Paige, who went to the Dominican Republic in 1937 for dictator Rafael Trujillo. Bankhead later played for the Homestead Grays. He was the oldest of five brothers who played Negro League baseball and was a highly respected teammate. Pitcher Wilmer Fields, a teammate of Bankhead with Homestead, wrote in his biography, *My Life in the Negro Leagues*, that Bankhead "was one of the greatest black ballplayers I was ever associated with . . . when he spoke, people listened. He would lift you up when you were down. If there was ever a black ballplayer who should be honored, it is Sam Bankhead."

Banks, Ben

Ben Banks was a second baseman for the Kansas City Monarchs in 1952.

Banks, Ernie

b. 1931

Ernie Banks, the Hall of Fame player known as "Mr. Cub," was born in Dallas, Texas, and got his start in the Negro Leagues with the San Antonio Sheepherders in 1949. He was signed by the Kansas City Monarchs in 1950, where he batted .255 with one home run and 20 RBIs in 53 games. The 6-foot-1, 185-pound Banks was scouted for the Cubs by former Monarchs' first baseman Buck O'Neil. Banks broke into the major leagues in 1953 as a shortstop, appearing briefly in 10 games. The following season, his first full year, Banks hit 19 home runs and drove in 79 runs. He would set a record for home runs by shortstops with 277 (since broken by

An infielder, outfielder, and pitcher, Sam Bankhead was a seven-time Negro League All-Star and is believed to have batted .346 during a 20-year career with the Homestead Grays, Pittsburgh Crawfords, Birmingham Black Barons, and Nashville Elite Giants. He scored the winning run for the Crawfords in the seventh and deciding game against the New York Cubans in the 1935 Negro League World Series. (NATIONAL BASEBALL HALL OF FAME LIBRARY, COOPERSTOWN, N.Y./McNeill Photo)

Cal Ripken, who would go on to hit 345 home runs). Banks played first base for the remainder of his 19-year career, retiring in 1971 with 512 home runs, 1,636 RBIs, and a .274 batting average. He was a two-time Most Valuable Player who led the league in home runs and runs batted in twice, and was a 10-time All-Star. From 1955 to 1960, Banks hit more home runs than any other major league player. Banks was inducted into the Hall of Fame in 1977.

Banks, Johnny

Johnny Banks was a pitcher for the Philadelphia Stars in 1950.

Ernie Banks's road to major league baseball, the Chicago Cubs, and the Hall of Fame began in the Negro Leagues, first with the San Antonio Sheepherders in 1949 and then with the Kansas City Monarchs in 1950. Banks was scouted for the Cubs by former Monarchs first baseman Buck O'Neil and broke into the major leagues with the Cubs in 1953 as a shortstop. (NATIONAL BASEBALL HALL OF FAME LIBRARY, COOPERSTOWN, N.Y.)

Banks, Norman
Norman Banks was a second baseman for the Newark Eagles in 1945.

Barbee, Lamb (Bud)
Lamb Barbee was a pitcher, first baseman, and later manager for the New York Black Yankees, Cincinnati Clowns, Indianapolis Clowns, Philadelphia Stars, Baltimore Elite Giants, Brooklyn Royal Giants, and Raleigh Tigers from 1937 to 1948.

Barbee, Quincy
Quincy Barbee was an outfielder for the Louisville Buckeyes in 1949.

Barber, Bull
Bull Barber was a second baseman for the Kansas City Monarchs, Hilldale baseball club, and Harrisburg Giants from 1920 to 1925.

Barber, John
John Barber was an outfielder for the Pittsburgh Crawfords in 1946.

Barber, Sam
b. 1920, d. 1999
Sam Barber was a pitcher for the Cleveland Clippers and the Cleveland Buckeyes from 1943 to 1950.

Barbour, Jess
Jess Barbour was a versatile player who played first, second, and third base and the outfield for the Philadelphia Giants, Chicago American Giants, Bacharach Giants, Detroit Stars, Pittsburgh Keystones, St. Louis Giants, Harrisburg Giants, Indianapolis ABC's, Chicago Giants, and Quaker Giants from 1909 to 1926. He was one of owner John Connors's favorite players. Connors twice signed Barbour away from rival owners—the first time in 1918, when Barbour jumped from Rube Foster's Chicago American Giants to Connors's Bacharach Giants, and again in 1921, when Barbour was part of a group of players signed away from the Ed Bolden's Hilldale baseball club by Connors for the New York Bacharachs.

Barker, Marvin
Marvin Baker was an infielder, outfielder, and manager for the New York Black Yankees and the Philadelphia Stars from 1936 to 1948.

Barnes, Ed
Ed Barnes was a pitcher for the Kansas City Monarchs in 1937 and 1938.

Barnes, Frank
b. 1928
Frank Barnes was a pitcher for the Indianapolis ABC's and Kansas City Monarchs from 1947 to 1950. He was born in Longwood, Missouri, and records show that he posted an 8-6 record with a 3.78 ERA in 1949 and 9-4 with a 2.41 in 1950, both with Kansas City. He pitched in the minor leagues from 1951 to 1957, having his best seasons in 1956 in Class AA, when the 6-foot, 180-pound Barnes posted a 13-5 mark with a 3.39 ERA, and in 1957, when he went 12-10 with a 2.41 ERA, both with Omaha. He was called up to the St. Louis Cardinals in 1957 and

spent parts of that year, the 1958 season, and the 1960 season with St. Louis, finishing his major league career with a 1-3 record and a 5.89 ERA. He went on to pitch in the Mexican League from 1962 to 1967 and posted a 6-5 mark with a 2.54 ERA in 12 games in his final season.

Barnes, Harry
Harry Barnes was a catcher for the Birmingham Black Barons, Atlanta Black Crackers, and Memphis Red Sox from 1935 to 1942 and again in 1949.

Barnes, Isaac
Isaac Barnes was a catcher for the Memphis Red Sox in 1955.

Barnes, Jimmy
Jimmy Barnes was a pitcher for the Baltimore Elite Giants in 1941 and 1942.

Barnes, Joe, Sr.
Joe Barnes pitched for the Kansas City Monarchs, Memphis Red Sox, and Indianapolis Clowns from 1950 to 1952.

Barnes, John
John Barnes was a pitcher for the Philadelphia Stars in 1952.

Barnes, John (Tubby)
John Barnes was a catcher for the Cleveland Browns, Cleveland Tate Stars, St. Louis Stars, Detroit Stars, Cleveland Tigers, Cleveland Hornets, Toledo Tigers, Memphis Red Sox, Cleveland Elites, and Indianapolis ABC's from 1921 to 1931.

Barnes, Ray
Ray Barnes was a pitcher for the Kansas City Monarchs in 1951.

Barnes, Tobias
Tobias Barnes was an infielder for the Chicago American Giants in 1937.

Barnes, William
William Barnes was a pitcher for the Memphis Red Sox, New York Black Yankees, Baltimore Elite Giants, and Indianapolis Clowns from 1937 to 1947.

Barnes, William H.
William H. Barnes was an officer with the Lord Baltimores in the League of Colored Base Ball Players in 1887.

Barnhill, Dave
b. 1914, d. 1983
Dave Barnhill was a strong right-handed pitcher and outfielder for the Miami Giants, Ethiopian Clowns, Zulu Cannibal Giants, New Orleans–Jacksonville Red Caps, St. Louis Stars, and New York Cubans from 1936 to 1949. He was born in Greenville, North Carolina, and the teams that Barnhill played with early in his career—the Miami Giants, the Ethiopian Clowns, and the Zulu Cannibal Giants—put on entertainment shows more than ball games, especially the Ethiopian Clowns and the Zulu Cannibal Giants: "We'd come to the park with paint on our faces like clowns," Barnhill said in an interview with author John Holway on file at the National Baseball Hall of Fame. "Even the batboy had his face painted, too. We wore clowning wigs and the big old clown uniforms with ruffled collars. My clowning name was 'Impo.' During batting practice we'd play 'shadow ball,' pretend to hit and throw without any ball at all. They'd 'hit' the ball to me. I'd run to field it. I'd jump, turn a flip and throw it like I'm throwing the ball to first base. Then when we were supposed to get to business, we pulled the clown suits off and we had regular baseball uniforms underneath. But we didn't change our faces. We played with our clown paint."

Barnhill became a legitimate Negro League baseball star when he joined the New York Cubans in 1941, reportedly posting a 16-3 record. He pitched in the East-West All-Star Game for three straight seasons, from 1941 to 1943. He defeated Satchel Paige in the 1942 All-Star Game. A 1943 newspaper report about another duel between Barnhill and Paige illustrated how big their rivalry was—a 2-0 shutout win by Barnhill's Cubans over Paige's Monarchs: "The fans saw a sensational pitching duel between Paige and Barnhill, which might still be going on had it not been for a fourth inning home run with a mate aboard by Brooks, a Cuban outfielder, which put the game on ice. . . . Statistics showed very little difference in the work of Barnhill and Paige, the latter pitching his first full game at [Yankee] Stadium. Barnhill fanned nine and walked two; Paige struck out eight and walked one. The Cubans got to Paige for eight hits, while Barnhill let the Kay See crowd down with only two."

In 1943, Barnhill was offered a tryout by Pittsburgh Pirates owner William Benswanger, but the offer was believed to be nothing more than an attempt to appease those pressuring the Pirates owner to integrate major league baseball, and nothing ever came of it, even though Barnhill agreed to the tryout, even with the conditions imposed that seemed to guarantee failure, such as suggesting low pay and starting at the bottom of the franchise's minor league system. "Benswanger chickened out," Barnhill said in the Holway interview. "Every owner was waiting for the others to make the first move. . . . I know I was ready. I played against quite a few big leaguers in Cuba. I pitched against Bob Lemon. I pitched to Johnny Mize." In 1947, the 5-foot-7, 150-pound Barnhill shut out the Cleveland Buckeyes to win the Negro League World Series. In 1949, Barnhill was

signed by the New York Giants, and pitched for their Class AAA team, the Minneapolis Millers, with an 11-3 record in 1950, helping the Millers win the American Association pennant. He was never brought up to the major league club, though, and retired after the 1953 season after playing in the Pacific Coast League and the Florida International League. In the Holway interview, Barnhill talked about his missed opportunity in 1950: "Durocher was going to call me and Ray [Dandridge] to finish the season," he said. "My manager told me that. But we had a shot at the playoffs, so they wouldn't call us up. I've never been so mad. I could have gone up to the majors and gotten a cup of coffee and come back. I could have told everybody, 'I played in the majors. I played for the New York Giants.'"

Barnhill, Herbert
Herbert Barnhill was a catcher for the Jacksonville Red Caps, St. Louis Stars, and New York Cubans from 1938 to 1945.

Baro, Bernardo
Bernardo Baro was an outfielder, first baseman, and pitcher, for the Cuban Stars from 1916 to 1929.

Barrow, Wesley
Wes Barrow managed the New Orleans Black Pelicans, Nashville Cubs, and Baltimore Elite Giants from 1945 to 1947.

Bartlett, Howard
Howard Bartlett was a pitcher for the Indianapolis ABC's, Bowser's ABC's and Kansas City Monarchs from 1911 to 1925.

Barton, Sherman
Sherman Barton was an outfielder and third baseman for the Columbia Giants, Cuban X Giants, Chicago Giants, and Leland Giants, Columbia Giants, Quaker Giants of New York, and the Chicago Union Giants from 1896 to 1911.

Baskin, William
William Baskin played second base for the Chicago Unions from 1890 to 1892.

Bass, Red
Red Bass was a catcher for the Homestead Grays in 1940.

Dave Barnhill began his career in 1936 as a member of the clowning black baseball teams—the Miami Giants, Ethiopian Clowns, and Zulu Cannibal Giants. But he would go on to become a top pitcher in the Negro Leagues, with the New Orleans–Jacksonville Red Caps, St. Louis Stars, and New York Cubans, compiling a 16-3 record in 1941 and pitching in the East West All-Star Game for three straight seasons, from 1941 to 1943. In 1947, the 5-foot-7, 150-pound Barnhill shut out the Cleveland Buckeyes to win the Negro League World Series. (NATIONAL BASEBALL HALL OF FAME LIBRARY, COOPERSTOWN, N.Y.)

Bassett, Lloyd P. (Pepper)

Lloyd Bassett was a catcher for the Philadelphia Stars, New Orleans Crescent Stars, Chicago American Giants, Pittsburgh Crawfords, Birmingham Black Barons, Cincinnati Clowns, Indianapolis Clowns, Homestead Grays, Toledo Crawfords, Detroit Stars, and Memphis Red Sox from 1934 to 1954.

Bassett entertained crowds by catching while sitting in a rocking chair during exhibition and nonleague games. A backup catcher for the Crawfords, Bassett became the Crawfords' everyday catcher when Josh Gibson held out in 1937. Bassett batted .444 and was the starting catcher in the East-West All-Star Game. He also batted .350 in 40 games in 1948.

Battle, Ray

Ray Battle played third base for the Homestead Grays in 1944, when he batted .294, and 1945.

Battle, William

William Battle was a pitcher for the Homestead Grays and Memphis Red Sox from 1947 to 1949.

Bauchman, Harry

Harry Bauchman was a second baseman and shortstop for the Chicago American Giants, Chicago Union Giants, and Chicago Giants from 1915 to 1923.

Bauza, Marcelino

Marcelino Bauza was a shortstop for the Cuban Stars in 1930.

Baxter, Al

Al Baxter was an outfielder for the Acme Colored Giants of Celeron, New York, in 1898.

Baylis, Henry

Henry Baylis was a third baseman for the Chicago American Giants, Birmingham Black Barons, Baltimore Elite Giants, and Kansas City Monarchs from 1948 to 1955. The 5-foot-10, 175-pound Baylis played for minor league clubs in El Paso and Tucson in 1956 and 1957. Records show that his best NEGRO NATIONAL LEAGUE season came in his rookie year with Chicago when he batted .320.

Baynard, Frank

Frank Baynard was a catcher and outfielder for the Newark Stars, Pennsylvania Red Caps, Havana Red Sox, Bacharach Giants, Hilldale baseball club, Cuban X Giants, and Lincoln Giants from 1913 to 1928.

Bea, Bill

Bill Bea was an outfielder for the New York Black Yankees and Philadelphia Stars in 1940.

Beal, Lefty

Lefty Beal pitched for the Newark Eagles in 1947.

Beale, Harry

Harry Beale was an officer with the Pittsburgh Crawfords from 1926 to 1930.

Beckwith, John
b. 1902, d. 1956

John Beckwith was nicknamed the "Black Bomber" because of his long home runs. He was a shortstop, third baseman, catcher, outfielder, and manager for the Chicago Giants, Chicago American Giants, Homestead Grays, Baltimore Black Sox, New York Lincoln Giants, Montgomery Grey Sox, Newark Browns, Hilldale Daisies, Harrisburg Giants, New York Black Yankees, Bacharach Giants, Newark Dodgers, and Brooklyn Royal Giants from 1921 to 1938. In 1921, his rookie season, Beckwith became the first player to ever hit a ball over the laundry roof at Crosley Field in Cincinnati. Reportedly, in 1927, the year that Babe Ruth hit 60 home runs, Beckwith hit 72, but most of them were in barnstorming and exhibition competition. About a dozen were reportedly in league competition. He won two league home run titles and finished second twice behind Oscar Charleston, and hit 71 career home runs in league play. According to some accounts, Beckwith hit his longest home run at Griffith Stadium in Washington when he blasted a shot that hit a sign on the left field fence that was 460 feet from home plate and 40 feet high. "John Beckwith hit the ball farther than anybody," said Negro Leaguer Holsey "Scrip" Lee in an interview with author John Holway on file at the National Baseball Hall of Fame. Lee pitched against Beckwith in the old Eastern Colored League in the late 1920s: "For power he was the hardest hitter I ever saw. I'd say Babe Ruth and Beckwith were about equal in power. Beckwith weighed about 230 pounds and used a 38-inch bat, but it looked like a toothpick when he swung it." Beckwith also hit for a high average. He batted .398 in his rookie season and hit as high as .494 in league play in 1930, albeit in only 19 games. His career league average was .348, and he is believed to have batted .320 in games against white major league players. Remarkably, this 230-pound slugger did this while playing shortstop for much of his career, though he also played the outfield, caught, and managed. He had a volatile temper and punched umpires, opponents, teammates, and owners alike.

Bejerano, Agustin

Agustin Bejerano was an outfielder for the Cuban Stars in 1928.

Bell, Charles

Charles Bell pitched for the Homestead Grays in 1948.

Bell, Clifford

Clifford Bell was a pitcher for the Kansas City Monarchs, Cleveland Cubs, Memphis Red Sox, and Nashville Elite Giants from 1921 to 1932. Bell played on the Negro League World Series championship 1924 Kansas City Monarchs team, with such Negro League greats as Newt Allen, Joe Rogan, and Dobie Moore.

Bell, Frank

Frank Bell was an outfielder for the Ansonia Cuban Giants, Philadelphia Giants, Cuban Giants, and New York Gorhams from 1888 to 1891.

Bell, Fred

Fred Bell was a left-handed pitcher for the St. Louis Stars, Birmingham Black Barons, Detroit Stars, Harrisburg Giants, Toledo Tigers, and Washington Potomacs from 1922 to 1927.

Bell, Herman

Herman Bell was a catcher for the Birmingham Black Barons from 1945 to 1949.

Bell, James (Steel Arm)

James Bell was a catcher for the Montgomery Grey Sox and Indianapolis Crawfords from 1933 to 1940.

Bell, James Thomas (Cool Papa)

b. 1903, d. 1991

James Bell was a pitcher early in his career but later a great center fielder for most of his tenure in Negro League baseball, a career that lasted from 1922 to 1946 with the St. Louis Stars, Pittsburgh Crawfords, Kansas City Monarchs, Detroit Wolves, Memphis Red Sox, Chicago American Giants, and Homestead Grays. Bell,

James "Cool Papa" Bell. (NATIONAL BASEBALL HALL OF FAME LIBRARY, COOPERSTOWN, N.Y.)

who was inducted into the National Baseball Hall of Fame in 1974, is most famous for his legendary speed, which was often described in colorful stories, such as the one that his teammate and roommate, Satchel Paige, would often tell: "He could turn out the light switch and be in bed before the room got dark," Paige said. He is also supposed to have once hit a ball up the middle and was hit by the ball as he slid into second base. Although those stories may be more lore than truth, the fact is that the 5-foot-11, 150-pound Bell, born in Starksville, Mississippi, was probably the fastest man in Negro League baseball—and likely in all of baseball in his time. In an interview with author John Holway on file at the National Baseball Hall of Fame, Negro Leaguer Newt Allen talked about Bell's speed: "The man ran so fast, we woke up to the fact that if he's on first and a man singles, he's gone and we'd have to throw to home plate. Many times he would score on a hit-and-run play when the ball was hit to right field."

After playing with black semipro teams known as the Compton Hill Cubs, along with four of his brothers, and East St. Louis Cubs, both in St. Louis, Bell broke into Negro League baseball at age 19 in 1922 with the St. Louis Stars, where he got his nickname for his ability to play under pressure—in particular, one time when he struck out the great Oscar Charleston. He was a perennial player in the EAST-WEST ALL-STAR GAME, and in the 1935 game scored from second on an infield hit by Boojum Wilson in a spectacular play. In another Holway interview, catcher Larry Brown, who was behind the plate for that play, described it: "I threw him [Bell] out at second, but Sammy T. Hughes dropped the ball, and that left him safe on second," Brown said. "The next man [Boojum Wilson] hit the ball over Bill Foster, the pitcher's, head, and Bill jumped at it. Willie Wells at shortstop went over to scoop the ball up and scoop it to Sammy T. at second. When Sammy looked up, Cool Papa was already coming home. That sucker slid by me. I dove and missed him and he beat us 1-0."

Bell remained one of the best hitters in Negro League baseball in his later years, batting .373 in 1945 and .412 the following year, according to some reports. Bell was offered a chance to play major league baseball with the St. Louis Browns in 1951 when he was nearly 48 years old but turned it down. Browns owner Bill Veeck said of Bell: "Defensively, he was the equal of Tris Speaker, Joe DiMaggio, or Willie Mays." Though he declined the Browns' invitation and talked about how happy he was the day that Jackie Robinson played for the Brooklyn Dodgers, it hurt Bell, like so many other Negro League players, that he didn't get a chance to play major league baseball in his prime: "They used to say, 'If we find a good black player, we'll sign him.' They was lying," Bell is quoted as saying.

James "Cool Papa" Bell, shown sliding in safely in a Negro League game, is considered by many to be the fastest player in the history of Negro League baseball. Bell said he stole 175 bases in 200 games one year, and one report had him running around the bases in 12 seconds. His speed allowed him to leg out many hits and turn others into extra bases, and he is believed to have batted .342 during a Negro League career with the St. Louis Stars, Pittsburgh Crawfords, Kansas City Monarchs, Detroit Wolves, Memphis Red Sox, Chicago American Giants, and Homestead Grays from 1922 to 1946.   (NATIONAL BASEBALL HALL OF FAME LIBRARY, COOPERSTOWN, N.Y./Robert Peterson)

Bell said he stole 175 bases in 200 games one year, and one report had him running around the bases in 12 seconds. His speed allowed him to leg out many hits, turn others into extra bases, and protect his pitchers by running down balls in center field. In Robert Peterson's book, *Only the Ball Was White*, shortstop Bill Yancey recalled his own experiences watching Bell in the 1920s: "I haven't seen anybody yet could run with Cool. When I was on the Lincoln Giants, we played in a little park in New York called the Catholic Protectory in the Bronx. That was our regular home field. Judy Johnson had been telling me about this guy that came to Cuba every winter, and Judy told me, if this guy hits the ball on two hops on the ground you won't be able to throw him out from shortstop. Now I could throw, and I said nobody can outrun a baseball. So the first time Cool Papa came to New York with the St. Louis Stars, he hit a ball into right field. Chino Smith was out there, and he could field a ball, and if you made a wide turn at first base he could throw you out trying to hustle back. I went out to get the throw, and when I looked up Cool Papa was slowing up going into third. And I said to myself, 'That sonofagun didn't touch second.' Next time up he hit another one about the same place. Now, nobody got a three-base hit in that little park, I don't care where they hit the ball. And I watched this guy run. Well, he came across second base and it looked like his feet weren't touching the ground."

Records show that Bell is believed to have batted .342 during his Negro League career. Negro Leaguer Dave Barnhill, in an interview with author John Holway on file at the National Baseball Hall of Fame, told a story about Bell's clubhouse antics: "Cool Papa Bell sitting in front of his locker," Barnhill said. "Take off one piece of clothing at a time, sit there a while. Take off another, sit there a while. Pull his pants off. Put his leg up on a stool, start wrapping it with gauze. When he got through, he looked like a mummy. 'The old man don't feel too good tonight,' he'd moan. Then he'd get out on the ball field, hit one of those high hoppers, and he's gone. Then he'd be standing on first, with this big old grin on his face."

In St. Louis, Bell played with such Negro League greats as Willie Wells and Mule Suttles. In Pittsburgh, he played with Paige, Charleston, and Josh Gibson. Bell also played winter baseball in Cuba, where he reportedly hit .316 lifetime, and in Mexico, where he batted 367 during his career there. Brown talked about how Bell dazzled Cubans with his speed and about his own experiences trying to stop the crafty base runner: "Cool Papa Bell was a trickeration base stealer," Brown said. "You know what I saw Cool Papa Bell do in Cuba? He was on second base and the man hit the ball to center field. He could run so fast he could back up all the way to home. He wouldn't have to run."

In 1937, Bell was one of a group of Negro players recruited by Dominican Republic dictator Rafael Trujillo to play one season in his country as part of the baseball political battle going on there. He also played on a team in the California Winter League in 1935—the only black team in the league that year, playing on a squad known as the Philadelphia Giants, along with Suttles and Turkey Stearnes. He also played for a barnstorming team that competed against white teams, with players like Dizzy Dean and Bob Lemon, and batted 392 against them. He spent his final years in baseball managing a team owned by Tom Baird and J. L. Wilkinson, co-owners of the Kansas City Monarchs, sometimes known as the Kansas City Stars, the Travelers, or actually billed as the Monarchs when they traveled outside the Midwest. Some of the players he managed on that team included Ernie Banks and Elston Howard. Bell was not only respected by his peers as a player but was also beloved for his warm personality. "Cool Papa Bell was an exciting baseball player and a lovely man," said John "Buck" O'Neil, former first baseman and manager of the Kansas City Monarchs. Pitcher Wilmer Fields called Bell a "role model" for teammates. "Cool was a modest man," Fields said. "I really enjoyed being around him. He was that kind of person."

Bell retired and worked for the city of St. Louis as a watchman and janitor until retiring in 1973. A month after his wife, Clara, passed away in 1991, Bell suffered a heart attack in February and died a week later.

Bell, Julian
d. 1992

Julian Bell was a pitcher for the Birmingham Black Barons, Detroit Stars, Memphis Red Sox, and Louisville White Sox from 1923 to 1931.

Bell, William

William Bell was a pitcher for the Philadelphia Giants from 1902 to 1904. He won one game against the Cuban X Giants in a Negro baseball East-West series in 1903, which was won by the Giants, five games to two. Bell also played the outfield.

Bell, William, Jr. (Lefty)

William Bell, Jr., was the son of Negro League pitcher William Bell, Sr., and, like his father, was also a pitcher, playing for the Kansas City Monarchs and Birmingham Black Barons from 1949 to 1954.

Bell, William, Sr.

William Bell, Sr., was a pitcher for the Kansas City Monarchs, New York Black Yankees, Homestead Grays, Newark Eagles, Newark Dodgers, Pittsburgh Crawfords, and Detroit Wolves from 1923 to 1948.

Benjamin, Jerry

Jerry Benjamin was an outfielder for the Detroit Stars, Memphis Red Sox, Homestead Grays, Birmingham Black Barons, New York Cubans, and Toledo Crawfords from 1932 to 1948. Records show that he batted .305 for Homestead in 1944 in 42 games and .329 in 43 games in 1945.

Bennett, Arthur

Arthur Bennett was an outfielder for the Kansas City Monarchs in 1955.

Bennett, Bradford

Bradford Bennett was an outfielder for the St. Louis Stars, New Orleans–St. Louis Stars, New York Black Yankees, and the Boston Blues from 1940 to 1946.

Bennett, Clyde

Clyde Bennett was a second baseman for the Kansas City Monarchs in 1952.

Bennett, Don

Don Bennett was a second baseman for the Cleveland Cubs, Dayton Marcos, Birmingham Black Barons, and Memphis Red Sox in 1926 and from 1930 to 1934.

Bennett, Frank

Frank Bennett managed the Bacharach Giants in 1918.

Bennett, James

James Bennett pitched for the Cincinnati-Indianapolis Clowns and the Indianapolis Clowns from 1945 to 1948.

Bennett, Jerry

Jerry Bennett was a pitcher for the Kansas City Monarchs in 1951.

Bennett, Sam

Sam Bennett was an outfielder and catcher for the St. Louis Stars from 1911 to 1925.

Bennett, Willie

Willie Bennett was a shortstop for the Kansas City Monarchs from 1952 to 1955.

Bennette, George

George Bennette was an outfielder for the Columbus Buckeyes, Memphis Red Sox, Indianapolis ABC's, De-troit Stars, Chicago Giants, and Chicago Union Giants from 1920 to 1936.

Benson, Augusta

Augusta Benson was a pitcher for the Washington Elite Giants and Memphis Red Sox from 1937 to 1940.

Benson, Eugene (Gene)

b. 1918, d. 1999

Eugene Benson was an outfielder for the Bacharach Giants, Brooklyn Royal Giants, Philadelphia Stars, Newark Eagles, and Pittsburgh Crawfords from 1933 to 1948. The 5-foot-8, 180-pound Benson was believed to have hit .300 throughout his career, and over a three-year period, 1944–46, records show he batted .327, .370 and .345. In

Like many black ballplayers, Eugene Benson played on a barnstorming team during the off season; one of the members of that team was Jackie Robinson before he went on to play for the Brooklyn Dodgers. Benson became close to Robinson and was his adviser. Benson was an outstanding player as well, an outfielder for the Bacharach Giants, Brooklyn Royal Giants, Philadelphia Stars, Newark Eagles, and Pittsburgh Crawfords from 1933 to 1948, batting more than 300 throughout his career and .327, .370, and .345 during a three-year period from 1944 to 1946.
(NATIONAL BASEBALL HALL OF FAME LIBRARY, COOPERSTOWN, N.Y.)

1947, Benson played on a black barnstorming team, along with Hilton Smith, Buck O'Neil, and Hank Thompson, playing against a white team led by Bob Feller that included Stan Musial and Mickey Vernon. Also playing on that team, before he would join the Brooklyn Dodgers in that historic 1947 season, was Jackie Robinson. Benson grew close to Robinson and became his adviser at the request of his manager on that team, Felton Snow: "Robinson was a very hard fellow to get along with in this respect—he had a temper and he'd fight at the drop of a hat," Benson told *The Sporting News* in 1998. "So we weren't such great friends at first. One night in the room, he got loud with me and I told him, 'Jackie, I'm trying to help you. You can't just fight every time you get mad. But if you want to fight me, you should know I'm a better boxer than my stepfather and he fought the champion Tiger Flowers to a draw. I'm telling you this because you're getting mad, and I want you to know you're going to get hurt as much as, and possibly more than, you're going to hurt me. I have no fear of you, Jackie. I'm here only to help you make the major leagues.' That took his nerve away. He calmed down and from then on we became the best of friends. Two or three days before he died, I went to see him and he looked awful. He said, 'Ben I'd have never made it if it weren't for you.'"

Benson retired from playing in 1948 and worked for the transportation department of the Philadelphia Board of Education until retiring in 1979. He remained involved in local youth baseball in Philadelphia as vice president of the Seven Philadelphia Stars Baseball Foundation and advised the Jackie Robinson Baseball League in the city. In an interview with the *Philadelphia Daily News* several years before he died, Benson said he still loved the game, even though he was denied a chance to play major league baseball: "A few guys who played in the Negro Leagues are very bitter," he said. "They don't want to hear nothing about baseball. I never was bitter then, and I'm glad I didn't grow bitter. You only hurt yourself."

Benson, Herbert

Herbert Benson was a first baseman for the Indianapolis Clowns in 1952.

Benswanger, Bill

Bill Benswanger was the owner of the Pittsburgh Pirates from 1932 to 1946 and, according to several accounts, flirted with the notion of breaking the color line in major league baseball. There were reports that Benswanger tried to sign black players several times, although they were disputed by the Negro press. As early as 1933, Benswanger wrote the *Pittsburgh Courier:* "I have seen any number of [Negro League] games and was impressed with the ability of some of the players. Such men as Charleston, Gibson, Washington, Scales, and Cannady and others appeared to be of the highest in calibre and worthy of the highest in baseball." There were reports that Benswanger tried to sign Josh Gibson and Buck Leonard in 1939 and also reportedly was going to set up tryouts in 1943 for Roy Campanella and Dave Barnhill but never carried through on the promise.

Benvenuti, Julius

Julius Benvenuti was an officer with the Chicago American Giants in 1939.

Bergin, Jim

Jim Bergin played first base for the Kansas City Monarchs in 1949.

Berkeley, Randolph

Randolph Berkeley was a catcher for the Hilldale baseball club in 1919.

Bernal, Pablo

Pablo Bernal was a pitcher for the New York Cuban Stars in 1941.

Bernard, Pablo

Pablo Bernard was a shortstop and second baseman for the Louisville Buckeyes and Cleveland Buckeyes in 1949 and 1950.

Berry, John

John Berry was a pitcher and first baseman for the St. Louis Stars and Kansas City Monarchs from 1935 to 1937.

Berry, Mike (Red)

Mike Berry was a pitcher for the Baltimore Elite Giants and Kansas City Monarchs from 1943 to 1947.

Betts, Russell

Russell Betts was a pitcher for the Kansas City Monarchs in 1950 and 1951.

Beverly, Charles

Charles Beverly was a pitcher for the Cleveland Browns, Birmingham Black Barons, Kansas City Monarchs,

Cleveland Stars, Pittsburgh Crawfords, New Orleans Crescent Stars, and Newark Eagles from 1924 to 1936.

Beverly, William (Fireball)
William Beverly was a pitcher for the New Orleans Eagles, Houston Eagles, Birmingham Black Barons, and Chicago American Giants from 1950 to 1955.

Bibbs, Rainey
Rainey Bibbs was an infielder for the Detroit Stars, Cincinnati Tigers, Chicago American Giants, Kansas City Monarchs, Indianapolis Crawfords, Chicago American Giants, and Cleveland Buckeyes from 1933 to 1944.

Bigby, Charles
Charles Bigby was an outfielder for the Indianapolis Clowns in 1953.

Big Gorhams
The Big Gorhams were a New York black team organized in 1891, primarily with former players from the York, Pennsylvania, Monarchs. They were considered the greatest black baseball team of the 19th century, according to former players and Negro League historian Sol White. Some of the players on the Big Gorhams included White, Arthur Thomas, Clarence Williams, George Stovey, and Frank Grant. They lasted just one season, disbanding in 1892.

Billings, William
William Billings was a pitcher for the Nashville Elite Giants in 1921.

Billingsley, John
John Billingsley was a catcher for the Memphis Red Sox in 1950.

Billingsley, Sam
Sam Billingsley pitched for the Memphis Red Sox in 1950.

Binder, James
James Binder was a second baseman and third baseman for the Memphis Red Sox, Indianapolis ABC's, Detroit Stars, Homestead Grays, and Washington Elite Giants from 1930 to 1936.

Binga, William
William Binga was a catcher and third baseman for the Page Fence Giants, Philadelphia Giants, Chicago Union Giants, Columbia Giants, St. Paul Gophers, and Kansas City Giants from 1895 to 1910. In his book, *History of Colored Baseball,* Negro League player and historian Sol White called Binga one of "the hardest hitters in the colored profession."

Bingham, Bingo
Bingo Bingham was an outfielder for the West Baden Sprudels, Chicago Giants, and Chicago Union Giants from 1910 to 1921. He also later coached for the Gilkerson Union Giants, a midwestern barnstorming team.

Biot, Charlie
Charlie Biot was an outfielder for Newark Eagles, New York Black Yankees, and Baltimore Elite Giants from 1939 to 1941.

Birmingham Black Barons
The Birmingham Black Barons, out of Birmingham, Alabama, were organized in 1920 as a member of the Negro Southern League. They joined the NEGRO NATIONAL LEAGUE in 1922 but later returned to the Southern League in 1931. The Barons joined the NEGRO AMERICAN LEAGUE in 1937 and would go on to be one of the premier franchises in the league. They won three Negro American League pennants but lost to the Homestead Grays in the Negro League World Series all three times. In 1948, the Black Barons played in the last Negro League World Series. The Negro National League would fold after the series. Winfield "Gus" Welch managed Birmingham in 1943 and 1944, and one of his star players was Lorenzo "Piper" Davis, who would later manage the 1948 squad. Some of the players on the Black Barons roster in the 1940s included Artie Wilson, Ed Steele, Bill Powell, Alfred Saylor, and a young outfielder named Willie Mays. The team continued playing until 1960 when it was one of the final four teams remaining in the Negro American League. First baseman James Canady played for the Black Barons. "We've gotten as high as 12,000 to 15,000 fans for a game in Birmingham," Canady said. "We never did get lower than 5,000 to 6,000."

Birmingham Giants
The Birmingham Giants played in Birmingham, Alabama, in the early 1900s. They were managed by Charles I. (C. I.) Taylor, considered to be among the finest managers in the history of black baseball, from

1904 until 1910, when the franchise moved to West Baden, Indianapolis, changing their name to the West Baden Sprudels.

Bissant, John L.

John Bissant was an infielder, outfielder, and pitcher for the Cole's American Giants, Shreveport Acme Giants, Chicago American Giants, Birmingham Black Barons, and Chicago Brown Bombers from 1934 to 1947. In a 1996 interview with *Sports Collectors Digest*, Bissant talked about the highlight of his Negro League career: "I guess the highlight of my career was the year they [the Chicago American Giants] made me captain of the team," he said. "We had quite a few young players coming in then, and to be a leader on that ball club was quite an honor." Bissant was a solid hitter, with his best season in 1945, when he hit .304. "In Chicago I think I was quite a hit with the fans because I hit real well," he said. "I was a decent hitter, and very fast." He also played running back in a semipro football league in Chicago during the winter.

Bissant, Robert
b. 1915, d. 2000

Robert Bissant was an infielder for the Zulu Cannibal Giants and Miami Ethiopian Clowns (two clowning teams), and the Nashville Cubs and New Orleans Black Pelicans from 1935 to 1940.

Black, Daniel
b. 1926, d. 1998

Daniel Black was a pitcher for the Cleveland Elites and Dayton Marcos in 1926.

Black, Howard

Howard Black was an infielder for the Brooklyn Cuban Giants in 1928.

Black, Joe
b. 1924, d. 2002

Joe Black, who would go on to become a star pitcher for the Brooklyn Dodgers, began his career as a pitcher in the Negro Leagues for Baltimore in 1943. He pitched for the Elite Giants until 1950, and from 1948 to 1950, Black posted a 29-15 record in 57 appearances. In an interview conducted by author John Holway on file at the National Baseball Hall of Fame, Negro Leaguer Pee Wee Butts, a teammate of Black's in Baltimore, talked about Black's powerful arm: "He was a pretty hard thrower," Butts said. "At first he wanted to be a shortstop, but [manager George] Scales said we had too many shortstops. He [Black] didn't have too good a curve, but he had a slider. He was big and strong. I think that's what kept him so long in the big leagues."

Black was signed by the Brooklyn Dodgers in 1950, and after pitching for the Dodgers' minor league clubs in Montreal and St. Paul, the 6-foot-2, 210-pound Black was called up to Brooklyn in 1952, and would pitch primarily as a reliever for the Dodgers, Cincinnati Reds, and Washington Senators until retiring after the 1957 season, posting a record of 30-12 with a 3.91 ERA. He was named National League Rookie of the Year at the age of 28 in 1952, when he won 15 games and saved 15. He started the first game of the 1952 World Series, defeating the New York Yankees 4-2—the only World Series win by a black pitcher until Mudcat Grant won for the Minnesota Twins in 1965. He lost the seventh game of that series, also by a 4-2 score. He would never have that kind of success again, running into control problems, and in 1954 was sent down to the Dodgers' Class AAA Montreal team after an 11.57 ERA in five appearances. Black also pitched in Venezuela and Cuba in winter ball.

Born in Plainfield, New Jersey, Black went on to work for the Greyhound corporation after baseball and became a vice president. Black also has served as the vice president of the Baseball Assistance Team, which helps players from prepension times who are in need.

In a 1993 interview with *Sports Collectors Digest*, Black talked about his frustration at not getting an earlier shot at major league baseball: "Like the other Negro League players, I was a little disappointed that I wasn't able to show what I could do during my younger years," he said. "When I was 19 and 20 years old, I could throw a ball consistently at about 98 or 99 miles per hour. I was really hurt and shocked that I couldn't play organized baseball because of my skin pigmentation, particularly because that was contrary to everything I had read about, studied and made to believe in school," said Black, who received an undergraduate degree from Morgan State University in Baltimore.

Blackburn, Hugh

Hugh Blackburn was a pitcher for the Kansas City Monarchs in 1920.

Blackman, Clifford

Clifford Blackman was a pitcher for the Birmingham Black Barons, Chicago American Giants, Memphis Red Sox, Indianapolis ABC's, New York Cubans, Homestead Grays, and New Orleans–St. Louis Stars from 1937 to 1941.

Blackman, Henry

Henry Blackman was a third baseman for the San Antonio Black Aces, Indianapolis ABC's, and Baltimore Black Sox from 1918 to 1924.

Blackman, Warren

Warren Blackman was a pitcher for the Memphis Red Sox in 1939.

Blackwell, Charles

Charles Blackwell was an outfielder for the West Baden Sprudels, Bowser's ABC's, Jewell's ABC's, St. Louis Giants, St. Louis Stars, Birmingham Black Barons, Indianapolis ABC's, Detroit Stars, and Nashville Elite Giants from 1915 to 1929. He was one of the top hitters in the NEGRO NATIONAL LEAGUE, leading the league in batting in 1921 while with the St. Louis Giants, with an average of .448. He also reportedly led the league with 13 doubles that season and hit 9 home runs, second to teammate Oscar Charleston who led the league with 14 home runs.

Blair, Garnett

Garnett Blair was a pitcher for the Homestead Grays from 1945 to 1948.

Blair, Lonnie

d. 1992

Lonnie Blair was a pitcher and second baseman for the Homestead Grays in 1949 and 1950.

Blake, Frank

Frank Blake was a pitcher for the New York Black Yankees, Baltimore Black Sox, and New York Cubans from 1932 to 1935.

Blake, William

William Blake was a pitcher for the Philadelphia Stars in 1952.

Blakely, Bert

Bert Blakely was a catcher for the Cincinnati Tigers in 1934.

Blakemore, William

William Blakemore was a catcher for the Kansas City Monarchs, Memphis Red Sox, and Louisville Black Colonels in 1954.

Blanchard, Chester

Chester Blanchard played shortstop for the Dayton Marcos from 1926 to 1933.

Blanco, Carlos

Carlos Blanco was a first baseman for the New York Cubans from 1938 to 1941.

Blanco, Herberto

Herberto Blanco played second base for the Cuban Stars and New York Cubans in 1941 and 1942.

Blattner, Frank

Frank Blattner was a first baseman and outfielder for the Kansas City Monarchs in 1921.

Blavis, Fox

Fox Blavis was a third baseman for the Homestead Grays in 1936.

Bleach, Larry

Larry Bleach was a second baseman for the Detroit Stars in 1937.

Blount, John (Tenny)

John Blount was the owner of the Detroit Stars in the late 1910s. He was also part of Rube Foster's NEGRO NATIONAL LEAGUE in the 1920s, serving as his vice president. But Blount, who was the king of the Detroit numbers racket, got into a dispute with Foster in 1924, and the following year he was out of black baseball.

Blueitt, Virgil

Virgil Blueitt was an umpire in the NEGRO AMERICAN LEAGUE from 1937 to 1949.

Blukoi, Frank

Frank Blukoi played second base for the Kansas City Monarchs in 1920.

Boada, Lucas

Lucas Boada pitched for the Cuban Stars from 1921 to 1924.

Bobo, Willie

Willie Bobo was a first baseman for the ALL NATIONS team, Kansas City Monarchs, St. Louis Stars, and Nashville Elite Giants from 1923 to 1930.

Boggs, George

George Boggs was a pitcher and outfielder for the Detroit Stars, Dayton Marcos, Milwaukee Bears, Cleveland Tigers, Cleveland Tate Stars, and Baltimore Black Sox from 1922 to 1934.

Bolden, Ed

Ed Bolden was a U.S. Post Office worker in Philadelphia who founded the Eastern Colored League and owned two of the greatest black baseball teams that played in the Philadelphia area—the Hilldale Daisies and Philadelphia Stars. Negro ballplayer and historian Sol White named Bolden as one of the greatest figures in black baseball in what he called the modern era, the early 20th century. White wrote in his *History of Colored Baseball* that Bolden "has worked from the ground up in the business end of the game. He has given people in his home city some of the greatest baseball playing of all times, and a home ground for his players." Bolden became owner of the Hilldale club, which played in a suburb of Philadelphia known as Darby, in 1916, while it was still a semipro club, playing at Hilldale Park. He turned it into a pro Negro baseball team the following season and won the Negro National League championship in 1921. Two years later, he formed the EASTERN COLORED LEAGUE, starting a war with NEGRO NATIONAL LEAGUE operator Rube Foster. His Hilldale team won three straight Eastern Colored League titles from 1923 to 1925—posting a record of 32-17 in 1923, a 47-22 mark the following year, and 52-15 in 1925, when they won the Negro World Series, defeating the Kansas City Monarchs. They dropped to third place in the league in 1926, with a 34-24 record, and suffered a losing season in 1927, with a 36-45 mark. The stress was too much for Bolden, and he suffered a nervous breakdown in 1927. The league collapsed the following year. Bolden created the American Negro League in 1929. Hilldale finished fourth with a 39-35 record, but the league folded before the 1930 season began. Hilldale continued to play as an independent club until 1931. Among the great players who were on Hilldale teams were Judy Johnson, Biz Mackey, and Otto Briggs.

In 1933, Bolden, with white booking agent Eddie Gottlieb as his financial backer, started the Philadelphia Stars. They won the Negro National League pennant in their first year in the league in 1934. Bolden ran the team until his death in 1950, and the club disbanded two years later. Some of the Negro baseball greats who played for Bolden on the Stars included Gene Benson, Bill Cash, and Barney Brown.

Bolden, James

James Bolden pitched for the Birmingham Black Barons in 1952.

Bolden, Otto

Otto Bolden was a catcher for the Leland Giants in 1910.

Bond, Timothy

Timothy Bond was an infielder for the Pittsburgh Crawfords, Newark Dodgers, and Chicago American Giants from 1935 to 1940.

Bonner, Robert

Robert Bonner was a first baseman, second baseman, and catcher for the Cleveland Tate Stars, St. Louis Stars, Toledo Stars, and Cleveland Elites from 1922 to 1926.

Booker, Billy

Billy Booker was a second baseman for the Acme Colored Giants of Celeron, New York, in 1898.

Booker, Dan

Dan Booker pitched for the Kansas City Royal Giants in 1909.

Booker, James (Pete)

James Booker was a catcher for the Philadelphia Giants, Leland Giants, Lincoln Giants, Chicago American Giants, Chicago Giants, Brooklyn Royal Giants, and Indianapolis ABC's from 1903 to 1919. Booker was on the 1905 Philadelphia Giants squad, considered one of the best of its time, along with Charles Grant, Sol White, and Grant Johnson.

Booker, Rich

Rich Booker was an outfielder for the Kansas City Monarchs in 1952.

Boone, Alonzo

Alonzo Boone was a pitcher and manager for the Cleveland Cubs, Birmingham Black Barons, Chicago American Giants, Cincinnati Buckeyes, Cleveland Buckeyes, and Louisville Buckeyes from 1931 to 1950.

Boone, Charles (Lefty)

Charles Boone was a pitcher for the New Orleans–St. Louis Stars, Harrisburg–St. Louis Stars, and Pittsburgh Crawfords from 1941 to 1945.

Boone, Oscar

Oscar Boone was a catcher and first baseman for the Indianapolis ABC's and Chicago American Giants from 1939 to 1942.

Boone, Robert

Robert Boone was an umpire in the NEGRO NATIONAL LEAGUE from 1923 to 1928 who returned for one appearance in a game in 1946.

Boone, Steve (Lefty)

Steve Boone pitched for the Memphis Red Sox in 1940.

Bostic, Joseph
d. 1988

Joseph Bostic was the editor of the *People's Voice*, a black newspaper in New York, and an outspoken critic of major league baseball's color barrier. Bostic reportedly forced Brooklyn Dodgers' general manager Branch Rickey to give tryouts to Terris McDuffie, a pitcher with the Philadelphia Stars, and Dave Thomas, an outfielder with the New York Cubans in March 1945—seven months before Rickey signed Jackie Robinson. According to Jules Tygiel, author of *Jackie Robinson and His Legacy*, Bostic, along with Baltimore African-American sportswriter Sam Lacy, were the most influential black sportswriters in promoting the movement to integrate the major leagues: "Bostic, a resident of Brooklyn and a writer for a Harlem-based weekly, represented a persistent thorn in the side of the three New York teams by leading delegations to their offices and challenging them in his columns. At Christmas in 1943, Bostic wrote a seasonal letter entitled, 'No Room at the Yankee Inn,' criticizing the club for its failure to employ blacks. The column garnered Bostic a writing award and banishment from the Yankees press box."

Bostock, Lyman, Sr.

Lyman Bostock, Sr., was a first baseman and outfielder for the Birmingham Black Barons, Chicago American Giants, and New York Cubans from 1940 to 1949.

Boston, Bob

Bob Boston was a third baseman for the Homestead Grays in 1948.

Bowe, Randolph

Randolph Bowe was a left-handed pitcher for the Kansas City Monarchs and Chicago American Giants in 1939 and 1940.

Bowen, Chuck

Chuck Bowen was an outfielder for the Indianapolis Athletics and Chicago Brown Bombers from 1937 to 1943.

Bower, Julius

Julius Bower was a catcher for the New York Black Yankees from 1947 to 1950.

Bowers, Chuck

Chuck Bowers was a shortstop and pitcher for the Baltimore Black Sox in 1926.

Bowman, Bill

Bill Bowman was a pitcher for the Cuban X Giants in 1903 and 1904.

Bowman, Emmett (Scotty)

Emmett Bowman was a third baseman, shortstop, catcher, outfielder, and pitcher for the Keystone Giants, Philadelphia Giants, Leland Giants, Brooklyn Royal Giants, and Chicago American Giants from 1903 to 1916. In his book, *History of Colored Baseball*, former Negro League player and historian Sol White said that Bowman, who was a member of the great Philadelphia Giants 1905 club, was one of a group of black pitchers in his time who were good enough to pitch in the major leagues.

Bowser, Thomas

Thomas Bowser was a white businessman who purchased the Indianapolis ABC's from Ran Butler in 1912. Two years later, Bowser would hire Charles I. Taylor, who had founded the Birmingham Giants in 1908, as manager and also gave him part ownership in the team.

Boyd, Benjamin
b. 1858

Benjamin Boyd began playing ball in 1874 as a third baseman for a Manhattan team, and second baseman for the Mutuals of Washington the following season. He also played for the Philadelphia Orions in 1885 and the following year signed to play outfield for the Original Cuban Giants. Boyd was part of the 1887 team that defeated major league players in Cincinnati and Indianapolis. In 1890, Boyd played with the Colored Monarchs of York, Pennsylvania, in the Eastern Interstate League. Records show that in three minor league seasons, Boyd batted .266 with 46 stolen bases and 121 hits in 102 games.

Boyd, Fred

Fred Boyd was an outfielder with the Cleveland Tate Stars in 1922.

Boyd, James

James Boyd pitched for the Newark Eagles in 1946.

Boyd, Lincoln

Lincoln Boyd was an outfielder for the Louisville Buckeyes and Indianapolis Clowns from 1949 to 1952. The 6-foot-3, 190-pound Boyd spent several years in the minor leagues before retiring after the 1956 season.

Boyd, Ollie

Ollie Boyd was a pitcher and outfielder of the Kansas City Monarchs in 1933.

Boyd, Robert

Robert Boyd was a first baseman with the Memphis Red Sox from 1947 to 1950.

Boyd, Willie

Willie Boyd was a pitcher for the Homestead Grays and Newark Eagles in 1943 and 1946.

Bracken, Herb

Herb Bracken was a pitcher for the Cleveland Buckeyes, Brooklyn Brown Dodgers, and New Orleans–St. Louis Stars in 1940 and from 1946 to 1947.

Bradford, Charles

Charles Bradford was a pitcher and outfielder for the Pittsburgh Giants and Lincoln Giants from 1910 to 1926.

Bradford, William

William Bradford was an outfielder for the Indianapolis ABC's, St. Louis Stars, Memphis Red Sox, and Birmingham Black Barons from 1938 to 1942.

Bradley, Frank

Frank Bradley was a pitcher for the Cincinnati Tigers and the Kansas City Monarchs from 1937 to 1943.

Bradley, Phil

Phil Bradley was a catcher and first baseman for the Brooklyn Royal Giants, Famous Cuban Giants, Philadelphia Giants, Mohawk Giants Lincoln Giants, Pittsburgh Colored Stars, and Pittsburgh Stars of Buffalo from 1909 to 1927.

Brady, John

John Brady was an outfielder for the Pittsburgh Keystones in 1887.

Bragaña, Ramon (El Profesor)
b. 1909

Ramon Bragaña was a Cuban pitching star who pitched for the Cuban Stars, Stars of Cuba, New York Cubans, and Cleveland Buckeyes from 1928 to 1937 and again in 1947. The 5-foot-11, 180-pound pitcher had his best years in the Mexican League with the Vera Cruz club, recruited to play in the new league in 1937. Until he retired in 1955, Bragaña posted a record of 211-162 in Mexican League play. Like many other Negro League players, Bragaña also played in the Dominican League in 1937, playing for the opponent of dictator Rafael Trujillo in that country's political struggle that was played out on the baseball field that year. He also played ball in Venezuela in the 1930s.

Bragg, Eugene

Eugene Bragg was a catcher for the Chicago American Giants in 1925.

Bragg, Jesse

Jesse Bragg was an infielder for the Cuban Giants, Genuine Cuban Giants, Mohawk Giants, Brooklyn Royal Giants, Philadelphia Giants, Lincoln Giants, and Pennsylvania Red Caps from 1908 to 1919.

Braithwaite, Alonzo

Alonzo Braithwaite was a second baseman for the Philadelphia Stars in 1948.

Braithwaite, Archie

Archie Braithwaite was an outfielder for the Newark Eagles and Philadelphia Stars from 1944 to 1947. Records show he batted .282 with Newark in 1944 and .277 for Philadelphia in 1947.

Branahan, J. Finis (Slim)

J. Finis Branahan was a pitcher for the Harrisburg Giants, Cleveland Tate Stars, Cleveland Elites, Detroit Stars, St. Louis Stars, Cleveland Hornets, Lincoln Giants, Indianapolis ABC's, and Toledo Tigers from 1922 to 1927 and again in 1931.

Branham, Luther
b. 1924

Luther Branham was a 5-foot-7, 150-pound infielder who played for the Birmingham Black Barons in 1949 and Chicago in 1950.

Brannigan, George

George Brannigan pitched for the Cleveland Elites and Cleveland Hornets in 1926 and 1927.

Brantley, Ollie

Ollie Brantley was a pitcher for the Memphis Red Sox from 1950 to 1953. Born in Lexon, Arizona, Brantley went on to play in the minor leagues until 1969. His best season was 1957, when he posted a 22-15 mark in 42 games with the Eugene club. In his last season in Orlando, the 6-foot-3, 180-pound Brantley compiled a 5-1 record.

Bray, James

James Bray was a catcher and outfielder for the Chicago Giants and Chicago American Giants from 1922 to 1930.

Brazelton, John Clarkson

John Brazelton was a catcher for the Chicago American Giants and Chicago Giants from 1915 to 1917.

Breakers Hotel

The Breakers Hotel was a luxurious oceanfront resort in Palm Beach, Florida, that fielded teams in a hotel league composed of black players, primarily from New York, who spent their winters there and worked at the hotel in the early 1900s. Some of the Negro League greats who played for the Breakers included Rube Foster, Pete Hill, Dick Redding, John Henry Lloyd, and Judy Johnson.

Breda, Bill

Bill Breda was an outfielder for the Kansas City Monarchs and Birmingham Black Barons from 1950 to 1954.

Bremmer, Eugene (Gene)
b. 1915

Gene Bremmer was a right-handed pitcher for the Cincinnati Tigers, Memphis Red Sox, New Orleans Crescent Stars, Cincinnati Buckeyes, Kansas City Monarchs, and Cleveland Buckeyes from 1932 to 1948. Born in New Orleans, Bremmer played most of his career for the Cleveland Buckeyes from 1942 to 1948. He had a career record of 46-26, with his best season in 1944, when he posted a 10-6 mark in 20 games with a 2.87 ERA. The 5-foot-8, 160-pound Bremmer also pitched for Monterrey in the Mexican League and finished his career in 1949 in minor league ball with Cedar Rapids.

Brewer, Chet
b. 1907, d. 1990

The Kansas City Monarchs had one of the most impressive staffs in Negro League baseball in the 1920s with Satchel Paige and Bullet Joe Rogan, and Chet Brewer fit right in with that rotation. Brewer began his career with the Monarchs in 1925 and posted a 12-1 record in 1926, his second season with the Monarchs, with eight complete games. Three years later, he led the league with a 16-3 record and during one stretch pitched 31 consecutive scoreless innings. One of his most legendary performances came in a 1-0 loss in 12 innings against Smokey Joe Williams and the Homestead Grays in 1930, known as the "Battle of the Butchered Balls," featuring both pitchers throwing their best "emory balls" and spit balls. Williams struck out 27, while the 6-foot-4, 180-pound Brewer struck out 19 and, at one point, 10 batters in a row. He won a total of 30 games that season, league and nonleague, and 33 in 1934, including 16 straight victories. He also threw two no-hitters in the Mexican League in 1939 and pitched for San Pedro de Macoris, an opponent of the team put together by Dominican Republic dictator Rafael Trujillo in 1937 as part of the baseball war that went on that year in the Dominican.

In addition to the Monarchs, Brewer pitched for the Chicago American Giants, Washington Pilots, Cleveland Buckeyes, Tennessee Rats, Philadelphia Stars, and New York Cubans, ending his career in 1948. Sammy Haynes, a catcher for the Atlanta Black Crackers and Kansas City Monarchs, said Brewer was among the best pitchers he ever faced in the Negro Leagues: "Chet was a great pitcher," Haynes said. "He had a good fast ball, a great curve ball and, above all, great control. I'd have to rank Chet up there with Bullet Joe Rogan and Hilton Smith."

Brewer once aptly described the life of a Negro League ballplayer: "We just eat and ride and play. That was the size of it. It wasn't easy street." Brewer would go on to become a Pittsburgh Pirates scout from 1957 to 1974, where he signed such major league players as pitcher Dock Ellis, and also worked for the Major League Scouting Bureau. But he remained frustrated over being denied a chance to play major league baseball and expressed that frustration in blunt terms once to a reporter when he brought up Pete Gray, the one-armed outfielder who played for the St. Louis Browns during World War II when major league rosters were depleted because of the war: "How do you think I felt when I saw a one-armed outfielder?" Brewer said. He would also go on to organize a winter semipro team called the Kansas City Royals, which played against major league players and included a player named Jackie Robinson. Brewer also organized neighborhood teams in South Central Los Angeles for young players and helped develop such future major league stars as Eddie Murray and Reggie Smith.

Brewer, Luther

Luther Brewer was a first baseman and outfielder for the Chicago Giants from 1918 to 1921.

Brewer, Sherwood

Sherwood Brewer was an infielder for the Indianapolis Clowns, Detroit Stars, and Kansas City Monarchs from 1949 to 1955. In 1950, he batted .298 with 18 doubles and 11 stolen bases in 81 games. Brewer, born in Clarksdale, Mississippi, also spent two seasons in the minor leagues with the San Angelo club.

Brewster, Sam

Sam Brewster was an outfielder for the Cleveland Buckeyes in 1950.

Bridgeforth, William

William Bridgeforth was an officer with the Baltimore Elite Giants and Birmingham Black Barons from 1950 to 1953.

Bridges, John

John Bridges pitched for the Memphis Red Sox in 1954.

Bridges, Marshall

b. 1931, d. 1990

Marshall Bridges was a pitcher for the Memphis Red Sox from 1951 to 1954.

Briggery, Bo

Bo Briggery played shortstop for the Atlanta Black Crackers in 1932.

Briggs, Otto

Otto Briggs was an outfielder and manager for the Dayton Marcos, West Baden Sprudels, the Hilldale baseball club, Atlantic City Bacharach Giants, Santop's Broncos, and Quaker Giants from 1914 to 1934. Briggs battled leadoff for the Hilldale baseball team starting in 1917 and played on the 1923 EASTERN COLORED LEAGUE championship team.

Bright, John M.

John Bright was a white businessman who took over the ownership of the Cuban Giants along with black manager S. K. Govern after owner Walter Cook died in 1887. Bright later moved the team to York, Pennsylvania, calling them the Monarchs of York and played in the Interstate League. In 1890, he changed the club back to the Giants and into a barnstorming squad. In 1891, Bright placed his team in the Connecticut State League, where it represented Ansonia, Connecticut, until the league disbanded after several months of play. In the late 1890s, when another team emerged called the Cuban X Giants—which defeated Bright's Cuban Giants in a best two-out-of-three playoff in 1897—Bright changed his team's name to the "Genuine" Cuban Giants.

Former Negro League great and historian Sol White listed Bright as one of the greatest figures in early Negro baseball history in a 1927 *Pittsburgh Courier* article. The article described Bright, known as "J. M. Bright," as "extremely selfish in his financial dealings and naturally shrewd. Whether under salary or working on the co-plan (cooperative plan, in which expenses were deducted from gross receipts and the balance distributed evenly among players), his players were always called upon to help him in an idea. When it came to money, J. M. was full of ideas. He held up many games after his team reached a ground with a packed stand and demanded a boost in his stipulated guarantee. He generally got what he asked for."

Brighton Athletic Club

The Brighton Athletic Club was a team that played in the early 1900s at the Brighton Oval, a park in Brooklyn, New York, that hosted a number of Negro baseball teams, including the Cuban Giants.

Brisker, William

William Brisker was a general manager of the Cleveland Buckeyes in 1950.

Britt, Charles

Charles Britt was a third baseman for the Homestead Grays from 1927 to 1933.

Britt, George

George Britt was a pitcher and infielder for the Dayton Marcos, Baltimore Black Sox, Columbus Buckeyes,

Hilldale baseball club, Homestead Grays, Columbus Elite Giants, Newark Dodgers, Jacksonville Red Caps, Washington Black Senators, Chicago American Giants, Brooklyn Royal Giants, Cleveland Buckeyes, Harrisburg Giants, and Detroit Wolves from 1920 to 1944. He was one of three Homestead pitchers to defeat the rival Pittsburgh Crawfords in a special four-game series in 1932. Britt also played in several East-West Negro baseball All-Star Games.

Britton, George

George Britton was a catcher for the Cleveland Buckeyes in 1943 and 1944. Records show that he batted .229 in 1944.

Britton, John

John Britton was a third baseman for the St. Louis Stars, Cincinnati Clowns, Birmingham Black Barons, and Indianapolis Clowns from 1940 to 1950.

Broadnax, Maceo

Maceo Broadnax pitched for the Kansas City Monarchs in 1932.

Broadnax, Willie

Willie Broadnax pitched for the Memphis Red Sox in 1929.

Broads of Savannah

The Broads of Savannah were a black baseball team out of Savannah, Georgia, that played in the Southern League in the late 1880s.

Brooklyn Atlantics

Brooklyn Atlantics were a black baseball team that played in the 1880s in Brooklyn, New York.

Brooklyn Brown Dodgers

The Brooklyn Brown Dodgers were a team that played in Brooklyn, New York, in the brief United States League, a black baseball league started by Brooklyn Dodgers general manager Branch Rickey in 1945. The Dodgers played at Ebbets Field, and former Negro League great Oscar Charleston managed the team. He enlisted the help of the former owner of the Pittsburgh Crawfords, Gus Greenlee, who had been forced out of the NEGRO NATIONAL LEAGUE and was looking to get back into the

game. At the time, the belief was that Rickey was using the league as a cover for his scouts to look for talent for the major league team and was positioning himself to have better access to black players when the color line would finally be broken in major league baseball. However, the player whom Rickey would finally sign for that historic moment—Jackie Robinson—never played in the league, going from the Kansas City Monarchs right to the Dodgers' minor league team in Montreal in 1946. Rickey pulled out of the UNITED STATES LEAGUE midway through the 1945 season, and the league folded by the end of the 1946 season.

Brooklyn Cuban Giants

The Brooklyn Cuban Giants were one of the many versions of the Cuban Giants squads that played Negro League baseball, playing in Brooklyn, New York, in the late 1920s.

Brooklyn Dodgers

Though not a Negro League team, this major league franchise has an important place in the history of black baseball. It was the first team to sign a black player to play major league baseball, crossing the color line when they signed Jackie Robinson, who broke in with the Dodgers in 1947 after spending a season playing with their minor league team in Montreal. But although the Dodgers' move, engineered by general manager Branch Rickey after pressure mounted from the black community and other supporters of the effort to integrate major league baseball—including the black and the communist press—was hailed as a long-overdue progressive decision, it was the death knell for black baseball. The Dodgers followed up the Robinson signing quickly by making deals with two other Negro League players, catcher Roy Campanella and pitcher Don Newcombe, and other major league clubs followed suit, thereby starting the exodus of the black players from the Negro Leagues, although that exodus was held back by what was believed to be quotas by teams, limiting the number of black players they would carry on a roster. The Dodgers were perhaps the right team for this kind of social change, a blue-collar team in one of the most ethnically mixed places in America—Brooklyn, New York.

The franchise began play in the borough in 1890, playing in Washington Park and after that played in Eastern Park from 1891 to 1897 and back to a new Washington Park from 1898 to 1912. In 1913, the owner, Charles Ebbets, moved into Ebbets Field, and would become an integral part of the borough's identity, from the hapless "Bums" of the 1930s to the National League championship teams led by Robinson, Campanella, and others in the late 1940s and early 1950s.

Another move by the Dodgers would have social implications—this one by owner Walter O'Malley, who moved the franchise to Los Angeles after the 1957 season, marking the beginning of major league baseball out west and contributing to the demise of Brooklyn as an economically healthy borough. The Dodgers, however, would be extremely successful under O'Malley in Los Angeles in their own privately owned ballpark, Chavez Ravine, often leading the National League in attendance, setting a club record in 1982 with 3.6 million fans coming to the ballpark.

Brooklyn Eagles

The Brooklyn Eagles were a black baseball team in Brooklyn, New York, started by Abe Manley, a numbers racketeer and nightclub owner, in 1935. Playing at Ebbets Field, the team included such players as pitcher Leon Day, pitcher-catcher Ted "Double Duty" Radcliffe, and outfielder Ted Page. The team would move to Newark the following year, merging with the Newark Dodgers, becoming the Newark Eagles.

Brooklyn Monitors

The Brooklyn Monitors were a black baseball team that played in the 1860s in Brooklyn, New York.

Brooklyn Remsens

The Brooklyn Remsens were a black baseball team that played in the 1880s in Brooklyn, New York.

Brooklyn Royal Giants

The Brooklyn Royal Giants were a team started in 1905 by John W. Connor, a black owner of the Royal Cafe and Palm Garden in Brooklyn, New York, who would be named by Negro League great and historian Sol White as one of the most important figures in early black baseball in a 1927 *Philadelphia Tribune* article. The Royal Giants, first managed by Grant "Home Run" Johnson, played in those early days at the Brighton Oval field, and later, in a dispute with Negro League boss Nat Strong over field fees, played at the Harlem Oval briefly until Strong gained control of the team and used it as a barnstorming team for a period of time. The franchise existed in one form or another until 1940, including part of Ed Bolden's EASTERN COLORED LEAGUE from 1923 to 1927. Some of the players who were on Royal Giant squads included pitchers Dick Redding and Joe Williams, shortstop John Henry Lloyd, catcher Louis Santop, and third baseman Oliver Marcelle.

Brooklyn Uniques

The Brooklyn Uniques were a black baseball team that played in the 1860s in Brooklyn, New York.

Brooks, Alex

Alex Brooks was an outfielder for the New York Black Yankees and Brooklyn Royal Giants from 1938 to 1940.

Brooks, Ameal

Ameal Brooks was a catcher for the Chicago American Giants, Cleveland Cubs, Cole's American Giants, Columbus Blue Birds, Cincinnati Clowns, New York Black Yankees, Cuban Stars, and New York Cubans from 1929 to 1945.

Brooks, Beattie

Beattie Brooks was an infielder and catcher for the Lincoln Giants, Brooklyn Royal Giants, and Philadelphia Giants from 1918 to 1921.

Brooks, Charles

Charles Brooks was a pitcher and second baseman for the St. Louis Giants and St. Louis Stars from 1919 to 1924.

Brooks, Chester

Chester Brooks was an outfielder for the Brooklyn Royal Giants from 1918 to 1933.

Brooks, Edward

Edward Brooks was a second baseman with the Houston Eagles in 1949 and 1950.

Brooks, Gus

Gus Brooks was an outfielder for the Page Fence Giants in 1895. Brooks collapsed during a game and died shortly after.

Brooks, Irvin

Irvin Brooks pitched for the Brooklyn Royal Giants from 1919 to 1924.

Brooks, Jess

Jess Brooks was a third baseman and outfielder with the Cleveland Red Sox and Kansas City Monarchs in 1936 and 1937. Brooks resurfaced briefly in 1946 with a tryout for the Tacoma minor league club in the Western International League, the same year Jackie Robinson played with Montreal in the International League.

Brooks, John

John Brooks pitched for the Memphis Red Sox in 1942.

Brooks, Moxie

Moxie Brooks was a pitcher for the Toledo Cubs in 1945.

Brooks, Wallace

Wallace Brooks pitched for the Baltimore Elite Giants in 1948.

Broome, J. B.

J. B. Broome was an outfielder for the New York Black Yankees in 1947.

Brown, Arnold

Arnold Brown was an infielder for the Atlantic City Bacharach Giants, Harrisburg Giants, and Hilldale baseball club from 1920 to 1922.

Brown, Barney

Barney Brown was a pitcher for the Cuban Stars, Philadelphia Stars, and New York Black Yankees from 1931 to 1949. Brown also spent the next two seasons in the Mexican League and played on the 1941 Vera Cruz championship team that was considered by some to be one of the greatest teams in the history of Mexican League baseball. Brown had a 16-5 record on that squad, which included Josh Gibson and Ray Dandridge. Brown returned to play for the Philadelphia Stars from 1942 to 1949 but then spent the next five years back in the Mexican League before retiring after the 1954 season. He also played a number of seasons of winter baseball in Cuba and Puerto Rico. Incomplete records show that his best season in Negro League baseball may have been 1946, when he posted an 8-4 record in 12 starts with Philadelphia.

Brown, Ben

Ben Brown was a pitcher for the Genuine Cuban Giants in 1900.

Brown, Benny

Benny Brown was a shortstop for the Newark Browns and Bacharach Giants in 1931 and 1932.

Brown, Carl

Carl Brown was a pitcher and shortstop for the Indianapolis Clowns, Detroit Stars, and Philadelphia Stars from 1951 to 1954.

Brown, Charles

Charles Brown was a pitcher for the Cuban Giants and Pittsburgh Keystones in 1886 and 1887.

Brown, Curtis

Curtis Brown played first base for the New York Black Yankees in 1947.

Brown, David
b. 1896–unknown

David Brown was a left-handed pitcher for the Chicago American Giants and New York Lincoln Giants from 1918 to 1925. From 1920 to 1923, he helped pitch Chicago to three championships. In 1921, his record was 11-3 with five shutouts, and he had a career mark of 41-18 over four years, from records available. Unfortunately, Brown's career ran afoul of the law. Rube Foster, the owner of the Chicago American Giants, put up a $20,000 bond to get him out of jail on robbery charges, and his career ended in 1925 when he disappeared after being a suspect in a New York murder.

Brown, Earl

Earl Brown was a pitcher and outfielder for the Lincoln Giants from 1923 to 1926.

Brown, Edward

Edward Brown was a pitcher for the Detroit Stars, Indianapolis ABC's, Chicago American Giants, and Chicago Giants from 1920 to 1923.

Brown, Elias (Country)

Elias Brown played second base, third base, and the outfield for the Brooklyn Royal Giants, Washington Potomacs, Atlantic City Bacharach Giants, and Hilldale baseball club from 1918 to 1933.

Brown, Elmore (Scrappy)

Elmore Brown was a shortstop for the Lincoln Giants, Washington Red Caps, Brooklyn Royal Giants, Hilldale baseball club, and Baltimore Black Sox from 1918 to 1932.

Brown, George

George Brown pitched on the Pythians of Philadelphia baseball club in 1867.

Brown, George

George Brown was an outfielder and third baseman for the St. Louis Giants, Indianapolis ABC's, Detroit Stars, Dayton Marcos, Columbus Buckeyes, and West Baden Sprudels from 1910 to 1928.

Brown, George

George Brown was an outfielder for the Chicago American Giants, Cleveland Buckeyes, Baltimore Elite Giants, and Philadelphia Stars from 1939 to 1945.

Brown, Hap

Hap Brown was a pitcher for the Cleveland Browns in 1924.

Brown, Hugh

Hugh Brown played for the Mutuals of Philadelphia baseball club in 1867.

Brown, Isaac (Ike)

b. 1942

Isaac Brown played shortstop, third base, and the outfield on the final Kansas City Monarchs team in 1960. Born in Memphis, Tennessee, Brown would spend the next nine seasons in the minor leagues before coming up with the Detroit Tigers in 1970. In six major league seasons, the 6-foot-1, 200-pound Brown batted .256 with 20 home runs and 65 RBIs in 280 games.

Brown, James

James Brown was a catcher, first baseman, and manager for the Montgomery Grey Sox, Louisville Black Caps, Cleveland Cubs, and Chicago American Giants from 1918 to 1942.

Brown, James

James Brown was a shortstop for the Monroe Monarchs in 1934.

Brown, Jerome

Jerome Brown was an infielder for the Houston Eagles in 1949.

Brown, Jesse

Jesse Brown was an infielder for the Lincoln Giants in 1890.

Brown, Jesse

Jesse Brown was a pitcher for the New York Black Yankees, Newark Eagles, and Baltimore Elite Giants from 1939 to 1941.

Brown, John W.

b. 1918, d. 1999

John Brown was a pitcher for the St. Louis Giants, Cleveland Buckeyes, and Houston Eagles from 1942 to 1949.

Brown, Joseph

Joseph Brown was the manager of the Washington Capital Citys in 1887.

Brown, Julius

Julius Brown was a pitcher for the Indianapolis Clowns in 1946.

Brown, Larry

b. 1905, d. 1972

Like Lou Gehrig and Cal Ripken, Jr., Larry Brown was nicknamed the "Iron Man" because he rarely took a day off from catching. Sometimes he would be behind the plate for three games in one day. According to reports, Brown caught 230 games in 1934. Brown played and later managed for the Pittsburgh Keystones, Birmingham Black Barons, Memphis Red Sox, Indianapolis ABC's, Chicago American Giants, Detroit Stars, Cole's American Giants, Philadelphia Stars, and New York Black Yankees from 1919 to 1949. Born in Pratt City, Alabama, Brown was considered one of the top defensive catchers in Negro League baseball history, with a strong arm and a habit of leaving his mask on when catching pop fly balls. He played in six Negro League All-Star games, and in 1928, he led the Red Sox in hits and doubles and batted .294. Some records show that his best years offensively were 1932 to 1935 in Chicago when he is believed to have batted .368 during that period, including a .429 average in 1935, when he also managed the team. He also batted .345 in exhibition competition against major league players. According to one report, Brown, while playing winter baseball in Cuba in 1924, was asked by major league players there if he would stay in Cuba, learn Spanish, and be willing to try to pass himself off as Cuban to be signed by the Detroit Tigers. Brown declined, fearful of being

Larry Brown was nicknamed the "Iron Man" because he rarely took a day off catching. One year he reportedly caught 230 games behind the plate. Brown was considered one of the best defensive catchers in Negro League history, and from 1919 to 1949 he played and managed for the Pittsburgh Keystones, Birmingham Black Barons, Memphis Red Sox, Indianapolis ABC's, Chicago American Giants, Detroit Stars, Cole's American Giants, Philadelphia Stars, and New York Black Yankees. (NATIONAL BASEBALL HALL OF FAME LIBRARY, COOPERSTOWN, N.Y.)

exposed by Tigers manager Ty Cobb, a well-known racist. According to newspaper accounts, Brown "did not trust Cobb's reaction and possible explosion once he had learned Brown was indeed a Negro. Criticized by this decision, and accused by his mates of having 'cold feet,' Brown stood his ground. He would have no part of a possible head-on with Cobb, a demoniac competitor." Brown was hardly afraid, though. Negro League baseball was very tough, and in an interview with author John Holway on file at the National Baseball Hall of Fame, Brown talked about how rough it was: "It was nothing else but a rough league then," he said. "We used to go in the clubhouse and a guy would be in there sharpening his spikes with a file. A catcher had to protect himself if he got the ball. If the runner and the ball connect [at home] at the same time, you have to look out for yourself to the extent of not being cut up." In a newspaper interview, Brown talked about the

many pitchers he had seen—Satchel Paige, Willie Foster, Bill Holland, Verdel Mathis—and how they all could have pitched in the major leagues: "Lots of pitchers I knew might have been up there," Brown said. "I could have been up there all right." One of his fellow Negro League catchers, Ted "Double Duty" Radcliffe, in the Holway interview, said that Brown was one of the all-time great Negro League catchers: "I'd have to rate Larry Brown and Frank Duncan as the two best catchers that came up with me," he said.

In the Holway interview, Brown talked about some of the skills he used behind the plate: "I could throw pretty good," he said. "The crowd used to roar to see me throw the men out. And I used to boot the ball and let it roll about eight or ten feet and go get it and throw the guy out. Make him run. We had a play I used to pull off when I was with the Chicago American Giants in 1935. A man on third and a man on second, I'd call for a pitchout and throw that to the man at third. That was just a decoy. The next pitch the second baseman is way over toward the bag as the runner is playing off. I throw the ball back to third and he takes it and shoots it to second and gets the guy off second. I used a whole lot of trickeration."

Brown, Lawrence
Lawrence Brown was a pitcher for the Claybrook Tigers and Memphis Red Sox from 1931 to 1940.

Brown, Maywood
Maywood Brown was a pitcher for the Indianapolis ABC's from 1921 to 1925.

Brown, Oliver
Oliver Brown was the business manager for the Newark Browns in 1932.

Brown, Oscar
Oscar Brown was a catcher for the Indianapolis ABC's and Baltimore Elite Giants in 1939.

Brown, Ossie
Ossie Brown was a pitcher for Cole's American Giants, Indianapolis Athletics, Indianapolis ABC's, and St. Louis Stars from 1935 to 1939.

Brown, Ralph
Ralph Brown was a second baseman and shortstop for the Birmingham Black Barons in 1954.

Brown, Ray

Ray Brown was a catcher for the Chicago American Giants and Brooklyn Royal Giants in 1939 and 1940.

Brown, Raymond

b. 1908

Raymond Brown was a knuckleball pitcher and outfielder for the Indianapolis ABC's, Dayton Marcos, Homestead Grays, and Detroit Wolves from 1930 to 1948. Brown, a knuckleballer, pitched a one-hit shutout for the Grays in that series. Born in Ashland Grove, Ohio, Brown married the daughter of the owner of the Homestead Grays, Cum Posey. He also played winter ball in Cuba and one season, 1936–1937, posted a remarkable 20-3 record. The 6-foot, 200-pound Brown also played in Mexico from 1946 to 1949 and the Canadian Provincial League from 1950 to 1953.

Brown, Richard

Richard Brown was an infielder for the Chicago American Giants in 1952.

Brown, Ronnie

Ronnie Brown was a first baseman for the Harrisburg–St. Louis Stars in 1943.

Brown, Roy

Roy Brown was a pitcher and outfielder for the Cleveland Cubs and Kansas City Monarchs from 1928 to 1932.

Brown, Theo

Theo Brown played third base for the Chicago Union Giants in 1911.

Raymond Brown, shown here crossing the plate after homering for the Homestead Grays, was better known for his pitching skills as a knuckleball hurler who also played the outfield for the Grays, Indianapolis ABC's, Dayton Marcos, and Detroit Wolves from 1930 to 1948. Brown married the daughter of Grays owner Cum Posey. (NATIONAL BASEBALL HALL OF FAME LIBRARY, COOPERSTOWN, N.Y.)

Brown, Tom

Tom Brown was a shortstop and third baseman for the Memphis Red Sox and Cleveland Buckeyes from 1939 to 1950.

Brown, Tom

Tom Brown pitched for the Chicago American Giants in 1919.

Brown, Tute

Tute Brown was a third baseman for the Washington Red Caps in 1918.

Brown, Ulysses (Buster)

Ulysses Brown was a catcher and outfielder for the Newark Eagles, Jacksonville Red Caps, and Cincinnati Buckeyes from 1937 to 1942.

Brown, Walter S.

Walter Brown was a former Pittsburgh correspondent for the *Cleveland Gazette*, a black weekly newspaper, and was the founder and president of the League of Colored Baseball Clubs in 1887, which consisted of the Resolutes of Boston, Keystones of Pittsburgh, Lord Baltimore of Baltimore, Gorhams of New York, Washingtonians of Washington, Pythians of Philadelphia, and Louisvilles of Louisville.

Brown, Willard (Home Run)

b. 1911, d. 1996

Willard Brown was a shortstop and outfielder for the Monroe Monarchs and Kansas City Monarchs from 1934 to 1952. Born in Shreveport, Louisiana, Brown was considered one of Negro League baseball's best hitters, batting more than .350 eight times, including .374 in 1948 and .420 in 1951. "I could hit the ball where ever it was pitched," Brown said in a newspaper interview. "I could hit a ball that was over my head over the fence, you know, bad pitches. I didn't care where it was."

A seven-time all-star, the 5-foot-11, 200-pound Brown, who began at shortstop but later moved to the outfield, was given the nickname "Home Run" by catcher and slugging great Josh Gibson, reportedly because Brown would outslug Gibson when the two played each other. Negro Leaguer Buck O'Neil said Brown was "the most talented player I ever saw. He was so natural that people thought he was lazy. He'd steal second standing up. He was a great talent."

Brown played in the 1942 and 1946 Negro Baseball World Series for the Monarchs and batted .304 with 14

A shortstop and outfielder, Willard Brown played for the Monroe Monarchs and Kansas City Monarchs from 1934 to 1952 and was considered one of the Negro League baseball's best hitters, batting more than .350 eight times over his career. He could hit for power as well and got the nickname "Home Run" from slugging great Josh Gibson because Brown would outslug Gibson when they played against each other.
(NATIONAL BASEBALL HALL OF FAME LIBRARY, COOPERSTOWN, N.Y.)

RBIs in the two series. He said he was scouted in 1943 by baseball scout Tom Greenwade: "I thought he was kidding when he asked me how I would like to play in the major leagues," Brown recalled in a newspaper interview. "I said, 'Okay, I'll be ready.' Then I went in the service." Brown did have a major league opportunity. In 1947, at the age of 34, he signed with the St. Louis Browns and played 21 games. He was the first black to hit a home run in the American League but batted just .179 and quit, going back to play for the Monarchs. One of his Browns teammates, Billy Hitchcock, remembered that home run, which came off the great Hal Newhouser, a two-time Most Valuable Player, in a 1997 newspaper interview: "Willard hit it deep into the center field bleachers," Hitchcock said. "Hal turned six different colors. He was so mad he stared at Willard all around the bases." In a 1985 newspaper interview, Brown recalled the reaction he received from one teammate in particular—Jeff Heath, whose bat Brown had used to hit the home run—after he hit it: "After I came back to the dugout, he [Heath] was going to see I wasn't going to use it no more. Everyone was shaking my hand. He took the bat and hit it on the dugout. Tore it all to pieces in splinters in the dugout. Now that's something. Now if you're a ballplayer and you play with me, and I use your bat and hit a home run, you get mad at me. . . . I wasn't use to that kind of baseball." Hitchcock said Brown was not a disciplined hitter, but Brown said he quit St. Louis for two reasons—the racism he encountered and because the Browns were simply not as good as the Monarchs: "The Browns couldn't beat the Monarchs no kind of way, only if we was all asleep."

Brown also played winter ball in Puerto Rico. Nicknamed "El Hombre," Brown batted .432 with 27 home runs and 86 RBIs in winter ball. He played minor league baseball with Dallas, Houston, and Austin in the Texas League from 1953 to 1956, slugging 95 home runs and driving in 437 runs in four seasons. He would return to the Monarchs for one year in 1958 before retiring.

Brown, William

William Brown was an assistant manager with the Chicago Leland Giants in 1906.

Brown, William

William Brown was an infielder for the Birmingham Black Barons in 1952.

Brown, William H.

William H. Brown played first base for the Pittsburgh Keystones in 1887.

Brown, William M.

William M. Brown was an officer with the Montgomery Grey Sox in 1931 and 1932.

Brown, Willie

Willie Brown was an infielder for the Indianapolis Clowns from 1953 to 1955.

Browns of Cincinnati

The Browns of Cincinnati were a black team that played in the League of Colored Base Ball Players in the Ohio city in 1887.

Bruce, Clarence
b. 1926, d. 1987

Clarence Bruce played second base for the Homestead Grays in 1947 and 1948. The 6-foot, 175-pound Bruce, born in Pittsburgh, Pennsylvania, batted .246 for the Grays in 1946.

Bruce, Lloyd

Lloyd Bruce pitched for the Chicago American Giants in 1940.

Bruton, Charles

Charles Bruton was a pitcher, infielder, and outfielder for the Philadelphia Stars, Cleveland Bears, New Orleans–St. Louis Stars, Cleveland Buckeyes, New York Black Yankees, and Birmingham Black Barons from 1928 to 1941 and again in 1950.

Bryant, Allen (Lefty)
d. 1992

Allen Bryant was a pitcher for the All Nations team, Kansas City Monarchs, and Memphis Red Sox from 1938 to 1946.

Bryant, Eddie

Eddie Bryant was a second baseman for the Pennsylvania Red Caps and Harrisburg Giants from 1925 to 1928.

Bryant, Johnnie

Johnnie Bryant was an outfielder for the Cleveland Buckeyes in 1950.

Buchanan, Chester

Chester Buchanan pitched for the Brooklyn Royal Giants, Atlantic City Bacharach Giants, and Philadelphia Stars from 1931 to 1943.

Buchanan, Floyd

Floyd Buchanan was a pitcher for the Hilldale baseball club in 1914.

Buckner, Harry

Harry Buckner was a pitcher and outfielder for the Columbia Giants, Chicago Unions, Cuban X Giants, Philadelphia Giants, Brooklyn Royal Giants, Lincoln Giants, Quaker Giants, Mohawk Giants, Louisville White Sox, and Chicago Giants from 1896 to 1918. He also played for the Royal Poinciana Hotel team in Florida during the winter months.

Buckner, Joseph

Joseph Buckner was a pitcher for the Boston Blues and Chicago American Giants in 1946.

Buffalo Giants

The Buffalo Giants were a black baseball team that played in Buffalo, New York, in the 1920s.

Bugle Field

Bugle Field was the one of the fields in Baltimore where the Baltimore Elite Giants played from 1938 to 1950.

Bumpus, Earl

Earl Bumpus was a pitcher and outfielder for the Kansas City Monarchs, Birmingham Black Barons, and Chicago American Giants from 1944 to 1948.

Bunch, Sidney

Sidney Bunch was an outfielder for the Birmingham Black Barons in 1954.

Burbage, Knowlington O. (O. K. and Buddy)
b. 1905, d. 1989

Knowlington Burbage was an outfielder for the Pittsburgh Crawfords, Hilldale baseball club, Homestead Grays, Baltimore Black Sox, Bacharach Giants, Washington Black Senators, Newark Dodgers, Philadelphia Stars, Brooklyn Royal Giants, and New York Black Yankees from 1928 to 1951. The 5-foot-6 Burbage didn't let his size hold him back, according to Negro Leaguer Bill Cash: "He was a good outfielder who could run real fast," Cash said in a 1989 newspaper interview. "He was small in stature but made up for that in his hustle." In another interview eight years earlier, Burbage recalled the demands that were placed on players when he played for Baltimore in 1929: "In those days we only carried 12 to 15 players," Burbage said. "If one car broke down on the way to a road game, utility men and pitchers would have to fill the vacant positions. Our players were more versatile then." Burbage said at the peak of his Negro League baseball career, he was making $400 a month. He also estimated that his batting average was around .333.

Burch, Alonzo

Alonzo Burch was a pitcher for the Chicago Union Giants and Indianapolis ABC's from 1914 to 1916.

Burch, John Walter

John Burch was a catcher and infielder for the Bacharach Giants, Cleveland Bears, Baltimore Black Sox, New Orleans Stars, St. Louis Stars, Cleveland Buckeyes, Cincinnati Buckeyes, Washington Pilots, Chicago American Giants, and Newark Dodgers from 1931 to 1946.

Burgee, Louis

Louis Burgee was a pitcher and second baseman for the Hilldale baseball club in 1910 and 1917.

Burgin, Ralph

Ralph Burgin was an infielder and outfielder for the Hilldale baseball club, New York Black Yankees, Philadelphia Stars, and Brooklyn Royal Giants from 1917 to 1940.

Burgos, Jose
b. 1928

Jose Burgos played shortstop for the Birmingham Black Barons in 1949 and 1950. The 5-foot-7, 160-pound Burgos batted .224 in 84 games in 1949 and .243 in 74 games in 1950. He went on to spend the next three seasons playing minor league baseball.

Burke, Ernest
b. 1924

Ernest Burke was born in Perryville, Maryland, and pitched for the nearby hometown team the Baltimore Elite Giants from 1946 to 1949, posting a 4-1 record in his final year with Baltimore. He went on to play minor league baseball as an outfielder and third baseman for Pough-Kingston in the Western League and St. Jean in the Canadian Province League. In two seasons with St. Jean, the 6-foot-1, 180-pound Burke posted a 15-3 record pitching in 1950, followed by an 8-8 mark the following year. He continued playing minor league baseball until 1956. In an interview, Burke said he played baseball in the U.S. Marines Corps against major league ballplayers when it was suggested he try to play Negro League baseball: "John Rigney of the Chicago White Sox told me that I should contact the Negro Leagues when I got out," Burke said. "I got out in 1946, and played on a local team in Havre de Grace, Maryland. We played a game at Bugle Field in Baltimore, and the Elite Giants saw me play and signed me to a contract. I played with Henry Kimbro, Joe Black, Jim Gilliam and Pee Wee Butts. I held my own. I was a better road pitcher than home pitcher. My biggest thrill came when I beat the Newark Eagles 3-2 in their home park in a game in 1947. They had some big guns, like Larry Doby and Monte Irvin. I threw a fastball, knuckleball, slider and curveball."

Burke, Ping

Ping Burke pitched for the Atlanta Black Crackers in 1937.

Burley, Dan

Dan Burley was a sportswriter for the Associated Negro Press whose work appeared in the black press all around the country, making him one of the most influential reporters covering Negro League baseball.

Burnett, Fred (Tex)

Fred Burnett was a catcher, first baseman, and outfielder who later became a manager for the Indianapolis ABC's, Lincoln Giants, Pittsburgh Keystones, Harrisburg Giants, New York Black Yankees, Baltimore Black Sox, Brooklyn Royal Giants, Homestead Grays, Brooklyn Eagles, Newark Eagles, Bacharach Giants, Pittsburgh Crawfords, Newark Dodgers, and Nashville Cubs from 1921 to 1946. One story about Burnett involves Oscar Charleston, who, according to the John Holway book *Blackball Stars,* seriously injured Burnett at a play at the plate: "Charleston just undressed him, just cut his shin guards off, his uniform, everything," Buck Leonard said. "Burnett was out for about a month."

Burnham, Willie (Bee)

Willie Burnham was a pitcher for the Monroe Monarchs from 1930 to 1934.

Burns, Cloyce

Cloyce Burns pitched for the Boston Blues in 1946.

Burns, Peter

Peter Burns was a catcher and outfielder for the Page Fence Giants, Chicago Unions, Columbia Giants, Philadelphia Giants, and Algona Brownies from 1890 to 1902.

Burns, William

William Burns was a pitcher for the Cincinnati-Indianapolis Clowns, Newark Dodgers, Memphis Red Sox, Baltimore Elite Giants, Chicago American Giants, Philadelphia Stars, Atlanta Black Crackers, New York Black Yankees, and Chicago American Giants from 1933 to 1944.

Burrell, George

George Burrell was a pitcher and catcher for the Baltimore Atlantics in 1884 and 1885.

Burris, Samuel

Samuel Burris pitched for the Memphis Red Sox and Birmingham Black Barons in 1939 and 1940.

Burrows, Al

b. 1932

Al Burrows was a pitcher and first baseman for the New York Black Yankees and Indianapolis Clowns from 1954 to 1962. The 6-foot-1, 180-pound Burrows, born in Washington, D.C., posted a 56-16 career mark, with an ERA of 3.00 and a .320 batting average. In an interview, Burrows said he was first offered a job with the Monarchs, but the Yankees offered him more money. "We had good times traveling," he said. "Even then, we couldn't stay in the big hotels, so we stayed in people's homes, and we met a lot of good people along the way."

Burton, Lefty

Lefty Burton was a pitcher for the Pittsburgh Crawfords in 1929 and 1930.

Busby, Maurice

Maurice Busby pitched for the Bacharach Giants and All Cubans team in 1920 and 1921.

Bushwick Park

Bushwick Park was a field in Brooklyn, New York, that hosted Negro League games, including the Lincoln Giants.

Bustamante, Luis

d. 1912

Luis Bustamante was a Cuban ballplayer who played in America for the Cuban Stars and Brooklyn Royal Giants from 1905 to 1911. Bustamante was a slick-fielding shortstop known as "El Anguila," or "The Eel." According to former Negro League player and historian Sol White, Bustamante was the "leading Cuban player, in the estimation of the American public." But he reportedly drank himself to death purposely in 1912, out of frustration over being denied a chance to play major league baseball because of the color of his skin and left the following suicide note: "I'll drink until I become stupified. Thus I will eliminate myself [from baseball] as useless, keeping deep within me the conviction of what I am worth but what they won't let me prove simply because I have had the immense misfortune of being a Negro."

Buster, Herbert

Herbert Buster was an infielder for Chicago American Giants in 1943.

Butler, Benjamin M. (Ben)

Benjamin Butler was the manager of the New York Big Gorhams in 1887.

Butler, Doc

Doc Butler was a catcher for the Memphis Red Sox in 1950.

Butler, Frank

Frank Butler was an outfielder and pitcher for the Chicago Unions in 1894 and 1895.

Butler, Ran

Ran Butler was a white bartender who owned the Indianapolis ABC's from 1908 to 1912.

Butler, Sol

Sol Butler was a pitcher for the Kansas City Monarchs in 1925.

Butts, Harry

Harry Butts was a pitcher for the Indianapolis Clowns from 1949 to 1951. Butts went 8-8 in 1950 and had a 6-1 mark with Indianapolis in 1951. He went on to pitch the next two seasons in the minor leagues.

Butts, Thomas (Pee Wee)

b. 1919, d. 1973

Thomas Butts, at 5-foot-9 and 145 pounds, was considered one of the best shortstops in Negro League baseball during the 1940s. Born in Sparta, Georgia, Butts played for the Indianapolis ABC's, Atlanta Black Crackers, Baltimore Elite Giants, Birmingham Black Barons, and Memphis Red Sox from 1938 to 1954. In 1940, Butts led the NEGRO NATIONAL LEAGUE in hitting with .391 average. One of his teammates with the Elite Giants was future Brooklyn Dodgers second baseman James "Junior" Gilliam. They were a strong double-play combination, and Butts is credited with the development of Gilliam into a major league second baseman. Records show that Butts was a six-time Negro League All-Star and batted .308 in 1944, .309 in 1945, .287 in 1946, and .321 in 1947. Baltimore teammate Roy Campanella said Butts was just as good as two of the great major league shortstops Campanella played with and against: "I'd compare Butts with [Pee Wee] Reese or [Phil] Rizzuto or anyone I've seen in the big leagues," Campanella said. "Butts could do everything. He just didn't get the opportunity to go to the majors."

Butts played with Baltimore through the 1950 season, then played minor league baseball in Winnipeg in 1951. Butts split time during the 1952 season between Birmingham in the NEGRO AMERICAN LEAGUE and minor league baseball in Lincoln, Nebraska. In between minor league stints the next two seasons, Butts would have a brief stay in 1954 with Memphis in the NAL and would finish playing organized baseball in 1955 with Texas City, batting .265 in 28 games.

His manager in Baltimore, Lenny Pearson, in an interview with author John Holway on file at the National Baseball Hall of Fame, said that Butts was heartbroken when Gilliam got the call to the major leagues with the Brooklyn Dodgers and he did not: "It broke Butts up. . . . I thought Butts would make it big. He was a tremendous shortstop and a pesky hitter, sprayed the ball everywhere." In another Holway interview, Butts talked about his missed opportunity: "If I had been 10 years younger, I think I could have made the major leagues," he said. "My two roommates, Roy Campanella and Junior Gilliam, both went to the majors from Baltimore. I was glad to

Thomas "Pee Wee" Butts was considered to be among the slickest shortstops ever to play the game and was just as slick with the bat, leading the Negro National League in hitting with a .391 average in 1940. He was a six-time Negro League All-Star and played from 1938 to 1954 for the Indianapolis ABC's, Atlanta Black Crackers, Baltimore Elite Giants, Birmingham Black Barons, and Memphis Red Sox. (NATIONAL BASEBALL HALL OF FAME LIBRARY, COOPERSTOWN, N.Y.)

see them get the chance, but if the doors had opened a little earlier, I think I'd have done pretty good. I could have been up there, too."

Byas, Richard T. (Subby)
Richard Byas was a catcher, first baseman, and outfielder for the Kansas City Monarchs, Cole's American Giants, Chicago American Giants, Newark Dodgers, and Memphis Red Sox from 1931 to 1941.

Byers, Henry
Henry Byers played second base for the Pittsburgh Keystones in 1887.

Byrd, James F.
James Byrd was an officer with the Hilldale baseball club from 1927 to 1930.

Byrd, Prentice
Prentice Byrd was an officer with the Cleveland Red Sox in 1934.

Byrd, William
b. 1908, d. 1991
William Byrd was a pitcher for Columbus Turfs, Columbus Blue Birds, Cleveland Red Sox, Columbus Elite Giants, Washington Elite Giants, Nashville Elite Giants, and Baltimore Elite Giants from 1932 to 1949. Byrd was one of the last pitchers to use the spitball legally before it was banned. Records show he was 10-6 with 79 strikeouts and 11 complete games. Also, as a switch-hitter, he batted .364 for the Cleveland Red Sox in 1934. Byrd also played winter ball in Puerto Rico.

Caballero, Luis
b. 1927

Luis Caballero played third base for the New York Cubans and Indianapolis Clowns from 1948 and 1950. The 5-foot-8, 160-pound Caballero batted .248 for the Clowns in 1948 and .209 for New York in 1950, records show. He also played in the Mexican League and minor league baseball in 1954 and 1955.

Cabañas, Armando

Armando Cabañas was a second baseman for the Cuban Stars in 1910.

Cabrera, Alfredo

Alfredo Cabrera was a first baseman for the All Cubans in 1905.

Cabrera, Clemente

Clemente Cabrera was a second baseman, third baseman, and outfielder for the New York Cubans from 1938 to 1941.

Cabrera, Lorenzo
b. 1920

Lorenzo Cabrera played first base for the New York Cubans from 1947 to 1950, batting .352 in 1947 and

.377 in 1949. The 6-foot, 200-pound Cabrera, who was born in Cuba, played one season of minor league baseball in 1951 and from there played in the Mexican League until 1956.

Cabrera, Luis

Luis Cabrera was a pitcher for the Indianapolis Clowns in 1948.

Cabrera, Rafael

Rafael Cabrera was a pitcher and outfielder for the Indianapolis Clowns and Birmingham Black Barons from 1944 to 1950.

Cabrera, Villa

Villa Cabrera was an outfielder for the Indianapolis Clowns in 1948.

Cade, Joe

Joe Cade was a pitcher and outfielder for the Bacharach Giants in 1929.

Caffie, Joseph
b. 1931

Joseph Caffie was an outfielder who played one season for the Cleveland Buckeyes in the NEGRO

AMERICAN LEAGUE in 1950, batting .203. The 5-foot-11, 180-pound Caffie, who was born in Ramer, Alabama, went on to play minor league baseball in the Cleveland Indians organization and was called up twice by the Indians, in 1956 and 1957. He played 44 major league games and batted .291 with three home runs and 11 RBIs.

Cain, Marlon (Sugar)

Marlon Cain was a pitcher for the Pittsburgh Crawfords, Brooklyn Royal Giants, and Indianapolis Clowns for the 1938 to 1949.

Calderon, Benito

Benito Calderon was a catcher for the Cuban Stars and Homestead Grays from 1926 to 1928.

Caldwell, Frank

Frank Caldwell was a pitcher for the Cleveland Buckeyes in 1947.

Calgary Black Sox

The Calgary Black Sox were a black baseball team organized by Rube Foster to represent Alberta, Canada, traveling through Wisconsin, Minnesota, North Dakota, and Canada in 1921.

Calhan, Rowland

Rowland Calhan was a pitcher for the Washington Black Senators in 1938.

Calhoun, Jim

Jim Calhoun played second base for the Toledo Tigers in 1923.

Calhoun, Walter (Lefty)

Walter Calhoun was a pitcher for the Birmingham Black Barons, Montgomery Grey Sox, Washington Black Senators, Pittsburgh Crawfords, Indianapolis ABC's, St. Louis Stars, New Orleans–St. Louis Stars, New York Black Yankees, Harrisburg–St. Louis Stars, and Cleveland Buckeyes from 1931 to 1946.

Calhoun, Wesley

Wesley Calhoun was an infielder with the Cleveland Buckeyes in 1950.

California Winter League

The California Winter League was a four-team league, owned and operated by Joe Pirrone and based in Los Angeles in the 1930s. Three of the teams were white, with one team an entry of Negro League players, giving black players the rare chance to compete in a league against white players, many of whom were major league players. The black team, often composed of Kansas City Monarchs, was usually called the Los Angeles Stars or Los Angeles White Sox. The league attracted some of the greatest players in Negro League baseball, such as Satchel Paige and a young infielder named Jackie Robinson.

Callis, Joseph

Joseph Callis was the manager of the Baltimore Lord Baltimores in 1887.

Calvin, Floyd

Floyd Calvin was a journalist who wrote about black baseball for the *Pittsburgh Courier*, a black newspaper in Pittsburgh, Pennsylvania, in the 1920s.

Calvo, Jacinto (Jack)

Jacinto Calvo was an outfielder for the Long Branch, New Jersey, Cubans from 1913 to 1915.

Campanella, Roy (Campy)
b. 1921, d. 1993

Roy Campanella followed Jackie Robinson onto the roster of the Brooklyn Dodgers in the 1948 season, becoming the first black catcher in major league baseball. Before that, he was a Negro League star, playing behind the plate for the Bacharach Giants in 1936 in Philadelphia, where Campanella was born and raised, when he was asked at the age of 15 by Tom Dixon, a catcher for the Bacharach Giants, if he wanted to play for them. Campanella's mother was reluctant to let him but agreed to let her son play on weekends while still going to school. Campanella said Dixon was a mentor, and in his autobiography, *It's Good to Be Alive*, he wrote that Dixon offered him a lesson that always stuck with him: "Let this stick in the bones of your head if nothing else I tell you does. Don't see yourself small. If you start off aiming small, you'll always be small. Aim for the bright lights back there. Aim for the big time and that big money. Reaching never hurt a man, no matter what his color is. Remember, success ain't gonna chase you. You got to go after it. You're still a kid, but you got a good head on your shoulders and you got a way with you behind the plate. You got it, kid."

He had it and went on to become one of the greats in Negro League baseball. Campanella played the following season for the Baltimore Elite Giants and stayed with the team until 1942, where he learned more about catching from another mentor, Negro League great "Biz" Mackey. In his book, Campanella noted how good the 1938 pennant-winning Elite Giant team was. "It was quite a team," he wrote. "I'll always remember that bunch. Jim West was the first baseman. Sammy Hughes was at second, Pee Wee Butts at short, and Felton Snow, who later was to manage the team, was at third. The outfield had Bill Wright in right field, Henry Kimbrough in center and Zollie Wright in left. Eggie Clark shared the catching with me." The squat (5-foot-9, 200-pound) catcher was the driving force behind the Elite Giants teams that defeated the Homestead Grays and Newark Eagles in postseason play. He was named Most Valuable Player in 1941 Negro EAST-WEST ALL-STAR GAME. In his book, Campanella wrote about the challenge of catching pitchers in Negro League baseball. "Anything went in the Negro National League. Spitballs, shine balls, emery balls; pitchers used any and all of them. They nicked and moistened and treated the ball to make it flutter and spin, dip and break. Not only were there no rules against it, there weren't enough spare baseballs around to substitute clean unmarked ones for the damaged ones, like they did in the big leagues. I was never sure what a ball would do once it left the pitcher's hand, even when he threw what I had called." He also described the differences between spring training for major league baseball and training for Negro League ball: "Man, we didn't just sop up sun and orange juice and run laps and play pepper and listen to the theory on the 'pickoff play' those first few days after reaching camp. No sir—regular exhibition games with the hat being passed. And often as not, those old boys were hard as iron and limber as a rubber tube right from the gun. The reason for that was because they'd never stopped playing ball, really, from the season before," referring to nearly all the Negro League players who played winter baseball in Cuba, Puerto Rico, Venezuela, and Mexico. Campanella said at the height of his Negro League career, he was earning about $3,000 a year playing Negro League baseball and another $2,000 playing winter ball in Latin America. After a dispute with owner Tom Wilson, Campanella played in the Mexican League in the second half of the 1942 season and the entire 1943 season. He was also one of several players who were supposedly offered a tryout in 1942 by Pittsburgh Pirates owner William Benswanger in a half-hearted attempt to break the major league baseball color line. Campanella said the letter he received from the Pirates inviting him for a tryout seemed to try to discourage him. "It contained so many buts that I was discouraged even before I had finished reading the letter: 'You must understand that you would have to start at the very bottom . . . you must come

Roy Campanella learned how to be a great major league catcher during his time in Negro League baseball: One of the all-time great Negro League catchers, Biz Mackey, guided Campanella as he got his start with the Baltimore Elite Giants. Campanella was voted the Most Valuable Player in the 1941 Negro League East-West All-Star Game.   (NATIONAL BASEBALL HALL OF FAME LIBRARY, COOPERSTOWN, N.Y.)

up through our minor league farm system in the conventional manner . . . it might take you years to reach the major leagues . . . the pay would be small . . . there is no guarantee that you would ever make it . . . your years of hard work might be for nothing." Campanella still responded to the letter, saying he was ready to try out, but he never heard anything more from the Pirates.

Campanella returned to Baltimore in 1944, leading the league in doubles, and then led the league in RBIs in 1945. Campanella tried to get a tryout with the Philadelphia Phillies in 1945, calling them to ask if they were interested in his service, but he was politely put off. His time would soon come, though, as Campanella was one of five black players signed by Dodgers general manager Branch Rickey in 1946 and played for the club's Class B farm team in Nashua, New Hampshire. His manager there was Walter Alston, who would go on to become Campanella's manager in Brooklyn. He batted .290, led the league in putouts, assists, and errors, and won the MVP award. He also might have been the first black manager in minor league baseball history when, during a July game, Alston was kicked out and handed the lineup card to Campanella to run the team for the remainder of the game.

In 1947, Campanella moved up to Montreal, the Dodgers' International League team, and again was named the MVP, batting .273. He started the 1948 season with the Dodgers—the second black player on the Brooklyn squad behind Jackie Robinson—but general manager Branch Rickey declared he was an outfielder, not a catcher, in an effort to downplay his presence. He went as far as ordering manager Leo Durocher from using Campanella as a catcher, according to the book *Jackie Robinson and His Legacy* by Jules Tygiel. Campanella was sent down on May 15 to the Dodgers' Class AA team in St. Paul. Tygiel wrote that Rickey sent Campanella to St. Paul to make him the first black player in the American Association, over Campanella's protests. "I'm a ballplayer, not a pioneer," Campanella said. "If you want me to play for St. Paul, that's where I'll play. Because it's in my contract. For no other reason." Campanella batted .325 with 39 RBI in 35 games before being called up again to Brooklyn on July 2. It was Campanella's reluctance to be a pioneer that created problems between him and Robinson. According to the John C. Chalberg book, *Rickey and Robinson*, Campanella, who was half-black and half-Italian, was the opposite of Robinson's temperament. "If Robinson was quick out of the batter's box and quick to take offense, Roy Campanella was forever calm and terminally good-natured," Chalberg wrote. "He also had the habit of good-naturedly doing what he could to calm others, Robinson included." However, the book also claims that their personality differences created tension between the two players. "To Roy, a liberated Jackie seemed to go out of his way to seek trouble. To Jackie, an accommodating Roy seemed to go out of his way to avoid it. The differences did not end there. Robinson was the racial trailblazer, who felt that Campanella should have been more grateful for what he had done. More than that, he was disappointed by the catcher's reluctance to be a fellow pioneer on the racial front. . . . For his part, Campanella saw himself as a baseball player first, last and always. If Jackie wanted to be a symbol—or could not avoid being cast as one—Campy wanted no part of it. He wasn't anybody's symbol; he was simply the Dodger's catcher."

He proved to be the best catcher in franchise history and was an integral part of the great Dodger teams that won National League pennants in 1949, 1952, 1953, and 1956, losing to the New York Yankees in each of those series, and 1955, when the Dodgers finally defeated the Yankees to win the World Series. Campanella became one of the greatest home-run-hitting catchers in major league baseball history. His best season came in 1953, when he batted .312 with 41 home runs, a league-leading 142 RBIs and 103 runs scored, and was named the National League's Most Valuable Player, an award he had won in 1951 and would win again in 1955. He was also a member of the league's All-Star team from 1949 to 1956. He would wind up with 242 career home runs, 856 RBIs, and a .276 batting average in 1,215 games.

On January 28, 1958, Campanella was seriously injured while driving home from his New York liquor store. His car crashed into a telephone pole, and Campanella, with a damaged spinal cord, was permanently disabled, living out the rest of his life in a wheelchair. The Dodgers moved to Los Angeles that year, and Campanella was honored on May 7, 1959, before an exhibition game between the Dodgers and the Yankees, with a record crowd of 93,103 fans coming to the Los Angeles Coliseum to honor him. He continued to display his remarkable spirit by working for the Dodgers in community relations and was inducted into the National Baseball Hall of Fame in 1969.

Campbell, Andrew

Andrew Campbell was a catcher for the Leland Giants and Chicago Union Giants from 1903 to 1906.

Campbell, Buddy

Buddy Campbell was a catcher for Cole's American Giants in 1932.

Campbell, David

David Campbell was a second baseman for the New York Black Yankees and Philadelphia Stars from 1938 to 1941.

Campbell, Grant

Grant Campbell was a second baseman and outfielder for the Chicago Unions from 1887 to 1893.

Campbell, Hunter

Hunter Campbell was a black man who was identified as the owner of the Ethiopian Clowns, one of the clowning Negro traveling baseball teams in the 1930s and 1940s that were actually owned and operated by Syd Pollock.

Campbell, Joe

Joe Campbell was a pitcher for the Chicago Unions from 1887 to 1893.

Campbell, Joseph

Joseph Campbell was an outfielder and third baseman for the Pittsburgh Keystones in 1922.

Campbell, Robert

Robert Campbell was a catcher for the Bacharach Giants, Cole's American Giants, and Pittsburgh Crawfords from 1931 to 1932.

Campbell, William (Zip)

William Campbell was a pitcher for the Washington Potomacs, Philadelphia Giants, Hilldale baseball club, and Lincoln Giants from 1923 to 1929.

Campini, Joe

Joe Campini, born in East Wareham, Massachusetts, was a 5-foot-10, 190-pound catcher for the Baltimore Elite Giants in 1948.

Camps, Manuel

Manuel Camps managed the Cuban Stars when they were first organized in 1905.

Campos, Tatica

Tatica Campos was a pitcher, infielder, and outfielder for the Cuban Stars, All Cubans, and New York Cuban Stars from 1915 to 1923 and again in 1930.

Canada, James

James Canada was a first baseman and later manager for the Birmingham Black Barons, Memphis Red Sox, Chattanooga Choo-Choos, Baltimore Elite Giants, and Jacksonville Red Caps from 1937 to 1945. He also managed Willie Mays. In an interview with author John Holway on file at the National Baseball Hall of Fame, Canada talked about how he first saw Mays play. "I first found Willie Mays in Fairfield, Alabama, playing on a little team called the Fairfield Stars. . . . When I first met Willie, he was playing shortstop. He'd get down on one knee to field the ball—he was just determined to be a good ballplayer. But I told him, 'You're not a shortstop, you're not a catcher and you're not a pitcher. You're an outfielder.' So I changed him to center field. . . . I carried Mays away to the Chattanooga Choo-Choos in 1948. I was managing there at the time. I managed there about two months and then left on account of finances. They couldn't pay me one Sunday morning and so Willie came over with me to Birmingham." In the Holway interview, Canada also talked about his own playing days. "They saw I was one of the best fielding first basemen in baseball," Canada said. "I learned from Jim West—Shifty West—and Showboat Thomas."

Canizares, Avelino

Avelino Canizares played shortstop for the Cleveland Buckeyes in 1945, batting .305. The 5-foot-7, 140-pound Canizares played winter baseball in Cuba—he was born in Havana—and also played in the Mexican League until 1958.

Cannady, Jesse

Jesse Cannady was a second baseman and third baseman for the Chicago American Giants, Homestead Grays, Indianapolis-Cincinnati Clowns, and New York Cubans from 1942 to 1945.

Cannady, Walter (Rev)

Walter Cannady played first base, second base, shortstop, third base, outfield, and pitcher and managed for the Columbus Buckeyes, Dayton Marcos, Cleveland Tate Stars, Homestead Grays, Harrisburg Giants, Hilldale baseball club, Lincoln Giants, Darby Daisies, Pittsburgh Crawfords, New York Black Yankees, Philadelphia Stars, Brooklyn Royal Giants, Chicago American Giants, Cincinnati-Indianapolis Clowns, and New York Cubans from 1921 to 1945.

Cannon, John

John Cannon was an outfielder for the Pythians of Philadelphia in the 1860s.

Cannon, Richard (Speed Ball)

Richard Cannon was a pitcher for the St. Louis Stars, Nashville Elite Giants, Birmingham Black Barons, and Louisville Red Caps from 1928 to 1934.

Capers, Lefty

Lefty Capers was a pitcher for the Louisville White Sox in 1931.

Capital Citys of D.C.

The Capital Citys of D.C. were a black baseball team in Washington, D.C., that was part of the National Colored Base Ball League in 1887. One of the players on the Capital Citys was Frank Leland, who would go on to be one of the most influential people in black baseball, organizing several teams.

Carabello, Esterio

Esterio Carabello was an outfielder for the Cuban Stars in 1939.

Carey, Carry

Carry Carey was a second baseman and third baseman for the Dayton Marcos and St. Louis Giants from 1916 to 1921.

Carlisle, Matthew

Matthew Carlisle was a second baseman and shortstop for the Birmingham Black Barons, Montgomery Grey Sox, Memphis Red Sox, and Homestead Grays from 1931 to 1946.

Carlisle, Sylvester

Sylvester Carlisle was an infielder for the Kansas City Monarchs in 1945.

Carney, Ted

Ted Carney was an infielder for the Washington Pilots in 1932.

Carpenter, Andrew

Andrew Carpenter was a pitcher for the Detroit Stars from 1954 to 1955.

Carpenter, Clay

Clay Carpenter was a pitcher for the Baltimore Black Sox and Philadelphia Giants from 1925 to 1926.

Carr, Ed

Ed Carr was an infielder for the Lincoln Giants in 1890.

Carr, George Henry (Tank)

George Carr was a first baseman, third baseman, outfielder, and catcher for the Kansas City Monarchs, Hilldale baseball club, Atlantic City Bacharach Giants, Philadelphia Stars, Lincoln Giants, Washington Pilots, and Baltimore Black Sox. He was a .300 hitter during much of his career, including a .339 average in 1921, .300 in 1924, and .370 in 1925. He played for Hilldale in the 1924 and 1925 Negro World Series. He also played winter ball in Cuba and for the Los Angeles White Sox in the integrated California Winter League.

Carr, Wayne

Wayne Carr was a pitcher for the Indianapolis ABC's, Baltimore Black Sox, St. Louis Giants, Bacharach Giants, Washington Potomacs, Newark Stars, Wilmington Potomacs, Lincoln Giants, and Brooklyn Royal Giants from 1920 to 1928.

Carrera, Sungo

Sungo Carrera played second base and outfield for the Cuban Stars in 1940 and 1941.

Carroll, Sonny

Sonny Carroll was a pitcher for the Baltimore Elite Giants in 1950.

Carruthers, Warren

Warren Carruthers was a pitcher for the Detroit Stars in 1955.

Carswell, Frank

Frank Carswell was a pitcher for the Cleveland Buckeyes from 1944 to 1946.

Carter, Alfred

Alfred Carter was an infielder and outfielder for the Nashville Elite Giants, New York Cubans, Pittsburgh Crawfords, and Philadelphia Stars from 1934 to 1940.

Carter, Art

Art Carter was a second baseman for the St. Louis Black Stockings in 1884.

Carter, Bill

Bill Carter was a pitcher for the Newark Eagles in 1948.

Carter, Bo

Bo Carter was president of the Chattanooga Black Lookouts in 1931.

Carter, Charles

Charles Carter was a pitcher for the Homestead Grays and Baltimore Elite Giants in 1943.

Carter, Charles (Kid)

Charles Carter was a pitcher for the Philadelphia Giants, Wilmington Giants, and Brooklyn Royal Giants from 1902 to 1906.

Carter, Clifford

Clifford Carter was a pitcher for the Baltimore Black Sox, Bacharach Giants, Harrisburg Giants, Philadelphia Tigers, Hilldale baseball club, and Philadelphia Stars from 1923 to 1934.

Carter, Elmer

Elmer Carter was a catcher, shortstop, and first baseman for the Birmingham Black Barons from 1930 to 1932 and again in 1937.

Carter, Ernest (Spoon)

Ernest Carter was a pitcher for the Pittsburgh Crawfords, Memphis Red Sox, Cleveland Red Sox, Toledo Crawfords, Indianapolis Crawfords, Newark Eagles, Philadelphia Stars, Homestead Grays, and Birmingham Black Barons from 1932 to 1949. Carter was one of the Negro Leaguers who played in the Dominican Republic in the 1937 baseball political war between dictator Rafael Trujillo and his opponents. Carter played for one of Trujillo's opponents, Santiago de los Caballeros.

Carter, Frank

Frank Carter was a pitcher for the St. Louis Giants in 1917.

Carter, Ike

Ike Carter was a second baseman for the St. Louis Black Stockings in 1884. He was considered to be one of the best second basemen in the country but reportedly was shot and killed by a St. Louis man whose house he broke into.

Carter, Jimmy

Jimmy Carter was a pitcher for the Philadelphia Stars from 1938 to 1939.

Carter, Kenneth

Kenneth Carter was a catcher for the Cleveland Buckeyes in 1950.

Carter, Mark

Mark Carter was a pitcher for the Detroit Stars and Louisville Black Colonels from 1954 to 1955.

Carter, Marlin (Pee Wee)

Marlin Carter was a second baseman and third baseman for the Shreveport Black Sports, San Antonio Black Indians, Monroe Monarchs, Cincinnati Tigers, Atlanta Black Crackers, Memphis Red Sox, Black Spiders, and Chicago American Giants from 1926 to 1950. He played his last season in 1950 with the minor league Class A Rochester Royals. In a 1993 interview with *Black Ball News*, Carter talked about the challenge of playing in the Texas Negro League in the early days of his career. "Competition in the league was always tough," Carter said. "Some of the best players at that time were down in Texas. It's hard to say that the teams in that league weren't as good as the teams that were playing in the Negro National League. Back then the Negro National League didn't have a whole lot of teams. There were a lot more great players than could play on those teams. There were great players, many who later became stars in the Negro National and American Leagues, that were playing in the Texas Negro League and the Southern League back then."

Carter, Paul

Paul Carter was a pitcher for the Hilldale baseball club, Darby Daisies, Philadelphia Stars, and New York Black Yankees from 1929 to 1936.

Carter, Robert

Robert Carter pitched for the Homestead Grays in 1947.

Carter, William

William Carter was a catcher for the Kansas City Monarchs and Detroit Stars from 1920 to 1922.

Carter, William

William Carter was a third baseman for the St. Louis Stars and Harrisburg–St. Louis Stars in 1937 and 1943.

Cartledge, Menske

Menske Cartledge was a pitcher for the Birmingham Black Barons and Philadelphia Stars from 1951 to 1955.

Cartmill, Alfred

Alfred Cartmill was a second baseman for the Kansas City Monarchs from 1949 to 1951 and again in 1955.

Cartwright, Clay

Clay Cartwright was an infielder for the Memphis Red Sox, Detroit Stars, and Louisville Black Colonels from 1953 to 1954.

Casanova, Paulino (Paul)
b. 1941

Paulino Casanova was a catcher who played for the Indianapolis Clowns in the NEGRO AMERICAN LEAGUE in 1960. Born in Colon, Cuba, the 6-foot-4, 190-pound

Casanova would go on to play 10 major league seasons for the Washington Senators and Atlanta Braves, retiring after the 1974 season with a .225 average in 859 games.

Casey, Joe

Joe Casey was a pitcher for the St. Louis Giants in 1920.

Casey, William

William Casey was a catcher and manager for the Baltimore Black Sox, Bacharach Giants, Philadelphia Stars, Washington Black Senators, New York Cubans, Cuban Stars, Baltimore Grays, and New York Black Yankees from 1931 to 1943.

Cash, Bill (Ready)

b. 1919

Bill Cash was a catcher, third baseman, and outfielder for the Philadelphia Stars from 1943 to 1950. His best recorded year was 1944, when the 6-foot-2, 200-pound Cash batted .282 in 41 games. He also batted .276 in 1947 and .268 in 1949. In an interview, Cash, born in Round Oak, Georgia, said he learned about handling pitchers and calling games behind the plate from two of the pitchers he caught, Chester Buchanan and Barney Brown. "I learned more from those two guys about catching and how to call a game." Cash had a strong throwing arm. "Webster McDonald, the manager who brought me to the Stars, said they never saw a catcher who could throw like me," said Cash, who threw from a crouching position. He went on to play minor league baseball in the Chicago White Sox organization but was passed over for promotions. He retired after the 1955 season. He also played winter ball in Cuba, Venezuela, and the Dominican Republic.

Cason, John

John Cason was a catcher, outfielder, and second baseman for the Brooklyn Royal Giants, Norfolk Stars, Hilldale baseball club, Lincoln Giants, Bacharach Giants, and Baltimore Black Sox from 1918 to 1932.

Castille, Irwin

Irwin Castille was a shortstop and third baseman for the Birmingham Black Barons from 1951 to 1953.

Castillo, Julian

Julian Castillo was a first baseman for the All Cubans and Cuban Stars in 1911 and 1912.

Castone, William

William Castone was a pitcher and outfielder for the Lincoln Giants and for another Lincoln team in the Nebraska State League and a team in Aspen, Colorado, from 1889 to 1892.

Castro, Antonio

Antonio Castro was a catcher for the Cuban Stars in 1929.

Cates, Joe

Joe Cates was a shortstop for the Louisville White Sox and Louisville Red Caps from 1931 to 1934.

Cathey, Willis

Willis Cathey pitched for the Indianapolis Clowns from 1948 to 1950.

Catholic Protectory Grounds

The Catholic Protectory Grounds was a field in the Bronx in New York where the Lincoln Giants and other black baseball teams played in the 1920s. There was reportedly a grandstand that held about 500 people and a small set of bleachers. Crowds would sometimes be as many as 1,500–2,000 for games.

Catling, Charles

Charles Catling was an umpire in the League of Colored Base Ball Players in 1887.

Cato, Harry

Harry Cato was a second baseman, pitcher, and outfielder for the Cuban X Giants and Cuban Giants from 1893 to 1896.

Catto, Octavius V.

b. 1840, d. 1871

Octavius Cato was a former U.S. Army major and teacher at the Institute for Colored Youth in Philadelphia who was the promoter for the Pythians of Philadelphia, a black baseball team in the 1860s. He tried unsuccessfully for the Pythians to be integrated into white baseball as part of the National Association of Base Ball Players and grew to be an influential politician in the black community in Philadelphia and an active proponent of civil rights. In 1871, Cato was shot and killed at the age of 31.

Cepeda, Pedro

Pedro Cepeda was an outfielder for the New York Cubans in 1941.

Cephus, Goldie

Goldie Cephus was an outfielder for the Philadelphia Giants and Bacharach Giants from 1926 to 1931.

Chacon, Pelayo

Pelayo Chacon was a shortstop and manager for the Cuban Stars and Havana Stars from 1910 to 1930.

Chambers, Arthur (Rube)

Arthur Chambers was a left-handed pitcher for the Lincoln Giants, Wilmington Potomacs, and Washington Potomacs from 1924 to 1927. He was found dead in a railroad boxcar in 1927.

Chandler, A. B. (Happy)

A. B. Chandler was selected by major league franchise owners as the commissioner of baseball in April 1945 to succeed Kenesaw Mountain Landis, who died of a heart attack in 1944. This change helped pave the way for the integration of major league baseball two years later with the arrival of Jackie Robinson. Landis had halted efforts to break the color barrier, but Chandler, a United States senator and former governor of the segregated state of Kentucky, supported the idea of blacks playing major league baseball. His famous quote on the subject—"If a black boy can make it on Okinawa and Guadalcanal, hell, he can make it in baseball"—alerted those in the black community who had been working to get a black player in the majors that the time was nearly at hand. However, he turned away efforts by Negro League teams to try to enter organized white baseball. When Negro League officials met with Chandler in 1945 to propose their entry into the game, Chandler said, "I will be glad to arrange an alliance between organized baseball and the Negro Leagues, when you can come to me with a clean bill of health. You must clean out the gamblers. You must establish your game on a fair and honest footing and develop your umpires to the levels of high respect which the decision callers hold in organized baseball." Chandler was succeeded by National League president Ford Frick in 1951.

Chaney, John

John Chaney was a pitcher for the Philadelphia Stars in 1952.

Chapman, Edward

Edward Chapman was a pitcher for the Chicago Columbia Giants and Detroit Stars in 1927 and 1931.

Chapman, Roy Lee

Roy Lee Chapman was a pitcher for the New York Black Yankees from 1949 to 1951.

Charleston, Benny

Benny Charleston played outfielder for the Homestead Grays in 1930.

Charleston, Oscar McKinley (The Hoosier Comet)
b. 1896, d. 1954

Oscar Charleston was inducted into the National Baseball Hall of Fame in 1976, recognizing his place as one of the best players and managers ever in Negro League baseball. According to Negro League records, Charleston, a left-handed hitter, batted over .400 twice, hit over .350 for nine consecutive seasons, and played and managed for the Indianapolis ABC's, Lincoln Stars, Chicago American Giants, St. Louis Giants, Harrisburg Giants, Hilldale baseball club, Homestead Grays, Pittsburgh Crawfords, Toledo Crawfords, Indianapolis Crawfords, Philadelphia Stars, Brooklyn Brown Dodgers, and Indianapolis Clowns from 1915 to 1954. Charleston also made his mark in winter baseball, and when he played in Cuba, Charleston had a career mark of .361. He also turned in some legendary performances in exhibitions against white major league ballplayers, such as blasting a home run off Lefty Grove in an exhibition contest in Philadelphia.

Charleston was a volatile player, often compared to Ty Cobb for his hard-nosed style of play. Like Cobb, the 5-foot-11 Charleston, whose weight ranged from 175 pounds to 240 pounds during his career, was also known for his fights both on and off the field and was one of the most feared players in Negro League baseball history. Some of the stories of his scraps include threatening to throw wrestling champion Jim Londos out of a train window. There were also tales about how Charleston could supposedly tear the cover off the ball with his bare hands. In John Holway's book *Blackball Stars*, former teammate Ted Page talked about Charleston's baseball and fighting prowess. "Oscar Charleston loved to play baseball," Page said. "There was nothing he liked to do better, unless it was fight. He didn't smoke, he didn't drink, but he enjoyed a good fight—with the opposition."

Charleston was born in Indianapolis, Indiana, and worked as a batboy for the Indianapolis ABC's, a team he would later play for and manage. Charleston ran away

from home at the age of 15 and joined the U.S. Army. He played baseball while stationed in the Philippines for the Negro 24th Infantry and also played in the white Manila League in 1914. In a 1915 exhibition game against a white team in Indianapolis, Charleston was thrown in jail and charged with assault and battery after he punched an umpire over a disputed call, starting a riot. He once got into a brawl with another volatile player, Oliver Marcelle, who bashed Charleston over the head with a baseball bat. But, like Cobb, his intensity and talent on the field made him, according to some, the greatest player in the history of the game. Negro League great Buck O'Neil, in his autobiography, *I Was Right On Time*, said Charleston was the best he had ever seen: "To this day, I always claim that Willie Mays was the greatest major league player I have ever seen . . . but then I pause and say that Oscar Charleston was even better. . . . He was like Ty Cobb, Babe Ruth and Tris Speaker rolled into one."

Charleston began his career as an outfielder with the Indianapolis ABC's in 1915 and was one of the team's star hitters. He hit .446 and 14 home runs and a .774 slugging percentage in 1921. The following season, Charleston returned to the Indianapolis ABC's and hit .370. He then played for the Harrisburg Giants in 1924–1927, hitting over .400 twice. He would go on to play for the Hilldale club and the Homestead Grays until 1932 when he joined Gus Greenlee's Pittsburgh Crawfords and remained with them until 1938, becoming part of probably the greatest team in the history of Negro League baseball—Charleston, Judy Johnson, Josh Gibson, Cool Papa Bell, Jimmy Crutchfield, Ted "Double Duty" Radcliffe, and Satchel Paige. He was the second-highest vote-getter in the first Negro Leagues All-Star Game, the EAST-WEST GAME, in 1934, trailing only Turkey Stearnes. Negro Leaguer Newt Allen, in an interview conducted by author John Holway on file at the National Baseball Hall of Fame, called Charleston a great outfielder. "Oscar Charleston was the best outfielder I've ever seen," Allen said. "Willie Mays was a good outfielder, so was DiMaggio, but this

Oscar Charleston was a hard-nosed player who was one of the most feared figures in Negro League history for his relentless style of play as well as his talent with the bat. A left-handed hitter, Charleston batted over .400 twice and hit over .350 for nine consecutive seasons, with a career mark of .361. From 1915 to 1954, he played and managed for the Indianapolis ABC's, Lincoln Stars, Chicago American Giants, St. Louis Giants, Harrisburg Giants, Hilldale baseball club, Homestead Grays, Pittsburgh Crawfords, Toledo Crawfords, Indianapolis Crawfords, Philadelphia Stars, Brooklyn Brown Dodgers, and Indianapolis Clowns. (NATIONAL BASEBALL HALL OF FAME LIBRARY, COOPERSTOWN, N.Y.)

man Charleston had, I don't know, something about him." One of his feats came against major league players in a barnstorming tour against the St. Louis Cardinals. He hit five home runs in five games and batted .458 against the Cardinals. Three times in the series after reaching first base, Charleston told opposing pitchers he would steal second on the next pitch. He kept his word all three times. He is believed to have batted about .400 in 20 seasons of barnstorming against major league players. In Robert Peterson's book *Only the Ball Was White*, Crutchfield told a story that illustrated Charleston's batting talents. "We were playing a major league All-Star team one night in Des Moines, Iowa—Bob Feller, Gus Suhr, Ival Goodman, Al Todd, Jimmy King, Big Jim Weaver, Johnny Mize, Jim Winford—they had a heckuva club," Crutchfield said. "Now this was 1936, when Charleston was big and fat. I heard him on the bench saying, 'I just don't get a thrill out of batting anymore unless there's someone on the bases.' He had popped up a couple of time. Sure enough, we got two men on against Big Jim Weaver, and Charleston said, 'Now this is what I've been waiting for.' And he doubled against the left-center-field wall and waddled into second base. That's the kind of guy Charleston was. If I had to pick the best player I saw in my time, it would be hard to pick between Charleston and Josh Gibson. When the chips were down and you needed somebody to bat in the clutch . . . even at his age, he was as good as anybody playing baseball."

Charleston was player-manager in Pittsburgh until 1941 when he took over as manager of the Philadelphia Stars. In 1945, Brooklyn Dodger's general manager Branch Rickey created the UNITED BASEBALL LEAGUE and hired Charleston to manage the Brooklyn Brown Bombers. He also scouted players for Rickey and urged him to sign a catcher named Roy Campanella. The United Baseball League dissolved in 1947, and Charleston, who umpired in the Negro Leagues East-West All-Star Game that same season, played for and managed the Indianapolis Clowns until he died in 1954. That year he led the Clowns to a Negro American League championship with a 43-22 record—the last year the league was in existence. Former Philadelphia Giants catcher Bill "Ready" Cash recalled that even as an aging player-manager, Charleston still had remarkable batting skills. "When he was manager, he was about 50 years old," Cash said. "He would dare any lefthander, give him two strikes and dare him to throw anything he wanted to throw, and he'd never get it by him for the third strike."

Charleston, Porter

Porter Charleston was a pitcher for the Hilldale baseball club, Darby Daisies, and Philadelphia Stars from 1927 to 1935.

Charleston, Red

Red Charleston was a catcher for the Nashville Elite Giants from 1929 to 1932.

Charleston Fultons

The Charleston Fultons were a team out of Charleston, South Carolina, that played in the Southern League of Colored Baseballists in 1886.

Charter, Bill

Bill Charter was a first baseman and catcher for the Chicago American Giants from 1943 to 1946.

Chatman, Edgar

Edgar Chatman was a pitcher for the Memphis Red Sox from 1944 to 1945.

Chattanooga Black Lookouts

The Chattanooga Black Lookouts were a black baseball team in Chattanooga, Tennessee, that played in the Negro Southern League in the 1920s.

Chattanooga Choo-Choos

The Chattanooga Choo-Choos were a black baseball team in Chattanooga, Tennessee, that played in the Negro Southern League in 1945.

Chattanooga White Sox

The Chattanooga White Sox were a black baseball team in Chattanooga, Tennessee, that played in the Negro Southern League in 1926.

Cherry, Hugh

Hugh Cherry was an officer for the Houston Eagles in 1949.

Chestnut, Joe

Joe Chestnut was a pitcher for the Indianapolis Clowns, Birmingham Black Barons, and Philadelphia Stars from 1950 to 1952.

Chicago American Giants

In 1909, a pitcher named Andrew "Rube" Foster, one of the stars of Frank Leland's Giants in Chicago, took over the ownership and operation of the team, forming a partnership with John Schorling, the brother-in-law of

Chicago White Sox owner Charles Comiskey, playing in the former White Sox ballpark on 39th and Wentworth. In that first year under Foster's ownership, the team reportedly won 109 games and lost just nine. He would later change their name to the Chicago American Giants, and through Negro baseball and barnstorming exhibition games against white ballplayers, the team became a legendary black franchise, with players in those early days such as John Henry Lloyd, Bruce Petway, and Frank Wickware. Foster, considered one of the driving forces in the development of Negro League baseball, formed the NEGRO NATIONAL LEAGUE in 1920, and his Giants were the prize franchise of the league. With outfielders like Cristobal Torriente and Jimmy Lyons, infielders Elwood "Bingo" DeMoss and Dave Malarcher, and pitcher Dave Brown, the Giants won the league title in its first three years of existence. In 1926, Malarcher would take over operation of the team after Foster was institutionalized; he won Negro National League championships in 1926 and 1927, winning the Negro baseball version of the World Series by beating the EASTERN COLORED LEAGUE champion Bacharach Giants both years. Foster fell on hard times and suffered from psychological problems as the Negro National League began to fall apart. He was declared incompetent and was institutionalized with dementia (he died in 1930), and the franchise was sold to a white businessman from Princeton, Illinois, named William Trimble after the 1927 season. But the franchise continued its downward spiral, and in 1932, after the Negro National League disbanded, the Chicago American Giants were purchased by Robert A. Cole and won the Negro Southern League pennants as Cole's American Giants. The Giants joined the revived Negro National League the following year and won that league's pennant as well. In 1934, Chicago won the league's first-half title but lost the season championship in a seven-game playoff. In 1937, the American Giants were sold to a black Chicago businessman and former owner of the Memphis Red Sox, Dr. J. B. Martin. The American Giants joined the NEGRO AMERICAN LEAGUE that year and played in that league until 1952. Some of the players on those American Giants teams included Norman "Turkey" Stearnes, George "Mule" Suttles, shortstop Willie Wells, pitcher Willie Foster, and catcher Larry Brown. Others who were members of the American Giants over their career included Oscar Charleston, Walter "Steel Arm" Davis, and Pythias Russ.

Chicago Brown Bombers

The Chicago Brown Bombers were the city's entry in Branch Rickey's United States League for black teams in 1945. They were managed by Bingo DeMoss.

Chicago Defender

The *Chicago Defender*, a black newspaper in Chicago, covered black baseball and the Negro Leagues. One of the reporters who covered Negro Leagues for the newspaper was Cary B. Lewis.

Chicago Giants

The Chicago Giants were a black baseball team that played in Chicago in the early 1900s. Owned by Chicago businessman Joseph Green, the Giants were one of the original teams in the NEGRO NATIONAL LEAGUE, formed in 1920.

Chicago Leland Giants

The Chicago Leland Giants were a black baseball team in Chicago, owned and operated by Frank Leland in the 1890s and early 1900s. In 1909, a pitcher for the Leland Giants named Andrew "Rube" Foster took over the ownership and operation of the team, forming a partnership with John Schorling, the brother-in-law of Chicago White Sox owner Charles Comiskey. Foster operated the team successfully, drawing such players as John Henry Lloyd and Grant "Home Run" Johnson to play there. Later Foster would changed the name to the Chicago American Giants.

Chicago Union Giants

The Chicago Union Giants were a black baseball team started in Chicago in 1901 by Frank Leland, who had managed the Chicago Unions and played in the early years of the 1900s. Rube Foster pitched for the Union Giants before going to the Leland Giants in 1910.

Chicago Unions

The Chicago Unions were a black baseball team in Chicago that started as an amateur team in 1886. They turned professional in 1896 and played into the 20th century, touring through Indiana, Wisconsin, Illinois, Iowa, and Michigan.

Childers, Wolf

Wolf Childers was a catcher for the Cincinnati Tigers in 1936.

Childs, Andy

Andy Childs was a pitcher and second baseman for the Indianapolis Athletics, Indianapolis ABC's, St. Louis Stars, and Memphis Red Sox from 1936 to 1945.

Chirban, Louis

Louis Chirban was a pitcher for the Chicago American Giants in 1950.

Chisholm, Joe

Joe Chisholm was a pitcher for the Philadelphia Stars in 1945.

Chism, Elijah

Elijah Chism was an outfielder for the Cleveland Buckeyes, Birmingham Black Barons, and St. Louis Stars in 1937 and again from 1946 to 1951.

Chisolm, Joe

Joe Chisolm played second base for the Memphis Red Sox in 1953.

Cholston, Bert

Bert Cholston was an umpire in the NEGRO NATIONAL LEAGUE in the 1920s.

Chretian, Ernest

Ernest Chretian was an infielder and outfielder for the Philadelphia Stars and Kansas City Monarchs in 1948 and 1950.

Christopher, Ted

Ted Christopher was a catcher for the New York Black Yankees and Homestead Grays in 1943 and 1949.

Christopher, Thad

Thad Christopher was an outfielder and first baseman for the Newark Eagles, Pittsburgh Crawfords, New York Black Yankees, Cincinnati Buckeyes, Cincinnati Clowns, and Cleveland Buckeyes from 1936 to 1945. He was one of a group of Negro Leaguers who played in the Dominican Republic in 1937 as part of the political baseball war being played out there between dictator Rafael Trujillo and his opponents. Christopher played for one of the opponents, San Pedro de Macoris.

Cincinnati Browns

The Cincinnati Browns were a black baseball team in the League of Colored Base Ball Players in 1887.

Cincinnati Buckeyes

The Cincinnati Buckeyes were a black baseball team that played in Cincinnati in the Negro American League in the 1940s.

Cincinnati Clowns

The Cincinnati Clowns were one of Syd Pollock's versions of his black baseball "Clowns" teams that split time playing from 1943 to 1945 in Cincinnati and Indianapolis.

Cincinnati Cubans

The Cincinnati Cubans were one of the many versions of the various black baseball teams that played Negro League baseball under the name *Cubans* that was based in Cincinnati in the 1920s in the Negro American League.

Cincinnati Dismukes

The Cincinnati Dismukes were a black baseball team operated by William "Dizzy" Dismukes, a former Negro League pitcher, in Cincinnati in the 1950s.

Cincinnati Tigers

The Cincinnati Tigers were a black baseball team that played in Cincinnati in the Negro American League in the 1930s.

Clarizio, Louis

Louis Clarizio was an outfielder for the Chicago American Giants in 1950.

Clark, Albert

Albert Clark was a pitcher for the Cleveland Tate Stars, Dayton Marcos, Indianapolis ABC's, Pittsburgh Keytones, Memphis Red Sox, and Cleveland Browns from 1919 to 1926.

Clark, Cleveland

Cleveland Clark was an outfielder for the New York Cubans from 1945 to 1950.

Clark, Dave

Dave Clark was the last owner of a version of the Clowns, the clowning black baseball team that finally folded in the early 1980s.

Clark, Dell

Dell Clark was a shortstop for the Brooklyn Royal Giants, Indianapolis ABC's, Lincoln Giants, and Washington Potomacs from 1914 to 1923.

Clark, Eggie

Eggie Clark was an outfielder for the Memphis Red Sox in 1928.

Clark, Estaban

Estaban Clark played first base for the Kansas City Monarchs in 1955.

Clark, Harry

Harry Clark was a pitcher for the Hilldale baseball club and Brooklyn Royal Giants from 1922 to 1925.

Clark, John L.

John L. Clark was a reporter for the black *Pittsburgh American* and *Pittsburgh Courier* newspapers. Clark was also the business manager and public relations man for the Pittsburgh Crawfords and Homestead Grays from 1932 to 1946.

Clark, Maceo

Maceo Clark was a pitcher and first baseman for the Washington Potomacs, Wilmington Potomacs, Bacharach Giants, and Indianapolis ABC's from 1923 to 1925.

Clark, Milton J., Jr.

Milton Clark was secretary for the Chicago American Giants in 1937.

Clark, Morten

Morten Clark was a shortstop for the Indianapolis ABC's and Baltimore Black Sox from 1915 to 1923.

Clark, Roy

Roy Clark pitched for the Newark Dodgers from 1934 to 1935.

Clarke, Allie

Allie Clarke was an infielder, outfielder, and catcher for the Washington Black Senators in 1938.

Clarke, Robert

Robert Clarke was a catcher and manager for the Richmond Giants, Baltimore Black Sox, New York Black Yankees, Philadelphia Stars, and Baltimore Elite Giants from 1922 to 1948.

Clarke, Vibert

Vibert Clarke was a pitcher for the Cleveland Buckeyes, Louisville Buckeyes, and Memphis Red Sox from 1946 to 1950.

Clarkson, James (Buster)

b. 1913, d. 1989

James Clarkson was a shortstop, second baseman, and outfielder for the Pittsburgh Crawfords, Toledo Crawfords, Indianapolis Crawfords, Newark Eagles, Philadelphia Stars, and Baltimore Elite Giants from 1937 to 1950. The 6-foot, 200-pound Clarkson, born in Hopkins, South Carolina, batted .421 for Toledo in 1939 and .428 for Newark in 1940. He was signed by the Boston Braves, and played several years of minor league baseball. He was called up to the Braves in 1951 and played 14 major league games, getting five hits in 25 at bats, scoring three runs and driving in one. He also played in the Mexican League and winter baseball in Puerto Rico.

Claxton, James

James Claxton pitched for the Cuban Stars in 1932.

Clay, Albert

b. 1924, d. 1998

Albert Clay was an outfielder for the New York Black Yankees from 1949 to 1950.

Clay, William (Lefty)

William Clay pitched for the Kansas City Monarchs in 1932.

Claybrook Tigers

The Claybrook Tigers were a team out of Claybrook, Arkansas, in the Negro Southern League owned by plantation owner J. C. Claybrook in the early 1930s. Marlin Carter, who played for the Tigers, said "The Claybrook Tigers were a first-class team. They won the Negro Southern League championship a couple of times." Ted "Double Duty" Radcliffe managed the Tigers for several seasons.

Clayton, Leroy

Leroy Clayton was a catcher and first baseman for the Chicago Brown Bombers, Bacharach Giants, Cole's

American Giants, Chicago American Giants, New York Black Yankees, Brooklyn Royal Giants, and Brooklyn Eagles from 1932 to 1944.

Clayton, Zach

Zach Clayton was a first baseman for the Bacharach Giants, Cole's American Giants, Chicago American Giants, and New York Black Yankees from 1937 to 1950.

Cleage, Pete

Pete Cleage was an umpire in the Negro National League in 1936.

Cleage, Ralph

Ralph Cleage was an outfielder for the St. Louis Stars in 1924 and an umpire in the Negro National League.

Clemente, Miguel

Miguel Clemente was a catcher for the Havana Cubans in 1917.

Cleveland, Howard (Duke)

Howard Cleveland was an outfielder for the Jacksonville Red Caps, Cleveland Bears, and Cleveland Buckeyes from 1938 to 1943.

Cleveland Browns

The Cleveland Browns were a black baseball team in Cleveland managed by former Negro League player and historian Sol White. They played in the Negro National League in 1924, finishing last in the league with a 15-34 record.

Cleveland Buckeyes

The Cleveland Buckeyes were a black baseball team formed in 1942 by Ernest Wright that played home games in both Cleveland and Cincinnati for that first season. Playing in League Park in Cleveland, the Buckeyes finished second in the NEGRO AMERICAN LEAGUE, with a record of 35-15. The following season the Buckeyes had a record of 27-12, but in 1943 they had a losing record of 40-41. The Buckeyes' best year was 1945 when they were league champions, winning both halves of a split season and defeating the Homestead Grays in the World Series in four straight games—a huge upset. Some of the players on that Buckeyes team included catcher-manager Quincey Trouppe, Sam Jethroe, and the pitchers-brothers George and Willie Jefferson. The team would win the

league title again in 1947 with a record of 54-23 but lose to the New York Cubans in five games in the World Series. Their final year was 1948—the year the Indians, with the second black player to cross the color line, Larry Doby, won the World Series. The Buckeyes had a record of 41-42 and moved to Louisville the following season but finished fifth in the league with a record of 15-51. Another Cleveland Buckeyes team was put together in 1950, but the team folded before the season ended, with a record of 3-39.

Cleveland Clippers

The Cleveland Clippers were a black baseball team in Cleveland that played in the short-lived United States League in 1945.

Cleveland Cubs

The Cleveland Cubs were a black baseball team in Cleveland that included pitcher Satchel Paige and played in the Negro Southern League in 1932, posting a record of 22-18 before the league folded that season.

Cleveland Elites

The Cleveland Elites were a black baseball team in Cleveland that played in the NEGRO NATIONAL LEAGUE in 1926 but went 7-41 and did not finish the season.

Cleveland Gazette

The *Cleveland Gazette* was a black newspaper in Cleveland that covered black baseball.

Cleveland Hornets

The Cleveland Hornets were a black baseball team in Cleveland that played in the NEGRO NATIONAL LEAGUE in 1927, finishing last with a 16-38 record.

Cleveland Indians

The Cleveland Indians were the first American League team to have a black player on the major league roster. Outfielder Larry Doby followed Jackie Robinson as the second black player in the major leagues, signing a contract with the Indians in July 1947.

Cleveland Red Sox

The Cleveland Red Sox were a black baseball team in Cleveland that played in the NEGRO NATIONAL LEAGUE in 1934.

Cleveland Stars

The Cleveland Stars were a team in Cleveland that formed in 1932 and played in the black East-West League.

Cleveland Tate Stars

The Cleveland Tate Stars were the first organized black team in Cleveland, formed in 1918. They joined the Negro National League in 1922 but had a record of 17-29 and folded before the end of the season.

Cleveland Tigers

The Cleveland Tigers were a black baseball team that played in the NEGRO NATIONAL LEAGUE in 1928, posting a record of 19-53.

Clifford, Luther

Luther Clifford was a catcher and outfielder for the Homestead Grays from 1949 to 1950.

Clifton, Nat (Sweetwater)

b. 1922, d. 1990

Nat Clifton was best known as a 6-foot-6, 220-pound basketball player for the Harlem Globetrotters and New York Knicks in the 1950s. But he also played Negro League Baseball for two seasons—in 1949, with the Chicago American Giants and in 1958 with the Detroit Stars, where he played 10 games as a first baseman, batting .286. He also played minor league baseball in 1949 and 1950.

Close, Herman

Herman Close was manager of the Philadelphia Pythians in the League of Colored Base Ball Players in 1887.

Cobb, Lorenzo S.

Lorenzo Cobb was the owner of the St. Louis Giants and one of the original members of the NEGRO NATIONAL LEAGUE, founded in 1920.

Cockerham, James

James Cockerham was a first baseman for the Indianapolis ABC's in 1939.

Cockrell, Phil

Phil Cockrell was a pitcher and outfielder who went on to become a Negro League umpire. Cockrell died tragically when he was shot in Philadelphia in 1946. He played for the Philadelphia Stars, Hilldale baseball club, Bacharach Giants, New York Lincoln Giants, Darby Daisies, and Havana Red Sox from 1913 to 1946. Cockrell's best seasons came when he led Hilldale to the Negro World Series against the Kansas City Monarchs in 1924 and 1925, winning 25 games during those two years. Cockrell, who relied on a spitball and a knuckle ball, and Leon Day pitched in a series of doubleheaders against a team of major league All-Stars called the Brooklyn Bushwicks, organized by Dizzy and Paul Dean in the 1930s, combining to win 13 of the 14 games played. He once pitched a no-hitter against the Chicago American Giants.

Coffey, Howard

Howard Coffey was a pitcher for the Indianapolis Clowns and Philadelphia Stars from 1951 to 1954.

Coffey, Marshall

Marshall Coffey played second base for the Chicago Unions in 1889.

Coffie, Clifford

Clifford Coffie was an outfielder for the Cleveland Buckeyes in 1950.

Cohen, James

b. 1918

James Cohen was a pitcher for the Indianapolis Clowns from 1948 to 1952. Cohen played with a young Hank Aaron and Harlem Globetrotters star Goose Tatum. In an interview, Cohen said he got his start pitching for a coal mining team in a western Pennsylvania town called Blairsville. "All coal mining towns had baseball teams then," he said. "When I went to get a job at the mine, they asked me if I played baseball, and they told me to bring my glove next time. I worked in the coal mine and played baseball for their team. There were a lot of good players on that team, some who could have played Triple A ball. I worked in the mines for about five years, and then I met the owner of the Clowns, Syd Pollock, who signed me to play. Actually, it was Buck Leonard who got me started there. Our coal mining team was playing the Homestead Grays, and after the game Buck pulled me aside and told me I should try to play professional ball. He would take the time with a young man to help him."

Coimbre, Al

Al Coimbre was an outfielder and second baseman for the Cuban Stars from 1940 to 1946.

Colas, Carlos

Carlos Colas was a catcher for the Memphis Red Sox and New York Cubans in 1941 and from 1949 to 1951.

Colas, Jose

Jose Colas was an outfielder and manager for the Memphis Red Sox from 1947 to 1952. Records show he batted .310 for Memphis in 1948, .247 in 1949, and .268 in 1950. He also played two seasons of minor league baseball and winter baseball in Cuba.

Cole, Cecil

Cecil Cole pitched for the Newark Eagles in 1946.

Cole, Ralph

Ralph Cole was an outfielder for the Jacksonville Red Caps, Cleveland Bears, and Cincinnati Clowns from 1939 to 1943.

Cole, Robert A.

Robert Cole was a black businessman from Chicago who bought the Chicago American Giants in 1932 and changed the name of the team to Cole's American Giants, playing in the Negro Southern League. He would rejoin a new version of the NEGRO NATIONAL LEAGUE, organized by Gus Greenlee in 1933, and served as league treasurer. He sold the team in 1937 to Dr. J. B. Martin.

Cole, William

William Cole was a catcher for the Cuban Giants in 1896.

Coleman, Benny

Benny Coleman pitched for the Chicago American Giants in 1950.

Coleman, Carl

Carl Coleman was a first baseman for the Chicago American Giants in 1951.

Coleman, Clarence

Clarence Coleman was a pitcher, catcher, outfielder, and first baseman for the Chicago Giants, Chicago Union Giants, Indianapolis ABC's, Columbus Buckeyes, Dayton Marcos, Lincoln Giants, and Cleveland Tates Stars from 1913 to 1926.

Coleman, Elliott

Elliott Coleman was a pitcher for the Birmingham Black Barons from 1954 to 1955.

Coleman, Gilbert

Gilbert Coleman was an infielder and outfielder for the Bacharach Giants, Newark Dodgers, Brooklyn Cuban Giants, and Newark Browns from 1928 to 1933.

Coleman, Joe

Joe Coleman was a pitcher for the Birmingham Black Barons in 1955.

Coleman, John

John Coleman was an outfielder for the Brooklyn Remsens in 1885.

Coleman, John (Lefty)

John Coleman was a pitcher for the Baltimore Elite Giants and Birmingham Black Barons from 1950 to 1954.

Coleman, Melvin

Melvin Coleman was a shortstop, catcher, and pitcher for the Birmingham Black Barons from 1937 to 1940.

Coleman, Tom

Tom Coleman pitched for the Baltimore Elite Giants in 1951.

Colliers, Leonard

Leonard Colliers was a pitcher for the Birmingham Black Barons and Cleveland Buckeyes in 1950 and 1951.

Collins, Eugene

b. 1925, d. 1998

Eugene Collins was a pitcher and outfielder for the Kansas City Monarchs from 1947 to 1951. His best season was 1951, when records show he batted .359. He also batted .299 in 1948. The 5-foot-8, 170-pound Collins, born in Kansas City, Missouri, went on to play minor league and Mexican baseball until 1961.

Collins, Frank

Frank Collins was a pitcher for the Birmingham Black Barons in 1934.

Collins, Fred (Nate)

Fred Collins pitched for the New York Gorhams and Philadelphia Giants in 1888 and 1889.

Collins, George

George Collins was an outfielder and second baseman for the New Orleans Crescent Stars and Milwaukee Bears from 1922 to 1933.

Collins, Jake

Jake Collins was a black pitcher who played for the Sioux Falls Canaries and in the white National Baseball Congress tournament in the 1920s.

Collins, Sonny

Sonny Collins was a pitcher for the New York Black Yankees and Bacharach Giants from 1934 to 1936.

Collins, Walter

Walter Collins pitched for the Chicago American Giants in 1947.

Collins, Willie

Willie Collins was an outfielder for the Nashville Elite Giants in 1933.

Collins, Willie P.

Willie P. Collins was a pitcher for the Birmingham Black Barons from 1950 to 1951.

Colloway, Andrew

Andrew Colloway, from London, West Virginia, was an umpire in 1932 in the East-West League.

Colored Union Club

The Colored Union Club were a black baseball team that played in New York in the 1860s.

Columbia Giants

The Page Fence Giants, a black baseball team from Adrian, Michigan, moved to Chicago in 1899 and played in Chicago into the 20th century. Former Negro league player and historian Sol White described the Columbia Giants as "an organization composed of Chicago's best business and professional men," and said the Giants were "the best-equipped colored team" of their time. They were owned by a businessman named Alvin Garrett, and its roster included players such as Harry Buckner and Billy Holland. However, after a power struggle for a place to play ball in Chicago with Frank Leland, the Columbia Giants had folded by 1901.

Columbia Park

Columbia Park was a baseball field in Chicago that hosted black baseball teams.

Columbus Blue Birds

When the dormant NEGRO NATIONAL LEAGUE was revived in 1933 by Gus Greenlee, the Columbus Blue Birds, out of Columbus, Ohio, were formed to be part of the new league. However, the franchise would fold before the end of the season. They finished in last place in the first half of the season. Some Blue Bird players included outfielder Herman Andrews, infielder Dewey Creacy, and catcher Ameal Brooks. They were managed by William "Dizzy" Dismukes.

Columbus Buckeyes

The Columbus Buckeyes competed for one season in Columbus, Ohio, 1921, in the NEGRO NATIONAL LEAGUE, finishing in sixth place with a record of 24-38. Some of the players on the Buckeyes included Negro baseball historian Sol White, a player-coach at the age of 60, reportedly playing in 12 games with a batting average of .167; John Henry "Pop" Lloyd; and William "Buck" Ewing.

Columbus Elite Giants

The Columbus Elite Giants, owned by Tom Wilson and a member of the NEGRO NATIONAL LEAGUE, lasted in Columbus, Ohio, for just one year, moving there from Nashville to Columbus in 1935. They finished second in the first-half standings behind the Pittsburgh Crawfords and wound up in fourth place in the second half of the season with an overall record of 27-21 for the year. Some of the players on that 1935 Columbus team included pitcher-outfielder Bill Byrd, infielder Sammy Hughes, and catcher Tommy Dukes. After the season they moved to Washington, D.C., and would later move to Baltimore.

Columbus Turfs

The Columbus Turfs played for just a half-year, replacing the Louisville Black Caps in the second half of the 1932 Negro Southern League season.

Colzie, Jim

Jim Colzie was a pitcher for the Cincinnati-Indianapolis Clowns and Indianapolis Clowns from 1946 to 1947.

Combs, Jack

Jack Combs pitched for the Detroit Stars from 1922 to 1925.

Comiskey, Charles

Charles Comiskey, the owner of the Chicago White Sox, had several connections to Negro League baseball. His brother-in-law, John Schorling, was partners with the legendary black baseball pitcher Andrew "Rube" Foster in the ownership and operation of the Chicago Leland Giants in the early 1900s, and Comiskey secretly was the owner of South Side Park, the field that would be leased to the Leland Giants.

Comiskey Park

Comiskey Park was the site of numerous Negro League baseball games, including the first Negro Leagues All-Star Game, the EAST-WEST GAME, in 1934, and subsequent games thereafter, sometimes drawing as many as 50,000 fans to the home of the major league Chicago White Sox.

Communist Party

The American Communist Party was one of the most vocal supporters of integrating major league baseball, with its newspaper, the *Daily Worker*, featuring numerous editorials and stories about the issue. According to Jules Tygiel's book, *Jackie Robinson and His Legacy*, the *Daily Worker*, led by its sports editor, Lester Rodney, "unrelentingly attacked the baseball establishment." The party lobbied for tryouts for black players and organized petitions and protests to force the issue.

Conners, Dock

Dock Conners was a shortstop for the Kansas City Monarchs in 1954.

Connors, John W.

John Connors was the owner of a Brooklyn restaurant called the Royal Cafe and formed the Brooklyn Royal Giants in 1905. He would lose the team later to rival Nat Strong but came back in 1918 as the co-owner of the Atlantic City Bacharach Giants, moving the team to Harlem in a partnership with Baron Wilkins, a Harlem gangster and owner of a nightclub called the Exclusive Club. But Connors failed in that effort, too, and the team was out of business by 1922.

Coogan's Smart Set of New York

Coogan's Smart Set of New York was a black baseball team that played in New York in the early 1900s.

Cook, Charlie

Charlie Cook was a pitcher for the Pittsburgh Crawfords in 1935.

Cook, Howard

Howard Cook was a pitcher for the Indianapolis Athletics in 1937.

Cook, Walter

Walter Cook was a businessman from Trenton, New Jersey, who owned the Cuban Giants in 1886 and 1887. Cook urged his black players to "act as if they were Cubans" so white fans also would come watch them play.

Cooke, James

James Cooke was a pitcher for the Baltimore Black Sox and Bacharach Giants in 1932 and 1933.

Cooley, Walter

Walter Cooley was a catcher and third baseman for the Birmingham Black Barons in 1931.

Cooper, Alex

Alex Cooper was an outfielder for the Philadelphia Tigers and Harrisburg Giants in 1928.

Cooper, Alfred (Army)

Alfred Cooper was a pitcher for the Kansas City Monarchs and Cleveland Stars from 1923 to 1932. He was the brother of another Negro League pitcher, Andy "Lefty" Cooper, who was a teammate on the Monarchs. He was also the manager of one of the teams in the EAST-WEST ALL-STAR GAME in 1938.

Cooper, Andy (Lefty)

Andy Cooper was a pitcher for the Detroit Stars, Chicago American Giants, St. Louis Stars, and Kansas City Monarchs from 1920 to 1941. He also pitched for the U.S. Army's 25th Infantry Team, along with Dobie

Moore and Joe Rogan. He was the brother of another Negro League pitcher, Alfred "Lefty" Cooper, who was a teammate on the Monarchs.

Cooper, Anthony

Anthony Cooper was a shortstop for the Birmingham Black Barons, Cleveland Stars, Baltimore Black Sox, and Cleveland Red Sox from 1929 to 1934.

Cooper, Bill

Bill Cooper was a catcher for the Atlanta Black Crackers and Philadelphia Stars from 1938 to 1942.

Cooper, Chief

Chief Cooper was an umpire in the NEGRO NATIONAL LEAGUE in 1928.

Cooper, Daltie

Daltie Cooper was a pitcher for the Nashville Elite Giants, Indianapolis ABC's, Harrisburg Giants, Lincoln Giants, Hilldale baseball club, Bacharach Giants, Homestead Grays, Baltimore Black Sox, and Newark Eagles from 1921 to 1940.

Cooper, George

George Cooper was a pitcher for the Boston Blues in 1946.

Cooper, Henry

Henry Cooper was a barber from St. Louis who also umpired in the NEGRO NATIONAL LEAGUE in the 1920s.

Cooper, James

James Cooper was a pitcher for the New York Black Yankees, Atlanta Black Crackers, Philadelphia Stars, and Newark Eagles from 1938 to 1947.

Cooper, Ray

Ray Cooper was a pitcher for the Hilldale baseball club from 1928 to 1929.

Cooper, Sam

Sam Cooper was a pitcher for the Baltimore Black Sox, Harrisburg Giants, Bacharach Giants, and Homestead Grays from 1926 to 1934.

Cooper, Thomas
b. 1927

Thomas Cooper was a catcher, outfielder, and first baseman for the Kansas City Monarchs from 1948 to 1953. Records show that he batted .269 in 1948, .279 in 1950, and .281 in 1952. The 6-foot, 180-pound Cooper also went on to play minor league baseball.

Copeland, Lawrence

Lawrence Cooper was an infielder for the Brooklyn Eagles in 1935.

Corbett, Charles

Charles Corbett was a pitcher for the Pittsburgh Keystones, Indianapolis ABC's, and Harrisburg Giants from 1922 to 1928.

Corcoran, Tom

Tom Corcoran pitched for the Homestead Grays in 1942.

Cordova, Pete

Pete Cordova was a shortstop and third baseman for the Toledo Tigers, Cleveland Tate Stars, Kansas City Monarchs, and Havana Cubans from 1917 to 1923.

Cornelius, Willie (Sug)

Willie Cornelius was a pitcher for the Nashville Elite Giants, Memphis Red Sox, Chicago American Giants, and Cole's American Giants from 1929 to 1946. He played in several Negro Leagues EAST-WEST ALL-STAR GAMES. In an interview with author John Holway on file at the National Baseball Hall of Fame, Cornelius, who was slight of build at 168 pounds, said he would win about 27–28 games every year in barnstorming and Negro League competition. He also talked about some of his matchups against Satchel Paige. "I know Satchel Paige and I used to have some awful pitching duels," he said. "I remember one particular game I think I pitched 10 2/3 innings. I had two men out in the 11th inning, and I gave up my first hit. I walked one man in that ball game. I think it was Cool Papa Bell. I remember I walked him, because I picked him off first base. Turkey Stearnes was playing right field for us, and he said to me, 'You couldn't see yourself pitching, but it was something to behold from where I was.' I don't think over three or four balls were hit to the outfield."

Cornelius also compared the quality of Negro League baseball to that of major league baseball. "We had the same thing whites had," he said. "We had good hitting and good fielding. They had good pitching, and we had it over here. Only thing I think, in our baseball we had better of everything. Let's put it this way, if it wasn't better, it was as good. At the time 250 to 500 good ballplayers. I mean players that could have made any club in the major leagues and could have stayed there. Now you take Jackie Robinson and [Roy] Campanella, they were in the Negro Leagues. Well, I don't think Campanella had two hits off me all the while he was over here. And Jackie Robinson had one single off me, as far I can remember. They went over there and they were .300-plus hitters. I say if a man could hit .200 in the league we were in, he'd be a .350–.375 hitter over there. We had some pitchers who were just as tough. You take Birmingham, you take Memphis, Nashville, Kansas City—all those clubs carried five pitchers, and whenever the manager said, 'You're pitching today,' you pitched nine innings. You always got a good pitched ball game."

Cornett, Harry

Harry Cornett was a catcher for the Indianapolis ABC's in 1913.

Correa, Marceline

Marceline Correa was a shortstop for the Cuban Stars and New York Cubans from 1926 to 1936.

Cortez, Aurelio

Aurelio Cortez was a catcher for the Cuban Stars from 1928 to 1931.

Cos, Celedonco

Celedonco Cos pitched for the Indianapolis Clowns in 1954.

Cottman, Darby

Darby Cottman was a third baseman for the Chicago Unions from 1887 to 1893.

Cotton, James

James Cotton was an officer for the Chattanooga Choo-Choos in 1945.

Cowan, Eddie

Eddie Cowan played shortstop for the Cleveland Tate Stars in 1919.

Cowan, John

John Cowan was a third baseman and second baseman for the Birmingham Black Barons, Cleveland Buckeyes, and Memphis Red Sox from 1934 to 1950.

Cox, Alphonse

Alphonse Cox was a pitcher for the Jacksonville Red Caps, Memphis Red Sox, and Cleveland Bears from 1938 to 1943.

Cox, Hannibal

Hannibal Cox was an outfielder for the Nashville Elite Giants in 1931.

Cox, Roosevelt

Roosevelt Cox was a shortstop, second baseman, and third baseman for the Detroit Stars, Kansas City Monarchs, New York Cubans, and Cuban Stars from 1937 to 1943.

Cox, Tom

Tom Cox was a pitcher for the Cleveland Cubs, Cleveland Tigers, and Lincoln Giants from 1928 to 1932.

Cozart, Harry

Harry Cozart was a pitcher for the Newark Eagles from 1939 to 1943.

Craig, Charles

Charles Craig was a pitcher for the Lincoln Giants and Brooklyn Cuban Giants from 1926 to 1928.

Craig, Dick

Dick Craig played first base for the Indianapolis Crawfords in 1940.

Craig, Homer

Homer Craig was a pitcher for the Newark Dodgers in 1934 and 1935.

Craig, John

John Craig was an umpire in the NEGRO NATIONAL LEAGUE from 1935 to 1946 and is credited with inventing the inside chest protector for umpires.

Craig, Joseph

Joseph Craig was an outfielder and first baseman for the Philadelphia Stars and Indianapolis Crawfords in 1940 and 1946.

Crawford, John

John Crawford was an umpire in the NEGRO NATIONAL LEAGUE in 1943.

Crawford, Sam

Sam Crawford was a pitcher and later managed for the New York Black Sox, Chicago Giants, Chicago American Giants, Chicago Union Giants, Detroit Stars, Kansas City Monarchs, Brooklyn Royal Giants, Birmingham Black Barons, Chicago Columbia Giants, Cole's American Giants, and Indianapolis Athletics from 1910 to 1937.

Crawford, Willie

Willie Crawford was an outfielder with the Birmingham Black Barons in 1934.

Crawford Colored Giants

The Crawford Colored Giants were a black baseball team in Pittsburgh owned by nightclub owner and numbers operator Gus Greenlee in the early 1930s and developed into the Pittsburgh Crawfords.

Crawford Grille

The Crawford Grille was the Pittsburgh nightclub owned by Gus Greenlee, the Pittsburgh numbers racketeer who started the Pittsburgh Crawfords, the legendary Negro League baseball team named after the nightclub. The club often featured such great performers as Cab Calloway and Duke Ellington. It burned down in 1951 and was rebuilt at a new location with new ownership.

Creacy, Dewey

Dewey Creacy played third base for the Kansas City Monarchs, St. Louis Stars, Detroit Wolves, Washington Pilots, Columbus Blue Birds, Cleveland Giants, Philadelphia Stars, and Brooklyn Royal Giants from 1924 to 1940.

Creek, Willie

Willie Creek was a catcher for the Brooklyn Royal Giants in 1930.

Crespo, Alejandro

Alejandro Crespo was a second baseman and third baseman for the Cuban Stars and Cuban Stars of Havana from 1918 to 1933.

Crespo, Alex

b. 1915

Alex Crespo, born in Guira de Melana, Cuba, played the outfield for the Cuban Stars and New York Cubans for two seasons, 1940, when he batted .278, and, 1946, batting .336, records show. He also played in the Mexican and Venezuelan leagues and in the Cuban Winter League from 1939 to 1954.

Crockett, Frank

Frank Crockett was an outfielder for the Brooklyn Royal Giants, Norfork Stars, and Bacharach Giants from 1916 to 1923.

Cromartie, Leroy

Leroy Cromartie was a second baseman for the Cincinnati-Indianapolis Clowns in 1945.

Crosby, Ralph

Ralph Crosby was an infielder for the Birmingham Black Barons in 1954.

Cross, Bennie

Bennie Cross was an outfielder for the Boston Resolutes in 1887.

Cross, Norman

Norman Cross pitched for Cole's American Giants in 1932.

Crossan, Frank

Frank Crossan was a pitcher for the Memphis Red Sox in 1954.

Crossen, George

George Crossen was a catcher for the Lincoln Giants in 1921.

Crowe, George Daniel

b. 1931

George Crowe played first base and the outfield for the New York Cubans from 1947 to 1949. The 6-foot-2, 220-

pound Crowe, born in Whiteland, Indiana, went on to play in the major leagues for the Boston and Milwaukee Braves, Cincinnati Reds, and St. Louis Cardinals, and in nine seasons, Crowe batted .270 with 81 home runs and 299 RBIs in 702 games. He also played winter baseball in Puerto Rico and Cuba, batting .375 and .396 in two years of winter ball in Puerto Rico in 1950–51 and 1951–52.

Crudup, Zeke

Zeke Crudup was a pitcher for the Philadelphia Giants from 1924 to 1928.

Crue, Martin

Martin Crue was a pitcher for the Homestead Grays, New Orleans Eagles, and New York Cubans from 1942 to 1951.

Crumbie, Ralph

Ralph Crumbie was a catcher for the Pittsburgh Crawfords in 1946.

Crumbley, Alex

Alex Crumbley was an outfielder and pitcher for the Atlanta Black Crackers, Pittsburgh Crawfords, Washington Black Senators, and New York Black Yankees from 1938 to 1939.

Crump, James

James Crump played second base for the Norfolk Giants, Norfolk Stars, Hilldale baseball club, and Philadelphia Giants from 1920 to 1938. He also worked as an umpire in the NEGRO NATIONAL LEAGUE.

Crump, Willis

Willis Crump was an outfielder and second baseman for the Bacharach Giants from 1916 to 1923.

Crutchfield, Jimmie

b. 1910, d. 1993

Jimmie Crutchfield was a solid outfielder who proved to be one of the most dependable ballplayers in Negro League baseball. He played for the Indianapolis ABC's, Birmingham Black Barons, Newark Eagles, Pittsburgh Crawfords, Indianapolis Crawfords, Toledo Crawfords, Cleveland Buckeyes, and Chicago American Giants from 1930 to 1945. He hit near .300 throughout his career and was adept at hitting the ball to all fields. In a 1992 interview with *Sports Collectors Digest*, Crutchfield, born in

Ardmore, Missouri, said he had to overcome his slight build to become a good hitter when he first started. "I was young and the smallest man on the field, so I almost had to hit," Crutchfield said. "Pitchers often thought they could just throw the ball by me because of my size. But I could pick that ball up. . . . I had good eyes. Plus I was pretty lucky. . . . I was a line-drive hitter who depended on speed and fielding. Plus, it was hard to get the third strike past me." He began his career with the Birmingham Black Barons in 1930, and batted .331 the follow-

Jimmie Crutchfield had a reputation in the Negro Leagues as a reliable and likable outfielder who hit near .300 throughout his career with the Indianapolis ABC's, Birmingham Black Barons, Newark Eagles, Pittsburgh Crawfords, Indianapolis Crawfords, Toledo Crawfords, Cleveland Buckeyes, and Chicago American Giants from 1930 to 1945. In Pittsburgh, Crutchfield played in one of the legendary outfields of Negro League baseball, alongside Ted Strong and Cool Papa Bell. (NATIONAL BASEBALL HALL OF FAME LIBRARY, COOPERSTOWN, N.Y.)

ing season. He also went on to play in one of the legendary outfields of Negro League baseball, in Pittsburgh alongside Ted Strong and Cool Papa Bell on the Pittsburgh Crawfords. Crutchfield also played in numerous Negro League All-Star Games, known as the EAST-WEST GAME. In the Robert Peterson book, *Only the Ball Was White,* Crutchfield spoke of the often loose financial arrangements that players lived with, talking about his playing days with Indianapolis: "We weren't getting paid. That would go on maybe for two months till we had a good gate. Then perhaps you got some of your back pay. Maybe one or two of the fellows would be getting something under the table, but most of us weren't being paid. So we were going to Pittsburgh to play, and when we got there the Crawfords gave me $25 or $50, so I stayed. That's how I went to the Pittsburgh Crawfords."

Fellow Negro Leaguer Monte Irvin, in a 1992 *Sports Collectors Digest* article, said that Crutchfield was a good player who was well liked by teammates and opponents alike. "Although he didn't have a lot of power, Jimmie was a real good fielder and had an adequate arm," Irvin said. "Plus he could run real well and was a great team player. Down through the years, Jimmie has always been loved by just about everyone in the Negro Leagues."

In a 1971 interview, Crutchfield looked back on his playing days with fond memories. "Once in a while I get a kick out of thinking that my name was mentioned as one of the stars of the East-West Game and little things like that," he said. "I don't know whether I'd feel better if I had a million dollars [but] I can say I contributed something [to baseball]."

Cuban Giants

The Cuban Giants were formed in 1885, the first black professional baseball team, according to former Negro League player and black baseball historian Sol White. They were formed by Frank P. Thompson, the headwaiter at the Argyle Hotel in Babylon, New York, during the summer of 1885. Thompson put together a team from the Negro waiters who worked at the hotel as entertainers for the hotel's guests. Walter Cook, a businessman from Trenton, New Jersey, took over operation of the team, turning them into a professional club in 1886, and encouraged them to act like Cubans, believing more white fans would come watch if they believed the players were Cubans instead of American blacks. Some of the great players who were on those Cuban Giant teams included pitcher George Stovey and Frank Grant. They continued to be a popular barnstorming team and were considered to be the best black team of their time.

Cook died in 1887, and John M. Bright took over the operation of the team. In 1889, the Giants joined the Middle States League, representing Trenton; two

years later the name of the team changed to the Monarchs of York (Pennsylvania), and the team became part of the Eastern Interstate League, the reorganization of the Middle States League. The team underwent another change in 1891, and they were then called the Big Gorhams and represented Ansonia, Connecticut, in the Connecticut State League. Accounts claim that the team won 100 games and lost just four. In 1900, they reverted back to a version of their original name, the Genuine Cuban Giants.

Cuban Stars

One version of the Cuban Stars, a black baseball team, was organized in 1905, coming out of Santiago, Cuba. Another surfaced the following year out of Havana. Both consisted of Cuban ballplayers who played as a Negro baseball team that barnstormed around the United States. Later, there was a Cuban Stars team that played out of New York, with their home field the Dyckman Oval in uptown Manhattan. They were owned by Nat Strong and operated by Harlem numbers operator Alex Pompez. The Stars were one of the original teams formed to create the NEGRO NATIONAL LEAGUE in 1920. In the 1930s, the Cubans would include such great players as Martin Dihigo. There would be other versions of the Cuban Stars in later years in different part of the country. They played until 1950, and won the Negro National League championship in 1947, with such players as pitchers Dave Barnhill and Luis Tiant, Sr., and a young outfielder named Minnie Minoso.

Cuban X Giants

The Cuban X Giants were a black baseball team founded by white businessman E. B. Lamar, Jr., in the 1890s and named to cash in on the popularity of the popular Cuban Giants. The Cuban Giants tried to sue the Cuban X Giants for using the name, but the suit failed. The Cuban X Giants, based out of New York where they played at the Brighton Oval and Dexter Park, were one of the top black teams in the country in the early 1900s. In 1903, the Cuban X Giants played the Philadelphia Giants, and Rube Foster, pitching for the Cuban X Giants, won four of the five games that the Cuban X Giants won in a seven-game series billed as "the colored championship of the world." In 1904, the Cuban X Giants lost a two-out-of-three series to Philadelphia, with Foster now pitching for the Philadelphia Giants. In 1906, the Cuban X Giants joined the Independent Professional Base Ball Clubs league, but the league collapsed after that season, and so did the Cuban X Giants. Other Negro League greats who played for the Cuban X Giants included John Henry Lloyd, Grant Johnson, and Charles Grant.

Cuella, Jose Luis

Jose Cuella was an outfielder for the Pittsburgh Crawfords in 1945.

Cuerira, Basilio

Basilio Cuerira was a pitcher and outfielder for the Cuban Stars and All Cubans from 1921 to 1922.

Culver, Culcra

Culcra Culver was a shortstop, third baseman, and outfielder for the Pittsburgh Stars, Pennsylvania Red Caps, Cuban Stars, and Lincoln Stars from 1916 to 1922.

Cummings, Hugh

Hugh Cummings was the manager of the Baltimore Lord Baltimores in 1887.

Cummings, Napoleon (Chance)

Napoleon Cummings was a first baseman and second baseman for the Duval Giants in Jacksonville, Florida, the Atlantic City Bacharach Giants, and Hilldale baseball club from 1916 to 1929. His nickname "Chance" was taken from major league first baseman Frank Chance. He later went on to work in the Atlantic City prosecutor's office and told Robert Peterson in his book *Only the Ball Was White* about how players worked at other jobs while playing ball. "Some of them came in here and got into politics and went from there," Cummings said. "We were only here [Atlantic City] a few days before we got registered to vote. I been in politics ever since. We came here on the fifth of May, and we played our first game on the eighth, and I registered on the ninth."

Cunningham, Earl

Earl Cunningham was a second baseman and outfielder for the Detroit Stars in 1955.

Cunningham, Harry

Harry Cunningham was a pitcher for the Memphis Red Sox and Birmingham Black Barons from 1930 to 1937.

Cunningham, Larry

Larry Cunningham was an outfielder for the New Orleans Eagles, Houston Eagles, and Memphis Red Sox from 1950 to 1951.

Cunningham, Marion

Marion Cunningham was a first baseman and manager for the Memphis Red Sox and Montgomery Red Sox from 1924 to 1926.

Cunningham, Robert

Robert Cunningham pitched for the Cleveland Buckeyes in 1950.

Curley, Earl

Earl Curley was an outfielder for the Memphis Red Sox in 1925.

Currie, Reuben (Rube)

Reuben Currie was a pitcher for the Chicago Unions, Kansas City Monarchs, Hilldale baseball club, Chicago American Giants, and Detroit Stars from 1919 to 1932.

Curry, Homer (Goose)

Homer Curry was an outfielder, pitcher, and manager for the Memphis Red Sox, Washington Elite Giants, New York Black Yankees, Newark Eagles, Baltimore Elite Giants, and Philadelphia Stars from 1930 to 1950.

Curry, Oscar

Oscar Curry was a pitcher for the Cuban Giants in 1887.

Curtis, Harry

Harry Curtis was a white businessman from southwestern New York who started the Acme Colored Giants in 1898, representing Celeron, New York, and joined the Iron and Oil League—a league of white teams. He folded the team after it went 8-49 and came back with a new version, this time with white players.

Custer's Baseball Club of Columbus

Custer's Baseball Club of Columbus was a black baseball team in Columbus, Ohio, that played in the 1920s.

Cyrus, Herb

Herb Cyrus was a third baseman for the Kansas City Monarchs from 1940 to 1943.

Dabney, John Milton

John Milton Dabney was an outfielder and pitcher for the Argyle Hotel and Cuban X Giants from 1885 to 1896.

Dailey, James

James Dailey was a pitcher for the Baltimore Elite Giants in 1948.

Daily Worker

The *Daily Worker* was the Communist Party newspaper, which pushed for the integration of major league baseball in the late 1930s and early 1940s.

Dallard, William (Eggie)

William Dallard was a first baseman, catcher, and outfielder for the Baltimore Black Sox, Wilmington Potomacs, Hilldale baseball club, Bacharach Giants, Darby Daisies, Quaker Giants, and Philadelphia Stars from 1925 to 1933.

Dallas, Bill

Bill Dallas was a white sportswriter who was hired by Hilldale baseball club owner Ed Bolden in 1925 to supervise the umpires of his Eastern League.

Dallas, Porter (Big Boy)

Porter Dallas was a third baseman for the Monroe Monarchs and the Birmingham Black Barons from 1929 to 1932.

Dallas Black Giants

The Dallas Black Giants were a black baseball team out of Dallas, Texas, that played in the Texas Negro League in the 1920s.

Dalton, Rossie

Rossie Dalton was an infielder for the Chicago American Giants and Birmingham Black Barons in 1940.

Dancer, Carl

Carl Dancer was an outfielder for the Detroit Stars in 1954.

Dandridge, John

John Dandridge was a pitcher for the Houston Eagles in 1949.

Dandridge, Ping

Ping Dandridge was an infielder and pitcher for the Havana Red Sox, St. Louis Giants, and Lincoln Giants from 1917 to 1920.

Dandridge, Ray Emmett (Hooks)
b. 1913, d. 1994

Ray Dandridge was considered one of the greatest third basemen in Negro League baseball history. He was known for his soft hands, strong arm, and bowed legs. He was selected by the Veterans Committee for the National Baseball Hall of Fame in 1987, with an overall lifetime mark of .319 in Negro League baseball. He is also a member of the Mexican Baseball Hall of Fame, with a league career average of .347, but was inducted there as a shortstop. He also played second base.

Born in Richmond, Virginia, Dandridge played third base, second base, and shortstop for the Paramount All-Stars, Nashville Elite Giants, Detroit Stars, Newark Eagles, Newark Dodgers, and New York Cubans from 1933 to 1949. Roy Campanella said of the 5-foot-8, 175-pound Dandridge: "I never saw anyone better as a fielder." Another Negro Leaguer who went on to play in the major leagues, Monte Irvin, also described Dandridge in John Holway's book *Blackball Stars* as the best third baseman he had ever seen. "Ray Dandridge was fantastic," Irvin said. "Best I've ever seen at third. I saw all the greats—Brooks, Nettles—but I've never seen a better third baseman than Dandridge. . . . I never saw Judy [Johnson] in his prime. I never saw [Oliver] Marcelle at all, but a lot of people who saw both would give it to Dandridge because of his hitting, his fielding, and his speed. Once you saw him, you never would forget him."

In a 1987 *Sports Illustrated* article, Dandridge talked about life on the road in the Negro Leagues: "We didn't make any money, but we had fun," he said. "Riding the buses, hanging our sweatshirts out the windows to dry for the next day's three games. We used to have quartets. We'd challenge each other as we went down the road. And when we'd meet another team, we'd have wrestling matches. We'd go over to their clubhouse and say, 'We've got the strongest man.'" He was a slap hitter who batted .436 in 1934, followed up by .368 in 1935. He had a career batting average of .355 in the NEGRO NATIONAL LEAGUE. Dandridge played much of his career in the 1930s with the Newark Eagles, where he, Dick Seay, Willie Wells, and Mules Suttles formed the legendary "million dollar infield" for the Eagles. He left to play in Mexico in 1940 but returned to Newark in 1944 and hit .370, leading the Negro National League in hits and runs scored. He went back to Mexico in 1945 as a player-manager, and in nine Mexican League seasons, Dandridge batted .343. His movement between the Negro Leagues and Mexican Leagues created some bitter feelings among Negro League baseball owners. According to Mark Ribowsky's book *A Complete History of the Negro Leagues*, Newark owner Effa Manley tried to pressure Dandridge to stay with Newark in 1945 by attempting to get his draft status upgraded to 1-A for leaving the country, but she was unsuccessful. Dandridge also played on an All-Star

Ray Dandridge was a star in the Mexican League, where he is a member of the Mexican Baseball Hall of Fame, but he made his mark as one of the greatest third basemen in Negro League history and has also been inducted into the National Baseball Hall of Fame in Cooperstown. Dandridge played much of his career in the 1930s with the Newark Eagles where he, Dick Seay, Willie Wells, and Mules Suttles formed the legendary "million dollar infield" for the Eagles. (NATIONAL BASEBALL HALL OF FAME LIBRARY, COOPERSTOWN, N.Y.)

team in Venezuela in 1947 that, in an exhibition game, defeated the New York Yankees, who would go on to win the World Series that season.

In 1948, he was player-manager of the New York Cubans. In 1949, Dandridge, at the age of 36, although according to Ribowsky's book Dandridge told the Giants he was 29, signed a contract with the New York Giants. Playing for their Class AA team in Minneapolis, Dandridge was the league's Most Valuable Player, batting .363 and leading the Minneapolis Millers to a championship. One of his teammates was a young Willie Mays. Dandridge played four years in the minor leagues, also playing with the Sacramento Solons and Oakland Oaks of the Pacific Coast League, with an overall average of .318. But he never got a call from the New York Giants to the major leagues, still a victim of racial policies that limited the number of black players coming into the major league game. He would eventually work for the Giants but as a scout after the team moved to San Francisco.

Dandridge, Troy
Troy Dandridge was a shortstop and third baseman for the Dayton Marcos and Chicago Giants from 1926 to 1929.

Daniels, Alonzo
Alonzo Daniels was a pitcher for the Newark Dodgers in 1935.

Daniels, Eddie
Eddie Daniels was a pitcher for the New York Cubans in 1947.

Daniels, Fred
Fred Daniels was a pitcher for the Birmingham Black Barons, St. Louis Giants, and Hilldale baseball club from 1919 to 1927.

Daniels, Hammond
Hammond Daniels was an officer with the Bacharach Giants from 1924 to 1926.

Daniels, Harry
Harry Daniels was a secretary with the Philadelphia Quaker Giants in 1908.

Daniels, James George (Schoolboy)
James Daniels was a pitcher for the Birmingham Black Barons in 1943.

Daniels, John
John Daniels was a pitcher for the Detroit Stars in 1955.

Daniels, Leon (Pepper)
Leon Daniels was a catcher and first baseman for the Harrisburg Giants, Detroit Stars, Brooklyn Eagles, and Cuban Stars from 1921 to 1935.

Darby, Eddy
Eddy Darby was an outfielder for the Philadelphia Giants in 1904.

Darden, Clarence
Clarence Darden was a third baseman for the Atlanta Black Crackers in 1938.

Darden, Floyd
Floyd Darden was a second baseman for the Baltimore Elite Giants in 1950.

Darnell, Herman
Herman Darnell was a first baseman for the Indianapolis Clowns in 1951.

Davenport, Lloyd (Ducky)
Lloyd Davenport was an outfielder and manager for the Monroe Monarchs, Philadelphia Stars, Cincinnati Tigers, Memphis Red Sox, Birmingham Black Barons, Chicago American Giants, Jacksonville Red Caps, Louisville Buckeyes, Pittsburgh Crawfords, Cleveland Buckeyes, and New Orleans Crescent Stars from 1934 to 1951.

Davidson, Charles (Specks)
Charles Davidson was a pitcher who played in 1939 and 1940 and then returned after World War II to play from 1946 to 1949 for the New York Black Yankees, Brooklyn Royal Giants, Memphis Red Sox, and Baltimore Elite Giants.

Davis, A. G.
A. G. Davis was an umpire in the League of Colored Base Ball Players in 1887.

Davis, Albert
Albert Davis was a pitcher for the Detroit Stars and Baltimore Black Sox from 1928 to 1937.

Davis, Ambrose
Ambrose Davis was the owner of the New York Gorhams from 1887 to 1891. Former Negro League player and historian Sol White called Davis one of the greatest figures in the history of early black baseball.

Davis, Charley
Charley Davis was a pitcher for the Memphis Red Sox from 1953 to 1955.

Davis, Dwight

Dwight Davis was a pitcher for the Detroit Stars and Pittsburgh Crawfords in 1931 and 1932.

Davis, Earl (Hawk)

Earl Davis was a second baseman for the Bacharach Giants, Hilldale baseball club, Indianapolis ABC's, Philadelphia Giants, and Newark Browns from 1927 to 1938.

Davis, Eddie (Peanuts)

Eddie Davis was a pitcher for the Cincinnati Clowns, Cincinnati-Indianapolis Clowns, and Indianapolis Clowns from 1942 to 1950.

Davis, Hy

Hy Davis was a first baseman for the Hilldale baseball club and Newark Dodgers in 1934.

Davis, Jack

Jack Davis was a third baseman for the Philadelphia Giants and Bacharach Giants from 1922 to 1925.

Davis, James

James Davis was a pitcher for the Chicago Giants, Lincoln Giants, and Kansas City Monarchs in 1920 and 1921.

Davis, John

John Davis was a pitcher for the Algona Brownies, Cuban Giants, Chicago Union Giants, Leland Giants, and Philadelphia Giants from 1903 to 1910.

Davis, John Howard (Cherokee)
b. 1917, d. 1982

John Davis was a pitcher and outfielder for the Newark Eagles and Houston Eagles from 1943 to 1950. Records show that Davis, born in Ashland, Virginia, had a five-year run of .300-plus batting averages in limited plate appearances, batting .405 in 48 at bats in 1941, .305 in 42 at bats in 1942, .344 in 154 at bats in 1943, .319 in 138 at bats in 1944 and .340 in 159 at bats in 1945. He also played in the Mexican League and minor league ball, including one year with San Diego in 1952 when Davis batted .263 with six home runs and 36 RBIs in 167 at bats.

Davis, Lee

Lee Davis was a pitcher for the Kansas City Monarchs in 1945.

Davis, Lonnie

Lonnie Davis was a first baseman for the Chicago American Giants in 1952.

Davis, Lorenzo (Piper)
b. 1917, d. 1997

Lorenzo Davis has a place in baseball history as being the first black player signed by the Boston Red Sox organization in 1950, though he would never reach the major league level. However, he did work for 25 years as a scout for three major league teams—the St. Louis Cardinals, the Detroit Tigers, and the Montreal Expos. The 6-foot-3 Davis was also one of a number of Negro League ballplayers who would also play basketball for the Harlem Globetrotters. Finally, Davis, as player-manager of the Birmingham Black Barons, would also be part of history by signing a 16-year-old outfielder named Willie Mays to play for the Black Barons.

Davis, born in Piper, Alabama, was a high school basketball star in Birmingham and won a scholarship to play at Alabama State University. He was forced to quit after one year, though, and to work to help support his family. He worked at a steel mill and played for the company's black baseball team in a city league. In 1936, Davis signed a contract to play for the Omaha Tigers, a barnstorming Negro baseball team but was back in Birmingham to play in the city league the following season after the Tigers had financial problems. He was signed by the Birmingham Black Barons, who were managed by Winfield Welch, who was also the head coach of the Harlem Globetrotters. Welch also signed Davis to play for the Globetrotters.

The Black Barons would go on to be one of the most powerful teams in Negro League baseball history, winning the NEGRO AMERICAN LEAGUE pennant in 1943 and 1944, only to lose in the World Series to the Homestead Grays. Playing first base, second base, and the outfield, Davis's best years with Birmingham were 1948, when he batted .353, and 1950, when he hit .383. The Black Barons would win a third pennant in 1948, with Davis as player-manager, and again lose to the Grays in the World Series.

Davis nearly joined Jackie Robinson in the major leagues in that historic 1947 season, as the St. Louis Browns also took out a 30-day option to sign Davis. He was passed over, though, in favor of Kansas City Monarchs' outfielders Hank Thompson and Willard Brown for the major league club. The door opened too late for Davis. "If he'd had a chance when he was young, he'd have been outstanding," said Brooklyn Dodger scout

Clyde Sukeforth, in Jules Tygiel's book *Jackie Robinson and His Legacy*. Davis was offered a minor league contract by the Browns, which he rejected.

In 1950, Davis signed a deal with the Boston Red Sox, a minor league contract with their Scranton, Pennsylvania, Class A team for $15,000. The Red Sox paid Birmingham owner Tom Hayes $7,500 for the rights to sign Davis, who, like many Negro Leaguers, told Boston he was 29 years old, two years younger than he really was. According to Tygiel, Red Sox general manager Joe Cronin told reporters that he had signed the "sleeper" of the season, and declared that Davis was just 26 years old. Davis described to Tygiel what happened after he reported to the Red Sox training camp in Cocoa, Florida: "I took the routine exercises, got ready to throw," he said. "I patted that ball around for a minute or more, but it felt like 15. Nobody spoke to me." Davis said because of local segregation laws, he could not live or eat with his teammates. He lived in a house with a group of black waiters in town. He ate with the waiters while his teammates ate together in the dining room. He played with the team's Class A club in Scranton and was batting .333 after 15 games when he was suddenly released for "economical reasons." Davis said that reason was "a joke, because [Red Sox owner] Tom Yawkey was one of the richest men in the East."

From 1951 to 1955, Davis played with the Oakland Oaks in the Pacific Coast League. His best season with Oakland was 1953, when he hit 13 home runs and had 97 RBIs with 90 runs scored and a .288 average. In 1956, Davis signed with the Brooklyn Dodgers, who assigned him to their Class AAA club in Los Angeles. The following season he was sent down to the Fort Worth Cats in Class AA ball and retired after the 1958 season. Davis was inducted into the Alabama Sports Hall of Fame in 1993.

Davis, Martin Luther

Martin Davis was a pitcher for the Chicago American Giants in 1945.

Davis, Nathaniel

Nathaniel Davis was a first baseman for the New York Black Yankees and Philadelphia Stars from 1947 to 1950.

Davis, Red

Red Davis was an outfielder for the Indianapolis ABC's in 1925.

Davis, Robert (Butch)

Robert Davis was an outfielder for the Atlanta Black Crackers and Baltimore Elite Giants from 1946 to 1950. In

1947, Davis batted .340 for Baltimore and followed that in 1949 with a .371 average. He also played in the Mexican League and minor league baseball, batting .319 in 257 at bats with Class AA Toledo and Charleston in 1952.

Davis, Roosevelt

Roosevelt Davis was a pitcher for the Columbus Blue Birds, St. Louis Stars, New York Black Yankees, Pittsburgh Crawfords, Memphis Red Sox, Philadelphia Stars, Baltimore Elite Giants, Brooklyn Royal Giants, Chicago Brown Bombers, Cincinnati Clowns, Cincinnati-Indianapolis Clowns, and Cleveland Buckeyes from 1924 to 1945.

Davis, Ross (Satchel)

Ross Davis was a pitcher for the Cleveland Buckeyes in 1947.

Davis, Saul Henry (Rareback)

Saul Davis was a shortstop, third baseman, and second baseman for the Cleveland Tigers, Birmingham Black Barons, Chicago American Giants, Memphis Red Sox, and Detroit Stars from 1925 to 1931.

Davis, Spencer (Babe)

Spencer Davis played shortstop, third base, and the outfield and managed for the Atlanta Black Crackers, Indianapolis ABC's, New York Black Yankees, Winston–Salem Giants, and Brooklyn Eagles from 1935 to 1948.

Davis, Walter (Steel Arm)

Walter Davis was an outfielder, pitcher, and first baseman for the Chicago American Giants, Detroit Stars, Chicago Columbia Giants, Nashville Elite Giants, and Cole's American Giants from 1923 to 1934.

Davis, William

William Davis was a third baseman and outfielder for the St. Louis Stars, Memphis Red Sox, Indianapolis ABC's, and Atlanta Black Crackers from 1937 to 1940.

Davis, William N.

William Davis was a pitcher for the Philadelphia Stars from 1945 to 1947.

Davis, Willie

Willie Davis was an officer with the Mobile Black Shippers in 1945.

Dawson, Johnny

Johnny Dawson was a catcher for the Memphis Red Sox, Kansas City Monarchs, Birmingham Black Barons, and Chicago American Giants from 1938 to 1942.

Dawson, Leroy

Leroy Dawson was the manager of the Philadelphia Stars in 1946.

Day, Eddie

Eddie Day was a shortstop for the Acme Colored Giants in Celeron, New York, in 1898.

Day, Guy

Guy Day was a catcher for the Argyle Hotel in Babylon, New York, in 1885.

Day, Leon

b. 1916, d. 1995

Leon Day is considered one of the top pitchers in Negro League baseball history—a seven-time All Star. Though not as colorful as the legendary Satchel Paige, Day would get the best of Paige in their four meetings, winning three of them. Some historians estimate Day won more than 300 games in his career and batted over .300, but the records are incomplete. Records show he batted .469 in 49 at bats in 1946, and .336 in 122 at bats in 1941. One report had Day going undefeated during the 1937 Negro League season, posting a 15-0 record during the 40-game season. He also posted a 12-4 mark in 1939 and 13-4 in 1946. Day spent much of his career with the Newark Eagles, also playing second base and the outfield. But it was as a pitcher that he made his mark. Former teammate Monte Irvin said Day "was always the best pitcher on every team he ever played for, and he was as good as or better than the starting center fielder on our team. That center fielder was me." Irvin compared Day's pitching style to that of St. Louis Cardinals pitcher Bob Gibson. Author Jules Tygiel wrote in his book *Jackie Robinson and His Legacy* that Day excelled at every position.

Born in Alexandria, Virginia, Day's family moved to Baltimore soon after his birth. He showed his baseball abilities at an early age, playing with a local men's team, the Mount Winan Athletic Club, when he was just 12 years old. He left school several years later to play ball for a semipro team called the Silver Moons, and, in 1934, at the age of 17, joined a pro team out of Chester, Pennsylvania, called the Black Sox. One year later the team folded, and Day went to play for the Brooklyn Eagles, who moved to Newark, New Jersey, a year later. His style of pitching was to deliver the ball from his hip, and his best pitch was a fastball, though he also had a strong change-up and good curveball. In 1942, Day struck out 18 pitching for the Baltimore Elite Giants at Bugle Field in Baltimore, which was considered to be the Negro National League single-game record. Day also pitched in winter ball in Mexico and Puerto Rico and held the Puerto Rican League record for strikeouts in a single game with 19.

Day joined the U.S. Army after the 1943 season, and two years later he pitched in an exhibition game at Nuremburg Stadium against a group of white major league ballplayers in front of more than 100,000 servicemen. Day allowed just four hits in a 2-1 win. He believed he suffered an arm injury while in the service and was not the same pitcher when he came back to the states. But he still managed to turn in his finest performance on opening day of 1946, hurling a no-hitter against the Philadelphia Stars at Newark's Ruppert Stadium. Day told friends that Jackie Robinson had tried to recruit him for the

To some Negro League historians, Leon Day was every bit as good a pitcher as Satchel Paige. He was a seven-time All Star, and there are some estimates that he won more than 300 games in his career and also batted over .300 as a pitcher and outfielder for the Brooklyn Eagles, Newark Eagles, and Baltimore Elite Giants from 1935 to 1946, including an undefeated 15-0 record in the 1937 season. (NATIONAL BASEBALL HALL OF FAME LIBRARY, COOPERSTOWN, N.Y.)

Brooklyn Dodgers' farm team in Montreal, but Day already had signed a contract to play for the Newark Eagles. He would never make the major leagues but did play with minor league teams in Toronto, Edmonton, and Scranton. In his last year, with the Boston Red Sox minor league team in Scranton, Day pitched well, with a 13-9 record and a 3.41 ERA. But no major league opportunities opened up, and he retired after the 1952 season. On March 7, 1995, Day became the 12th Negro League player elected to the National Baseball Hall of Fame. He died of heart failure after battling diabetes, six days after he was voted in.

Day, Wilson C. (Connie)

Wilson Day was a second baseman, shortstop, and third baseman for the Baltimore Black Sox, Indianapolis ABC's, Harrisburg Giants, and Bacharach Giants from 1920 to 1932.

Dayton Chappies

The Dayton Chappies were a black baseball team that played in Dayton, Ohio, in the early 1900s.

Dayton Giants

The Dayton Giants were a black baseball team that played in Dayton, Ohio, in the early 1900s.

Dayton Marcos

The Dayton Marcos were a black baseball team in Dayton, Ohio, that played in the early 1900s and was one of the original teams in the NEGRO NATIONAL LEAGUE. However, they moved to Columbus after the 1920 season and folded after the 1921 season.

Dean, Charlie

Charlie Dean was a pitcher for the New York Black Yankees in 1947.

Dean, Jimmy

Jimmy Dean was a pitcher for the Philadelphia Stars, New York Cubans, and New York Black Yankees from 1946 to 1950.

Dean, Nelson

Nelson Dean was a pitcher for the Cleveland Hornets, Kansas City Monarchs, Cleveland Tigers, Detroit Stars, and Cleveland Stars from 1925 to 1932.

Dean, Robert

Robert Dean was a pitcher for the St. Louis Stars in 1939 and 1940.

Dean, Robert

Robert Dean was a second baseman and third baseman for the Lincoln Giants and Pennsylvania Red Caps from 1925 to 1933.

Deane, Alpheus

Alpheus Deane was a pitcher for the New York Black Yankees in 1947.

Deas, James Alvin (Yank)

James Deas was a catcher for the Bacharach Giants, Lincoln Giants, Philadelphia Giants, Pennsylvania Giants, Richmond Giants, and Hilldale baseball club from 1916 to 1928. He caught for such Negro League pitching greats as Smokey Joe Williams and Dick Redding.

Deberry, C. I.

C. I. Deberry was the manager of the Greensboro Red Wings and vice president of the Negro American Association in 1948.

Debran, Roy

Roy Debran was an outfielder for the New York Black Yankees in 1940.

Decker, Charles (Dusty)

Charles Decker was an infielder and manager for the Detroit Stars, Louisville Black Colonels, Indianapolis ABC's, Montgomery Grey Sox, and Memphis Red Sox from 1932 to 1938.

Decuir, Lionel

Lionel Decuir was a catcher for the Kansas City Monarchs in 1939 and 1940.

Dedeaux, Russ

Russ Dedeaux was a pitcher for the Newark Eagles and New York Black Yankees in 1941 and 1946.

Defiance team

The Defiance team was a black baseball team in Philadelphia in 1907.

Delaware County Athletic Park

The Delaware County Athletic Park was a ball field in Delaware County, Pennsylvania, outside of Philadelphia, where the Philadelphia Giants played in 1919.

Delgado, Felix Rafael

Felix Delgado was a first baseman and outfielder for the New York Cubans from 1936 to 1941.

DeMoss, Elwood (Bingo)

b. 1889, d. 1965

Elwood DeMoss was a standout second baseman, considered to be among the best in Negro League baseball history, and a great batsman, skilled as a bunter and in executing the hit-and-run. He also played second base, pitched, and managed from 1905 to 1944 for the Topeka Giants, West Baden Sprudels, Kansas City Giants, Detroit Stars, Oklahoma Giants, Chicago American Giants, Indianapolis ABC's, Cleveland Giants, St. Louis Giants, and Bowser's ABC's and played one winter for the Poinciana Hotel in Florida as part of the hotel winter league there.

DeMoss began his career as a shortstop with the Topeka Giants in 1905 but moved to second base after suffering an arm injury. In 1915, playing for the Indianapolis ABC's, DeMoss was involved in a brawl in a game against a white major league All-Star team that resulted in a riot and DeMoss, along with Oscar Charleston, was jailed on assault charges. But he was considered a great second baseman by his peers. In Robert Peterson's book *Only the Ball Was White*, a teammate, Jelly Gardner, said that DeMoss "could make all the plays at second. He was a good hitter and a good sacrifice man. He batted second and I led off for the American Giants, and I could run anytime I wanted to with him at bat. He'd save you. If he thought you'd be out trying to steal, he'd foul off the pitch if he couldn't hit it well. He could hit them anywhere he wanted to." Rival Newt Allen, in an interview with author John Holway on file at the National Baseball Hall of Fame, said that DeMoss was one of the greatest second basemen he ever saw: "He was a great ballplayer, a good double play man and a smart baseball player." However, he did not compile a high batting average, with a career .236 mark throughout his Negro League career. Allen said that DeMoss was a great bunter: "He did something I've never seen anybody else do," Allen said. "He stuck his head down under the ball and bunted the ball when it came over his shoulder. Who knows how he did it? For years I tried to learn how the man could just duck down and take his bat and bunt the ball." DeMoss finished his career as a manager for the Chicago Brown Bombers and the Brooklyn Brown Dodgers in Branch

Rickey's UNITED STATES LEAGUE in 1945, the only season the league was in existence.

Dennard, Rick

Rick Dennard was an outfielder for the Toledo Cubs in 1945.

Dennis, Wesley (Doc)

b. 1918, d. 2001

Wesley Dennis was a first baseman and outfielder for the Birmingham Black Barons, Baltimore Elite Giants, and Philadelphia Stars from 1944 to 1948 and is believed to have batted around the .300 mark for much of his career. Born in Nashville, Tennessee, Dennis, in a 1984 newspaper interview, said that he believed he could have been a major league ballplayer in his prime: "Our league was just as good," he said. "We used to barnstorm against major league teams when the regular season was over. In all, I would say that we split the games that we played against them. But things were so bad for blacks back then. Branch Rickey [president and general manager of the Brooklyn Dodgers] picked Jackie Robinson in 1947 because he felt Jackie could handle the pressure of breaking the color barrier. It was a smart move on Rickey's part. Jackie was an intelligent man and a fine athlete. People think Jackie was the best ballplayer in the Negro Leagues because he was the first black in the majors. But as good as Jackie was, there were guys who were better."

Dent, Carl J.

Carl Dent was a shortstop for the Philadelphia Stars and Indianapolis Clowns from 1950 to 1952.

Dequindre Park

Dequindre Park was a ballpark in Detroit where the 1937 version of the Detroit Stars played.

Despert, Harry (Denny)

Harry Despert was an outfielder for the Philadelphia Giants, Lincoln Giants, and Brooklyn Royal Giants from 1914 to 1916.

Detroit Black Sox

The Detroit Black Sox were a black baseball team that played in Detroit in the late 1930s and early 1940s and whose roster included such players as Turkey Stearnes.

Detroit Chronicle

The *Detroit Chronicle* was a black newspaper in Detroit that covered black baseball.

Detroit Motor City Giants

The Detroit Motor City Giants were a black baseball team in Detroit that was part of Brooklyn Dodgers general manager Branch Rickey's United States League in 1945.

Detroit Senators

The Detroit Senators were a black baseball team that played in Detroit in 1947 and were managed by Cool Papa Bell.

Detroit Stars

The Detroit Stars were formed by Andrew "Rube" Foster, the founder of the NEGRO NATIONAL LEAGUE, as part of the new league in 1920, with local black gambler John T. "Tenny" Blount as Foster's front man for ownership. Blount operated the team, which played at Mack Park in Detroit, at the corner of Mack and Fairview Avenues. J. Preston "Pete" Hill, a former player on Foster's Chicago American Giants, was the team's first manager. Some of the players on the Stars included pitchers Frank Wickware and Jose Mendez and catcher Bruce Petway. One of the best hitters in Negro League history, Norman "Turkey" Stearnes, joined the Stars in 1923. They reportedly had a record of 35-23 in their first season in the Negro National League, finishing second behind the Chicago American Giants. They never won a championship but posted winning records until 1929 when they went 39-42. In 1930, a fire damaged Mack Park, so the Stars played in Hamtramck Stadium. The Stars also played in the integrated Michigan Semi-Pro Championship tournament, winning five straight titles, starting in 1919. Their last year in the Negro National League was 1931, only their second losing season in the league. Second baseman Elwood "Bingo" DeMoss managed the team in its final four seasons in league. The Stars dissolved when the league was disbanded and had several reincarnations. In 1933, the Stars played in a newly formed Negro National League but folded after one season. The name was resurrected again with a new team in 1937, with an aging Stearnes on the roster, but it lasted just one year, playing in Dequindre Park. In 1954, a Grand Rapids businessman named Ted Rasberry brought back another version of the Stars but changed the name to the Clowns in 1958, and it lasted just two more seasons. In the final season in 1960 they were called the Detroit–New Orleans Stars.

Detroit Wolves

The Detroit Wolves were a black baseball team in Detroit formed in 1932, after the collapse of the Stars, by Pittsburgh businessman and owner Cum Posey as part of the East-West League. He assembled a remarkable roster of talent, including Willie Wells, Newt Allen, Cool Papa Bell, Ray Brown, Smokey Joe Williams, and Mule Suttles. They had a record of 29-13 when the team was disbanded because of financial problems. Another version of the Wolves played in 1947 for one year.

Devoe, J. R.

J. R. Devoe was business manager for the Cleveland Tate Stars in 1922.

Dewitt, Fred

Fred Dewitt was an infielder and catcher for the Kansas City Monarchs and the Hilldale baseball club from 1922 to 1930.

Dewitt, S. R. (Eddie)

S. R. Dewitt was a third baseman for the Dayton Marcos, Dayton Giants, Columbus Buckeyes, Indianapolis ABC's, Cleveland Tigers, Toledo Tigers, and Memphis Red Sox from 1917 to 1930.

Dexter Park

Dexter Park was a ballpark in Brooklyn, New York, that hosted a number of black baseball teams, including the Cuban Giants, Cuban Stars, and Cuban X Giants. Owner Nat Strong owned the fields, sold permits to teams to use the fields, and also used the fields for his own team, the Brooklyn Royal Giants.

Diago, Miximo

Miximo Diago was a catcher for the Kansas City Monarchs in 1952.

Dial, Kermit

Kermit Dial was a second baseman and pitcher for the Columbus Blue Birds, Detroit Stars, Cole's American Giants, and Cincinnati Buckeyes from 1932 to 1940.

Dials, Lou (Alonzo Odem)

Lou Dials, like many Negro League players, was a star in two countries, a standout outfielder and first baseman in the NEGRO NATIONAL LEAGUE and in the North Mexican League. He began his career with the Chicago American Giants in 1925 and is believed to have won the NNL batting championship, playing for the Detroit Stars, in 1931 with a .382 average. Dials nearly became the first black player to play organized minor league baseball in the 20th century when he and pitcher Chet Brewer were about to be signed to the Los Angeles Angels in the Pacific Coast League in 1943. Pressure from major league owners, though, scuttled the plan. "Wrigley [Phil Wrigley, owner of the Chicago Cubs, the parent organization of the Angels] wouldn't let me sign and that was final," Dials said in a newspaper interview. "He told me there was no place for me in their organization no matter how good I was. I'll tell you, if I had gone to spring training, I would have been in the majors that year. I know I would have." He continued playing until 1946. Dials was also a perennial .300 hitter in the North Mexican League and managed the Torrion team to two league titles. Besides Chicago and Detroit, Dials played for the Memphis Red Sox, Hilldale, Columbus Blue Birds, Akron, Cleveland Giants, Homestead Grays, and New York Black Yankees.

Diaz, Fernando

Fernando Diaz was an outfielder for the New York Cubans in 1950.

Diaz, Heliodoro (Yoyo)

Heliodoro Diaz was a pitcher, first baseman, and outfielder for several versions of the Cuban Stars and the New York Cubans from 1926 to 1939.

Diaz, Pablo

Pablo Diaz was a catcher and first baseman for the Cuban Stars from 1930 to 1932.

Diaz, Pedro (Manny)

Pedro Diaz was a shortstop and catcher for the New York Cubans from 1945 to 1950.

Dibut, Pedro

Pedro Dibut was a pitcher for the Cuban Stars in 1923.

Dickerson, John Fount (Babe)

John Dickerson was a pitcher for the Chicago American Giants and Homestead Grays in 1950.

Dickerson, Lou

Lou Dickerson was a pitcher for the Hilldale baseball club in 1921.

Dickey, Bill

Bill Dickey was a pitcher for the Kansas City Monarchs in 1953.

Dickey, John (Steel Arm)

John Dickey was a pitcher for the Montgomery Grey Sox, St. Louis Stars, and St. Louis Giants from 1921 to 1922.

Diggs, Leon

Leon Diggs was an outfielder for the Indianapolis Clowns in 1953.

Dihigo, Martin
b. 1905, d. 1971

Martin Dihigo was a Cuban baseball star known as "El Inmortal" in his homeland and "El Maestro" in Mexico. He also became one of the greatest and best all-around ballplayers in Negro League baseball and was elected to the National Baseball Hall of Fame in 1977. He has also been inducted into halls of fame in Cuba, Mexico, and Venezuela. In John Holway's book *Blackball Stars*, Negro League pitching great Hilton Smith described Dihigo as a great, versatile player. "Dihigo could do everything—pitcher, good hitter, good fielder," Smith said. "He was a big guy, looked like Joe DiMaggio. Weighed 200 pounds, a big, tall guy. That man could play the outfield, and ooh, could he throw. You better not try to stretch a hit—he could throw. And pitching, he threw everything, overhand or sidearm. . . . Had he come along today, he'd lead the major leagues in winning. Would have hit .300, too. Tremendous power."

Dihigo was born in Matanzas, Cuba, and began playing organized basebll at the age of 17 for the Havana Reds. The following year Dihigo came to the United States and began his Negro League career, playing from 1923 to 1945, for the Cuban Stars, Homestead Grays, Hilldale Daisies, Baltimore Black Sox, and New York Cubans. A versatile player, Dihigo played all over the field, at first base, second base, third base, shortstop, the outfield, and pitcher, and he also managed. Negro Leaguer Holsey "Scrip" Lee said Dihigo was an outstanding outfielder. "He had an arm like a cannon," Lee said in a 1973 story in *Black Sports*. "Oh, yeah, stronger than Ruth, Musial and DiMaggio. Anytime he got his hands on the ball, it was as good as where he wanted to throw it."

Dihigo began his Negro League baseball career with the Cuban Stars in the EASTERN COLORED LEAGUE, and the 6-foot-1, 200-pound Dihigo led the league in home runs in 1926 and tied for the league lead the following season with 18, along with Oscar Charleston. Records also show that he finished second in the AMERICAN NEGRO LEAGUE with 19 home runs in 1929 and also batted .386. The following season, Dihigo batted .434. In 1935, as a player-manager for the Cubans, Dihigo came out on the losing side in a legendary seven-game series to the Pittsburgh Crowfords. He also played in the EAST-WEST ALL-STAR GAME that season, starting in center field

Martin Dihigo may have been the greatest international player in the history of baseball. A star in his homeland of Cuba (where he was known as "El Inmortal"), in Mexico (where he was called "El Maestro") and in Venezuela, he was inducted into each country's baseball hall of fame. Dihigo made his mark in the United States as a great player in the Negro Leagues, where he was a pitcher, hitter, and versatile fielder from 1923 to 1945 for the Cuban Stars, Homestead Grays, Hilldale Daisies, Baltimore Black Sox, and New York Cubans. He batted .434 in 1930 and .391 in 1936, winning the Negro National League batting title, and was inducted into the National Baseball Hall of Fame in 1977. (NATIONAL BASEBALL HALL OF FAME LIBRARY, COOPERSTOWN, N.Y.)

and finishing as a pitcher. In 1936, he won the NEGRO NATIONAL LEAGUE batting crown with a .391 average. He also was part of the group of players that was recruited to go to the Dominican Republic in 1937 to play for a political opponent of dictator Rafael Trujillo in that country's baseball–political war. In 1938, pitching in Mexico and Cuba, Dihigo posted a combined record of 32-4. He would continue to play in Mexico, batting over .300 from 1937 to 1942. At the age of 41, Dihigo batted .316 while posting an 11-4 record on the mound in the Mexican League.

After returning to Cuba that winter of 1946, he retired and was a national hero in that country and a favorite of Fidel Castro, serving as minister of sports until his death. Overall, in competitive play in the United States and abroad, Dihigo is believed to have batted .304 lifetime, with a won-loss pitching mark of 256-136.

Dilworth, Arthur

Arthur Dilworth was a pitcher, catcher, and outfielder for the Bacharach Giants, the Hilldale baseball club, and the Lincoln Giants from 1916 to 1918.

Direaux, Jimmy

Jimmy Direaux was a pitcher for the Washington Elite Giants and Baltimore Elite Giants from 1937 to 1939.

Dismukes, William (Dizzy)

b. 1890, d. 1961

William Dismukes was a pitcher and manager for the East St. Louis Imperials, Brooklyn Royal Giants, Philadelphia Giants, Indianapolis ABC's, Mohawk Giants, Dayton Marcos, Chicago American Giants, Memphis Red Sox, Pittsburgh Keystones, Cincinnati Dismukes, St. Louis Stars, Detroit Wolves, Columbus Blue Birds, Homestead Grays, Kansas City Monarchs, and Birmingham Black Barons from 1913 to 1950. He was also the Monarchs director of player personnel from 1942 to 1952 and signed a number of players who would go on to become major league stars, including Jackie Robinson, Ernie Banks, and Elston Howard. Dismukes scouted for the New York Yankees in 1953 and 1954 and for the Chicago White Sox in 1955 and 1956.

Dixon, Ed (Bullet)

Ed Dixon was a pitcher for the Atlanta Black Crackers, Indianapolis ABC's, and Baltimore Elite Giants in 1938 and 1939.

Dixon, George (Tubby)

George Dixon was a catcher for the Indianapolis ABC's, Chicago American Giants, Cleveland Hornets, Birmingham Black Barons, and Cleveland Tigers from 1917 to 1928.

Dixon, Glenn

Glenn Dixon was a pitcher and outfielder for the St. Louis Stars in 1937.

Dixon, Herbert Albert (Rap)

Herbert Dixon was a outfielder for the Baltimore Black Sox, Harrisburg Giants, Darby Daisies, Chicago American Giants, Philadelphia Stars, Pittsburg Crawfords, Homestead Grays, and Brooklyn Eagles from 1922 to 1937. He also played part of the 1927 season in Japan. Dixon, born in Kingston, Georgia, was known as a power hitter, and, according to reports, slammed three home runs into the right field stands at Yankee Stadium in the first game ever played there between Negro League teams. His brother Paul was his teammate in Baltimore and Philadelphia.

Dixon, John

John Dixon was a pitcher and shortstop for the Detroit Stars, Cleveland Tigers, Cuban Stars, Cleveland Red Sox, and Cleveland Giants from 1928 to 1934.

Dixon, John

John Dixon was a pitcher for the Birmingham Black Barons and Chicago American Giants in 1950.

Dixon, Paul Perry

Paul Dixon was the brother of power-hitting outfielder Herbert "Rap" Dixon and played the outfield for the Bacharach Giants, Baltimore Black Sox, Washington Pilots, New York Cubans, Philadelphia Stars, and Newark Browns from 1931 to 1938. He was a teammate of his brother Rap in Baltimore and Philadelphia.

Dixon, Randy

Randy Dixon was a sportswriter for the *Philadelphia Tribune,* a black newspaper that covered Negro League baseball in the 1930s.

Dixon, Tom

Tom Dixon was a pitcher and catcher for the Bacharach Giants, Baltimore Black Sox, Washington Pilots, Hilldale baseball club, and Baltimore Elite Giants from 1932 to 1940.

Dobbins, Ed

Ed Dobbins was a second baseman for the Chicago American Giants in 1952.

Dobbins, Nat

Nat Dobbins was a shortstop for the Hilldale baseball club in 1921.

Doby, Larry

Larry Doby was a historic figure in both Negro League and major league baseball for his role in the integration of the game, following Jackie Robinson as the second black player in the major leagues and the first in the American League, signing with the Cleveland Indians

in July 1947. Doby, who would also be the first black to be named to the American League All-Star team in 1949, did not perceive himself as a pioneer, according to a 1997 interview with *USA Today Baseball Weekly.* "I never thought of myself as being second," he said. "I never thought of myself as anything except a baseball player. I was just happy to be part of the progress." Unlike Robinson, who spent a season with the Dodgers minor league team in Montreal before coming up to the majors, Doby, who was signed by Indians owner Bill Veeck, went straight from the Negro Leagues to the Indians within one day.

Like Robinson, the 6-foot-1, 185-pound Doby was the target of prejudice from both teammates and opposing players. In a 1997 *New York Times* interview, Doby spoke of the first time he met his teammates: "Some of the players shook my hand, but most of them didn't," he said. "It was one of the most embarrassing moments of my life." Doby defended himself several times when he felt he was being purposely thrown at by opposing pitchers. "If a guy wants to brush you back, that's baseball," Doby said in Jules Tygiel's book *Jackie Robinson and His Legacy.* But Doby went on to say that "headhunting for a Negro isn't baseball." In fact, in 1957 Doby punched pitcher Art Ditmar after being hit with a pitch, which

Larry Doby (NATIONAL BASEBALL HALL OF FAME LIBRARY, COOPERSTOWN, N.Y.)

Larry Doby followed Jackie Robinson as the second black player in the major leagues and the first in the American League, signing with the Cleveland Indians in July 1947. Doby was signed right from the Negro Leagues, where he starred for the Newark Eagles, and is shown here on the right, sitting on the dugout steps with Newark teammate Monte Irvin, who would also go on to the major leagues. In 1946, Doby batted .341 and led the Eagles to a Negro League World Series win over the Kansas City Monarchs. (NATIONAL BASEBALL HALL OF FAME LIBRARY, COOPERSTOWN, N.Y.)

moved Washington sportswriter Shirley Povich to write that this marked "the complete emancipation of the American Negro in America's national game," the first time "a Negro had thrown the first punch in a player argument."

Born in 1924 in Camden, South Carolina, his father died when Doby was just eight years old, and he and his mother moved from South Carolina to Paterson, New Jersey. Doby became a star athlete at East Side High School and earned a basketball scholarship from Long Island University, where legendary basketball coach Clair Bee ran the program. He attended L.I.U. for three months before signing a baseball contract with the Newark Eagles in 1943. He later enlisted in the U.S. Navy and played baseball for the all-black Great Lakes Naval Station Training team, which often played teams that included white major league players.

When the war ended, Doby returned to the Eagles, where he played second base in the 1946 season under the direction of manager and former Negro League great Raleigh "Biz" Mackey. Doby batted .341 and led the Eagles to a Negro League World Series win over the Kansas City Monarchs. He would also play for the Indians in the 1948 World Series (he batted .318 with a game-winning home run against the Boston Braves) and the 1954 World Series, making him one of four players, along with Willie Mays, Satchel Paige, and Monte Irvin, to play in both the Negro League World Series and the major league baseball World Series.

Doby was batting .458 with 13 home runs for the Eagles when he was signed by Cleveland in July. The Indians were not the only team interested in Doby. The Dodgers had considered signing him as well. Doby had his difficulties on the field—and off as well, facing the battle against racism. Some opposing players voiced their strong dislike for playing on the same field with Doby, and some hotels on the road refused to let him stay with the team. On the field, Doby struck out six times in his first 13 at bats and managed just five hits in 32 at bats for the rest of the season. "I struck out a lot because I tried too hard," said Doby, who saw little playing time for the rest of 1947, as the Indians worked to change him into an outfielder. Doby began to turn things around in 1948, batting .301 with 14 home runs, 66 RBIs, and 83 runs scored in 121 games. He would go on to become a top run producer, and in 13 major league seasons—10 with the Indians, two with the Chicago White Sox, and part of one year with the White Sox and Detroit Tigers—Doby hit 253 home runs, drove in 969 runs, and batted .283 before retiring after the 1959 season. Nearly 20 years later, Doby became another pioneer, following Frank Robinson's debut as the first black manager, when Doby was named manager of the Chicago White Sox in 1978, also by Veeck, then owner of the White Sox. Doby held the job for 87 games, posting a 37-50 record. He was inducted into the National Baseball Hall of Fame in 1998.

Donaldson, John Wesley

Born in Glasglow, Missouri, in 1892, John Wesley Donaldson started his baseball career with the Tennese Rats in 1912. He then played for the All Nations team organized by J. L. Wilkinson from 1913 to 1917 and then pitched for the Chicago American Giants, Indianapolis ABC's, Detroit Stars, Brooklyn Royal Giants, Lincoln Giants, Donaldson All-Stars, House of David, Los Angeles White Sox, and Kansas City Monarchs from 1912 to 1923. Reports claim that Donaldson once struck out 35 batters in one 18-inning game, and in another 12-inning contest he reportedly struck out 27 hitters. He is also believed to have thrown three consecutive no-hitter against semipro teams. According to Robert Peterson's book *Only the Ball Was White*, the *Chicago Defender* reported in 1917 that Donaldson was offered $10,000 by a New York State League baseball manager to go to Cuba, change his name, and return as a "Cuban" pitcher for his team. He declined the offer. He would go on to become a scout for the Chicago White Sox.

Donaldson, W. W. (Billy)

W. W. Donaldson was an umpire in the NEGRO NATIONAL LEAGUE from 1923 to 1927.

Donnell, Herman

Herman Donnell was an outfielder for the Indianapolis Clowns in 1952.

Donoso, Lino
d. 1991

Lino Donoso was a pitcher for the New York Cubans from 1947 to 1949.

Dorsey, F. T.

F. T. Dorsey was an infielder for the Baltimore Atlantics in 1884 and 1885.

Dougherty, Charles
b. 1879, d. 1940

Charles Dougherty was a pitcher for the Leland Giants, Chicago American Giants, and Chicago Giants from 1909 to 1915. He was born in Summmerdale, Kansas, and his nickname was the "Black Marquad," referring to major league pitcher Rube Marquad.

Dougherty, Leon

Leon Dougherty was a pitcher for the Brooklyn Eagles in 1935.

Dougherty, Romeo

Romeo Dougherty was a reporter for the New York *Amsterdam News* who wrote about black baseball in the 1920s.

Douglas Club

The Douglas Club were a black baseball team in Washington, D.C., in the 1880s.

Douglas, George

George Douglas was an outfielder for the Brooklyn Remsens in 1885.

Douglas, Jesse

Jesse Douglas was an infielder and outfielder for the Chicago American Giants, New York Black Yankees, New Orleans Eagles, Kansas City Monarchs, Birmingham Black Barons, and Memphis Red Sox from 1937 to 1950. Born in Longview, Texas, Douglas's best seasons were 1941, when he batted .389 for Birmingham, and 1950, when he hit .331 for Chicago in 169 at bats.

Douglass, Charles R.

Charles R. Douglass played for the Mutuals of Philadelphia, a black baseball team that played in Philadelphia in the 1860s. He was the son of Frederick Douglass, one of the leaders of the abolitionist movement.

Douglass, Eddie
Eddie Douglass was a first baseman and manager for the Brooklyn Royal Giants and Lincoln Giants from 1918 to 1929. He also played in Cuba in the winter of 1923–1924, playing for a Santa Clara team with an infield consisting of Douglass and other Negro League greats, such as Frank Warfield, Oliver Marcelle, and Dobie Moore—one of the best infields ever put together.

Douse, Joseph Solomon
Joseph Douse was a pitcher and outfielder for the Kansas City Monarchs from 1952 to 1953.

Downer, Fred
Fred Downer was an outfielder for the Baltimore Black Sox and Pittsburgh Keystones from 1921 to 1922.

Downs, McKinley (Bunny)
McKinley Downs was a shortstop, second baseman, third baseman, and manager for the Bacharach Giants, St. Louis Giants, Hilldale baseball club, Brooklyn Royal Giants, Brooklyn Cuban Giants, Philadelphia Tigers, Cincinnati Clowns, and Indianapolis Clowns from 1916 to 1951. In Indianapolis, Downs managed a young outfielder named Hank Aaron.

Drake, Andrew
Andrew Drake was a catcher for the Chattanooga Black Lookouts, Cole's American Giants, Birmingham Black Barons, Louisville Black Caps, and Nashville Elite Giants from 1930 to 1932.

Drake, Verdes
Verdes Drake was an outfielder for the Cuban Stars, Cincinnati-Indianapolis Clowns, and Indianapolis Clowns from 1945 to 1954.

Drake, William (Plunk)
b. 1895
William Drake was a pitcher for the Tennessee Rats, ALL NATIONS team, St. Louis Stars, St. Louis Giants, Indianapolis ABC's, Kansas City Monarchs, and Detroit Stars from 1916 to 1927. The 6-foot, 205-pound Drake, born in Sedalia, Missouri, in 1895, got the nickname "Plunk" because he was aggressive in throwing at hitters. He is believed to have won 82 games and lost 62 in organized Negro League play, and in 1921, records show Drake posted a 20-10 mark. In an interview con-

ducted by author John Holway on file at the National Baseball Hall of Fame, Monarchs teammate Newt Allen said that Drake "threw a good, hard curveball." In another Holway interview, Drake said that Paige learned from him. "I met Satchel the first year he came out in 1926," Drake said. "He was with Chattanooga, and I was with Memphis. He had just come out of reformatory school, about 17 or 18 years old. I used to call it a 'delayed' pitch—stride and then throw. Satchel called it a 'hesitation' pitch. Whether Satchel copied it from me or some other fellow, I don't know. I wouldn't say definitely that he learned it from me, but if he didn't, he learned it from someone who learned it from me. I don't remember anyone who was doing it before me, and I started pitching in 1913."

Drake began his career with the Tennessee Rats. "We had a baseball team and a minstrel show," he said. "We played a game in the afternoon and put on a minstrel show in the evening and traveled around. My salary was $12.50 a week. I played a whole season and my salary was $144." Drake also addressed his reputation for throwing at hitters. "I kind of got a bad name for knocking men down," he said. "If you got a toe hold on me, down you went. That was my plate up there, don't crowd me. One time we played in Fort Worth. Old Bib Haines, a first baseman there, he'd say, 'Go on, you old ballplayers on the Kansas City Monarchs.' I turned his cap bill around like that with a pitch. He nearly died. Next time he came up, you could drive a team of horses between him and home plate." Drake had a bitter rivalry with fellow Negro League pitcher Joe Rogan, which he revealed to Holway: "Deep down in my heart, I don't believe Rogan ever saw the day he could pitch as much baseball as I could pitch," Drake said.

Dreke, Valentin
Valentin Dreke was an outfielder for the Cuban Stars from 1919 to 1928.

Drew, John M.
John Drew was a black politician in Delaware County, Pennsylvania, who was an officer for the Darby Daisies and the Hilldale baseball club in 1931 and 1932.

Duany, Claro
Claro Duany was an outfielder for the New York Cubans from 1944 to 1947. Born in Santiago, Cuba, he is believed to have hit .300 for the Cubans in 80 at bats in 1944 and .297 in 182 at bats in 1947. He also played in the Cuban and Mexican winter baseball leagues, as well as some minor league baseball.

Dubisson, D. J.

D. J. Dubisson was an officer with the Little Rock Grays in 1932.

Duckett, Mahlon

Mahlon Duckett was a shortstop, second baseman, and third baseman for the Philadelphia Stars from 1940 to 1950, part of a standout double-play combination with Frank Austin. He had signed a contract with the New York Giants and reported to training camp in 1951 in Phoenix, Arizona. But Duckett developed rheumatic fever, and his career was over. In a 1996 interview with *Sports Collectors Digest,* Duckett talked about the unique challenges facing a young player in the Negro Leagues: "When you came in our league, you played on your natural ability," Duckett said. "We had no one to teach us. Like when I came in the league at the age of 17, just about all the ballplayers, they were mean and that was their livelihood. They all had families and they didn't want anyone to take their jobs. They wouldn't tell us anything. You just went out there, and I tried to learn as I went along. I played in the Negro Leagues for 11 years, and as I went along, I picked up different things. That wasn't only me. That's the way any fellow that came in the league had to do it."

Ducy, Eddie

Eddie Ducy was a second baseman for the Homestead Grays in 1947.

Dudley, C. A.

C. A. Dudley was an outfielder for the St. Louis Giants and St. Louis Stars from 1920 to 1922.

Dudley, Edward

Edward Dudley was a pitcher for the Lincoln Giants and Brooklyn Royal Giants from 1926 to 1928.

Duff, Ernest

Ernest Duff was an outfielder for the Cleveland Elites, Indianapolis ABC's, Cleveland Tigers, Cleveland Hornets, and Cuban Stars from 1925 to 1932.

Dukes, Tommy

Tommy Dukes was a third baseman and catcher for the Memphis Red Sox, Chicago American Giants, Columbus Elite Giants, Nashville Elite Giants, Toledo Crawfords, Homestead Grays, and Indianapolis Crawfords from 1928 to 1945.

Dula, Louis

Louis Dula was a pitcher for the Homestead Grays from 1934 to 1937.

Dumas, Jim

Jim Dumas was a pitcher for the Memphis Red Sox in 1940 and 1941.

Dumpson, Bill

Bill Dumpson was a pitcher for the Indianapolis Clowns and Philadelphia Stars in 1950.

Dunbar, Ashby

Ashby Dunbar was an outfielder for the Lincoln Stars, Brooklyn Royal Giants, Pennsylvania Red Caps, Indianapolis ABC's, and Lincoln Giants from 1909 to 1919.

Dunbar, Frank

Frank Dunbar was an outfielder for the Philadelphia Giants in 1908.

Dunbar, Vet

Vet Dunbar was an infielder and catcher for the Memphis Red Sox and Indianapolis Athletics in 1937.

Duncan, Charlie

Charlie Duncan was a pitcher for the Atlanta Black Crackers, Indianapolis ABC's, and St. Louis Stars from 1938 to 1940.

Duncan, Frank

Frank Duncan was an outfielder and manager for the Philadelphia Giants, Leland Giants, Chicago American Giants, Detroit Stars, Chicago Giants, Toledo Tigers, Cleveland Elites, Cleveland Hornets, and Cleveland Tigers from 1909 to 1928.

Duncan, Frank, Jr.

b. 1901, d. 1973

Frank Duncan, Jr., was a catcher, outfielder, and manager for the Chicago Giants, Kansas City Monarchs, New York Black Yankees, Pittsburgh Crawfords, Homestead Grays, New York Cubans, and Chicago American Giants from 1920 to 1948. Duncan helped the Monarchs defeat the Hilldales of the EASTERN COLORED LEAGUE in the 1924 Negro World Series, the first such World

Series ever held. Duncan, who was one of the players voted on the historic first Negro Leagues All-Star Game, the EAST-WEST GAME, in 1934, was considered one of the finest defensive catchers in Negro League history, though he was an average hitter with a career batting mark around .260. In an interview conducted by author John Holway on file at the National Baseball Hall of Fame, teammate Newt Allen, who grew up with Duncan in Kansas City, called Duncan "an awfully smart receiver and one of the greatest defensive receivers. The pitchers would really pitch to him." In another Holway interview, pitcher Bill Drake said that Duncan was at the top of all the catchers he played with. "Frank Duncan was the cream of the crop at catcher," Drake said. "He could catch every game every day, he didn't care. He was the best catcher I ever saw throwing to second base."

Dizzy Dean believed that Duncan, who caught Dean in barnstorming exhibitions, was as good as his own catcher with the Cubs, Gabby Hartnett. "I sure got a kick out of Duncan," Dean said. "One time when Duncan catches me, he has a glove that makes the ball pop, and it makes my pitch sound like a rifle shot, and Duncan keeps telling them hitters, 'Boy, don't get near that plate, Don't let that ball hit you or it'll kill you.'" Duncan also spent time touring Japan in 1927, playing baseball with other Negro League greats. Duncan went on to manage the Monarchs in the 1940s and was Jackie Robinson's first professional baseball manager in 1945. "Jackie wasn't the best player on the club," Duncan said. "No, he wasn't. I knew I had a little kid named Bonnie Surrell at second—slender and hit, oh man he could hit that ball downtown and he wasn't bigger than a midget."

Duncan, Frank, III
b. 1920, d. 1999
Frank Duncan III was a pitcher for the Kansas City Monarchs and Baltimore Elite Giants in 1941 and from 1945 to 1949. Duncan had the distinction of playing Negro League baseball with his father, catcher Frank Duncan, Jr., when he first started with the Kansas City Monarchs in 1940. Duncan III left the Monarchs for military service in 1942, returning two years later to play for the Baltimore Elite Giants. Duncan later played minor league baseball with the San Angelos Colts in the West Texas–New Mexico League and played for Cordoba in the Mexican League.

Duncan, Joe
Joe Duncan was a catcher for the Bacharach Giants in 1927.

Duncan, Joseph
Joseph Duncan was a pitcher and first baseman for the Indianapolis Clowns in 1954.

Duncan, Melvin
Melvin Duncan was a pitcher for the Kansas City Monarchs from 1949 to 1950.

Duncan, Warren
Warren Duncan was a catcher and outfielder for the Bacharach Giants from 1922 to 1927.

Frank Duncan, Jr., was an outstanding Negro League catcher and manager and was Jackie Robinson's first professional baseball manager in 1945 for the Kansas City Monarchs. Before that, Duncan was an All-Star defensive catcher and outfielder for the Monarchs, Chicago Giants, New York Black Yankees, Pittsburgh Crawfords, Homestead Grays, New York Cubans, and Chicago American Giants. Duncan helped the Monarchs defeat the Hilldales of the Eastern Colored League in the 1924 Negro World Series. (NATIONAL BASEBALL HALL OF FAME LIBRARY, COOPERSTOWN, N.Y.)

Dunkin, Ishkooda (Stringbean)

Ishkooda Dunkin was a pitcher for the Pittsburgh Crawfords from 1936 to 1937.

Dunlap, Herman

Herman Dunlap was an outfielder for the Chicago American Giants from 1937 to 1939.

Dunn, Alphonse (Blue)

Alphonse Dunn was a first baseman and outfielder for the Detroit Stars, New York Cubans, and Birmingham Black Barons from 1937 to 1943.

Dunn, Jake

Jake Dunn was a shortstop, second baseman, outfielder, and manager for the Detroit Stars, Washington Pilots, Nashville Elite Giants, Baltimore Black Sox, and Philadelphia Stars from 1930 to 1941.

Dunn, Willie

Willie Dunn was a pitcher for the Jacksonville Red Caps in 1942.

Dunville, Larry

Larry Dunville, from Indianapolis, Indiana, umpired in the NEGRO NATIONAL LEAGUE.

Durham, Winn

Winn Durham was an outfielder for the Chicago American Giants in 1952.

Dwight, Eddie (Pee Wee)

Eddie Dwight was an outfielder for the Tennessee Rats, Indianapolis ABC's and Kansas City Monarchs from 1925 to 1937. The 5-foot-6 Dwight was one of the Monarchs' most popular players and was chosen to play in the 1937 EAST-WEST ALL-STAR GAME. Sometimes, as a sideshow, Dwight, who was a speedster, would run races against Jesse Owens.

Dyckman Oval

Dyckman Oval was a ball field in upper Manhattan that hosted a number of black baseball teams, including the New York Bacharachs, New York Lincoln Giants, and New York Cuban Stars.

Dykes, John

John Dykes was an officer with the Washington Pilots in 1932.

Dyll, Frank

Frank Dyll was a shortstop for the Chicago American Giants in 1950.

Dysoin, Major

Major Dysoin was a shortstop for the New York Black Yankees in 1950.

Earle, Charles Babcock

Charles Earle was a pitcher, outfielder, and manager for the Cuban Giants, Wilmington Giants, Brooklyn Royal Giants, Philadelphia Giants, Bacharach Giants, Lincoln Giants, and Pennsylvania Red Caps from 1906 to 1919.

Earle, James

James Earle was an infielder for the Detroit Stars in 1954.

Easter, Luscious (Luke)
b. 1915, d. 1979

Luke Easter was an outfielder and first baseman for the Cincinnati Crescents and Homestead Grays from 1946 to 1948. Easter, a huge slugger at 6-feet-5 and 240 pounds, hit 10 home runs and batted .311 in 219 at bats in 1947 and 13 home runs and a .363 average in 215 at bats in 1948. At the age of 34, Easter signed a contract with the Cleveland Indians and played for the Indians for six years, from 1949 to 1954, batting .274 with 93 home runs and 340 RBIs in 491 games. But a broken foot and knee problems held back his major league career.

Born in Jonestown, Mississippi, Easter had both of his legs broken in 1941 in a car accident, and his legs never fully recovered. However, Easter would still become a minor league baseball legend for his home run hitting, hitting 269 home runs and driving in 919 runs in 13 seasons with San Diego in the Pacific Coast League, Indianapolis and Charleston in the American Association, and Ottawa, Buffalo, and Rochester in the International League. In his autobiography, *I Was Right on Time*, Negro Leaguer Buck O'Neil named Easter as his first baseman on his second-team of all-time Negro League greats. "He might have been a big star if he hadn't broken his foot," O'Neil said. "He had real major-league power. We had some good hitters among the first basemen in our league, guys like Jim West and Showboat Thomas, but they couldn't hit the long ball like Luke." Easter's size, hitting prowess, and flamboyant attitude made him a legendary baseball figure. In *Jackie Robinson and his Legacy*, author Jules Tygiel wrote that "Luscious Easter was a figure of Bunyanesque proportions. His massive six-foot, four-inch frame radiated awesome strength, yet he charmed people with his gentle manner and humor. Easter's tastes in fashion included 'racy pinstripe suits' and a diamond ring that resembled 'the headlight of the Santa Fe Chief.' . . . Luke Easter was the most spectacular of the wave of black athletes who entered organized baseball in 1949." His play on the field made him a fan favorite when he first broke into minor league baseball in the Pacific Coast League. Tygiel wrote that sportswriters "compared

Luke Easter was a legendary slugger both in Negro League history and in minor league baseball. A foot injury and other physical problems kept him from a successful major league career, but, after successful stints with the Cincinnati Crescents and Homestead Grays in Negro League baseball, Easter became a minor league star, hitting 269 home runs and driving in 919 runs in 13 seasons. He was a fan favorite, a larger-than-life figure, at 6 foot 5, 240 pounds with a personality that fans loved, particularly in Rochester with the Class AAA Red Wings. (COURTESY ROCHESTER RED WINGS)

his batting and drawing power to Babe Ruth. 'When he takes his turn at batting practice,' described sportswriter Frank Finch, noting the unusually early crowd arrival, 'the other players, the sportswriters, the goober salesmen and fans rivet their eyes on the batting cage to watch Luke powder the ball.'" There were numerous stories of his long home runs blasts. Reportedly, while playing for the Grays, Easter hit a ball into the center field bleachers in the vast Polo Grounds and also another against the top wall of the bleachers at Yankee Stadium. Then there is the legend of the 1,000-mile home run. Supposedly, while playing minor league baseball in Charleston, West Virginia, Easter hit a home run that landed in a coal car and traveled 1,000 miles.

Easter's life ended tragically on March 29, 1979, when he was shot and killed by two men outside a bank in Euclid, Ohio. According to a 1997 *Cleveland Plain Dealer* article, Easter, a union steward at TRW Inc. had just cashed more than $40,000 of his coworkers' paychecks for them, which he did every week, when two men came out of a parked car, shot him, grabbed the money, and ran. They were captured, and one was sentenced to life in prison, while the other got 15 years to life. An estimated 4,000 mourners filed past Easter's coffin for his viewing, and more than 1,000 attended his funeral service. The city of Cleveland renamed a park to honor Easter.

Easterling, Howard

Howard Easterling was a second baseman, shortstop, and third baseman for the Chicago American Giants, Cincinnati Tigers, New York Cubans, and Homestead Grays from 1936 to 1949.

Eastern Colored League

The Eastern Colored League was originally founded as the Mutual Association and started in 1923 by Ed Bolden, owner of the Hilldale baseball club, to compete against Rube Foster's NEGRO NATIONAL LEAGUE. Other teams in the league included the Atlantic City Bacharach Giants, Brooklyn Royal Giants, Philadelphia Stars, New York Lincoln Giants, Baltimore Black Sox, and Cuban Stars. In its second season, the league added the Harrisburg Giants and Washington Potomacs. The league champions began playing a World Series against the Negro National League champions in 1924, with Hilldale facing the Kansas City Monarchs—considered to be the first black World Series. The Monarchs won a 10-game series. The league disbanded in 1928, and a version of it surfaced under Bolden the following year called the American Negro League. Some of the stars who played in the Eastern Colored League included Raleigh "Biz" Mackey, McKinley "Bunny" Downs, Phil Cockrell, Frank Warfield, Clint Thomas, and George Scales.

Eastern Sportswriters Association

The Eastern Sportswriters Association was an organization of black sportswriters that covered Negro League baseball.

East St. Louis Cubs

The East St. Louis Cubs were a black baseball team that played in East St. Louis, Missouri, in the 1920s. One of the members of the Cubs was Negro League great James "Cool Papa" Bell.

East-West Game

The East-West Game was the Negro League's All-Star Game. It was started by Gus Greenlee, owner of the Pittsburgh Crawfords, in 1934, the same year major league baseball began its All-Star Game. It was played in Comiskey Park in Chicago, the home of the Chicago White Sox, and pitcher Bill Foster, representing the East, beat Lefty Streeter, representing the West, 11-7. The players were selected through voting by fans in black newspapers. The game would sometimes draw as many as 50,000 fans and outdrew the major league All-Star Game in 1938, 1942, 1943, 1946 (two East-West Games were held in 1946, the second at Griffith Stadium in Washington), and 1947. In his autobiography, *I Was Right on Time,* Negro Leaguer Buck O'Neil said that playing in an East-West Game "was something very special. That was the greatest idea Gus ever had, because it made black people feel involved in baseball like they'd never been before. While the big leagues left the choice of players up to the sportswriters, Gus left it up to the fans. After reading about great players in the [Chicago] *Defender* and the [Pittsburgh] *Courier* for so many years, they could cut out that ballot in the black papers and have a say. That was a pretty important thing for black people to do in those days, to be able to vote, even if it was just for ballplayers, and they sent in thousands of ballots. It was like an avalanche. Right away it was clear that our game meant a lot more than the big league game. Theirs was, and is, more or less an exhibition. But for black folks, the East-West Game was a matter of racial pride. Black people came from all over Chicago every year—that's why we outdrew the big-league game some years, because we always had 50,000 people, and almost all of them were black people. . . . The weekend was always a party. All the hotels on the South Side were filled. All the big nightclubs were hopping."

Monte Irvin, in Mark Ribowsky's book *A Complete History of the Negro Leagues,* called the East-West games "a joyful experience. They put red, white and blue banners up all over the park, and a jazz band would play in between innings. People would come from all over the country to be part of this spectacle. The games were good. The players were great. If you could have picked one all-star team from the two squads, it surely could have rivaled any white major league all-star team of all time. That team would have been as good as any all-star team that's ever played."

Some of the other great Negro League players who were voted to play in the East-West Game included Josh Gibson, Oscar Charleston, Satchel Paige, Martin Dihigo, Cool Papa Bell, Willie Wells, Ray Dandridge, Mule Suttles, and O'Neil. The game, in a watered-down version after the integration of major league baseball, continued until the final game was played in 1963 in Kansas City.

East-West League

The East-West League was a Negro League started by Homestead Grays owner Cumberland Posey in 1932 and included the Washington Pilots, Cleveland Stars, Newark Browns, Hilldale baseball club, Detroit Wolves, Baltimore Black Sox, and a Midwest version of the Cuban Stars. The league lasted just one season.

Ebbets Field

Ebbets Field was the home of the Brooklyn Dodgers, the Brooklyn, New York, ballpark where Jackie Robinson made his 1947 debut to break major league baseball's color line. It also hosted Negro League teams, such as the Brooklyn Eagles, Brooklyn Brown Dodgers, and New York Bacharachs.

Echevarria, Rafael

Rafael Echevarria was a second baseman for the New York Cubans in 1938.

Echols, Joseph

Joseph Echols was an outfielder for the Newark Eagles in 1939.

Echols, Melvin Jim (Sunny)

Melvin Echols was an outfielder and pitcher for the Atlanta Black Crackers in 1943.

Eckelson, Juan

Juan Eckelson was a pitcher for the Cuban Stars in 1925.

Edgar Thompson Steel Works Club

The Edgar Thompson Steel Works Club was a sports club in Pittsburgh that fielded teams in numerous sports, including baseball, to offer recreation for black steel workers. Some players would often go on to play Negro League baseball, and the teams would also include former Negro League players as well. According to *Sandlot Seasons: Sport in Black Pittsburgh*, by Rob Ruck, a number of players from the Pittsburgh Monarchs team went to play for the Edgar Thompson club after the Monarchs folded in 1924. The club played baseball from 1923 to the mid-1940s.

Edsall, George

George Edsall was an outfielder for the Celeron, New York, Acme Colored Giants in 1898.

Edwards, Chancellor (Pep)

Chancellor Edwards was a catcher for the Cleveland Tigers in 1928.

Edwards, Frank

Frank Edwards was a catcher, second baseman, and shortstop for the Cincinnati Tigers and St. Louis Stars in 1936 and 1937.

Edwards, George

George Edwards was a shortstop for the Baltimore Elite Giants and Boston Blues in 1946 and 1951.

Edwards, James (Smokey)

James Edwards was a pitcher, catcher, and outfielder for the Lincoln Stars, Mohawk Giants, Philadelphia Giants, Pennsylvania Red Caps, Bacharach Giants, Louisville White Sox, and Lincoln Giants from 1913 to 1922.

Edwards, Jesse

Jesse Edwards was a pitcher, second baseman, and outfielder for the Birmingham Black Barons, Nashville Elite Giants, Detroit Stars, and Memphis Red Sox from 1923 to 1931.

Edwards, Osee

Osee Edwards was an outfielder for the New York Black Yankees in 1950.

Edwards, Prince

Prince Edwards, from Wichita, Kansas, was an umpire in the Western League of Colored Baseball Clubs in the 1920s.

Edwards, William

William Edwards was a pitcher for the Kansas City Monarchs in 1944.

Eggleston, Macajah (Mack)

Macajah Eggleston was an outfielder, third baseman, and catcher for the Dayton Marcos, Dayton Giants, Indianapolis ABC's, Detroit Stars, Columbus Buckeyes, Washington Potomacs, Wilmington Potomacs, Baltimore Black Sox, Harrisburg Giants, New York Black Yankees, Bacharach Giants, Homestead Grays, Washington Pilots, Lincoln Giants, and Nashville Elite Giants from 1917 to 1934.

Eggleston, William

William Eggleston was a shortstop for the Argyle Hotel in Babylon, New York, in 1885.

Elam, James

James Elam was a pitcher and infielder for the Newark Eagles and Bacharach Giants from 1932 to 1943.

Ellerbe, Lacey

Lacey Ellerbe was an infielder for the Baltimore Elite Giants in 1950.

Elliott, Joseph

Joseph Elliott was a pitcher for the Memphis Red Sox, Louisville Black Colonels, and Detroit Stars in 1954 and 1955.

Ellis, Albert

Albert Ellis was a pitcher for the Cleveland Buckeyes in 1950.

Ellis, James

James Ellis was a first baseman and third baseman for the Nashville Elite Giants, Dayton Marcos, Memphis Red Sox, and Cleveland Browns from 1921 to 1925.

Ellis, Rocky

Rocky Ellis was a pitcher and outfielder for the Philadelphia Stars, Hilldale baseball club, Jacksonville Red Caps, Homestead Grays, Bacharach Giants, Baltimore Grays, and Birmingham Black Barons from 1925 to 1942.

Else, Harry (Speedy)

Harry Else was a catcher for the Kansas City Monarchs, Monroe Monarchs, New Orleans Crescent Stars, and Chicago American Giants from 1931 to 1940.

Embry, William (Cap)

William Embry was an umpire in the NEGRO NATIONAL LEAGUE in 1923.

Emery, Jack

Jack Emery was an outfielder and pitcher for the Philadelphia Giants, Brooklyn Colored Giants, Pittsburgh Colored Stars, Smart Set, Brooklyn Royal Giants, and Pittsburgh Stars of Buffalo from 1906 to 1922.

Emery, Sims

Sims Emery was a first baseman and catcher for the Philadelphia Pythians and New York Gorhams from 1887 to 1889.

English, Louis

Louis English was an outfielder and catcher for the Louisville Black Caps, Louisville White Sox, Louisville Red Caps, Detroit Stars, Nashville Elite Giants, and Memphis Red Sox from 1929 to 1934.

Ensley, Frank

Frank Ensley was an outfielder for the Indianapolis Clowns and Kansas City Monarchs from 1952 to 1954.

Ervin, Willie

Willie Ervin was a pitcher for the New York Black Yankees in 1948.

Estrada, Oscar

Oscar Estrada was a pitcher and outfielder for the Cuban Stars in 1924 and 1925.

Etchegoven, Carlos

Carlos Etchegoven was a third baseman and outfielder for the Cuban Stars from 1930 to 1932.

Ethiopian Clowns

The Miami, Florida, Giants changed their name to the Ethiopian Clowns. They were a clowning baseball team, dressing in costumes and putting on shows while playing barnstorming baseball. In an interview with author John Holway on file at the National Baseball Hall of Fame, pitcher Dave Barnhill talked about his days with the clowns: "We'd come to the park with paint on our faces like clowns," he said. "Even the batboy had his face painted, too. We wore clowning wigs and the big old clown uniforms with ruffled collars. My clowning name was Impo. During batting practice we'd play 'shadow ball,' pretend to hit and throw without any ball at all. They'd 'hit' the ball to me. I'd run to field it. I'd jump, turn a flip and throw it like I'm throwing the ball to first base. Then when we were supposed to get to business, we pulled the clown suits off and we had regular baseball uniforms underneath. But we didn't change our faces. We played with our clown paint." Although a black man named Hunter Campbell was listed as the owner of the Clowns, they were owned by white promoter Sydney Pollock.

Evans, Boots

Boots Evans was an umpire from Philadelphia in the Eastern Colored League in 1925.

Evans, Charles Alexander

Charles Evans was a pitcher for the Pennsylvania Red Caps, Bacharach Giants, and Baltimore Black Sox from 1921 to 1927.

Evans, Clarence

Clarence Evans was a pitcher for the Homestead Grays in 1949.

Evans, Claude

Claude Evans was an outfielder for the Pittsburgh Crawfords in 1937.

Evans, Felix (Chin)

Felix Evans was a pitcher for the Atlanta Black Crackers, Indianapolis ABC's, Memphis Red Sox, Birmingham Barons, Baltimore Elite Giants, and Newark Eagles from 1934 to 1949.

Evans, Frank

Frank Evans was a third baseman and outfielder for the ALL NATIONS team, Kansas City Giants, and Kansas City Monarchs from 1908 to 1920.

Evans, Frank

Frank Evans was an outfielder for the Birmingham Black Barons, Cleveland Buckeyes, and Philadelphia Stars from 1950 to 1955.

Evans, John

John Evans was a second baseman for the Indianapolis Clowns in 1954.

Evans, Robert

Robert Evans was a pitcher for the Newark Eagles, Newark Dodgers, New York Black Yankees, Jacksonville Red Caps, Homestead Grays, and Philadelphia Stars from 1933 to 1943.

Evans, Tom

Tom Evans was a pitcher for the Philadelphia Stars in 1939.

Evans, Ulysses

Ulysses Evans was a pitcher for the Cincinnati Clowns, Louisville Red Caps, and Chicago Brown Bombers in 1933 and 1943.

Evans, William

William Evans was an outfielder and catcher for the Philadelphia Giants in 1903.

Evans, William Demont (Happy)

William Evans was an outfielder, shortstop, third baseman, and pitcher for the Louisville White Sox, Brooklyn Royal Giants, Chicago American Giants, Cleveland Hornets, Dayton Marcos, Indianapolis ABC's, Gilkerson Union Giants, St. Louis Stars, Washington Pilots, Homestead Grays, Cincinnati Tigers, Detroit Wolves, and Memphis Red Sox from 1918 to 1936. Born in Louisville, Kentucky, in 1899, Evans also played for the Poinciana Hotel black team in Florida during the winters of 1927, 1928, and 1929. "That's where all the money was made, in Florida," Evans said in a 1975 interview in *Black Sports*. "We had a syndicate, just certain groups would go. The rest would go to Cuba, but I couldn't hardly do that, because down in Florida they paid you $40 a month, room and board. If you wanted to wait tables, you could. If you wanted a crap game, things like that, you could do that. Then we played games during the week."

Evans, W. P.

W. P. Evans was a pitcher and outfielder for the Chicago American Giants, Baltimore Black Sox, and Lincoln Stars from 1920 to 1925.

Everett, Clarence

Clarence Everett was a shortstop for the Detroit Stars and Kansas City Monarchs in 1927.

Everett, Curtis

Curtis Everett was an outfielder and catcher for the Kansas City Monarchs from 1950 to 1951.

Everett, Dean

Dean Everett was a pitcher for the Lincoln Giants in 1929.

Everett, James

James Everett was a pitcher and outfielder for the Cincinnati Clowns, Pennsylvania Red Caps, Memphis Red Sox, Newark Browns, and Newark Eagles from 1931 to 1943.

Ewell, Russell

Russell Ewell was an infielder for the New Orleans Eagles in 1951.

Ewell, Wilmer

Wilmer Ewell was a catcher for the Cincinnati Tigers and Indianapolis ABC's from 1925 to 1934.

Ewing, William (Buck)

William Ewing was a catcher for the Columbus Buckeyes, Chicago American Giants, Homestead Grays, Indianapolis ABC's, Cleveland Tate Stars, and Lincoln Giants from 1920 to 1930.

Excelsiors of Philadelphia

The Excelsiors of Philadelphia were a black baseball team that played in Philadelphia in the 1880s.

Fabelo, Julian
Julian Fabelo was an infielder and outfielder for the Havana Stars, Cuban Stars, and New York Cuban Stars from 1916 to 1923.

Fabors, Thomas
Thomas Fabors was a pitcher for the Baltimore Elite Giants in 1942.

Fabre, Isidro
Isidro Fabre was a pitcher and outfielder for the New York Cubans, Cuban Stars, and All Cubans team from 1918 to 1939.

Fagan, Bob
Bob Fagan was a second baseman for the Kansas City Monarchs and St. Louis Stars from 1920 to 1923. In military service in 1917, Fagan also played for the Fort Huachuca 25th Infantry all-black baseball team that included such Negro League players as shortstop Dobie Moore, "Heavy" Johnson in the outfield, and Bullet Joe Rogan and Andy Cooper on the mound.

Fagan, Gervis
Gervis Fagan was an infielder for the Jacksonville Red Caps, Philadelphia Stars, and Memphis Red Sox in 1942 and 1943.

Fairfield Stars
The Fairfield Stars were a black baseball team that played in Fairfield, Alabama, in the 1940s.

Fallings, John
John Fallings was a pitcher for the New York Black Yankees in 1947.

Falls City of Louisville
The Falls City of Louisville were a black baseball team out of Louisville, Kentucky, that played in the League of Colored Base Ball Players in 1887.

Farmer, Greene
Greene Farmer was an outfielder for the New York Cubans, Cincinnati Clowns, Jacksonville Red Caps, and New York Black Yankees from 1942 to 1947.

Farrell, Jack
Jack Farrell was the owner of the Baltimore Black Sox in the 1930s.

Farrell, Luther (Red)
Luther Farrell was a pitcher and outfielder for the Lincoln Giants, Atlantic City Bacharach Giants,

Chicago Giants, New York Black Yankees, Hilldale baseball club, Chicago American Giants, Gilkerson's Union Giants, St. Louis Giants, Johnson Stars, and Indianapolis ABC's from 1920 to 1934. He led the EASTERN COLORED LEAGUE in batting in 1926 with a .359 average. As a pitcher, he went 17-8 in 1927 for Atlantic City, second-best record in the league, and on October 8, 1927, in game three of the Negro League World Series against the Chicago American Giants, Farrell allowed no hits in a seven-inning game that was called on account of rain, with the Bacharach Giants winning 3-2 (Chicago scored on walks and errors). Farrell came back to win the next game as well on two days' rest, 8-1. In 1928, he compiled a 15-11 record and batted .357. According to John Holway's book *Blackball Stars*, Farrell played on a black all-star team in Baltimore that played against white players that included pitcher Lefty Grove, who won 24 games that season, Max Bishop, Spud Davis, Johnny Neunn, and a group of Baltimore Orioles players from the International League. Farrell won the game 9-3. He would go on to post a 10-0 mark in 1930, based on incomplete records, and bat .529. "He could hit the ball out of the park easier than anyone you ever saw," Negro Leaguer Eugene Benson said. "It looked like he would just sweep it out, didn't swing hard at all, and that ball would go. That's the way he played first base, too—easy."

Favors, Thomas
Thomas Favors was a first baseman and outfielder for the Kansas City Monarchs in 1947.

Felder, James
James Felder was a shortstop for the Indianapolis Clowns in 1948.

Felder, Kendall (Buck)
Kendell Felder was a third baseman for the Chicago American Giants, Memphis Red Sox, and Birmingham Black Barons from 1944 to 1946.

Felder, William (Benny)
b. 1925
William Felder was a third baseman and shortstop for the Newark Eagle and Philadelphia Stars in 1946 and 1951.

Felix, James
James Felix was a pitcher for the Chicago American Giants in 1952.

Fennar, Al
Al Fennar was a shortstop for the Cuban Stars, Brooklyn Royal Giants, New York Black Yankees, and Bacharach Giants from 1932 to 1934.

Fernandez, Bernard
Bernard Fernandez was a pitcher for the Jacksonville Red Caps, Atlanta Black Crackers, New York Black Yankees, New York Cubans, and Pittsburgh Crawfords from 1938 to 1939 and from 1946 to 1949.

Fernandez, Emanuel
Emanuel Fernandez was a pitcher and outfielder for the New York Cubans in 1941.

Fernandez, Jose Maria, Sr.
Jose Fernandez, Sr., was a catcher, first baseman, and manager for the Cuban Stars, New York Cubans, Havana Stars, New York Cuban Stars, Chicago American Giants, and Cuban Stars of Havana from 1916 to 1950. His son, Jose, Jr., played catcher for the New York Cubans from 1948 to 1950.

Fernandez, Jose Maria, Jr. (Pepe)
Jose Fernandez, the son of Jose Fernandez, Sr., was a catcher for the New York Cubans from 1948 to 1950.

Fernandez, Renaldo
Renaldo Fernandez was an outfielder for the New York Cubans in 1950.

Fernandez, Rodolfo
Rodolfo Fernandez was a pitcher who played for the Cuban Stars, Cincinnati Cubans, and New York Cuban Stars from 1916 to 1923.

Fernandez, Rodolfo (Rudy)
b. 1911, d. 2000
Rodolfo Fernandez was a pitcher for the Cuban Stars, New York Cubans, and New York Black Yankees from 1932 to 1946. In a 1996 interview with *Sports Collectors Digest*, Fernandez talked about his Negro League playing days: "I played with the New York Cubans," he said. "Before that I played with the other team named the Cuban Stars. But the Cuban Stars don't play in the Negro League. They played independent baseball. In 1935, I played for the New York Cubans. We don't make money, and we play everywhere. Sometimes we play in Mexico

and Venezuela. I pitched for more than 15 years, and we needed to play around the year because we didn't make any money . . . everybody in the colored league, you don't have a room to sleep in. We sleep all the time on the bus. It was pretty rough. We used to wear only one uniform."

Fernandez also played in the Cuban League, starting with the Almendares club in Havana, and he was elected to the Cuban Hall of Fame in Miami in 1985. He also played winter baseball in Venezuela, Puerto Rico, and the Dominican Republic. His most memorable moments came in the spring of 1937 when he shut out the defending National League champion New York Giants and the Brooklyn Dodgers and lost to the Cincinnati Reds 2-1 in exhibition games. He would go on that year to be one of a number of Negro Leaguers who pitched in the Dominican Republic as part of the political baseball war going on between Rafael Trujillo and his opponents. His brother, Jose Maria Fernandez, Sr., and nephew, Jose M. Fernandez, Jr., both played Negro League baseball.

Ferrell, Howard (Toots)
Howard Ferrell was a pitcher for the Newark Eagles and Baltimore Elite Giants from 1948 to 1950.

Ferrell, Willie (Red)
Willie Ferrell was a pitcher for the Chicago American Giants, Homestead Grays, Birmingham Black Barons, Cincinnati Clowns, Cleveland Bears, and Jacksonville Red Caps from 1937 to 1943.

Ferrer, Efigenio (Al)
Efigenio Ferrer was a second baseman and shortstop for the Chicago American Giants and Indianapolis Clowns from 1946 to 1951.

Ferrer, Pedro
Pedro Ferrer was a second baseman for the Cuban Stars from 1922 to 1925.

Fiall, George
George Fiall was a shortstop and third baseman for the Harrisburg Giants, Lincoln Giants, Birmingham Black Barons, Baltimore Black Sox, and Pennsylvania Red Caps of New York from 1918 to 1929.

Fiall, Tom
Tom Fiall was an outfielder, third baseman, and catcher for the Brooklyn Royal Giants, Cuban Giants, Pennsyl-

vania Red Caps of New York, Hilldale baseball club, and Lincoln Giants from 1917 to 1925 and again in 1931.

Fields, Benny
Benny Fields was a second baseman and outfielder for the Cleveland Cubs, Memphis Red Sox, Cleveland Stars, and Birmingham Black Barons from 1930 to 1936.

Fields, Clifford
Clifford Fields was an outfielder for the Chicago American Giants in 1950.

Fields, Tom
Tom Fields was a pitcher for the Homestead Grays in 1946.

Fields, Wilmer (Red)
b. 1922
Wilmer Fields was a pitcher, third baseman, and outfielder for the Homestead Grays from 1939 to 1950. Born in Manassas, Virginia, in 1922, the 6-foot-3, 215-pound Fields, who had a football scholarship to Virginia State College, compiled an outstanding record of 104-21 on the mound in Negro League baseball competition. In an interview, Fields said he was playing sandlot baseball in Fairfax, Virginia, when he was discovered by the Grays. "Vic Harris saw me and arranged for me to pitch in Boston, Virginia, for a tryout game," Fields said. "We won 9-3, but I made a lot of mistakes. But they asked me to bring enough clothes to last me for two weeks. I would go to school in the winter and play ball in the summer."

His best years at the plate were 1947, when Fields batted .286 for Homestead, and the following season, when he hit .311 for the Grays, who won eight pennants while Fields was on the roster. He played with such Negro League greats as Josh Gibson and Buck Leonard. But it was on the mound where fields was a dominating player, posting a 16-1 record in 1948—the year Fields also pitched in the Negro League World Series. "We played Birmingham, and I won the first and fifth game of that series," Fields said. He also played for Toronto in the International League from 1951 to 1954, and Fields was the team's Most Valuable Player in three of those seasons, batting .381 and posting a 9-1 pitching record in 1951, a .379 average and an 8-2 mark in 1953, and a .425 average and a 6-1 record in 1954. He also played winter baseball in Mexico, Puerto Rico, and Venezuela.

In his autobiography, *My Life in the Negro Leagues*, Fields talked about the challenges he faced when he first joined the Grays: "If you were a youngster trying to make it in the Negro Leagues in the 1930s and 1940s, you didn't complain about anything at any time," Fields said. "You had to be able to ride in a bus all night, and then go out and produce on the field the next day. That was a must. Being able to deal within that structure was a big part of whether or not you would mature into a good ballplayer. The older members of the team set examples of how things were done, and then the younger ballplayers were expected to follow them. No excuses. People often don't believe me when I tell them about some of the things we had to go through when I played ball—like being escorted from the field by policemen after things got out of hand. Spectators would bet on what every player would do in a game, and if you didn't meet their expectations you would sometimes be abused. When we'd arrive at a ballpark, we'd have to enter by the gate in center field. We weren't allowed to go into the park through the front gate, where the home team entered. Our manager would complain to the other team's

Wilmer Fields has made Negro League baseball his life's work from the time he was discovered on a sandlot in Fairfax, Virginia, in 1939 to his current work as president of the Negro League Baseball Players Association. From 1939 to 1950, Fields was a third baseman, outfielder, and an outstanding pitcher for the Homestead Grays, who won eight pennants with Fields pitching. He posted a pitching record of 104-21 against Negro League competition, including a 16-1 record in 1948. (NATIONAL BASEBALL HALL OF FAME LIBRARY, COOPERSTOWN, N.Y.)

manager and he'd promise it wouldn't ever happen again. Sometimes when I look back, it's hard to believe some of the horrible things we had to endure. But that was the way it was in the 1930s, 1940s and 1950s."

Fields was a light-skinned, and had the job of going into restaurants to order takeout food for the team, with his hat pulled low. Sometimes the disguise didn't work, and he would be ordered out of the restaurant. He had strong nerve on and off the mound as well. "Most pitchers can't come back when you get three or four hits off them, but he could," said Negro Leaguer Pee Wee Butts. "Most fellows get shaky and blow up, but it looked like he came back with more. That's what I called hanging in there. Had a chance to win his own game at bat, too."

Fields had a number of offers to play major league baseball, but he turned them down. He said that at that point in his career, he had already reached what he believed was the pinnacle of his professional career by playing with the Grays, and the money was not good enough. "I had to ask myself if switching would benefit my family," Fields said. "I decided it would not. It wasn't worth the risk of jeopardizing my family's well being, because at that point I was playing three or four games weekly for a salary (including winter ball) that exceeded most major league salaries." In an interview, Fields said he could make as much money playing two months of winter ball as he could playing an entire season of minor league ball.

He went on to become president of the Negro League Baseball Players Association, promoting the history of Negro League baseball.

Figarola, Jose Rafael

Jose Figarola was a catcher and first baseman for the All Cubans, Stars of Cuba, and Cuban Stars from 1904 to 1915.

Figueroa, Enrique

Enrique Figueroa was a pitcher for the Baltimore Elite Giants in 1946. His brother, Jose Figueroa, pitched for the New York Cubans in 1940.

Figueroa, Jose (Tito)
b. 1914

Jose Figueroa was a pitcher for the New York Cubans and the Baltimore Elite Giants in 1940 and 1946. He was born in Mayaguez, Puerto Rico, in 1914 and was a track star as well as an outstanding baseball pitcher. In the Carribean Olympics, he pitched Puerto Rico to a win over Cuba in 1938 and turned around and set an all-time record in the javelin throw in the games. He started opening day for the Cubans in 1940 at Yankee Stadium, and defeated the New York Black Yankees 8-1. However, he developed a sore arm that year and did not return to the Negro Leagues, instead playing for the Mayaguez Indians until 1946 and pitching his final year in 1947 for Caguas Guayama. In a 1995 interview with *Sports Collectors Digest*, Figueroa said his best pitch was a "drop ball" that he said he learned as a child. "Then Leon Day and Satchel Paige helped me improve it." His brother, Enrique Figueroa, pitched for the Baltimore Elite Giants in 1946. Tito Figueroa is a member of the Puerto Rican Professional Baseball Hall of Fame.

Fillmore, Joseph
d. 1992

Joseph Fillmore was a pitcher for the Philadelphia Stars from 1941 to 1952.

Finch, Rayford
Rayford Finch was a pitcher for the Louisville Buckeyes and Cleveland Buckeyes in 1949 and 1950. He went on to pitch in the minor leagues from 1950 to 1953.

Finch, Robert
Robert Finch was a pitcher for the Madison Stars from 1920 to 1921 and the New York Lincoln Giants in 1926.

Finley, Thomas
Thomas Finley was a catcher, shortstop, second baseman, and third baseman for the Lincoln Giants, Bacharach Giants, Pennsylvania Red Caps of New York, Atlantic City Bacharach Giants, Brooklyn Royal Giants, New York Black Yankees, Darby Daisies, New York Harlem Stars, Philadelphia Stars, Baltimore Black Sox, Washington Potomacs, and Wilmington Potomacs from 1922 to 1934. His career came to a tragic end in 1933 when he died from an infection as a result of a spiking accident while playing for the Philadelphia Stars.

Finner, John
John Finner was a pitcher for the St. Louis Stars, St. Louis Giants, Birmingham Black Barons, and Milwaukee Bears from 1919 to 1925. He had an 11-7 record with the Giants in 1921.

Finney, Ed
b. 1924, d. 1997

Ed Finney was a third baseman for the Baltimore Elite Giants from 1948 to 1950. He played minor league baseball and also in the Canadian League in 1951. Born in Akron, Ohio, Finner batted .278, .320, and .333 for Baltimore.

Fisher, George
George Fisher was an outfielder for the Washington Braves, Richmond Giants, and Harrisburg Giants from 1922 to 1923.

Fishue, Pete
Pete Fishue was a catcher for the New York Gorhams in 1886.

Fleet, Joseph
Joseph Fleet was a pitcher for the Chicago American Giants in 1930.

Flemming, Frank
Frank Flemming was a pitcher for the Cleveland Buckeyes in 1946.

Flood, Jess
Jess Flood was a catcher for the Cleveland Tate Stars in 1919.

Flores, Conrad
Conrad Flores was a pitcher for the Kansas City Monarchs in 1954.

Florida Clippers
The Florida Clippers were a black baseball a team out of Jacksonville, Florida, that played in the Southern League of Colored Baseballists in 1886.

Flourney, Fred
Fred Flourney was a catcher for the Pennsylvania Red Caps of New York and Brooklyn Cuban Giants from 1928 to 1933.

Flourney, Willis (Pud)
Willis Flourney was a pitcher for the Baltimore Black Sox, Brooklyn Royal Giants, Hilldale baseball club, Pennsylvania Red Caps of New York, and Bacharach Giants from 1919 to 1934.

Flowers, Jake
Jake Flowers was an infielder for the New York Black Yankees from 1941 to 1943.

Floyd, Earle

Earle Floyd was a first baseman and outfielder for the Detroit Stars in 1954 and 1955.

Floyd, Irv

Irv Floyd was a pitcher and outfielder for the Detroit Stars in 1954.

Floyd, J. J.

J. J. Floyd was an officer with the Little Rock Greys in 1932.

Footes, Robert

Robert Footes was a catcher for the Philadelphia Giants, Chicago Unions, Brooklyn Royal Giants, and Chicago Union Giants from 1895 to 1909.

Forbes, Frank

Frank Forbes was an infielder for the Lincoln Giants in the 1910s and 1920s. Forbes went on to become an umpire and business manager for the New York Cubans from 1929 to 1943.

Forbes, Joseph

Joseph Forbes was a shortstop, outfielder, and third baseman for the Pennsylvania Red Caps of New York, Lincoln Giants, Brooklyn Royal Giants, Bacharach Giants, Philadelphia Giants, and Lincoln Stars from 1911 to 1927.

Forbes Field

Forbes Field, the ballpark in Pittsburgh that was home to the Pittsburgh Pirates, also hosted Negro League baseball games with teams such as the Homestead Grays, Pittsburgh Crawfords, and Lincoln Giants. John Holway, in *Blackball Stars,* wrote that the Crawfords played twilight baseball games at Forbes Field in 1932 and 1933—after the Pirates played day games—and white major leaguers often stayed and watched. Babe Herman of the Brooklyn Dodgers recalled watching Oscar Charleston playing at Forbes Field. "Hit the ball a mile," he said. During one game at Forbes Field, Negro Leaguer Vic Harris punched a white umpire over a disputed call, setting off a riot in the ballpark.

Force, William

William Force was a pitcher for the Baltimore Black Sox, Brooklyn Royal Giants, and Detroit Stars from 1920 to 1930.

Ford, Bubber

Bubber Ford was an officer with the Jacksonville Eagles in 1947.

Ford, Carl

Carl Ford was an officer with the Shreveport Tigers in 1947.

Ford, Erwin

Erwin Ford was a second baseman for the Indianapolis Clowns from 1951 to 1954.

Ford, Frank

Frank Ford was a catcher for the Hilldale baseball club and Pennsylvania Giants from 1915 to 1918.

Ford, James

James Ford was a third baseman and second baseman for the St. Louis Stars, Memphis Red Sox, New York Black Yankees, New Orleans–St. Louis Stars, Philadelphia Stars, Cincinnati Clowns, Harrisburg–St. Louis Stars, Baltimore Elite Giants, Nashville Elite Giants, and Washington Black Senators from 1931 to 1946.

Ford, Roy

Roy Ford was a second baseman and pitcher for the Harrisburg Giants and Baltimore Black Sox from 1916 to 1925.

Foreman, Sylvester (Hooks)

Sylvester Foreman was a pitcher and catcher for the Indianapolis ABC's, Kansas City Monarchs, Washington Pilots, Homestead Grays, Milwaukee Bears, and Cleveland Browns from 1920 to 1933.

Foreman, Zack

Zack Foreman was a pitcher for the Kansas City Monarchs in 1921.

Forge, Willie

Willie Forge was a catcher for the Louisville Black Colonels and Kansas City Monarchs in 1954 and 1955.

Forkins, Marty

Marty Forkins was an officer with the New York Black Yankees in 1931.

Formenthal, Pedro

Pedro Formenthal was an outfielder for the Memphis Red Sox from 1947 to 1950. Records show he batted .341 in 1949 and .264 the following season for Memphis. Born in Baguanos, Cuba, in 1915, the 5-foot-11, 200-pound Formenthal also played baseball in the Mexican League, Dominican League, and Cuban Winter League and played two seasons for Havana in the International League in 1954 and 1955.

Forrest, Joseph

Joseph Forrest was a pitcher for the New York Black Yankees in 1949.

Forrest, Percy

Percy Forrest was a pitcher for the Newark Eagles, Chicago American Giants, Indianapolis Clowns, and New York Black Yankees from 1938 to 1949.

Fort Worth Wonders

The Fort Worth Wonders were a black baseball team that played out of Forth Worth, Texas, in the 1920s.

Foster, Albert (Red)

Albert Foster was a first baseman for the Kansas City Giants in 1910.

Foster, Andrew (Rube)

b. 1879, d. 1930

Andrew Foster was one of the greatest pitchers in the history of Negro League baseball and also became known as the father of black baseball for his career as a team owner and founder of the NEGRO NATIONAL LEAGUE. Born in Calvert, Texas, Foster pitched and managed for the Waco Yellowjackets, Fort Worth Colts, Chicago Union Giants, Cuban X Giants, Leland Giants, Philadelphia Giants, Leland Giants, and Chicago American Giants from 1898 to 1926. He was believed to have been given the nickname "Rube" after he defeated George "Rube" Waddell and the Philadelphia Athletics in an exhibition game.

Foster was a big (6-foot-4, 200+ pound), hard-throwing right-hander who became a pitching legend. He is believed to have struck out 18 batters pitching for the Philadelphia Giants in game one of a three-game series against the Cuban X Giants in 1904 and allowed just two hits in game three, clinching the series. He was also Philadelphia's leading hitter over the three games, batting .400, and played on the 1906 Giants squad that was considered by many to be the best black team in the early part of the 20th century, with players such as Home Run

Andrew "Rube" Foster was known as the father of black baseball as both owner of the famous Chicago American Giants and founder of the Negro National League, considered to have been the most competitive and stable of the Negro Leagues that were formed. He was also an outstanding pitcher and all-around player and is believed to have put together a record of 111-31 against Negro League teams from 1903 to 1917. He pitched and managed for Waco Yellowjackets, Fort Worth Colts, Chicago Union Giants, Cuban X Giants, Leland Giants, Philadelphia Giants, Leland Giants, and Chicago American Giants from 1898 to 1926. He passed away at the age of 51 in 1930 after suffering from a series of mental illnesses.
(NATIONAL BASEBALL HALL OF FAME LIBRARY, COOPERSTOWN, N.Y.)

Johnson, Pete Hill, Sol White, Bill Francis, and James Booker, along with Foster. According to some accounts, Foster won 51 games that year. However, pitching against Negro League teams in his career, records show that Foster went 111-31 from 1903 to 1917. He was also 26-11 in the Cuban Winter League.

He wrote an article in Sol White's guide to Negro League baseball titled, "How to Pitch"—Foster's dissertation on the art of pitching: "I have a theory of pitching that has helped me considerably. A pitcher should have control of every ball he pitches. But it matters not how good a pitcher is, he will become wild at times and can't get over them. Do not become disheartened at that. Don't slacken your speed to get a ball over the plate, but teach yourself to master the weakness."

Foster was considered a pioneer of baseball strategy, credited with coming up with the hit-and-run bunt and often called upon by New York Giants manager John McGraw to work with pitchers. He was a talented manager as well. In his autobiography, *I Was Right on Time*, Buck O'Neil wrote about the unique way he gave signals to his player. "He was something to watch, even from the dugout. He smoked a meerschaum pipe and signaled his players and coaches with smoke rings. I spent a lot of time trying to figure out his system, but I couldn't. . . . Rube was way ahead of his time in the psychological side of the game— we didn't even know there was one. He was always trying to fool the other team, and most of the time he did."

Foster's influence on baseball would go far beyond the pitching mound. He became an influential operator in Negro baseball, starting by taking over the booking duties for the Leland Giants as well as pitching for them, and his influence and power grew. By 1909, he had formed a partnership with John C. Schorling, a Chicago businessman and brother-in-law of Chicago White Sox owner Charles Comiskey, taking over the ownership of Frank Leland's Giants and playing in the former White Sox ballpark on 39th and Wentworth. In that first year under Foster's ownership the team reportedly won 109 games (and lost just 9). He would later change their name to the Chicago American Giants, and, through Negro baseball and barnstorming exhibition games against white ballplayers, Foster continued to become the driving force in Negro baseball. Former Negro Leaguer Dave Malarcher, who played third base for Foster's team and later succeeded him as Chicago manager, said in an interview with *Baseball in Chicago* that Foster ran an impressive team. "I never saw such a well-equipped ball club in my whole life," Malarcher said. "Every day they came out in different uniforms, all kinds of bats and balls, all the best kinds of equipment. The American Giants traveled everywhere. No other team traveled as many miles as the American Giants. When Rube gave them the name American Giants, he really selected a name. That was a good idea, because it became the greatest ballclub there ever was." Some of the players who played for Foster's early teams included John Henry Lloyd, Bruce Petway, and Frank Wickware.

In 1919, Foster formed the NEGRO NATIONAL LEAGUE. He said the purpose of the league was to "create a profession that would equal the earning capacity of other professions, and keep colored baseball from the control of whites." He also said he wanted to "do something concrete for the loyalty of the race." However, he quietly enlisted the financial support of white businessmen behind the scenes. The league, which began play in 1920, consisted of eight teams—Chicago Giants, Chicago

American Giants, Cuban Giants (a team without a home field), Detroit Stars, Dayton Marcos, Indianapolis ABC's, Kansas City Monarchs, and St. Louis Giants. Foster's American Giants would dominate the league, winning the league's first three pennants with such players as Oscar Charleston, Dave Malacher, and pitcher Dave Brown. According to Robert Peterson's book *Only the Ball Was White*, Foster was a smart but ruthless businessman: "His hold over league affairs is illustrated by the story, possibly apocryphal, that at a league meeting after the 1920 season, John Matthews, owner of the Dayton Marcos, indulged in a catnap and awoke to find that he had lost his franchise and his players, whom Rube had distributed among other teams. Whether true or not, the tale reflects the reality; it is a fact that Dayton was not in the league in 1921 . . . but if he was stern and domineering, Rube Foster was also a responsible businessman, and there is no question that his efforts alone kept the league afloat during its infancy. He shored up shaky franchises with his own money, paid transportation costs for some clubs, and guaranteed hotel bills for teams stranded far from home because games were rained out and they had no money."

Within four years, the league was drawing a total of more than 4 million fans but then found themselves competing with a new league called the EASTERN COLORED LEAGUE, formed by businessman Ed Bolden. The competition and financial pressures weighed heavily on Foster, who would show signs of mental illness that would result in his being placed in the Illinois State Hospital in Kanakee in 1926. Four years later he died at age 51. His funeral was a major event in Chicago, with thousands viewing his body and more than 3,000 people attending the ceremonies. Foster was inducted into the National Baseball Hall of Fame in 1981.

Foster, James

James Foster was an officer with the Chicago Brown Bombers in 1945.

Foster, Leland

Leland Foster was a pitcher for the Monroe Monarchs from 1932 to 1936.

Foster, Leonard

Leonard Foster was an infielder for the Atlanta Black Crackers in 1938.

Foster, William Hendrick (Bill)
b. 1904, d. 1978

William Foster, like his half brother, Rube, was one of the all-time great Negro League pitchers, playing and managing for the Chicago American Giants, Memphis Red Sox, Kansas City Monarchs, Homestead Grays, Birmingham Black Barons, Cole's American Giants, and Pittsburgh Crawfords from 1923 to 1937. A left-hander, Foster helped his half brother's team, the Chicago American Giants, win the Negro League World Series in 1926, when he is believed to have won 28 or 29 games, and 1927, with an 18-3 won-loss mark in 1927. Remarkably, in 1926, Foster won both ends of a doubleheader against the Kansas City Monarchs to win the championship. In a 1974 interview with *Black Sports*, Foster talked about his dominance on the mound over that period: "That year [1926] they said I was one of the greatest pitchers of all time," he said. "I think I won 28 or 29 ball games that year, and I didn't lose but about three or four. For the eight years I was with

Chicago, I don't think I lost over five ball games in each year, and I pitched two ball games in every series of five." Foster would also pitch the decisive seventh game in the 1932 playoffs for Chicago, throwing a 2-0 shutout against the Nashville Elite Giants. Foster pitched for the West in the first two EAST-WEST ALL-STAR GAMES in 1933 and 1934, winning in 1933 and losing a tough 1-0 decision to Satchel Paige in 1934. Foster talked about his matchups over the years against Paige. "I think, as near as I can remember, we faced each other around 13 or 14 times," Foster said. "I think I got the edge of Satchel when I beat him in a doubleheader in Pittsburgh one Saturday—5-0 and 1-0. I think that put me one ball game ahead of him in our career. But I'll tell you something: if Satchel got one run first, he would beat you; if I got one run first, he was beat."

Willie Foster's arm led the Chicago American Giants—the team owned by his half brother, Negro National League founder Rube Foster—to greatness in the 1920s. A left-handed pitcher, Foster pitched the Chicago American Giants to the Negro League World Series in 1926, where he is believed to have won 28 or 29 games. Foster won both ends of a doubleheader against the Kansas City Monarchs to win the championship. Foster played and managed for the American Giants, Memphis Red Sox, Kansas City Monarchs, Homestead Grays, Birmingham Black Barons, Cole's American Giants, and Pittsburgh Crawfords from 1923 to 1937. (NATIONAL BASEBALL HALL OF FAME LIBRARY, COOPERSTOWN, N.Y.)

Foster is believed to have won 137 games over his career (while losing 62) against Negro League teams, the most ever recorded, and also had 34 shutouts. According to Robert Peterson's book *Only the Ball Was White*, Negro League owner Cum Posey called Foster "the greatest left-hander Negro baseball ever saw," and Dave Malacher, Foster's teammate and manager with Chicago, said that Foster's greatness "was that he had this terrific speed and a great, fast-breaking curve ball and a drop ball, and he was really a master of the change of pace. He could throw you a real fast one and then use the same motion and bring it up a little slower, and then a little slower yet. And then he'd use the same motion again, and Z-zzz! He was really a great pitcher."

Foster, who was born in Calvert, Texas, finished his playing career after spending his last season in 1938 with the Washington Browns, a black team in Yakima, Washington, and a white semipro team in Elgin, Illinois. He would go on to become head baseball coach and dean of men at Alcorn College, his alma mater. Despite being one of the greatest pitchers of all time, yet never having the opportunity to play in the major leagues and make large sums of money, Foster said he wasn't bitter: "I'm not bitter that I didn't make $75,000 or $80,000," he said. "What would I have done with it anyway. I don't know whether it would have done me any good or not. They say, 'You should have waited 20 years before you were born, you would have been in good financial shape.' Yeah, in that respect, but what about other respects? I might have been born with one lame leg and couldn't walk. . . . I didn't have to be born strong and healthy like I am. I could have been born deformed in some way. But no, I came in a healthy kid, so I appreciate that. I take it as it comes." Foster was inducted into the National Baseball Hall of Fame in 1996.

Fowler, J. W. (Bud)
b. 1858

J. W. Fowler is believed to be professional baseball's first black player. Fowler, a pitcher, infielder, outfielder, catcher, and manager, played from 1872 to 1899 for a number of both white and black teams as a star attraction and drawing card in both organized games and barnstorming exhibitions. Fowler's real name was John W. Jackson, and he was born in Fort Plain, New York, in 1858. He grew up in Cooperstown, New York—now the home of the National Baseball Hall of Fame. He was playing for a white team in New Castle, Pennsylvania, when he was just 14 years old. Fowler also played for teams in Stillwater in the Northwestern League; Keokuk and Topeka in the Western League; Binghampton in the International League; Crawfordsville, Terre Haute, and Galesburg in the Central Interstate League; Lafayette, Indiana; Greenville in the Michigan League;

Sterling and Davenport in the Illinois-Iowa League; Evansville; New York Black Gorhams; All-American Black Tourists; Page Fence Giants (which Fowler founded); Adrian in the Michigan State League; Lansing in the Michigan State League; Lynn in the International Association; Lincoln-Kearney in the Nebraska State League; Galesburg in the Illinois-Iowa League; Burlington in the Illinois-Iowa League; Pueblo in the Colorado League; Worchester in the New England Association; Santa Fe in the New Mexico League; and Montpelier in the Vermont League.

Records are sporadic at best from this era, but Fowler is believed to have batted .309 in 1886 and .350 in 1887. Through 10 minor league seasons, Fowler batted .308 with 455 runs scored, 112 doubles, 38 triples, 7 home runs, and 190 stolen bases in 465 games and 2,039 at bats.

He moved around often and in 1899 started one of his barnstorming teams, the All-American Black Tourists. The team would hold a pregame parade dressed in formal wear, with white vests, swallow-tail coats, opera hats, and silk umbrellas, and Fowler made the following offer: "By request of any club, we will play the game in these suits." He also organized the Page Fence Giants in 1895. According to Robert Peterson's book *Only the Ball Was White*, Fowler could play any position, "but it was as a second baseman that he excelled. He was recognized by white sportswriters as the equal of any of his contemporaries at that position, but he had no chance to test his talents against them at the highest level, the National League."

Fowler is also credited with developing what would become the modern day shin guards, only Fowler used them—wooden guards—to protect himself at second base because of the number of white players who would come into the base sliding with the intention of spiking him. In a March 1889 edition of the *Sporting News*, an unidentified International League player said Fowler was a target. "He knew that about every other player that came down to second base on a steal had it in for him, and would, if possible, throw the spikes into him," the player said. "He [Fowler] was a good player, but left the base every time there was a close play in order to get away from the spikes. I've seen him muff balls intentionally, so that he would not have to try to touch runners, fearing that they might injure him." Fowler eventually was banned from playing for white teams as the 19th century came to a close, and the movement to ban blacks from white organized ball would unfortunately be successful. An 1895 quote from Fowler in Peterson's book illustrates the closing opportunities for him: "It was hard picking for a colored player this year," he said. "I didn't pick up a living; I just existed. I was down in the lower Illinois country and in Missouri, cross-roading with teams in the little towns . . . my skin is against me. If I had not been quite so black, I might have caught on as a Spaniard or something of that kind. The race prejudice is so strong that my black skin barred me."

Fowlkes, Erwin

Erwin Fowlkes was a shortstop for the Homestead Grays and Chicago American Giants from 1947 to 1948.

Fowlkes, Samuel

Samuel Fowlkes was a pitcher for the Cleveland Buckeyes and Kansas City Monarchs in 1950.

Fox, Orange

Orange Fox was an outfielder for the Chicago Unions in 1887.

Francis, Del

Del Francis was a second baseman for the Indianapolis ABC's in 1911 and from 1917 to 1920.

Francis, James H.

James Francis was a former cricket player who, along with Francis Wood, formed the Pythians of Philadelphia, a black baseball team based in Philadelphia in the 1860s.

Francis, William (Brodie)

William Francis was a third baseman and shortstop for the Cuban Giants, Brooklyn Royal Giants, Wilmington Giants, Lincoln Giants, Philadelphia Giants, Chicago American Giants, Bacharach Giants, Hilldale baseball club, Chicago Giants, Cleveland Browns, and Mohawk Giants from 1904 to 1925. The Brooklyn Royal Giants team on which he played in 1906 won 134 games and lost just 21. In the John Holway book *Blackball Stars*, Judy Johnson recalled his former teammate and mentor, Francis: "He was close to the ground," Johnson said. "He could get to ground balls easily, and hit pitches at his eyes." Francis also played winter ball on the Breakers Hotel team in Florida in 1914. He is believed to have batted .270 through his career and had several big years at the plate, batting .396, .344, and .324.

Franklin, William B.

William Franklin was the manager of Louisville Falls City in 1887.

Frazier, Albert

Albert Frazier was a second baseman and third baseman for the Jacksonville Red Caps, Montgomery Grey Sox, and Cleveland Bears from 1932 to 1940.

Frazier, Oran

Oran Frazier was an infielder for the Montgomery Grey Sox in 1932.

Frazier, Sam

Sam Frazier was an infielder for the Montgomery Grey Sox in 1932.

Freeman, Buck

Buck Freeman was an umpire in the NEGRO NATIONAL LEAGUE in 1925.

Freeman, Charles

Charles Freeman was president of the Hilldale baseball club in 1927.

Freeman, William

William Freeman was a pitcher for the Cuban Stars and Indianapolis ABC's in 1925 and 1933.

Freeman, William

William Freeman was a third baseman for the Chicago Unions from 1886 to 1889.

Freihofer, William

William Freihofer was president of the International League of Independent Professional Base Ball Clubs in 1906.

Frye, Jack

Jack Frye was a pitcher, outfielder, catcher, and first baseman. Frye played both minor league organized white baseball and Negro League baseball for Reading, Pennsylvania, in the Interstate League; Lewiston in the Pennsylvania State League; York Giants in the Middle States League; Ansonia Cuban Giants in the Connecticut State League; New York Gorhams and York Colored Monarchs from 1883 to 1896. Records show that in 1890, Frye batted .303 for the Cuban Giants. Through five minor league seasons, Frye batted .253 with 87 runs scored, 23 doubles, seven triples, three home runs, and 27 stolen bases in 124 games and 446 at bats.

Fulcer, Robert

Robert Fulcer was a pitcher for the Chicago American Giants and Birmingham Black Barons in 1940.

Fuller, James

James Fuller was a catcher for the Bacharach Giants, Cuban Giants, Lincoln Stars, and Philadelphia Giants from 1912 to 1922.

Fuller, W. W. (Chick)

W. W. Fuller was a shortstop and second baseman for the Cuban Giants, Bacharach Giants, Cleveland Tate Stars, Pennsylvania Giants, Brooklyn Colored Giants, Hilldale baseball club, Pennsylvania Red Caps of New York, and New York Colored Giants from 1908 to 1919.

Fulton, Sam

Sam Fulton was a pitcher for the Birmingham Black Barons in 1955.

Gadsen, Gus
Gus Gadsen was an outfielder for the Hilldale baseball club in 1932.

Gaines, George (Lefty)
George Gaines was a pitcher for the Baltimore Elite Giants, Newark Eagles, Washington Elite Giants, Philadelphia Stars, and Chicago American Giants from 1937 to 1951.

Gaines, Willy
Willy Gaines was a pitcher for the Philadelphia Stars and Indianapolis Clowns from 1950 to 1955.

Galata, Domingo
Domingo Galata was a pitcher for the New York Cubans from 1949 to 1950. Galata also played in the Mexican League from 1951 to 1964.

Galata, Raul
b. 1930
Raul Galata was a pitcher for the Indianapolis Clowns from 1949 to 1953. Born in Cuba, the 5-foot-9, 170-pound Galata also played in the Mexican League until 1964 and played winter baseball in Puerto Rico and Venezuela.

Gall, J. E.
J. E. Gall was the co-owner, along with J. L. Wilkinson, of the ALL NATIONS teams, the barnstorming team in the early 1900s that consisted of blacks, Cubans, Mexicans, Orientals, and even female players.

Galloway, Bill (Hippo)
Bill Galloway was an outfielder and second baseman for the Cuban Giants, Cuban X Giants, and Famous Cuban Giants from 1899 to 1906.

Galvez, Cuneo
Cuneo Galvez was a pitcher for the Cuban Stars and the Cuban House of David from 1928 to 1932.

Gans, Robert (Judy)
Robert Gans was a pitcher, outfielder, and manager for the Madison Stars, Smart Set, Cuban Giants, Lincoln Giants, Chicago American Giants, Lincoln Stars, Chicago Giants, Cleveland Tigers, and Mohawk Giants from 1910 to 1938. He also umpired in the East-West League and the NEGRO NATIONAL LEAGUE. In Madison, Gans was a teammate of a young third baseman named William Johnson and took the young player under his wing, giving him, for some unknown reason, the nickname "Judy," as

in Judy Johnson, who would go on to become one of the greatest third basemen in Negro League history.

Garay, Martiniano (Jose)

Martiniano Garay was a pitcher and outfielder for the New York Cubans from 1948 to 1950.

Garcia, Antonio Maria

Antonio Garcia was a catcher and first baseman for the Cuban Stars, Cuban X Giants, and All Cubans from 1904 to 1912. According to *Baseball's Other All-Stars*, by William F. Mitchell, Garcia was "arguably the greatest Cuban League player for the 19th century. In addition to his defensive capabilities, Garcia was a powerful hitter who won four Cuban League baseball titles, with his highest average of .448 in 1888. By the time he came to the United States to play in the Negro Leagues, he was well past his prime." He was elected to the Cuban Baseball Hall of Fame in its first year in 1939.

Garcia, Atires (Angel)

Atires Garcia was a pitcher for the Cincinnati-Indianapolis Clowns and the Indianapolis Clowns from 1945 to 1953.

Garcia, John

John Garcia was a catcher for the Cuban Giants in 1904.

Garcia, Juan

Juan Garcia was an infielder for the Indianapolis Clowns in 1952.

Garcia, Manuel (Cocaina)

Manuel Garcia was an outfielder and pitcher for the New York Cubans and Cuban Stars from 1926 to 1936. Garcia, a 5-foot-8, 185-pound left-hander, was nicknamed "Cocaina" because supposedly his pitching would leave batters unfocused and confused, as if in a cocaine-induced state. In his autobiography, *I Was Right on Time*, Negro Leaguer Buck O'Neil said that Garcia got his nickname "from his wicked curveball, which made all us hitters go numb." He also played baseball in leagues in his homeland of Cuba, and in Mexico, the Dominican Republic, and Venezuela. He is a member of the Cuban and Venezuelan baseball hall of fames.

Garcia, Regino

Regino Garcia was a catcher for the All Cubans in 1905.

Garcia, Romando

Romando Garcia was a second baseman for the Lincoln Giants and Bacharach Giants from 1926 to 1927.

Garcia, Silvio

b. 1914

Silvio Garcia was an infielder for the New York Cubans from 1940 to 1947, with a career batting average of .322. He also played in the Mexican League and the Cuban Winter League. The 6-foot, 195-pound Garcia was born in Limonar, Cuba, in 1914 and was elected to the Cuban Baseball Hall of Fame in 1975.

Gardner, Floyd (Jelly)

1895–1977

Floyd Gardner was an outfielder and first baseman for the Chicago American Giants, Detroit Stars, Homestead Grays, and Lincoln Giants from 1919 to 1933. Born in Russellville, Arkansas, Gardner helped lead the Chicago American Giants to four pennants during his career. The 5-foot-7, 170-pound Gardner batted left-handed but threw right-handed. In his best years with Chicago, Gardner batted .367 in 1924 and .333 in 1926. "We played everywhere," Gardner said in an interview on file at the National Baseball Hall of Fame. "Wisconsin, Milwaukee, Sheboygan, Racine . . . these would be against white semipro teams. We used a bus on short trips. On longer trips, we used a private car or a train. We used trains for trips to St. Louis, Kansas City, Detroit. . . . The American Giants park had a wooden grandstand, and it would hold about 8,000 or 9,000. . . . We usually played about five days a week. Every year in the fall we made a swing through the East. In the early 1920's, we played the Bacharach Giants at Ebbets Field. The first time 40,000 people were there."

Gardner said he was nicknamed Jelly as a child. "I used to be a little stout when I was small," he said. Gardner also talked about the satisfaction they got out of barnstorming games against major league players. "We did quite a bit of barnstorming every year against big leaguers until [baseball commissioner] Judge [Kenesaw Mountain] Landis made that ruling [forbidding teams from playing Negro League teams]," he said. "We beat the Detroit Tigers three out of four, and Judge Landis made a ruling that they couldn't play intact anymore. The Tigers had everybody but Ty Cobb."

Kansas City rival Newt Allen, in an interview conducted by author John Holway on file at the National Baseball Hall of Fame, said Gardner was an outstanding center fielder. "There was another Willie Mays. If the ball stayed in the playing field, he caught it, and he could throw it after he got it. He was a great baserunner, too."

Floyd "Jelly" Gardner was an outfielder and first baseman who helped lead the Chicago American Giants to four pennants during his career, batting .367 in 1924 and .333 in 1926. The 5-foot-7, 170-pound Gardner played from 1919 to 1933 for the American Giants, Detroit Stars, Homestead Grays, and Lincoln Giants. (NATIONAL BASEBALL HALL OF FAME LIBRARY, COOPERSTOWN, N.Y.)

Gardner, Grover (Gus)

Gus Gardner was a catcher and outfielder for the New Orleans Caufield Ads and Chicago American Giants from 1921 to 1923.

Gardner, James (Chappy)

James Gardner was a third baseman and second baseman for the Havana Red Sox, Brooklyn Royal Giants, Brooklyn Colored Giants, and Cuban Giants from 1908 to 1917.

Gardner, Kenneth (Steel Arm)

Kenneth Gardner was a pitcher for the Brooklyn Royal Giants, Washington Red Caps, Philadelphia Royal Stars, Hilldale baseball club, Harrisburg Giants, Lincoln Giants, Cleveland Tigers, Bacharach Giants, Newark Browns, and Baltimore Black Sox from 1918 to 1932.

Garner, Horace

b. 1925

Horace Garner was an outfielder for the Indianapolis Clowns in 1949. The 6-foot-3, 200-pound Garner went on to play minor league baseball in Jacksonville, Cedar Rapids, Augusta, Evansville, and Eau Claire.

Garrett, Alvin

Alvin Garrett, a black Chicago businessman, was the owner of the Columbia Giants in the late 1890s. In a battle with Frank Leland's Giants, Garrett was eventually forced to dissolve the team shortly after the turn of the 20th century when they were unable to find a permanent place to play.

Garrett, Soloman

Soloman Garrett was a second baseman for the New York Black Yankees in 1950.

Garrett, William

William Garrett was an officer for the New York Black Yankees in 1943.

Garrido, Gil

Gil Garrido was an infielder for the New York Cubans from 1944 to 1946.

Garrison, Robert

Robert Garrison was a pitcher for the St. Paul Gophers in 1909.

Garrison, Ross

Ross Garrison was a third baseman and shortstop for the New York Gorhams, York-Cuban Giants, and Cuban Giants from 1889 to 1897.

Garvin, Leedell

Leedell Garvin was a pitcher for the Philadelphia Stars in 1942.

Gary, Charles

Charles Gary was a third baseman for the Homestead Grays from 1948 to 1950.

Gaston, Hiram

Hiram Gaston was a pitcher for the Birmingham Black Barons in 1952 and 1953.

Gaston, Robert

Robert Gaston was a catcher for the Homestead Grays and Brooklyn Brown Dodgers from 1932 to 1949.

Gatewood, Bill

Bill Gatewood was a pitcher and manager for the Philadelphia Giants, Cuban X Giants, Leland Giants, Brooklyn Royal Giants, Chicago American Giants, Chicago Giants, Detroit Stars, St. Louis Giants, Toledo Tigers, St. Louis Stars, Birmingham Black Barons, Albany Giants, Milwaukee Bears, Memphis Red Sox, Lincoln Giants, and Indianapolis ABC's from 1905 to 1928. He is believed to have killed another pitcher, Bill Lindsay, with a ball while pitching batting practice in 1914. According to Mark Ribowsky's book *A Complete History of the Negro Leagues*, Gatewood had an act on the mound that consisted of drinking a bottle of corn whiskey before he pitched as the crowd and the other team watched; however, Gatewood later said that it was an act to psych out the hitters and incite the crowd and that the bottle was actually filled with water. As manager of the St. Louis Stars, Gatewood is believed to have given his outfielder James Thomas Bell the nickname "Cool Papa."

Gatewood, Ernest

Ernest Gatewood was a first baseman and catcher for the Brooklyn Royal Giants, Lincoln Giants, Harrisburg Giants, Bacharach Giants, Mohawk Giants, and Lincoln Stars from 1914 to 1927.

Gatson, Robert

Robert Gatson was a catcher for the Homestead Grays in 1942.

Gautier, John

John Gautier was a pitcher for the Kansas City Monarchs in 1955.

Gay, Herbert

Herbert Gay was a pitcher and outfielder for the Birmingham Black Barons, Chicago American Giants, and Baltimore Black Sox from 1929 to 1930.

Gee, Richard

Richard Gee was a catcher and outfielder for the Lincoln Giants and New Orleans Crescent Stars from 1922 to 1929.

Gee, Sammy

Sammy Gee was a shortstop for the Detroit Stars in 1955.

Gee, Tom

Tom Gee was a catcher for the Newark Stars and Lincoln Giants from 1925 to 1926.

Genuine Cuban Giants

The Genuine Cuban Giants were one of the many versions of the Cuban Giants in black baseball. They were a descendant of the original Cuban Giants and played in the early 1900s in various cities, including New York; Trenton and Hoboken, New Jersey; York, Pennsylvania; and Ansonia, Connecticut.

George, John

John George was a shortstop for the Chicago Giants, New Orleans Crescent Stars, Chicago American Giants, Harrisburg Giants, Bacharach Giants, and New Orleans Caufield Ads from 1921 to 1925.

Georgia Champions

The Georgia Champions were a black baseball team out of Atlanta, Georgia, that played in the Southern League of Colored Baseballists in 1886.

Gerald, Alphonso

Alphonso Gerald was an infielder and outfielder for the New York Black Yankees, Chicago American Giants, and Indianapolis Clowns from 1945 to 1949. He went on to play minor league baseball until 1953 and played in the Puerto Rico Winter League.

Gholston, Bert

Bert Gholston was an umpire in the NEGRO NATIONAL LEAGUE and the East-West League from 1923 to 1943. Gholston also wrote articles for the *Kansas City Call*, one of which, in 1926, expounded on the importance of purpose and principles to Negro League baseball: "If every club in the colored baseball league would fulfill the purposes of its organization and existence, it must be a force in the betterment and upbuilding of colored baseball," Gholston wrote. "Colored leagues can live and flourish only upon that basis. Interest cannot be maintained in a club or league without high purposes and definite principles as a foundation is bound to persist. There can be no higher motives than the betterment and upbuilding of colored baseball. There must be and there are, motives which constantly actuate men to put forth their best efforts towards the progress of the game. Substantial improvement of the game increases and enhances the opportunities and pleasures of all individuals who take part in it or who are affected by the influence. Individual clubs' betterment means league betterment. It is a big task, but all of the clubs of the different leagues must earnestly and honestly set themselves to it."

Giant Collegians

The Giant Collegians were also known as the Singing Baseball Team, a group of traveling black baseball players that was started in 1930 at the Piney Woods Country Life School in Jackson, Mississippi. The squad played against a number of teams in the Negro Southern League and included such players as Howard Easterling, who would go on to become a star in Negro League baseball for the Homestead Grays in the 1940s. They would also go by the name of the St. Louis Blues. They entertained crowds with singing quartets.

Gibbons, John

John Gibbons was a pitcher for the Philadelphia Stars in 1941.

Gibbons, Walter Lee

Walter Lee Gibbons was a pitcher for the Indianapolis Clowns from 1948 to 1949.

Gibson, Jerry

Jerry Gibson was an outfielder and pitcher for the Cincinnati Clowns, Cincinnati Tigers, and Cincinnati Buckeyes from 1935 to 1943. He was the brother of Negro League catching great Josh Gibson, Sr.

Gibson, Joshua, Jr. (Josh)
b. 1930

Josh Gibson, Jr., was the son of Negro League catching great Josh Gibson and was an infielder for the Homestead Grays in 1949 and 1950. He went on to play briefly for Youngstown in the Middle Atlantic League.

Gibson, Joshua, Sr. (Josh)
b. 1911, d. 1947

Josh Gibson was known as the Babe Ruth of black baseball for his home run power. He was a stocky catcher, at 6 foot 2, 210 pounds, and one of the Negro League's biggest attractions. Gibson was considered one of the Negro League players who likely would have been a major league baseball star as well. He was born in Buena Vista, Georgia, and his family moved to Pittsburgh when he was 12. He grew up a young star athlete, playing at the age of 16 for an all-Negro amateur team known as the Gimbels A. C., and later worked in a manufacturing plant that made air brakes in Pittsburgh. He was unable to get a shot at playing for the Homestead Grays, so he organized a semipro team called the Crawford Colored Giants until his chance came in June 1930 when the Grays' regular catcher, Buck Ewing, hurt his finger during a game. Gibson was in the stands and went down to the clubhouse and put on a Grays uniform. He would go on to become one of the legendary players on a team that won nine straight Negro League pennants. His first wife, Helen, died in childbirth while she delivered twins the same year he began playing for the Grays. His son, Josh, Jr., would join him as a teenager on the Grays at the end of his career. Gibson would also go on to play for the Pittsburgh Crawfords as Satchel Paige's catcher, one of a number of Grays lured away from Cum Posey by Crawfords owner Gus Greenlee. Gibson also played with such Negro League greats as Ted Page and Buck Leonard. Gibson and Leonard were known as the "Heavenly Twins" when they played together on the Homestead Grays because of their skills with the glove and bat. Hall of Fame catcher Roy Campanella, who would go on to play for the Brooklyn Dodgers with Jackie Robinson, played against Gibson when Campanella played for the Baltimore Elite Giants in the Negro Leagues and said that Gibson was "not only the greatest catcher but the greatest ballplayer I ever saw."

However, while his slugging prowess came naturally, Gibson had to work to become a great catcher. In interviews conducted by John Holway on file at the National Baseball Hall of Fame, former Negro League players talked about Gibson's skills and accomplishments. Ted Page said when Gibson first broke in, he "couldn't catch a sack of balls. On foul balls he was terrible. We used to call him 'boxer' because he'd catch like he was wearing a boxing glove." Third baseman Judy Johnson taught Gibson how to get under foul balls and handle bad pitches. "He would come to me and say, 'Jing [a Johnson nickname], what did I do wrong today?' and I'd say, 'Josh, you caught a real nice game.' That boy was game. I've seen the time Josh had his finger split and tied a piece of tape around it and played just as though nothing had happened." Buck Leonard said he honed his skills as a catcher in winter ball. "Down there in those winter leagues you can work out all morning on your weakness, whatever it is, hitting, running, pop flies, anything," Leonard said. "Josh would work by the hour perfecting his catching."

It was his bat, though, that made Gibson a star. Pitcher Willie "Sug" Cornelius said major league baseball fans missed out on a chance to see a great player. "The American people were denied the right to see a superstar perform, because in the world of stars, you'd have to put Josh in the superstar category," Cornelius said. "Had he been given the right to participate in the American or National League, I bet he'd have hit 75 home runs. I mean, with his strength and power." Gibson was the Mark McGwire of his time, a player who people came to watch take batting practice for his monstrous blasts. One remarkable story, told by Pittsburgh Crawford's teammate Harold Tinker in the book *Sandlot Seasons: Sport in Black Pittsburgh,* tells about the time Gibson was facing a white team outside of Pittsburgh. "That team got ahead of us some kind of way and they stayed there until about the sixth inning," Tinker noted. "They were two runs ahead and I was the first man up and I got on base. The next man up hit an infield single and moved me over to second. Josh was due up. He was the clean-up batter. Quite naturally, you know, you walk a man when you got an open base. They didn't have no open base, but they knew Josh. So the man threw two pitch-outs, Josh called time and he called over to me. I met him there on the infield grass and he said, 'Can I hit the ball?' I said, 'What do you mean, Josh? The man is giving you the intentional walk and we need two runs to tie.' Josh said, 'I don't know, the man is pitching out too close to the plate.' I said, 'Josh, you mean to tell me you could reach out and hit the ball where he's throwing it?' Josh smiled and said, 'I can hit it.' I said, 'Well, Josh, if you feel you can hit it, you go ahead and hit it.' I walked back to second base, and the next pitch-out that boy threw him was a pitch-out on the outside, way out, and Josh didn't hit that ball over the right field fence . . . he hit it over the center field fence. The people went crazy. I couldn't believe it."

Gibson was known for rolling up his left sleeve to display his muscles. His home run power produced a number of legendary tales: When Gibson played for the Homestead Grays, who played their home games at Edgar Thompson Field in Pittsburgh, a large greenhouse was behind the center field fence, more than 400 feet from home plate. The story goes that when the Grays played their home games, workers at the greenhouse had a pool to see how many glass panes in the roof Gibson would shatter with his home runs. Another story is that Gibson hit a home run so hard once that it shattered a wooden

bleacher seat when it landed. He once hit a ball that struck the rooftop facade at Yankee Stadium, about 580 feet from home plate, nearly going out of the park. New York Yankee outfielder Mickey Mantle was the only other player to ever hit the facade at the stadium. At old Forbes Field in Pittsburgh, where the Pirates played, Gibson is believed to be the first player ever to hit a home run over the center field fence over the 450-foot mark, blasting a shot in the 1930 Negro World Series in his rookie year. Again, the only other player to have done that was Mantle in the 1960 Pirates-Yankees World Series. In another Holway interview, Negro Leaguer Newt Allen talked about Gibson's slugging: "The ball parks were too small for him," Allen said. "He could hit to all fields, and hit just as hard to right field as he did to left field. If he hit to center field, it would be either up against the fence or in the bleachers. He could hit any kind of pitchers." In another Holway interview with Dave Barnhill, the pitcher marveled at Gibson's power: "Ain't no man in the world could hit a ball farther or harder than Josh Gibson," Barnhill said. "Every time we left a town, some young kid would way, 'Hey, see over there? Josh done hit one right there.' And that was about four blocks from the ballpark where he was pointing. One Sunday we were playing the Grays. There was a cemetery beyond the fence. I threw Josh a curve ball. When the ball broke, his hand slipped off the bat and he just followed through with his right hand and hit the ball in the cemetery."

Gibson played with Satchel Paige for five years on the Crawfords and combined to be the biggest draw in Negro League baseball, and the two of them often dictated the outcomes of games—and the success of the Crawfords. One game in particular was an exhibition game against a championship team from the U.S. Marines. According to newspaper accounts, the Crawfords led 12-0, and the Marines were at bat with two outs in the ninth inning. Gibson went out to the mound to talk to Paige, and they concluded that the Marines had to score at least one run. When Gibson got behind the plate, he told the Marine coming up to hit, "You're gonna be the hero." Paige delivered a slow, fat pitch to hit, but the Marine was so surprised he barely got his bat on the ball, hitting it just a few feet in front of home plate. Gibson grabbed it and threw the ball 30 feet over the first baseman's head. By the time the ball was retrieved, the Marine was rounding third on his way home. The throw in from the outfield hit Gibson's chest protector and bounced high into the air. When the dust cleared, Gibson told the Marine, "I had a feeling you were gonna be the hero."

Gibson and Paige were an impact duo even after Paige left the Crawfords and played for Kansas City. Then the draw of Gibson and Paige became the games when the two would face each other. Those battles became Negro League legend, with Paige sometimes striking out

There may have been no better player in the history of the Negro Leagues than Josh Gibson, a slugger who many observers believed was on par with the great Babe Ruth. A catcher, Gibson played for the Homestead Grays and the Pittsburgh Crawfords over the course of his career, which began in 1930 and ended in 1946 with his untimely death. The numbers that Gibson put up over that period are so astounding they have been the subject of much debate. Some statistics have Gibson batting .391 through 17 seasons, with varied estimates in career home runs, from 821 to as high as 962, with supposedly 75 in the 1931 season. Some reports claim Gibson actually never hit more than 22 home runs in a regular Negro League season, and 209 over his Negro League career. Inducted into the National Baseball Hall of Fame in 1972, the plaque in Gibson's honor credits him with nearly 800 home runs. (NATIONAL BASEBALL HALL OF FAME LIBRARY, COOPERSTOWN, N.Y.)

Gibson and Gibson sometimes tagging Paige, as he did in one game when he went 4 for 4 against Paige in Chicago. Joe Greene, Paige's catcher in Kansas City, said in an interview conducted by historian John Holway on file at the National Baseball Hall of Fame that he believed Paige got the best of Gibson more often than not. "Satchel could get him out, never had any trouble with him," Greene said. "We played Josh's team, the Washington-Homestead Grays, in the Negro World Series in 1942 and beat them in four straight games. Satchel just handcuffed Josh. When Willard Brown and I were down in

Puerto Rico in 1941, they had Josh on a radio interview, and they asked him how did he stack up with Satchel as a hitter. Josh said he hit Satchel about like he did the rest of the pitchers. Well, we didn't like it too much, so we told Satchel about it. That same year we were playing the Grays in the World Series, and when Josh came up in the first game, Satchel said, 'You talk about the way you hit me. I heard all about it. Come up here, you big so-and-so, and see how you can hit may fast one.' Naturally Josh was looking for a curveball, but Satchel blazed number one, the fast ball, down the middle for strike one. Josh

looked at it. Satchel waved his hand at Josh, and on the next pitch he threw him another fast ball. Josh made an attempt to hit it but he was too late. He just barely tipped it and I caught it for strike two. Satchel came walking about halfway in and said, 'Get ready to hit, you can't hit with the bat on your shoulder. I'm not going to waste anything on you, get ready to hit.' And on the next pitch he threw him another fast ball and Josh looked at it for strike three. All the time he was looking for the curveball, he was thinking that Satchel would throw a curve. He was crossed up by the way Satchel was talking to him. And the crowd just roared. Next time Josh came up, Satchel says, 'Get ready, I'm going to throw you one belt-high, so don't crowd the plate.' Then, 'I'm going to throw you one outside and low on the corner. You better swing.' I noticed Josh set his left foot closer to the plate, to hit that outside pitch, and I told him, 'You know you don't hit like that. Get your foot back.' But I know why he was doing it, and Satchel knew, too. Satchel would show him a curveball, but he never did let him hit it. And the people roared. They wanted to see those two tangle up." Ted "Double Duty" Radcliffe believed Gibson got the better of Paige from what he saw. "Josh hit three homers one day off Satchel in Wrigley Field," he said. "Then he tripled off the top of the right centerfield fence. Josh would hit anybody."

Gibson's legend spread not only among baseball fans in the United States but in Cuba and Mexico as well, where people would often talk about the long home runs they saw Gibson hit. He was named Most Valuable Player of the Puerto Rican League in 1941 and is one of only three American players to be inducted into the Mexican Baseball Hall of Fame. He also played on an all-star team recruited by Dominican dictator Rafael Trujillo in 1937.

The stories of Gibson's batting records, like many Negro League baseball records, have been disputed, perhaps more than any other player, because some of those numbers are among the best recorded in organized baseball. Some statistics have Gibson batting .391 through 17 seasons, with varied estimates in career home runs, from 821 to as high as 962, with supposedly 75 in the 1931 season. Those records are not recognized by some baseball historians, though, and some reports claim Gibson actually never hit more than 22 home runs in a regular Negro League season and 209 over his Negro League career. The leagues averaged between 40 to 50 official games during a season, with the rest considered semipro or exhibition baseball on the many barnstorming tours the Negro League players took part in. The National Baseball Hall of Fame credits Gibson with nearly

800 home runs on the plaque in his honor installed when he was inducted in 1972. The Negro Leagues Baseball Museum credits Gibson with a career batting average of .347.

In a 1974 interview with *Black Sports*, Negro League pitching great Bill Foster talked about pitching to Gibson: "When Gibson turned that cap bill up and got in that crouch at the plate, you had your problems," Foster said. In 1942, Gibson was invited by Washington Senators owner Clark Griffith to meet to talk about the possibility of playing in the major leagues, and the following year, Pittsburgh Pirates owner Bill Benswanger reportedly signed Gibson to a contract in 1943—four years before Jackie Robinson broke the color line with the Brooklyn Dodgers—but the deal was stopped by baseball Commissioner Kenesaw Mountain Landis. During his peak earning years in the early 1940s, Gibson was reportedly earning $1,000 a month, behind only Paige as the top money-maker in Negro League baseball.

Gibson died at the age of 35. His cause of death remains in dispute. Some reports had Gibson, who suffered from alcohol abuse, dying of a stroke, others of a brain tumor, and then there were stories that he died of a drug overdose. He was a troubled man, based on this 1945 report in *Beisbol Magazine*, based in Mexico City: "The magnificent colored ballplayer, Josh Gibson, has been confined in a hospital in Puerto Rico, in order to find out why he has not been in his right mind," the article stated. Also, there were reports about Gibson being hospitalized on numerous occasions at St. Elizabeth's, a mental institution in Washington. Many attribute his decline to a married woman he met in Washington named Grace Fournier, a reputed drug addict and alcoholic. However, in his autobiography, *I Was Right on Time*, Negro Leaguer Buck O'Neil said that being passed over for the first player to break the color barrier in major league baseball broke Gibson's heart. "By the time Jackie was signed, it was too late for Josh, and he never got over the fact that he didn't get the chance 10 years earlier, when he was the best hitter in the game." There has been little argument that Gibson was one of the greatest hitters of his time, on any level of baseball. He was inducted into the National Baseball Hall of Fame in 1972.

Gibson, Paul

Paul Gibson was a pitcher for the Homestead Grays and Newark Dodgers from 1934 to 1935.

Gibson, Ralph

Ralph Gibson was a second baseman and shortstop for the Louisville Black Colonels, Birmingham Black Barons, and Memphis Red Sox from 1951 to 1955.

Gibson, Ted

Ted Gibson was a catcher and infielder for the Chicago American Giants, Columbus Buckeyes, Birmingham Black Barons, and Cincinnati Buckeyes from 1940 to 1942.

Gibson, Welda

Welda Gibson was a pitcher for the Houston Eagles from 1949 to 1950.

Gilcrest, Dennis

Dennis Gilcrest was a second baseman and catcher for the Columbus Blue Birds, Indianapolis ABC's, Brooklyn Eagles, Cleveland Red Sox, and Homestead Grays from 1931 to 1935.

Giles, Cornelius

Cornelius Giles was a pitcher for the Indianapolis Clowns in 1954.

Giles, George
b. 1909, d. 1992

George Giles was a first baseman and manager for the St. Louis Stars, Philadelphia Stars, Detroit Stars, Kansas City Monarchs, Baltimore Elite Giants, Kansas City Royal Giants, New York Black Yankees, Pittsburgh Crawfords, Gilkerson Union Giants, Satchel Paige All-Stars, and Brooklyn Eagles from 1927 to 1938. Giles played from 1929 to 1931 for one of the best Negro baseball teams ever assembled, the St. Louis Stars, a team that defeated a major league All-Star team six games to two in an eight-games series in 1930. Giles was a lifetime .300 hitter in Negro League baseball.

Gilkerson, Robert P.

Robert Gilkerson was a first baseman, owner, and operator of a number of black baseball teams, including the Union Giants that traveled though Iowa, Illinois, and Wisconsin in 1919 and an interracial team known as the Spring Valley (Illinois) Giants in 1918 that would later be called the Gilkerson Union Giants.

Gill, William

William Gill was an outfielder, first baseman, and third baseman for the Louisville Red Caps, Detroit Stars, Indianapolis Athletics, and Homestead Grays from 1931 to 1937.

Gillard, Albert

Albert Gillard was a pitcher for the Chicago American Giants, St. Louis Giants, Birmingham Giants, and West Baden Sprudels from 1909 to 1914.

Gillard, Luther

Luther Gillard was a first baseman and outfielder for the Chicago American Giants, Memphis Red Sox, Birmingham Black Barons, Indianapolis Crawfords, Kansas City Monarchs, and St. Louis Stars from 1934 to 1942.

Gillespie, Henry

Henry Gillespie was a pitcher and outfielder for the Hilldale baseball club, Pennsylvania Giants, Bacharach Giants, Lincoln Giants, Quaker Giants, Philadelphia Tigers, Baltimore Black Sox, New York Black Yankees, Madison Stars, and Harrisburg Giants from 1917 to 1934.

Gillespie, Murray

Murray Gillespie was a left-handed pitcher for the Nashville Elite Giants, Memphis Red Sox, and Monroe Monarchs from 1930 to 1932.

Gilliam, James (Junior)

b. 1928, d. 1978

James Gilliam was a second baseman for the Nashville Black Vols and the Baltimore Elite Giants from 1945 to 1951, batting .253 for Baltimore in 71 games in 1946, .301 in 88 games in 1948, and .265 in 42 games in 1950. Born in Nashville, Tennessee, Gilliam went on to play for the Brooklyn and Los Angeles Dodgers for 14 major league seasons, batting .265 in 1,956 games, with 1,889 hits and 203 stolen bases. Gilliam also batted .211 with 15 runs scored and 12 RBI in 39 World Series games. In an interview with author John Holway on file at the National Baseball Hall of Fame, Negro Leaguer Othello Renfroe said that Pee Wee Butts—Gilliam's partner in their double-play combination in Baltimore—was responsible for the development of Gilliam as a major league second baseman. "Butts is responsible," Renfroe said. "Butts worked with him just like he was his own son and developed him into one of the top infielders in the Negro National League." Baltimore manager Lenny Pearson said that Gilliam and Butts "were out of sight as a double-play combination. Good hands, both of them, and both of them loved the game." His manager in Nashville, James Canady, talked about Gilliam's early days as a Negro League player in

Junior Gilliam was one of a number of Brooklyn Dodgers players who got their start in Negro League baseball. He played second base for the Nashville Black Vols and the Baltimore Elite Giants from 1945 to 1951 and then went on to play 14 seasons for the Dodgers. He joined up with Pee Wee Butts in Baltimore to make an outstanding double-play combination. (NATIONAL BASEBALL HALL OF FAME LIBRARY, COOPERSTOWN, N.Y.)

another Holway interview: "I had Junior Gilliam on my team in Nashville," Canady said. "Gilliam was about 17, a nice, quiet guy. Junior had been playing third, but he had a weak arm and we put him on second. I thought he could get rid of the ball better at second. He was a good team man, so I decided that we would shift him over. Pee Wee Butts was the guy who made him. Butts really could play shortstop, and after the team moved to Baltimore, that combination of Butts and Gilliam clicked."

Gillis, Louis

Louis Gillis was a catcher for the Birmingham Black Barons in 1951.

Gilmore, James

James Gilmore was a pitcher for the Kansas City Monarchs from 1953 to 1955.

Gilmore, Quincy

Quincy Gilmore was the business manager for the Kansas City Monarchs, secretary-treasurer for the NEGRO NATIONAL LEAGUE, and president of the Texas-Oklahoma-Louisiana League from 1922 to 1937.

Gilmore, Speed

Speed Gilmore was a pitcher for the Lincoln Giants from 1926 to 1928.

Gipson, Alvin

Alvin Gipson was a pitcher for the Birmingham Black Barons, Chicago American Giants, and Houston Eagles from 1941 to 1950.

Gisentaner, Willie

Willie Gisentaner was a left-handed pitcher and outfielder for the Washington Potomacs, Columbus Buckeyes, Harrisburg Giants, Kansas City Monarchs, Lincoln Giants, Newark Stars, Louisville White Sox, Cuban Stars, Nashville Elite Giants, Pittsburgh Crawfords, Homestead Grays, Louisville Red Caps, Louisville Black Caps, Philadelphia Giants, Brooklyn Royal Giants, and Chicago American Giants from 1921 to 1939.

Givens, Oscar

Oscar Givens was a shortstop for the Newark Eagles from 1946 to 1948.

Gladstone, Granville

b. 1925

Granville Gladstone was an outfielder for the Indianapolis Clowns in 1950, batting .240 in 64 games. Born in Panama, Gladstone went on to play minor league baseball for Portland in the Pacific Coast League and St. Paul in the American Association until 1957. The 5-foot-11, 170-pound Gladstone also played in the Mexican League and in Panama.

Glass, Carl Lee

Carl Glass was a left-handed pitcher and manager for the Cincinnati Tigers, Memphis Red Sox, Birmingham Black Barons, St. Louis Stars, Kansas City Monarchs, Chicago American Giants, Louisville White Sox, St. Louis Giants, and Kansas City Monarchs from 1921 to 1936.

Glenn, Hubert

Hubert Glenn was a pitcher for the Indianapolis Clowns, Philadelphia Stars, New York Black Yankees, and Brooklyn Brown Dodgers from 1943 to 1949.

Glenn, Oscar

Oscar Glenn was a third baseman for the Atlanta Black Crackers from 1937 to 1938.

Glenn, Stanley

b. 1926

Stanley Glenn was a catcher for the Philadelphia Stars from 1944 to 1950. In an interview, Glenn, born in Wachapreague, Virginia, said that the Stars scouted him and signed him while he was playing high school baseball at John Bartram High School in Philadelphia: "In 1944, my senior year, I was having a pretty good year," Glenn said. "The Stars were watching me, but I didn't know it. They asked me to come to their ballpark, at 44th and Parkside, and they signed me to a contract right there in June 1944. I played with teammates like Gene Benson, Frank

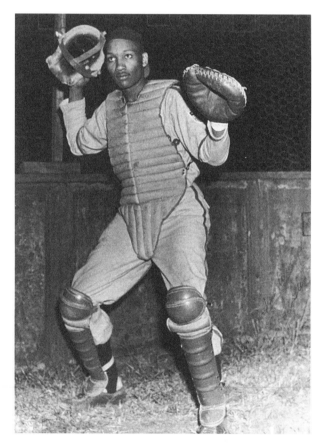

Stanley Glenn was the anchor behind the plate for the Philadelphia Stars from 1944 to 1950, known for his ability to handle pitchers and his knowledge of Negro League hitters. The 6-foot-3, 200-pound Glenn was signed by the Boston Braves in 1950 and played for Hartford for several years. He also went on to play minor league baseball in Canada and retired after the 1955 season. (NATIONAL BASEBALL HALL OF FAME LIBRARY, COOPERSTOWN, N.Y.)

Austin and Harry Simpson. I caught Wilmer Harris, who I've known since high school in Philadelphia. I was known for handling pitchers well. I got my real joy out of getting pitchers through games with the least amount of damage possible. I learned the hitters very well. I also hit with power. I batted around .265 in may career, but my strength was the long ball. I figure I hit about 191 home runs over my Negro League and minor league career. We played sometimes two or three games a day, and you could lose 15 pounds in one day behind the plate. Traveling was hard, too, because there were very few hotels to stay in and eating was tough because we weren't allowed to go into certain restaurants. Down south it was even difficult to buy gasoline. But it was a good time. It was a way of life, a good life. We loved it so much we would have probably played for nothing, and almost did play for nothing." The 6-foot-3, 200-pound Glenn was signed by the Boston Braves in 1950 and played for Hartford for several years. He also went on to play minor league baseball in Canada and retired after the 1955 season. Glenn also played winter baseball in Venezuela and Puerto Rico.

Glover, Thomas Moss
Thomas Glover was a left-handed pitcher for the Cleveland Red Sox, Birmingham Black Barons, Washington Elite Giants, New Orleans Black Pelicans, Baltimore Elite Giants, Columbus Elite Giants, and Memphis Red Sox from 1934 to 1945.

Godinez, Manuel
Manuel Godinez was a pitcher for the Cincinnati-Indianapolis Clowns and Indianapolis Clowns from 1946 to 1949.

Goines, Charles
Charles Goines was a catcher and outfielder for the Indianapolis ABC's and Bowser's ABC's from 1915 to 1916.

Golden, Clyde
Clyde Golden was a pitcher for the Houston Eagles, Newark Eagles, New Orleans Eagles, Chicago American Giants, and Cleveland Buckeyes from 1948 to 1952.

Goliath, Fred
Fred Goliath was an outfielder for the Chicago Giants in 1920.

Gomez, David
David Gomez was a pitcher for the Cuban Stars from 1925 to 1928 and in 1932.

Gomez, Domingo
Domingo Gomez played catcher for the Philadelphia Tigers, Harrisburg Giants, and Baltimore Black Sox from 1926 to 1929.

Gomez, Joseph
Joseph Gomez was a catcher and pitcher for the Cuban Stars and Bacharach Giants from 1929 to 1933.

Gonzalez, Gervasio
Gervasio Gonzalez was a catcher for the Long Branch Cubans and Cuban Stars from 1910 to 1917.

Gonzalez, Hiram Rene
b. 1923
Hiram Gonzalez was an outfielder for the New York Cubans in 1950. The 6-foot-2, 205-pound Gonzalez, born in Cuba, batted .302 with 21 RBIs in 32 games.

Gonzalez, Luis
Luis Gonzalez was a pitcher for the Cuban Stars in 1910.

Gonzalez, Miguel Angel (Cordero) (Mike)
b. 1890, d. 1977
Miguel Angel Gonzalez, born in Cuba, was a first baseman and catcher for the Cuban Stars from 1911 to 1914 and went on to be one of the few Cubans who would be able to play major league baseball because of his light skin color. Under the name Mike Gonzalez, he played 17 years, spanning the period from 1912 to 1932 for five major league clubs—the Boston Braves, Cincinnati Reds, New York Giants, Chicago Cubs, and three stints with the St. Louis Cardinals—batting .253 with 717 hits in 1,042 games. He also appeared in two games in the 1929 World Series. He coached in the major leagues and also managed the Cardinals in interim periods in 1938 and 1940, with a career record of 9-13.

Good, Cleveland
Cleveland Good was a pitcher for the Newark Eagles in 1937.

Gooden, Ernest (Pud)
Ernest Gooden was a second baseman and third baseman for the Toledo Tigers, Pittsburgh Keystones, Chicago American Giants, Detroit Stars, and Cleveland Tate Stars from 1922 to 1933.

Goodgame, John

John Goodgame was a pitcher for the Chicago Giants in 1917.

Goodrich, Joseph

Joseph Goodrich was a shortstop, second baseman, and third baseman for the Wilmington Potomacs, Washington Potomacs, Philadelphia Giants, and Harrisburg Giants from 1923 to 1926.

Goodson, M. E.

M. E. Goodson was an officer for the New York Black Yankees from 1931 to 1932.

Gordon, Charlie

Charlie Gordon was an outfielder for the Philadelphia Stars and New York Black Yankees from 1939 to 1941.

Gordon, Harold (Beebop)

Harold Gordon was a pitcher for the Detroit Stars and Chicago American Giants from 1950 to 1954.

Gordon, Herman

Herman Gordon was an outfielder, pitcher, and second baseman for the Birmingham Black Barons, Toledo Tigers, St. Louis Stars, Cleveland Browns, and Kansas City Monarchs from 1920 to 1924.

Gordon, Sam

Sam Gordon was an infielder and outfielder for the Chicago Union Giants, Genuine Cuban Giants, Cuban Giants, New York Stars, Indianapolis ABC's, Lincoln Giants and Brooklyn All-Stars from 1905 to 1915. Gordon had a reputation as one of the "comedians" of the diamond.

Gorhams of New York

The Gorhams were a black baseball team in New York in the 1880s and were one of the teams to join the League of Colored Baseball Clubs in 1887. Two years later, they were part of the Middle States League.

Goshay, Sam

Sam Goshay was an outfielder for the Kansas City Monarchs in 1949.

Gottlieb, Eddie

Eddie Gottlieb was a white sports promoter who got his start with a semipro basketball team in Philadelphia, the South Philadelphia Hebrew All-Stars, and also owned a baseball field. He wound up a partner with Negro League operator Nat Strong to lease the field to black baseball teams, and their efforts would hurt rival Negro League owner Cumberland (Cum) Posey, who started the East-West League and needed a place to play in the Philadelphia market. Gottlieb went on to create a baseball team similar to the South Philadelphia Hebrew All-Stars and then took over the operation of the Philadelphia Stars in 1933, though he allowed former Hilldale baseball club owner Ed Bolden to purchase a minority portion and serve as the black majority owner in the public eye. He was an officer in the second version of the NEGRO NATIONAL LEAGUE. Gottlieb was also a booking agent and got into a dispute with Newark Eagles owners Abe and Effa Manley over the promotional fees Gottlieb received for securing places to play. He also owned a basketball team called the Philadelphia Warriors and refused to let blacks play on the team, which drew the wrath of *Pittsburgh Courier* sportswriter Wendell Smith: "He refuses to give them a chance to play on his team," Smith wrote. "He contends he can't find a Negro good enough. He hasn't tried to find one, of course, and we all know that. 'Brother Eddie' has been disrobed as a liberal. Today he's a prejudiced, biased man. He's a traitor of sorts in the world of sports. He will have nothing to do with Negro basketball players in the winter months. When baseball season starts, however, 'Brother Eddie' will be back with us. He'll be operating his Philadelphia Stars and raking in the dough of Negro baseball fans." Booking agents like Gottlieb and Abe Saperstein, who sought 40 percent of the gate receipts, controlled much of Negro League baseball with their stranglehold on game locations and schedules.

Gould, John

John Gould was a pitcher for the Philadelphia Stars from 1947 to 1948.

Govantes, Manuel

Manuel Govantes was a second baseman and outfielder for the Stars of Cuba and Cuban Stars from 1909 to 1910.

Govern, S. K.

S. K. Govern was the manager of the Philadelphia Pythians in 1887 and 1888 and the Cuban Giants in 1896. In a *Pittsburgh Courier* article in 1927, Negro League player and historian Sol White named Govern as one of the greatest figures in the history of Negro League baseball.

Grace, Ellsworth

Ellsworth Grace was a second baseman for the New York Black Yankees in 1950.

Grace, Willie

b. 1919

Willie Grace played the outfield for the Cincinnati–Cleveland Buckeyes, Cleveland Buckeyes, Louisville Buckeyes, and Houston Eagles from 1942 to 1950. Records show that Grace's best season was 1948, when he batted .322 for Cleveland. The 6-foot, 170-pound Grace, born in Memphis, Tennessee, also batted .305 in 1944 and .301 the following season. Grace played minor league baseball in Erie, Pennsylvania, in 1951, batting .299.

Graham, Dennis

Dennis Graham was an outfielder for the Bacharach Giants, Washington Red Caps, St. Louis Stars, Pittsburgh Crawfords, and Homestead Grays from 1918 to 1931.

Graham, Vasco

Vasco Graham was an outfielder and catcher for the Page Fence Giants, Colored Capital All-Americans, Cuban Giants, and teams in Adrian and Lansing, Michigan, from 1895 to 1899.

Gransberry, William

William Gransberry was a first baseman and outfielder for the Chicago Giants and Chicago American Giants.

Grant, Art

Art Grant was a catcher for the Richmond Giants and Baltimore Black Sox from 1920 to 1922.

Grant, Charles

d. 1932

Charles Grant was a second baseman for the Page Fence Giants, Cuban X Giants, Columbia Giants, New York Black Sox, Philadelphia Giants, Quaker Giants, Lincoln Giants, and Cincinnati Stars from 1896 to 1916. According to Mark Ribowsky's book *A Complete History of the Negro Leagues*, Grant nearly became the first black major leaguer to follow Fleet Walker. Grant, born in Cincinnati, had light skin and in 1901 was working as a porter in Hot Springs, Arkansas, where the Baltimore Orioles were training. Orioles manager John McGraw got a look at Grant's talent and came up with a plan to sneak him into the major leagues. He would be identified as a native American, a full-blooded Cherokee named "Chief Tokohoma." Grant played in spring training games, but Cap Anson, retired but still part of the Chicago White Sox organization, strongly objected to Grant's presence. McGraw abandoned his plan.

In *The American League Story*, author Lee Allen described in detail how McGraw purportedly tried to get Grant on the Orioles squad: "In March 1901 Grant was one of a group of Cincinnati Negroes working as bellboys at the Eastland Hotel in Hot Springs, Arkansas," Allen wrote. "To fill their idle time they formed a baseball team, and McGraw, watching them play, recognized immediately that Grant had enough class to perform in the major leagues. But there was an unwritten law that barred Negroes from the professional game, and McGraw wondered how on earth he could circumvent it. Then one day, while examining a large wall map just off the lobby at the Eastland, he was seized with an inspiration. Calling Grant over, he said, 'Charlie, I've been trying to think of some way to sign you for the Baltimore club, and I think I've got it. On this map there's a creek called Tokohoma. That's going to be your name from now on, Charlie Tokohoma, and you're a full-blooded Cherokee.'" But word got out who Grant really was, and McGraw abandoned the plan when Anson and the White Sox protested. Grant died in 1932 after being struck by a car after a tire blew out.

Grant, Leroy

Leroy Grant was a first baseman for the Lincoln Giants, Chicago American Giants, Cleveland Browns, Indianapolis ABC's, and Mohawk Giants from 1911 to 1925.

Grant, Ulysses F. (Frank)

b. 1868, d. 1937

Ulysses Grant was one of the black pioneers of organized integrated baseball; he played with Meriden in the Eastern League from 1883 to 1886 and then with the Buffalo Bisons in the International League from 1886 to 1889. Born in Pittsfield, Massachusetts, Grant was called the "Black Dunlap," after St. Louis Browns second base star Fred Dunlap. He was a star second baseman and shortstop who was among the league leaders during his International League tenure in average (batting .340 in 1886), home runs, stolen bases, and total bases and had an average of .337 in six total minor league seasons. The 5-foot-8, 160-pound Grant, who began his career as a pitcher for the Graylocks of Pittsfield in 1865, later fell victim to the ban of black players in the International League in the late 1880s and would go on to play for the Cuban X Giants, Philadelphia Giants, Trenton Cuban Giants, Ansonia Cuban Giants, Colored Capital All-Americans (Lansing, Michigan), New York Gorhams, and Philadelphia Giants. While he played organized white ball, Grant, like the handful of other black players who did the same, was a target of white opponents and, like Bud Fowler, was forced to wear splints on his lower legs to protect them from vicious slides. "The runners chased him off second base," according to an anonymous International

League player in an 1888 *Sporting Life* article. "They went down so often trying to break his legs that he gave up his infield position and played right field." According to Robert Peterson's book *Only the Ball Was White*, Grant's white teammates on the Buffalo club refused to sit with him for the team photograph. However, his teammates in Harrisburg were willing to stand up for Grant, according to a newspaper account of a stay in Wilmington, Delaware: "The Harrisburg Base Ball Club's negro player was barred out of the Clayton House on account of his color this morning," the article stated. "The same team was here a few days ago and all the members, including Grant, the negro player, were quartered at the Clayton. Grant took his meals in the dining room with the rest of the guests, and was assigned a sleeping apartment on the guest's hall. The boarders protested against being obliged to eat in the same dining room with a colored man, and threatened to leave the house unless the dusky-hued ball player was turned out. Mr. Pyle [the owner], however, allowed him to stay with his fellow players while they remained here. This morning the club returned and with them Grant. They applied at the hotel for board and Proprietor Pyle informed them he would accommodate all but the colored man. The white players determined to stick by their sable-hued companion and all marched out of the hotel in high dudgeon over the refusal to accommodate Grant."

Most of his teammates respected his ability as a player. Historian Sol White, a teammate of Grant's, wrote in *History of Colored Base Ball* that Grant was one of several black ballplayers who "possessed major league qualifications. Grant and [Bud] Fowler had no equal in the International League. . . . Frank Grant was a baseball marvel. His playing was a revelation to his fellow teammates, as well as the spectators. In hitting, he ranked with the best and his fielding bordered on impossible. Grant was a born ballplayer. He started as a catcher when very young and it is said during a game in Plattsburg, N.Y., while catching, he ran to a telegraph pole and climbing up about eight feet caught a foul ball. Otherwise it would have gone out of his reach over an embankment. Grant was always quiet and unassuming on the ball field, never protesting a decision of an umpire, nor resenting the action of an opposing player. He was the greatest card in the profession."

Graves, Lawrence

Lawrence Graves was a pitcher for the Harrisburg Giants in 1923.

Graves, Robert

Robert Graves was an outfielder and pitcher for the Indianapolis Athletics and Indianapolis ABC's from 1932 to 1937.

Graves, Wesley

Wesley Graves was the owner of the Little Rock Black Travelers baseball team in the 1940s.

Graves, Whitt

Whitt Graves was a pitcher for the Indianapolis Clowns from 1950 to 1951.

Gray, Chester

Chester Gray was a catcher for the New York Black Yankees, St. Louis Stars, Kansas City Monarchs, Harrisburg–St. Louis Stars, Boston Blues, and Toledo Cubs from 1940 to 1946.

Gray, Howard

Howard Gray was an infielder for the New Orleans Eagles in 1951.

Gray, Roosevelt

Roosevelt Gray was a pitcher and first baseman for the Toledo Tigers, Cleveland Tate Stars, Kansas City Monarchs, and Dayton Marcos from 1920 to 1923.

Gray, William

William Gray was an outfielder for the Baltimore Atlantics and Baltimore Lord Baltimores from 1884 to 1887.

Gray, Willie

Willie Gray was a pitcher and outfielder for the Homestead Grays, Cleveland Tate Stars, Pennsylvania Red Caps of New York, Lincoln Giants, Pittsburgh Keystones, Dayton Marcos, Columbus Buckeyes, and Newark Browns from 1920 to 1933.

Greason, William

William Greason was a pitcher for the Birmingham Black Barons from 1948 to 1951.

Green, Alphonse

Alphonse Green was an outfielder for the New York Cubans in 1942.

Green, Alvin

Alvin Green was an infielder for the Baltimore Elite Giants in 1950.

Green, Charles

Charles Green was an outfielder, manager, and owner for the Leland Giants, Chicago Giants, Chicago American Giants, Columbia Giants, Union Giants, and Philadelphia Giants from 1902 to 1931.

Green, Curtis

Curtis Green was an outfielder and first baseman for the Brooklyn Cuban Giants and Birmingham Black Barons from 1923 to 1928.

Green, Dave

Dave Green was an outfielder for the Baltimore Elite Giants in 1950.

Green, Henryene P.

Henryene Green was the owner of the Baltimore Elite Giants from 1949 to 1950.

Green, Herman

Herman Green was an outfielder for the Detroit Stars in 1954 and 1955.

Green, Honey

Honey Green was a pitcher for the Memphis Red Sox, Cleveland Bears, and Boston Royal Giants from 1939 to 1942.

Green, James

James Green was a third baseman for the New York Black Yankees in 1950.

Green, Joseph

Joseph Green was a second baseman for the Chicago Leland Giants in the early 1900s. According to Mark Ribowsky's book *A Complete History of the Negro Leagues*, Green became a black baseball legend when, in a 1909 exhibition game against the Chicago Cubs, Green suffered a broken leg stealing third base: When the ball got away from the third baseman, Green got up and hopped toward home in a failed effort to score. He also managed the Leland Giants.

Green, Julius

Julius Green was an outfielder for the Detroit Stars and Memphis Red Sox from 1929 to 1930.

Green, Leslie (Chin)

Leslie Green was an outfielder for the New York Black Yankees, Memphis Red Sox, and St. Louis Stars from 1939 to 1946.

Green, Peter

Peter Green was a pitcher and outfielder for the Brooklyn Royal Giants, Pittsburgh Giants, Philadelphia Giants, and Brooklyn Colored Giants from 1908 to 1920.

Green, Vernon

Vernon Green was the owner of the Baltimore Elite Giants in the 1940s.

Green, William

William Green was an outfielder and third baseman for the Chicago Union Giants and Chicago Giants from 1911 to 1923.

Green, Willie

Willie Green was a pitcher and catcher for the St. Louis Giants and Pittsburgh Giants from 1910 to 1912.

Greene, James Elbert (Joe)

James Greene was a catcher for the Kansas City Monarchs, Cleveland Buckeyes, Atlanta Black Crackers, and Homestead Grays from 1932 to 1948. In an interview with historian John Holway on file at the National Baseball Hall of Fame, Greene talked about his days with Kansas City and how a tight-knit unit led to the Monarchs' success: "We had a good bunch of fellow on the Monarchs," Greene said. "We had a good team. Frank Duncan was a good manager. He was temperamental, but we all liked him. We all got along so well. We didn't allow anything to get between us and our baseball and winning. We liked to win. They say he had a 'syndicate' there. We admitted it, too. We wanted certain guys on the ball club, and if one man wasn't the right kind of guy, five or six of us on the ball team had ways and means of getting him off the team. And he knew it. The team wasn't going to join him, he's going to join the team. He's got to weave himself into the team. We had good youngsters, but they had to have good discipline and everything else. Some guys would get a little money in his pocket, go out and stay all night. He can't play ball the next day. We would tell him things that were coming and how he should carry himself." Greene also talked about the most challenging pitchers he faced in his career: "The toughest pitcher for me to hit was Gentry Jessup of Chicago," he said. "He had a good sinker and good curveball. What made him so good was good control. . . . He was tough for me. I just never could hit him successfully. Another guy playing on Memphis, a submarine pitcher, Porter Ross, pretty well baffled me for a couple of years. . . . I built myself up as a curveball hitter. If a pitcher's got a good curve, he wants to rely on it as his best pitch because most hitters can't hit the curveball. The reason I could hit the white pitchers was because they pitched low, and I could hit low pitches. Sometimes they'd say, 'Joe Greene, you were on your knees when you hit that.' Sometimes I would go almost down on my right knee. But I'd hit it in the stands. When they tried to pitch high, I used a 36" bat. I had three weights in that bat. I stood back off the plate, and I always swung fast."

Greene began his career as a first baseman with the Black Crackers at the age of 21 in 1933 but soon switched to behind the plate. "They [Atlanta] had fellows like Donald Reed, Red Moore, Pee Wee Butts, Babe Davis, Red Hatley, James Kemp, Ping Burt and Oscar Glenn," Greene said. "We were in the Negro Southern League, and I was playing first base. One night we were playing in Anniston, Alabama, and a guy by the name of Tish, who had played in the colored leagues about 13 or 14 years, told me, 'You play all right over there at first base. You're going to make a good ball player. You're big, got good weight on you, but you throw like a catcher. Can you catch?' I said, 'I'm not scared to get back there, but I don't know how to catch. If you teach me how to catch, I'll catch.' It didn't make any difference to me where I played as long as I played. I figured right quick if he was managing the ball club and if he was an ex-catcher, I'd have a better chance than anybody on the team of getting all the information that I wanted. . . . The manager at the time was Jones, and he was an ex-catcher. For a while Nish Williams, another catcher, managed the team. He was Donn Clendennon's stepfather. Donn was a tiny little baby then, and he raised him."

Greene, John

John Greene was an infielder for the Chicago American Giants in 1951.

Greene, Walter

Walter Greene was an outfielder and first baseman for the Bacharach Giants and Brooklyn Cuban Giants in 1928.

Greene, Will

Will Greene was a pitcher for the Pittsburgh Giants in 1912.

Greenidge, Victor

Victor Greenidge was a pitcher for the New York Cubans from 1941 to 1945.

Greenlee, Charles

Charles Greenlee was the younger brother of Gus Greenlee, who purchased the majority interest of the Pittsburgh Crawfords from his older brother in 1939 and then turned around and sold the club to a group of white businessmen in Toledo, Ohio.

Greenlee, William A. (Gus)
b. 1897, d. 1948

William Greenlee was a Pittsburgh nightclub owner and numbers racketeer who owned one of the greatest teams in Negro League baseball history, the Pittsburgh Crawfords. Born in Marion, North Carolina, Greenlee came to Pittsburgh in 1916 and worked as a cabdriver, undertaker, and fireman. He served in World War I, and when he returned to Pittsburgh, Greenlee, nicknamed "Big Red," drove a taxi and began building an illegal liquor empire by bootlegging and later opening a speakeasy. Greenlee took over a local amateur team called the Pittsburgh Crawfords in 1930 and made an immediate impact on black baseball. Greenlee raided much of the hometown rival Homestead Grays, bringing in such stars as Josh Gibson, William "Judy" Johnson, and Jud Wilson, joining other Negro baseball stars such as Satchel Paige, Jimmy Crutchfield, and James "Cool Papa" Bell, putting together perhaps the most talented team in Negro baseball history, with the legendary Oscar Charleston as manager.

A flamboyant underworld figure and big man, at 6 foot 2 and about 230 pounds, Greenlee, whose friends included another numbers racketeer in Pittsburgh named Art Rooney and a number of local politicians, also managed a number of fighters, including world light heavyweight title champion John Henry Lewis, which made Greenlee the first black man to manage a black champion. One of Greenlee's nightclubs, the Crawford Grille, featured such stars as Duke Ellington, Count Basie, and Lena Horne, among others. Greenlee was fondly recalled as a stylish, memorable figure by Negro Leaguer Dick Seay in *Blackball Stars* by John Holway: "He looked like the racketeer that he was," Seay said. "Dressed neat, big expensive hats, always a big crowd around him. I imagine he was something like Diamond Jim Brady, you know, always had a crowd."

After playing an independent schedule for two seasons, Greenlee's team joined the East-West League in 1932. After first playing games at Ammon Field, the owner also built a ballpark, called Greenlee Field, at an estimated cost of $100,000. The following year, Greenlee formed and presided over the NEGRO NATIONAL LEAGUE. He also organized the first Negro All-Star Game that same year, the same season major league baseball, under the direction of Chicago sportswriter Arch Ward, started its All-Star Game. Both games were played at Comiskey Park in Chicago. In his autobiography, *I Was Right on Time*, Negro Leaguer Buck O'Neil said that playing in an EAST-WEST GAME "was something very special. That was the greatest idea Gus ever had, because it made black people feel involved in baseball like they'd never been before. While the big leagues left the choice of players up to the sportswriters, Gus left it up to the fans. After reading about great players in the [Chicago] *Defender* and the [Pittsburgh] *Courier* for so many years, they could cut out that ballot in the black papers and have a say. That was a pretty important thing for black people to do in those days, to be able to vote, even if it was just for ballplayers, and they sent in thousands of ballots. It was like an avalanche. Right away it was clear that our game meant a lot more than the big league game. Theirs was, and is, more or less an exhibition. But for black folks, the East-West Game was a matter of racial pride."

Greenlee's raid of the Homestead team made him the enemy of Grays' owner Cum Posey, and Posey brought in a partner in 1935 to compete against Greenlee and his Crawfords—a rival numbers operator in Pittsburgh, Rufus "Sonnyman" Jackson, and the Grays joined Greenlee's NNL that year. In 1937, Crawford's team took a huge hit when Dominican Republic dictator Rafael Trujillo persuaded Paige, Gibson, and a host of other players to come to the Dominican Republic to play for his Santo Domingo team. Greenlee never recovered from the moves. The players came back to the United States that same year but not to the Crawfords. In fact, Gibson came back to play for Homestead and led the Grays to the NNL pennant that season, also posting an overall mark against all competition of 152-11.

Greenlee sold the team in 1939. The Crawfords moved to Toledo in 1939 and Indianapolis the following year. Another Pittsburgh Crawfords team was formed by Greenlee in the mid-1940s but did not last long. He also was partners with Branch Rickey in the short-lived UNITED STATES LEAGUE in 1945 and 1946. Greenlee became the target of government prosecution for income tax problems, and his Crawford Grille was destroyed by fire in 1951. He died the following year.

Greenlee Field

Greenlee Field was the ballpark built by Pittsburgh Crawfords owner Gus Greenlee in 1932 on Bedford Avenue in the Hill neighborhood of Pittsburgh at an estimated cost of $100,000. In addition to serving as the home field for the Crawfords, the field also hosted a number of other sporting events, including college football games and boxing shows. However, the ballpark was demolished in 1939 by the city's Housing Authority for a housing project.

Greensboro Red Wings

The Greensboro Red Wings were a black baseball team in Greensboro, North Carolina, that played in the late 1940s.

Greer, J. B.

J. B. Greer was an officer for the Jacksonville Red Caps, Knoxville Red Caps, and Cleveland Bears from 1939 to 1942.

Greyer, George

George Greyer was a first baseman for the Baltimore Black Sox from 1916 to 1922.

Grier, Claude (Red)

Claude Grier was a pitcher for the Atlantic City Bacharach Giants, Wilmington Potomacs, and Washington Potomacs from 1924 to 1928. He pitched a no-hitter for the Bacharach Giants in the 1926 Negro League World Series against the Chicago American Giants, the first one in the history of the series. It was the same year that Grier had a won-loss record of 11-6. He posted a 7-4 record in his rookie season, followed by a 7-9 mark in 1925. He was finished shortly after that, putting together a 1-2 mark in 1927 before he left the game after he developed an illness. In an interview with the *Atlantic City Press*, Judy Johnson recalled Grier as "a good-sized boy, with a very good fastball. But he was wild, as most young pitchers are. He was wild as the devil. Didn't know where the ball was going." Macajah Eggelston told the *Press* that Grier was the best left-hander he ever saw. "Lefty Grove was one of the best pitchers I ever hit against," Eggelston said. "But Grier was the best left-hand pitcher I ever saw. If Grier had been in the same league with Grove, you'd have to rate him just as high as Grove."

Griffin, James

James Griffin was a second baseman for the Nashville Elite Giants, Cuban Giants, Philadelphia Giants, Pittsburgh Giants, and Cuban X Giants from 1911 to 1921.

Griffin, Robert

Robert Griffin was a pitcher for the St. Louis Stars and Chicago Columbia Giants from 1931 to 1937.

Griffith, Clark

Clark Griffith, the owner of the Washington Senators, leased his ballpark, Griffith Stadium, to the Homestead

Grays for home games. Griffith was considered a supporter of Negro League baseball, and at one point, in 1942, there were reports that Griffith called Josh Gibson and Buck Leonard in for a meeting to talk about possibly signing black players, but nothing ever came of it.

Griffith, Robert Lee (Schoolboy)

Robert Griffith was a pitcher for the Columbus Elite Giants, Nashville Elite Giants, Baltimore Elite Giants, Washington Elite Giants, Philadelphia Stars, New York Black Yankees, and Indianapolis Clowns from 1934 to 1952.

Griffith Stadium

Griffith Stadium, the Washington, D.C., home of the Washington Senators in major league baseball, also served as the home field for the Homestead Grays when the Grays were splitting their home dates between Pittsburgh and Washington. In 1942, the Grays drew an estimated 102,000 fans for 10 games at Griffith Stadium. It also hosted several Negro League EAST-WEST ALL-STAR games. In his autobiography, Grays pitcher Wilmer Fields wrote about the popularity of the Grays at Griffith Stadium: "The Washington Senators would draw 7,500 fans to Griffith Stadium for their game, and then the Grays would come into town and bring in up to 20,000," Fields said. "Most of the fans were black, although we had white fans in attendance. I think the black fans came to the stadium to put all their worries behind them. They were such good fans that they would even applaud a good play in practice. Griffith Stadium was one of my favorite places to play."

Griggs, Acie

Acie Griggs was an outfielder for the Birmingham Black Barons in 1951.

Griggs, Wally

Wally Griggs was an infielder for the Detroit Stars in 1954.

Griggs, Willie

Willie Griggs was an infielder for the Houston Eagles, Birmingham Black Barons, New Orleans Eagles, Cleveland Buckeyes, and Louisville Black Colonels from 1948 to 1955.

Gross, Ben

Ben Gross was an outfielder for the Pittsburgh Keystones in 1887.

Guerra, Juan

Juan Guerra was a catcher, first baseman, and outfielder for the Cuban Stars, New York Cuban Stars, Stars of Cuba, and Cincinnati Cubans from 1910 to 1924.

Guerra, Marcelino

Marcelino Guerra was a first baseman for the Cuban Stars in 1916.

Guice, Lacey

Lacey Guice was an outfielder for the Chicago American Giants and New Orleans Eagles from 1951 to 1952.

Guilbe, Felix

Felix Guilbe was an outfielder for the Baltimore Elite Giants in 1946 and 1947.

Guilbe, Juan

Juan Guilbe was a pitcher and outfielder for the Baltimore Elite Giants, Indianapolis Clowns, and New York Cubans from 1940 to 1947.

Guinn, Napoleon

Napoleon Guinn was a catcher for the Cleveland Buckeyes from 1943 to 1945.

Gulley, Napoleon

b. 1924, d. 1999

Napoleon Gulley was a pitcher and outfielder for the Kansas City Monarchs, Birmingham Black Barons, Chicago American Giants, Cleveland Buckeyes, and Newark Eagles from 1943 to 1947. He went on to play minor league baseball. The 6-foot, 170-pound Gulley, born in Huttig, Arizona, also played with the baseball version of the Harlem Globetrotters, a black barnstorming team formed by Abe Saperstein, owner of the better-known basketball team, and in fact left the Buckeyes before the end of the 1945 season—in which the Buckeyes won a championship—to play for the Globetrotters, who were managed by Ted "Double Duty" Radcliffe. In a 1999 interview with *Sports Collectors Digest*, Gulley said that he enjoyed his time with the Globetrotters most of all. "That was the happiest time of my life," he said. "I had a chance to tour the West—Montana and Idaho, and see Yellowstone. I had been worn out with the cities. We toured the country all the way into Canada out to Vancouver and then back to California and then back across the states again. I didn't know the Buckeyes had won the championship until the spring. I was so happy and had so much fun and made more money and I wasn't even interested in what Cleveland was doing."

Gurley, James

James Gurley was an outfielder, first baseman, and pitcher for the Memphis Red Sox, St. Louis Stars, Montgomery Red Sox, Chicago American Giants, Birmingham Black Barons, Nashville Elite Giants, Cleveland Hornets, Indianapolis ABC's, and Harrisburg Giants from 1922 to 1932.

Guthrie, Wallace

b. 1922, d. 1999

Wallace Guthrie was a pitcher for the Birmingham Black Barons and Kansas City Monarchs in 1953.

Gutierrez, Luis

Luis Gutierrez was an outfielder for the Cuban Stars in 1926.

Guy, Wesley

Wesley Guy was a pitcher for the Chicago Giants from 1927 to 1929.

Guyton, Miller

Miller Guyton was a third baseman for the Philadelphia Stars and Kansas City Monarchs in 1951.

Hackley, Albert

Albert Hackley was an infielder and outfielder for the Chicago Unions from 1887 to 1896.

Hadley, Red

Red Hadley was a catcher and outfielder for the Atlanta Black Crackers in 1937 and 1938.

Haggins, Billy Ray

Billy Ray Haggins was an outfielder for the Memphis Red Sox from 1953 to 1955.

Hairston, Harold

Harold Hairston was a pitcher for the Birmingham Black Barons and Homestead Grays from 1946 to 1947 and again in 1953.

Hairston, Napoleon

Napoleon Hairston was an outfielder for the Indianapolis Crawfords, Pittsburgh Crawfords, and Toledo Crawfords from 1938 to 1940.

Hairston, Richard

Richard Hairston was a pitcher and outfielder for the Indianapolis Clowns from 1953 to 1954.

Hairston, Samuel

b. 1920, d. 1997

Samuel Hairston was a third baseman and catcher for the Birmingham Black Barons, Cincinnati-Indianapolis Clowns, and Indianapolis Clowns from 1945 to 1950. Some press reports say that Hairston, born in Crawford, Mississippi, led the NEGRO AMERICAN LEAGUE in 1950 with a .424 average in 70 games. He would go on to play for the Chicago White Sox in 1951. Officially, he is listed as the first black player for the White Sox, appearing in just four games. However, Minnie Minoso actually played with Chicago three months before Hairston played for the White Sox. Hairston went on to have a career in the minor leagues, playing for Colorado Springs, Sacramento, and Charleston, retiring after the 1960 season. Hairston would go on to work for the White Sox organization as a scout and coach. Years later, his son, Jerry, played 12 major league seasons, primarily for the White Sox, and then went on to manage the team. A third generation Hairston, Jerry Jr., played for the Baltimore Orioles.

Hairstone, J. B.

J. B. Hairstone was a catcher, outfielder, and manager for the Baltimore Black Sox and Bacharach Giants from 1916 to 1922.

Hale, Red

Red Hale was a shortstop for the Detroit Stars and Chicago American Giants from 1937 to 1939.

Haley, Red

Red Haley was a second baseman and third baseman for the Birmingham Black Barons, Cuban Stars, and Chicago American Giants from 1928 to 1933. Haley also played with an integrated semipro team in Jamestown, North Dakota, with Ted "Double Duty" Radcliffe, Quincy Trouppe, and other Negro Leaguers in 1934.

Hall, Blainey

Blainey Hall was an outfielder for the Lincoln Giants, Mohawk Giants, Philadelphia Giants, and Baltimore Black Sox from 1913 to 1925.

Hall, Charley

Charley Hall was an infielder and outfielder for the Kansas City Monarchs in 1948.

Hall, Emory

Emory Hall was a second baseman for the Philadelphia Pythians in 1887.

Hall, Horace

Horace Hall, a Chicago businessman, was an officer with the Chicago American Giants from 1933 to 1942 and also served as a vice president of the NEGRO AMERICAN LEAGUE.

Hall, Joseph W.

Joseph Hall was an officer with the Hilldale baseball club in 1945.

Hall, Perry

Perry Hall was a third baseman, pitcher, and outfielder for the Milwaukee Bears, St. Louis Giants, Memphis Red Sox, Chicago Giants, Cleveland Tigers, Chicago Columbia Giants, Indianapolis Athletics, Detroit Stars, and Birmingham Black Barons from 1921 to 1937.

Hall, Sellers McKee (Sell)

Sellers Hall was a pitcher for the Homestead Grays, Pittsburgh Colored Giants, and Chicago American Giants from 1916 to 1920.

Hall, Thomas

Thomas Hall was a shortstop for the Washington Pilots in 1934.

Hamilton, Arthur Lee

Arthur Lee Hamilton was a catcher for the Indianapolis Clowns from 1953 to 1954.

Hamilton, George

George Hamilton was a catcher for the Birmingham Black Barons, Memphis Red Sox, and Washington Pilots from 1923 to 1932.

Hamilton, James

James Hamilton was a shortstop for the Kansas City Monarchs in 1946.

Hamilton, J. C.

J. C. Hamilton was a pitcher for the Homestead Grays from 1939 to 1942.

Hamilton, J. H.

J. H. Hamilton was an infielder for the Birmingham Black Barons, Washington Potomacs, Cleveland Elites, Indianapolis ABC's, and Wilmington Potomacs from 1924 to 1927.

Hamilton, Theron

Theron Hamilton was a vice president with the Homestead Grays in 1934.

Hamman, Edward

Edward Hamman was the owner of the Indianapolis Clowns, taking over for Syd Pollock in the 1960s.

Hammond, Don

Don Hammond was a shortstop and third baseman for the Cleveland Browns, Toledo Tigers, and Cleveland Tate Stars in 1923 and 1924.

Hampton, Eppie

Eppie Hampton was a pitcher and catcher for the New Orleans Crescent Stars, Washington Pilot, Memphis Red Sox, Cleveland Tigers, Cleveland Tate Stars, and Birmingham Black Barons from 1922 to 1938.

Hampton, Lewis

Lewis Hampton was a pitcher for the Bacharach Giants, Indianapolis ABC's, Columbus Buckeyes, Wilmington Potomacs, Detroit Stars, Lincoln Giants, and Washington Potomacs from 1921 to 1928.

Hampton, Lionel

Lionel Hampton gained worldwide acclaim as a big-band leader and jazz musician. But he was also a baseball fanatic and sometimes worked as a first base coach for the Kansas City Monarchs in the late 1940s.

Hampton, Wade

Wade Hampton was a pitcher for the Pennsylvania Giants and Hilldale baseball club from 1918 to 1924.

Hamtramck Stadium

Hamtramck Stadium was a ballpark in Detroit that served as the home field for the Detroit Stars and hosted a number of Negro League games.

Hancock, Art

Art Hancock was a first baseman and outfielder for the Cleveland Hornets and Cleveland Elites from 1926 to 1927.

Hancock, Charles

Charles Hancock was a catcher for the St. Louis Giants in 1921.

Hancock, Eddie

Eddie Hancock was a pitcher for the Memphis Red Sox from 1952 to 1955.

Hancock, Gene

Gene Hancock was an outfielder for the Memphis Red Sox in 1954.

Hancock, John

John Hancock was a pitcher for the New Orleans Eagles in 1951.

Hancock, Leroy

Leroy Hancock was a pitcher and outfielder for the Memphis Red Sox, New Orleans Eagles, and Chicago American Giants from 1951 to 1954.

Handy, George

George Handy was an infielder for the Houston Eagles and Memphis Red Sox from 1946 to 1949. Records show that Handy batted .326 for Memphis in 1949. Born in 1924, the 5-foot-6, 175-pound Handy went on to play minor league baseball in Bridgeport, Miami Beach, and Winston–Salem, among other teams, retiring after the 1955 season.

Handy, William Oscar (Buck)

William Handy was an infielder for the Brooklyn Royal Giants, New York Black Sox, Lincoln Giants, St. Louis Giants, Philadelphia Royal Giants, and Bacharach Giants from 1910 to 1927.

Hannibal, Leo Jack

Leo Hannibal was a pitcher for the Indianapolis Athletics, Indianapolis ABC's, and Homestead Grays in 1932, 1937, and 1938.

Hanson, Harry

Harry Hanson was vice president of the Negro Southern League in 1926.

Hardaway, Curtis

Curtis Hardaway was a third baseman for the Indianapolis Clowns in 1952 and 1953.

Harden, James

James Harden was a pitcher for the Homestead Grays in 1947.

Harden, John

John Harden was an officer with the Atlanta Black Crackers, New York Black Yankees, and Indianapolis ABC's from 1939 to 1948. He also served as treasurer of the Negro Southern League.

Harden, Lovell

Lovell Harden was a pitcher for the Cleveland Buckeyes from 1943 to 1945.

Harding, Hallie

Hallie Harding was a shortstop, second baseman, and third baseman for the Detroit Stars, Indianapolis ABC's, Chicago Columbia Giants, Kansas City Monarchs, Baltimore Black Sox, and Bacharach Giants from 1926 to 1931.

Harding, Roy

Roy Harding was a pitcher for the Philadelphia Stars in 1937.

Harding, Tom

Tom Harding was an outfielder for the Indianapolis Crawfords in 1940.

Hardy, Arthur

Arthur Hardy was a pitcher for the Kansas City Giants, Topeka Giants, Leland Giants, and Union Giants from 1906 to 1912. In Robert Peterson's book *Only the Ball Was White*, Hardy talked about barnstorming around the Midwest: "When I was barnstorming with the Kansas City, Kansas, Giants, we got around any way we could," Hardy said. "I have ridden between towns, especially out in Kansas and Nebraska where they were off the railroads—there weren't any buses then—in a farm wagon. Any kind of transportation. I've ridden in a wagon 15 or 20 miles and then slept all night in a railroad station to catch a train to get into the next place. We used to carry our clothes in a roll, and whenever we got caught out, like in a railroad station or someplace, we'd unroll that for a pallet to sleep on. . . . We played baseball every day. We started in Topeka and we played up through Kansas, Iowa and into Illinois and Chicago. And then we played back in those little country towns. Now that was a very interesting experience. We carried eight players and three pitchers. I pitched today; tomorrow I'd be on the gate, the day after that would be my rest day, or maybe I'd play in the outfield."

Hardy also talked about clowning for the Topeka Giants: "We did some clowning on the field," he said. "But it was done like this. . . . Some people might resent what they might consider you making fun of them, and so [manager] Topeka Jack Johnson would always talk to the local people. He'd say, 'Now what about you folks here? Do you want us to put on some kind of funny act? Or do you think they would resent it.' Here was one of the stunts: the pitcher would throw the ball and maybe it would be a little low but the umpire would call it a strike; all right, you'd get down on your knees at the plate. Or some guy would hit the ball out of the park and run to third base and around the bases backward, that sort of thing. Well, now, unless the local people would approve, we would never do it. Johnson always insisted that we didn't want to humiliate anybody. After all, we were pros and the other teams were fellows who were playing once a week. Of course, if they wanted to come out and measure arms with us, all right! But if the local people thought clowning would help any and add a little to it, okay, but not unless they gave their consent. And that's the way we handled it. Now, of course, the team that was noted for clowning a little later was the Indianapolis Clowns. That was part of their business, although most of their humor was directed at themselves."

Hardy, Doc

Doc Hardy was an infielder for the Cleveland Buckeyes in 1950.

Hardy, Paul
b. 1911, d. 1979

Paul Hardy was a catcher for the Detroit Stars, Montgomery Grey Sox, Birmingham Black Barons, Baltimore Elite Giants, Columbus Elite Giants, Kansas City Monarchs, Chicago American Giants, Nashville Elite Giants, and Memphis Red Sox from 1931 to 1952. He also played for the Harlem Globetrotters baseball team and went on to work for the Globetrotters for 37 years.

Hardy, Walter

Walter Hardy was a shortstop and second baseman for the New York Cubans and New York Black Yankees from 1945 to 1950. Records show that the 5-foot-11, 160-pound Hardy, born in 1927, batted .267 in 1949 and .252 in 1950. He went on to play until 1955 for St. Jean in the Provincial League.

Harland, Bill

Bill Harland was a pitcher for the Lincoln Giants in 1929.

Harlem Globetrotters

The Harlem Globetrotters, named after the famous traveling black basketball team, were a barnstorming black baseball team formed by Globetrotters owner Abe Saperstein and managed by Ted "Double Duty" Radcliffe. Its players included Nap Gulley.

Harlem Oval

The Harlem Oval was a ball field in Harlem in New York City at the intersection of 125th Street and Lenox Avenue that hosted a number of Negro League games, including those of the Brooklyn Royal Giants.

Harmon, Charlie (Chuck)
b. 1926

Charlie Harmon was an outfielder for the Indianapolis Clowns in 1947. Harmon, born in Washington, Indiana, went on to play minor league baseball and several seasons of major league ball with the Cincinnati Reds, St. Louis Cardinals, and Philadelphia Phillies. In four major league seasons, the 6-foot-2, 175-pound Harmon batted .238 with 141 hits in 592 at bats and 289 games. His last season of organized ball was with Hawaii in the Pacific Coast League in 1961. He also played winter baseball in Puerto Rico.

Harness, Robert

Robert Harness was a pitcher for the Chicago Giants from 1927 to 1928.

Harney, George

George Harney was a pitcher for the Chicago Columbia Giants, Chicago Giants, and Chicago American Giants from 1923 to 1931.

Harper, Chick

Chick Harper was a pitcher, shortstop, and outfielder for the Norfolk Stars, Hilldale baseball club, Detroit Stars, and Kansas City Monarchs from 1920 to 1925.

Harper, David

David Harper was a pitcher and outfielder for the Philadelphia Stars, Birmingham Black Barons, and Kansas City Monarchs from 1943 to 1946.

Harper, John

John Harper was a pitcher for the Bacharach Giants, Lincoln Giants, and Richmond Giants from 1922 to 1926.

Harper, Walter

Walter Harper was a first baseman and catcher for the Birmingham Black Barons, Chicago American Giants, and Chicago Columbia Giants from 1929 to 1932.

Harpson, Fred

Fred Harpson was an infielder for the Brooklyn Cuban Giants and Lincoln Giants in 1923 and 1928.

Harrell, William

William Harrell was a shortstop and third baseman for the Birmingham Black Barons in 1951. Born in 1928 in Norristown, Pennsylvania, the 6-foot-1, 180-pound Harrell went on to play minor league baseball, including two seasons with Rochester in the International League, where Harrell hit 32 home runs and drove in 147 runs during two seasons. He also played four major league seasons with the Cleveland Indians and Boston Red Sox, batting .231 with 79 hits in 342 at bats and 173 games. His final season was with Toronto in the International League in 1966.

Harris, Ananias

Ananias Harris was a pitcher for the Harrisburg Giants, Brooklyn Royal Giants, and Hilldale baseball club from 1921 to 1923.

Harris, Andy

Andy Harris was a third baseman and manager for the Pennsylvania Red Caps of New York, Hilldale baseball club, Pennsylvania Giants, Pittsburgh Stars of Buffalo, Newark Stars, and Cleveland Elites from 1917 to 1926.

Harris, Charlie

b. 1909, d. 1998
Charlie Harris was an infielder for the Chicago Brown Bombers and Cincinnati Clowns in 1943.

Harris, Chick

Chick Harris was a first baseman and outfielder for the Kansas City Monarchs, Detroit Wolves, Cleveland Stars, and New Orleans Crescent Stars from 1931 to 1936.

Harris, Cornelius

Cornelius Harris was an outfielder and third baseman for the Pittsburgh Crawfords from 1928 to 1931.

Harris, Curtis

Curtis Harris was a catcher and infielder for the Philadelphia Stars, Pittsburgh Crawfords, and Kansas City Monarchs from 1931 to 1940.

Harris, Elander (Vic)

b. 1905
Elander Harris was a left-handed-hitting outfielder, manager, and coach for the Cleveland Browns, Cleveland Tate Stars, Homestead Grays, Chicago American Giants, Pittsburgh Crawfords, Baltimore Elite Giants, Toledo Tigers, Birmingham Black Barons, and Detroit Wolves from 1923 to 1950. Born in Pensacola, Florida, Harris would go on to be manager of the great Homestead teams that included Josh Gibson and Jud Wilson. As an outfielder for the Grays, Harris made an outstanding running catch in the first contest between the Grays and the rival Pittsburgh Crawfords in July 1930 to give Homestead the victory, according to Mark Ribowsky's book *A Complete*

History of the Negro Leagues. Harris was part of that great 1931 Homestead team, considered perhaps the most talented team in Negro League history, though Harris told John Holway, in his book *Blackball Stars*, that he believed the 1930 Grays team was their best. "That's when we beat the Monarchs when they came out East with their lights," Harris said. "They'd beaten everybody. They were the team out West, and the Grays were the team out East. We took them, lights and all. They won one ball game out of the 12 we played."

In 1932, while managing the Grays, Harris once punched umpire Jimmy Ahearn during a dispute in a game. Ahearn filed assault and battery charges, but they were later dropped. In a 1975 article in *Dawn* magazine, several Negro Leaguers talked about Harris's aggressiveness and temper: "He'd cut you in a minute," said second baseman Dick Seay, talking about Harris sliding into second. "Cut you and laugh . . . and he'd fight, too." Apparently, he would even fight his teammates, according to Jake Stephens, who told a story about a fellow Homestead Gray who was traveling in a car with Harris and said something to upset him. "Vic told him to get out," Stephens said. "He worked him over good, beat the living hell out of him. Vic was quick with his fists."

His temper didn't stop him from being a successful manager, as Harris managed the Grays from 1936 to 1948 and led the Grays to championships from 1937 to 1943. Harris managed some great players on those Grays teams, and in the *Dawn* magazine article, talked about the challenge of managing those players: "There were a lot of stars on that team, but I didn't have any trouble managing them," Harris said. "I would never ask them to do more than I would myself. They knew I liked to win. That's the main thing. They liked to win, too. Jud Wilson was supposed to be temperamental, but he was no problem. He was out to win, same as I was. And there was no one easier to handle than Josh Gibson. But there are a lot of problems in managing. You got to put down your discipline and stick to it. You can't let your star do one thing and one of your so-so players, give him the devil for doing the same thing your star did. You can't do that. You've got to treat them all alike, stars and all."

Harris also was a coach for the Baltimore Elite Giants in 1949 and managed the Birmingham Black Barons in 1950.

Harris, Frank

Frank Harris was a pitcher for the Argyle Hotel baseball team in 1885.

Harris, George

George Harris was a second baseman for the Louisville Red Caps and Louisville Black Caps from 1932 to 1938.

Harris, Henry

Henry Harris was a shortstop for the Baltimore Black Sox, Louisville White Sox, Memphis Red Sox, and Louisville Black Caps from 1928 to 1934.

Harris, Isaiah

Isiah Harris was a pitcher for the Memphis Red Sox from 1949 to 1955.

Harris, James

James Harris was an outfielder and manager for the Baltimore Atlantics and Baltimore Lord Baltimores from 1884 to 1887.

Harris, Joe

Joe Harris was a pitcher for the Bacharach Giants in 1933.

Harris, Lefty

Lefty Harris was a pitcher for the New York Cubans in 1941.

Harris, Leon

Leon Harris was a pitcher for the Kansas City Monarchs in 1954.

Harris, Lonnie

Lonnie Harris was an outfielder for the Memphis Red Sox and Louisville Black Colonels from 1954 to 1955.

Harris, Nathan

Nathan Harris was an outfielder and second baseman for the Leland Giants, Chicago Giants, Philadelphia Giants, Columbia Giants, and Cuban Giants from 1901 to 1911. Harris was recruited by Sol White to play on the Philadelphia Giants in 1906; that team is believed to have posted a 134-21 record and were crowned the champions of Negro League baseball.

Harris, Raymond (Moe)

Raymond Harris was a second baseman and outfielder for the Homestead Grays and Pittsburgh Crawfords from 1916 to 1943. He also worked as an umpire in the East-West League and the NEGRO NATIONAL LEAGUE.

Harris, Roger

Roger Harris was an infielder for the Birmingham Black Barons in 1942.

Harris, Samuel
Samuel Harris was a pitcher and outfielder for the Monroe Monarchs, Birmingham Black Barons, and Chicago American Giants in 1932 and 1940.

Harris, Sonny
Sonny Harris was an infielder and outfielder for the Cincinnati Tigers and Cincinnati–Cleveland Buckeyes from 1935 to 1942.

Harris, Tommy
Tommy Harris was a catcher for the Louisville Buckeyes and Cleveland Buckeyes from 1946 to 1949.

Harris, Virgil (Schoolboy)
Virgil Harris was a second baseman, pitcher, and outfielder for the Cincinnati–Cleveland Buckeyes and Cincinnati Tigers from 1935 to 1937.

Harris, William
William Harris was a catcher for the Monroe Monarchs, St. Louis Stars, Memphis Red Sox, and Indianapolis ABC's from 1929 to 1932.

Harris, William A.
William A. Harris was an outfielder for the Homestead Grays and Pittsburgh Crawfords from 1928 to 1931.

Harris, Willie
Willie Harris was a pitcher for the Detroit Stars in 1955.

Harris, Willie
Willie Harris was an outfielder for the Memphis Red Sox, Louisville Black Colonels, and Philadelphia Stars from 1951 to 1955.

Harris, Wilmer
b. 1924
Wilmer Harris was a pitcher for the Philadelphia Stars from 1945 to 1952. With a strong curveball, Harris posted a career record of 85-30, with his best year in 1946, when he posted a 16-4 mark. Born in Philadelphia, Harris learned how to play baseball on the sandlots of that city, playing semipro ball with and against white players as well as black. Playing as the lone black on an all-white team, Harris caught the attention of the Stars by defeating a powerful black semipro team known as the Black Meteors. "The first game I pitched for the Stars was in Yankee Stadium, against Satchel Paige, before a crowd of about 45,000 people," Harris said in an interview. They pitched three-inning stints at that time, and Harris said they lost 2-1 to Paige. "Ignorance was bliss," Harris said. "I just threw the ball and didn't worry about it." Harris said he faced some of the great Negro League hitters, such as Josh Gibson at the end of his career, Monte Irvin, Larry Doby, and a young Jackie Robinson in 1945. "The first time I faced Jackie Robinson I struck him out on three curveballs. The worst thing you can do is to try to pull a curveball and that's what he did. I saw him play in 1947, and he was hitting those pitches to right center field, a sign that he had become a good curveball hitter." Harris played with Robinson's barnstorming teams in 1947 and 1951. He developed a sore arm in 1947, and it hurt him again in 1950 when he got a tryout with the Boston Braves, he said.

Harris, Win
Win Harris was a shortstop and first baseman for the Homestead Grays from 1922 to 1928.

Harrisburg Giants
The Harrisburg Giants, out of Harrisburg, Pennsylvania, were first formed in the latter part of the 1880s and played in the Middle States League, named league champions in 1888. Another version was formed in 1922, started by a local businessman named "Colonel" Strothers. They played their games at Island Park in Harrisburg and also at Rossmere Ball Park in Lancaster. They were managed by Oscar Charleston in 1925, finishing second in the Eastern Colored League behind Hilldale. Charleston, who along with Josh Gibson were the greatest sluggers in Negro baseball history, was joined in the outfield by Herbert "Rap" Dixon and Clarence "Fats" Jenkins. According to John Holway's book *Blackball Stars,* catcher William "Big C" Johnson called that trio of outfielders "the best I ever played with. Dixon was fast, maybe the best of the three, but all were accurate. I caught more men trying to come home after fly balls the two years I was in Harrisburg than in all my other years put together." Also on that team were infielders Walter "Rev" Cannady and Ben Taylor. In 1927, John Beckwith, another great Negro baseball slugger, joined the Giants. During that season, records show that Beckwith batted .361 with nine home runs, while Charleston hit .335 with 12 home runs and 18 doubles. They disbanded in 1928 and were organized again in 1932 but lasted just one season.

Harrisburg Stars
The Harrisburg Stars, out of Harrisburg, Pennsylvania, played in the NEGRO NATIONAL LEAGUE for one season in 1943.

Harrison, Abraham

Abraham Harrison was a shortstop for the Argyle Hotel, Cuban Giants, Trenton Cuban Giants, York Cuban Giants, and York Colored Monarchs from 1885 to 1897. In his book *History of Colored Base Ball,* Negro Leaguer and historian Sol White described Harrison as one of the game's "comedians." In 1891, playing for the Cuban Giants, Harrison reportedly batted .267.

Harrison, Tomlini

Tomlini Harrison was a pitcher for the Kansas City Monarchs and St. Louis Stars from 1927 to 1930.

Harriston, Clyde

Clyde Harriston was an infielder for the Cincinnati-Indianapolis Clowns and Birmingham Black Barons in 1944.

Hart, Frank

Frank Hart was a shortstop for the St. Louis Black Stockings in 1884.

Hartman, Garrel

Garrell Hartman was an infielder and outfielder for the Philadelphia Stars in 1944.

Hartman, J. C.

b. 1934

J. C. Hartman was a shortstop for the Kansas City Monarchs in 1955. Born in Cottonton, Alabama, Hartman went on to play minor league baseball and played two seasons for the Houston Astros, in 1962 and 1963, batting .185 with 44 hits in 238 at bats and 90 games.

Harvey, Charles

Charles Harvey was a shortstop for the Cleveland Buckeyes in 1950.

Harvey, David William

b. 1908, d. 1989

David Harvey was a pitcher for the Pittsburgh Crawfords, Memphis Red Sox, Cleveland Red Sox, Baltimore Elite Giants, Indianapolis Crawfords, Toledo Crawfords, Cleveland Giants, and Monroe Monarchs from 1932 to 1945. The 5-foot-8, 175-pound Harvey, born in Clarksdale, Mississippi, also played in the Mexican League and for Youngstown in the Mid-Atlantic League in 1950.

Harvey, Frank

Frank Harvey was a pitcher and outfielder for the Brooklyn Royal Giants, St. Louis Giants, Lincoln Giants, Lincoln Stars, Philadelphia Giants, and Bacharach Giants from 1912 to 1924.

Harvey, James

James Harvey was a catcher for the Chicago Union Giants in 1911.

Harvey, Robert

Robert Harvey was an outfielder for the Houston Eagles, New Orleans Eagles, and Newark Eagles from 1943 to 1951.

Haslett, Claude

Claude Haslett was a pitcher for the Memphis Red Sox and Indianapolis Athletics from 1936 to 1937.

Havana Cuban Stars

The Havana Cuban Stars were a team consisting primarily of Cuban players who played Negro League baseball in 1904. They lasted two seasons, going bankrupt in the 1906 season.

Havana Red Sox

The Havana Red Sox were a black baseball team that was primarily a "clowning" team operated by white promoter Syd Pollock in the 1930s. Like many clowning teams, the Red Sox were considered an attraction for white fans and an insult to black fans. One *Pittsburgh Courier* sportswriter described the Red Sox as "a collection of chattering jackasses."

Havis, Chester

Chester Havis was a pitcher for the Memphis Red Sox in 1947.

Hawkins, John

John Hawkins was a shortstop for the New York Black Yankees in 1940.

Hawkins, Lemuel

Lemuel Hawkins was a first baseman and outfielder for the Kansas City Monarchs, Los Angeles White Sox, Chicago American Giants, and Chicago Giants from 1919 to 1928. Hawkins also played on the U.S. Army's

25th Infantry team prior to his Negro League tenure, a team that included a number of talented black players, such as Dobie Moore and Oscar Johnson.

Hayes, Buddy

Buddy Hayes was a catcher for the Indianapolis ABC's, Chicago American Giants, Cleveland Browns, Pittsburgh Keystones, Milwaukee Bears, St. Louis Giants, and Toledo Tigers from 1916 to 1924.

Hayes, Burnalle James (Bun)

Burnalle Hayes was a pitcher and manager for the Washington Pilots, Baltimore Black Sox, Newark Dodgers, Chicago American Giants, Jacksonville Red Caps, Brooklyn Eagles, and Pittsburgh Crawfords from 1929 to 1935.

Hayes, Jimmy

Jimmy Hayes was a catcher for the Kansas City Monarchs in 1949.

Hayes, John

John Hayes was a catcher who played from 1934 to 1951 for the Newark Eagles, Newark Dodgers, Boston Blues, New York Black Yankees, Pittsburgh Crawfords, Philadelphia Giants, and Baltimore Elite Giants from 1934 to 1951.

Hayes, John W.

John W. Hayes was a shortstop and second baseman for the St. Louis Stars and Philadelphia Stars in 1940.

Hayes, Thomas H., Jr.

Thomas Hayes was an officer with the Birmingham Black Barons in the 1940s. Hayes, a black funeral home operator, was also vice president of the NEGRO AMERICAN LEAGUE.

Hayes, Wilbur

Wilbur Hayes was the general manager with the Cincinnati Buckeyes and Cleveland Buckeyes from 1942 to 1950.

Hayman, Charles

Charles Hayman was a pitcher and first baseman for the Philadelphia Giants from 1909 to 1916.

Haynes, Sammy

Sammy Haynes was a catcher for the Atlanta Black Crackers and Kansas City Monarchs from 1937 to 1938 and from 1943 to 1945. Years later, Haynes founded an organization called the International Society of Athletes to counsel at-risk students and dropouts.

Haynes, Willie

Willie Haynes was a pitcher for the Harrisburg Giants, Dallas Giants, Hilldale baseball club, Bacharach Giants, and Baltimore Black Sox from 1921 to 1924.

Haywood, Albert (Buster)

Albert Haywood was a catcher and manager for the New York Cubans, Birmingham Black Barons, Indianapolis Clowns, Cincinnati-Indianapolis Clowns, Memphis Red Sox, Cincinnati Clowns, and Brooklyn Eagles from 1935 to 1965. Haywood managed the Clowns when a young outfielder named Hank Aaron played for the team in 1952, and Haywood is given credit for changing Aaron's unorthodox cross-handed hitting style.

Head, John

John Head was an outfielder for the Kansas City Monarchs in 1951.

Heard, Jehosie (Jay)
b. 1920

Jehosie Heard was a pitcher who played for the Birmingham Black Barons, Houston Eagles, Memphis Red Sox, and New Orleans in the NEGRO AMERICAN LEAGUE from 1946 to 1951. He posted a 6-1 record for Birmingham in 1948 as part of the Barons' pennant-winning team. Heard's best Negro League baseball season on record was with New Orleans in 1951 when he went 17-9. He played minor league baseball in 1952 and 1953 with Victoria, where he had a 20-12 record, and Portland, where he went 16-12. The 5-foot-8, 150-pound Heard, born in Atlanta, Georgia, broke into the major leagues with the Baltimore Orioles in 1954 but would pitch just three innings in two games before being sent down to the minors. He finished the 1954 season with Portland, going 3-3 as a reliever in 19 appearances. Heard finished his career with Charleston and Seattle in 1955.

Heffner, Arthur

Arthur Heffner was an outfielder for the Philadelphia Stars and New York Black Yankees from 1947 to 1949.

Henderson, Armour

Armour Henderson was a pitcher for the Mohawk Giants from 1914 to 1915.

Henderson, Arthur (Rats)

Arthur Henderson was a pitcher for the Bacharach Giants, Detroit Stars, and Richmond Giants from 1922 to 1931. In an interview with author John Holway on file at the National Baseball Hall of Fame, Negro Leaguer Newt Allen said that Henderson was a great curveball pitcher: "He was what they'd call a curveball artist," Allen said. "He could throw five curveballs at you before one hit the bat, because he had pretty good control, some of the best control for a curveball pitcher." In 1927, Henderson reportedly won 19 games for the Atlantic City Bacharach Giants, who won their second straight Eastern Colored League championship.

Henderson, Ben (Rabbit)

Ben Henderson was a pitcher for the Birmingham Black Barons and St. Louis Stars in 1936 and 1937.

Henderson, Curtis

Curtis Henderson was a shortstop and third baseman for the New York Black Yankees, Philadelphia Stars, Toledo Crawfords, Washington Black Senators, Chicago American Giants, Indianapolis Crawfords, Brooklyn Royal Giants, and Homestead Grays from 1936 to 1942.

Henderson, George (Rube)

George Henderson was a third baseman, outfielder, and pitcher for the Toledo Tigers, Cleveland Tate Stars, Chicago Giants, and Detroit Stars from 1920 to 1923.

Henderson, James (Duke)

James Henderson was an outfielder for the Kansas City Monarchs from 1949 to 1953.

Henderson, Lenon

Lenon Henderson was a shortstop and third baseman for the Louisville Black Caps, Montgomery Grey Sox, Birmingham Black Barons, Nashville Elite Giants, and Indianapolis ABC's from 1930 to 1933.

Henderson, Long

Long Henderson was a first baseman for the Nashville Elite Giants in 1932.

Henderson, Louis

Louis Henderson was a pitcher and outfielder for the Bacharach Giants in 1925.

Henderson, Neale

Neale Henderson was an infielder for the Kansas City Monarchs in 1949.

Hendrix, Stokes

Stokes Hendrix was a pitcher for the Nashville Elite Giants in 1934.

Henry, Alfred

Alfred Henry was an outfielder for the Philadelphia Stars and Baltimore Elite Giants from 1950 to 1951.

Henry, Charlie

Charlie Henry was a pitcher and manager for the Harrisburg Giants, Hilldale baseball club, Bacharach Giants, Detroit Stars, Detroit Black Sox, and Louisville Black Colonels from 1922 to 1942. He was also the promoter for the Zulu Cannibal Giants, a clowning black baseball team. In his autobiography, *I Was Right on Time*, Negro Leaguer Buck O'Neil said that the Zulu Cannibal Giants "painted their faces, put rings in their noses and played in straw dresses. They looked like extras in a Tarzan movie, and Charlie gave them phony African names, like Bebop and Sheba and Limpopo."

Henry, Joe

Joe Henry was a second baseman for the Memphis Red Sox from 1950 to 1952 and the Detroit Stars in 1958. Henry batted .284 with Memphis in 1951 and batted .284 with Detroit in 1958. He also played two seasons for Mt. Vernon in the Mississippi-Ohio Valley League in 1953 and 1954.

Henry, Leo (Preacher)

Leo Henry was a pitcher for the Cleveland Bears, Jacksonville Red Caps, Indianapolis Clowns, and Cincinnati Clowns from 1938 to 1951.

Henry, Otis

Otis Henry was a second baseman and third baseman for the Monroe Monarchs, Memphis Red Sox, and Indianapolis Athletics from 1931 to 1937.

Hensley, Logan (Eggie)

Logan Hensley was a pitcher for the Toledo Tigers, St. Louis Stars, Detroit Stars, Indianapolis ABC's, Chicago

American Giants, Cleveland Giants, Cleveland Browns, and Cleveland Tate Stars from 1922 to 1939. He reportedly won 17 games for the Detroit Stars in 1930.

Heredia, Ramon
b. 1917

Ramon Heredia was a third baseman and shortstop for the New York Cubans from 1939 to 1945. The 6-foot, 200-pound Heredia, born in Cuba, also played in the Mexican League until 1949.

Hernandez, Alberto

Alberto Hernandez was an outfielder for the New York Cubans in 1941.

Hernandez, Jose

Jose Hernandez was a pitcher and outfielder for the Cuban Stars from 1920 to 1922.

Hernandez, Ramon

Ramon Hernandez was a third baseman for the Cuban Stars from 1929 to 1930.

Hernandez, Ricardo

Ricardo Hernandez was a second baseman and third baseman for the Cuban Stars, ALL NATIONS team, and All Cubans from 1909 to 1916.

Herrera, Juan (Pancho)
b. 1934

Juan Herrera was a first baseman and third baseman for the Kansas City Monarchs from 1953 to 1954. Born in Santiago, Cuba, records show that the 6-foot-3, 220-pound Herrera batted .280 for the Monarchs in 1953 and .328, with 13 home runs and 48 RBIs, in 1954. He went on to play minor league baseball from 1955 until 1972, and spent three seasons—1958, 1960, and 1961—playing for the Philadelphia Phillies, batting .271 with 31 home runs and 128 RBIs in 975 at bats and 300 games.

Herrera, Ramon

Ramon Herrera was a second baseman and third baseman for the Cuban Stars, Long Branch, New Jersey, Cubans, Jersey City Cubans, and Cincinnati Cubans from 1916 to 1928.

Herron, Robert Lee

Robert Lee Herron was an outfielder for the New Orleans Eagles and Houston Eagles from 1950 to 1951.

Heslip, Jesse

Jesse Heslip was an officer with the Toledo Cubs in 1945.

Hewitt, Joe

Joe Hewitt was a shortstop, second baseman, outfielder, and manager for the Lincoln Stars, Birmingham Black Barons, Dayton Marcos, St. Louis Stars, Detroit Stars, Lincoln Giants, St. Louis Giants, Brooklyn Royal Giants, Philadelphia Giants, Chicago American Giants, Cleveland Cubs, Milwaukee Bears, and Nashville Elite Giants from 1910 to 1932.

Heywood, Charlie

Charlie Heywood was a pitcher for the Lincoln Giants in 1925 and 1926.

Hickle, James

James Hickle was an outfielder for the Detroit Stars in 1955.

Hicks, Buddy

Buddy Hicks was an outfielder for the Indianapolis Clowns in 1951.

Hicks, Eugene

Eugene Hicks was a pitcher for the New York Cuban Stars and Homestead Grays in 1940 and 1941.

Hicks, Wesley

Wesley Hicks was an outfielder for the Memphis Red Sox, Chicago American Giants, and Kansas City Monarchs from 1927 to 1931.

Hidalgo, Heliodoro

Heliodoro Hidalgo was an outfielder and third baseman for the Stars of Cuba, Cuban Stars, and All Cubans from 1905 to 1913.

Higdon, Barney

Barney Higdon was a pitcher for the Cincinnati Clowns in 1943.

Higgins, Robert

Robert Higgins was a pitcher for the Syracuse Cuban Giants in 1887, 1888, and 1896. As a rookie at the age of 19, Higgins was one of the black players who played with white teams, and was involved in a controversy when several of his teammates reportedly botched plays on purpose to sabotage Higgins's debut, a 22-8 loss to Toronto in 1887. Higgins left the team for a period during that season, according to a *Sporting News* report: "Robert Higgins, the colored pitcher . . . is in a state of insubordination. He is tired of baseball, and after failing to obtain his release decided to desert the club, give up his $200 a month, and return to his barbershop in Memphis, Tenn." Higgins was reportedly fined $100 for his departure and returned to the team and was described as "the very much homesick colored pitcher," according to Robert Peterson's book *Only the Ball Was White*. Higgins still went on to win 20 games that year in the International League. In 54 minor league games during two seasons, Higgins won 37 games and lost 14, striking out 207 batters and walking 107 in 473 innings.

Hightower, James

James Hightower was a first baseman for the Lincoln, Nebraska, Giants in 1890.

Hill, Ben

Ben Hill was a pitcher for the Philadelphia Stars and Pittsburgh Crawfords in 1943 and 1946.

Hill, Charley (Lefty)

Charley Hill was an outfielder and pitcher for the Dayton Marcos, Chicago Union Giants, St. Louis Giants, Detroit Stars, West Baden Sprudels, and Chicago American Giants from 1910 to 1924.

Hill, Gilbert

Gilbert Hill was a pitcher for the Pittsburgh Crawfords from 1928 to 1929.

Hill, Herb

Herb Hill was a pitcher and outfielder for the Philadelphia Stars in 1949.

Hill, James (Lefty)

James Hill was a pitcher for the Newark Eagles from 1938 to 1945.

Hill, John

John Hill was a shortstop and third baseman for the Cuban X Giants, Philadelphia Giants, Genuine Cuban Giants, and Brooklyn Royal Giants from 1900 to 1907.

Hill, Johnson

Johnson Hill was an infielder and outfielder for the Detroit Stars, Milwaukee Bears, St. Louis Giants, and Brooklyn Royal Giants from 1920 to 1928.

Hill, Jonathan

Jonathan Hill was an outfielder and pitcher for the St. Louis Stars and Atlanta Black Crackers in 1937.

Hill, J. Preston (Pete)

b. 1880, d. 1951

J. Preston Hill was an outfielder, second baseman, and manager for the Leland Giants, Philadelphia Giants, Detroit Stars, Chicago American Giants, Madison Stars of Philadelphia, Baltimore Black Sox, Milwaukee Bears, and Cuban X Giants from 1903 to 1925. He is believed to have had a career batting average of .307. He also played winter ball in Cuba for the Havana Reds. In his later years, Hill also formed a team known as the Buffalo Red Caps. In John Holway's book *Blackball Stars*, Negro Leaguer Norman "Turkey" Stearnes said that Hill "was about one of the finest hitters in colored baseball at that time." Reportedly Hill hit in 115 out of 116 games in 1911, and, at the age of 41 in 1921, Hill batted .388. He played winter baseball in Cuba, batting .307 in six seasons and led the Cuban Winter League with a .365 average in the winter of 1910–1911. Author William F. McNeil, in his book *Baseball's Other All-Stars*, wrote that Hill "was one of baseball's first superstars, excelling in all phases of the game. He was the Willie Mays of the dead ball era. A fast, aggressive center fielder, he had a great glove, and a cannon for a throwing arm. He could do it all at the plate; hit to any field; go for the long ball if necessary, or drag a bunt down the first base line to keep the infielders on their toes. On the bases, he played like Jackie Robinson, constantly moving, and daring the opposing pitcher to catch him." One of the stories about Hill was the time he was involved in a riot while playing for the American Giants in 1915 in a game in Indiana against the ABC's. An argument about whether or not to call the game because of bad weather turned into a melee, and, according to reports, an umpire pulled out a gun and hit Hill in the nose, breaking it.

Hill managed Crush Holloway on the ABC's in 1924 and 1925, and Holloway, in a Holway interview on file at the National Baseball Hall of Fame, credited Hill for his hitting lessons: "He was a great manager," Holloway said. "He played left field, too. He was a left-handed hitter and hit to left field. He's the man who taught me how to hit to left field."

Hill, Sam

Sam Hill was an outfielder and first baseman for the Chicago American Giants, Detroit Stars, and Memphis

Red Sox in 1937, 1947, 1948, 1952, and 1958. Records show he batted .313 with Chicago in 1948 and in his last season batted .227 in 1958. The 6-foot-2, 180-pound Hill also played minor league baseball from 1950 to 1958 in the Manitoba-Dakota League, the Eastern League and the Northern League.

Hill, William

William Hill was a pitcher for the Kansas City Monarchs in 1955.

Hill, W. R.

W. R. Hill was a shortstop for the Brooklyn Remsens in 1885.

Hilldale baseball club

The Hilldale baseball club (also called the Hilldale Daisies) were owned by Ed Bolden, a businessman who was influential in the development of Negro League baseball and battled Rube Foster in the early 1920s in a power struggle in black baseball. Bolden created the Eastern Colored League in 1923 to compete with Foster's NEGRO NATIONAL LEAGUE. The Hilldale Field Club was an amateur baseball team formed in 1910 in Darby, Pennsylvania, a suburb of Philadelphia. Bolden, a post office clerk, took over operation of the team in 1911, and it turned professional in 1917 under the auspices of the Hilldale Baseball and Exhibition Co. They played at a field that would be called Hilldale Park. In Robert Peterson's book *Only the Ball Was White*, third baseman Judy Johnson recalled playing at the ballpark: "We usually filled it," Johnson said. "Mr. Bolden told me one Decoration Day that we had already made enough money to pay off our salaries for the rest of the year. So what we made from Decoration Day on was velvet. We had the best infield that the big league players had ever played on—that's what they told us. The dirt—I don't know what it was, but it shone like silver. And it could rain for an hour like everything and if you sat around for half an hour you couldn't see a bit of water anyplace. The dirt looked like ground-in glass. A ball would very seldom take a bad hop unless someone dug a hole with his spikes. You could just smooth it over and you wouldn't have any trouble. The big league boys always liked to come out there and play because they could make big money. They would never take a guarantee. They'd take 60 or 40 percent—60 for winning, 40 for losing. They were willing to take it because of the crowds we were having. One year I remember we played the Athletics intact and the field was so crowded we had to have special ground rules. You couldn't get a home run unless the ball went out of the park, because the people were so crowded in the outfield. They were up so close the centerfielder was almost playing second base."

Hilldale also played some games at Shibe Park in Philadelphia and also played in Darby and Yeadon in suburban Philadelphia and at Passon Field and Pennar Park in Philadelphia. Bolden brought in established ballplayers such as outfielder Spotswood Poles, outfielder Otto Briggs and pitcher Frank "Doc" Sykes, and Louis Santop and Phil Cockrell the following season. They also had a young third baseman named William "Judy" Johnson, who would go on to become one of the all-time Negro baseball greats. Later, Oliver Marcelle and Bill Pettus would also play for Hilldale.

Foster tried to recruit Bolden to join his Negro National League in 1920, but Bolden refused. As a result, Foster refused to allow teams in his league to play Hilldale, which meant Bolden's black team played primarily white teams, some of which were barnstorming white All-Star teams that included Babe Ruth. Bolden made an agreement with Foster to be an "associate" member of the NNL prior to the 1921 season, and Hilldale played the Kansas City Monarchs in 1921. The six-game series ended with Hilldale defeating Kansas City three games to two, with one tie.

Two years later, Bolden formed the Eastern Colored League in 1923, made up of Hilldale, now known as the Giants, the New York Lincoln Giants, the Atlantic City Bacharach Giants, the Cuban Stars, the Brooklyn Royal Giants, the Washington Potomacs, and the Baltimore Black Sox. The Hilldale Daisies won the league's first three pennants from 1923 through 1925, posting a record of 32-17 in that inaugural 1923 season in the league, with an overall record of 137-43-6 against all competition. In 1924, the Daisies played the NNL champions, the Kansas City Monarchs, in Negro baseball's first World Series. They lost the series but came back in 1925 to beat the Monarchs in a rematch. Some of the players on those pennant-winning Hilldale teams included player-manager Frank Warfield, pitchers Nip Winters, Judy Johnson, catcher Raleigh "Biz" Mackey, and outfielder Clint Thomas.

In 1927, the pressures of trying to operate a successful baseball franchise and the business battles would finally take their toll on Bolden, and he checked himself into a hospital, putting the operation of the franchise in the hands of Charles Freeman. The following year Bolden pulled his Hilldale team from the league, but was wooed back into the league at the end of the 1928 season, with Hilldale being part of a newly formed league, the American Negro League. The league lasted just one year, and Bolden finally left the club in 1930. He had become the target of protests for his failure to use black workers at the ballpark and black umpires and was criticized in a 1929 *Philadelphia Tribune* editorial: "It is a reflection on the ability and intelligence of colored people," the *Tribune* editorial stated. "Are we still slaves? Is it possible that colored players are so dumb that they will resent one of their own race umpiring the game? Or is it that the management of Hilldale is so steeped in racial inferiority that it has no faith in Negroes. Aside from the economic unfairness of such a position the employment of white umpires at Negro games brands Negroes as inferior. It tells white people in a forceful manner that colored people are unable to even play a ball game without white leadership. It is a detestable mean attitude."

Bolden was forced to leave the club, and others tried to keep the Hilldale Field Club running in 1930 with a barnstorming tour, but it was sporadic after that. Black businessman John Drew took over operation of the club in 1931, and the following year it became part of Cum Posey's new East-West League. But Drew closed down the club for good in 1932. Another version was briefly resurrected in 1945 as part of Branch Rickey's short-lived UNITED STATES LEAGUE.

Hilldale Park

Hilldale Park was a ballfield in Darby, Pennsylvania, just outside of Philadelphia, that Hilldale baseball club owner Ed Bolden expanded to 8,000 seats in 1917 and renamed Hilldale Park, the home field for the Hilldale Daisies.

Hilltop Stadium

Hilltop Stadium was a ballpark in New York that hosted Negro League ball games.

Hines, C. W.

C. W. Hines was manager of the Louisville Falls City team in 1887.

Hines, John

John Hines was a catcher and outfielder for the Chicago American Giants and Cole's American Giants from 1924 to 1934. He reportedly batted .328 for the Giants in 1926.

Hinesman, Robert

Robert Hinesman was a pitcher for the Detroit Stars and Chicago American Giants from 1951 to 1954.

Hinson, Frank

Frank Hinson was a pitcher for the Cuban Giants and Cuban X Giants in 1896.

Hinson, Roland

Roland Hinson was a pitcher and infielder for the Baltimore Elite Giants from 1945 to 1946.

Hoagland, F. B.

F. B. Hoagland was secretary with the Brooklyn Remsens in 1885.

Hobgood, Fred (Lefty)

Fred Hobgood was a pitcher, infielder, and outfielder for the New York Black Yankees, Newark Eagles, and Philadelphia Stars from 1941 to 1946.

Hobson, Charles

Charles Hobson was a pitcher, outfielder, and shortstop for the Bacharach Giants, Lincoln Giants, and Richmond Giants from 1922 to 1925.

Hoch, L. W.

L. W. Hoch was a white businessman from Adrian, Michigan, who was the co-owner of the Page Fence Giants, a black baseball team in the 1890s.

Hocker, Bruce

Bruce Hocker was an outfielder and first baseman for the Lincoln Stars, Bowser ABC's, Louisville White Sox, Dayton Marcos, Hilldale baseball club, Chicago American Giants, and West Baden Sprudels from 1913 to 1920.

Hodges, William

William Hodges was a pitcher and outfielder for the Baltimore Black Sox and Lincoln Giants from 1917 to 1925.

Hogan, Julius

Julius Hogan was a catcher and outfielder for the Bacharach Giants in 1932.

Holder, Clyde

Clyde Holder was a pitcher for the New Orleans Eagles in 1951.

Holder, William

William Holder was a shortstop for the Kansas City Monarchs and Indianapolis Clowns in 1953 and 1954.

Holland, Bill

Bill Holland was a pitcher and manager for the Chicago American Giants, Detroit Stars, Brooklyn Royal Giants, Lincoln Giants, Philadelphia Stars, Hilldale baseball club, and New York Black Yankees from 1920 to 1941. The 5-foot-8, 175-pound Holland reportedly posted an 11-1 mark for the Lincoln Giants in 1930, though Holland has told writers he went 29-2 that season. He was considered one of the top Negro League pitchers of his time by his peers. In Robert Peterson's book *Only the Ball Was White*, Negro Leaguer Bill Yancey gave the ultimate compliment to Holland: "On certain days, our Negro National or Negro American League clubs could have been major leaguers," he said. "If we played with Bill Holland pitching, we were major league." In an interview with author John Holway on file at the National Baseball Hall of Fame, Holland talked about breaking new ground at Yankee Stadium: "I was the first colored pitcher to pitch in Yankee Stadium," Holland said. "I was pitching for the New York Lincoln Giants against the Baltimore Elite Giants in 1930 when they opened Yankee Stadium to a Negro team for the first time, and I was the one to toe the mound. We had 15,000 fans that day, and I won the game, 15-4. That was a big day for me." He credited catcher Bruce Petway for helping him develop as a pitcher: "I guess Petway's the cause of me pitching as long as I did," Holland said. "They used to say my fast ball was my best pitch. I had a curveball, drop ball and change-up, but my best pitch was my fast ball. We had an older pitcher on our team [Detroit] named Bill Gatewood who knew all the tricks—spitball and emery ball—and he taught me how to throw the emery ball. You make the ball break down, break up, break in or break out. But Petway told me, 'With the stuff you've got, you don't have to fool around with those trick pitches. You just hand me the ball where I ask for it. That's all you need.' I went on from there."

Holland, William

William Holland was a pitcher, outfielder, and third baseman for the Chicago Unions, Page Fence Giants, Algona Brownies, Leland Giants, and Chicago Columbia Giants from 1894 to 1908. He also umpired in the Negro National League in 1923.

Holliday, Charles

Charles Holliday was a pitcher and outfielder for the Atlanta Black Crackers in 1938.

Hollimon, Ulysses

Ulysses Hollimon was a pitcher for the Birmingham Black Barons and Baltimore Elite Giants from 1950 to 1954.

Hollingsworth, Curtis

Curtis Hollingsworth was a pitcher for the Birmingham Black Barons from 1946 to 1950.

Holloway, Crush
b. 1896–unknown

Crush Holloway was an outfielder for the Waco Black Navigators, San Antonio Black Aces, Baltimore Black Sox, Indianapolis ABC's, Detroit Stars, Hilldale baseball club, Brooklyn Eagles, Bacharach Giants, Brooklyn Royal Giants, Baltimore Elite Giants, and New York Black Yankees from 1921 to 1939. Born in Hillsboro, Texas, Holloway was known as a fierce competitor, and former Negro Leaguer Newt Allen, in an interview by author John Holway on file at the National Baseball Hall of Fame, said that he had particular problems with Holloway's style of play, even though they were friends: "Crush Holloway was a friend of mine, a good base runner, but a nasty slider," Allen said. "He came in with his spikes up. If you're down low, he was liable to stick his spikes right in your neck somewhere." Pitcher Bill Foster echoes those remarks. "Crush Holloway was fast, but he was rough, too," Foster said. "He'd put his spikes right there, in your mouth, if you opened it. But he was always nice. He'd hurt you and jump up and say, 'Hey, I'm sorry,' I'd say, 'Get out of here, Holloway.'" In a Holway interview, Holloway did nothing to dispel those notions. "Yeah, I made them jump down there on second base," he said. "They were scared of me because I'd say, 'I'm gonna jump on you.' I wouldn't really jump on them, just trying to scare them. I didn't want to hurt anybody. But I filed my spikes, that's true. Most fast men did that. We didn't intend to hurt anybody, though. Just scare them, that's all. I wouldn't hurt anybody for anything in the world, unless it's necessary. Now you see, the only place you could score was home plate. All these other bases were just temporary. But if someone gets in your way there—at home plate—when you're trying to get there, you'd jump every way, you're trying to score! Yeah, better get out of the way. That was baseball in those days." Not surprising, Holloway said his hero was Ty Cobb—ironically, one of the most outspoken racists in the game. "Ever since I was 10 years old my hero was Ty Cobb," he said. "His picture used to come in Bull Durham tobacco. Showed the way he's slide. . . . I said, 'I want to slide like Ty Cobb. I want to run bases like him.'" Holloway said that Crush was his real name, not a nickname. "The day I was born, September 16, 1896, down in Hillsboro, Texas, my father was fixing to go see a 'crash,' a collision. They'd take two old locomotive engines and crash them together for excitement, sort of a fair, and my father was going to see it. Before he got on the train, somebody pulled him off and said, 'Your wife is about to have a child.' And when I turned out to be a boy, he named me Crush."

Holmes, Benjamin Franklin (Ben)

b. 1858

Benjamin Holmes was a third baseman for the Douglas Club of Washington, Trenton Cuban Giants, Argyle Hotel, and Cuban Giants from 1885 to 1889. In his book "History of Colored Base Ball," Negro League player, manager, and historian Sol White wrote that Holmes was good enough to play major league baseball. An article in the May 10, 1886, *Trenton Times* described Holmes, as "a fair batsman and good base runner."

Holmes, Eddie

Eddie Holmes was a pitcher for the Baltimore Black Sox in 1932.

Holmes, Frank (Sonny)

Frank Holmes was a pitcher for the Philadelphia Stars, Bacharach Giants, Washington Elite Giants, Lincoln Giants, and Washington Black Senators from 1929 to 1938.

Holmes, Leroy

Leroy Holmes was a shortstop for the Cleveland Bears, Jacksonville Red Caps, Kansas City Monarchs, Atlanta Black Crackers, New York Black Yankees, Cincinnati-Indianapolis Clowns, and Brooklyn Eagles from 1934 to 1945.

Holscroff, William

William Holscroff was an infielder for the Birmingham Black Barons in 1954.

Holsey, Robert (Frog)

Robert Holsey was a pitcher for the Chicago Columbia Giants, Chicago American Giants, Nashville Elite Giants, and Cleveland Cubs from 1928 to 1932.

Holt, Johnny

Johnny Holt was an outfielder for the Toledo Tigers and Pittsburgh Keystones from 1922 to 1923.

Holt, Joseph

Joseph Holt was an outfielder for the Brooklyn Cuban Giants in 1928.

Holtz, Eddie

Eddie Holtz was a shortstop and second baseman for the St. Louis Stars, St. Louis Giants, Lincoln Giants, and Chicago American Giants from 1919 to 1924.

Homestead Grays

The Homestead Grays were one of the legendary franchises in Negro League baseball history. The Grays were born out of a sandlot team called the Blue Ribbon Nine around 1900 by black workers at U.S. Steel in Homestead, Pennsylvania, a steel town just outside of Pittsburgh on the Monongahela River. They would later become the Murdock Grays in 1909. Two years later, Cum Posey joined the team and would later become the manager in 1918 and owner in the 1920s. From 1912 through 1928 the Grays, who played many of their games in Forbes Field in Pittsburgh, were an independent team, not affiliated with any league, and played all kinds of competition, from sandlot to barnstorming white teams. They trained in Orlando or Daytona Beach, Florida, and barnstormed their way back up the East Coast before opening day. Posey said his team had a record of 130-28 in 1925 and won 43 straight the following season, according to Mark Ribowsky's book *A Complete History of the Negro Leagues*. They were the dominant force in black baseball in Pittsburgh. In *Sandlot Seasons—Sport in Black Pittsburgh*, Rob Ruck wrote about Posey and the Grays' influence: "Posey put up with little interference off the field. . . . By the 1930s he held sway over black baseball in the area. As the Grays evolved from a Homestead club of industrial workers playing in their free time to the toast of the Pittsburgh sandlots, they became an excellent draw, the best and most popular local black team. The Grays were in great demand by white tri-state semipro and sandlot clubs, which realized that when the Grays played the fans came in droves."

In 1929, Homestead joined the American Negro League and had a record of 34-29. They went back to independent play for the next two seasons; they also played NEGRO NATIONAL LEAGUE competition and in 1931 fielded what is considered to have been the best Negro League baseball team ever when they posted a record of 136-17 in independent play. It was the second year that the great Josh Gibson was a member of the Grays and, according to some reports, hit 75 home runs that year against various levels of competitive teams. The 1931 team included other greats such as Oscar Charleston, Jud Wilson, Ted Page, George Scales, and Vic Harris. The pitching staff included Smokey Joe Williams, Willie Foster, and Ted "Double Duty" Radcliffe.

In 1932, the Grays joined the new league organized by Posey, the East-West League, and compiled a record of 29-19 before the league folded. The Grays wound up being raided by their new rivals, Gus Greenlee's Pittsburgh Crawfords, who signed away a number of Posey's players, including Josh Gibson. In Robert Peterson's book *Only the Ball Was White*, Buck Leonard recalled the way the Grays conducted some of their business: "On the Grays we had to pay our own expenses at home, and when we were on the road we were getting 60 cents a day on which to eat," Leonard said. "And we could eat two good meals in 1934 with 60 cents. Ham and eggs, toast and coffee cost you about 20 to 25 cents; dinner would cost you about 30 or 35 cents. So when we were on the road they paid our lodging in a hotel and gave us that 60 cents. Now all of us maintained a room in Pittsburgh and later in Homestead when they made us move there because we weren't behaving ourselves in Pittsburgh. I was paying $6 a week for my room in Homestead. Sometimes we would leave Homestead and be gone three weeks, and when we got back I would still owe because I had kept the room. Later on they went up to 75 cents a day for meal money, then a dollar, then they went to a dollar and a half per day, and the last year the Grays played in 1950 we were getting $2 a day on which to eat. Now there were some fellas on the Pittsburgh Crawfords who used to get $80 a month, but they got their expenses at home and on the road. But with us, I was getting $125 but I had to pay my expenses while I was at home."

Greenlee revived a new version of the Negro National League, and in 1933, Homestead joined the NNL, but dropped out before the end of the season. Two years later, the Grays were part of the NNL again, posting a record of 23-23, followed by a 22-27 mark in 1936. In 1937, the Grays began playing home games in both Pittsburgh and Washington, D.C., playing in Griffith Stadium in the District. In John Holway's book *Blackball Stars*, Negro Leaguer Buck Leonard described how they split time between the two cities: "We would play in Washington when the Senators were on the road and in Pittsburgh when the Pirates were away. We would leave Pittsburgh after midnight some Sunday morning to play a doubleheader in Washington. That was 263 miles over the Pennsylvania Turnpike. We would get in Washington, I would say around a quarter to eleven or eleven o'clock, go out, and get a sandwich, and at that time we had to be at the ballpark by 11:30. They would say, 'If you're not here at 11:30, we're not going to open the gates, unless we're sure you're here.' With the traveling we were doing, we weren't sure whether we were going to get there or not. One time I remember our bus broke down near Hagerstown, Maryland, and we had to call Washington and tell them to send three taxicabs out there to pick us up to get in Washington to start the game at two o'clock. We'd play a semipro team, say, in Rockville, Maryland, in the afternoon and a league game in Griffith Stadium that night. . . . Sometimes we'd stay in hotels that had so many bedbugs you had to put a newspaper down between the mattress and the sheets. Other times we'd rent rooms in a YMCA, or we'd go to a hotel and rent three rooms. That way you got the use of the bath, by renting three rooms. All the ballplayers would change clothes in those three rooms, go to the ball park and play a doubleheader—nine innings the first game, seven innings the second. The second game would be over about 6:15. We'd come back to the hotel and take a bath, then go down in the street and get back in the bus to go to Pittsburgh."

The travel did not seem to hurt the team's winning ways. The 1937 season began a run of nine straight Negro National League championships to 1945, with Gibson, who returned to the Grays after Greenlee's Crawfords began to collapse, Wilson, Buck Leonard, and Cool Papa Bell featured on teams during that period. The 1938 team, led by player-manager Vic Harris, was anchored by the pitching duo of Raymond Brown and Edsall Walker. Infielders Lick Carlisle and Jelly Jackson were also members of that squad, which was sometimes referred to as "The Gashouse Gang," a reference to the hard-nosed style of play of the St. Louis Cardinals in the early 1930s. In 1943, the Grays, managed by Candy Jim Taylor with a pitching staff led by Brown, Roy Partlow, and Johnny Wright, won their first Negro World Series when they defeated the NEGRO AMERICAN LEAGUE champion Birmingham Black Barons four games to three, with the games played in six different cities—Columbus, Chicago, Washington, Birmingham, Indianapolis, and Montgomery, Alabama. Other members of that squad included Sam Bankhead, Jerry Benjamin, and Howard Easterling. The 1944 club defeated Birmingham in five games, and in 1945, the Grays lost the world championship to the Cleveland Buckeyes.

The demise of the franchise began in 1946 with the death of Posey, followed by Gibson's death in 1947. Homestead would rise for one more title run in 1948, winning the last Negro National League pennant, led by Leonard, the league leader in batting, and Luke Easter, who tied Leonard for the home run title. Wilmer Fields was the ace of that pitching staff, which helped defeat Birmingham in the last Negro World Series ever played. Luis Marquez and Bob Thurman were also on that 1948 roster. Two years later the franchise folded.

Hood, Charles

Charles Hood was a catcher for the Kansas City Monarchs in 1945.

Hooker, Leniel
b. 1919

Leniel Hooker was a pitcher for the Newark Eagles and Houston Eagles from 1940 to 1949. The 6-foot-2, 170-pound Hooker also played winter baseball in Cuba and minor league baseball in the Provincial League in 1950 and 1951.

Hopkins, George

George Hopkins was a pitcher and second baseman for the Page Fence Giants, Chicago Unions, and Algona

Brownies from 1890 to 1902. In his book *History of Colored Base Ball*, Negro League player, manager, and historian Sol White wrote that Hopkins "frequently struck out 12 and 15 men in games with strong amateur and semi-professional teams of Chicago."

Horn, Herman (Doc)
Herman Horn was an outfielder for the Kansas City Monarchs from 1951 to 1954.

Horn, William
William Horn was a pitcher for the Philadelphia Giants, Leland Giants, Chicago Unions, and Algona Brownies from 1896 to 1905.

Horne, William
William Horne was a shortstop and second baseman for the Chicago American Giants, Monroe Monarchs, Cleveland Buckeyes, Cincinnati Buckeyes, and the Harrisburg–St. Louis Stars from 1938 to 1946.

Horton, Clarence (Slim)
Clarence Horton was a pitcher for the Pittsburgh Crawfords in 1930.

Hoskins, David
b. 1925, d. 1970
David Hoskins was a pitcher and outfielder for the Homestead Grays, Louisville Buckeyes, Chicago American Giants, and Cincinnati Clowns from 1942 to 1949. Records show that the 6-foot-1, 180-pound Hoskins, born in Greenwood, Mississippi, batted .355 for Homestead in 1944 and .278 in 1945. He also posted a 5-3 record on the mound for Newark in 1943 and 8-9 in 1944. He went on to play minor league baseball—the first black to play in the Texas League and the Central League, posting a 22-10 record in the Texas League in 1952, with a 2.12 ERA in 280 innings pitched. He finished third in the league in hitting with a .328 average. He went on to play two major league seasons with the Cleveland Indians, posting a 9-3 record in 1953 but just 0-1 in 1954. In Jules Tygiel's book *Jackie Robinson and His Legacy*, Hoskins said that he became a full-time pitcher in 1950 after being hit by a pitch in the head and was hospitalized in critical condition. "I was tired of having pitches thrown at me," Hoskins said. "I made up my mind I would start throwing at other guys."

Hoskins, William
William Hoskins was an outfielder for the Memphis Red Sox, Detroit Stars, New York Black Yankees, Baltimore Elite Giants, Kansas City Monarchs, St. Louis Stars, Washington Black Senators, and Chicago American Giants from 1937 to 1946.

Hotton, Jimmy
Jimmy Hotton operated a black baseball team known as Jimmy Hotton's Colored All-Stars in 1928 and 1929.

Houleward, Mike
Mike Houleward was a pitcher for the Birmingham Black Barons in 1954.

House, Charles (Red)
Charles House was a third baseman for the Detroit Stars in 1937.

Houston, Bill
Bill Houston was a pitcher for the Homestead Grays from 1941 to 1942.

Houston, Nathanial (Jess)
Nathanial Houston was a pitcher and infielder for the Cincinnati Tigers, Memphis Red Sox, and Chicago American Giants from 1930 to 1939.

Houston, William
William Houston was a shortstop and catcher for the West Baden Sprudels in 1910.

Houston Black Buffaloes
The Houston Black Buffaloes were a black baseball team out of Houston, Texas, that played in the Texas Negro League in the 1920s.

Houston Eagles
The Houston Eagles were a black baseball team out of Houston, Texas, that played in the Negro American League in 1949 and 1950.

Howard, Carl
Carl Howard was an outfielder for the Pittsburgh Crawfords and Birmingham Black Barons from 1935 to 1936.

Howard, Carranza (Schoolboy)
Carranza Howard was a pitcher for the Indianapolis Clowns, New York Cubans, and New York Black Yankees from 1940 to 1950.

Howard, Charles

Charles Howard was a pitcher, infielder, and outfielder for the Cuban Giants and Cuban X Giants from 1897 to 1899.

Howard, Elston Gene

b. 1929, d. 1980

Elston Howard was a catcher, first baseman, and outfielder for the Kansas City Monarchs from 1948 to 1950. He batted .283 for the Monarchs in 1948, .270 in 1949, and .319 in 1950. The 6-foot-2, 200-pound Howard, born in St. Louis, Missouri, played for manager Buck O'Neil in Kansas City, and in his autobiography, *I Was Right on Time*, O'Neil talked about how he pushed Howard when the scouts came looking for players: "We had Earl Taborn as our catcher at the time, but when I saw Elston hit one over the scoreboard at Municipal Stadium in his first game, I found a place for him in the outfield," O'Neil wrote. "Later, when Taborn left to try out for the majors, I put Elston behind the plate. When Tom Greenwade, the scout for the New York Yankees who signed Mickey Mantle, came through in 1950 to check out Willard Brown, I told him, 'Willard can play for your club, but the player you should be looking at is our young catcher. He can play the outfield, too, and besides, he's a fine person.' So that's how Elston Howard became the first black player for the Yankees." Howard went on to have a standout major league career for the Yankees, playing on four World Championship teams. In 14 major league seasons, 13 with the Yankees and one with the Boston Red Sox, from 1955 to 1968, Howard batted .274 with 167 home runs and 762 RBIs in 1,605 games.

Howard, Herb

Herb Howard was a pitcher and outfielder for the Kansas City Monarchs in 1948.

Howard, Herman (Red)

Herman Howard was a pitcher for the Atlanta Black Crackers, Memphis Red Sox, Washington Elite Giants, Indianapolis Athletics, Jacksonville Red Caps, Indianapolis ABC's, Little Rock Grays, Cleveland Bears, Little Rock Black Travelers, Birmingham Black Barons, and Chicago American Giants from 1932 to 1946.

Howard, Percy

Percy Howard was an outfielder and catcher for the Indianapolis Clowns and Detroit Stars in 1954 and 1955.

Howard, William

William Howard was an infielder for the Birmingham Black Barons from 1931 to 1933.

Howell, Henry

Henry Howell was a pitcher for the Bacharach Giants, Pennsylvania Giants, Brooklyn Royal Giants, and Pennsylvania Red Caps of New York from 1918 to 1921.

Hoyt, Dana

Dana Hoyt was a first baseman for the Bacharach Giants in 1932.

Hubbard, DeHart

DeHart Hubbard was an officer with the Cleveland–Cincinnati Buckeyes and Cincinnati Tigers from 1934 to 1937 and also in 1942.

Hubbard, Jesse James (Mountain)

Jesse Hubbard was a pitcher and outfielder for the Brooklyn Royal Giants, Bacharach Giants, Hilldale baseball club, Baltimore Black Sox, New York Black Yankees, and Homestead Grays from 1919 to 1934.

Hubbard, Larry

Larry Hubbard was an infielder and outfielder for the Kansas City Monarchs in 1946.

Hubbie, Butch

Butch Hubbie was a pitcher for the Birmingham Black Barons in 1951.

Huber, Hubert

Hubert Huber was a catcher and outfielder for the Birmingham Black Barons, Memphis Red Sox, and Nashville Elite Giants from 1930 to 1931.

Huber, John (Hubert)

John Huber was a pitcher and catcher for the Birmingham Black Barons, Chicago American Giants, Memphis Red Sox, Cincinnati Clowns, and Philadelphia Stars from 1939 to 1950.

Hubert, Willie (Bubber)

Willie Hubert was a pitcher for the Baltimore Elite Giants, Newark Eagles, Cincinnati Buckeyes, Baltimore Grays, Pittsburgh Crawfords, Homestead Grays, Brooklyn Brown Dodgers, Cleveland Buckeyes, Philadelphia Stars, Newark Dodgers, and New York Black Yankees from 1935 to 1946.

Hudson, Charles
Charles Hudson was a pitcher for the Louisville White Sox and Milwaukee Bears in 1923 and 1930.

Hudspeth, Robert (Highpockets)
Robert Hudspeth was a first baseman for the San Antonio Black Aces, Columbus Buckeyes, Indianapolis ABC's, Bacharach Giants, Brooklyn Royal Giants, Lincoln Giants, New York Black Yankees, and Hilldale baseball club from 1920 to 1932.

Hueston, William C.
William Hueston, a former judge in Gary, Indiana, later moved to Washington to practice law and became president of the NEGRO NATIONAL LEAGUE from 1926 to 1931.

Huff, Eddie
Eddie Huff was a catcher, outfielder, and manager for the Dayton Marcos and Bacharach Giants from 1923 to 1932.

Hughbanks, Hugh
Hugh Hughbanks was a second baseman for the Lincoln, Nebraska, Giants in 1890.

Hughes, Charlie
Charlie Hughes was a second baseman for the Columbus Blue Birds, Cleveland Red Sox, Washington Pilots, Washington Black Senators, Homestead Grays, and Pittsburgh Crawfords from 1928 to 1938.

Hughes, Frank
Frank Hughes was a pitcher for the Atlanta Black Crackers and Indianapolis Athletics in 1937.

Hughes, Lee
Lee Hughes was a pitcher for the Kansas City Monarchs in 1950.

Hughes, Robert
Robert Hughes was a pitcher for the Louisville White Sox in 1931.

Hughes, Samuel T.
b. 1910, d. 1981
Sammy Hughes was a second baseman for the Nashville Elite Giants, Louisville White Sox, Washington Elite Giants, Columbus Elite Giants, Washington Pilots, and Baltimore Elite Giants from 1930 to 1946. Records show he batted .322 in his NEGRO NATIONAL LEAGUE career, and Negro League baseball historian James A. Riley wrote that Hughes, "in addition to his picture-perfect work afield, he was also a good base runner and a solid hitter. The 6-foot-3, 190-pound Hughes was a consistent contact hitter who excelled on the hit-and-run play and was a good bunter." After World War II with the Elite Giants, Hughes became a mentor for a young second baseman named James "Junior" Gilliam. Hughes had been touted, along with Roy Campanella, as a possible choice to break the color barrier in the major leagues when the Pirates said they were considering signing a black player, but nothing came of it, and the effort was seen as less than sincere.

Hull, Horace G.
Horace Hull was president of the NEGRO AMERICAN LEAGUE when it was formed in 1937.

Humber, Tom
Tom Humber was a second baseman for the Baltimore Elite Giants and Newark Eagles in 1945 and 1950.

Humes, John
John Humes was a pitcher for the Newark Eagles in 1937.

Humphreys, Carey
Carey Humphreys was an outfielder for the Kansas City Monarchs in 1952.

Hundley, Johnny Lee
Johnny Lee Hundley was a catcher and outfielder for the Cleveland Buckeyes in 1943.

Hunt, Grover
Grover Hunt was a catcher for the Chicago American Giants in 1946.

Hunt, Leonard
b. 1929
Leonard Hunt was an outfielder for the Kansas City Monarchs from 1949 to 1953. Records show that the 5-foot-9, 170-pound Hunt batted .315 for Kansas City in 1949. He went on to play minor league baseball in the Big State League, South Atlantic League, and Northern League until 1957.

Hunter, Bertrum (Nate)
Bertrum Hunter was a pitcher for the Detroit Wolves, St. Louis Stars, Kansas City Monarchs, Pittsburgh Crawfords, Homestead Grays, and Philadelphia Stars from 1931 to 1937.

Hunter, Eugene
Eugene Hunter was a pitcher for the Memphis Red Sox and Cleveland Browns in 1924.

Hunter, Willie
Willie Hunter was a pitcher for the Akron Black Tyrites in 1933.

Husband, Vincent
Vincent Husband was a pitcher for the Chicago American Giants, Indianapolis Clowns, and New Orleans Eagles from 1951 to 1954.

Hutchinson, Fred (Hutch)
Fred Hutchinson was an infielder for the Chicago American Giants, Leland Giants, Indianapolis ABC's, Bowser's ABC's, and Bacharach Giants from 1910 to 1925.

Hutchinson, Willie
Willie Hutchinson was a pitcher for the Memphis Red Sox and Kansas City Monarchs from 1939 to 1950.

Records show that Hutchinson went 6-10 with a 3.19 ERA in 26 games with Memphis in 1944 and 8-8 with a 3.81 ERA in 18 games in 1949. He also played for Danville in the Mississippi–Ohio Valley League in 1953, posting a 4-2 mark with a 3.71 ERA.

Hyde, Cowan (Bubba)
b. 1908
Cowan Hyde was an outfielder and second baseman for the Memphis Red Sox, Cincinnati Tigers, Indianapolis Athletics, Chicago American Giants, Birmingham Black Barons, and Houston Eagles from 1927 to 1930 and again from 1937 to 1951. Born in Pontotac, Mississippi, Hyde's best recorded seasons were 1941, with a .357 average; 1942, batting .313; and 1943, when he hit .405. The 5-foot-8, 160-pound Hyde, who also played in the Mexican League, played until his 40s with minor league clubs in the early 1950s in Farnham, Rhode Island, and Winnipeg, Canada, and several other teams, retiring after the 1953 season.

Hyde, Harry
Harry Hyde was a third baseman and first baseman for the Chicago Unions and Chicago Union Giants from 1896 to 1904.

I

Illidge, Eric

Eric Illidge was the traveling secretary for the Newark Eagles in the late 1930s.

Incera, Victor

Victor Incera was an outfielder for the Kansas City Monarchs in 1955.

Indianapolis ABC's

The Indianapolis ABC's were a black baseball team based in Indianapolis, Indiana, that fielded some of the greatest teams in Negro League baseball history. They were named after the American Brewing Company and began play in the 1890s. The ABC's were bought by a white bartender named Ran Butler and they played in their early years at Northwestern Park on 17th Street in Indianapolis. They also played some of their later games at Perry Stadium, later called Bush Stadium, and at ABC's Field on Route 40. The team was purchased in 1912 by Thomas Bowser, a white bail bondsman. In 1914, Negro League managing great C. I. Taylor, came to Indianapolis from Birmingham, Alabama, where he had managed the Birmingham Giants, and moved that team briefly to West Baden, Indiana, where they were called the Sprudels. He purchased a half-interest in the ABC's and stocked the team with many of his players from the Sprudels and Giants.

The ABC's were known as a tough team, and in 1915, they were in the middle of a legendary riot in a game against a white major league All-Star team. Second baseman Bingo DeMoss tried to punch an umpire who called a white player safe on a play at second, and the powerful Oscar Charleston charged in from center field and connected with a punch that knocked the umpire down. Fans poured on the field, and nearly 20 police were called in to stop the brawling. Charleston and DeMoss were jailed and charged with assault and battery.

In 1916, the ABC's won what was referred to as the "Colored World Championship," defeating Rube Foster's Chicago American Giants in what turned out to be a bitter rivalry. That squad included such players as Charleston, who was a batboy for the ABC's and broke in as a rookie, DeMoss, Ben Taylor, and George Shively; William "Dizzy" Dismukes was the pitching ace. But there were two versions of the ABC's that year after a dispute within the club. In 1920, the ABC's were stocked with a group of players that came up from the San Antonio Black Aces. In an interview with author John Holway on file at the National Baseball Hall of Fame, Crush Holloway, a former Ace who went on to play for the ABC's, talked about the exodus north: "[Biz] Mackey and about six other guys went up to Indianapolis in 1920. Old man Bellinger . . . Charlie Bellinger, he was a rich millionaire and a politician in San Antonio. He was a friend of C. I. Taylor of the Indianapolis ABC's, and he'd look out for ballplayers for him. Mackey, [Henry] Blackman, [High Pockets] Hudspeth, [Laymon] Washington and two other players—Morris Williams and Bob McClure—went to Indianapolis that year. It broke our club all to pieces. . . . The next year C. I. sent for me to join his team and that was the greatest team I ever played on. . . . They had somebody who could do everything. Six good pitchers—[Tony] Mahoney, Louis Hampton, [Cecil] Rose, Dickie Johnson, [James] Jeffries and Wayne Carr. Mackey and Mac Eggleston were the catchers. Ben Taylor played first base, Connie Day second, Marty Clark played short and [Henry] Blackman at third. I call that the million dollar infield. I wouldn't call the outfield a million dollars, because I was on it. But it was a great outfield, too. Had some good hitters, everybody could hit that ball. I was in right, Laymon Washington in left and Oscar Charleston in center."

The ABC's joined the NEGRO NATIONAL LEAGUE in 1920. Indianapolis's best season would come in 1922, posting a 46-33 mark. The ABC's winter team was in Florida, where the Breakers Hotel team represented the ABC's in the 1920s. Taylor died after the 1922 season, and the following year the ABC's had a 45-34 record. In 1924, they pulled out of the NNL after their club was decimated by the loss of a number of players to the Eastern Colored League. They rejoined the NNL in 1925, but they were not the same team, posting a losing mark of 17-57. In 1926, Indianapolis rebounded slightly with a 43-45 record but left the NNL after that year and disbanded.

There would be several more versions of the Indianapolis ABC's in 1931 and again in 1938, but it was difficult financially. In Robert Peterson's book *Only the Ball Was White*, Negro Leaguer Jimmy Crutchfield talked about the problems he had on the club in 1931: "We weren't getting paid," Crutchfield said. "That would go on maybe for two months until we had a good gate. Then perhaps you got some of your back pay. Maybe one or two of the fellows would be getting something under the table, but most of us weren't being paid. So we were going to Pittsburgh to play, and when we got there the Crawfords gave me $25 or $50, so I stayed. That's how I went to the Pittsburgh Crawfords."

The ABC's suffered a tragedy in 1935, a by-product of the difficult travel schedules Negro League teams had to endure. Returning from a game in Evansville, Indianapolis, a car with six ABC's overturned, and first baseman Carl Lewis was killed. Some of the other players who played for the ABC's during its tenure included Raleigh "Biz" Mackey, George Dixon, and Dave Malarcher. They moved to Toledo in 1939, then back to Indianapolis in 1940 and disbanded again.

Indianapolis Athletics

The Indianapolis Athletics were a black baseball team that operated out of Indianapolis, Indiana, that played in the NEGRO AMERICAN LEAGUE in 1937 and disbanded during that same season. They played at ABC's Field on Route 40.

Indianapolis Clowns

The Indianapolis Clowns were a black baseball team that operated out of Indianapolis, Indiana, that played in the NEGRO AMERICAN LEAGUE from 1946 to 1955. They were born out of the old Ethiopian Clowns, owned and operated by promoter Syd Pollock. That team, based in Miami, Florida, made its reputation with its clown antics on the field, barnstorming around the country. Pollock, seeking stability, joined the Negro American League in 1943 and moved the team north, splitting its home games between Cincinnati and Indianapolis, and changed its identity to a more legitimate brand of baseball. However, while the clowning was cut back, it did not disappear, as the team still promoted its showmanship and gave nicknames to players, such as "King Tut." In 1946, the Clowns made Indianapolis their full-time home, playing at ABC's Field on Route 40 and went on to be a force in the Negro American League, winning the pennant in 1950 and 1951. The Clowns defeated the Birmingham Black Barons in a 12-game championship series, seven games to five, in 1952 and won another league title with a 43-22 record in 1954, with Negro League great Oscar Charleston as manager.

"The Clowns had some good ball players, but most of them were brought in from Cuba," said Negro Leaguer Othello Renfroe, in an interview with author John Holway on file at the National Baseball Hall of Fame: "Hank Aaron was their best player, I guess. When you played against them and they did the same thing every night, they still kept you in stitches laughing every night. They were a show within themselves, plus they had a good ball team. They paid the salary for the league, because any team able to barnstorm with the Clowns made money. They packed them in, small towns or large towns." Shortly after, the league disbanded and the Clowns went back to barnstorming, continuing in one version or another until the 1980s. Edward Hamman took over ownership of the franchise after Pollock, and Dave Clark was the final owner of what was left of the Clowns at the end. One of its players was a young outfielder named Hank Aaron. Other noteworthy players for the Clowns during the years included two female players, Toni Stone and Connie Morgan in 1953 and 1954, and Harlem Globetrotter star Goose Tatum. Satchel Paige pitched for the Clowns in 1967, his last year as a player.

Indianapolis Freeman

The *Indianapolis Freeman* was a black newspaper that covered black baseball in Indianapolis.

Indianapolis Recorder

The *Indianapolis Recorder* was a black newspaper that covered black baseball in Indianapolis.

Indianapolis-Toledo Crawfords

The Indianapolis-Toledo Crawfords were a black baseball team that operated out of Indianapolis, Indiana, that played in the NEGRO AMERICAN LEAGUE in 1939 and 1940. They played at ABC's Field on Route 40.

Ingram, Alfred

Alfred Ingram was a pitcher for the Jacksonville Red Caps in 1942.

International League of Independent Professional Base Ball Clubs

The International League of Independent Professional Base Ball Clubs was a league founded by E. B. Lamar in the early 1900s.

Irvin, Irwin (Bill)

Irwin Irvin was a third baseman, outfielder, and manager for the Leland Giants and Cleveland Tate Stars in 1906 and 1919.

Irvin, Monford Merrill (Monte)

b. 1919

Monford Irvin, who would go on to become a star for the New York Giants, was an outfielder, shortstop, and third baseman for the Newark Eagles from 1937 to 1948. Born in Columbus, Alabama, in 1919, Irvin first began playing pro baseball under the name "Jimmy Nelson" to protect his amateur status while playing at Lincoln University in Oxford, Pennsylvania. He had turned down a football scholarship at the University of Michigan to play with his friend, future Negro League teammate Max Manning, at Lincoln. Irvin grew up in New Jersey and was a top high school athlete, earning 16 letters and all-state honors in four sports. In 1938, he suffered a near-fatal infection from a scratch he received in a basketball game. He also played for the Orange Triangles, a semipro team. In a 1991 interview with *Sports Collectors Digest*, Irvin said that he signed with the Eagles for a chance to play with the great players on that team. "The reason I signed was because of Willie Wells, Ray Dandridge, and Leon Day.

Leon Day was the Bob Gibson of our league. Dandridge was one of the best third basemen I've ever seen."

With Newark, Irvin batted .361 and .380 in 1940 and 1941. After World War II, he returned to bat .401 in 1946, leading the Eagles to a win over the Kansas City Monarchs in the 1946 Negro League World Series, batting .462 with three home runs and scoring the winning run in the seventh game.

After World War II, Dodgers general manager Branch Rickey contacted Irvin and put some sort of claim on him for the major leagues before Jackie Robinson made his debut. But Rickey did not act on it, refusing to pay Eagles owner Effa Manley for his contract, and gave up his rights to the New York Giants for $5,000. Irvin came back in 1947 and hit 14 home runs with a .317 av-

Monte Irvin got the attention of major league baseball fans when he batted .458 in six games in the 1951 World Series for the New York Giants in their loss to the New York Yankees. Before that, Irvin was well known to Negro League baseball fans who saw him play the outfield, shortstop, and third base for the Newark Eagles from 1937 to 1948, with a break in between to serve in World War II. Irvin batted .361 and .380 in 1940 and 1941 and after returning from the war batted .401 in 1946. He led the Eagles to a win over the Kansas City Monarchs in the 1946 Negro League World Series, batting .462 with three home runs and scoring the winning run in the seventh game. (NATIONAL BASEBALL HALL OF FAME LIBRARY, COOPERSTOWN, N.Y.)

erage in 1947 for Newark. After signing with the New York Giants organization following the 1948 season, the 6-foot-1, 195-pound Irvin batted .373 with 52 RBIs in 63 games with Jersey City in the International League.

He was called up to New York in 1949 and in 1951 had a breakthrough season, batting .312 with 24 home runs and leading the National League with 121 home runs. He, along with Willie Mays and Hank Thompson, were the first all-black outfield in the major leagues. He also made an unsuccessful run in politics in 1951, seeking an assembly seat in New Jersey, trying a run as a Democrat in staunch Republican Essex County. During an exhibition game the following spring, Irvin seriously hurt his ankle while sliding into third base and was never the same. He went on to bat .293 with 99 home runs and 443 RBIs in 764 games in eight seasons, including his final year with the Chicago Cubs in 1956. Irvin batted .458 in six games in the 1951 World Series loss to the Yankees but hit just .222 in the 1954 series against the Cleveland Indians, which the Giants swept in four games. He would play four games for Los Angeles in the Pacific Coast League in 1957 before retiring. Irvin also played winter baseball in Puerto Rico and Cuba.

In an interview with author John Holway on file at the National Baseball Hall of Fame, Negro Leaguer Pee Wee Butts talked about Irvin's versatility: "Monte Irvin of Newark was an all-around athlete," Butts said. "He could play almost anything." Irvin would go on to scout for the New York Mets and work in the commissioner's office as a public relations specialist for 16 years until 1984. He was inducted into the National Baseball Hall of Fame in 1973.

Israel, Clarence (Pint)
d. 1987
Clarence Israel was a second baseman and third baseman for the Homestead Grays and Newark Eagles from 1940 to 1947.

Israel, Elbert Willis
Elbert Israel was an infielder for the Philadelphia Stars in 1950.

Ivory, Buddy
Buddy Ivory was a shortstop for the Louisville Black Colonels and Detroit Stars in 1954 and 1955.

J

Jackman, Bill (Cannonball)

b. 1898

Bill Jackman was a right-handed submarine pitcher for the Houston Buffalos, Philadelphia Giants, Lincoln Giants, Brooklyn Eagles, Quaker Giants, Newark Eagles, and Boston Royal Giants from 1925 to 1942. In a 1971 newspaper interview, Jackman, born in Carter, Texas, said that his father discouraged him from being a ballplayer. "My father was a Baptist minister and didn't want me playing ball Sundays," Jackman said. "But that was the big day. I just knew I could be some kind of ballplayer. So I left home at 17." He also talked about the demands of playing Negro League baseball. "I remember days when I played three games in the same uniform," Jackman said. "If an arm or leg hurt, you just wrapped something around it and kept playing. There was no such thing as a whirlpool. We were lucky to get showers. Whenever we found a place with hot water we were delighted. It didn't happen often."

Like so many Negro League pitchers, Jackman used his matchup against Satchel Paige as a measure of his ability. "I beat every man I pitched against at least twice," he said. "I went up against Paige twice, and we split. I had good stuff, but when I could have helped a major league team, none wanted me." New York Giants manager John McGraw wanted Jackman and in a newspaper interview lamented the color barrier that prevented him from signing the pitcher. "I never predict pennants, but I saw a young fellow the other day, and if I had him things would look so much better," McGraw said. When asked by the reporter why he wouldn't try to trade for the player, McGraw replied, "Young man, I wish I could. His name is Jackman, and he's a Negro, but if there wasn't a color line, Jackman could be a regular on any major league team in the United States. That young fellow has the speed and curve for a major league pitcher, but he'd probably be like Babe Ruth. I would probably go crazy deciding whether to use his big bat every day, or have him pitch every four days. Either way he would be a star. I have tried using Cubans, and some of them were good, too, but this Jackman is the greatest natural, all-around baseball player I ever saw."

Jackson, Andrew

Andrew Jackson was a third baseman for the Cuban Giants; New York Gorhams; Lansing, Michigan, Colored Capital All-Americans; York Cuban Giants; and Cuban X Giants from 1887 to 1899.

Jackson, Bozo

Bozo Jackson was a third baseman for the Homestead Grays and Philadelphia Stars from 1943 to 1945.

Jackson, Carlton

Carlton Jackson was an officer with the Harrisburg Giants in 1928.

Jackson, Dallas

Dallas Jackson was an infielder for the Cleveland Buckeyes in 1950.

Jackson, Daniel

Daniel Jackson was an outfielder for the Homestead Grays in 1949.

Jackson, Edgar

Edgar Jackson was a catcher for the Little Rock Grays and Memphis Red Sox from 1932 to 1937.

Jackson, Fred

Fred Jackson was an outfielder for the Birmingham Black Barons in 1955.

Jackson, George

George Jackson was an infielder for the New York Black Yankees in 1950.

Jackson, Gumbo

Gumbo Jackson was a third baseman for the New Orleans Crescent Stars in 1922.

Jackson, Guy

Guy Jackson was an infielder for the Chicago Union Giants and Chicago Giants from 1911 to 1915.

Jackson, Isaiah (Ike)

Isaiah Jackson was a catcher and outfielder for the Kansas City Monarchs from 1951 to 1953. He also played minor league baseball in the Longhorn League and Southwestern League from 1952 to 1956.

Jackson, Jack

Jack Jackson was an outfielder for the Baltimore Black Sox and Bacharach Giants from 1927 to 1928.

Jackson, Jackie

Jackie Jackson was an outfielder for the Homestead Grays in 1950.

Jackson, John W., Jr. (Stony)

John W. Jackson, Jr., was a pitcher for the Houston Eagles and Kansas City Monarchs from 1950 to 1953.

Jackson, Lefty

Lefty Jackson was a pitcher for the Brooklyn Royal Giants and Philadelphia Giants from 1926 to 1931.

Jackson, Lester E.

Lester Jackson was a pitcher for the Newark Eagles and New York Black Yankees from 1938 to 1941.

Jackson, Lincoln

Lincoln Jackson was a first baseman for the Washington Pilots, Cuban Stars, Bacharach Giants, and Baltimore Black Sox from 1933 to 1935.

Jackson, Major Robert R.

Major Robert R. Jackson was a Chicago black businessman who became partners with Frank Leland in the Chicago Unions and was named manager of the Unions in 1894. He lasted just one season and would later be team secretary. He was named commissioner of the NEGRO AMERICAN LEAGUE in 1936 and served until 1941. The following year, Jackson formed a new league called the Negro Major Baseball League of America, but it folded before the season was out.

Jackson, Matthew

Matthew Jackson was a third baseman and shortstop for the Birmingham Black Barons, Montgomery Grey Sox, Chicago American Giants, and Cincinnati Tigers from 1932 to 1936.

Jackson, Norman (Jelly)

Norman Jackson was a second baseman and shortstop for the Homestead Grays, Cleveland Red Sox, Pittsburgh Crawfords, and Washington Elite Giants from 1934 to 1945.

Jackson, Oscar

Oscar Jackson was an outfielder and first baseman for the Cuban X Giants, New York Gorhams, Cuban Giants, York Cuban Giants, and Philadelphia Giants from 1887 to 1903.

Jackson, Richard

Richard Jackson was an infielder for the Harrisburg Giants, Baltimore Black Sox, Hilldale baseball club, and Bacharach Giants from 1921 to 1931.

Jackson, Robert

Robert Jackson was a first baseman, catcher, and outfielder for the Cuban X Giants, New York Gorhams, York

Colored Giants, and Ansonia Cuban Giants from 1886 to 1896.

Jackson, Robert

Robert Jackson was a catcher for the Chicago Unions from 1897 to 1900.

Jackson, R. T.

R. T. Jackson was the owner of the Birmingham Black Barons in the 1920s and 1930s.

Jackson, Rufus (Sonnyman)
b. 1902

Rufus Jackson was a numbers racketeer in Pittsburgh who became partners in the Homestead Grays with Cum Posey in 1935 and was named team president. Jackson also served on the board of directors of the NEGRO NATIONAL LEAGUE. Jackson, born in Columbus, Georgia, was a rival in the numbers racket in Pittsburgh with Posey's main rival in black baseball, Pittsburgh Crawfords owner Gus Greenlee. Jackson, like Greenlee, also owned a nightclub in the city, the Skyrocket Cafe. In John Holway's book *Blackball Stars,* former Negro Leaguer Buck Leonard described the underworld connections of Jackson's numbers operation: "They had a 'night roll,'" Leonard said. "Jackson had a pool room, some fellow would come in there at 9 at night and roll some dice on the table and get a number, and they would pay off on that. He had two or three gambling houses—shoot crap, play poker, blackjack, all kinds of games. Every time you bet, the man would rake out so much for his cut. Then he had a beer tavern called the Skyrocket. Oh, a big place. Sold beer, wine, whiskey and everything. Had a restaurant in the back. He finally ended up with a lot of 'piccolos'—nickelodeons, jukeboxes. He had about 400 or 500 up and down the Allegheny and Monongahela rivers. That's where his money came from . . . the baseball team was covering for his undercover stuff. Baseball was just a cover-up. Both of them [Jackson and Greenlee] had a baseball team. That was to keep the law off them, see. They weren't making any money with the baseball teams. The numbers business and the rackets, that was their business."

Jackson, Sam

Sam Jackson was a catcher for the Pittsburgh Keystone in 1887.

Jackson, Sam

Sam Jackson was a catcher for the Cleveland Elites in 1926.

Jackson, Samuel

Samuel Jackson was a pitcher and first baseman for the Chicago American Giants from 1942 to 1947.

Jackson, Stanford

Stanford Jackson was an infielder and outfielder for the Chicago American Giants, Memphis Red Sox, Birmingham Black Barons, and Chicago Columbia Giants from 1923 to 1931.

Jackson, Thomas

Thomas Jackson was an Atlantic City, New Jersey, politician who, along with another Atlantic City politician, Henry Tucker, purchased the Jacksonville, Florida, Duval Giants and moved them to Atlantic City in 1916. They became the Atlantic City Bacharach Giants, named after the city's mayor, Harry Bacharach. Jackson was an officer with the Bacharach Giants from 1916 to 1928.

Jackson, Thomas Walter

Thomas Jackson was a pitcher for the Cleveland Tigers, St. Louis Stars, Nashville Elite Giants, Louisville White Sox, and Memphis Red Sox from 1924 to 1931.

Jackson, Tommy

Tommy Jackson was a pitcher for the Birmingham Black Barons, Cleveland Clippers, and Louisville Black Colonels in 1946, 1953 and 1954.

Jackson, Verdell

Verdell Jackson was a pitcher for the Memphis Red Sox in 1950.

Jackson, William

William Jackson was a catcher, outfielder, and second baseman for the Cuban X Giants, Cuban Giants, Famous Cuban Giants, Ansonia Cuban Giants, and York Cuban Giants from 1890 to 1906.

Jackson, William (Ashes)

William Jackson was a third baseman for the Kansas City Royal Giants, Kansas City Giants, and Kansas City Colored Giants from 1910 to 1917.

Jackson Cubs

The Jackson Cubs were a black baseball team based in Jackson, Mississippi, that played in the Negro Southern League in 1952.

Jacksonville Athletics

The Jacksonville Athletics were a black baseball team in Jacksonville, Florida, that played in the Southern League of Colored Baseballists in 1886.

Jacksonville Duval Giants

The Jacksonville Duval Giants were a black baseball team in Jacksonville, Florida, that was purchased and moved in 1916 to Atlantic City, New Jersey, where they became the Bacharach Giants.

Jacksonville Eagles

The Jacksonville Eagles were a black baseball team in Jacksonville, Florida, that played in the 1940s.

Jacksonville Macedonias

The Jacksonville Macedonias were a black baseball team out of Jacksonville, Florida, that played in the Southern League of Colored Baseballists in 1886.

Jacksonville Red Caps

The Jacksonville Red Caps were a black baseball team out of Jacksonville, Florida, that played in the Southern Negro League in 1920 and the NEGRO AMERICAN LEAGUE in 1938, 1941, and 1942.

Jacksonville Young Receivers

The Jacksonville Young Receivers were a black baseball team in Jacksonville, Florida, that played in the late 1890s and early 1900s.

Jamerson, Londell

Londell Jamerson was a pitcher for the Kansas City Monarchs in 1950 and 1951.

James, Gus

Gus James was a second baseman, catcher, and outfielder for the Lincoln Giants, Mohawk, New York, Giants, Smart Set, Philadelphia Giants, Louisville White Sox, Cuban X Giants, Pittsburgh Stars of Buffalo, Pop Watkins Stars, Brooklyn Royal Giants, and Bacharach Giants from 1905 to 1920.

James, Livingston

Livingston James was a shortstop for the Cincinnati Clowns, Cincinnati Buckeyes, Cleveland Buckeyes, Chicago American Giants, and Memphis Red Sox from 1936 to 1942.

Jamison, Caesar

Caesar Jamison was an umpire in the NEGRO NATIONAL LEAGUE from 1923 to 1932.

Jamison, Eddie

Eddie Jamison was a catcher for the Cleveland Buckeyes in 1950.

Jarmon, Don

Don Jarmon was a pitcher for the Columbus Blue Birds in 1933.

Jefferson, Edward

Edward Jefferson was a pitcher for the Philadelphia Stars from 1942 to 1947.

Jefferson, George

George Jefferson was a pitcher for the Cleveland Buckeyes, Jacksonville Red Caps, and Louisville Buckeyes from 1942 to 1950. He was a key member of the 1945 Buckeyes Negro League World Series championship team.

Jefferson, Ralph

Ralph Jefferson was an outfielder for the Bacharach Giants, Indianapolis ABC's, Washington Potomacs, Philadelphia Royal Stars, Peter's Chicago Union Giants, and Philadelphia Giants from 1918 to 1932.

Jefferson, Willie

Willie Jefferson was a pitcher for the Memphis Red Sox, Cincinnati Tigers, Cleveland Buckeyes, and Cincinnati Buckeyes from 1937 to 1950.

Jeffreys, Frank

Frank Jeffreys was an outfielder and second baseman for the Chicago Giants from 1917 to 1920.

Jeffries, Harry

Harry Jeffries was a catcher, shortstop, third baseman, first baseman, and manager for the Chicago American Giants, Chicago Giants, Cleveland Tigers, Detroit Stars, Bacharach Giants, Chicago Columbia Giants, Knoxville

Giants, Toledo Tigers, Baltimore Black Sox, Baltimore Panthers, Harrisburg Giants, Cleveland Browns, Newark Dodgers, Cleveland Tate Stars, Brooklyn Royal Giants, and Washington Potomacs from 1920 to 1948.

Jeffries, James

James Jeffries was a pitcher for the Baltimore Black Sox, Indianapolis ABC's, Harrisburg Giants, Birmingham Black Barons, and Chicago American Giants from 1913 to 1931.

Jeffries, Jeff

Jeff Jeffries was a pitcher for the Homestead Grays and Brooklyn Royal Giants in 1940.

Jenkins, Clarence

Clarence Jenkins was a catcher for the Detroit Stars and Philadelphia Giants from 1925 to 1929.

Jenkins, Clarence R. (Fats)

b. 1903, d. 1968

Clarence Jenkins was an outfielder and manager for the Harrisburg Giants, Lincoln Giants, Baltimore Black Sox, Bacharach Giants, Philadelphia Stars, New York Black Yankees, Brooklyn Royal Giants, Brooklyn Eagles, Toledo Crawfords, Pittsburgh Crawfords, and Penn Red Caps of New York from 1920 to 1940. The 5-foot-9, 165-pound Jenkins was also a great professional basketball player, a captain and star guard with the Renaissance team, and a member of the Basketball Hall of Fame. Statistics show that Jenkins batted .319 in 1924 and .307 in 1925 for Harrisburg, .358 for the Bacharach Giants in 1929, and .305 in 1935 for Brooklyn, also stealing nine bases that year.

Jenkins, George

George Jenkins was a pitcher for the Detroit Stars in 1955.

Jenkins, Horace

Horace Jenkins was an outfielder and pitcher for the Chicago Giants, Chicago Union Giants, and Chicago American Giants from 1911 to 1925.

Jenkins, James (Pee Wee)

James Jenkins was a pitcher for the New York Cubans, Cincinnati-Indianapolis Clowns, Birmingham Black Barons, and Indianapolis Clowns from 1944 to 1954.

Clarence "Fats" Jenkins and Bill Yancey shared the same uniform as teammates on the New York Black Yankees, where Jenkins played the outfield and Yancey played shortstop. They shared something else as well, as they were both members of the Renaissance Five basketball team in the 1930s, and were inducted as part of that team into the National Basketball Hall of Fame in 1963. (NATIONAL BASEBALL HALL OF FAME LIBRARY, COOPERSTOWN, N.Y.)

Jenkins, Jimmy

Jimmy Jenkins was an outfielder for the Detroit Stars in 1954.

Jennings, Thurman (Jack)

Thurman Jennings was a shortstop, second baseman, and outfielder for the Chicago Giants from 1914 to 1927.

Jessup, Charles

b. 1915, d. 1998

Charles Jessup was a pitcher for the Chicago Union Giants in 1911.

Jessup, Gentry

Gentry Jessup was a pitcher for the Birmingham Black Barons and Chicago American Giants from 1940 to 1949.

Jethroe, Sam (Jet)

b. 1922, d. 2001

Sam Jethroe was an outfielder for the Indianapolis Clowns, Cincinnati Buckeyes, and Cleveland Buckeyes from 1942 to 1948. He played in four EAST-WEST ALL-STAR GAMES, batted a league-leading .393 in 1946, and compiled a career Negro League average of .340. He was a member of the 1945 Buckeyes club that won the Negro League World Series. Born in East St. Louis, Illinois, Jethroe was one of the early black players who followed Jackie Robinson into major league baseball. He had received a tryout with the Boston Red Sox in 1945, along with Robinson and Marvin Williams, but it was not a serious opportunity. In 1948, Jethroe was sold by the Buckeyes to the Brooklyn Dodgers for $5,000, and two years later Dodgers general manager Branch Rickey sold Jethroe's contract to the Boston Braves for $100,000. With four black players already on the Dodgers, some speculated that Rickey sold Jethroe's contract to the Braves rather than promote him to Brooklyn, for fear of having too many black players on the major league team. With Boston, Jethroe was National League Rookie of the Year in 1950 when he batted .273 with 18 home runs, a league-leading 35 stolen bases, and 100 runs scored. The following season Jethroe batted .280, with 18 home runs, 35 stolen bases, again leading the league, and 101 runs scored. But in 1952, his numbers dropped to a .232 batting average, 13 home runs, 28 stolen bases, and 79 runs scored as Jethroe developed some problems with his eyesight. He spent the 1953 season with Toledo in the International League and hit 28 home runs, drove in 74 runs, had a .309 average, 113 runs scored, and 27 stolen bases but would play just two more major league games in his career, in 1954 with the Pittsburgh Pirates at the age of 32. He finished his baseball career after five seasons with the Toronto Maple Leafs in the International League, putting up solid numbers but never getting another chance at major league baseball, finally retiring after the 1958 season. In *Jackie Robinson and His Legacy*, by Jules Tygiel, Jethroe talked about the early struggles of black players in the major leagues, even after Jackie Robinson broke the color barrier in 1947: "Jackie may have broken the barrier to playing," Jethroe said. "But I knew when I arrived there was more required for me to do than a white player. It still was a hard thing to go through." When the Braves purchased Jethroe's contract, they followed up by drafting a player named Luis Angel Marquez in the next minor league draft, reportedly to have a black teammate for Jethroe to room with on the road.

Jimenez, Bienvenido (Hooks)

Bienvenido Jimenez was a second baseman for several versions of the Cuban Stars, the Havana Cubans, and Cincinnati Cubans from 1915 to 1929.

Jimenez, Eugenio

Eugenio Jimenez was an outfielder for the Cuban Stars, Philadelphia Giants, and Cincinnati Cubans from 1920 to 1921.

Johnson, Al

Al Johnson was a pitcher for the Washington Black Senators and Baltimore Elite Giants from 1938 to 1940.

Johnson, Allen

Allen Johnson was an officer with the St. Louis Stars, Harrisburg–St. Louis Stars, New York Black Yankees, Indianapolis ABC's, and Boston Blues from 1938 to 1946.

Johnson, Ben

Ben Johnson was a pitcher for the Bacharach Giants from 1916 to 1923.

Johnson, Bill

Bill Johnson was a third baseman for the Akron Tyrites and Cleveland Red Sox in 1933.

Johnson, Byron (Mex)

Byron Johnson was a shortstop for the Kansas City Monarchs from 1937 to 1940.

Johnson, Cecil

Cecil Johnson was a first baseman, third baseman, pitcher, and shortstop for the Philadelphia Tigers, the Hilldale baseball club, Baltimore Black Sox, Philadelphia Royal Stars, Norfolk Stars, Newark Stars, Cuban X Giants, Bacharach Giants, and Newark Browns from 1916 to 1931.

Johnson, Charles

Charles Johnson was a third baseman for the Memphis Red Sox and Cleveland Buckeyes from 1949 to 1950.

Johnson, Charles B.

Charles B. Johnson was an officer with the Bacharach Giants from 1925 to 1926.

Johnson, Charlie

Charlie Johnson was a pitcher for the Indianapolis Clowns in 1952.

Johnson, Claude

Claude Johnson was an infielder for the Pittsburgh Crawfords from 1928 to 1931.

Johnson, Claude (Hooks)

Claude Johnson was a shortstop, second baseman, third baseman, and pitcher for the Harrisburg Giants, Baltimore Black Sox, Birmingham Black Barons, Detroit Stars, Cleveland Tate Stars, Memphis Red Sox, Brooklyn Royal Giants, Nashville Elite Giants, Hilldale baseball club from 1919 to 1932.

Johnson, Clifford (Connie)

b. 1922

Clifford Johnson was a pitcher for the Indianapolis Crawfords and Kansas City Monarchs from 1940 to 1950. The 6-foot-4, 200-pound Johnson, born in Stone Mountain, Georgia, was a member of the Monarchs team that defeated the Homestead Grays in 1942 to win the Negro World Series and posted a 3-0 record that season. He left the Monarchs after 1942 for military service and then came back to Kansas City in 1946. Johnson went on to pitch for the Monarchs until 1950, putting together an 11-2 mark that year before moving on to minor league baseball in Colorado Springs and Charleston. He finally saw major league action in 1953 with the White Sox, appearing in 14 games, with a record of 4-4 with a 3.54 ERA. He was sent down to Toronto in the International League in 1954 where he went 17-8 with a 3.72 ERA in 34 games. He returned to Chicago in 1995 and went 7-4 but found himself back down in Toronto the same year, and continued to pitch well, posting a 12-2 mark with a 3.05 ERA. He was back with the White Sox in 1956 but this time was traded to the Baltimore Orioles and finished the season with a 9-11 record. Johnson went 20-20 for the Orioles in the next two seasons but returned to the minor leagues in 1959 with Vancouver in the Pacific Coast League, finishing the season with an 8-4 record and a 3.16 ERA. He pitched just one game for Vancouver in 1960 and finished his professional career with Marianao in the Mexican League in 1961, posting a 12-11 mark with a 3.30 ERA in 31 games.

Johnson, Curtis

Curtis Johnson was a pitcher for the Kansas City Monarchs in 1950.

Johnson, Dan

Dan Johnson was a pitcher who played for the Brooklyn Royal Giants, Bacharach Giants, Hilldale baseball club, Lincoln Giants, and Indianapolis ABC's from 1916 to 1925.

Johnson, Don

Don Johnson was a third baseman and second baseman for the Birmingham Black Barons, Baltimore Elite Giants, and Chicago American Giants from 1948 to 1953.

Johnson, Donald

Donald Johnson was a pitcher for the Birmingham Black Barons in 1953.

Johnson, Dud

Dud Johnson was a shortstop, outfielder, and second baseman for the Brooklyn Royal Giants and Philadelphia Giants from 1914 to 1919.

Johnson, Ernest (Schoolboy)

b. 1931

Ernest Johnson was an outfielder and pitcher for the Kansas City Monarchs from 1949 to 1953. The 6-foot-3, 165-pound Johnson batted .296 and .288 in his final two seasons with the Monarchs and went on to play minor league baseball in the Provincial League, Pioneer League, South Atlantic League, and Western League until retiring after the 1959 season.

Johnson, Frank

Frank Johnson was an outfielder and manager for the Memphis Red Sox and Monroe Monarchs from 1932 to 1937.

Johnson, Furman

Furman Johnson was a pitcher for the Indianapolis Clowns in 1954.

Johnson, George (Chappie)

George Johnson was a catcher, first baseman, and manager for the Chicago Union Giants, Columbia Giants, Leland Giants, Brooklyn Royal Giants, St. Louis Giants, Chicago Giants, Dayton Chappies, Philadelphia Royal Stars, Algona Brownies, Norfolk Stars, Page Fence Giants, Philadelphia Giants, Mohawk Giants, Louisville White Sox, Pennsylvania Red Caps of New York, Cuban X Giants, Quaker Giants, and Chappie Johnson's Stars from 1896 to 1939. In *History of Colored Base Ball*, former Negro League player and historian Sol White listed Johnson among the black players who he believed could play in the major leagues.

Johnson, George Washington (Dibo)

b. 1888

George Johnson was a pitcher and outfielder for the Kansas City Giants, Fort Worth Wonders, Hilldale baseball club, Brooklyn Royal Giants, Philadelphia Tigers, Lincoln Giants, and Bacharach Giants from 1909 to 1931. Born in San Marcos, Texas, Johnson suffered a

In his book *History of Colored Base Ball,* former Negro League player and historian Sol White listed George Johnson among the black players who he believed could play in the major leagues. He would never get that chance, though, as his time came and went long before Jackie Robinson broke the color line in 1947. Johnson was a catcher, first baseman, and manager from 1896 to 1939 for a number of teams, including several that used his name to promote them, such as Chappie Johnson's All-Stars. (NATIONAL BASEBALL HALL OF FAME LIBRARY, COOPERSTOWN, N.Y.)

broken leg late in his career. Until then, Johnson was considered one of the premier outfielders in Negro League baseball, and batted as high as .390 in 1923, records show.

Johnson, Grant (Home Run)
b. 1874

Grant Johnson was a second baseman, shortstop, and manager for the Columbia Giants, Leland Giants, Page Fence Giants (that he helped organize), Cuban X Giants, Brooklyn Royal Giants, Lincoln Giants, Philadelphia Giants, Pittsburgh Colored Stars, Lincoln Stars, Chicago Unions, Brooklyn Colored Giants, Mohawks Giants, Buffalo Giants, and Chicago Giants from 1894 to 1922. Johnson, born in Findlay, Ohio, was considered one of the greatest

hitters of the dead ball era, and while playing winter ball in Cuba in 1910, he reportedly outhit Ty Cobb. In *History of Colored Base Ball,* former Negro League player and historian Sol White listed Johnson among the black players who he believed could play in the major leagues.

In White's book, Johnson also wrote an article titled "The Art and Science of Hitting": "There are a number of requisites that a player should possess to be a first-class hitter, but in my opinion, two of the greatest and most essential ones are confidence and fearlessness. If, because of the reputation of the pitcher opposing you, your confidence in your ability to hit him is lacking, or you fear being hit by his wonderful speed or have the least fear in your heart at all, your success at such a time is indeed doubtful. If you possess both of these essentials, then it is an easy matter for the earnest student of hitting to acquire the science and judgement. Most young players make the natural mistake of trying to become home-run hitters and hit the ball with all the force at their command at all times with a full swing of the bat. This is a serious mistake and a great detriment to good batting. In swinging the bat with all your might, you in a measure, lose sight of the ball and also change the course you intended the bat to go, and even if only a fraction of an inch, it will not meet the ball fairly, which results as a rule, in a comparatively easy chance for the opposing fielders. At a critical period of the game the experienced pitcher would far prefer pitching to the mighty swinger to the cool, steady batter who tries to meet the ball and place it to the best advantage. My advice to young players is secure a bat which you can handle perfectly, catch well upon it and in taking your position at the plate, be sure and stand firmly and face the pitcher, thinking you are going to hit without the least atom of fear about you. Seldom strike at the first ball pitched, as in letting it pass you get a line on the speed or curve of the pitcher. As he delivers one to your liking, try to meet it fairly, and when successful you will be surprised, and gratified, at the distance of the hit, with only ordinary force behind the swing. To improve the eye, I find bunting to be very effective, and should be practiced before each game as a player who can both hit and bunt is a very valuable man to any team." Johnson batted near .400 up to the final years of his career, and he played until he was 58 years old with the Buffalo Giants.

Johnson, Hamp
Hamp Johnson was an outfielder for the Birmingham Black Barons in 1933, 1934, and 1946.

Johnson, Harry
Harry Johnson was a second baseman, outfielder, and catcher for the Cuban Giants and Trenton Cuban Giants

from 1886 to 1889. According to a May 10, 1886, article in the *Trenton Times*, Johnson, born in Burlington, New Jersey, in 1860, was a good fielder: "[Johnson] first came before the public as a ball player in 1883, signing with the Post Office club, then with the Department League of Washington, D.C. He is a second Dunlap, covering more ground than ever was seen by any colored second baseman on the road, fair batsman, good base runner and expert thrower."

Johnson, Jack

Jack Johnson was a third baseman for the Toledo Crawfords, Cincinnati Buckeyes, and Homestead Grays from 1938 to 1940.

Johnson, Jack

Jack Johnson, the former heavyweight champion of the world, reportedly played first base for the Philadelphia Giants in 1903 and 1904 and used Rube Foster's Chicago American Giants as a cover to flee the country in 1913 to avoid prosecution on charges the fighter violated the Mann Act.

Johnson, Jack (Topeka Jack)

Jack Johnson was a first baseman and outfielder for the Topeka Giants, which he formed, the Kansas City Royal Giants, Philadelphia Giants, and Kansas City Giants from 1903 to 1904 and from 1909 to 1910. He changed his name to Jack Johnson after the heavyweight champion of the world, as Topeka Jack was also a fighter as well as a baseball player and manager. Topeka Jack Johnson fought the real Jack Johnson in an exhibition while the former heavyweight champion was in prison in Chicago.

In an interview with historian Robert Peterson, Arthur Hardy, one of the Topeka Giants' players, described their barnstorming tours: "We always liked to get into town at least by the middle of the morning for advertising purposes," he said. "As a rule, when we went into a town, we would placard it and uniform up and go out and practice so the people could get it noised around that we were in town. Sometimes they set up a parade. Both teams paraded. That was in Smith Center and Blue Rapids and Frankfort, Kansas. That was the regular program. They had very good bands. Most of those little towns had a municipal band, you know—the band concert once a week was a big event then—and they would lead the parade and we'd march out to the baseball park. In those little towns, we would average $15, $20 a man for a game. The admission charge was 50 cents or 75 cents, kids a quarter . . . and expenses were at minimum. In those days you could get a good meal for 25 cents and you could get lodging for 50 cents. We did some clowning on the field. But it was done like this: as you know, some people might resent what they might consider you making fun of them. . . . Johnson always insisted that we didn't want to humiliate anybody. . . . After all, we were pros and the other teams were fellows who were playing once a weekend . . . and so Topeka Jack would always talk to the local people. He'd say, 'Now what about you folks here? Do you want us to put on some funny kind of acts? Or do you think they would resent it.'"

Johnson, James

James Johnson was a catcher and outfielder for the Page Fence Giants in 1898.

Johnson, James

James Johnson was a pitcher for the Kansas City Monarchs, Philadelphia Stars, and Birmingham Black Barons from 1950 to 1953.

Johnson, Jim

Jim Johnson was a shortstop for the Newark Dodgers, Hilldale baseball club, and Bacharach Giants from 1932 to 1934.

Johnson, Jimmy (Jeep)

Jimmy Johnson was a shortstop for the Homestead Grays and Pittsburgh Crawfords in 1946 and 1947.

Johnson, Jimmy (Slim)

Jimmy Johnson was a pitcher for the Indianapolis Crawfords, Toledo Crawfords, Newark Eagles, New York Black Yankees, and Philadelphia Stars from 1938 to 1943.

Johnson, Joe

Joe Johnson was a pitcher and catcher for the Baltimore Atlantics from 1884 to 1885.

Johnson, John B.

John Johnson was the president and manager of the Brooklyn Cuban Giants from 1925 to 1928.

Johnson, Rev. John H.

The Rev. John H. Johnson was president of the NEGRO NATIONAL LEAGUE from 1947 to 1948.

Johnson, Johnny

Johnny Johnson was a pitcher for the Homestead Grays, Birmingham Black Barons, Baltimore Elite Giants, New

York Black Yankees, New York Cubans, and Cleveland Buckeyes from 1939 to 1946.

Johnson, John Wesley (Smokey)

John Johnson was a pitcher for the Cleveland Elites, Cleveland Tate Stars, Cleveland Browns, Cleveland Tigers, Chicago American Giants, and Lincoln Giants from 1922 to 1930.

Johnson, Joseph

Joseph Johnson was an officer with the Indianapolis Athletics in 1937.

Johnson, Joshua (Brute)

Joshua Johnson was a catcher, pitcher, and outfielder for the New York Black Yankees, Homestead Grays, Cincinnati Tigers, and Brooklyn Royal Giants from 1934 to 1942.

Johnson, Leaman

Leaman Johnson was an infielder for the Newark Eagles, Memphis Red Sox, New York Black Yankees, and Birmingham Black Barons from 1941 to 1946.

Johnson, Lee

Lee Johnson was a catcher for the Birmingham Black Barons in 1941.

Johnson, Lefty

Lefty Johnson was a pitcher, outfielder, and first baseman for the Memphis Red Sox from 1929 to 1933.

Johnson, Leonard

Leonard Johnson was a pitcher for the Chicago American Giants and Kansas City Monarchs from 1947 to 1948.

Johnson, Leroy

Leroy Johnson was a pitcher for the Birmingham Black Barons from 1950 to 1951.

Johnson, Lou (Sweet Lou)

b. 1934

Lou Johnson was an outfielder for the Kansas City Monarchs in 1955. Johnson, born in Lexington, Kentucky, went on to play major league baseball for the Chicago Cubs, Los Angeles Dodgers, Milwaukee Braves, and California Angels from 1960 to 1969. The 5-foot-11, 170-pound Johnson played 677 games, with a .258 average, 48 home runs, 232 RBIs, and 529 hits. In 11 World Series games for the Dodgers in 1965 and 1966, Johnson batted .286 with two home runs and four RBIs.

Johnson, Louis

Louis Johnson was a pitcher, manager, and coach for the Chicago American Giants, Twin City Gophers, Detroit Stars, Indianapolis ABC's, Pittsburgh Keystones, Toledo Tigers, Bowser's ABC's, Milwaukee Bears, and Louisville White Sox from 1911 to 1925.

Johnson, Mamie (Peanut)

Mamie Johnson was one of three women who played for the Indianapolis Clowns in 1954, signed by owner Syd Pollock, the other women being Toni Stone and Connie Johnson. The Clowns were a team known for gimmicks and showmanship, and much of Negro League baseball had been decimated by integration into the major leagues by 1954. Johnson, a pitcher, had been reportedly studying engineering and medicine at New York University before signing to play with the Clowns. In a newspaper interview, Johnson said she got some pitching tips from Satchel Paige: "He showed me how to grip the ball to keep from throwing my arm away because I was so little," she said. Paige also taught her a curveball, and after she learned that, Johnson said, "I was damn good."

Johnson, Monk

Monk Johnson was a pitcher, first baseman, second baseman, and outfielder for the Lincoln Giants, Pennsylvania Red Caps of New York, Brooklyn All-Stars, and Indianapolis ABC's from 1914 to 1926.

Johnson, Nate

Nate Johnson was a pitcher who played for the Brooklyn Royal Giants, Harrisburg Giants, Cleveland Browns, and Bacharach Giants from 1922 to 1924.

Johnson, Oscar (Heavy)

Oscar Johnson was an outfielder, catcher, and second baseman for the Baltimore Black Sox, Kansas City Monarchs, Cleveland Tigers, Harrisburg Giants, Dayton Marcos, and Memphis Red Sox from 1922 to 1933. Johnson was also part of the 25th Infantry team with the U.S. Army in 1915, along with fellow Negro Leaguers Joe Rogan, Lemuel Hawkins, Andy Cooper, and Dobie Moore, a team known as The Wreckers. In an interview with author James Holway on file at the National Baseball Hall of Fame, Negro Leaguer Bill Drake told one unusual story about Johnson's power: "I remember one time he was sleeping on the bench, and they woke him up to go in and pinch hit," Drake said. "So he reached down and got a fungo bat and went out there and hit a home run." Records show that Johnson batted .323 in 1926 and .399 the following season.

Johnson, Oziah

Oziah Johnson was an outfielder for the Boston Blues in 1946.

Johnson, Pearley (Tubby)

d. 1992

Pearley Johnson was a pitcher, infielder, and outfielder for the Brooklyn Royal Giants and Baltimore Black Sox from 1920 to 1927 and again in 1942.

Johnson, Ralph

Ralph Johnson was a pitcher for the Philadelphia Stars in 1940, 1941, and 1945.

Johnson, Ralph

Ralph Johnson was a shortstop for the Kansas City Monarchs and Indianapolis Stars from 1950 to 1952.

Johnson, Ray

Ray Johnson was an outfielder for the St. Louis Stars in 1923.

Johnson, Richard

Richard Johnson was a black catcher and outfielder who played in the white Ohio State League for Zanesville in late 1880s, batting .296 in 1887. He also played for Springfield and Peoria in the Central Interstate League.

Johnson, Robert

Robert Johnson was an infielder and outfielder for the Philadelphia Tigers, Brooklyn Cuban Giants, Washington Pilots, and Brooklyn Royal Giants from 1928 to 1937.

Johnson, Robert

Robert Johnson was an outfielder for the New York Black Yankees from 1939 to 1940.

Johnson, Robert

Robert Johnson was a pitcher for the Kansas City Monarchs in 1944.

Johnson, Roy

Roy Johnson was a first baseman and second baseman for the Kansas City Monarchs and St. Louis Giants from 1920 to 1922.

Johnson, Rudy

Rudy Johnson was an outfielder for the Cleveland Buckeyes in 1950.

Johnson, Sampson

Sampson Johnson was a catcher for the Pittsburgh Giants, Bacharach Giants, Homestead Grays, Pennsylvania Giants, and Philadelphia Giants from 1913 to 1922.

Johnson, Thomas

Thomas Johnson was a pitcher for the Chicago American Giants, Indianapolis ABC's, Mohawk Giants, and Pittsburgh Keystones. He was also an umpire in the NEGRO NATIONAL LEAGUE from 1914 to 1925.

Johnson, Tom

Tom Johnson was a pitcher for the Chicago American Giants and St. Louis Stars from 1937 to 1942.

Johnson, Tommy

Tommy Johnson was a pitcher for the Indianapolis Clowns in 1950.

Johnson, William H. (Big C)

d. 1988

William Johnson was a catcher, outfielder, and manager for the Hilldale baseball club, Homestead Grays, Pennsylvania Red Caps of New York, Philadelphia Tigers, Harrisburg Giants, Wilmington Potomacs, Dayton Marcos, and Washington Potomacs from 1920 to 1934.

Johnson, William Julius (Judy)

b. 1899, d. 1989

William Johnson was a third baseman, shortstop, and manager for the Madison Stars, Homestead Grays, Hilldale baseball club, and Pittsburgh Crawfords from 1918 to 1938. Born in Snow Hill, Maryland, the 5-foot-11, 155-pound Johnson would go on to become one of the all-time third basemen in Negro League baseball history. He gained his nickname "Judy" while playing for the Madison Stars, given to him by teammate Robert "Judy" Gans, who looked like Johnson. After his first year with Hilldale was disappointing—a .227 batting average—

Johnson broke out and became a top hitter. He batted .391 in 1923, leading Hilldale to an Eastern Colored League pennant, and followed that up with a .324 average, with Hilldale playing Kansas City in the Negro League World Series where Johnson led all batters with a .364 average, with eight RBIs. He also developed into a top-notch fielder at third base, learning how to play the corner from veteran Bill "Brodie" Francis. In August 1926, Johnson was hit by a pitch, and it took its toll on him, as his average fell to .268 in 1927 and .224 the following year. But Johnson came back in 1929, batting .390. In 1935, Johnson became the captain of the legendary Crawfords team, with Satchel Paige, Josh Gibson, and Cool Papa Bell, that would post a 35-15 record and go on to defeat the New York Cubans in a postseason series for the NEGRO NATIONAL LEAGUE championship.

He also played for and managed the rival Homestead Grays—he was Josh Gibson's first manager in 1930—and, in Robert Peterson's book *Only the Ball Was White*, Johnson described life on the road with the Grays: "The Grays traveled all season long. Every day you were going, you'd go and ride over those hills. Every two hours you had to average 100 miles. With nine men in the car! That's what we averaged. The cops all knew us; we had 'Homestead Grays' on the side and they'd call, 'Hey, Homestead Grays!' and we'd be going like a bat out of hell. We never got stopped once until we got in the South. We were treated pretty rough down there at times."

Johnson also played winter baseball in Cuba and batted .331 there, as well as playing in the Florida winter hotel league. Johnson coached a semipro basketball team in Delaware to a state championship in 1937 and would later do scouting for the Philadelphia Athletics, Philadelphia Phillies, and Milwaukee Braves. He tried to get Connie Mack to sign another Negro League third baseman who followed Johnson, the great Ray Dandridge, and he was also credited with signing Richie Allen for the Phillies and Bill Bruton, who would later become Johnson's son-in-law, for the Braves.

In an interview conducted by author John Holway on file at the National Baseball Hall of Fame, Negro Leaguer Newt Allen said Johnson was a "great ballplayer, and he was a gentleman. He was a gentleman all through those baseball years when baseball was just as rough as it

William "Judy" Johnson was considered to be among the greatest third basemen in the history of Negro League baseball, and he was honored for his place in that history by being inducted into the National Baseball Hall of Fame in Cooperstown in 1975. Nicknamed "Judy" by teammate Robert "Judy" Gans, who looked like Johnson, Judy Johnson was a perennial .300-plus hitter and batted .391 in 1923, leading the Hilldale baseball club to an Eastern Colored League pennant. Johnson played for the Madison Stars, Homestead Grays, Hilldale baseball club, and Pittsburgh Crawfords from 1918 to 1938.   (NATIONAL BASEBALL HALL OF FAME LIBRARY, COOPERSTOWN, N.Y.)

could be. He was the type of fellow that didn't try to hurt anyone. He just went along and played the game. You have to respect a man like that. And in all those years he was never hurt, because the ballplayers respected him as a ballplayer. Never argued with you about anything."

Another Holway interview, this one with Ted Page published in Holway's book *Blackball Stars*, described Johnson's intelligence on the field and how he was an unselfish, contact hitter who used a 40-ounce bat and would do anything to get on base: "Judy Johnson was the smartest third baseman I ever came across," Page said. "A scientific ballplayer, did everything with grace and poise. Played a heady game of baseball, none of this just slugging the ball, a man on first base, and he just dies there because you didn't hit the ball up against the wall. Judy would steal your signals. He should have been in the major leagues 15 or 20 years as a coach. They talk about Negro managers. I always thought that Judy should have made a perfect major league manager."

In another Holway interview, this one with Johnson, the Negro League great talked about his introduction to baseball as a young boy: "My dad liked sports," Johnson said. "He was an athletic director of the Negro Settlement House [in Wilmington, Delaware]. Our backyard had everything you'd find in a gym. I could do a lot of things you see in a circus now. My daddy wanted me to be a prize fighter. My sister was my sparring partner. She boxed me all over the place. She said, 'Defend yourself?' How am I gonna defend myself against a girl? Where could I hit her? I wanted to play baseball. It was my first love. I lived on the West Side on Delmar Place right in back of the park they dedicated to me, Judy Johnson Park. I could come right out of my backyard and into the park. That's where I started playing baseball. Mostly it was a pasture. A gentleman lived a few blocks away, had cows and horses that grazed there. We would clean it off. When we came home from school, we'd play ball there, and we'd play until dark." Johnson was inducted into the National Baseball Hall of Fame in 1975.

Johnson, Willie

Willie Johnson was a catcher for the Philadelphia Stars in 1945.

Johnson, Willie

Willie Johnson was a pitcher for the Chicago American Giants in 1952.

Johnson, Willie

Willie Johnson was a catcher for the New York Black Yankees and Chicago American Giants from 1938 to 1939.

Johnston, Bert (Bucky)

Bert Johnston was an outfielder for the Baltimore Black Sox, Newark Dodgers, Washington Pilots, Birmingham Black Barons, and Newark Eagles from 1932 to 1938.

Johnston, Tom

Tom Johnston was an umpire in the NEGRO NATIONAL LEAGUE in 1923.

Johnston, Wade

Wade Johnston was an outfielder and pitcher for the Kansas City Monarchs, Cleveland Tate Stars, Baltimore Black Sox, Pennsylvania Red Caps of New York, and Detroit Stars from 1920 to 1933.

Jones, Aaron

Aaron Jones was a pitcher for the Detroit Stars in 1954 and 1955.

Jones, Abe

Abe Jones was a catcher and manager for the Chicago Unions from 1887 to 1894.

Jones, Albert

Albert Jones was a pitcher for the Memphis Red Sox and Chicago American Giants from 1944 to 1946.

Jones, Alvin

Alvin Jones was an officer with the Harrisburg Giants in 1928.

Jones, Archie

Archie Jones was a pitcher for the Philadelphia Stars and New York Cubans from 1939 to 1941.

Jones, Arthur

Arthur Jones was a pitcher for the Birmingham Black Barons in 1925 and 1934.

Jones, Bailey

Bailey Jones was a catcher for the New Orleans Eagles in 1951.

Jones, Ben

Ben Jones was a shortstop for the New York Black Yankees in 1950.

Jones, Benny

Benny Jones was a catcher, infielder, and outfielder for the Cleveland Red Sox, Newark Dodgers, Brooklyn Eagles, Pittsburgh Crawfords, and Hilldale baseball club from 1932 to 1935.

Jones, Bert

Bert Jones was a pitcher and outfielder for the Chicago Unions and Algona Brownies from 1896 to 1903.

Jones, Charles

Charles Jones was a third baseman for the Cleveland Buckeyes in 1950.

Jones, Clinton (Casey)

Clinton Jones was a catcher for the Memphis Red Sox from 1940 to 1955.

Jones, Country

Country Jones was a catcher and second baseman for the Brooklyn Royal Giants from 1932 to 1933.

Jones, Curtis

Curtis Jones was a pitcher for the Cleveland Buckeyes in 1946.

Jones, Edward (Yump)

Edward Jones was a catcher for the Chicago Giants, Chicago American Giants, Bowser's ABC's, Chicago Union Giants, and Bacharach Giants from 1915 to 1929.

Jones, Ernest

Ernest Jones was a first baseman for the Cleveland Bears, Jacksonville Red Caps, Boston Royal Giants, and Philadelphia Stars from 1934 to 1942.

Jones, Eugene

Eugene Jones was a pitcher for the Homestead Grays and Baltimore Elite Giants in 1943.

Jones, Fate

Fate Jones was an outfielder for the Birmingham Black Barons in 1950.

Jones, Hank

Hank Jones was an outfielder for the Kansas City Monarchs in 1955.

Jones, Hurley

Hurley Jones was a pitcher for the Birmingham Black Barons in 1931.

Jones, James

James Jones was an outfielder and first baseman for the Philadelphia Stars from 1949 to 1952.

Jones, John

John Jones was a pitcher for the New Orleans Eagles in 1951.

Jones, John (Nippy)

John Jones was an outfielder and first baseman for the Indianapolis ABC's, Detroit Stars, Washington Pilots, Bacharach Giants, Baltimore Black Sox, and Homestead Grays from 1922 to 1934.

Jones, Lee

Lee Jones was an outfielder for the Brooklyn Colored Giants, Dallas Giants, and Brooklyn Royal Giants from 1908 to 1922.

Jones, Marvin

Marvin Jones was a pitcher for the Kansas City Monarchs in 1954 and 1955.

Jones, Ollie

Ollie Jones was a third baseman for the St. Louis Giants in 1919.

Jones, Paul
b. 1929

Paul Jones was a pitcher for the Cleveland Buckeyes and Louisville Buckeyes in 1949 and 1950 and for the Memphis Red Sox in 1958. The 6-foot-3, 220-pound Jones also played minor league baseball in the Central League and Western International League.

Jones, Reuben

Reuben Jones was an outfielder and manager for the San Antonio Black Indians, Mineola Black Spiders, Birmingham Black Barons, Dallas Giants, Chicago American Giants, Indianapolis ABC's, Memphis Red Sox, Little Rock Black Travelers, Cleveland Red Sox, and Houston Eagles from 1918 to 1949.

Jones, Robert

Robert Jones was an outfielder for the Memphis Red Sox from 1933 to 1934.

Jones, Samuel (Toothpick Sam)

b. 1925, d. 1971

Sam Jones was a pitcher for the Cleveland Buckeyes and Homestead Grays from 1946 to 1948. Jones, born in Stewartsville, Ohio, posted a 4-2 record for Cleveland in 1947 and 9-8 in 1948. The 6-foot-4, 190-pound Jones played major league baseball for 12 seasons, from 1951 to 1964, for the Cleveland Indians, Chicago Cubs, St. Louis Cardinals, San Francisco Giants, Detroit Tigers, and Baltimore Orioles, with a career record of 102-101 and a 3.59 ERA. He played minor league baseball with Columbus in the International League until 1967 before retiring. Jones also played winter baseball in Puerto Rico, Venezuela, and Nicaragua.

Jones, Stuart (Slim)

b. 1914, d. 1939

Stuart Jones was a tall, thin fastball pitcher for the Philadelphia Stars and Baltimore Black Sox from 1932 to 1938. Sometimes called "the left-handed Satchel Paige," Jones was the starting pitcher for the East team in the 1935 East-West Negro League All-Star team. Jones had won 25 games with Philadelphia in 1934. However, Jones's career ended prematurely because of alcoholism. In his book, *I Was Right on Time*, Negro Leaguer Buck O'Neil wrote that Jones may have turned out to be the best pitcher in Negro League history, if his career wasn't cut short by alcoholism. "Slim Jones may have turned out to be the best, but for a bad drinking habit that destroyed him," O'Neil wrote. "Slim, who looked a lot like Satchel and pitched like him, too, beat Satchel three times in 1936. But his drinking got so bad that, by 1938, he couldn't pitch anymore." He died the following year, freezing to death on the streets of Philadelphia.

Jones, Tom

Tom Jones was a catcher for the Philadelphia Stars in 1946.

Jones, William (Fox)

William Jones was a pitcher and catcher for the Chicago Giants, Chicago American Giants, Hilldale baseball club, Chicago Union Giants, and Bacharach Giants from 1915 to 1930.

Jones, Willis

Willis Jones was a shortstop and outfielder for the Leland Giants, Chicago Unions, Algona Brownies, and Gilkerson's Union Giants from 1895 to 1911. In Robert Peterson's book *Only the Ball Was White*, Carter Wilson, a teammate of Jones on the Union Giants, talked about Jones's clowning antics on the field: "Sometimes he might go out to his position in the outfield with a newspaper and cut a little hole through and pretend he was reading it," Wilson said. "And if a ball was hit to him and the game was lopsided in our favor, he wouldn't run after the ball. The centerfielder would have to go and get it."

Jordan, Henry

Henry Jordan was an outfielder and catcher for the Baltimore Black Sox, Pittsburgh Stars of Buffalo, and Harrisburg Giants from 1921 to 1925.

Jordan, Larnie

Larnie Jordan was a shortstop for the New York Black Yankees, Philadelphia Stars, Bacharach Giants, and Brooklyn Royal Giants from 1936 to 1942.

Jordan, Maynard

Maynard Jordan was an outfielder for the Houston Eagles in 1950.

Jordan, Robert

Robert Jordan was a first baseman and catcher for the Cuban Giants, Cuban X Giants, Brooklyn Royal Giants, and Philadelphia Giants from 1896 to 1907.

Jordan, William F.

William Jordan was the manager of the Baltimore Giants in 1899.

Joseph, Walter Lee (Newt)

Walter Joseph was a second baseman, third baseman, and manager for the Birmingham Black Barons, Kansas City Monarchs, and Satchel Paige's All-Stars from 1922 to 1939. In an interview conducted by author John Holway on file at the National Baseball Hall of Fame, teammate Newt Allen said Joseph was a smart player: "He was a great signal catcher. He'd watch everybody on the other ball club—the bench, the pitchers down in the bullpen, the coaches, the managers—and in three innings, if there was any kind of signs, he had one or two of them." Joseph was also part of the 25th Infantry team with the U.S. Army in 1915, along with fellow Negro Leaguers Joe Rogan, Lemuel Hawkins, Andy Cooper, and Dobie Moore, a team known as The Wreckers. Joseph also owned a taxi business in Kansas City known as Newt Joseph's Monarch Cab Company. In his book *I Was Right on Time*, Negro Leaguer Buck O'Neil said Joseph was one of his mentors: "When I got to know him, he was running a very successful cab stand downtown. I would hang around that cab stand for hours, talking baseball with Newt. In his day, he was a great sign-stealer, and he taught me some of his tricks. He also gave me scouting reports on all the players and pitchers in the league, what to look for from certain pitchers, where to play certain hitters, which catchers I could steal on. What he taught me not only helped me as a new player in the league but also as a manager later on."

Josephs, William

William Josephs was a shortstop for the Cleveland Browns, Indianapolis ABC's, and Birmingham Black Barons in 1924 and 1925.

Joyner, William

William Joyner was a shortstop for the Chicago Union Giants and Chicago Unions from 1893 to 1902. He had a reputation as a player who did a lot of clowning on the field.

Juncos, Jose

Jose Juncos was a pitcher for the Cuban Stars, Cuban Stars East, and Cuban Stars of Havana from 1912 to 1922.

Jupiter, Al

Al Jupiter was the manager of the Boston Monarchs in 1893.

Juran, Eli

Eli Juran was a pitcher for the Newark Stars and Birmingham Black Barons from 1923 to 1926.

Juran, Johnny

Johnny Juran was a pitcher for the Birmingham Black Barons in 1923.

Justice, Charley

Charley Justice was a pitcher for the Detroit Stars and Akron Tyrites in 1933 and 1937.

Kaiser, Cecil
Cecil Kaiser was a pitcher for the Homestead Grays and Pittsburgh Crawfords from 1945 to 1949.

Kansas City Call
The *Kansas City Call* was a black newspaper in Kansas City, Montana, that covered the Kansas City Monarchs and other black baseball teams.

Kansas City Giants
The Kansas City Giants were a black baseball team that played in the early 1900s in Kansas City, Kansas. According to Robert Peterson's book *Only the Ball Was White*, the Giants were originally a team made up of doctors around the early 1900s that was formed to create a rivalry with the Kansas City Monarchs in Missouri—the original Kansas City Monarchs, a team primarily consisting of former college athletes. But the Giants, owned by Tobe Smith, couldn't defeat the Monarchs, so they brought in the Topeka Giants, run by Topeka Jack Johnson, and transformed them into the Kansas City Giants.

Kansas City House of David
The Kansas City House of David was one of the versions in the early 1930s teams born out of the barnstorming Jewish House of David baseball club, featuring players with long beards and named after the religious colony in Harbor, Michigan, originating in 1903.

Kansas City Monarchs
The Kansas City Monarchs were one of the legendary Negro League clubs, emerging in the 1920s as a force in black baseball. Owned by white businessman J. L. Wilkinson (later joined by co-owner Tom Baird in 1929), the Monarchs, who played at Muelebach Field and Municipal Stadium in Kansas City, won a total of 10 Negro League pennants, which tied them with the Homestead Grays for the most among Negro League teams. The Monarchs were originally a black team in the early 1900s consisting of former college athletes and professionals, such as doctors, who played recreationally. But the version of the Monarchs that became the well-known legendary black baseball team was the one that began as the ALL NATIONS team from Des Moines, Iowa, in 1912 and moved to Kansas City in 1915. They established a legacy of baseball excellence and began to win over Kansas City baseball fans when, in 1921, they challenged the white Kansas City Blues of the American Association to a series and split two games. The following year, the Blues, who were the American Association champions, played the Monarchs again, this time in a longer series, and the Monarchs won five out of six games. The Monarchs were declared "the new city

champions" by the *Kansas City Star*. "There can be little doubt that the best team won," the *Star* proclaimed. "The series speaks for itself, baseball men who saw the set of six games declare. The Monarchs outplayed the Blues in five of the sextet of exhibitions and are so entitled to their full share of tribute and glory."

The Monarchs were considered the class team of Negro League baseball, the black version of the New York Yankees, a team seen as the standard for excellence and professionalism. The *Kansas City Call* wrote that the Monarchs "have done more than any other single agent in Kansas City to break down the damnable outrage of prejudice that exists in this city." The Monarchs won three straight NEGRO NATIONAL LEAGUE championships from 1923, when they went 57-33, to 1925, when they posted a 62-23 mark. In 1924, the Monarchs, who had a record of 55-22 that year, defeated the Eastern Colored League champion Hilldale baseball club five games to four, with one tie, in what was recognized as the first Negro League World Series. The following season the Monarchs defeated the St. Louis Stars in a seven-game playoff series to win the league title but lost to Hilldale five games to one in the series. Those Monarch teams, managed by Jose Mendez, included such great Negro League players as pitcher Bullet Joe Rogan and infielders Newt Allen and Dobie Moore. In 1926, they posted a record of 57-21, winning the Negro National League first-half title, but lost to the Chicago American Giants, the second-half champions, in the championship game. In 1929, with Joe Rogan managing the team, Kansas City won another Negro National League pennant with a record of 62-17, led by a strong pitching staff that included Andy and Army Cooper and Chet Brewer. In 1930, the Monarchs became the first team to play under the lights, using a portable light system.

In an interview by author John Holway on file at the National Baseball Hall of Fame, Newt Allen talked about the parks the Monarchs played in and how popular the team was: "They used the park of the old Western League white club at 20th and Olive. . . . In right field they had a 25-foot to 30-foot screen up there, like you have in Boston," Allen said. "But in left field the bleachers went all around from the railroad tracks clear around to 21st Street, from left field to center field. At that time, the capacity was around 25,000. It was single deck, all-wood, nothing was concrete. We used to draw 14,000 to 15,000 people during those times, 18,000 to 19,000 on a Sunday, and ladies night, my goodness, we'd have lots of people."

In 1931, the Monarchs left the Negro National League and began extensive barnstorming tours, with an occasional return to league play, until 1937. Kansas City joined the new NEGRO AMERICAN LEAGUE in 1937 and won five out of six league titles, with Newt Allen as

manager and the great Satchel Paige (joining the club in 1940) on the mound, drawing record crowds. Also during this time there was an offshoot of the Monarchs team, a barnstorming unit called the Little Monarchs, also sometimes called the Traveling Monarchs, the Travelers, and later, the Satchel Paige All-Stars.

In 1942, Kansas City defeated the Homestead Grays in the Negro League World Series, the first such series since 1927. That 1942 squad, managed by Frank Duncan, included such Negro League great players as first baseman Buck O'Neil, outfielder Ted Strong, infielders Jesse Williams and Willie Sims, and a pitching staff consisting of Paige, Lefty LaMarque, Connie Johnson, and Hilton Smith. In 1945, Kansas City did not make the playoffs for the third straight season but came from a losing season the year before (23-42) to put together a winning record of 32-30, led by a group of returning war veterans that included a former UCLA baseball star named Jackie Robinson, who played one season with the Monarchs before joining the Brooklyn Dodgers organization in 1946.

The Monarchs won the 1946 Negro American League pennant, with O'Neil leading the league in batting and joined in the lineup by Williard Brown and Hank Thompson. Paige, Johnson, and Hilton Smith anchored the pitching staff. Kansas City lost in seven games to the Newark Eagles that year in the Negro League World Series, as Paige and Strong left the team five games into the series. In 1948, the Monarchs won the Negro American League second-half championship but lost to the Birmingham Black Barons in the playoffs. The Monarchs won the first-half title the following year, but there was no playoff against the second-half champion. In 1950, Kansas City won both the first and second-half titles in the Negro American League western division, with a record of 51-20. The franchise remained intact in various barnstorming forms, under new owner Ted Rasberry, a Kansas City businessman, until finally folding in the 1960s.

Over the years, some of the other players who were on the Monarchs roster included Cool Papa Bell, Elwood "Bingo" DeMoss, Cristobal Torrienti, John Donaldson, William "Dizzy" Dismukes, Willie Foster, Ted "Double Duty" Radcliffe, Ernie Banks, and Elston Howard.

Kansas City Pullman Colts

The Kansas City Pullman Colts were a black baseball team that played in Kansas City, Montana, in the early 1900s.

Keane, John

John Keane was an outfielder for the Chicago American Giants in 1952.

Keenan, James J.

James J. Keenan was co-owner and business manager of the New York Lincoln Giants from 1919 to 1930 and secretary-treasurer of the Eastern Colored League. Negro League player, manager, and historian Sol White, in a 1927 article in the *Pittsburgh Courier*, listed Keenan among the greatest figures in modern Negro League baseball. In a 1930 article in the *Amsterdam News*, White wrote that the Lincoln Giants, under Keenan's stewardship, had the highest-paid black baseball players in the country.

Keeton, Eugene

Gene Keeton was a pitcher for the Cleveland Tate Stars, Dayton Marcos, and Indianapolis ABC's from 1921 to 1926.

Kelley, Palmer

Palmer Kelley was a pitcher for the Chicago Giants and Chicago Union Giants from 1916 to 1918.

Kelley, Richard A.

Richard Kelley was an infielder for Danville in the Illinois-Indiana league and Jamestown in the Pennsylvania–New York League from 1889 to 1891.

Kellman, Edric
b. 1927

Edric Kellman was a third baseman for the Louisville Buckeyes, Cleveland Buckeyes, Indianapolis Clowns, and Memphis Red Sox from 1946 to 1953. The 5-foot-11, 170-pound Kellman, born in Panama, batted .297 in his first year with Cleveland in 1946, followed by a .306 average the following season, .307 in 1948, .254 with Louisville in 1949, and his career year—a .329 average—in 1950 with Memphis. Kellman played winter baseball in Panama and also went on to play in the Mexican League until 1958.

Kelly, Walter

Walter Kelly was a pitcher for the Memphis Red Sox, Cleveland Buckeyes, and Birmingham Black Barons from 1950 to 1953.

Kelly, William

William Kelly was a third baseman for the Celeron, New York, Acme Colored Giants in 1898.

Kelly, William

William Kelly was a catcher for the New York Black Yankees and Homestead Grays from 1944 to 1947.

Kemp, Ed (Ducky)

Ed Kemp was an outfielder for the Norfolk Stars, Norfolk Giants, Philadelphia Royal Giants, Lincoln Giants, and Baltimore Black Sox from 1914 to 1928.

Kemp, George

George Kemp was an outfielder for the Hilldale baseball club in 1917.

Kemp, James (Gabby)

James Kemp was a second baseman for the Jacksonville Red Caps, Atlanta Black Crackers, and Indianapolis ABC's from 1937 and 1939. Kemp also later umpired Negro League baseball games.

Kemp, John

John Kemp was an outfielder for the Birmingham Black Barons and Memphis Red Sox from 1923 to 1928.

Kendricks, L. H.

L. H. Kendricks was a pitcher for the Atlanta Black Crackers in 1943.

Kennard, Dan

Dan Kennard was a catcher for the Chicago American Giants, Atlanta Black Crackers, Lincoln Giants, St. Louis Giants, Detroit Stars, St. Louis Stars, West Baden Sprudels, and Bowser's ABCs from 1914 to 1925.

Kennedy, Ernest D.

Ernest Kennedy was an infielder for the Memphis Red Sox in 1950.

Kennedy, James

James Kennedy was a first baseman for the Birmingham Black Barons in 1951.

Kennedy, John
b. 1930, d. 1998

John Kennedy was a third baseman and shortstop for the Birmingham Black Barons in 1954 and 1955, batting .273 in 1954. Born in Sumter, South Carolina, the 5-foot-10, 175-pound Kennedy went on to play for the Philadelphia Phillies organization—the first black ballplayer in a Phillies uniform—appearing in five major league games in 1957, scoring one run with no hits. He continued playing minor league baseball with Des

Moines in the Three I League and Asheville and Jacksonville in the South Atlantic League until 1961.

Kennedy, Ned

Ned Kennedy was a pitcher for the Kansas City Monarchs in 1954.

Kennedy, Robert

Robert Kennedy was a pitcher for the Boston Blues in 1946.

Kennedy, Walter

Walter Kennedy was an outfielder for the Chicago American Giants in 1950.

Kent, Richard

Richard Kent was a numbers racketeer who owned the St. Louis Stars from 1922 to 1931.

Kenyon, Harry C.

Harry C. Kenyon was a pitcher, second baseman, outfielder, and manager for the Hilldale baseball club, Brooklyn Royal Giants, Chicago American Giants, Indianapolis ABC's, Detroit Stars, Lincoln Giants, Memphis Red Sox, and Kansas City Monarchs from 1919 to 1929.

Key, Ludie

Ludie Key was president of the Birmingham Black Barons in 1934.

Keyes, Garvin

Garvin Keyes was an infielder for the Philadelphia Stars in 1943.

Keyes, Robert

Robert Keyes was a pitcher for the Memphis Red Sox and Cleveland Buckeyes from 1941 to 1946.

Keyes, Steve (Zeke)

Steve Keyes was a pitcher for the Philadelphia Stars, Memphis Red Sox, Cincinnati Clowns, Indianapolis Crawfords, and Cleveland Buckeyes from 1940 to 1948.

Keys, Dr. George B.

Dr. George B. Keys was an officer for the St. Louis Stars from 1922 to 1932 and also an officer in the NEGRO NATIONAL LEAGUE.

Keystone Athletics

The Keystone Athletics were a black baseball team in Philadelphia that was first organized in May 1885 by F. P. Thompson and moved two months later to Babylon, New York.

Kimbro, Arthur (Jess)

Jess Kimbro was a second baseman and third baseman for the St. Louis Giants, Bowser's ABCs, Louisville White Sox, Lincoln Giants, Hilldale baseball club, and West Baden Sprudels from 1914 to 1918.

Kimbro, Henry (Kimmie)

b. 1912, d. 1999

Henry Kimbro was an outfielder and manager for the Baltimore Elite Giants, Washington Elite Giants, Birmingham Black Barons, New York Black Yankees, and Philadelphia Stars from 1937 to 1953. Born in Nashville, Tennessee, Kimbro was among the most talented hitters of his time in Negro League baseball, a six-time All Star who batted .350 in 1946 and 1947 and also won the Cuban Winter League batting title in 1947 with a .346 average. He was considered a problem player, though, and Ted "Double Duty" Radcliffe said that Kimbro was "the wildest man I ever saw in baseball and absolutely the hardest to manage." In a 1999 interview with *Sports Collectors Digest*, former Negro Leaguer Nap Gulley talked about Kimbro's power at the plate: "He wasn't known as a home run hitter, but if you happened to get the ball in the wrong place, you could forget about it because he'd hit the ball out of the ballpark." Kimbro said he once hit a ball out of Briggs Stadium in Detroit, but the credit in the newspaper the next day had been given to another player. In a 1997 interview with *Sports Collectors Digest*, Kimbro said he was a fast base runner: "I was real fast on my feet. I don't know how many bases I stole, but I sure could run. I was real fast, and had a strong arm and a good eye at the plate. "Kimbro also said he had problems getting along with people because he felt intimidated by his lack of education. "That had its effect on me," Kimbro said. "I couldn't say the things that I wanted to say because I didn't go to school. It just tore me to pieces. So I didn't talk too much. I think that's where this 'evilness' came from."

Kimbro, Howard

Howard Kimbro was a pitcher for the Pittsburgh Crawfords from 1928 to 1932 and again in 1945.

Kimbrough, Jim

Jim Kimbrough was a pitcher for the Philadelphia Stars and Homestead Grays from 1945 to 1948.

Henry "Kimmie" Kimbro was one of those players with talent and trouble. An outfielder and manager for the Baltimore Elite Giants, Washington Elite Giants, Birmingham Black Barons, New York Black Yankees, and Philadelphia Stars from 1937 to 1953, Kimbro was a six-time All Star who batted over .350 in 1946 and 1947, but, according to Ted "Double Duty" Radcliffe, Kimbro was "the wildest man I ever saw in baseball and absolutely the hardest to manage." (NATIONAL BASEBALL HALL OF FAME LIBRARY, COOPERSTOWN, N.Y.)

Kimbrough, Larry

Larry Kimbrough was a pitcher for the Philadelphia Stars from 1942 to 1946.

Kinard, Roosevelt

Roosevelt Kinard was a third baseman for the Washington Pilots in 1932.

Kincannon, Harry

Harry Kincannon was a pitcher for the Pittsburgh Crawfords, Philadelphia Stars, Washington Black Senators, New York Black Yankees, and Toledo Crawfords from 1929 to 1939.

Kindle, William

William Kindle was a shortstop, second baseman, and outfielder for the Indianapolis ABC's, Brooklyn Royal Giants, Chicago American Giants, Lincoln Giants, Lincoln Stars, New York Stars, Cuban Giants, and West Baden Sprudels from 1910 to 1920.

King, Baby

Baby King was an umpire in the NEGRO NATIONAL LEAGUE in 1928.

King, Brendan

Brendan King was a pitcher for the Cincinnati Clowns in 1943.

King, Clarence

Clarence King was an outfielder for the Birmingham Black Barons from 1947 to 1954.

King, Ezell

Ezell King was a first baseman for the Detroit Stars in 1955.

King, Lee

Lee King was an officer for the Birmingham Black Barons in 1923.

King, Leonard

Leonard King was an outfielder for the Kansas City Monarchs in 1921.

King, Paris

Paris King was a catcher for the Memphis Red Sox in 1955.

King, Wilbur (Dolly)

Wilbur King was a shortstop and second baseman for the Cleveland Buckeyes, Memphis Red Sox, Homestead

Grays, Chicago American Giants, and New York Black Yankees from 1944 to 1947.

King, William

William King was a shortstop for the Chicago Unions from 1890 to 1892.

Klepp, Eddie

Eddie Klepp was a pitcher for the Cleveland Buckeyes in 1946. Klepp was a novelty in Negro League baseball—a white ballplayer—and, ironically, he ran into the same racism that black players did but in a perverse way. When Cleveland went on barnstorming tours through the South, Klepp could not eat or sleep with his teammates because of the separate accommodations that existed in the South. In one incident in Birmingham, city officials wouldn't let Klepp take the field with his team.

Knight, Dave (Mule)

Dave Knight was a first baseman, outfielder, and pitcher for the Baltimore Black Sox and Chicago American Giants from 1921 to 1922 and also in 1930.

Knox, Elwood C.

Elwood Knox was a reporter for the *Indianapolis Freeman*, a black newspaper in Indianapolis, Indiana, that wrote about Negro League baseball. He was one of several reporters who attended the meeting Rube Foster called in February 1920 in Kansas City to form the NEGRO NATIONAL LEAGUE.

Knoxville Grays/Smokies

The Knoxville Grays/Smokies were a black baseball team that played in Knoxville, Tennessee, in 1945 in the Negro Southern League.

Kuebler Park

Kuebler Park was a baseball field in St. Louis that served as the home field for the St. Louis Giants in the early 1930s.

Lackey, Obie

Obie Lackey was a shortstop, second baseman, and third baseman for the Hilldale baseball club, Philadelphia Giants, Pittsburgh Crawfords, Bacharach Giants, Baltimore Black Sox, Homestead Grays, Brooklyn Royal Giants, Philadelphia Stars, New York Black Yankees, and Santop's Broncos from 1927 to 1943.

Lacy, Raymond

Raymond Lacy was an outfielder for the Houston Eagles from 1949 to 1950.

Lacy, Sam
b. 1904

Sam Lacy was a sportswriter and editor for the Afro-American newspapers in Baltimore and Washington. Lacy was very instrumental in keeping the pressure on major league baseball to integrate. Lacy first began working for the *Washington Tribune* in 1937 and later wrote for the *Chicago Defender* before taking the position where he would make his mark as one of the legends of sportswriting in the 20th century at the Afro-American newspapers. Lacy tried to get Washington Senators owner Clark Griffith to give a tryout to black players in 1937 but was unsuccessful. "He told me the time wasn't right," Lacy said in a newspaper interview. "He tried to tell me that if a Negro came in, there will be constant confrontations

and that it would break up the Negro Leagues and cost 400 jobs. I told him when Abraham Lincoln signed the Emancipation Proclamation, he put 400,000 of my people out of jobs, and life went on."

Lacy didn't give up, though. He was the driving force behind the major leagues' creation of an advisory panel known as the Major League Baseball Committee on Baseball Integration in 1945. One of those committee members was Brooklyn Dodgers general manager Branch Rickey, who was already planning his own integration of the game by signing a young black player on the Kansas City Monarchs named Jackie Robinson. In 1945, Lacy wrote what turned out to be the blueprint for Rickey to follow in selecting a candidate to be the first black player: "With us, the first man to break down the bars must be suited in every sense of the word," Lacy wrote. "We can't afford to have any misfits pioneering for us, and for obvious reasons. Unwilling as they are to employ Negro players, they will be quick to draw the old cry: 'We gave 'em a chance and look what we got.'"

Although a champion of the cause of black players' entry into major league baseball, Lacy was not a cheerleader for Negro League baseball, as was the perception of some black sportswriters. His reporting was considered fair and objective. Lacy was also instrumental in reporting the treatment that Robinson received in the South during spring training for the Dodgers, when many of the white mainstream newspapers failed to report incidents such as cities refusing to allow games to take place if Robinson was on the field. He also suffered the same indignities and was barred from some press boxes. In New Orleans, he had to sit on the roof of a press box to cover a game. Reportedly, a halfdozen white writers joined him there. Lacy was elected to the National Baseball Hall of Fame in 1998.

Laduna, Phil

Phil Laduna was a pitcher for the Indianapolis Clowns from 1954 to 1955.

Laflora, Louis

Louis Laflora was an outfielder for the Kansas City Monarchs in 1925.

Lain, William

William Lain was a third baseman and shortstop for the Chicago American Giants and Chicago Giants in 1911.

Lamar, Clarence

Clarence Lamar was a shortstop and second baseman for the Cleveland Bears, St. Louis Stars, Indianapolis ABC's, Jacksonville Red Caps, and Birmingham Black Barons from 1937 to 1942.

Lamar, E. B., Jr.

E. B. Lamar, Jr., was a white businessman who was manager and club officer for the Cuban Stars, Cuban X Giants, Harrisburg Giants, Brooklyn Cuban Giants, and Cuban Stars from 1895 to 1926. He founded the Cuban X Giants, using primarily American blacks from Philadelphia under the promotion of a Cuban team, first in 1895, using a variation of the already existing Cuban Giants names. His Cuban X Giants defeated the Cuban Giants in a three-game series in New Jersey in 1897 in what was referred to as the unofficial "colored" championship. Lamar's X Giants later played Frank Leland's Chicago Unions in a 14-game series in Chicago in 1898, and Lamar's X Giants won nine of the 14 games. Some of the great players that were on Lamar's teams included Charlie Grant, Home Run Johnson, and a big pitcher who would eventually change Negro League baseball—Rube Foster, who led the X Giants to a championship in a seven-game series against the Philadelphia Giants, as Foster won four of the five games the X Giants won. Lamar also started the International League of Independent Professional Base Ball Clubs in 1906, but the league failed and was gone after one season.

LaMarque, James Harding (Lefty)
b. 1920, d. 2000

James LaMarque was a left-handed pitcher for the Kansas City Monarchs from 1942 to 1951. Born in Potosi, Montana, LaMarque was a two-time All-Star pitcher in the Negro EAST-WEST GAME, and in 1946 helped the Monarchs win the NEGRO AMERICAN LEAGUE pennant. His best years were 1947, when LaMarque had a record of 12-2 with a 3.79 ERA; 1948, when he posted a 15-5 record and led the league with a 1.96 ERA; and 1949, when he went 13-7 with a 3.08 ERA. In 1951, pitching for Mexico City in the Mexican League, LaMarque had a 19-6 record. He also spent the winter of 1946–47 pitching in Havana. In a July 1999 interview with *Sports Collectors Digest*, LaMarque talked about his missed opportunity to play major league baseball: "I used to belong to the Monarchs, which was owned by a man named [J. L.] Wilkinson at first and his partner was named Tom Baird. I had talked to the chief scout of the Yankees at that time. His name was Tom Greenwade. After Tom Baird found out that they might want me, he hiked the price on me, so Greenwade told me, 'At your age, I can't pay this kind of money.' So I didn't go with him.'" About his pitching, LaMarque said, "I won most of my games. I learned to have real good control. I guess my top speed was maybe 80 or 85 miles per hour. As I was in baseball, I was learning more how to pitch, but my fastball always moved. I couldn't throw a straight fastball, it just moved. I guess just the movement on the ball kept the hitters from hitting it as well as they could if it came straight at them. I think I was a pretty fair pitcher. Well, most people said I was. I hit fairly good as a pitcher. My lifetime average was .333."

Landers, John

John Landers was a pitcher for the Indianapolis ABC's in 1917.

Landers, Robert Henry
b. 1931, d. 1998

Robert Landers was a pitcher for the Kansas City Monarchs from 1949 to 1952.

Landis, Kenesaw Mountain

Kenesaw Landis, commissioner of baseball from 1921 to 1944, was an ardent opponent of baseball integration, refusing to allow it to ever be considered or discussed among baseball owners and discouraging tryouts that had been attempted. Landis went so far as to refuse to allow major league teams to play exhibition games against Negro League teams, an off-season practice that had been common before Landis, a former federal judge selected to give baseball credibility after the 1919 "Black Sox" scandal, took office.

Lane, Alto (Big Train)

Alto Lane was a pitcher for the Indianapolis ABC's, Memphis Red Sox, Louisville White Sox, Cincinnati Tigers, Louisville Black Caps, and Kansas City Monarchs from 1929 to 1934.

Lane, Isaac

Isaac Lane was a pitcher, third baseman, and outfielder for the Dayton Marcos, Dayton Giants, Detroit Stars, and Columbus Buckeyes from 1917 to 1924.

Lang, John

John Lang was a white businessman who was manager of the Argyle Hotel and Cuban Giants from 1885 to 1886.

Langrum, E. L.

Dr. E. L. Langrum was an officer with the Cleveland Red Sox in 1934.

Lanier, A. S.

A. S. Lanier was an officer for the Cuban Stars in 1921.

Lansing, Wilbur

Wilbur Lansing was a pitcher for the Houston Eagles and Newark Eagles in 1948 and 1949.

Lantiqua, Enrique

Enrique Lantiqua was a catcher for the New York Cubans in 1935. Lantiqua was also considered one of the greatest catchers in the history of baseball in the Dominican Republic.

Lanuza, Pedro

Pedro Lanuza was a catcher for the Cuban Stars and House of David Cubans from 1931 to 1932.

Larrinago, Perez

Perez Larrinago was a shortstop and second baseman for the Cleveland Buckeyes in 1946.

Lattimore, Alphonso

Alphonso Lattimore was a catcher for the Brooklyn Royal Giants, Baltimore Black Sox, and Columbus Blue Birds from 1929 to 1933.

Laurent, Milfred
b. 1903, d. 1996

Milfred Laurent was an infielder, outfielder, pitcher, and catcher for the Cleveland Cubs, Memphis Red Sox, New Orleans Crescent Stars, Nashville Elite Giants, and Birmingham Black Barons from 1922 to 1935. In a December 1995 interview with *Sports Collectors Digest*, Laurent talked about his versatility: "Every team I played with, I played well," he said. "I played well. I could do it all . . . everything, pitch, catch, play the outfield or the infield. . . . I guess I was a jack of all trades, boss of none. . . . I was a fair hitter. I knew how to bunt, which is something these players now have no idea how to do."

Lawson, L. B. (Flash)

L. B. Lawson was a pitcher for the Philadelphia Stars and Washington Pilots in 1934 and 1940.

Lawyer, Floyd

Floyd Lawyer was an outfielder for the Mohawk Giants in 1913.

Layton, Cliff

Cliff Layton was a pitcher for the Indianapolis Clowns in 1954.

Layton, Obie

Obie Layton was a pitcher for the Hilldale baseball club and Bacharach Giants in 1931.

Lazaga, Agipito

Agipito Lazaga was a pitcher and outfielder for the Cuban Stars and the New York Cuban Stars from 1916 to 1922.

League of Colored Base Ball Clubs

The League of Colored Base Ball Clubs was an organized league of black baseball teams formed in 1887. Teams were placed in New York, Boston, Baltimore, Philadelphia, Pittsburgh, Louisville, and Washington. However, the league folded shortly after the season began.

Leak, Curtis

Curtis Leak was an officer with the New York Black Yankees from 1940 to 1948.

Leavelle, Harry

Harry Leavelle was a first baseman and catcher for the Cuban Giants, Cuban Stars, and Genuine Cuban Giants from 1908 to 1912.

LeBlanc, Julio

Julio LeBlanc was a pitcher and outfielder for the Cuban Stars and Cincinnati Cubans from 1919 to 1921.

Lee, Dick

Dick Lee was an outfielder for the Chicago Union Giants from 1917 to 1918.

Lee, Ed

Ed Lee was a shortstop for the Chicago Union Giants and Chicago Giants in 1911 and 1916.

Lee, Fred

Fred Lee was an outfielder for the Kansas City Giants in 1908 and 1915.

Lee, Holsey (Scrip)
b. 1899, d. 1974

Holsey Lee was a pitcher, outfielder, and first baseman for the Philadelphia Stars, Norfolk Stars, Hilldale baseball club, Norfolk Giants, Baltimore Black Sox, Richmond Giants, Cleveland Red Sox, Bacharach Giants, and Philadelphia Giants from 1920 to 1943. Born in Washington, Lee, as a young pitcher, started the ninth game of the series in the historic 1924 Negro League Series between Hilldale and the Kansas City Monarchs. Pitching for Hilldale, Lee lost to veteran Jose Mendez. However, he would help Hilldale win the 1927 Negro League world championship. Lee also umpired in the NEGRO NATIONAL LEAGUE. In an interview with author John Holway on file at the National Baseball Hall of Fame, Lee said that the Hilldale club he pitched for was the best team he ever saw: "We played the Philadelphia Athletics three or four seasons, and the last time we played them, in 1926, we beat them five out of six," Lee said. "The only one they beat us, I lost 1-0. . . . We used to play big leaguers in Baltimore every fall. Heinie Manush led the league in hitting in 1926, I think, and that year, when he played against us, he got three hits in six games. And they weren't well-hit balls, either. Frank Warfield and Jake Stephens got mixed up on one ball and it hit the ground between them. My fast ball he'd hit on the ground to an infielder. And then he wondered how he won the batting championship and didn't get but three hits against us. It might have been because he developed a slump or something, the only thing I could see."

Lee said he grew up with Duke Ellington in Washington and also said he enlisted in the National Guard in 1916, going to Mexico to fight Pancho Villa later to France to fight in World War I where he was wounded in battle.

He went on to play Negro League baseball, where he developed his specialized submarine delivery. "I just figured, 'Well, I'll try it.' It seemed to work out and I got so I could control it, and I said, 'Well, I'll pitch that way altogether.' My curveball, I'd start almost down here at my ankles, and it would come up. My fast ball was different, it would break down. I'd start it here at my thigh, and then when it got to home plate it was liable to be at the knee or below. That's why I had a lot of balls hit directly back to me. A man had to hit it close to nine feet in the air to get it over second base, or I'd stop it, just like that. You had to get a lot of wood on it to get it past me."

Lee said his greatest thrill came in the 1924 Negro League World Series, against the Kansas City Monarchs: "The first four Monarchs got doubles and they took our starter out and put me in," Lee said. "I won the game in the 10th inning. There were men on second and third and one out, and I stepped out of the batter's box and hitched up my pants, the signal for the hit-and-run bunt. Judy Johnson was the runner on third. Frank Warfield, our manager, was coaching at first. He didn't want me to do it, but I looked at him as if to say, 'Yes, come on, they're not looking for it' and gave the signal again. Well, he nodded okay. I bunted toward the pitcher, Johnson slid over home plate safe, and that was my greatest thrill."

Lee, Lown

Lown Lee was a pitcher for the Kansas City Royal Giants in 1909.

Lee, William

William Lee was a shortstop for the Chicago Unions in 1888.

Lee, Willie

Willie Lee was a pitcher and outfielder for the Kansas City Monarchs in 1955.

Leftwich, John

John Leftwich was a pitcher for the Homestead Grays in 1945.

Leland, Frank C.

Frank Leland was an outfielder and manager for the Washington Capital Citys, Chicago Union Giants, Leland Giants, and Chicago Giants from 1887 to 1912. He was a graduate of Fisk College in Memphis and used his education, along with his baseball skills, to not just play but organize teams as well. He founded the Chicago Unions in 1889. He also gained a partner, Major R. R. Jackson, a

Chicago black politician. Leland built up the Unions to be a powerful force in Negro League baseball that played in Chicago at Auburn Park, among other fields in the city. After beating down the competing Columbia Giants and their owner, Alvin Garrett, Leland changed the name of his team in 1901 to the Chicago Union Giants.

Some of the players on Leland's team included Billy Holland, William Binga, and a big young pitcher named Rube Foster, who would go on to become one of the most influential figures in Negro League baseball history. Foster left Leland shortly after to play for the Philadelphia Giants but would later return. In 1905, Leland changed the name again to the Leland Giants, and they are believed to have put together a record of 112-10 that year, with Leland as manager. However, he ran into some tough times on the business side and asked Foster, who had been a drawing card, to come back in 1907. Leland went on to become a local politician, a clerk in the circuit court, a deputy sheriff, and a member of the Cook County Board of Commissioners in 1908. While Leland was devoting his interests outside of baseball, Foster was building up his interests in the game—and the Leland Giants. Eventually, he would battle Leland in court for ownership of the Leland Giants. Foster won the name, but Leland kept the players. Foster, along with Leland's former financial backers, formed a new version of the Leland Giants, while Leland used his players to form a new team called the Chicago Giants. Leland's money woes continued, and in 1914 he died of a heart attack at the age of 45.

Lenox Oval

Lenox Oval was a field in the Bronx in New York where black baseball teams played in the early 1900s.

Leon, Isidore

Isidore Leon was an outfielder for the New York Cubans in 1948.

Leonard, James (Bobo)

James Leonard was a pitcher, outfielder, and first baseman for the Cleveland Browns, Cleveland Tate Stars, Cleveland Hornets, Cleveland Tigers, Chicago American Giants, Toledo Giants, Lincoln Giants, Bacharach Giants, Baltimore Black Sox, Pennsylvania Red Caps of New York, Homestead Grays, Indianapolis ABC's, and Brooklyn Royal Giants from 1919 to 1936.

Leonard, Walter (Buck)
b. 1907, d. 1997

Walter Leonard was a left-handed-hitting outfielder and first baseman for the Chattanooga Black Lookouts, Bal-

timore Stars, Homestead Grays, and Brooklyn Royal Giants from 1934 to 1950. Born in Rocky Mount, North Carolina, the 5-foot-10, 190-pound Leonard was a perennial .300-plus hitter. His best years were 1934, his rookie season, when he batted .400, .383 average in 1940, .410 in 1946, and .395 in 1947, when he also hit 13 home runs in 47 recorded Negro League games. The National Baseball Hall of Fame and *The Baseball Encyclopedia* list Leonard's career batting average at .324. Leonard, in an interview on file at the Hall of Fame, said that he nearly gave up trying to play organized baseball before he finally broke into the Negro Leagues: "I was 25 when I got up there," Leonard said. "I had almost given up baseball. I had gotten too old to play semipro ball. I could always hit, and that was the reason I got up there. But I learned to field when I got there. When I came up, I practiced fielding. I would let them hit me a lot of balls, and playing winter ball helped." It was Leonard's bat, though, that made him a Negro League star, and along with Josh Gibson, he was known as one of the "Thunder Twins" in the Grays lineup. He helped lead Homestead to nine straight NEGRO NATIONAL LEAGUE pennants from 1937 to 1946 and reportedly batted .419 in series play. In an interview with author John Holway, Leonard said the 1948 Grays team he played on that defeated Birmingham in the Negro League World Series "was maybe our greatest team. . . . Gibson wasn't with us. He was dead. But we had Luke Easter, Luis Marquez and Roy Welmaker. Easter and Welmaker went to the Cleveland Indians and Marquez went to the Boston Braves."

At the age of 45, Leonard got into 10 games for Portsmouth in the Piedmont League in 1953, getting 11 hits in 33 at bats for a .333 average. Leonard also played in the Mexican League until 1955 and winter baseball in Cuba, Venezuela, Mexico, and Puerto Rico. In an August 1991 article in *Sports Collectors Digest*, Leonard talked about the demands of playing baseball year-round: "We'd play about 200 games a year. After the season was over we would play white barnstorming teams or travel to Cuba, Mexico or South America. The least amount of money I made was $85 a month when I first started playing. The most I ever made was $1,000 a month later on. None of us made enough that we didn't have to work in the winter."

In a 1996 interview with *Sports Collector Magazine*, Negro Leaguer John Bissant talked about what a sportsman Leonard was: "Once, after getting a hit against the Grays pitcher, Buck told me when I got to first, 'You're a good hitter, but you're not using all of your power.' Even though he was on the opposite team, he was still trying to help me. They beat us that day, but I still remember Buck's words. Buck was a great ballplayer, one of the greatest ever, especially when it came to hitting."

Pitcher Wilmer Fields in his autobiography, *My Life in the Negro Leagues*, cited Leonard as one of the leaders of the Grays when he played: "There was no playing around in the dugout of the Homestead Grays," Fields wrote. "Players such as Buck Leonard and Sam Bankhead saw to that. . . . I can sincerely say that I was brought up the right way both at home and then with the Grays. . . . Buck Leonard would always remind me what I needed to do to have a successful inning. He would tell me, 'You got to stop them from hitting.' When he'd stop talking I knew I was doing a good job. He is a true Hall of Famer."

Leonard's name had been mentioned as a possible candidate to break major league baseball's color barrier. Wendell Smith of the *Pittsburgh Courier* wrote in 1939 that Leonard and Josh Gibson had been promised try-outs with the Pittsburgh Pirates by owner Bill Benswanger, but there was a dispute over whether Grays owner Cum Posey stopped the tryouts or if Benswanger truly intended to do it. Leonard also received a tentative offer for a tryout in 1943 from Washington Senators owner Clark Griffith, but like the other offers, it didn't materialize. In a 1995 interview with *Sports Collectors Digest*, Leonard spoke of the tryout offer from Griffith: "We didn't ever know what happened," he said. "He asked us would we like to play in the major leagues and we told him yes. He asked us if we thought we could make the major leagues and we told him we were trying. He told us we would hear from him and we didn't ever hear from him again. Later Bill Veeck asked me to try out with a team. I told him, 'No, I can't try out with a new team. I'm too old now.' I was in my 40s."

In the Holway interview, Leonard addressed the prejudice that kept him from playing in the major leagues: "I never thought about race prejudice much," Leonard said. "I felt, regardless of what color you were, if you could play baseball, you ought to be allowed to play anywhere that you could play. I thought integration would come, but I didn't think it would come like it did, as quickly. I thought they still were going to keep pushing it back. Even when they took [Jackie] Robinson, I said, 'If he doesn't make it, they're going to be through with us for the next five or 10 years. But if he does make it, maybe they are going to keep him in the minors for a long time.' But we were wrong. . . . I can't understand how we could have gone about protesting. We didn't have time to demonstrate. We were playing every day, so to speak. We were satisfied. We were doing what we liked to do, what we loved, and getting a little pay. . . . I don't know of anything that we could have done to speed it up." But Leonard recognized that once the color line was broken, that was the end of Negro League baseball. "It starting dropping off in 1949, and in 1950 the attendance was so poor around the league that the Homestead Grays got out of the Negro National League and got into a league in Greensboro and Raleigh," Leonard said. "I don't know what the name of the league was, it was just in North Carolina. We just decided we would get out of the Negro National League and go south because we could make more money. We had lost most of our ballplayers to white teams, and all the young players that didn't make the majors went to the minors. We just couldn't compete." Leonard was elected to the National Baseball Hall of Fame in 1972.

Lett, Roger

Roger Lett was a pitcher for the Cincinnati Clowns in 1943.

Leuschner, William J.

William Leuschner was an officer with the New York Black Yankees, working for Nat Strong and taking over Strong's baseball enterprises when Strong died in 1935. He continued with the Black Yankees until 1943.

Levis, Oscar

Oscar Levis was a pitcher for the Darby Daisies, Cuban Stars, Hilldale baseball club, All Cubans, and Baltimore Black Sox from 1921 to 1934.

Lewis, A. D.

A. D. Lewis was a first baseman for the Louisville Black Colonels and Birmingham Black Barons from 1937 to 1938.

Lewis, Bernard

Bernard Lewis was a pitcher for the Atlanta Black Crackers in 1943.

Lewis, Cary B.

Cary Lewis was a reporter for the *Chicago Defender*, a black newspaper in Chicago that covered Negro League baseball. He was one of a group of newspapermen that Rube Foster invited to a 1920 meeting to form the NEGRO NATIONAL LEAGUE.

Lewis, Charles

Charles Lewis was a shortstop for the Philadelphia Giants and Lincoln Giants from 1925 to 1926.

Lewis, Clarence (Foots)

Clarence Lewis was a shortstop for the Cleveland Red Sox, Memphis Red Sox, Pittsburgh Crawfords, Nashville Elite Giants, Cleveland Giants, and Akron Tyrites from 1931 to 1937.

Lewis, Earl

Earl Lewis was a pitcher for the Indianapolis ABC's in 1923.

Lewis, George

George Lewis was a pitcher for the Bacharach Giants and Lincoln Giants from 1917 to 1922.

Lewis, Grover

Grover Lewis was a third baseman for the Homestead Grays in 1928.

Lewis, Henry

Henry Lewis was the manager, officer, and owner of the Atlanta Black Crackers and Knoxville Black Smokies from 1943 to 1945.

Lewis, Ira

Ira Lewis was the secretary with the Pittsburgh Keystones in 1922. He was also a reporter for the *Pittsburgh Courier,* a black newspaper in Pittsburgh that covered Negro League baseball.

Lewis, James

James Lewis was a pitcher for the Memphis Red Sox in 1953.

Lewis, Jerome

Jerome Lewis was a first baseman for the West Baden Sprudels from 1910 to 1913.

Lewis, Jim

Jim Lewis was a second baseman for the Indianapolis Clowns in 1953.

Lewis, Jim (Slim)

Jim Lewis was a pitcher for the Chicago Brown Bombers and New York Black Yankees in 1943 and 1947.

Lewis, Joseph (Sleepy)

Joseph Lewis was a third baseman, catcher, and manager for the Washington Potomacs, Baltimore Black Sox, Hilldale baseball club, Homestead Grays, Quaker Giants, Lincoln Giants, Bacharach Giants, Darby Daisies, Brooklyn Royal Giants, and Norfolk–Newport News Royals from 1919 to 1936 and again in 1946.

Lewis, Milton

Milton Lewis was an infielder who played from 1922 to 1928 for the Bacharach Giants, Wilmington Potomacs, Harrisburg Giants, Richmond Giants, and Philadelphia Giants from 1922 to 1928.

Lewis, Robert S. (Bubble)

Robert Lewis was an officer with the Memphis Red Sox and the NEGRO NATIONAL LEAGUE from 1923 to 1928.

Lewis, Rufus

b. 1919, d. 1999

Rufus Lewis was a right-handed pitcher for the Pittsburgh Crawfords, Newark Eagles, and Houston Eagles from 1936 to 1950. Lewis's best years were with the Newark Eagles, when he posted an 18-3 record in 1946. Born in Hattiesburg, Mississippi, Lewis finished his career in Mexico from 1950 to 1952. He also spent the winter of 1947–48 and pitching in Havana.

Lewis, Tuck

Tuck Lewis was a second baseman for the Chicago Giants in 1916.

Liggons, James

James Liggons was a pitcher and outfielder for the Memphis Red Sox, Monroe Monarchs, and Little Rock Black Travelers from 1932 to 1934.

Ligon, Rufus C.

Rufus Ligon was a pitcher for the Memphis Red Sox from 1944 to 1946.

Lillard, Joseph

Joseph Lillard was a pitcher, catcher, and outfielder for the Chicago American Giants, Cole's American Giants, Birmingham Black Barons, and Cincinnati Tigers from 1932 to 1937 and again in 1944.

Linares, Abel

Abel Linares was owner and president of the All Cubans team, Cuban Stars, and Cincinnati Cubans from 1911 to 1921.

Linares, Rogelio (Ice Cream)

Rogelio Linares was an outfielder and first baseman for the Cuban Stars and New York Cubans from 1940 to 1946.

Lincoln, James
James Lincoln was a third baseman and shortstop for the Lincoln Giants in Nebraska and the Adrian Page Fence Giants from 1890 to 1895.

Lincoln Giants
The Lincoln Giants were a black baseball team based in Lincoln, Nebraska, that played in the early 1890s. Former Negro Leaguer and historian Sol White in his book *History of Colored Base Ball* wrote that the Lincoln Giants "were strong in batteries, hard hitters and fast runners. They were hard to beat unless a strong pitcher was against them." There was another team called the Lincoln Giants, but they were often referred to as the New York Lincoln Giants, based in New York City.

Lindsay, Bill (Kansas City Cyclone)
Bill Lindsay was a pitcher for the Kansas City Giants, Leland Giants, and Chicago American Giants from 1908 to 1914. He was reportedly killed by a pitch from Bill Gatewood in batting practice in 1914.

Lindsay, Charles
Charles Lindsay was a shortstop for the Bacharach Giants, Richmond Giants, Wilmington Potomacs, Baltimore Black Sox, Penn Red Caps of New York, Philadelphia Giants, Washington Pilots, and New York Lincoln Giants from 1920 to 1935.

Lindsay, James
James Lindsay was an infielder for the Birmingham Black Barons in 1943.

Lindsay, Leonard
Leonard Lindsay was a pitcher, first baseman, and third baseman for the Birmingham Black Barons, Cincinnati Clowns, and Indianapolis Clowns from 1942 to 1946.

Lindsay, Merf
Merf Lindsay was an outfielder for the Kansas City Giants in 1910.

Lindsay, Robert (Frog)
Robert Lindsay was a shortstop for the Kansas City Giants and the Kansas City Colored Giants from 1908 to 1917.

Lindsey, Ben
Ben Lindsey was a shortstop for the Bacharach Giants in 1929.

Lindsey, Bill
Bill Lindsey was a second baseman, shortstop, and outfielder for the Dayton Marcos, Lincoln Giants, and Washington Potomacs from 1924 to 1926.

Lindsey, James
James Lindsey was an outfielder for the Pittsburgh Keystones in 1887.

Lindsey, Robert
Robert Lindsey was a pitcher, outfielder, and first baseman for the Indianapolis ABC's in 1931.

Linton, Ben
Ben Linton was an officer with the Detroit Giants in 1945.

Lipsey, Henry
Henry Lipsey was a pitcher for the Memphis Red Sox in 1942.

Lisby, Maurice C.
Maurice Lisby was a pitcher for the Bacharach Giants and Newark Dodgers in 1934.

Listach, Nora
Nora Listach was an outfielder for the Cincinnati Buckeyes and Birmingham Black Barons from 1940 to 1941.

Little, William
William Little was an officer with the Chicago American Giants from 1937 to 1950.

Little Rock Black Travelers
The Little Rock Black Travelers were a black independent baseball team out of Little Rock, Arkansas, that played in the 1920s. There was also a version of the Black Travelers that played in the Negro Southern League in 1945.

Little Rock Grays

The Little Rock Grays were a black baseball team out of Little Rock, Arkansas, that played in the Negro Southern League in 1932.

Littles, Ben

Ben Littles was an outfielder for the New York Black Yankees, Philadelphia Stars, and Homestead Grays from 1947 to 1951.

Livingston, Curtis

Curtis Livingston was an outfielder for the Cleveland Buckeyes in 1950.

Livingston, Lee

Lee Livingston was an outfielder for the New York Black Yankees, Kansas City Monarchs, Pennsylvania Red Caps of New York, Pittsburgh Crawfords from 1928 to 1933.

Lloyd, John Henry (Pop)

b. 1884, d. 1965

John Henry Lloyd was a first baseman, second baseman, shortstop, catcher, and manager for the Jacksonville Old Receivers, Cuban X Giants, Macon Acmes, Leland Giants, Philadelphia Giants, Chicago American Giants, Lincoln Giants, Columbus Buckeyes, Brooklyn Royal Giants, Hilldale baseball club, Bacharach Giants, Kansas City Monarchs, Lincoln Stars, and New York Black Yankees from 1905 to 1932. He was often referred to as the "black Honus Wagner," and Wagner himself had this to say about the comparison: "They called John Henry Lloyd 'The Black Wagner,' and I was anxious to see him play," Wagner said. "Well, one day I had an opportunity to go see him play, and after I saw him I felt honored that

John Henry "Pop" Lloyd was sometimes called the "black Honus Wagner" for his skill on the field at shortstop and at the plate during his Negro League career as a first baseman, second baseman, shortstop, catcher, and manager from 1905 to 1932. In 1911, the 6-foot, 180-pound Lloyd played for and managed the New York Lincoln Giants and reportedly batted .475. He led the Giants to a 1913 championship win over the Chicago American Giants. The following season he joined the Chicago club, leading the American Giants to three west titles and two championships. He also won the 1924 batting title with a .433 average and is believed to have batted .564 for the Lincoln Giants in 1928, which is the all-time Negro League record for hitting in one season. (NATIONAL BASEBALL HALL OF FAME LIBRARY, COOPERSTOWN, N.Y.)

they would name such a great player after me." Others echoed those sentiments. Negro Leaguer Judy Johnson said that Connie Mack once told him that Lloyd was the equal of Wagner at shortstop: "He said the two best shortstops that he had ever seen were Hans Wagner and John Henry Lloyd," Johnson said. "He said you could put them in a bag and shake them up and either one you'd pull out, you wouldn't go wrong. Lloyd must have been a marvel because when I saw him he was sliding downhill. He was a great man and a great teacher."

Lloyd, born in Palatka, Florida, was a slick-fielding shortstop and considered to be among the greatest base runners in Negro baseball history. In 1911, the 6-foot, 180-pound Lloyd played for and managed the New York Lincoln Giants and reportedly batted .475. He led the Giants to a 1913 championship win over the Chicago American Giants. The following season he joined the Chicago club, leading the American Giants to three West titles and two championships. He also won the 1924 batting title with a .433 average. Like other Negro League players, Lloyd also played some games for an organized team from The Breakers Hotel in Palm Beach, Florida.

A left-handed hitter, Lloyd maintained a batting average of over .360 for most of his 27-year career, playing until the age of 48 in Negro League baseball and continuing to play semipro ball for the Atlantic City Johnson Stars, the Farley Stars, and other teams until he was 58. He is believed to have batted .564 for the Lincoln Giants in 1928 at age 44, which is the all-time Negro League record for hitting in one season.

During his career Lloyd played with such Negro baseball greats as Judy Johnson, Raleigh "Biz" Mackey, and Bingo DeMoss and was also managed by Sol White. He also gained a reputation as a mercenary player and unabashedly was quoted as saying, "Where the money was, that's where I was." However, he had the admiration and respect of his fellow players. "He was a gentleman," Negro Leaguer Napoleon "Chance" Cummings said in *Blackball Stars*, the John Holway book. "Everybody who knew him liked him. He was a man practically everybody could get along with."

Lloyd also spent 12 winters playing ball in Cuba and was given the nickname "El Cuchara" (the shovel), because he would scoop up handfuls of dirt when he fielded ground balls. Like many Negro League ballplayer playing in Cuba, Lloyd often competed against barnstorming white major league players. In 1909, he is believed to have batted .546 against major league competition. In a Holway interview on file at the National Baseball Hall of Fame, Negro Leaguer Ted Page said that Lloyd was a "scientific hitter. He was the kind of a hitter that if the ball was pitched in on him, he would pull the ball to right field. He didn't try to force the ball to his field. He would try to hit the ball where it was pitched. If the ball is out-

side, you can hit the ball to the left better than you can pull it, because this is where you pop up so much. . . . I never saw Lloyd hit skyrockets—although he must have. But he hit line drives, he could just lay the bat on his shoulder and just lean in on it."

In a 1953 article in *Our World*, Lloyd, in an article with his byline but written by Alvin White, wrote about his playing days: "Thirty years ago, Negro baseball players were not only as good as today's highly paid stars, they were better," Lloyd said. "Besides, during the 25 years I played baseball, there were more good Negro ball players than there are today. I know. I played with and against them."

Lloyd became a favorite son of Atlantic City, working as a janitor in the school system, befriending generations of schoolchildren, and also serving as the city's Little League commissioner. A field in the New Jersey shore town is named after Lloyd, and when it was dedicated in 1949, Lloyd said, "I do not consider that I was born at the wrong time. I felt it was the right time, for I had a chance to prove the ability of our race in this sport, and because many of us did our very best to uphold the traditions of the game and of the world of sport, we have given the Negro a greater opportunity now to be accepted into the major leagues with other Americans." Lloyd was inducted into the National Baseball Hall of Fame in 1977.

Locke, Clarence

Clarence Locke was a pitcher and first baseman for the Chicago American Giants from 1945 to 1948.

Locke, Eddie
b. 1923

Eddie Locke was a left-handed-hitting third baseman and pitcher for the Kansas City Monarchs, Cincinnati Clowns, Chicago American Giants, and New York Black Yankees from 1943 to 1951. The 6-foot, 180-pound Locke batted .297 with Kansas City in 1944. He also went on to play minor league baseball in the Longhorn League, West Texas–New Mexico League, Western International League, Big State League, and Mississippi–Ohio Valley League, as well as in the Mexican League, until 1959 and again for one year in 1967.

Locke, James

James Locke was an umpire in the Negro Leagues in the 1920s.

Lockett, Lester (Buck)
b. 1912

Lester Lockett was a second baseman, third baseman, and outfielder for the Birmingham Black Barons,

Chicago American Giants, Cincinnati-Indianapolis Clowns, Memphis Red Sox, Baltimore Elite Giants, Cincinnati Buckeyes, St. Louis Stars, and Philadelphia Stars from 1937 to 1950. Born in Princeton, Indiana, Lockett, playing for Birmingham, batted .328 in 1941, .315 in 1942, and a career-high .408 in 1953. Lockett played minor league baseball with Farnham, Winnipeg, and Carman from 1951 through 1953 and finished his playing career in the winter of 1953 with Torreon in the Mexican League, where he batted .351 in eight games.

Lockett, Monroe
Monroe Lockett was a pitcher for the Indianapolis ABC's in 1938.

Lockett, Willie
Willie Lockett was a pitcher for the Indianapolis ABC's in 1938.

Lockhart, A. J.
A. J. Lockhart was a pitcher and third baseman for the Philadelphia Giants and Wilmington Potomacs from 1924 to 1926.

Lockhart, Joe
Joe Lockhart was a pitcher for the Chicago American Giants, Wilmington Potomacs, and Bacharach Giants from 1923 to 1929.

Logan, Carl
Carl Logan was infielder for the Philadelphia Stars and Bacharach Giants in 1934 and 1940.

Logan, Fred
Fred Logan was an outfielder for the New York Black Yankees in 1950.

Logan, Nick
Nick Logan was a pitcher for the Baltimore Black Sox from 1920 to 1925.

Long, Buck
Buck Long was a catcher for the Memphis Red Sox in 1950.

Long, Carl
Carl Long was an outfielder for the Birmingham Black Barons and Philadelphia Stars in 1952 and 1953.

Long, Earnest (The Kid)
Earnest Long was a pitcher for the Louisville Buckeyes and Cleveland Buckeyes from 1948 to 1950.

Long, Emory (Bang)
Emory Long was an outfielder and third baseman for the Indianapolis Athletics, Atlanta Black Crackers, Chicago American Giants, Philadelphia Stars, Washington Black Senators, and Kansas City Monarchs from 1932 to 1940 and again in 1945.

Long, Tom
Tom Long was a catcher for the Kansas City Monarchs in 1926.

Longest, Bernell
Bernell Longest was a second baseman and third baseman for the Chicago American Giants and Chicago Brown Bombers from 1942 to 1947. He also went on to play in the Mexican League and played minor league baseball in the Manitoba-Dakota League and Provincial League until 1955.

Longest, Charles
Charles Longest was an outfielder for the Detroit Stars in 1954.

Longest, Jimmy
Jimmy Longest was a first baseman for the Chicago Brown Bombers in 1942.

Long Island Alpines
The Long Island Alpines were a black baseball team based in Long Island, New York, in the 1880s.

Longley, Wayman (Red)
Wayman Longley was a catcher, infielder, and outfielder for the Little Rock Black Travelers, Chicago American Giants, Memphis Red Sox, New Orleans Eagles, and Washington Elite Giants from 1932 to 1951.

Looney, Charlie
Charlie Looney was a second baseman for the Akron Tyrites and Louisville Black Colonels in 1933 and 1938.

Lopez, Cando

Cando Lopez was a third baseman and outfielder for the Cuban Stars and the New York Cubans from 1920 to 1926.

Lopez, Justo

Justo Lopez was a first baseman for the Cuban Stars in 1939.

Lopez, Pedro

Pedro Lopez was an outfielder for the Cuban Stars from 1938 to 1939.

Lopez, Raul

Raul Lopez was a pitcher for the New York Cubans from 1948 to 1950.

Lopez, Vidal

Vidal Lopez was a pitcher for the Cuban Stars from 1923 to 1929.

Lorenzo, Jesus

Jesus Lorenzo was a pitcher for the Cuban Stars from 1928 to 1930.

Los Angeles Stars/Los Angeles White Sox

The Los Angeles Stars/Los Angeles White Sox were a black baseball team in Los Angeles, sometimes called the Stars, other times the White Sox, that played in the integrated (black teams against white teams) four-team California Winter League in the 1930s.

Los Dragones

Los Dragones was the Dominican Republic team owned by dictator Rafael Trujillo that raided Negro League baseball in 1937, luring stars like Satchel Paige, Josh Gibson, and Cool Papa Bell to leave the Negro Leagues and play in the Dominican Republic that year in what was a baseball war between Trujillo and his political opponents who also owned teams.

Lott, Benjamin

Benjamin Lott was a second baseman and third baseman for the New York Black Yankees and Indianapolis Clowns from 1949 to 1951. The 5-foot-11, 170-pound Lott, born in 1927, batted .304 with Indianapolis in 1950. He went on to play minor league baseball in the Western League, Three I League, Manitoba-Dakota League, Texas League, and Longhorn League until 1955. He also played in the Dominican Summer League in 1952.

Lott, Raymond

Raymond Lott was an outfielder for the Philadelphia Stars in 1950.

Louden, Louis

b. 1919, d. 1989

Louis Louden was a catcher for the Birmingham Black Barons and New York Cubans from 1942 to 1950. Louden, born in West Point, Virginia, had his best years with New York in 1946, when he batted .290, and in 1950, when he batted .311. He also played minor league baseball in the Manitoba-Dakota League and the Southwestern League until 1957. Louden also played in the Mexican League and played winter baseball in Puerto Rico and Cuba.

Louisville Black Caps

The Louisville Black Caps were a black baseball team out of Louisville, Kentucky, that played in the Negro Southern League in the 1930s.

Louisville Black Colonels

The Louisville Black Colonels were a black baseball team out of Louisville, Kentucky, that played from the 1930s to the 1950s.

Louisville Buckeyes

The Louisville Buckeyes were a black baseball team out of Louisville, Kentucky, that played in the NEGRO AMERICAN LEAGUE in 1949.

Louisville Cubs

The Louisville Cubs were a black baseball team out of Louisville, Kentucky, that played in the early 1900s.

Louisville White Caps

The Louisville White Caps were a black baseball team out of Louisville, Kentucky, that played in the NEGRO NATIONAL LEAGUE in 1930.

Louisville White Sox

The Louisville White Sox were a black baseball team out of Louisville, Kentucky, that played in the NEGRO AMERICAN LEAGUE in 1931.

Love, William

William Love was a catcher and outfielder for the Memphis Red Sox, Detroit Stars, and Toledo Cubs from 1930 to 1931 and again in 1945.

Low, Nat

Nat Low was sports editor of the *Daily Worker*, the Communist Party newspaper. Low wrote numerous articles calling for major league baseball to integrate and organized a tryout for several Negro League players, including catcher Roy Campanella and pitcher Dave Barnhill, for Pittsburgh Pirates owner William Benswanger in 1943.

Lowe, William

William Lowe was an infielder, outfielder, and manager for the Detroit Stars, Memphis Red Sox, Chattanooga Black Lookouts, Nashville Elite Giants, and Indianapolis ABC's from 1921 to 1933.

Lucas, Miles (Pepe)

Miles Lucas was an outfielder and pitcher for the Cuban Stars, Cuban Stars of Havana, Harrisburg Giants, and New Orleans Crescent Stars from 1919 to 1927.

Lucas, Scotty (Smitty)

Scotty Lucas was a Philadelphia nightclub owner and numbers operator who owned and operated the Philadelphia Tigers in the late 1920s.

Luga, Orlando

Orlando Luga was an infielder for the Indianapolis Clowns in 1954.

Lugo, Leo

Leo Lugo was an outfielder for the Cincinnati-Indianapolis Clowns and Indianapolis Clowns from 1943 to 1946.

Lumkins, Lefty

Lefty Lumkins was a pitcher for the Newark Browns from 1931 to 1932.

Lundy, Dick (The King)

b. 1899, d. 1965

Dick Lundy was a shortstop, second baseman, third baseman, and manager for the Brooklyn Royal Giants, Jacksonville Eagles, Newark Eagles, New York Cubans, Newark Dodgers, Philadelphia Stars, Baltimore Black Sox, Hilldale baseball club, Lincoln Giants, Duval Giants, Bacharach Giants, and Havana Red Sox from 1916 to 1948. A brilliant fielding shortstop who also played second and third base, the 5-foot-11, 180-pound Lundy was part of the "million-dollar infield" of the Baltimore Black Sox in 1929, along with Oliver Marcelle, Frank Warfield, and Jud Wilson. In John Holway's book *Blackball Stars*, another shortstop, Jake Stephens, said Lundy "had great range. He could shoot you out from left field."

Born in Jacksonville, Florida, Lundy began his career with the Jacksonville Eagles in 1915 and then moved with the club to New Jersey the following season when the Eagles became the Atlantic City Bacharach Giants, where he had his best seasons. Lundy, a switch hitter, batted .484 in 1921 and led the Eastern Colored League in home runs with 13 in 1924 with a .360 average. The following year, he became player-manager and in 1926 led the Giants to the league pennant and also batted .329. Facing the Chicago American Giants in the Negro League World Series, the Giants would lose, but Lundy drove in six runs, scored four, stole six bases, and batted .325. He played for the Black Sox in 1929, moved to the Philadelphia Stars in 1933, and managed and played for the East squad in the first EAST-WEST ALL-STAR GAME. He retired from playing in 1937, and records show that in about 2,800 at bats over his career, Lundy batted .321. Lundy also played winter baseball in Cuba for eight seasons, batting .341.

The October 1934 edition of *Colored Baseball & Sports Monthly* called Lundy "one of the greatest single gate attractions in baseball. His playing personality naturally makes ball players on his team put forth their utmost to win for him. He is a natural leader and has the respect of practically all the ball players everywhere. Dick represents a great type of sportsman and gentleman. The spectacular playing that he delivers with so much ease and grace electrifies the fans. Wherever he goes and plays he leaves a lasting impression on the fans. . . . Whenever Lundy has played or managed he has been a financial success. He has always produced winners. . . . Lundy, [John Henry] Lloyd and Babe Ruth will go down in history as the greatest of all time."

Luque, Adolfo (Dolf)

b. 1890, d. 1957

Adolfo Luque was an outfielder and pitcher for the Cuban Stars and Long Branch Cubans from 1912 to

1913. Luque was able to break through to major league baseball as a Cuban player, getting a tryout with the Boston Braves in 1914, and went on to post a 193-179 record for the Braves, Cincinnati Reds, Brooklyn Dodgers, and New York Giants, with a 3.24 ERA, including a 27-8 record in 1923 with Cincinnati. He also pitched and managed in winter ball in Cuba.

Lyles, John

John Lyles was an infielder, outfielder, and catcher for the Cleveland Buckeyes, Cincinnati Buckeyes, Chicago American Giants, St. Louis Stars, Cleveland Bears, Homestead Grays, Indianapolis ABC's, New Orleans–St. Louis Stars, and Indianapolis Clowns from 1932 to 1943.

Lynch, Thomas

Thomas Lynch was an outfielder, third baseman, and second baseman for the West Baden Sprudels, Dayton Marcos, and Indianapolis ABC's from 1914 to 1919.

Lyons, Bennie

Bennie Lyons was a first baseman, outfielder, and catcher for the Dayton Marcos, Jewell's ABC's, Bowser's ABC's, and Indianapolis ABC's from 1911 to 1918.

Lyons, Chase

Chase Lyons was a pitcher for the Cuban Giants and Genuine Cuban Giants from 1899 to 1905.

Lyons, Granville

Granville Lyons was a pitcher and first baseman for the Louisville Black Caps, Nashville Elite Giants, Louisville Red Caps, Detroit Stars, Memphis Red Sox, Philadelphia Stars, and Baltimore Elite Giants from 1931 to 1942.

Lyons, James

James Lyons was an outfielder and manager for the Chicago American Giants, Indianapolis ABC's, Brooklyn Royal Giants, Chicago Giants, St. Louis Giants, Lincoln Giants, Washington Potomacs, Louisville Black Caps, Cleveland Browns, Detroit Stars, and Bowser's ABC's from 1910 to 1932. In an interview with author John Holway on file at the National Baseball Hall of Fame, Negro League great Dave Malarcher talked about a unique compliment Lyons once received from an unlikely source: "Jimmy Lyons was one of those who went to war with me," Malarcher said. "We were in the AEF league together in 1919, and we played against a team in Le Mans, France, on which was a fellow who was Ty Cobb's brother. He said that Jimmy was the greatest ballplayer he had ever seen, not his brother. Wasn't that something?"

Lytle, Clarence

Clarence Lytle was a pitcher for the Leland Giants and Chicago Union Giants from 1901 to 1906.

Maben, Ben

Ben Maben was an infielder for the Memphis Red Sox in 1952.

Mack, John

John Mack was a pitcher for the Kansas City Monarchs in 1945.

Mack, Paul

Paul Mack was a third baseman and outfielder for the Jersey City Colored Giants and Bacharach Giants from 1916 to 1917.

Mack, Robert

Robert Mack was a pitcher for the New York Black Yankees in 1945.

Mackey, Raleigh (Biz)

b. 1897, d. 1959

Raleigh Mackey was a catcher, shortstop, third baseman, and manager for the San Antonio Giants, Hilldale baseball club, Darby Daisies, Indianapolis ABC's, Washington Elite Giants, Baltimore Elite Giants, Philadelphia Stars, Philadelphia Royal Giants, Newark Eagles, Newark Dodgers, and Nashville Elite Giants from 1918 to 1947. Mackey was born in Seguin, Texas, the same town as Negro pitching great Smokey Joe Williams. Mackey batted .319 through his career, including a .353 average in 1922, .364 in 1923, and .363 in 1924 when Mackey, catching for the Hilldale Daisies, played in what was acknowledged as the first black World Series, batting .360 in the series in a five-games-to-four losing effort to the Kansas City Monarchs. Mackey's Hilldale club met the Monarchs for the second straight time in 1925, and Mackey batted .375, leading Hilldale to the series title. He went on to have an illustrious Negro League career, and in 1941, he was named by fans as the top catcher in the Negro League EAST-WEST ALL-STAR GAME history. He had been the first starting catcher in the East-West Game in 1933, beating out Josh Gibson. Mackey played a number of seasons of winter baseball in the California winter league, and he also played in Japan in 1932. In 1945, at the age of 48, Mackey reportedly batted .307 for the Newark Eagles.

Among the players he managed or instructed were Roy Campanella, Larry Doby, and Monte Irvin. In John B. Holway's book *Blackball Stars*, Irvin described the teaching skills of Mackey: "He was the dean of teachers," Irvin said. "He taught Campanella how to think like a catcher, how to set a hitter up—throw a hitter his favorite pitch at a time when he's not expecting it, and he'd just stand there and take it." Campanella himself acknowledged Mackey's contribution in an interview: "In

Raleigh "Biz" Mackey was a catcher, shortstop, third baseman, and manager during his Negro League career, but he was best known for his ability behind the plate. He was the first starting catcher in the East-West Game in 1933, beating out Josh Gibson, and later as a manager taught Roy Campanella how to catch in the Negro Leagues in Baltimore. Mackey was also an outstanding hitter, batting .319 through a career that spanned 1918 to 1947 for the San Antonio Giants, Hilldale baseball club, Darby Daisies, Indianapolis ABC's, Washington Elite Giants, Baltimore Elite Giants, Philadelphia Stars, Philadelphia Royal Giants, Newark Eagles, Newark Dodgers, and Nashville Elite Giants.
(NATIONAL BASEBALL HALL OF FAME LIBRARY, COOPERSTOWN, N.Y.)

my opinion, Biz Mackey was the master of defense of all catchers," Campanella said. "When I was a kid in Philadelphia I saw both Mackey and Mickey Cochrane in their primes, but for real catching skills, I didn't think Cochrane was the master of defense that Mackey was. When I went under his direction at Baltimore, I was 15 years old. I gathered quite a bit from Mackey, watching how he did things, how he blocked low pitches, how he shifted his feet for an outside pitch, how he threw with a short, quick, accurate throw without drawing back. I got all this from Mackey at a young age." In a 1999 interview with *Sports Collectors Digest*, former Negro Leaguer Nap Gulley said that Mackey was "a gentle giant and one of the finest managers I had the privilege of

playing for. He could help a ballplayer to become a better player. Without him, Larry Doby, Monte Irvin, Don Newcombe and those guys would have never seen the major leagues."

One of his earliest teammates was Crush Holloway, on the Black Aces, and in another Holway interview on file at the National Baseball Hall of Fame, Holloway called Mackey the "greatest catcher I ever saw. I mean fielding, throwing, everything. He taught Campanella how to throw. He was a big fast man for his size. Mackey weighed 235 in his playing days, in shape. Biz was a great catcher, but he pitched, caught and played the infield then. He was a good pitcher, too." In another Holway interview, Negro League pitcher Bill Holland also compared Mackey to Cochrane: "Biz Mackey was great," Holland said. "I'd classify him with Mickey Cochrane or anybody. I think Mickey Cochrane outhit him a little. Mackey was a good hitter, but I don't think he was as good as Cochrane. . . . Mackey was a big guy, weighed around 219 to 220 pounds, in condition. A great arm, he didn't have to stride to throw. He'd just raise up and that ball would go down there to second. He and Frank Warfield used to put on a show in infield practice. Mackey would throw down to second, Warfield would catch it and say, 'Ow, Mackey, you're gonna kill somebody!'"

Holsey "Scrip" Lee, another teammate of Mackey's, said he remembered that the big man had remarkable stamina: "He was the best catcher in the world, bar none," Lee said. "I never worried about fielding a bunted ball. Mackey would go down both lines. Mackey weighed about 230 pounds and he had more stamina than any man on the ball club. While we were having batting practice, he'd be out there playing shortstop. Then when the game started, he'd catch the ball game. He didn't care how hot it was, he'd play."

In a *Pittsburgh Courier* readers' poll in 1954, Mackey was named the greatest catcher in Negro League history, ahead of Josh Gibson. Mackey died shortly after being honored at Roy Campanella Day in Los Angeles in 1959.

Macon Acmes
The Macon Acmes were a black baseball team in Macon, Georgia, in the early 1900s.

Maddix, Ray
Ray Maddix was a pitcher for the Indianapolis Clowns from 1949 to 1953.

Maddox, Arthur
Arthur Maddox was a pitcher for the Cincinnati Tigers from 1935 to 1936.

Madison, Robert

Robert Madison was an outfielder, pitcher, and third baseman for the Memphis Red Sox, Kansas City Monarchs, Indianapolis Athletics, and Birmingham Black Barons from 1935 to 1942.

Madison Stars

The Madison Stars were a black baseball team in the early 1900s that served as a farm club for the Hilldale baseball club in Darby, Pennsylvania, a suburb of Philadelphia.

Magee, Sherry

Sherry Magee was an umpire in the Negro Leagues in the 1920s.

Magrinat, Hector

Hector Magrinat was an outfielder for the Cuban Stars of Havana, All Cubans, and Cuban Stars from 1906 to 1918.

Mahoney, Tony

Tony Mahoney was a pitcher for the Baltimore Black Sox, Indianapolis ABC's, Norfolk Giants, Norfolk Stars, and Brooklyn Royal Giants from 1920 to 1923.

Mainor, John J., III (Hank)

John Mainor was a pitcher for the Philadelphia Stars and Baltimore Elite Giants from 1950 to 1951.

Major League Committee on Baseball Integration

The Major League Committee on Baseball Integration was an advisory group formed in 1945 by major league baseball to study the issue of bringing black players into the major leagues. Its members included Joseph P. Rainey, a Philadelphia court magistrate and Pennsylvania State Athletic Commissioner, Brooklyn Dodgers general manager Branch Rickey, and New York Yankees general manager and former Dodgers owner Larry MacPhail. Afro-American sportswriter Sam Lacy was the driving force behind the committee, but little came of it.

Makell, William

William Makell was a catcher for the Baltimore Elite Giants, Newark Eagles, and Philadelphia Stars from 1944 to 1949.

Malarcher, Dave (Gentleman Dave)

Dave Malarcher was an outfielder, second baseman, third baseman, and manager for the Detroit Stars, Indianapolis ABC's, Cole's American Giants, Chicago American Giants, and Chicago Columbia Giants from 1916 to 1934. In an interview with author John Holway on file at the National Baseball Hall of Fame, Malarcher talked about how he wound up joining the Negro Leagues: "C. I. Taylor's Indianapolis ABC's had been to Cuba during the winter of 1915 and 1916, and they barnstormed back through New Orleans and played against my city team, the Eagles," Malarcher said. "They had Jimmy Lyons and Todd Allen; Morton Clark played shortstop; Ben Taylor was on first, George Shively in the outfield. Their second baseman, Bingo DeMoss, had left, he had gone to Jewell's ABC's in Indianapolis—they split—and the ABC's needed a second baseman. They saw me play and offered me a job. When C. I. offered me $50 a month, that was a lot of money, $50. I could give my mother half of that and still get along. So I went with him that summer, and went to school [New Orleans University] in the winter."

Malarcher also remembered some of his finest moments in baseball: "I made three plays in my career when fans came out and carried me around on their shoulders," he said. "The game in Detroit was my first year, 1916. We were barnstorming against the American Giants, and we played in Detroit in Navin Field, the Tigers' park. Bruce Petway was the guy that hit the ball, one of those long drives, a hard, long high fly. I guess I nearly ran a mile. I finally reached up and caught it with one hand, my left hand, over my right shoulder. We played 16 innings 1-1 and it was called on account of darkness. We had white umpires, and they made quite a few mistakes, we thought. We didn't argue with them, but after the game they came in and said, 'Definitely, fellows, we made some mistakes, but we have never seen this kind of baseball before.' The next morning the newspaper came out and said if the National and American leagues could play this kind of baseball that we saw today, they would have to enlarge their seating capacity. . . . In 1917 and 1918 they were calling me the best third baseman in the world. Once we were playing the Cubans in 1918 in Kokomo. The ABC's had a great record in Indiana. We liked to play in Anderson, Kokomo and all around there, in Ohio and that area. C. I. had all that area, and we beat those semi-pro clubs all the time. They loved the ABC's, all over the state. We were the favorites, even over the home team. This was a twilight game at Kokomo, and you know there are very few colored people in Kokomo. Just masses of white people out there, and they loved the ABC's. C. I. loved to win in Kokomo; that was his territory. We were playing the Cuban Stars, and it was getting late in the afternoon. They had one run behind in the ninth, and it was getting dark. I came to bat in the ninth inning and tripled. Rodriguez was the Cubans' catcher, kind of a proud fellow, a big, tall fellow—a good catcher. I was on third, the pitcher pitched, and I didn't even give Rodriguez time to throw it back. When he lobbed the ball back, I went home. Safe. On the first throw back to the pitcher—he didn't have any idea I was going home. I took the chance, because the next guy might fly out, then we would lose the ball game. C. I. was so happy, he ran out and grabbed me and kissed me. He gave me $5 right there on the field—$5 was a lot of money in those days."

Dave Malarcher was a brilliant baseman and showed skills both on the field and in the dugout when, as a manager, he led the famous Chicago American Giants to the Negro League World Series championship in 1926, defeating the Bacharach Giants in nine games. He did so again the following year, this time defeating the Giants in eight games. During a career that spanned 1916 to 1934, Malarcher was an outfielder, second baseman, third baseman, and manager for the American Giants, Detroit Stars, Indianapolis ABC's, Cole's American Giants, and Chicago Columbia Giants. (NATIONAL BASEBALL HALL OF FAME LIBRARY, COOPERSTOWN, N.Y.)

Malarcher also played for the great Chicago American Giant teams of Rube Foster's and talked about how they dominated the NEGRO NATIONAL LEAGUE. "From 1920, when the league started, the first four years we had a powerful team," he said. "Because we had gotten together the speed, the daring, the men that could really hit, a good pitching staff, and good catching. Rube was smart enough, a genius, to know how to pick men to fit into his plays, and he used to say this all the time, 'If you haven't got intelligence enough to fit into this play, you can't play here.' That's all there was to it." After Foster became ill, Malarcher took over managing the American Giants. "All the time I managed the American Giants I was never out of my seat on the bench, not a day, not a ball game," he said. "Every play started with me. And the ballplayers liked it. You have no trouble directing them if they know you are smarter than they are. When a man is under direction, he doesn't have to figure out what he should do. All he has to do is execute. If you know what to tell him to do, and he gets a great deal of success out of it, every time he comes up he's looking for the order. Every play started with me. That's the way Rube did it, and that's the way I did it."

Malarcher led the American Giants to a Negro League World Series championship in that 1926 season, defeating the Bacharach Giants in nine games and did so again the following year, this time in eight games. Like many Negro Leaguers and other baseball observers, Malarcher believes many of the players he played with and against could have played major league baseball: "From after the Civil War until the end of World War II, we had star ballplayers that could have measure up with any team in the major leagues. . . . Propaganda is a terrible thing. The propaganda of segregation and bigotry is evil. It deceives people. I used to have Negroes occasionally tell me, 'Do you think Negroes can play in the major leagues?' And do you know what I would say to them? I would say, 'Do you think so and so here, who is a barber, can cut hair like a white man?' I would say, 'Do you think Doctor so-and-so, who is teaching in a medical school, can teach a white professor? Well, certainly.' And I would say, 'What's baseball that I can't play it like a white?' The whole point is that the propaganda of keeping the Negro out of the major leagues made even some of the Negroes think that we didn't have the ability. It started them to thinking it too."

Malone, William

William Malone was a pitcher, first baseman, third baseman, and outfielder for the New York Gorhams, Cuban Giants, Pittsburgh Keystones, York Cuban Giants, Page Fence Giants, Pythians of Philadelphia, York Colored Monarchs, and Trenton Cuban Giants from 1886 to 1897. Partial records show that Malone batted .215 in 1890.

Manhattan baseball club of Washington

The Manhattan baseball club of Washington were a black baseball team that played in the 1880s in Washington, D.C.

Manley, Abe

Abe Manley was co-owner of the Brooklyn Eagles and Newark Eagles from 1935 to 1948 and vice president and treasurer of the NEGRO NATIONAL LEAGUE. Manley, like many other Negro League owners and operators, was heavily involved in the numbers racket. His wife, Effa, was the driving force behind the operation of the teams and sold the Newark franchise after the 1948 season.

Manley, Effa
b. 1900, d. 1981

Effa Manley was the wife of Abe Manley, co-owner of the Brooklyn Eagles and Newark Eagles from 1935 to 1948 and the primary presence behind the franchises. She also served as secretary of the NEGRO NATIONAL LEAGUE. She was the driving force behind the Eagles and found herself in several well-publicized business battles, both with players and major league owners. Several of her players, including Ray Dandridge, had left to play in Mexico, and Effa Manley went to court to try to stop them. She also tried to ban them from Negro League baseball when they returned. She got into feuds over influence in the Negro National League with white booking agent Eddie Gottlieb. Her influence extended to the field of play, where she would send signals to her managers about strategy during the game. Manley also battled Branch Rickey when the Brooklyn Dodgers' general manager began signing black players such as Don Newcombe and Monte Irvin, knowing it would be the demise of Negro League baseball. In Jules Tygiel's book *Jackie Robinson and His Legacy*, Effa Manley talked about their inability to get what they felt was proper compensation from Rickey when he began signing players away from Newark and how they had little recourse to fight it: "We were in no position to protest and he [Rickey] knew it," she said. "He had us over a barrel in a way. The fans would have never forgiven us [for holding players back from major league opportunities], plus it would have been wrong to have prevented the players from going to the major leagues." She sold the Eagles in 1948 to Memphis businessman W. H. Young and left the game.

Manning, John

John Manning was an outfielder for the Philadelphia Giants from 1902 to 1904.

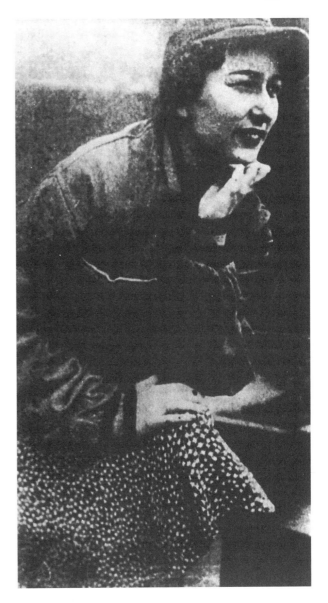

Effa Manley was probably the most powerful woman in the history of Negro League baseball. She was the wife of Abe Manley, co-owner of the Brooklyn Eagles and Newark Eagles from 1935 to 1948, but was the driving force behind the teams. She was also the secretary of the Negro National League and was an influential voice in league affairs. (NATIONAL BASEBALL HALL OF FAME LIBRARY, COOPERSTOWN, N.Y.)

Manning, Max
b. 1918

Max Manning was a pitcher for the Houston Eagles and Newark Eagles from 1938 to 1949. In a December 1992 interview with *Sports Collectors Digest*, Manning talked about the special challenge Negro League ballplayers felt when they took the field: "Each Negro League team felt they had something to prove," Manning said. "There was a tremendous amount of pride. Every athlete had in him

Max Manning was a standout pitcher in the Negro Leagues, posting a 51-29 career record in league competition while pitching for the Newark Eagles and Houston Eagles from 1938 to 1949 and playing with such future major league greats as Larry Doby and Monte Irvin. (NATIONAL BASEBALL HALL OF FAME LIBRARY, COOPERSTOWN, N.Y.)

the desire to play to the best of his ability. . . . We loved the game. We were thrilled to be playing baseball because we loved the game." Manning had the benefit of playing for Negro League great John Henry Lloyd on Johnson's All Stars in New Jersey as a young high school player. He was also a college teammate of Monte Irvin at Lincoln University in Pennsylvania. He also played winter baseball in Venezuela and Cuba and played minor league baseball in Canada in 1951. He posted a career won-loss record of 51-29 in Negro League baseball.

Manolo, Manno

Manno Manolo was a first baseman and pitcher for the Cincinnati Cubans, New York Cuban Stars, Cuban Stars, and All Cubans from 1916 to 1924.

Mapp, Dick

Dick Mapp was a shortstop for the Boston Royal Giants in 1942.

Mara, Candido

Candido Mara was a third baseman for the Memphis Red Sox in 1948.

Marcelle, Everett (Ziggy)
b. 1916, d. 1990

Everett Marcelle was a catcher for the Newark Eagles, Chicago American Giants, New York Black Yankees, Baltimore Elite Giants, Homestead Grays, and Kansas City Monarchs from 1939 to 1948. Records show that the 6-foot-2, 200-pound Marcelle batted .229 for Baltimore in 1947 and went on to play for Farnham in the Provincial League in 1950, batting .272. Marcelle also played basketball for the Harlem Globetrotters. He was the son of Negro League great Oliver Marcelle.

Marcelle, Oliver (Ghost)
b. 1897, d. 1949

Oliver Marcelle, one of the greatest third basemen in Negro baseball history, played for the New Orleans Black Eagles, New York Lincoln Giants, Atlantic City Bacharach Giants, Brooklyn Royal Giants, Miami Giants, Detroit Stars, and Baltimore Black Sox from 1918 to 1933. He was part of the "million dollar infield" of the Black Sox in 1929, along with Dick Lundy, Frank Warfield, and Jud Wilson.

Born in Thibedeaux, Louisiana, Marcelle batted .315, according to Negro League records, batting .379 for the Bacharach Giants in 1922, .352 in 1924, and .324 in 1927, and played in two Negro World Series in 1926 and 1927. He also played winter baseball in Cuba from 1923 to 1930 and batted .393 in the 1923–1924 season, leading the winter league. Marcelle is also believed to have hit .365 in 17 exhibition games against major league ballplayers. The *Pittsburgh Courier* once named Marcelle the best black third baseman of all time. "Oliver Marcelle could do everything!" the *Courier* stated. "A fielding gem who could go to his right or left with equal facility, could come up with breath-taking plays on bunts . . . he was a ballplayer's ballplayer and the idol of fandom." In John Holway's book *Blackball Stars*, pitcher Holsey "Scrip" Lee said that Marcelle was the best third baseman he had ever seen: "He made some of the greatest stops you've ever seen."

However, Marcelle's reputation was tarnished by a bad temper, as he got into numerous fights with opponents, umpires, and teammates. According to one story, during the winter baseball season in Cuba in 1927–1928, Marcelle got into a nasty brawl with Warfield and had a piece of his nose bit off and also once hit legendary baseball strongman Oscar Charleston over the head with a bat during a game. Buck O'Neil, in his autobiography, *I Was Right on Time*, recalled how Marcelle got his nickname: "We called Ollie the Ghost, because he was something of a loner on the road," O'Neil wrote. "He'd disappear after the games were over, and then he'd show up when we were ready for the next one. We'd see him and say, 'Well, here comes the Ghost!' He was a Creole from New Orleans, a handsome man who took pride in his looks."

After he was done playing after 1930, Marcelle tried managing in 1932 in Wilmington on what was a farm club for the Hilldale baseball club, wearing a patch on his nose. There, too, he got into one fight after another and was not cut out for managing. He came back in 1933 to play for the Miami Giants and spent his remaining years barnstorming and working as a laborer. His son, Everett "Ziggy" Marcelle, also played Negro League baseball.

Markham, John Matthew

John Markham was a left-handed knuckleball pitcher for the Kansas City Monarchs, Monroe Monarchs, and Birmingham Black Barons from 1930 to 1945. As a rookie in 1930, Markham, in a win over a team in Waco, became the first pitcher ever to throw a no-hitter in night baseball when the Monarchs, under owner J. L. Wilkinson, became the first club to play organized professional baseball under the lights.

Markham, Melvin

Melvin Markham was a pitcher for the Brooklyn Eagles and Newark Eagles from 1935 to 1936.

Maroto, Enrique

Enrique Maroto was a pitcher and outfielder for the Kansas City Monarchs from 1954 to 1955.

Marquez, Luis
b. 1925, d. 1988

Luis Marquez was an infielder and outfielder for the Homestead Grays, New York Black Yankees, and Baltimore Elite Giants from 1945 to 1948. Born in Puerto Rico, the 5-foot-10, 180-pound Marquez batted .309 in 81 at bats for Baltimore and Homestead in 1946, and hit .417 for Homestead in 1947 in 230 plates appearances, with 29 stolen bases. His career Negro League batting average was .389. Marquez went on to sign a contract with the New York Yankees in 1949 and was assigned to play with Newark in the International League, batting .246. He didn't stay with the Yankees organization, though, after contract problems came up and played with Portland in the Pacific Coast League in 1950 and 1951, batting .294 and .311. While with Portland, Marquez found himself the target of brushback pitches and other slights and attacks believed to be racially motivated and got into several well-publicized brawls with other players. Marquez played minor league baseball until 1961, his last year with Williamsport in the Eastern League, and had two brief stints in the major leagues, appearing in 68 games

with the Boston Braves in 1951, hitting .197, and then in 1954 with the Chicago Cubs and Pittsburgh Pirates, batting just .095 in 31 games. He finished his playing career in the Mexican League in 1963. Marquez also played winter baseball in Puerto Rico from 1945 to 1962. He was shot to death during a family argument in the Dominican Republic.

Marsans, Armando
b. 1887, d. 1960

Armando Marsans was an outfielder for the Cuban Stars and All Cubans in 1905 and 1923. In between his Negro League stints, the 5-foot-10, 160-pound Marsans, born in Matanzas, Cuba, played for the Cincinnati Reds, St. Louis Browns, and New York Yankees for eight seasons, from 1911 to 1918, getting 612 hits in 655 games, scoring 267 runs, driving in 221 runs, and batting .269, with 171 stolen bases.

Marsellas, David, Jr.

Dave Marsellas, Jr., was a catcher for the New York Black Yankees in 1941.

Marsh, Lorenzo

Lorenzo Marsh was a catcher for the Cleveland Buckeyes in 1950.

Marshall, Bobby

Bobby Marshall was a first baseman and manager for the Leland Giants, St. Paul Gophers, Twin City Gophers, and Chicago Giants from 1909 to 1911.

Marshall, Hiram

Hiram Marshall was a pitcher and third baseman for the Boston Blues in 1946.

Marshall, Jack

Jack Marshall was a pitcher for the Detroit Stars, Kansas City Monarchs, Chicago American Giants, and Birmingham Black Barons from 1920 to 1929.

Marshall, William (Jack)
b. 1907

William Marshall was an infielder for Gilkerson's Union Giants, Dayton Marcos, Cole's American Giants, Chicago Columbia Giants, Philadelphia Stars, Chicago American Giants, Kansas City Monarchs, and Cincinnati-Indianapolis Clowns from 1926 to 1944.

Born in Montgomery, Alabama, Marshall was a fast runner and known as a good bunter. In his final year of baseball, with the Indianapolis Clowns in 1944, Marshall batted .311. In Robert Peterson's book *Only the Ball Was White*, Marshall recalled some barnstorming independent clowning days: "In 1929, I organized a troupe—ballplayers, show and band—for a white Canadian named Rod Whitman out of Lafleche, Saskatchewan," Marshall said. "He came to Chicago and he wanted two Negro ballclubs, he wanted a minstrel show, and he wanted a band. In Canada he had a midway or carnival, and he would show in different towns, so he wanted two ballclubs—specifically, he wanted one named the Texas Giants and one named the New York All Stars. So I organized this group for him, and I got a five-piece band and six other people as the minstrel show. We traveled from Fort Williams, Ontario, to Vancouver, British Columbia, as far north as Prince Albert and as far south as Medicine Hat. We had four trucks—they looked like old covered wagons. We had a tent where the performers lived. When we got into a small town, they'd set up a tent where the other tents were for the midway, and some of the performers would sleep there. Then, when we got into a town big enough to have a hotel, the ballclubs would stop in the hotel. And at twelve o'clock every day, Rod would put up $500 to the local team to play the all-stars—a team that would be selected from the Texas Giants and New York All Stars. And if they won the game, they'd get the $500. Well, we never lost a game under those conditions because we had our own umpires. We weren't there to lose. So he'd charge admission for that, and then, when the ballgame was over, he would open up the midway. At six o'clock the Texas Giants and the New York All Stars would play a game and that's another admission. Now, when this ballgame was over, then the midway would open up again. While the midway was open, he would put this colored minstrel show on. With the midway and the minstrel show going on at one time, this man is coining the money! Now, when the midway closes, then the band would play for the dance. That's another admission, and the dance would go till one o'clock. Damnedest operation you ever saw! Whitman was just selling entertainment, no patent medicine or anything like that. All the ballplayers were semi-pros from Chicago. At that time, in 1929, you might call me a pro. Anyway, I organized the thing. We had a payroll of $1,800 a month for 24 players."

Martin, Ed

Ed Martin was a pitcher for the Philadelphia Stars from 1951 to 1952.

Martin, Jim (Pepper)

Jim Martin was an infielder for the Brooklyn Eagles in 1935.

Martin, John B.
(b. 1884, d. 1973)

Dr. John B. Martin was owner and officer from 1929 to 1950 for the Chicago American Giants and Memphis Red Sox and also served as president of the NEGRO AMERICAN LEAGUE, Negro Southern League, and Negro Dixie League.

Martin, William (Stack)

William Martin was a first baseman, outfielder, and catcher for the Detroit Stars, Indianapolis ABC's, Wilmington Potomacs, and Dayton Marcos from 1925 to 1928.

Martinez, Francisco

Francisco Martinez was a pitcher for the Cuban Stars in 1939.

Martinez, Horacio (Rabbit)

Horacio Martinez was a third baseman and shortstop for the New York Cubans from 1935 to 1947. Martinez was a weak-hitting but slick-fielding shortstop who was recognized during his time as one of the best shortstops in Negro League baseball and is among the greatest shortstops to ever come out of the Dominican Republic, a hotbed for shortstop prospects. He is a member of the Dominican Republic Sports Hall of Fame.

Martinez, Pasquel

Pasquel Martinez was a pitcher for the Cuban Stars and All Cubans from 1920 to 1928.

Martini, Jose

Jose Martini was a pitcher for the New York Cubans in 1928 and 1935.

Martin Park

Martin Park in Memphis, Tennessee, was the home of the Memphis Red Sox from 1923 to 1950, named after the Martin family that owned the club.

Maryland Park

Maryland Park was a ballpark in Baltimore, Maryland, that was home to the Baltimore Black Sox in the 1920s.

Marvarez, Fernando

Fernando Marvarez was an infielder for the Pittsburgh Crawfords in 1945.

Marvin, Alfred

Alfred Marvin was a pitcher for the Kansas City Monarchs in 1938.

Marvray, Charles (Hawk)

b. 1929, d. 1998

Charles Marvray was an outfielder for the Louisville Buckeyes and Cleveland Buckeyes from 1949 to 1950.

Mason, Charles (Suitcase)

Charles Mason was a pitcher and outfielder for the Bacharach Giants, Richmond Giants, Newark Stars, Homestead Grays, and Lincoln Giants from 1922 to 1929.

Mason, Henry

b. 1931

Henry Mason was a right-handed pitcher for the Kansas City Monarchs from 1951 to 1954. The 6-foot, 185-pound Mason, born in Marshall, Missouri, went on to pitch for the Philadelphia Phillies in 1958 and 1960, appearing in a total of four games, 10 2/3 innings with a 10.13 ERA.

Mason, James

James Mason was a pitcher for the Pittsburgh Keystones in 1887.

Mason, Jim

Jim Mason was an outfielder and first baseman for the Cuban Stars, Memphis Red Sox, and Washington Pilots from 1931 to 1934.

Mason, Marcelius

Marcelius Mason was an officer with the Cleveland Bears from 1939 to 1940.

Mason, William

William Mason was an infielder and outfielder for the Cleveland Clippers in 1946.

Massip, Armando

Armando Massip was a first baseman and outfielder for the Memphis Red Sox, Washington Pilots, New York Cubans, and Cuban Stars from 1920 to 1926.

Matchett, Clarence (Jack)

Clarence Matchett was a pitcher for the Kansas City Monarchs from 1940 to 1945 and helped lead Kansas City to a win over the Homestead Grays in the 1942 Negro World Series.

Mathis, Verdell (Lefty)

b. 1921, d. 1998

Verdell Mathis was a pitcher, outfielder, and first baseman for the Memphis Red Sox and Philadelphia Stars from 1940 to 1950. In a 1999 interview with *Sports Collectors Digest*, former Negro Leaguer Nap Gulley said that Mathis "was the best pitcher of our time. He should have been in the Hall of Fame. . . . Verdell could win. Just give him one run and he wouldn't have a problem. He beat Satchel more than Satchel beat him." In an interview with author John Holway on file at the National Baseball Hall of Fame, Mathis said that he grew up as a young boy reading about the exploits of Paige. In 1940, as a 19-year-old rookie, Mathis faced his boyhood hero Paige and beat him 1-0 in 11 innings in a game in New Orleans. He also drove in the winning run against Paige on Satchel Paige Day in Chicago before 30,000 fans. Mathis felt a strong kinship to Paige and said he tried to talking pitching with his idol whenever their clubs faced each other: "I was trying to get information, because I didn't want anybody to beat me," Mathis said. "I had determination."

He also talked about facing another legend, Josh Gibson: "Any good hitter, just rare [sic] back and throw the best pitch," he said. "If they hit it, they hit it. Now the only thing you have to do with a man like Gibson, you have to be careful and don't make no mistakes. You try to throw the ball where you want to. I always used the screwball on Gibson, low and away. He never hit a home run off me."

Mathis also pitched in several EAST-WEST Negro League ALL-STAR GAMES and talked about his success in those contests played in Chicago: "I didn't ever lose a game in Chicago," he said. "That was really my park. I started three East-West games there. They would put Gibson and Campanella in the lineup together. They wanted all the right-handed power they could get. They would put Campanella on third and let Gibson catch. But that didn't make no difference to me. I was happy. Right-handers didn't hit me because of my screwball. I was happy if they put eight right-handers in the lineup. I knew I had a good chance of winning that game. And in those East-West game, ain't nobody made a score on me."

In a 1975 interview with the *Memphis Commercial Appeal*, Mathis gave his version of how he believed major league baseball finally integrated: "We used to play in all the big white parks when they [major league

Verdell Mathis grew up as a young boy reading about the exploits of the great Negro League pitcher Satchel Paige. In 1940, as a 19-year-old rookie, Mathis faced his boyhood hero Paige and beat him 1-0 in 11 innings in a game in New Orleans. It was the start of a solid career as a pitcher, outfielder, and first baseman for the Memphis Red Sox and Philadelphia Stars from 1940 to 1950. (NATIONAL BASEBALL HALL OF FAME LIBRARY, COOPERSTOWN, N.Y.)

150,000 a year. They support my park, if you want to know the truth. Naw, we won't do that.' Well, Rickey wasn't getting any of that money so he decided to hurt the others where it hurt the most—in their pocketbooks. He went after a black. Took a year researching the black leagues and finally came up with Robinson, a college man, a man he felt could handle the pressure. Oh, Lordy, there must have been 30 guys playing then who were better than Robinson. But he was the right man for handling what was to come."

Matlock, Leroy
b. 1907, d. 1968

Leroy Matlock was a pitcher for the Detroit Wolves, St. Louis Stars, Homestead Grays, Washington Pilots, New York Cubans, and Pittsburgh Crawfords from 1929 to 1942. Matlock had a remarkable year in 1935, going 17-0 and leading the Crawfords to the first-half Negro National League championship. However, he fell to 3-2 in 1936 and never matched his 1935 season. Matlock was also one of the players who left the Crawfords in 1937 to play in the Dominican Republic for dictator Rafael Trujillo in the political baseball war that was being waged there. He also played for Vera Cruz in the Mexican League with Josh Gibson, Ray Dandridge, and Willie Wells in 1941.

Matthews, Clifford

Clifford Matthews was the owner of the New York Black Pelicans in 1945.

Matthews, Dell

Dell Matthews was a pitcher and outfielder for the Chicago Union Giants and Leland Giants from 1904 to 1905.

Matthews, Dick

Dick Matthews was a pitcher for the Monroe Monarchs and New Orleans Crescent Stars in 1932 and 1933.

Matthews, Francis Oliver

Francis Matthews as a first baseman for the Boston Royal Giants, Newark Eagles, Baltimore Elite Giants, and New York Cubans from 1938 to 1945.

Matthews, Jack

Jack Matthews was a third baseman for the Toledo Tigers in 1923.

teams] were out of town," he said. "We used to play in all but one—Ebbets Field in Brooklyn. But we used the Polo Grounds and Yankee Stadium and didn't need Ebbets. Branch Rickey [Brooklyn Dodgers general manager] soon discovered we, the blacks, were filling the stadiums every time we played. He saw Clark Griffith [Washington Senators owner] and asked him about it. Mr. Rickey asked Griffith why the major leagues couldn't buy up all the black franchises and gain the best players off those teams. I'm told that Mr. Griffith just leaned back in his chair and said, 'Naw, we won't do that.' Rickey asked him why not. He said, 'Branch, my friend, I can sit home with my legs crossed and those black players draw

Matthews, Jesse

Jesse Matthews was an infielder for the Birmingham Black Barons in 1942.

Matthews, John T. (Big)

John T. Matthews was the owner of the Dayton Marcos from 1919 to 1933, although it is not clear what form of the Marcos Matthews owned after 1920. According to one story in Robert Peterson's book *Only the Ball Was White*, Matthews lost his players after the 1920 season when, at a NEGRO NATIONAL LEAGUE meeting, he fell asleep and woke up to find that league president Rube Foster had dropped the Marcos from the league and sent his players to other teams. The Marcos were not part of the league in 1921.

Matthews, William

d. 1928

William Matthews was a shortstop and second baseman for Burlington in the Vermont League and the New York Black Sox from 1905 to 1910. According to Robert Peterson's book *Only the Ball Was White*, Matthews played baseball at Harvard from 1902 to 1905. There were reports that a National League team was going to try to sign Matthews to a major league contract. However, that never happened, and Matthews, after suffering from a number of racially motivated incidents in the Vermont League, left baseball and went on to be an attorney. He died in 1928.

Maupin, Frank

Frank Maupin was a catcher and third baseman for the Lincoln Giants and Plattsmouth in the Nebraska League from 1890 to 1902.

Maxwell, Zearlee

Zearlee Maxwell was a third baseman and second baseman for the Memphis Red Sox and Monroe Monarchs from 1931 to 1938.

Mayo, George (Hot Stuff)

George Mayo was an outfielder and first baseman for the Pittsburgh Giants, Pittsburgh Colored Stars, Pittsburgh Stars of Buffalo, and Hilldale baseball club from 1911 to 1917.

Mays, Dave

Dave Mays was an outfielder for the Kansas City Monarchs in 1937.

Mays, Roy (Cat)

Roy Mays, the father of Willie Mays, played for the Birmingham Black Barons in the 1930s. In an interview with author John Holway on file at the National Baseball Hall of Fame, Negro Leaguer James Canady talked about playing with Roy Mays and how he discovered Willie Mays: "I first found Willie Mays in Fairfield, Alabama, playing on a little team called the Fairfield Stars," he said. "I played with his daddy, Roy Mays. He had played a little bit with the Birmingham Black Barons. He was a center fielder, like Willie, and he was fast—he was faster than Willie. I don't think Willie could play any better outfield than Roy could, because he caught everything out there. He was shorter than Willie and a little lighter. He wasn't a natural hitter like Willie, but he could drag that ball. He couldn't hit much, but he could catch everything."

Mays, Willie

b. 1931

Willie Mays, considered perhaps the greatest all-around player in the history of major league baseball, began his career as an outfielder for the Chattanooga Choo-Choos and Birmingham Black Barons, playing Negro League baseball from 1948 to 1950. Mays would go on to play 22 major league seasons, from 1951 to 1973, for the New York Giants and then, after moving the team to the West Coast after the 1957 season, the San Francisco Giants and finishing his final year back in New York with the Mets. He was equally as great at the plate and in center field. Mays hit 660 home runs over his career, third behind Hank Aaron and Babe Ruth on the all-time home run list. In 2,992 career games, Mays had 3,283 hits—only one of three players (Aaron and Eddie Murray being the two others) to have hit more than 500 home runs and more than 3,000 hits. He also drove in 1,903 runs, scored 2,062 runs, stole 338 bases, and retired with a lifetime batting average of .302. He is considered the greatest center fielder ever to play major league baseball and is best known for the historic over-the-shoulder catch he made on a Vic Wertz long drive to center field in the 1954 World Series.

Before he became a major league legend, the 5-foot-11, 170-pound Mays, born in Westfield, Alabama, got his start in Negro League baseball. Records show that in 25 games with Birmingham in 1948, Mays batted .262 while he was still in high school at the time. The following year Mays hit .311 in 75 games, and with the Black Barons in 1950, Mays hit .330 in 27 games. Ironically, there was some interest in Mays from the Red Sox organization—the last baseball franchise to integrate. The Black Barons used a field owned by the Red Sox minor league club in Birmingham, and the team had sent several scouts to watch Mays after hearing about his play. But, according to Jules Tygiel in his book

Jackie Robinson and His Legacy, one scout failed to show up after several games were rained out, and another scout didn't want to make the drive for his assignment, so they never got the look at Mays that Red Sox management believed they had, although it's doubtful that they would have signed him.

In an interview with author John Holway on file at the National Baseball Hall of Fame, Negro Leaguer James Canada talked about how he first saw Mays play: "I first found Willie Mays in Fairfield, Alabama, playing on a little team called the Fairfield Stars. . . . When I first met Willie, he was playing shortstop. He'd get down on one knee to field the ball—he was just determined to be a good ballplayer. But I told him, 'You're not a shortstop, you're not a catcher and you're not a pitcher. You're an outfielder.' So I changed him to center field. . . . I carried Mays away to the Chattanooga Choo-Choos in 1948. I was managing there at the time. I managed there about two months and then left on account of finances. They couldn't pay me one Sunday

morning and so Willie came over with me to Birmingham." Mays was signed away from Birmingham by Giants scout Ed Montague, and he played for the Minneapolis minor league club before moving on to play for the Giants. In Minneapolis he befriended Negro League great Ray Dandridge, who was also playing for Minneapolis but by this time was considered too old by the Giants to call him up. Dandridge was instrumental in the development of Mays while in Minneapolis: "Ray Dandridge was like my father," Mays said in Holway's book *Blackball Stars*.

At a 1981 Hall of History reunion in Ashland, Kentucky, Mays credited his Negro League playing days for preparing him for success in major league baseball. "I'm proud that these fellows sent me to the majors," Mays said. "I learned baseball from these people. I learned how to hit certain pitches, how to control my mind, how to get knocked down and get up and hit again. I learned all these things before I came to the majors. The majors were easy for me. I have no reason to say I was a major league

Willie Mays was one of the greatest all-around players in the history of major league baseball. He hit 660 career home runs, 3,283 hits, drove in 1,903 runs, scored 2,062 runs, and had a batting average of .302 for most of his career with the New York and San Francisco Giants. He got his start in Negro League baseball as an outfielder for the Chattanooga Choo-Choos and Birmingham Black Barons from 1948 to 1950. Mays has credited his Negro League playing days with preparing him for success in major league baseball. (NATIONAL BASEBALL HALL OF FAME LIBRARY, COOPERSTOWN, N.Y.)

ballplayer by myself." Mays was inducted into the National Baseball Hall of Fame in 1979.

Mayweather, Eldridge (Head)

Eldridge Mayweather was a first baseman for the Monroe Monarchs, Kansas City Monarchs, St. Louis Stars, New Orleans–St. Louis Stars, Boston Blues, New York Black Yankees, and Brooklyn Eagles from 1934 to 1946.

Mayweather, Elliott

Elliott Mayweather was a pitcher for the Memphis Red Sox from 1928 to 1929.

Mazaar, Robert

Robert Mazaar was an officer for the Hilldale baseball club in 1945.

McAdoo, Dudley

Dudley McAdoo was a first baseman for the Topeka Giants, Kansas City Giants, St. Louis Stars, St. Louis Giants, Chicago American Giants, Cleveland Browns, Chicago Union Giants, and Chicago Giants from 1907 to 1927.

McAllister, Frank (Chip)

Frank McAllister was a pitcher for the St. Louis Stars, Indianapolis ABC's, New York Black Yankees, New Orleans–St. Louis Stars, Harrisburg–St. Louis Stars, Cleveland Clippers, and Brooklyn Brown Dodgers from 1938 to 1946.

McAllister, George

George McAllister was a pitcher for the Chicago American Giants, Birmingham Black Barons, Memphis Red Sox, Indianapolis ABC's, Homestead Grays, Detroit Stars, Cuban Stars, and Cleveland Red Sox from 1923 to 1934.

McAllister, Mike

Mike McAllister was an outfielder for the Kansas City Monarchs in 1921.

McBride, Fred

Fred McBride was a pitcher and outfielder for the Chicago American Giants, Indianapolis ABC's, and Birmingham Black Barons from 1931 to 1940.

McCall, Butch

Butch McCall was a first baseman for the Birmingham Black Barons, Chicago American Giants, and Indianapolis Athletics from 1936 to 1938.

McCall, Henry

Henry McCall was an outfielder for the Chicago American Giants in 1945.

McCall, William L.

William McCall was a pitcher for the Birmingham Black Barons, Pittsburgh Keystones, Chicago American Giants, Kansas City Monarchs, Detroit Stars, Indianapolis ABC's, Cleveland Tigers, Toledo Tigers, and Cleveland Tate Stars from 1922 to 1931.

McCarey, Willie

Willie McCarey was a pitcher for the Cleveland Buckeyes from 1943 to 1945.

McCarthy, C. H.

C. H. McCarthy was president of the Southeastern Negro League in 1921.

McCary, James

James McCary was an umpire in the NEGRO NATIONAL LEAGUE in 1925.

McCauley, Ben

Ben McCauley was an outfielder for the Kansas City Monarchs in 1953.

McClain, Edward (Boots)

Edward McClain was an infielder and pitcher for the Cleveland Tates Stars, Dayton Marcos, Toledo Tigers, Detroit Stars, Cleveland Browns, Columbus Buckeyes, Columbus Bluebirds, and Indianapolis ABC's from 1920 to 1933.

McClellan, Dan (Little)

Dan McClellan was a left-handed pitcher and manager who played from 1902 to 1931 for the Philadelphia Giants, Cuban X Giants, Lincoln Giants, Quaker Giants, Smart Set, Washington Potomacs, Wilmington Potomacs, and Brooklyn Royal Giants from 1902 to 1931. According to former Negro League player, manager, and historian Sol White, McClellan was the first black pitcher in Negro League competition to pitch a perfect game, blanking the York, Pennsylvania, club on July 17, 1903, before a crowd of about 600.

McClinnic, Nat
Nat McClinnic was an outfielder for the Cleveland Buckeyes from 1946 to 1948.

McClure, Bob
Bob McClure was a pitcher for the Baltimore Black Sox, Cleveland Tate Stars, Indianapolis ABC's, Toledo Tigers, Brooklyn Royal Giants, and Bacharach Giants from 1920 to 1930.

McClure, Will
Will McClure was an officer with the Chattanooga Choo-Choos in 1947.

McCollum, Frank
Frank McCollum was a pitcher for the Birmingham Black Barons and Louisville Black Colonels from 1954 to 1955.

McCord, Clinton
b. 1925

Clinton McCord was an infielder for the Chicago American Giants and Baltimore Elite Giants from 1947 to 1950. Born in Nashville, Tennessee, the 5-foot-11, 170-pound McCord hit .269 in 55 games with Baltimore in 1949 and .368 in 31 games with the Elite Giants and the American Giants in 1950. He went on to play minor league baseball until 1961. His best minor league seasons were with Paris in the Mississippi–Ohio Valley League, where McCord hit 16 home runs, drove in 118 runs, and batted .363 in 1951 and 15 home runs, 109 RBI, and batted .392 in 1952.

McCovey, Willie
b. 1938

Willie McCovey was a left-handed-hitting first baseman for the Birmingham Black Barons in 1958 who would go on to become one of the all-time home run hitters in major league baseball, playing first base primarily for the San Francisco Giants from 1959 to 1980, with three seasons with the San Diego Padres and the Oakland Athletics mixed in from 1974 to 1976. Born in Mobile, Alabama, the 6-foot-4, 200-pound McCovey went on to hit 521 career home runs and drive in 1,555 runs in 2,588 games. Manager and former Negro Leaguer James Canada in an interview with author John Holway on file at the

Willie McCovey was a Hall of Fame slugger for the San Francisco Giants, hitting 521 home runs and driving in 1,555 runs in 2,588 major league games. But he was one of the last black major league players to come from the Negro Leagues, spending one season with the Birmingham Black Barons in 1958, more than 10 years after Jackie Robinson broke the color barrier in baseball. (NATIONAL BASEBALL HALL OF FAME LIBRARY, COOPERSTOWN, N.Y.)

National Baseball Hall of Fame, said that McCovey "can't play first base. He could swing a bat, though."

McCoy, Frank
Frank McCoy was a catcher for the Newark Dodgers, Newark Browns, Bacharach Giants, and Harrisburg–St. Louis Stars from 1931 to 1943.

McCoy, Roy
Roy McCoy was an officer with the Washington Pilots in 1932.

McCoy, Walter
Walter McCoy was a pitcher for the Chicago American Giants from 1945 to 1948.

McCrary, George

George McCrary was a pitcher for the New York Black Yankees in 1943.

McCray, William

William McCray was a pitcher for the Louisville Black Colonels in 1954.

McCreary, Fred

Fred McCreary was an umpire in the NEGRO NATIONAL LEAGUE from 1938 to 1949.

McCree, Earl

Earl McCree was a pitcher for the Kansas City Monarchs in 1952.

McCurine, James (Big Jim and Big Stick)
b. 1921, d. 2002

James McCurine was an outfielder for the Chicago American Giants from 1946 to 1949. McCurine was a powerfully built player with a strong throwing arm who hit a career high .296 in 1946.

McDaniels, Booker T.
b. 1912, d. 1974

Booker T. McDaniels was a pitcher and outfielder for the Kansas City Monarchs and Memphis Red Sox from 1940 to 1952. A right-handed reliever, the 6-foot-2, 200-pound McDaniels, born in Morrilton, Arizona, posted a 7-0 record in 1942 on the Monarchs' Negro League World Series championship team and followed that with a 9-1 mark. He slumped to 2-5 in 1944 and bounced back with a 6-3 record in 21 appearances in 1945. In 1946, McDaniels pitched for San Luis in the Mexican League and posted a 14-18 mark. He came back to Kansas City in 1947 briefly but also pitched in Mexico for Vera Cruz (14-14) and again for San Luis (12-12) in 1948. He made another stop with the Monarchs in 1949, appearing in nine games and going 4-2. While pitching for the Monarchs, McDaniels sometimes was asked to pose as Satchel Paige in barnstorming promotional tours when Paige wasn't available, according to Mark Ribowsky's book *A Complete History of the Negro Leagues: 1884–1955*. McDaniels also broke into the Pacific Coast League in 1949, pitching for Los Angeles for two seasons. After one more stint in Mexico, McDaniels finished his career with Kansas City in 1952. He also played winter ball in Cuba from 1945 to 1950.

McDaniels, Fred

Fred McDaniels was an outfielder for the Kansas City Monarchs, Memphis Red Sox, Houston Eagles, and New Orleans Eagles from 1940 to 1951.

McDevitt, Dan

Dan McDevitt was an umpire in the NEGRO NATIONAL LEAGUE in the 1920s.

McDevitt, John J.

John McDevitt was an officer with the Baltimore Black Sox in 1922.

McDonald, Earl

Earl McDonald was an officer with the Washington Black Senators in 1938.

McDonald, Luther (Vet)

Luther McDonald was a pitcher for the Chicago American Giants, St. Louis Stars, Chicago Columbia Giants, Detroit Stars, Cole's American Giants, and Memphis Red Sox from 1927 to 1937.

McDonald, Webster
b. 1900, d. 1982

Webster McDonald was a pitcher with an underhand delivery and was a manager for the Richmond Giants, Philadelphia Giants, Madison Stars, Hilldale baseball club, Darby Daisies, Chicago American Giants, Washington Pilots, Wilmington Potomacs, Philadelphia Stars, Detroit Stars, Homestead Grays, Baltimore Black Sox, Norfolk Stars, and Lincoln Giants from 1918 to 1945. Born in Wilmington, Delaware, McDonald impressed Philadelphia Athletics owner and manager Connie Mack so much after he watched McDonald pitch in a 1935 exhibition game against Dizzy Dean that Mack said, "I'm sorry to say that, but I'd give half my ball club for a man like you," according to Jules Tygiel's book, *Jackie Robinson and His Legacy*. In one year, the 1923 season, McDonald reportedly had a record of 27-3 and went 17-2 in 1925.

In an interview with author John Holway on file at the National Baseball Hall of Fame, McDonald spoke about his pitching prowess: "Jimmy Foxx used to say all I have to do is throw my curve out there and they're beat," McDonald said. "He used to hit the curve in the American League like nobody's business, but I'd throw him a change-up that looked like you could catch it with your bare hands, and the umpire would call a strike. The next pitch I'd push him back a little with a fast one. Biz Mackey, my catcher, would tell Foxx what was coming,

Webster McDonald, shown here with an Italian newspaperman and Philadelphia's Anthony Angelo, had an unorthodox underhanded pitching delivery that made him one of the toughest pitchers for batters to face in Negro League baseball. In 1923, McDonald is believed to have posted a record of 27-3 and he also went on to become a Negro League manager. (NATIONAL BASEBALL HALL OF FAME LIBRARY, COOPERSTOWN, N.Y.)

and Foxx would say, 'Throw me something I can hit. Don't throw me that bender.' . . . I was strictly a submarine pitcher, a lot of junk. I had a good fast one, but I didn't throw it when I didn't have to. With the hard hitters, I'd time them. I'd throw mixed pitches—56 varieties, they used to call me. And then when I'd show them a good fast ball they weren't ready for it. I'd say, 'See, you weren't ready.'" McDonald also talked about his days as a manager: "The ballplayers believed in me," he said. "They trusted and respected me. If I told them something, they could depend on it, and I made the owners live up to their agreements . . . and I never used bad language. In fact, I got rid of a lot of good ballplayers because they used bad language. I'd trade them, give them away. I didn't like that kind of language."

McDougal, James

James McDougal was an outfielder for the Chicago American Giants in 1952.

McDougal, Lem

Lem McDougal was a pitcher for the Indianapolis ABC's, Chicago American Giants, and Chicago Giants from 1917 to 1920.

McDuffie, Terris

Terris McDuffie was a pitcher and outfielder for the Baltimore Black Sox, Birmingham Black Barons, Newark Eagles, New York Black Yankees, Philadelphia Stars, Homestead Grays, Brooklyn Eagles, Newark Dodgers, Bacharach Giants, Pennsylvania Red Caps, Cuban Stars, and Hilldale baseball club from 1930 to 1945. Records show the 6-foot-2, 200-pound McDuffie batted .290 for Birmingham in 61 games in 1930, and .333 in 1932 in 11 games for Baltimore, the Cuban Stars, and Bacharach Giants. McDuffie, along with Dave "Showboat" Thomas, had a private tryout before Brooklyn Dodgers general manager Branch Rickey in the spring of 1945 at the Dodgers training camp in Bear Mountain, New York, after pressure from Joe Bostic, sports editor of the *People's Voice*. Nothing came of the tryout. The year before, McDuffie, at the end of his career, posted a 5-6 record. According to Mark Ribowsky's book *A Complete History of the Negro Leagues: 1884–1955*, McDuffie was a self-pro-

Terris McDuffie, a pitcher and outfielder, once had a tryout for the Brooklyn Dodgers before general manager Branch Rickey in 1945, but nothing came of it. McDuffie played from 1930 to 1945 for the Baltimore Black Sox, Birmingham Black Barons, Newark Eagles, New York Black Yankees, Philadelphia Stars, Homestead Grays, Brooklyn Eagles, Newark Dodgers, Bacharach Giants, Pennsylvania Red Caps, Cuban Stars, and Hilldale baseball club. (NATIONAL BASEBALL HALL OF FAME LIBRARY, COOPERSTOWN, N.Y.)

moter who called himself "The Great McDuffie." The *New Jersey Herald News* said McDuffie was "Negro baseball's Dizzy Dean." Reports are that McDuffie's finest moment may have come on July 4, 1938, when he pitched a complete-game victory over the New York Black Yankees and then came into the second game with one out in the first inning and went on to pitch 8 2/3 innings to win his second game of the day.

McFarland, John

John McFarland was a pitcher for the New York Black Yankees from 1944 to 1947.

McGee, Horace

Horace McGee was the manager of the Cincinnati Browns in 1887.

McGowan, Curtis

Curtis McGowan was a pitcher for the Memphis Red Sox in 1950.

McGowan, Malcolm

Malcolm McGowan was the owner-officer of the Bacharach Giants from 1923 to 1941.

McHaskell, J. C.

J. C. McHaskell was a first baseman for the Memphis Red Sox from 1926 to 1929.

McHenry, Henry

Henry McHenry was a pitcher for the New York Black Yankees, Philadelphia Stars, Indianapolis Clowns, Pennsylvania Red Caps, Newark Browns, Bacharach Giants, and Kansas City Monarchs from 1930 to 1950.

McIntosh, James

James McIntosh was a catcher for the Detroit Stars in 1937.

McKelvin, Fred

Fred McKelvin was a pitcher for the Cincinnati–Cleveland Buckeyes and Jacksonville Red Caps in 1942.

McKenzie, Herbert

Herbert McKenzie was a catcher for the New York Black Yankees in 1950.

McKinnis, Gready (Lefty)
b. 1913

Gready McKinnis was a pitcher for the Chicago American Giants, Pittsburgh Crawfords, and Birmingham Black Barons from 1941 to 1949. Born in Bullock County, Alabama, McKinnis's best season came in 1949 with Birmingham, when he had a 12-7 record with a 2.35 ERA in 31 games. McKinnis played minor league baseball with Tampa in 1952 and 1953 and St. Petersburg in 1955, his final season in professional baseball, when he went 5-8 with a 4.58 ERA in 28 games.

McLain, Bill

Bill McLain was a pitcher for the Columbus Blue Birds in 1933.

McLaurin, Felix

Felix McLaurin was an outfielder for the Jacksonville Red Caps, New York Black Yankees, Chicago American Giants, and Birmingham Black Barons from 1942 to 1952.

McMahon, Ed

Ed McMahon was a boxing and wrestling promoter and a partner with his brother, Jess McMahon, who both owned and operated the Philadelphia Quaker Giants from 1906 to 1909 and the Lincoln Giants in New York from 1911 to 1916. The brothers were named by former Negro League player, manager, and historian Sol White on a list of "great modernists" of Negro League baseball in the early part of the 20th century.

McMahon, Jess

Jess McMahon was a boxing and wrestling promoter who, along with his brother, Ed McMahon, owned and operated the Philadelphia Quaker Giants from 1906 to 1909 and then the Lincoln Giants in New York from 1911 to 1916. His son, Vince McMahon, became a prominent wrestling promoter on the East Coast, and Jess McMahon's grandson, Vince McMahon, Jr., built his father's wrestling promotional company into the multimillion-dollar World Wrestling Entertainment. The brothers were named by former Negro League player, manager, and historian Sol White on a list of "great modernists" of Negro League baseball in the early part of the 20th century.

McMeans, Willie

Willie McMeans was a pitcher for the Chicago American Giants in 1945.

McMillan, Earl Thomas
b. 1901, d. 1999

Earl McMillan was an outfielder for the Toledo Tigers in 1923.

McMullin, Clarence
Clarence McMullin was an outfielder for the Houston Eagles and Kansas City Monarchs from 1945 to 1949.

McMurray, William
William McMurray was a catcher for the St. Louis Giants, St. Paul Gophers, and West Baden Sprudels from 1909 to 1914.

McNair, Hurley
Hurley McNair was a pitcher and outfielder for the Gilkerson Union Giants, Chicago Giants, Chicago American Giants, Chicago Union Giants, Detroit Stars, Kansas City Monarchs, ALL NATIONS team, and Cincinnati Tigers from 1911 to 1946. He also played with a black army team based at Fort Huachuca in California and played for the U.S. Army's 25th Infantry team in 1922. McNair was also an umpire in the NEGRO AMERICAN LEAGUE.

McNeal, Clyde
Clyde McNeal was a shortstop for the Chicago American Giants from 1945 to 1950. Records show that the 6-foot, 190-pound McNeal hit. 251 in 72 games for Chicago in 1948, .266 in 85 games in 1949, and .286 in 1950. He went on to play minor league baseball until 1957.

McNeal, Rufus (Zippy)
Rufus McNeal was a pitcher for the Indianapolis Clowns from 1953 to 1955.

McNeil, William (Red)
William McNeil was an outfielder and pitcher for the Louisville Black Caps, Louisville White Sox, Louisville Red Caps, and Nashville Elite Giants from 1930 to 1933.

McQueen, Pete
Pete McQueen was an outfielder for the New York Black Yankees, Memphis Red Sox, Pittsburgh Crawfords, and Little Rock Grays from 1932 to 1945.

McRee, Joe
Joe McRee was a pitcher for the Detroit Stars in 1955.

Meade, Fred (Chick)
Fred Meade was a shortstop, third baseman, and outfielder for the Pittsburgh Stars of Buffalo, Pittsburgh Colored Stars, Hilldale baseball club, Bacharach Giants, Baltimore Black Sox, Indianapolis ABC's, Harrisburg Giants, New York Stars, Brooklyn All Stars, Philadelphia Giants, and Cuban Giants from 1914 to 1922.

Meadows, Helburn
Helburn Meadows was an outfielder for the Cincinnati Tigers from 1934 to 1935.

Meadows, Hilburn
Hilburn Meadows was an outfielder for the Philadelphia Stars in 1953.

Means, Lewis
Lewis Means was a first baseman, second baseman, and catcher for the Bacharach Giants and Birmingham Black Barons from 1920 to 1928.

Means, Thomas
Thomas Means was a pitcher for the Chicago Unions and Chicago Union Giants from 1900 to 1904.

Mederos, Jesus
Jesus Mederos was a pitcher and outfielder for the All Cubans, Bacharach Giants, and Cuban Stars from 1910 to 1920.

Medina, Lazaro
Lazaro Medina was a pitcher for the Indianapolis Clowns and Cincinnati-Indianapolis Clowns from 1944 to 1946.

Medina, Pedro
Pedro Medina was a pitcher and catcher for the Cuban Stars from 1905 to 1907.

Medley, Calvin
Calvin Medley was a pitcher for the New York Black Yankees in 1946.

Mellix, Ralph (Lefty)
Ralph Mellix was a pitcher and manager for the Newark Browns, Brooklyn Brown Bombers, Homestead Grays,

Newark Dodgers, and Pittsburgh Crawfords from 1943 to 1946.

Mello, Harry

Harry Mello was an infielder for the Chicago American Giants in 1946.

Melton, Elbert (Babe)

Elbert Melton was an outfielder for the Lincoln Giants, Brooklyn Cuban Giants, Brooklyn Royal Giants, and Baltimore Black Sox from 1928 to 1929 and again in 1936.

Memphis Eclipses

The Memphis Eclipses were a black baseball a team out of Memphis, Tennessee, that played in the Southern League of Colored Baseballists in 1886. According to news accounts, they won the league championship that year.

Memphis Eurekas

The Memphis Eurekas were a black baseball team out of Memphis, Tennessee, that played in the Southern League of Colored Baseballists in 1886.

Memphis Grey Sox

The Memphis Grey Sox were a black baseball team out of Memphis, Tennessee, that played in the Negro Southern League in 1945.

Memphis Red Sox

The Memphis Red Sox were a black baseball team out of Memphis, Tennessee, that played in the Negro National League from 1924 to 1925 and 1927 to 1930, the Negro Southern League in 1926, 1932, and 1945, and the NEGRO AMERICAN LEAGUE from 1937 to 1962. Pitcher-catcher Ted "Double Duty" Radcliffe was one of the Negro League greats who played for and managed the Red Sox. Some of the players for the Red Sox included Neil "Shadow" Robinson, Cowan "Bubba" Hyde, Lloyd "Ducky" Davenport, Verdell Mathis, Marlin Carter, Gene Bremmer, and Porter Moss. In 1938, the Red Sox won the first-half NAL title, but in the playoffs against the second-half champions, the Atlanta Black Crackers, the series was canceled after two games.

Mendez, Jose (The Black Diamond)
b. 1887, d. 1927

Jose Mendez was a pitcher, infielder, and manager for the Cuban Stars, Stars of Cuba, ALL NATIONS baseball team, Chicago American Giants, Los Angeles White Sox, Kansas City Monarchs, and Detroit Stars from 1909 to 1926. Mendez, born in Cardenas, Cuba, was one of the great pitchers in Cuban baseball history who also made his mark in America in Negro League baseball, both as a player and as a manager. During his tenure as manager of the Kansas City Monarchs from 1920 to 1926, Mendez led the Monarchs to three straight Negro National League pennants from 1923 to 1925. While managing, Mendez would still take the field and had a 20-4 record with seven saves in his career with Kansas City, combining with Bullet Joe Rogan in 1923 to pitch a no-hitter, with Mendez pitching the first five innings, while Rogan finished the final four. Mendez was instrumental both in the dugout and on the mound in the Monarchs' 1924 Negro World Series championship victory over Hilldale, posting a record of 2-0 with a 1.42 ERA, including, at the age of 38, pitching a three-hit, 5-0 shutout victory in the final game of the series, which the Monarchs won five games to four, with one tie. In Cuba, Mendez had a record of 62-17 before he developed arm problems in 1914. His final pitching record in Cuban baseball was believed to be 74-25 in 157 appearances until he stopped after the 1926–1927 season. He came to America with a Cuban All-Star team in 1909, posting a 44-2 record against various levels of competition. One story goes that Mendez threw so hard that he once killed a teammate with a pitch in batting practice.

From 1912 to 1916, Mendez played for the All Nations team of Kansas City, a barnstorming club made up of ballplayers of various races and nationalities, a circus-style team that included a traveling orchestra in which Mendez played the cornet, according to Buck O'Neil's autobiography, *I Was Right on Time*.

In exhibition games against major league ballplayers, Mendez is believed to have won eight games and lost seven, defeating pitcher Eddie Plank and splitting showdowns against Christy Mathewson. At one time he was used by New York Giants manager John McGraw to coach Giant pitchers, who said that "Jose Mendez is better than any pitcher except Mordecai Brown and Christy Mathewson—and sometimes I think he's better than Matty."

In John Holway's book *Blackball Stars*, Negro Leaguer Judy Johnson said that Mendez was an intelligent player: "Mendez was smart," he said. "He was a small guy, a Bobby Shantz sort of pitcher. He had everything, and he knew how to use it." In another Holway interview on file at the National Baseball Hall of Fame, Negro Leaguer Dave Malarcher talked about Mendez's courage on the mound: "Jose Mendez of Kansas City was one of those courageous guys," he said "They said he became such a good pitcher during the years when Cobb and all of those white fellas went to Cuba. He struck them out. He became a national hero in Cuba." Mendez was elected to the Cuban Baseball Hall of Fame in 1939. He is believed to have died of tuberculosis.

Mendieta, Inocente

Inocente Mendieta was a second baseman for the Cuban Stars and Long Branch (New Jersey) Cubans from 1912 to 1913.

Merchant, Henry (Speed)

Henry Merchant was a pitcher and outfielder for the Indianapolis Clowns, Cincinnati-Indianapolis Clowns, and Chicago American Giants from 1940 to 1954.

Meredith, Buford

Buford Meredith was a shortstop and second baseman for the Nashville Elite Giants, Birmingham Black Barons, and Memphis Red Sox from 1923 to 1931.

Meredith, Zeke

Zeke Meredith was an outfielder for the Memphis Red Sox in 1954.

Merritt, William

William Merritt was a pitcher and outfielder for the Lincoln Giants and Brooklyn Royal Giants from 1905 to 1917.

Mesa, Andres

Andres Mesa was an outfielder for the Indianapolis Clowns in 1948.

Mesa, Pablo (Champion)

Pablo Mesa was an outfielder for the All-Cubans and Cuban Stars from 1921 to 1927.

Meyers, George (Deacon)

George Meyers was a pitcher and first baseman for the Dayton Marcos, St. Louis Stars, St. Louis Giants, and Toledo Tigers from 1921 to 1926.

Miami Giants

The Miami Giants were a black baseball team that played in Miami, Florida, in the 1930s and were owned by two liquor bootleggers, Buck O'Neal and John Pierce. Negro Leaguer Buck O'Neil, in his autobiography, *I Was Right on Time*, talked about his playing days with the Miami

Giants: "The Miami Giants were sort of an unofficial minor league team of the Negro National League. . . . Though there were no formal agreements, we supplied younger players to the big clubs." Later the team would change its name to the Ethiopian Clowns and begin wearing costumes, specializing in baseball clowning.

Miarka, Stanley

Stanley Miarka was a second baseman and pitcher for the Chicago American Giants in 1950. He was one of a group of white players who were signed by Giants president J. B. Martin in their battle to stop major league players from signing black ballplayers.

Mickey, James

James Mickey was a shortstop and third baseman for the Birmingham Black Barons and Chicago American Giants in 1940.

Mickey, John

John Mickey was a third baseman and shortstop for the Celeron, New York, Acme Colored Giants in 1898.

Miles, Jack

Jack Miles was an outfielder and third baseman for the Chicago American Giants from 1934 to 1939.

Miles, John (The Mule)

John Miles was an outfielder for the Chicago American Giants from 1946 to 1949. One report was that Miles hit 11 home runs in 11 straight games in 1947. He was given the nickname "The Mule" by his manager, "Candy" Jim Taylor, because Miles hit "as hard as a mule kicks." Miles played minor league baseball in Texas with teams in Laredo and San Antonio before retiring in 1952.

Miles, Jonas

Jonas Miles was a pitcher for the Cincinnati Buckeyes in 1940.

Miles, Tom

Tom Miles was a pitcher, first baseman, and outfielder for the Chicago American Giants, Philadelphia Stars, and Cleveland Clippers from 1934 to 1946.

Miles, Willie

Willie Miles was an outfielder, first baseman, and third baseman for the Memphis Red Sox, Toledo Tigers, Cleveland Browns, Cleveland Tate Stars, and Cleveland Elites from 1923 to 1927.

Miles, Zell

Zell Miles was an outfielder for the Chicago American Giants in 1951.

Miller, Bob

Bob Miller was a second baseman and third baseman for the Memphis Red Sox and Birmingham Black Barons from 1923 to 1928.

Miller, Charlie

Charlie Miller was an infielder and pitcher for the New Orleans Crescent Stars, Nashville Elite Giants, Cincinnati Tigers, Louisville Black Caps, and St. Louis Stars from 1932 to 1937.

Miller, Dempsey

Dempsey Miller was a pitcher and manager for the Cleveland Tigers, Cleveland Hornets, Detroit Stars, Detroit Giants, Nashville Elite Giants, Birmingham Black Barons, Cleveland Cubs, Kansas City Monarchs, Memphis Red Sox, Cleveland Elites, and Newark Browns from 1926 to 1945.

Miller, Eddie

Eddie Miller was a pitcher, shortstop, and third baseman for the Indianapolis ABC's, Chicago American Giants, Chicago Columbia Giants, and Homestead Grays from 1924 to 1931.

Miller, Eugene

Eugene Miller was an outfielder for the St. Paul Gophers in 1909.

Miller, Frank

Frank Miller was a pitcher and outfielder for the Cuban Giants, Cuban X Giants, Pittsburgh Keystones, New York Gorhams, Trenton Cuban Giants, and Philadelphia Giants from 1887 to 1897.

Miller, Hank

Hank Miller was a pitcher for the Newark Eagles and Philadelphia Stars from 1938 to 1949.

Miller, Hub

Hub Miller was a pitcher and outfielder for the St. Louis Giants and West Baden Sprudels from 1912 to 1916.

Miller, Jasper

Jasper Miller was a pitcher for the New Orleans Crescent Stars, Memphis Red Sox, and St. Louis Stars from 1930 to 1940.

Miller, Joseph

Joseph Miller was a pitcher and outfielder for the Lincoln (Nebraska) Giants, Columbia Giants, Page Fence Giants, and Chicago Union Giants from 1890 to 1903.

Miller, Leroy

Leroy Miller was a shortstop and second baseman for the New York Black Yankees and Newark Dodgers from 1935 to 1943.

Miller, Ned

Ned Miller was a first baseman for the Indianapolis Athletics in 1937.

Miller, Otto

Otto Miller was an infielder for the Indianapolis Clowns in 1951.

Miller, Percy

Percy Miller was a pitcher and outfielder for the Nashville Elite Giants, St. Louis Giants, St. Louis Stars, Detroit Stars, Kansas City Monarchs, and Chicago Giants from 1921 to 1934.

Miller, Ray

Ray Miller was a first baseman for the Detroit Stars in 1954.

Milliner, Eugene

Eugene Milliner was an outfielder for the St. Paul Gophers, Chicago Union Giants, Kansas City Royal Giants, and Brooklyn Royal Giants from 1903 to 1910.

Mills, Charles

Charles Mills was an owner and officer with the St. Louis Giants and St. Louis Black Sox from 1909 to 1924.

Milton, Edward

Edward Milton was an outfielder and second baseman for the Cleveland Tigers and Cleveland Elites from 1926 to 1928.

Milton, Henry (Streak)

Henry Milton was an outfielder for the Indianapolis ABC's, Chicago Giants, Chicago American Giants, Brooklyn Royal Giants, Kansas City Monarchs, Brooklyn Eagles, and New York Black Yankees from 1932 to 1943.

Milwaukee Bears

The Milwaukee Bears were a black baseball team out of Milwaukee, Wisconsin, that played in the NEGRO NATIONAL LEAGUE in 1923.

Mimes, Joseph

Joseph Mimes was a pitcher for the Detroit Stars in 1955.

Mineola Black Spiders

The Mineola Black Spiders were a black barnstorming baseball team based in Mineola, Texas, in the 1930s.

Minor, George

George Minor was an outfielder for the Cleveland Buckeyes, Chicago American Giants, and Louisville Buckeyes from 1944 to 1949.

Minoso, Saturnino Orestes Armas (Arrieta) (Minnie)
b. 1922

Saturnino Minoso was a third baseman for the New York Cubans from 1945 to 1948 before he went on to have an illustrious major league career. Born in Havana, Cuba, Minoso broke in with the Cleveland Indians, signed by owner Bill Veeck, in 1949 and played 17 seasons with the Indians, Chicago White Sox, St. Louis Cardinals, and Washington Senators. He made a brief two-game appearance with the Chicago White Sox in 1980, thanks to another Veeck signing, after retiring in 1976, giving him the distinction of playing in five decades. In 1,841 games, the 5-foot-10, 175-pound Minoso hit 186 home runs, drove in 1,023 runs, scored 1,136 runs, and had a career batting average of .298. During his brief tenure in Negro League baseball, records show Minoso batted .260 in 33 games in 1946 and .294 in 55 games in 1947. He played in the Negro baseball All-Star Game, the EAST-WEST GAME, in 1947. In an interview with author John Holway on file at the National Baseball Hall of Fame, Negro

League pitcher Dave Barnhill talked about Minoso's skills: "He was a great ballplayer," Barnhill said. "When the ball was hit to him, the pitcher had to lie down on the ground because Minoso threw the ball all the way [from third base] to first base about four feet off the ground."

Mirabel, Juan

Juan Mirabel was a pitcher for the Cuban Stars and New York Cuban from 1922 to 1934.

Mirable, Autorio

Autorio Mirable was a catcher for the New York Cuban Stars from 1939 to 1940.

Miro, Pedro

Pedro Miro was a second baseman for the New York Cubans from 1945 to 1948.

Missouri, Jim

Jim Missouri was a pitcher for the Philadelphia Stars from 1937 to 1941.

Mitchell, Alonzo (Fluke and Hooks)

Alonzo Mitchell was a pitcher, first baseman, and manager for the Jacksonville Red Caps, Cleveland Bears, Atlanta Black Crackers, Indianapolis ABC's, Baltimore Black Sox, Atlantic City Bacharach Giants, Harrisburg Giants, Birmingham Black Barons, and Akron Tyrites from 1921 to 1941.

Mitchell, Arthur

Arthur Miller was an infielder for the New York Black Yankees in 1939.

Mitchell, Bob
b. 1932

Bob Mitchell was a pitcher for the Kansas City Monarchs from 1954 to 1957. Born in West Palm Beach, Florida, Mitchell played in the Florida State Negro League in high school and for the Florida Cubans in 1952 and 1953. They were playing an exhibition game against the Monarchs in Lakeland, Florida, in 1952, and Mitchell impressed Monarchs manager Buck O'Neil: "I had my fast ball working that night," Mitchell said in an interview. "Buck O'Neil said they wanted to sign me and they would get in touch with me." Mitchell went on to play for the West Palm Beach Lincoln Giants, and in 1952 the Monarchs sent him a ticket to meet them for spring training in Newport News, Virginia. He posted a 25-23 record and sometimes would pitch behind Satchel Paige. Mitchell recalled one incident while traveling in Florida: "We were traveling south of St. Augustine and our bus caught fire," Mitchell said. "We lost the bus and our things, including our equipment. We were on Route A1A about 15 miles south of St. Augustine when the highway patrol drove by and refused to help us, calling us names. Our owner had to send another bus to take us to Miami."

Mitchell, Bud

Bud Mitchell was an outfielder, catcher, and pitcher for the Darby Daisies, Hilldale baseball club, Washington Pilots, Bacharach Giants, Newark Stars, Philadelphia Stars, and Baltimore Black Sox from 1926 to 1934.

Mitchell, Charlie

Charlie Mitchell was a catcher for the Boston Royal Giants in 1942.

Mitchell, George

George Mitchell was a pitcher and manager for the Indianapolis ABC's, Chicago American Giants, Cleveland Cubs, Montgomery Grey Sox, St. Louis Stars, New Orleans–St. Louis Stars, Harrisburg–St. Louis Stars, New York Black Yankees, Cleveland Stars, Houston Eagles, Kansas City Monarchs, and Houston Eagles from 1924 to 1949.

Mitchell, Jessie

Jessie Mitchell was an outfielder for the Birmingham Black Barons in 1954 and 1955.

Mitchell, John

John Mitchell was a catcher and outfielder for the Montgomery Grey Sox in 1932.

Mitchell, Joseph

Joseph Mitchell was a pitcher for the Chicago American Giants in 1951.

Mitchell, Leonard

Leonard Mitchell was a second baseman for the Louisville White Sox, Birmingham Black Sox, and Louisville Black Colonels from 1930 to 1938.

Mitchell, Robert

Robert Mitchell was an outfielder and catcher for the St. Louis Stars and Birmingham Black Barons from 1923 to 1924.

Mitchell, Robert L.

Robert L. Mitchell was a pitcher for the Cleveland Buckeyes and Kansas City Monarchs from 1950 to 1955.

Mobile Black Bears or Shippers

The Mobile Black Bears or Shippers were a black baseball team out of Mobile, Alabama, that played in the Negro Southern League in 1945.

Mobile Tigers

The Mobile Tigers were a black baseball team that played in Mobile, Alabama, in the 1910s and 1920s. Satchel Paige pitched his first professional game for the Tigers in 1924.

Mobley, Ira

Ira Mobley was a second baseman, shortstop, and outfielder for the Kansas City Monarchs in 1954.

Moles, Lefty

Lefty Moles was a pitcher for the Philadelphia Stars in 1935.

Molina, Augustin

Augustin Molina was an outfielder, first baseman, catcher, and manager for the Cuban Stars, Cuban Giants, and Cincinnati Cubans from 1906 to 1931.

Monarchs of York, Pennsylvania

The Monarchs of York, Pennsylvania, were a black baseball team that played in the 1880s and 1890s, winning the Eastern State League pennant in 1890. They were managed by J. Monroe Kreider and included such players as Ben Boyd, Oscar Jackson, Abe Harrison, and Sol White.

Mongin, Sam

Sam Mongin was a second baseman and third baseman for the Lincoln Stars, Lincoln Giants, Brooklyn Royal Giants, St. Louis Giants, Bacharach Giants, Philadelphia Giants, and Chicago Giants from 1907 to 1922.

Monitor Club of Jamaica

The Monitor Club of Jamaica were a black baseball team in the 1860s in New York.

Monitors of Brooklyn

The Monitors of Brooklyn were a black baseball team that operated out of Brooklyn, New York, in the 1880s and 1890s.

Monroe, Al

Al Monroe was secretary for the NEGRO AMERICAN LEAGUE in 1937. He was also a sportswriter for the *Chicago Defender*.

Monroe, Bill

Bill Monroe was a third baseman and shortstop for the Pittsburgh Stars of Buffalo and Baltimore Black Sox from 1920 to 1927.

Monroe, Bill (Diamond Bill)

Bill Monroe was a third baseman and second baseman for the Philadelphia Giants, Chicago Unions, Brooklyn Royal Giants, Cuban X Giants, Chicago American Giants, and Chicago Giants from 1896 to 1914. Monroe had a reputation as one of the clowns of the game during his time. In his book *History of Colored Baseball*, former Negro League player, manager, and historian Sol White described Monroe's style: "Monroe, third baseman of the Royal Giants of Brooklyn is the leading fun-maker of the colored profession of today," he wrote. "His comic sayings and actions while on the field, together with his ability as a fielder, hitter and runner has earned him a great reputation as a ballplayer."

Monroe Monarchs

The Monroe Monarchs were a black baseball team based in Monroe, Louisiana, owned by businessman Fred Stovall, that played in the Negro Southern League in the 1920s and 1930s.

Monrovia Club of Harrisburg

The Monrovia Club of Harrisburg were a black baseball team that played in Harrisburg, Pennsylvania, in the 1860s.

Montalvo, Estaban

Estaban Montalvo was an outfielder and first baseman for the Lincoln Giants and Cuban Stars from 1923 to 1928.

Montgomery, Grady

Grady Montgomery was an infielder for the Chicago American Giants in 1952.

Montgomery, Joseph

Joseph Montgomery was an outfielder for the Detroit Stars in 1954 and 1955.

Montgomery, Lou

Lou Montgomery was a pitcher, infielder, and outfielder for the Cincinnati Clowns in 1942.

Montgomery Blues

The Montgomery Blues were a black baseball team out of Montgomery, Alabama, that played in the Southern League of Colored Baseballists in 1886.

Montgomery Grey Sox

The Montgomery Grey Sox were a black baseball team out of Montgomery, Alabama, that played in the Negro Southern League in 1926 and 1932.

Moody, Frank

Frank Moody was a pitcher for the Birmingham Black Barons in 1940.

Moody, Lee
b. 1917, d. 1998

Lee Moody was a first baseman for the Kansas City Monarchs and Birmingham Black Barons from 1944 to 1947. Records show Moody batted .251 in 48 games in 1944 and .325 in 45 games with Kansas City in 1945. He played two seasons of minor league baseball, with Cairo in the Kitty League in 1950 and Three Rivers in the Provincial League in 1951.

Moody, Willis

Willis Moody was an outfielder for the Homestead Grays and Pittsburgh Keystones from 1921 to 1929.

Moore, Charles

Charles Moore was an umpire in the NEGRO NATIONAL LEAGUE in 1943.

Moore, Clarence

Clarence Moore was manager and owner of the Ashville Blues from 1945 to 1948 and president of the Negro American Association.

Moore, Excell

Excell Moore was a pitcher for the New Orleans Eagles, Indianapolis Clowns, and Cleveland Buckeyes from 1950 to 1952.

Moore, Harry

Harry Moore was a first baseman, third baseman, and outfielder for the Algona Brownies, Chicago Unions, Cuban X Giants, Leland Giants, Philadelphia Giants, Chicago Giants, Chicago Union Giants, and Lincoln Giants from 1894 to 1913.

Moore, Henry

Henry Moore was an officer for the St. Louis Stars and Birmingham Black Barons in 1937 and 1938.

Moore, Jack

Jack Moore was an outfielder for the Cleveland Bears in 1939.

Moore, James Robert (Red)

James Moore was a first baseman for the Newark Eagles, Baltimore Elite Giants, Atlanta Black Crackers, and Indianapolis ABC's from 1936 to 1940.

Moore, John

John Moore was a shortstop for the Birmingham Black Barons in 1929.

Moore, Johnny

Johnny Moore was a first baseman for the Pittsburgh Crawfords from 1928 to 1930.

Moore, Ralph

Ralph Moore was a pitcher and first baseman for the Kansas City Monarchs, Memphis Red Sox, Cleveland Tigers, Cleveland Hornets, Cleveland Tate Stars, Chicago American Giants, Cleveland Elites, and Birmingham Black Barons from 1920 to 1928.

Moore, Shirley

Shirley Moore was a pitcher for the Bowser ABC's and Louisville White Sox from 1914 to 1916.

Moore, Walter (Dobie)

Dobie Moore was one of the top shortstops in Negro League baseball history. The 5-foot-11, 230-pound Moore played from 1920 to 1926 for the Kansas City Monarchs, leading them to three pennants from 1923 to 1925. He was the NEGRO NATIONAL LEAGUE batting leader in 1924 with a .470 batting average and eight home runs in 59 games and also helped the Monarchs win a World Series title that year, batting .324 in the series. He played alongside second baseman Newt Allen to make a strong double-play combination. In an interview conducted by author John Holway on file at the National Baseball Hall of Fame, Allen talked about the skills of his double-play partner: "He was a great ballplayer, with awfully big hands," Allen said. "You've heard of Honus Wagner? Well, Dobie's hands were just like his. He could reach a batted ball and grab it right out of the air with his palm down. Dobie taught me a lot about playing the infield. In the first Negro World Series, we made six double plays in one game. Two of them came in the eighth and ninth innings. The last one ended the ball game with what would have been the winning run crossing the plate."

Casey Stengel once declared that Moore, also known as "The Black Cat," was "one of the best shortstops that will ever live." Moore, who also had played with the all-black 25th Infantry Wreckers Army team, batted .359 in six seasons with the Monarchs, batting .367 in 1922 and .358 in 1923. He was part of a great team put together in Cuba during the winter of 1923–1924, playing with Oscar Charleston, Oliver Marcelle, and Frank Warfield, and Moore is believed to have batted .380 during that winter.

Born in Georgia in 1893, Moore's career ended prematurely in 1926 when he was hurt in a shooting accident. There are disputed reports about what exactly happened. The incident occurred in May 1926. The Monarchs were having a team party celebrating a winning streak, but Moore was with a woman at her home. An argument resulted in the woman shooting Moore. His leg was shattered and his career with it.

Morales, Ismael

Ismael Morales was an outfielder for the Cuban Stars in 1932.

Moran, Francisco

Francisco Moran was an outfielder and third baseman for the Cuban Stars and All Cubans from 1911 to 1914.

Morefield, Fred

Fred Morefield was an outfielder for the Pittsburgh Crawfords from 1945 to 1946.

Morehead, Albert

Albert Morehead was a catcher for the Cleveland Cubs, Chicago Giants, Chicago Brown Bombers, and Birmingham Black Barons in 1925, 1932, and 1943.

Moreland, Nate

Nate Moreland was a pitcher for the Kansas City Monarchs and Baltimore Elite Giants from 1940 to 1945. Moreland, along with Jackie Robinson, once asked for a tryout with the Chicago White Sox in 1942 at their Pasadena, California, training camp. Manager Jimmy Dykes allowed Moreland and Robinson to work out with the team, but it was not a formal tryout. He would later pitch for the independent El Centro Imperials in California, and, according to Jules Tygiel's book *Jackie Robinson and His Legacy*, Moreland "was ready for anybody's league" but never rose above the independent minor leagues. He also went on to manage in those leagues.

Morgan, Connie

Connie Morgan was one of three women who were brought into Negro League baseball to boost attendance. Morgan was an infielder for the Indianapolis Clowns in 1954.

Morgan, John

John Morgan was an outfielder for the Memphis Red Sox and Indianapolis Athletics in 1937.

Morgan, William (Wild Bill)

William Morgan was a pitcher for the Baltimore Elite Giants, Memphis Red Sox, and Birmingham Black Barons from 1945 to 1949.

Morin, Eugenio

Eugenio Morin was a second baseman, third baseman, and catcher for the Cuban Stars and Cincinnati Cubans from 1910 to 1923.

Morney, Leroy

Leroy Morney was an infielder for the Monroe Monarchs, Columbus Blue Birds, Homestead Grays, Cleveland Giants, Toledo Crawfords, Pittsburgh Crawfords, Cincinnati Clowns, Columbus Elite Giants, Birmingham Black Barons, Washington Elite Giants, Chicago American Giants, New York Black Yankees, Philadelphia Stars, and Nashville Elite Giants from 1931 to 1944.

Morris, Al

Al Morris was a second baseman and outfielder for the Louisville White Sox and Nashville Elite Giants from 1927 to 1930.

Morris, Barney

Barney Morris was a pitcher for the Monroe Monarchs, New Orleans Crescent Stars, Pittsburgh Crawfords, Newark Eagles, New York Cubans, and Toledo Crawfords from 1932 to 1948.

Morris, Harold

Harold Morris was a pitcher for the Detroit Stars, Kansas City Monarchs, Monroe Monarchs, and Chicago American Giants from 1924 to 1936.

Morrison, Roy

Roy Morrison was a pitcher for the Bacharach Giants in 1934.

Morton, Ferdinando

Ferdinando Morton was a New York City Civil Service official who was named commissioner of the NEGRO NATIONAL LEAGUE from 1935 to 1938.

Morton, John

John Morton was an outfielder for the Pittsburgh Crawfords and Brooklyn Eagles from 1935 to 1937.

Morton, Sidney

Sidney Morton was a shortstop and second baseman for the Pittsburgh Crawfords, Philadelphia Stars, Newark Eagles, and Chicago American Giants from 1940 to 1947.

Moseley, Beauregard

Beauregard Moseley was a black attorney and politician in Chicago who became an officer for the Leland Giants in 1910 and 1911.

Moses, Joe

Joe Moses was a catcher for the Birmingham Black Barons in 1955.

Mosley, C. D. (Gatewood)

C. D. Mosley was a pitcher for the Homestead Grays, New Orleans Crescent Stars, and Kansas City Monarchs from 1934 to 1944.

Mosley, Lou

Lou Mosley was a pitcher for the Cuban Stars and Bacharach Giants in 1932.

Mosley, William

William Mosley was an officer for the Detroit Stars in 1932.

Moss, Porter

Porter Moss was a pitcher for the Cincinnati Tigers and Memphis Red Sox from 1934 to 1944.

Mothell, Carroll (Dink)

Carroll Mothell was an outfielder, infielder, and catcher for the Kansas City Monarchs, All Nations, Cleveland Stars, Topeka Giants, and Chicago American Giants from 1918 to 1934.

Motley, Bob

Bob Motley was an umpire in the Negro Leagues.

Motor City Giants

The Motor City Giants were a black baseball team that played in the UNITED STATES LEAGUE in Detroit in 1945.

Muehlebach Field

Muehlebach Field was a ballpark in Kansas City, Missouri, that was home for the Kansas City Monarchs from 1923 to 1955. It was also later known as Ruppert Stadium from 1938 to 1942, Blues Stadium from 1943 to 1954, and Municipal Stadium from 1955, the Monarchs' final season there, until 1976. It had a seating capacity of 17,476 in 1923.

Munoz, Joe

Joe Munoz was a pitcher and outfielder for the Stars of Cuban, Jersey City Cubans, Cuban Stars, All Cubans, Long Branch (New Jersey) Cubans, and Cuban X Giants from 1904 to 1916.

Munroe, Elmer

Elmer Munroe was a pitcher for the Boston Royal Giants in 1942.

Murdock Grays

The Murdock Grays were a black semipro baseball team of steelworkers from Homestead Steel, based in Homestead, Pennsylvania, and other steel mills in and around Pittsburgh that would later become the Homestead Grays, under the direction of Cum Posey.

Murphy, Al

Al Murphy was a pitcher for the Birmingham Black Barons, Indianapolis Athletics, and Cincinnati Tigers from 1936 to 1937.

Murray, Clay

Clay Murray was a pitcher for the Bacharach Giants in 1934.

Murray, Mitchell

Mitchell Murray was a catcher for the Dayton Marcos, Chicago American Giants, Cleveland Tate Stars, St. Louis Stars, Toledo Tigers, Indianapolis ABC's, and Columbus Buckeyes from 1919 to 1932. According to Mark Ribowsky's book *A Complete History of the Negro Leagues: 1884–1955*, Murray batted against Satchel Paige in Paige's first recorded professional game on June 27, 1927. Paige had hit the first three batters he faced, with Murray the third hitter, and Murray chased Paige around the field with a bat. He threw it at Paige, missed, and Paige picked the bat up and chased Murray with it. Both benches and fans poured onto the field, and the police were called to stop what had become a full-scale riot.

Murryall, Johnny

Johnny Murryall was a pitcher for the Indianapolis Clowns in 1952.

Mutuals of Washington

The Mutuals of Washington were a black baseball team that played out of Washington, D.C., in the 1880s.

Napier, Euthumn (Eudie)
b. 1915

Euthumn Napier was a catcher from 1935 to 1950 for the Pittsburgh Crawfords, Bacharach Giants, and Homestead Grays. The 5-foot-9, 190-pound Napier batted .286 in 119 at bats for Homestead in 1947. He also played minor league baseball for Farnham in the Provincial League in 1951, batting .285 with eight home runs, 42 RBIs, and 47 runs scored in 93 games.

Napoleon, Lawrence

Lawrence Napoleon was a pitcher for the Kansas City Monarchs from 1946 to 1947.

Naranjo, Pedro

Pedro Naranjo was a pitcher for the Kansas City Monarchs, Indianapolis Clowns, and Nashville Elite Giants from 1950 to 1954.

Nashville Black Volunteers

The Nashville Black Volunteers were a black baseball team from Nashville, Tennessee, in the Negro Southern League in the 1940s.

Nashville Elite Giants

The Nashville Elite Giants had several different lives. They were started as a semipro team called the Nashville Standard Giants, owned by numbers operator Thomas T. Wilson. They became the Nashville Elite Giants in 1921. The team moved to Cleveland after the 1930 season and became the Cleveland Cubs. In 1931, that team disbanded before the season was over. Another version of the Nashville Elite Giants was formed by Wilson, and they would join the second version of the NEGRO NATIONAL LEAGUE in the second half of the 1933 season after two of the original teams, the Homestead Grays and the Indianapolis ABC's, dropped out. Negro League greats who played for the Nashville Elite Giants included Sam Bankhead. The Nashville Elite Giants moved to Columbus, Ohio, then to Washington, D.C., in 1936 and would later wind up playing in Baltimore in 1938.

Nashville Standard Giants

The Nashville Standard Giants were a black baseball team from Nashville, Tennessee, in the 1920s.

National Association of Colored Base Ball Clubs

The National Association of Colored Base Ball Clubs was formed by Rube Foster along with the NEGRO NATIONAL LEAGUE in 1920. The association was the governing body of the Negro National League. The association included not only black baseball teams in the Negro National League, but independent teams and clubs in smaller leagues as well, such as the Negro Southern League.

National Association of Colored Base Ball Clubs of the United States and Cuba

The National Association of Colored Base Ball Clubs consisted of black baseball teams both in the United States and just one team from Cuba in the early 1900s—the Cuban Stars of Santiago de Cuba. The association was formed by Nat Strong, a white promoter from New York, and headed by Walter "Slick" Schlichter, the sports editor of the white *Philadelphia Item* newspaper and the founder of the Philadelphia Giants.

National League of Colored Base Ball Clubs

The National League of Colored Base Ball Clubs was league of black baseball teams formed in 1908.

Navarrette, Ramundo

Ramundo Navarrette was a pitcher for the New York Cubans in 1950.

Navarro, Emilio
b. 1905

Emilio Navarro, born in Patillas, Puerto Rico, was an infielder who became Puerto Rico's first player in the Negro Leagues, playing for the Cuban Stars in 1928 and 1929. The 5-foot-5, 160-pound shortstop batted .337 in 1928. He also played in the Puerto Rico Winter League from 1938, when it began, to 1943.

Navarro, Raymond

Raymond Navarro was an infielder, outfielder, and catcher for the Indianapolis Clowns and Cincinnati-Indianapolis Clowns from 1945 to 1946.

Neal, Charlie
b. 1931

Charlie Neal was an infielder for the Atlanta Black Crackers in 1949. He went on to play minor league baseball from 1950 to 1955 before being called up by the Brooklyn Dodgers in 1956. The 5-foot-10, 160-pound Neal played for the Dodgers for seven years from 1956 until being selected by the New York Mets in the 1961 expansion draft. Born in Longview, Texas, Neal batted .259, with 87 home runs, 391 RBIs, and 461 runs scored in 970 games over eight seasons. In two World Series—1956 with Brooklyn and 1959 in Los Angeles—Neal had two home runs, drove in six runs, and batted .323 in seven games. In a 1995 interview with *Sports Collectors Digest*, Neal talked about how he was discovered by the Black Crackers: "They [the Black Crackers] were playing in Longview [Texas] and they needed a shortstop," Neal said. "Their shortstop got hurt and so I played with them that night, so they got permission from my mom and dad to let me travel with them to Atlanta and I would stay with one of the adults. When the season was over, they would send me back home. A lot of great players came out of the Negro Leagues. I'm just happy that I played with some of them. There was a catcher in Atlanta named Dave Perkins. He was a real good player. Then I played against Satch [Satchel Paige]. When he was throwing hard, he'd just throw the ball by me."

Neal, George

George Neal was a second baseman for the Chicago Giants and Kansas City Giants from 1910 to 1911.

Neal, William (Willie)

William Neal was an infielder for the Memphis Red Sox in 1952.

Negro All Stars

The Negro All Stars were a group of the top players in Negro League baseball in 1936 who competed in the annual *Denver Post* baseball tournament and won it. Some of the players on that team included Satchel Paige, Josh Gibson, Cool Papa Bell, and Buch Leonard.

Negro American Association

The Negro American Association consisted of black baseball teams in Virginia and North Carolina in the late 1940s and early 1950s, and in 1950 it included a version of the Homestead Grays.

Negro American League

The Negro American League was organized in 1937 by J. L. Wilkinson, owner of the Kansas City Monarchs, and consisted of the Monarchs, Chicago American Giants, Memphis Red Sox, Atlanta Black Crackers, Birmingham Black Barons, Detroit Stars, St. Louis Stars, Indianapolis Athletics, and Cincinnati Tigers. Wilkinson, a white businessman, officially was listed as vice president and installed two black men to serve as the league officials—Horace G. Hull as president and Major R. R. Jackson as commissioner. In 1937, the Black Crackers played the

Red Sox in the league championship series. However, after Memphis took a three game to two lead over Atlanta, the series was canceled after financial and scheduling disputes, and the Black Crackers left the league after that season. The franchise moved to Indianapolis briefly but then returned to Atlanta and reentered the Negro American League in 1938. They won the second-half title of the split season, but the championship series, again against Memphis, the first-half champions, was canceled after just two games. Kansas City went on to win five out of six league titles, with Newt Allen as manager and the great Satchel Paige (joining the club in 1940) on the mound. The 1942 squad, managed by Frank Duncan, included such great Negro League players as first baseman Buck O'Neil, outfielder Ted Strong, infielders Jesse Williams and Willie Sims, and a pitching staff consisting of Paige, Lefty LaMarque, Connie Johnson, and Hilton Smith. The Monarchs won the 1946 Negro American League pennant, with O'Neil leading the league in batting and joined in the lineup by Williard Brown and Hank Thompson. Paige, Johnson, and Hilton Smith anchored the pitching staff. Kansas City lost in seven games to the Newark Eagles that year in the Negro League World Series as Paige and Strong left the team five games into the series. In 1948, the Monarchs won the Negro American League second-half championship but lost to the Birmingham Black Barons in the playoffs. The Monarchs won the first-half title the following year, but there was no playoff against the second-half champion. In 1950, Kansas City won both the first- and second-half titles in the Negro American League western division with a record of 51-20. The Monarchs won four straight Negro American League pennants, from 1939 to 1942, and in 1942, in the first Negro World Series since 1927, the Monarchs swept the Homestead Grays, the NEGRO NATIONAL LEAGUE champions, in four games. The Monarchs also won the NAL title in 1946 and played the Negro National League champion Newark Eagles in the Negro World Series, losing in seven games. Other teams that would later join the Negro American League included the Baltimore Elite Giants, Philadelphia Stars, New York Cubans, Indianapolis Clowns, Toledo Crawfords, and the Cleveland Buckeyes. Tom Wilson, owner of the Baltimore Elite Giants, would serve as president of the league in its later years as would Dr. J. B. Martin, owner and officer of the Memphis Red Sox. The NAL continued in various forms until 1960.

Negro Major Baseball League of America

Major Robert R. Jackson, a Chicago black businessman and former partner with Frank Leland in the Chicago Unions and former commissioner of the NEGRO NA-

TIONAL LEAGUE, formed the Negro Major Baseball League of America in 1942. However, the league did not last out the season.

Negro Midwest League
The Negro Midwest League was a league of black baseball teams formed in 1942 by white promoter Abe Saperstein.

Negro National League
In 1920, Rube Foster, owner of the Chicago American Giants, formed the Negro National League. He said the purpose of the league was to "create a profession that would equal the earning capacity of other professions, and keep colored baseball from the control of whites." He also said he wanted to "do something concrete for the loyalty of the race." However, he quietly enlisted the financial support of white businessmen behind the scenes. The league consisted of eight teams—Chicago Giants, Chicago American Giants, Cuban Giants (a team without a home field) Detroit Stars, Dayton Marcos, Indianapolis ABC's, Kansas City Monarchs, and St. Louis Giants. The Monarchs won three straight Negro National League championships from 1923, when they went 57-33, to 1925, when they posted a 62-23 mark. In 1924, the Monarchs, who had a record of 55-22 that year, defeated the Eastern Colored League champion Hilldale baseball club five games to four, with one tie, in what was recognized as the first Negro League World Series. The following season the Monarchs defeated the St. Louis Stars in a seven-game playoff series to win the league title but lost to Hilldale five games to one in the series. Those Monarch teams, managed by Jose Mendez, included such great Negro League players as pitcher Bullet Joe Rogan and infielders Newt Allen and Dobie Moore. In 1926, they posted a record of 57-21, winning the Negro National League first-half title, but lost to the Chicago American Giants, the second-half champions, in the championship game. In 1929, with Joe Rogan managing the team, Kansas City won another Negro National League pennant with a record of 62-17, led by a strong pitching staff that included Andy and Army Cooper and Chet Brewer.

After Foster died in 1930, the league folded one year later. However, Gus Greenlee, the Pittsburgh numbers boss who owned the Pittsburgh Crawfords, resurrected another version of the Negro National League in 1933. The league later included the Homestead Grays, who won the league championship in 1942. The Newark Eagles were the NNL champions in 1946 and won the Negro World Series by defeating Kansas City in seven games. This last version of the Negro National League folded after the 1948 season.

Negro Southern League

The Negro Southern League was a league of black baseball teams from the South that played in the 1920s to the 1940s. Some of the teams that played in the league were the Jacksonville Red Caps, Montgomery Grey Sox, Mobile Black Bears, New Orleans Black Volunteers, Knoxville Grays, and Nashville Elite Giants.

Negro West Coast League

The Negro West Coast League was formed in the 1940s with teams in California, Oregon, and Washington.

Neil, Ray

Ray Neil was an infielder for the Indianapolis Clowns and Cincinnati Clowns from 1942 to 1954.

Nelson, Clyde

Clyde Nelson was an infielder for the Chicago American Giants, Chicago Brown Bombers, Indianapolis Clowns, Cleveland Buckeyes, and Indianapolis ABC's in 1939 and from 1943 to 1949.

Nelson, Everett (Ace)

Everett Nelson was a pitcher for the Detroit Stars and Montgomery Grey Sox in 1922 and from 1931 to 1933.

Nelson, John

John Nelson was a pitcher and outfielder for the Cuban X Giants, New York Gorhams, Philadelphia Gorhams, Philadelphia Giants, Trenton Cuban Giants, Ansonia Cuban Giants, and Adrian Page Fence Giants from 1887 to 1903.

Nevelle, Gus

Gus Nevelle was a pitcher for the Pittsburgh Crawfords in 1930.

Newark Browns

The Newark Browns were a black baseball team that were one of the original franchises to join Cum Posey's East-West League in 1932.

Newark Dodgers

The Newark Dodgers, a black baseball team based in Newark, New Jersey, owned by Charles Tyler, a chicken farmer, began play in 1934 in the NEGRO NATIONAL LEAGUE. However, the team went out of business in 1936, folding along with another struggling franchise, the Brooklyn Eagles, by new owners Abe and Effa Manley to form the Newark Eagles.

Newark Eagles

The Newark Eagles were a black baseball team based in Newark, New Jersey, that were formed in 1936 by putting together two franchises in trouble, the Brooklyn Eagles and the Newark Dodgers, by owner Abe Manley, a numbers racketeer, and his wife, Effa, who was the true driving force behind the franchise. In 1937, the Eagles put together a tremendous infield—Ray Dandridge, Willie Wells, Dick Seay, and Mule Suttles. In 1946, the Eagles broke the Homestead Grays' nine-straight NEGRO NATIONAL LEAGUE pennant streak by winning the league title, capturing both halves of the split season and defeating the Kansas City Monarchs and Satchel Paige in a seven-game World Series, with a roster that included such players as Monte Irvin, Don Newcombe, Larry Doby, and Leon Day and manager Biz Mackey. The Eagles also won the first-half pennant in the league in 1947. They played many of their home games at Ruppert Stadium. Effa Manley sold the Newark franchise after the 1948 season, and it moved to Houston.

Newark Stars

The Newark Stars were a black baseball team that was managed by Negro League baseball player, manager, and historian Sol White and played in the Eastern Colored League in 1926.

Newberry, Henry

Henry Newberry was a pitcher for the Chicago American Giants in 1947.

Newberry, James Lee (Jimmie)

James Newberry was a pitcher for the Birmingham Black Barons from 1943 to 1950.

Newberry, Richard
b. 1926

Richard Newberry was a shortstop for the Chicago American Giants in 1947. The 5-foot-8, 170-pound Newberry went on to play minor league baseball for Duluth in the Northern League from 1951 to 1954. His best season was 1954, when he batted .330 in 93 games playing second base and third base.

Newcombe, Donald (Big Newk)
b. 1926

Donald Newcombe was a right-handed pitcher for the Newark Eagles in 1944 and 1945. He posted a 14-4 record in 1945 before he was signed by the Brooklyn Dodgers, where he would eventually join Jackie Robinson and Roy Campanella to form the nucleus of the Dodger National League championship teams of the early 1950s. However, sportswriter Wendell Smith is quoted in Jules Tygiel's book *Jackie Robinson and his Legacy,* saying that Newcombe was probably not the best pitcher in black baseball but the right choice for Dodgers general manager Branch Rickey: "He wasn't by any means the best pitcher in Negro baseball," Smith wrote. "But Rickey signed him because he's young, big and has all the natural ability necessary to get him into the big leagues." In John Holway's book *Blackball Stars,* Newcombe credited Negro League veteran Biz Mackey, his manager at Newark, for having a strong influence on his career: "He was one of the most knowledgeable baseball men that I ever knew," Newcombe said.

Born in Madison, New Jersey, the 6-foot-4, 220-pound Newcombe was called up to the Dodgers in 1949 and posted a 17-8 record with a 3.17 ERA in 38 appearances. Newcombe played 10 years in the major leagues, primarily with the Dodgers, although he spent parts of his three final seasons with the Cincinnati Reds before retiring after the 1960 season. His career record was 149-60 with a 3.56 ERA, including three 20-plus-win seasons. His best year was 1956, when he went 27-7 with a 3.06 ERA in 38 appearances. In three World Series, Newcombe went 0-4 in five pitching appearances with an 8.59 ERA.

In a 1994 interview with *Sport's Collectors Digest,* Newcombe credited the Negro Leagues for giving him an opportunity to be a major league player: "The Negro Leagues were a beginning, a chance for a poor kid to get out of the ghetto and a chance to become famous," he said. "Even in the Negro Leagues, you were famous if you were playing on a Negro League team. It turned out okay for me because I got a chance to play major league baseball with the Dodgers. Without Negro League baseball there wouldn't have been a Jackie Robinson or Roy Campanella or Willie Mays or Hank Aaron—or Don Newcombe. It's just too bad that at the time, the Negro Leagues weren't more organized and didn't have more power so they could protect some of the players from just getting scooped away by major league teams. I was scooped away by the Dodgers, and the Dodgers didn't pay even 10 cents for me. That was because the Negro League teams didn't have any muscle. What they should have done was, at least pay the Negro League teams a reasonable amount of money."

On his way to becoming a star pitcher for the Brooklyn Dodgers, Don Newcombe pitched for the Dodgers's minor league club in Nashua, New Hampshire (opposite). But before that Newcombe got his start in professional baseball in the Negro Leagues, pitching for the Newark Eagles from 1944 to 1945. He credited those seasons with Newark for putting him in position to be ready for the major leagues when the color line was broken in 1947. Two years later he was playing with Jackie Robinson on the Dodgers. (NATIONAL BASEBALL HALL OF FAME LIBRARY, COOPERSTOWN, N.Y.)

Newkirk, Alexander
Alex Newkirk was a pitcher for the New York Cubans, New York Black Yankees, and Boston Blues from 1946 to 1949.

New Orleans Black Eagles
The Black Eagles were a black baseball team in New Orleans, Louisiana, that played in the early 1900s. Negro League great Oliver Marcelle got his start with the Black Eagles in 1915.

New Orleans Black Pelicans
The Pelicans were a black baseball team in New Orleans, Louisiana, that played in the early 1900s through

(NATIONAL BASEBALL HALL OF FAME LIBRARY, COOPERSTOWN, N.Y.)

the 1930s. Satchel Paige was one of the players who had a stint with the Black Pelicans in 1926.

New Orleans Caufield Ads
The Caufield Ads were a black baseball team that played in New Orleans, Louisiana, in the 1920s.

New Orleans Crescent Stars
The Crescent Stars were a black baseball team that played in New Orleans, Louisiana, in the 1920s in the Negro Southern League.

New Orleans Eagles
The Eagles were a black baseball team—originally a semi-pro team in the early 1900s—that played in New Orleans, Louisiana, in the 1950s.

New Orleans Pinchbacks
The Pinchbacks played in the 1880s in New Orleans, Louisiana, and were named after P. B. S. Pinchback, a Louisiana governor and senator.

New Orleans Smart Nine
Black entertainers often got involved in Negro League baseball, and the New Orleans Smart Nine, in New Orleans, Louisiana, are an example of the connections between the two worlds. Louis Armstrong owned the New Orleans Smart Nine.

New Orleans Unions
The New Orleans Unions were a black baseball team out of New Orleans, Louisiana, that played in the 1880s.

New Orleans Zulus
The New Orleans Zulus were a black baseball team out of New Orleans, Louisiana, that played in the 1930s. They

were one of a series of black teams that used baseball clowning as a marketing pitch.

Newsome, Omer

Omer Newsome was a pitcher for the Washington Potomacs, Indianapolis ABC's, Dayton Marcos, Detroit Stars, Wilmington Potomacs, and Memphis Red Sox from 1923 to 1929.

New York All Stars

The All Stars were a barnstorming black baseball team formed in 1929 by Negro Leaguer Jack Marshall as part of a tour and show sponsored by a Canadian named Rod Whitman, according to Robert Peterson's book *Only the Ball Was White*. Marshall told the story about the birth of the All Stars: "He [Whitman] came to Chicago and he wanted two Negro ballclubs, he wanted a minstrel show, and he wanted a band. In Canada he had a midway or carnival, and he would show in different towns, so he wanted two ballclubs—specifically, he wanted one named the Texas Giants and one named the New York All Stars. So I organized this group for him, and I got a five-piece band and six other people as the minstrel show. We traveled from Fort Williams, Ontario, to Vancouver, British Columbia, as far north as Prince Albert and as far south as Medicine Hat. We had four trucks—they looked like old covered wagons. We had a tent where the performers lived. When we got into a small town, they'd set up a tent where the other tents were for the midway, and some of the performers would sleep there. Then, when we got into a town big enough to have a hotel, the ballclubs would stop in the hotel. And at twelve o'clock every day, Rod would put up $500 to the local team to play the all-stars—a team that would be selected from the Texas Giants and New York All Stars. And if they won the game, they'd get the $500. Well, we never lost a game under those conditions because we had our own umpires. We weren't there to lose. So he'd charge admission for that, and then, when the ballgame was over, he would open up the midway. At six o'clock the Texas Giants and the New York All Stars would play a game and that's another admission. Now, when this ballgame was over, then the midway would open up again. While the midway was open, he would put this colored minstrel show on. With the midway and the minstrel show going on at one time, this man is coining the money! Now, when the midway closes, then the band would play for the dance. That's another admission, and the dance would go till one o'clock. Damnedest operation you ever saw! Whitman was just selling entertainment, no patent medicine or anything like that. All the ballplayers were semi-pros from Chicago. At that time, in 1929, you might call me

a pro. Anyway, I organized the thing. We had a payroll of $1,800 a month for 24 players."

New York Bacharach Giants

The Bacharach Giants were born in Atlantic City, New Jersey, in 1916 after the Duval Giants moved from Jacksonville, Florida. However, a faction of the team broke away in 1919 and formed the New York Bacharach Giants. One of the Negro League greats who played for the New York Bacharach Giants was Dick Lundy.

New York Black Yankees

A black baseball team that grew out of the New York Lincoln Giants, the Black Yankees began play in 1931 as an independent team. Their biggest claim to fame was probably their owner for a period of time—Bill "Bojangles" Robinson, the black dancer, another instance of black entertainers' interest in Negro League baseball. One year later, though, Bojangles sold the team to James "Soldier Boy" Semler, a numbers operator from Harlem. The Black Yankees, who played at Yankee Stadium among their home ballparks, joined the Negro National League in 1936 and were part of the league through the 1948 season. In their final two years of existence, 1949 and 1950, they were an independent team again. Some of the players who were part of the Black Yankees squads included Ted "Double Duty" Radcliffe, George "Mule" Suttles, and John Henry "Pop" Lloyd.

New York Boston Giants

The New York Boston Giants were a black baseball team based in New York and organized by Negro Leagues baseball manager and historian Sol White in 1912. The club lasted one season.

New York Colored Club

The Colored Club was a black baseball team based in New York in the 1880s.

New York Cuban Giants

The first black professional baseball team that paid salaries to players is believed to be the New York Cuban Giants, a team formed from the Argyle Hotel squad of waiters in 1885 founded by Frank P. Thompson. They were considered the colored champions in 1887 and 1888 and also were the Eastern champions in 1894. They played in the Middle States League from 1889 to 1890 and the Connecticut State League in 1991.

New York Cubans

The New York Cubans, one of the many variations of black baseball teams that used the theme of Cuban players as its marketing tool, played in New York in the 1930s and 1940s. In 1935, with Negro League great Martin Dihigo serving as player-manager for the team, the Cubans narrowly lost a seven-game Negro baseball World Series to the Pittsburgh Crawfords. In 1947, the New York Cubans won the NEGRO NATIONAL LEAGUE pennant and beat the Cleveland Buckeyes in the Negro League World Series, with Luis Tiant, Sr., and Dave Barnhill on the mound. Silvio Garcia, Lorenzo Cabrera, and a young player named Orestes "Minnie" Minoso were part of that team. According to Robert Peterson in his book *Only the Ball Was White*, the 1949 New York Cubans, with Negro League great Ray Dandridge as the manager, was the only black team to become a farm club for a major league franchise when they signed a working agreement with the major league New York Giants. The Cubans played their home games at the Giants' ballpark, the Polo Grounds.

New York Cuban Stars

The New York Cuban Stars were one of the many clubs in Negro League baseball that used the idea of Cuban players as a promotional gimmick, although most of the players on the teams over the years were not Cubans. They played in the early 1900s and later were part of the East-West League formed by Cum Posey in 1932. They were also owned by Alex Pompez, a numbers racketeer.

New York Giants

This version of the New York Giants, with the same name as the major league franchise, was a black baseball team based in New York in the early 1900s.

New York Harlem Stars

The Harlem Stars were a black baseball team that played in the early 1900s and named after the black neighborhood in New York.

New York Lincoln Giants

One of the descendants of professional wrestling promoter Vince McMahon was Roderick "Jess" McMahon, and he, along with his brother, Ed, both New York city promoters, formed the New York Lincoln Giants in 1911. According to Mark Ribowsky's book, *A Complete History of the Negro Leagues: 1884–1955*, the McMahons had previously owned a minority share of the Philadelphia Giants. They were a dominant team in eastern Negro League baseball from 1911 through 1913 and were led by player-manager John Henry Lloyd, catcher Louis Santop, second baseman "Home Run" Johnson, and pitchers Smokey Joe Williams and Dick

Redding. According to Robert Peterson's book *Only the Ball Was White*, the Lincoln Giants, who played at Olympic Field in Harlem, were performers as well players: "The Lincoln Giants was one of the first black teams to add burlesque to baseball," he wrote. "In pregame practice they juggled the ball, hid it and performed all sorts of acrobatics in throwing and catching. In addition they had a pantomine act in which an imaginary ball flew from bat to glove and then went zipping around the infield." There was no denying their talent, though, as the Lincoln Giants reportedly posted a record of 101-6 in 1913 against all competition, including wins in exhibition games over several white major league teams. They were considered one of the best black baseball teams of their time. The McMahons sold the Giants in 1914 to two white businessmen, Charles Harvey and James Keenan. The Lincoln Giants would later join the Eastern Colored League in 1923 and continue to play until 1930 when they fielded another great club, including Lloyd, John Beckwith, Chino Smith, and Fats Jenkins. That 1930 squad lost to the Homestead Grays in a World Series, six games to four. That would be their final season, and the club was later called the New York Black Yankees.

New York Lincoln Stars

The New York Lincoln Stars grew out of the Lincoln black baseball team in 1915, as former Lincoln Giants' owners Jess and Ed McMahon formed the club consisting of some former Giants players. They were out of business by 1918.

New York Tigers

The New York Tigers had little to do with New York, except in name. They were a traveling black baseball team in 1935 that included such players as Oliver Marcelle, Bill Riggins, and Buck O'Neil. "We had nothing to do with New York, but we figured the name would get us some attention from the people fascinated with Harlem," O'Neil wrote in his book, *I Was Right on Time*. "Out west where we were headed, nobody was going to know the difference."

Nicholas, William

Bill Nicholas was a pitcher for the Newark Eagles in 1935 and 1936.

Nichols, Charles

Charles Nichols was an outfielder for the Argyle Hotel baseball team, consisting of black waiters who worked at the hotel, in 1885.

Nimmons, Ernie
Ernie Nimmmons was an outfielder for the Indianapolis Clowns in 1952.

Nix, Nathaniel (Tank)
Nathaniel Nix was a pitcher for the Bacharach Giants and Brooklyn Royal Giants in 1938 and 1939.

Nixon, William
Bill Nixon was an outfielder for the Jacksonville Red Sox and Birmingham Black Barons from 1940 to 1941.

Noble, Carlos
Carlos Noble was a pitcher for the New York Cubans in 1950.

Noble, Rafael (Ray)
b. 1919, d. 1998
Rafael Noble was born in Central Hatillo, Cuba, but got his start in the United States as a catcher for the New York Cubans from 1945 to 1950. The 6-foot, 210-pound Noble batted .325 in 1947 and was signed by the New York Giants after the 1948 season. Noble played minor league baseball in Jersey City in 1949, batting .259 and went on to play portions of three seasons of major league baseball from 1951 to 1953. In 107 games for the Giants, Noble batted .218 with nine home runs and 40 RBIs. He played in the International League for Havana, Columbus, Buffalo, and Houston from 1954 to 1961, and his best season was in 1958 with Buffalo when he hit 15 home runs, drove in 68 runs, and batted .294. He also played winter baseball in the Cuban Winter League.

Noel, Eddie
Eddie Noel was a pitcher for the Nashville Giants in 1950.

Norfolk Giants
The Norfolk Giants were a black baseball team based in Norfolk, Virginia, in the early 1900s. One of the Negro League greats who played for the Giants was pitcher Jesse "Nip" Winters in 1919.

Norfolk Red Stockings
The Norfolk Red Stockings were a black baseball team based in Norfolk, Virginia, in the late 1880s.

Norfolk Stars
The Stars were a black baseball team based in Norfolk, Virginia, in the late 1800s and early 1900s.

Norman, Alton (Ed)
Alton Norman was a shortstop for the Cleveland Elites, Cleveland Tate Stars, and Lincoln Giants from 1920 to 1926.

Norman, Bud
Bud Norman was a pitcher for the Indianapolis Crawfords in 1940.

Norman, James
Jim Norman was an infielder and manager for the Kansas City Giants and Kansas City Royal Giants from 1907 to 1910.

Norris, Slim
Slim Norris was a third baseman for the Louisville White Sox in 1930.

Northwestern Park
Northwestern Park was a ball field in Indianapolis, Indiana, that was the home field for the Indianapolis ABC's in the early 1900s.

Norwood, Walter
Walt Norwood was an officer in the Detroit Stars front office in 1933.

Nunez, Dagoberto (Berto)
Dagoberto Nunez was a first baseman for the Memphis Red Sox in 1934.

Nuttal, Bill
Bill Nuttal was a pitcher for the Bacharach Giants and Lincoln Giants from 1924 to 1926.

Nutter, Isaac
Ike Nutter was an officer in the Bacharach Giants front office and also served as president of the Eastern League in 1927 and 1928.

O'Bryant, Willie
Willie O'Bryant played shortstop for the Washington Pilots in 1932.

O'Dell, John Wesley
John Wesley O'Dell was a pitcher for the Houston Eagles in 1949 and 1950.

Oden, Johnny Webb
Johnny Oden was an outfielder and shortstop from 1927 to 1932 for the Louisville Black Caps, Knoxville Giants, Birmingham Black Barons, and Memphis Red Sox.

O'Donnell, Charles
Charlie O'Donnell was an officer and manager with the Pittsburgh Keystones in 1887.

O'Farrill, Estaban Orlando
Estaban O'Farrill played shortstop from 1949 to 1951 for the Baltimore Elite Giants, Philadelphia Stars, and Indianapolis Clowns.

Offert, Mose
Mose Offert was a pitcher for the Indianapolis ABC's from 1925 to 1926.

Oklahoma Monarchs
The Oklahoma Monarchs were a black baseball team that played in Oklahoma in the early 1900s.

Oldham, Jimmy
Jimmy Oldham was a pitcher for the St. Louis Stars and St. Louis Giants from 1920 to 1923.

Oliver, Hudson
Hudson Oliver played second base for the Brooklyn Royal Giants in 1911.

Oliver, James (Pee Wee)
James Oliver played shortstop for the Indianapolis Clowns, Cincinnati-Indianapolis Clowns, and Birmingham Black Barons from 1943 to 1946.

Oliver, John
John Oliver played third base for the Brooklyn Remsens in 1885.

Oliver, John Henry
John Henry Oliver played shortstop for the Cleveland Buckeyes and Memphis Red Sox in 1945 and 1946.

Oliver, Leonard

Leonard Oliver was a shortstop for the Philadelphia Giants and Pittsburgh Giants from 1911 to 1913.

Oliver, Martin

Martin Oliver was a catcher for the Memphis Red Sox, Birmingham Black Barons, and Louisville Black Caps from 1930 to 1934.

Olympic Field

Olympic Field was a ballpark in Harlem in New York where the Lincoln Giants and other black baseball teams played in the early 1900s.

Omaha Tigers

The Omaha Tigers were a black baseball team that played in Omaha, Nebraska, in the mid-1930s.

Oms, Alejandro

Alejandro Oms was an outfielder from 1917 to 1935 for the New York Cubans, All Cubans, and Cuban Stars. Partial records show that Oms batted .345 in 904 at bats during his Negro League career, including a .385 average in 1929 and .381 in 1925. The Cuban-born star was known as a great outfielder and played on the Cubans in one of the great outfields of Negro League history, along with Martin Dihigo and Pablo Mesa. The 5-foot-9, 195-pound Oms had the third-highest career batting average in Cuban Winter League history, batting .351. He is in the Cuban Baseball Hall of Fame.

O'Neil, John Jordan (Buck)

b. 1911

John O'Neil was a great Negro League first baseman and has emerged as a modern-day spokesman for the history of the game, immortalized in Ken Burns's documentary series on baseball. He was a first baseman and manager from 1934 to 1955 for the Tampa Black Smokers, Miami Giants, Shreveport Acme Giants, Memphis Red Sox, and Kansas City Monarchs. One of his accomplishments was to be the first black coach in major league baseball, named as a coach for the Chicago Cubs in 1962 after working for six years as a scout for the organization (he managed Ernie Banks in Negro League ball and signed him as a scout for the Cubs). He played in Miami for an owner named Buck O'Neal. That was how O'Neil got his nickname, when promoter Syd Pollock, promoting the Zulu Cannibal Giants, a clowning team for which O'Neil played, got O'Neil's name confused with the owner and started listing the young first baseman as "Buck" O'Neil.

He would find a home eventually in Kansas City as a mainstay for the Monarchs, both as a player and later as a manager. In his book *I Was Right on Time*, O'Neil wrote about what it meant to play for the Monarchs: "There I was, John Jordan O'Neil, heading off in the spring of 1938 to play first base for the Kansas City Monarchs," he wrote. "It had the same meaning as the New York Yankees would have for a boy 40 years ago. Just to tell the fellas back home, very cool-like, mind you, 'Yeah, I'm going to be playing for the Kansas City Monarchs,' was quite a thrill." He wrote about the two Monarchs who influenced him early in his career—Newt Joseph and Bullet Joe Rogan: "Newt Joseph was a fun-loving guy who actually managed the Monarchs for a while; there's a wonderful picture of Newt holding a gun on his players to keep them in line. When I got to know him, he was running a very successful cab stand downtown. I would hang around that cab stand for hours, talking baseball with Newt. In his day he was a great sign-stealer, and he taught me some of his tricks. He also gave me scouting reports on all the players and pitchers in the league, what to look for from certain pitchers, where to play certain hitters, which catchers I could steal on. What he taught me not only helped me as a new player to the league but also as a manager later on. My other mentor was Wilbur 'Bullet Joe' Rogan. He had just finished his pitching career when I arrived and was dividing his time between umpiring and working in the post office. As good a pitcher as Rogan was, he was adept at the plate—in 1924 he led the National League in wins and finished second in batting [.411]. Wilbur taught me a lot about hitting. I had problems handling pitches on the inside part of the plate, and it didn't take pitchers long to figure this out, so I was seeing a lot of balls thrown at my hands. Wilbur and I would go out to the ballpark early, and he would throw batting practice to me before anybody else got there. He taught me to stand back in the batter's box and away from the plate."

O'Neil played in the Negro League All-Star Game, the EAST-WEST GAME, three times. He won the NEGRO AMERICAN LEAGUE batting title in 1946 with a .350 average, coming back after three years of military service in World War II to lead the Monarchs to an NAL pennant. Later he would manage the Monarchs and win five pennants and manage in four straight All-Star Games from 1951 to 1954. O'Neil also wrote about the pride of playing in the Negro Leagues: "We might not have played in the major leagues, but we kept faith and cleared the path for Jackie Robinson," O'Neil wrote. "We might not have batted against Lefty Grove or pitched to Ted Williams, but we had to stand in against Bullet Joe Rogan and face Josh Gibson. It's like I said at Satchel's funeral in 1982. People say it's a shame he never pitched against the best. But who's to say he didn't."

John "Buck" O'Neil was a pioneer among Negro League ballplayers in his own right. He became the first black coach in major league baseball when he was named as a coach for the Chicago Cubs in 1962. The organization was calling on the expertise O'Neil gained when he was a first baseman and manager in the Negro Leagues from 1934 to 1955 for the Tampa Black Smokers, Miami Giants, Shreveport Acme Giants, Memphis Red Sox, and Kansas City Monarchs. He was a three-time Negro League All-Star and won the Negro American League batting title in 1946 with a .353 average. (NATIONAL BASEBALL HALL OF FAME LIBRARY, COOPERSTOWN, N.Y.)

O'Neill, Charles

Charles O'Neill was a catcher for the Bacharach Giants, Columbus Buckeyes, Chicago American Giants, Kansas City Monarchs, and Toledo Tigers.

Ora, Clarence

Clarence Ora was an outfielder for the Cleveland Cubs in 1932.

Orange, Grady

Grady Orange played shortstop, second base, and third base from 1925 to 1931 for the Cleveland Tigers, Detroit Stars, Kansas City Monarchs, and Birmingham Black Barons.

Oriole Park

Oriole Park was a ballpark in Baltimore that hosted some Baltimore Elite Giant games.

Orleans Eagles

The Orleans Eagles were a black baseball team based in New Orleans in the early 1900s.

O'Rourke, John

John O'Rourke was the secretary of the International League of Colored Base Ball Teams in 1906.

Ortiz, Julio

Julio Ortiz was an outfielder and shortstop for the Cincinnati-Indianapolis Clowns, and Kansas City Monarchs in 1944 and 1945.

Ortiz, Rafaelito

Rafaelito Ortiz was a pitcher for the Chicago American Giants in 1948. He was a star in the Puerto Rican Winter League and was elected to the Puerto Rico Baseball Hall of Fame in 1992.

Osorio, Alberto

Alberto Osorio was a pitcher for the Louisville Buckeyes in 1949.

Otis, Amos

Amos Otis was an outfielder for the Nashville Giants in 1920.

Ousley, Guy

Guy Ousley was a shortstop, second baseman, and third baseman for the Cleveland Cubs, Memphis Red Sox, and Chicago Columbia Giants in 1931 and 1932.

Overton, Albert

Albert Overton was a pitcher in 1937 and 1944 for the Philadelphia Stars and Cincinnati-Indianapolis Clowns.

Overton, John

John Overton was an officer with the Indianapolis ABC's in 1925.

Owen Bush Stadium

Owen Bush Stadium, in Indianapolis, Indiana, was the home of the Indianapolis Clowns in 1944 and from 1946 to 1950. It was named after Owen Bush, a former major league player who later owned and managed the minor league Indianapolis Indians.

Owens, Albert

Al Owens was a pitcher for the Nashville Elite Giants in 1930 and 1931.

Owens, Alphonso (Buddy)

Alphonso Owens played third base for the Chicago American Giants in 1951 and 1952.

Owens, Arthot

Arthot Owens was a pitcher for the Detroit Stars in 1954.

Owens, Aubrey

Aubrey Owens pitched for the Indianapolis ABC's, New Orleans Caufield Ads, Chicago Giants, and Chicago American Giants from 1920 to 1926.

Owens, Dewitt

Dewitt Owens was an outfielder and second baseman for the Indianapolis ABC's, Birmingham Black Barons, Philadelphia Stars, and Indianapolis Crawfords from 1936 to 1942.

Owens, Jack

Jack Owens was a pitcher for the Detroit Stars and Chicago American Giants from 1950 to 1954.

Owens, Lane

Lane Owens was an infielder for the Indianapolis Clowns in 1952.

Owens, Oscar (Iron Man)

Oscar Owens was a pitcher, first baseman, and outfielder for the Pittsburgh Keystones, Indianapolis ABC's, and Homestead Grays from 1913 to 1931.

Owens, Raymond (Smokey)

Raymond Owens was a pitcher and outfielder for the Cleveland Buckeyes, Cleveland Bears, New Orleans–St. Louis Stars, Cincinnati Buckeyes, Cincinnati Clowns, and Jacksonville Red Caps from 1939 to 1942.

Owens, William

b. 1901, d. 1999

William Owens was a shortstop, second baseman, and pitcher for the Chicago American Giants, Washington Potomacs, Dayton Marcos, Indianapolis ABC's, Memphis Red Sox, Birmingham Black Barons, Harrisburg Giants, Cleveland Elites, Detroit Stars, Wilmington Potomacs, and Brooklyn Royal Giants from 1923 to 1933. He was a defensive standout but batted around .250 throughout much of his career.

Pace, Benjamin

Benjamin Pace was a catcher for the Pittsburgh Keystones and Homestead Grays from 1921 to 1925.

Pace, Ed

Ed Pace was an outfielder for the Nashville Elite Giants in 1930.

Padrone, Juan

Juan Padrone was a pitcher, outfielder, and second baseman from 1909 to 1926 for the Smart Set, Chicago American Giants, Long Branch Cubans, Cuban Stars, Lincoln Stars, Brooklyn Royal Giants, Indianapolis ABC's, All Cubans, Birmingham Black Barons, Cuban Stars of Havana, Cuban Stars, Cincinnati Cubans, and Havana Cubans.

Page, Allen

Allen Page was vice president and treasurer of the Negro Southern League and also an officer with the New Orleans Creoles from 1945 to 1950.

Page, Theodore (Ted)

b. 1903, d. 1984

Theodore Page was an outfielder and first baseman for the Buffalo Giants, Homestead Grays, Newark Stars, New York Black Yankees, Pittsburgh Crawfords, Philadelphia Stars, Newark Eagles, Baltimore Black Sox, Brooklyn Royal Giants, Brooklyn Eagles, and Quaker Giants from 1926 to 1937. Page, who was born in Glasgow, Kentucky, said he failed to make the Toledo Tigers, a black baseball team in Toledo, Ohio, in 1923, just after he graduated from high school. In an interview with author John Holway on file at the National Baseball Hall of Fame, Page said he passed up a football scholarship to Ohio State University—he had been a star halfback in high school in Youngstown, Ohio. He wound up playing with the Buffalo Giants, managed by Home Run Johnson, at the end of the 1923 season. Page also played winter baseball in the Florida hotel league, playing for the Breakers Hotel in Palm Beach. Later he played for a team in Montreal managed by Chappie Johnson in 1928 and credited Johnson for teaching him the value of bunting: "I give Chappie credit for bringing me into the position where I could hold a job as a baseball player," Page said. "Somehow Chappie was a good con man, and he conned me into realizing that I was very fast. He taught me one thing for sure: if you're not hitting the ball—and who can hit ever time constantly, without running into a slump—there is another way to get on base. Bunt, and push the ball, if you're able to run. Heck, I could get two or three base hits out of a ball game without the ball going out of the infield. He taught me to drag the ball or push the ball, and I had a double offense, whether the ball was going down the third base line or the first base line. . . . I could run, and I could run bases good. When I was on second and the pitcher would make his delivery, I would tear. I'm halfway to home by the time they let the ball go, because I had rounded third, and my destination was home plate, on the bunt. The bunt would be down the third base line. Dick Seay would bunt the ball. He was almost perfect. And Jakes Stephens was good at it—perfect."

After he left baseball, Page went on to be a force in bowling in the Pittsburgh area, owning and operating his own alley. He was also the lone black member of the board of directors of the Greater Pittsburgh Bowling Proprietors Association. Looking back on his career, Page said he had no regrets about his days in the Negro Leagues: "I can look back and say that at least I played with and against some great players. And to have been on either of these teams, the Crawfords and the Grays, is an honor in itself." Page was inducted into the Pennsylvania Hall of Fame and also the Greater Pittsburgh Bowling Hall of Fame.

Page Fence Giants

A company called the Page Wire and Fence Co., owned by white businessmen L. W. Hoch and Rolla Taylor, in Adrian, Michigan, in 1890 sponsored a black baseball team called the Page Fence Giants. Their featured player was John "Bud" Fowler, and they barnstormed around the Midwest, and used clowning to help market their team, although they were a very good baseball club. Sol White played second base for the Giants, and in his book *History of Colored Base Ball* wrote that the Page Fence Giants were "a fine baseball team. They were hard to beat in 1895, as their pitchers were among the best and their fielding excellent. . . . The Giants were formidable opponents to any team." The Page Fence Giants defeated the Cuban Giants in a 15-game series in 1896 for what was then considered the black baseball championship. Other players who played for the Page Fence Giants were George Wilson and Charlie Grant. They moved to Chicago after the 1898 season and became the Columbia Giants.

Ted Page might have become a college football star running back. He passed up a football scholarship at Ohio State University in 1923 for a chance to play baseball, the game he loved, in the Negro Leagues. Page was an outfielder and first baseman for the Buffalo Giants, Homestead Grays, Newark Stars, New York Black Yankees, Pittsburgh Crawfords, Philadelphia Stars, Newark Eagles, Baltimore Black Sox, Brooklyn Royal Giants, Brooklyn Eagles, and Quaker Giants.

(NATIONAL BASEBALL HALL OF FAME LIBRARY, COOPERSTOWN, N.Y.)

Paige, LeRoy Robert (Satchel)
b. 1906, d. 1982

While there were many great ballplayers in Negro League baseball history, no one single player has been identified with Negro League baseball more than LeRoy "Satchel" Paige, considered by many to be the greatest pitcher of all time. The 6-foot-4, 180-pound hard-throwing Paige, born in Mobile, Alabama, was certainly the biggest draw in black baseball, playing from 1924 to 1955 for the Mobile Tigers, Birmingham Black Barons, Chattanooga Black Lookouts, Pittsburgh Crawfords, Cleveland Cubs, New York Black Yankees, Kansas City Monarchs, Philadelphia Stars, Satchel Paige's All-Stars (Paige's own barnstorming team), Cuban House of David, Baltimore Black Sox, Memphis Red Sox, Chicago American Giants, and St. Louis Stars.

Like most Negro League records, the statistics for Paige's black baseball career are incomplete and do not match his stature in the game. Some reports have Paige, one of 11 children, spending five years in a reform school for youths—from 1918 to 1923—for stealing, truancy, and other youth problems. When he got out, he tried out for a baseball team that his brother Wilson was playing for, the Mobile Tigers, and is believed to have won nearly 30 games in 1924 for the Tigers. In his first three years with Birmingham, from 1927 to 1929, Paige went 31-18. In his autobiography, *Maybe I'll Pitch Forever*, Paige recalled the first time he pitched for Birmingham: "I guess I was pretty confident," he wrote. "In my first ball game with Birmingham I even thought of calling in the outfield like I had done in Chattanooga, to build up the crowds. But I didn't think [Birmingham manager] Bill Gatewood would put up with it. Then I hit on another gimmick. I yelled over to the other team, 'I'm gonna strike out the first six guys up against me.' You should have seen those guys burn. They shook their bats at me. Well, after I'd struck out the first five, one of their guys pulled out a white towel and waved it back and forth. The sixth batter came up, and I grinned at him and threw quick. He popped out. George Perkins [Paige's catcher] cornered me at the bench. 'You didn't get those six in a row like you said you would.' I told him, 'They'd already surrendered. When old Satch needs a strikeout, he gets it.'"

After pitching for the Black Barons, Paige signed with Gus Greenlee and the Pittsburgh Crawfords in 1931, and records show he posted a 14-8 mark with Pittsburgh in 1932 and 13-3 in 1934, his two best-recorded seasons. "Before I started cutting loose around Pittsburgh in 1931, there was no big money for anybody in the Negro Leagues," Paige told the *Saturday Evening Post*. "Then they started getting nice, fat checks. I got the fans out." He also left the Crawfords in 1934 to pitch for a semipro barnstorming team—with a number of white players—in Bismarck, North Dakota, sponsored by a car dealer, and also pitched some for the Cuban House of David team. Paige had been banned by Pittsburgh Crawfords owner Gus Greenlee for leaving the Crawfords to play in Bismarck but was allowed back in 1936.

Again, in 1937, Paige left the Crawfords, and this time he took about nine teammates with him to the Dominican Republic to play for dictator Rafael Trujillo's baseball team in the Dominican baseball political war. Trujillo convinced Paige to come play for his team with a lucrative offer and got him to recruit other players such as Josh Gibson to accompany him. Trujillo's political opponent also had a team and had also recruited numerous Negro League baseball players for his team. The prestige that came with winning these games was considered an important political victory as well. Paige and his teammates found themselves under army guard constantly and played an important series at gunpoint, with soldiers lining the field. In a 1953 *Colliers* article, Paige described the consequences he believed he was facing if he lost the final game of the series: "I had it fixed with Mr. Trujillo's police," Paige said. "If we win, their whole army is gonna run out and escort us from the palace. . . . If we lose . . .

there is nothing to do but considered myself and my boys as passed over Jordan." They did not lose.

When Paige came back to the states, he was again considered persona non grata by the Negro Leagues. But he was too much of a box office draw to keep out of the game and would return to pitch for the Kansas City Monarchs. Paige went 7-1 with Kansas City in 1941 and 8-3 in 1942. He was also the winning pitcher in the East-West Negro League All-Star Game in 1943 but reportedly refused to play in 1944 because organizers would not donate receipts to the World War II effort.

The stories about Paige indicate he won many more games against all sorts of competition, including exhibitions against white major league barnstorming teams. He would finally get a chance to play major league baseball when Cleveland Indians owner Bill Veeck signed him to a contract in 1948, and Paige, at the age of 42, became the oldest rookie in major league baseball history. One year earlier, when Jackie Robinson had broken the color barrier, Paige expressed disappointment that he wasn't the first black in major league baseball in the 20th century. "Somehow I figured it would be me," he said. "Maybe it happened too late, and everybody figured I was too old. Maybe that's why it was Jackie and not me."

In six major league seasons with Cleveland and the St. Louis Browns, Paige posted a 28-31 record with a 3.29 ERA. His best year came in 1952 when he went 12-10. He came back to pitch in black baseball for the Monarchs and also signed with Abe Saperstein's Harlem Globetrotters (the baseball version of the famous clowning basketball team) for a barnstorming tour in 1954. He pitched minor league baseball in the International League, Pacific Coast League, and Carolina League until 1966, at the age of 60, and had come back to pitch one major league game in 1965 for the Kansas City Athletics. Owner Charlie Finley brought him back for that appearance, using it as a promotion, providing Paige with a rocking chair in the bullpen and a nurse who massaged his right arm. He still had something left, though, as he gave up just one hit in three innings pitched. In 1968, he put on a major league uniform again, this one for the Atlanta Braves, when it was discovered he was only 158 days short of qualifying for an annual $7,000 pension, and he was designated as a coach for the Braves in order to qualify. He also pitched in several spring training camps for the Braves in 1969. Paige also pitched winter baseball in Cuba and Puerto Rico.

A 1958 scouting report by Nap Reyes on file at the National Baseball Hall of Fame, while Paige was pitching for the Miami Marlins in the International League, said that Paige was "the best control pitcher in this league," but also described one of his faults by noting, "he pitches when he wants to pitch." The report said Paige was a winning player but not a good hustler and did not have good habits. The report rated Paige excellent for poise, brains,

There is probably no greater name in the history of Negro League baseball than Satchel Paige. The tall, lanky right-handed pitcher was the star of Negro League baseball for more than two decades, starting with the Mobile Tigers in 1924 to the Kansas City Monarchs in 1955. He pitched on some of the all-time great Negro League teams, including the Pittsburgh Crawfords, and was by far black baseball's biggest attraction. It is estimated that during his career, pitching against a variety of competition, Paige pitched in more than 2,500 games, winning about 2,000. One year he said he pitched in 153 games; he estimated that he probably threw about 100 no-hitters.
(NATIONAL BASEBALL HALL OF FAME LIBRARY, COOPERSTOWN, N.Y.)

to 20 days in jail in April by a local judge for two traffic violations. The sentence was deferred until the season was over, and there could be a day taken off his sentence for every game he wins, every run he scores, and, according to a newspaper report, "every time he strikes out Luke Easter of the Buffalo Bisons." It was certainly an interesting year because it was the same time Paige flirted with a career in Hollywood. He got a small role in the film *The Wonderful Country*, starring Robert Mitchum and Julie London. But that was the beginning and the end of his film career, although Paige was always a performer, even as a young boy.

Paige said his original family name was Page, but he told one interviewer that his family added the *i* to make themselves sound more "hightoned." He also said he got the name Satchel when he was seven years old while carrying baggage at the railroad depot in Mobile. He said he invented a device to carry more bags: "I rigged up ropes around my shoulders and my waist, and I carried a satchel in each hand and one under each arm," he told one reporter. "I carried so many satchels that all you could see were satchels. You couldn't see no LeRoy Paige."

Whether he was toting satchels or pitching, Paige always had style. In an interview conducted by author John Holway on file at the National Baseball Hall of Fame, Negro Leaguer Newt Allen talked about Paige's flair for showmanship: "He really was a showman," Allen said. "He used to make some of those ballplayers so mad that they'd want to shoot him. And if he knew that he was getting under your skin, he'd really have your skin rolling up." In another Holway interview, catcher Larry Brown said catching Paige was always interesting and fun: "You could catch him in a rocking chair, because he wasn't wild," Brown said. "One time we were playing a game in Los Angeles in 1931, and we were only leading 2-1 against Joe Pirrone's All-Stars—Babe Herman, Walter Berger, Fred Haney—big men. Anyway, Satchel called the outfield in on the grass and struck out the next two men coming up, Frank Damaree and Walter Berger. And we were only leading 2-1. He did it against major

and guts. It also noted that he "is older than his age." Another scouting report the same year by Tony Pacheco said that Paige "sleeps too much and is always late." It was a difficult year in Miami for Paige. He had been sentenced leaguers, I know, because I was catching. The other guys kept hollering, 'Come on, get on there, he ain't got nothing but a fastball.' But it was so fast they couldn't hit it. The main thing about it, his ball wasn't a hard ball, but the speed was so rapid, it would take off."

Fellow Negro League pitcher Willie "Sug" Cornelius said that if Paige had the opportunity to pitch his entire career in the major leagues, he would have been the best of all time. "If Satchel had been in the majors in his prime, he would have broken all the records," Cornelius said. "I'm not exaggerating. The man could throw in a cup. Satchel's control was so fine." Crush Holloway also spoke of Paige's control: "He could throw the ball anywhere he wanted it," Holloway said. "He used to throw it over a soda water bottle top. He'd used that for home plate when he was warming up on the sidelines. That's why his control was so good." However, one Negro Leaguer, Jelly Gardner, said that he could remember a time when Paige's control was not so good. "He was all right, but it was worth half your life to hit against him when he came up," Gardner said in another interview. "One time at you, one time behind you, the next time at your feet. You had to be an acrobat when he first came up, and I saw him the first day he was in the ballpark in Birmingham."

In another Holway interview, Negro Leaguer James Canada said Paige was a mercenary ballplayer: "Satchel was out there for the money," Canada said. "If you didn't give it to him, he didn't play. He had to have $500 down payment, or 20 percent. . . . He used to throw change up in the air and the ballplayers would scramble for it. He did that in the EAST-WEST GAME in 1944. When he'd get new luggage, he'd take the old luggage and give it away. I used to ride with him in the car. He'd be late for every ball game. You know how he was, he was a showman."

Paige had a pitch called the "hesitation pitch," which fellow Negro League pitcher Bill Drake, in another Holway interview, said Paige learned from him: "I met Satchel the first year he came out in 1926," Drake said. "He was with Chattanooga, and I was with Memphis. He had just come out of reformatory school, about 17 or 18 years old. I used to call it a 'delayed' pitch—stride and then throw. Satchel called it a 'hesitation' pitch. Whether Satchel copied it from me or some other fellow, I don't know. I wouldn't say definitely that he learned it from me, but if he didn't, he learned it from someone who learned it from me. I don't remember anyone who was doing it before me, and I started pitching in 1913."

One of Paige's greatest rivals was pitcher Bill Foster, who talked about his matchups against Paige in a 1974 interview with *Black Sports:* "One of the greatest pitchers I've ever seen, I think, was Satchel Paige," he said. "Now he didn't know how to throw a curveball for a long

time, so I knew him as a good fast ball pitcher. In the night time it looked like one of these zuzu biscuits, about the size of a 50 cent piece. That's the way it looked. I think, as near as I can remember, we faced each other around 13 or 14 times, and I think I got the edge on Satchel when I beat him in a doubleheader in Pittsburgh one Saturday—5-0 and 1-0. I think that put me one ball game ahead of him in our career. But I'll tell you something: if Satchel got one run first, he would beat you; if I got one run first, he was beat."

Joe Greene, Paige's catcher in Kansas City, in another Holway interview on file at the Hall of Fame, talked about how Paige thrived on attention: "Satchel like excitement and created it," Greene said. "Satchel always wanted to be noticed. He was one of those pitchers who wanted to attract an audience. Satchel would be down on a street corner with a big crowd around him talking about baseball. He always got the conversation going—and it gets late. He calls down that he wants a police escort, and sometimes our owner would be with us and Satchel doesn't show up—and he's got to pitch the first three innings—and it's 15-20 minutes to game time and Satchel hasn't shown up yet. . . . You hear some sirens outside the park and there'd be some police on motorcycles, he'd be in a cab coming to the ball park. He did all those kind of things. . . . He'd pitch three innings a day Mondays, Tuesdays, Wednesdays, Thursdays, Fridays, be off Saturday and pitch one game Sunday."

Paige's battles with fellow Negro League great Josh Gibson, who was Paige's teammate in Pittsburgh but later faced him when Paige played in Kansas City, became Negro League legend, with Paige sometimes striking out Gibson and Gibson sometimes tagging Paige, as he did in one game when he went 4 for 4 against Paige in Chicago. Greene said he believed Paige got the best of Gibson more often than not: "Satchel could get him out, never had any trouble with him," Greene said. "We played Josh's team, the Washington-Homestead Grays, in the Negro World Series in 1942 and beat them in four straight games. Satchel just handcuffed Josh. When Willard Brown and I were down in Puerto Rico in 1941, they had Josh on a radio interview, and they asked him how did he stack up with Satchel as a hitter. Josh said he hit Satchel about like he did the rest of the pitchers. Well, we didn't like it too much, so we told Satchel about it. That same year we were playing the Grays in the World Series, and when Josh came up in the first game, Satchel said, 'You talk about the way you hit me. I heard all about it. Come up here, you big so-and-so, and see how you can hit my fast one.' Naturally Josh was looking for a curveball, but Satchel blazed number one, the fast ball, down the middle for strike one. Josh looked at it. Satchel waved his hand at Josh, and on the next pitch he threw him another fast ball. Josh made an attempt to hit it but he was too late. He just barely tipped it, and I caught it for strike two. Satchel came walking about halfway in and said, 'Get ready to hit, you can't hit with the bat on your shoulder. I'm not going to waste anything on you, get ready to hit.' And on the next pitch he threw him another fast ball and Josh looked at it for strike three. All the time he was looking for the curveball, he was thinking that Satchel would throw a curve. He was crossed up by the way Satchel was talking to him. And the crowd just roared. Next time Josh came up, Satchel says, 'Get ready, I'm going to throw you one belt-high, so don't crowd the plate.' Then, 'I'm going to throw you one outside and low on the corner. You better swing.' I noticed Josh set his left foot closer to the plate, to hit that outside pitch, and I told him, 'You know you don't hit like that. Get your foot back.' But I know why he was doing it, and Satchel knew, too. Satchel would show him a curveball, but he never did let him hit it. And the people roared. They wanted to see those two tangle up."

Nearly every Negro Leaguer has a Satchel Paige story, and Jack Marshall of the Chicago American Giants told one in Robert Peterson's book *Only the Ball Was White* that credits Paige with introducing the use of plastic batting helmets. "In 1936 we had a Negro National League All-Star team we took to Denver to play in the Denver Post tournament," Marshall said. "I played third base. Chester Williams played shortstop; Sammy T. Hughes played second base. Buck Leonard first base, Josh Gibson and Hardy was catching. Raymond Brown, Sam Streeter, and somebody else was pitching—and Satchel. And Wild Bill Wright, Cool Papa Bell, and another boy in the outfield. That was the team we had. We didn't lose a game. We won seven straight games. And when we came up to play Borger, Texas, a white team—we were the only colored team in the tournament—these boys sent back to Borger and had these helmets made to go around in their caps because they didn't want to get hurt with Satchel's speed. And that was the very first time anybody ever put that kind of protection on their heads in baseball. Satchel must have struck out about 21 men and never threw a ball higher than a person's belt line. Well, for three innings he called in the outfield. . . . He was the fastest I ever saw."

The stories about Satchel Paige and his exploits seem to be limitless, and it is often difficult to sort out the myth from the truth. But Peterson put together a summary of Paige's accomplishments that included Paige's 1961 estimate of pitching in more than 2,500 games, winning about 2,000, and he still pitched in several hundred games after that; from 1929 through 1958 Paige played both summer and winter baseball, and one year said he pitched in 153 games; he estimated that he probably threw about 100 no-hitters; he earned three to four times as much money as any other player in the Negro Leagues, making as much as $40,000 in some years with the

Monarchs. Paige claimed to have a list of rules to live by that contributed to his lengthy baseball career:

"Avoid fried meats, which angry up the blood.
If your stomach disputes you, lie down and pacify it with cool thoughts.
Keep the juices flowing by jangling around gently as you move.
Go very light on the vices, such as carrying on in society. The social rumble ain't restful.
Avoid running at all times.
Don't look back. Something might be gaining on you."

Paine, Henry

Henry Paine was an outfielder for the Brooklyn Remsens in 1885.

Paine, John

John Paine was an outfielder for the Philadelphia Pythians in 1887.

Palm, Robert (Spoony)

Robert Palm was a catcher from 1927 to 1946 for the St. Louis Stars, Birmingham Black Barons, Cleveland Giants, Detroit Stars, Brooklyn Eagles, Homestead Grays, Philadelphia Stars, New York Black Yankees, Akron Tyrites, Cole's American Giants, Chicago American Giants, and Pittsburgh Crawfords. Palm was one of many Negro League players who went to the Dominican Republic in 1937 to play in that country's baseball war between political factions. Palm played for San Pedro, one of the teams owned by an opponent of dictator Rafael Trujillo.

Palmer, Curtis

Curtis Palmer was an outfielder for the New York Black Yankees in 1949 and 1950.

Palmer, Earl

Earl Palmer was an outfielder for the Lincoln Giants and Chicago Union Giants in 1918 and 1919.

Palmer, Leon

Leon Palmer was an outfielder for the Louisville White Sox and Dayton Marcos in 1926 and 1930.

Palomino, Emilio

Emilio Palomino was an outfielder for the Cuban X Giants and All Cubans team from 1904 to 1906.

Pape, Ed
Ed Pape was an outfielder for the Homestead Grays in 1946.

Pareda, Monk
Monk Pareda was a pitcher and first baseman from 1910 to 1921 for the Cincinnati Cubans, Stars of Cuba, and Cuban Stars.

Parego, George
George Parego was a first baseman, outfielder, and pitcher for the Argyle Hotel team, Cuban Giants, Philadelphia Keystones, Trenton Cuban Giants, and Cuban Stars from 1885 to 1888. An article in the *Trenton Times* on May 10, 1886, praised Parego's fielding, noting that he "played right field with great credit for the Cuban Giants in the season of 1885 and 1886, making some very difficult catches with great style and ease."

Parker, Jack
Jack Parker was an infielder for the New York Black Yankees and Pittsburgh Crawfords in 1938.

Parker, Sonny
Sonny Parker was a pitcher for the Kansas City Monarchs, Harrisburgh–St. Louis Stars, and Chicago Brown Bombers in 1942 and 1943.

Parker, Thomas (Tom)
Thomas Parker was a pitcher, outfielder, and manager for the Indianapolis ABC's, Memphis Red Sox, Homestead Grays, Monroe Monarchs, New York Black Yankees, New Orleans–St. Louis Stars, New York Cubans, Indianapolis Athletics, Boston Blues, Columbus Elite Giants, Nashville Elite Giants, Toledo Crawfords, and Birmingham Black Barons from 1929 to 1948.

Parker, Willie
Willie Parker was a left-handed pitcher for the Baltimore Black Sox and Lincoln Giants from 1917 to 1920.

Parker, Willie
Willie Parker was a first baseman for the Philadelphia Stars in 1952.

Parkinson, Parky
Parky Parkinson was a pitcher for the Houston Eagles in 1950.

Parks, Charles (Charlie)
1987

Charles Parks was a catcher for the Newark Eagles from 1940 to 1947.

Parks, John
John Parks was an outfielder and catcher for the Newark Eagles and New York Black Yankees from 1939 to 1947.

Parks, Joseph (Joe)
Joe Parks was a shortstop, catcher, and outfielder for the Philadelphia Giants, Cuban Giants, Pennsylvania Red Caps of New York, Bacharach Giants, and Brooklyn Royal Giants from 1909 to 1919.

Parks, Sam
Sam Parks was an officer and owner with the Little Rock Black Travelers and Memphis Grey Sox in 1945 and 1946.

Parks, William (Bill)
William Parks was an outfielder, second baseman, and shortstop for the Lincoln Giants, Chicago Giants, Lincoln Stars, Chicago American Giants, Philadelphia Giants, Chicago Union Giants, and Pennsylvania Red Caps of New York from 1910 to 1920.

Parnell, Roy (Red)
Roy Parnell was an outfielder, first baseman, and manager for the Birmingham Black Barons, New Orleans Crescent Stars, Monroe Monarchs, Philadelphia Stars, Columbus Elite Giants, Houston Eagles, Nashville Elite Giants, and Pittsburgh Crawfords from 1926 to 1950. In an interview with author John Holway on file at the National Baseball Hall of Fame, Negro Leaguer Ted Page said that Parnell was a good all-around player: "He could do everything—hit, throw and run," Page said. Records show that Parnell batted .343 for Philadelphia in 1936, .224 in 1938, .304 in 1939, .305 in 1940 and .247 in 1941.

Parpetti, Augustin (Gus)
Gus Parpetti was an outfielder and first baseman for the Bacharach Giants, Kansas City Monarchs, Cuban Stars, Havana Cubans, and Richmond Giants from 1909 to 1923.

Parris, Jonathan
Jonathan Parris was a first baseman, third baseman, and outfielder for the Louisville Buckeyes, New York Black Yankees, and Philadelphia Stars from 1946 to 1949.

Parsons, Augustus (Gus)

Augustus Parsons was the business manager of the Page Fence Giants, a black baseball team based in Adrian, Michigan, in the 1890s.

Partlow, Roy (Silent Roy)

b. 1912, d. 1987

Roy Partlow was a left-handed pitcher for the Memphis Red Sox, Cincinnati Tigers, Philadelphia Stars, and Homestead Grays from 1934 to 1946 and again from 1947 to 1950. The 6-foot, 180-pound Partlow, born in Washington, Georgia, had 9-4 record for Philadelphia in 1945. Pitcher Don Newcombe said of Partlow, "There's no man I can think of who had better stuff than Roy Partlow when he wanted to pitch," according to Jules Tygiel in his book *Jackie Robinson and His Legacy*. Tygiel wrote that press reports claimed Partlow was 30 years old when the Dodgers signed him, but he was actually 36—a common problem when the color line in major league baseball began to break down. Tygiel wrote that the Dodgers appeared to sign Partlow just to take some of the pressure off Jackie Robinson—to keep him company and not have him as the sole black player on the Montreal Royals—and was never intended for promotion to the major leagues. He never went past the Dodgers' minor league club in Montreal, and also played minor league baseball in the Provincial League. He also played in the Dominican Summer League, Mexican League and winter baseball in Cuba and Puerto Rico.

Passon, Harry

Harry Passon was an officer with the Bacharach Giants in 1934.

Pate, Archie

Archie Pate was a catcher and outfielder for the Chicago Giants, St. Paul Gophers, Bowser's ABC's and New York Stars from 1909 to 1917.

Patterson, Andrew (Pat)

Andrew Patterson was an infielder and outfielder for the Cleveland Red Sox, Pennsylvania Red Caps, Kansas City Monarchs, Pittsburgh Crawfords, Newark Eagles, Philadelphia Stars, Homestead Grays, and Houston Eagles from 1934 to 1949. Patterson was one of many Negro League players who went to the Dominican Republic in 1937 to play in that country's baseball war between political factions.

Patterson, Gabriel (Gabe)

Gabriel Patterson was an outfielder and catcher for the Homestead Grays, Pittsburgh Crawfords, Philadelphia Stars, and New York Black Yankees from 1941 to 1950.

Patterson, John W. (Pat)

John Patterson was a shortstop, outfielder, second baseman, and manager for the Page Fence Giants, Lincoln Giants, Philadelphia Giants, Columbia Giants, Cuban Giants, Cuban X Giants, Brooklyn Royal Giants, Quaker Giants, and Chicago Union Giants from 1890 to 1907. He was known as a fast run and good base stealer.

Patterson, Joseph (Joe)

Joseph Patterson was an outfielder for the Kansas City Monarchs in 1955.

Patterson, William

William Patterson was the manager of the Austin Senators, Houston Black Buffaloes, and Birmingham Black Barons from 1914 to 1925.

Patterson, Willie Lee (Pat)

Willie Patterson played first base, third base, and catcher for the Birmingham Black Barons, New York Cubans, Memphis Red Sox, Philadelphia Stars, Louisville Black Colonels, Chicago American Giants, Detroit Stars, and Pittsburgh Crawfords from 1945 to 1955.

Payne, Andrew (Jap)

Andrew Payne was an outfielder for the Cuban X Giants, Philadelphia Giants, Chicago American Giants, Leland Giants, New York Central Red Caps, Chicago Union Giants, Pennsylvania Red Caps of New York, Brooklyn Royal Giants, Chicago Giants, Lincoln Giants, and Lincoln Stars from 1902 to 1922.

Payne, Ernest (Rusty)

Ernest Payne played the outfield for the Cincinnati Tigers and Indianapolis Crawfords in 1937 and 1940.

Payne, James

James Payne was an outfielder for the Cuban Giants and Baltimore Lord Baltimores in 1887 and 1888.

Payne, Tom

Tom Payne was an outfielder for the Baltimore Black Sox, Pittsburgh Crawfords, and Homestead Grays in 1933.

Payne, William (Doc)

William Payne was an outfielder for the Celeron, New York, Acme Colored Giants in 1898.

Peace, William

William Peace was a pitcher for the Newark Eagles from 1945 to 1948.

Peak, Rufus

Rufus Peak was an officer with the Detroit Stars in 1931.

Pearson, Frank

Frank Pearson was a pitcher for the Chicago American Giants, Memphis Red Sox, New York Cubans, Louisville Black Colonels, and New York Black Yankees from 1945 to 1954.

Pearson, Jimmy

Jimmy Pearson was a pitcher for the New York Cubans in 1949.

Pearson, Leonard (Lenny)

Leonard Pearson was an infielder, outfielder, and manager for the Baltimore Elite Giants, St. Louis Stars, and Newark Eagles from 1936 to 1950. In an interview with author John Holway on file at the National Baseball Hall of Fame, Negro Leaguer and Elite Giants teammate Pee Wee Butts talked about Pearson's arrival in Baltimore in 1949 in a trade with Newark: "I think if I'd been Newark, I'd have kept him and sent another ballplayer," Butts said. "I wish we had Pearson on our team all the time, because every time he hit the ball it would come my way. He could hit it hard, too. You had to be on the ball when he came to bat. . . . Pearson played first base for us and managed. . . . He was a cool operator. He never did say too much."

Pearson, Rutledge

Rutledge Pearson was a first baseman for the Chicago American Giants in 1952.

Peatros, Maurice (Baby Face)

b. 1927

Maurice Peatros was a first baseman and outfielder for the Pittsburgh Crawfords, Atlanta Black Crackers, and Homestead Grays from 1945 to 1947. He also played minor league baseball in Canada, was signed to a contract by the Brooklyn Dodgers in 1949, and spent four years in the Dodgers minor league system. Peatros, who was born in Pittsburgh, told one interviewer that, like many Negro League players, he took a reduction in pay to play minor league baseball: "All of us took a cut in pay to go to the minors," Peatros said. "You better go or the neighborhood wouldn't let you back. You're invited to sing at the Met, you sing."

Pedroso, Eustaquio

Eustaquio Pedroso was a pitcher, outfielder, catcher, and first baseman for the Cuban Stars and All Cubans from 1910 to 1930. Pedroso was an outstanding pitcher in Cuba and had legendary performances against white clubs that came to Cuba to play winter baseball. According to author John Holway, in his book *Blackball Stars*, Pedroso pitched an 11-inning no-hitter against the Detroit Tigers, and he and Jose Mendez combined to beat Christy Mathewson 7-4. The Cuban-born Pedroso was elected to the Cuban Hall of Fame in 1962.

Peeples, Nat

b. 1926

Nat Peeples was a catcher and outfielder for the Indianapolis Clowns and Kansas City Monarchs from 1949 to 1951. The 6-foot-2, 180-pound Peeples, born in Memphis, Tennessee, batted .302 for Kansas City in 1949 and .252 for Kansas City and Indianapolis in 1950. He went on to play minor league baseball in the Eastern League, Three I League, California League, Western League, Southern League, South Atlantic League, Texas League, Big State League, American Association, and Mexican League until 1960.

Peete, Charles

b. 1929, d. 1956

Charles Peete was an outfielder for the Indianapolis Clowns in 1950, batting .314. The 5-foot-10, 190-pound Peete, born in Franklin, Virginia, went on to play in the International League, American Association, and in 1956 played 23 games with the St. Louis Cardinals, batting just .192.

Pelham, William

William Pelham was a shortstop and outfielder for the Atlanta Black Crackers and Bacharach Giants from 1933 to 1938.

Pelican Stadium

Pelican Stadium was a ballpark in New Orleans, Louisiana, that was the home of the New Orleans Black Pelicans from 1945 to 1958 and the New Orleans Stars in 1941. It opened in 1915 as the home of the New Orleans Pelicans of the Southern Association.

Pendleton, James (Jim)

b. 1924

James Pendleton was a shortstop for the Chicago American Giants in 1948, batting .361 in 75 games. The 6-foot, 185-pound Pendleton, born in St. Charles, Missouri, went on to play in the American Association, International League and eight years in the major leagues for the Milwaukee Braves, Pittsburgh Pirates, Cincinnati Reds and Houston Astros, retiring after the 1962 season. He had a career major league batting average of .255 in 444 games. He played one more year of minor league baseball in 1963 in the Pacific Coast League and Texas League. Pendleton also played winter baseball in Venezuela and Cuba.

Pennington, Arthur (Art)

b. 1923

Art Pennington was an outfielder, first baseman, and second baseman for the Pittsburgh Crawfords, Chicago American Giants, and Birmingham Black Barons from 1940 to 1951. The 5-foot-10, 190-pound Pennington, born in Memphis, Tennessee, had his best-recorded Negro League seasons in 1944 and 1945 with Chicago when he batted .299 and .359, respectively, and in 1950, when he batted .350. Pennington also played in the Mexican League and minor league baseball in the Pacific Coast League, Three I League, Dominican Summer League, Florida State League, Western International League, and California League until 1959.

Penno, Dan

Dan Penno was an outfielder, pitcher, and second baseman for the Cuban Giants, Cuban X Giants, and Boston Resolutes from 1887 to 1896.

Pennsylvania League

The Pennsylvania League was made up of black baseball teams, including the Cuban Giants, New York Gorhams (who played in Easton, Pennsylvania, at this time), and Pennsylvania teams from York, Norristown, Harrisburg, Lancaster, Lebanon, and Hazleton, formed in 1889. The league disbanded in July 1890.

Pennsylvania Red Caps of New York

The Pennsylvania Red Caps of New York were a black baseball team that played in New York in the early 1920s. They were supposedly Red Cap workers, but, according to Dick Seay who got his start in Negro League baseball with the Red Caps, their main occupation was baseball: "We weren't really Red Caps; we just played ball," Seay said. "The only time we'd work was maybe the day before a holiday. We'd probably make $15 to $20 for that day. Mostly the players were college kids going through school. Chino Smith played with us. He went to school in South Carolina; in the summer he came up and worked as a Red Cap and then he went back to school. He played second base and I played shortstop. Most of the players went on to become doctors and lawyers. I guess the only two that went into baseball professionally were Chino and myself."

Peoples, Eddie

Eddie Peoples was a pitcher for the Memphis Red Sox in 1933.

Perdue, Frank M.

Frank Perdue was an officer with the Birmingham Black Barons and president of the Negro Southern League from 1920 to 1934.

Pereira, Jose

Jose Pereira was a pitcher for the Baltimore Elite Giants in 1947.

Perez, Javier

Javier Perez was a third baseman for the New York Cubans from 1942 to 1945.

Perez, Jose

Jose Perez was a pitcher, catcher, and infielder for the Harrisburg Giants, Cuban Stars, Hilldale baseball club, Bacharach Giants, Homestead Grays, New York Cubans, Madison Stars, and Brooklyn Eagles from 1911 to 1937.

Perkins, William George (Cy)

George Perkins was a catcher, outfielder, and manager for the Cleveland Cubs, Birmingham Black Barons, Cleveland Stars, Pittsburgh Crawfords, Baltimore Elite Giants, Philadelphia Stars, Homestead Grays, and New York Black Yankees from 1928 to 1948. Perkins was Satchel Paige's favorite catcher in Pittsburgh, according to Mark Ribowsky in his book A Complete History of the Negro Leagues: 1884–1955. He also accompanied Paige and other Crawford teammates to the Dominican Republic in 1937 to play for the team owned by dictator Rafael Trujillo in that country's political baseball war that year. Negro Leaguer Ted Page, a teammate of Perkins's with the Crawfords, told author John Holway in an interview on file at the National Baseball Hall of Fame that Perkins may have been a better catcher than Josh Gibson: "There were some ballplayers who as catchers were better catchers than

Josh," Page said. "George Perkins on the Crawfords was one. We stole Perkins out from under the sheriff's watch dogs in Dawson, Georgia. Perkins was the idol of the town. They had built a ball park for him out of old logs and broken down doors. Everybody came to watch the ball games, and the sheriff was the ticket taker. Well, we went down in spring training and saw him and wanted to take him back north, but the sheriff said, 'No, he has to stay here. We built a ball park for him.' He said if we left town in the morning and his man—he didn't say man, I'll let you guess what he said—if his man wasn't there, we better not be in Georgia. And we weren't. We hid Perkins in the bus and drove right past the sheriff sitting in front of a store. . . . Perkins was a terrific catcher, but he had the misfortune of being on the team with Josh. And nobody else could have gotten Perkins. [Crawfords owner] Gus Greenlee just wasn't going to let him go. Gus kept him, played him in the outfield, on first base, or catch part of a doubleheader. But Josh was the attraction." Later in his career, with the Baltimore Elite Giants, he helped tutor a young catcher named Roy Campanella. Records show that Perkins batted .335 with Pittsburgh in 1932, .379 in 1935, .375 in 1936, .392 with Philadelphia in 1938, .225 with Philadelphia in 1939, and .270 with Baltimore in 1940. He finished his Negro League career with a .304 batting average.

Perry, Alonzo
b. 1923

Alonzo Perry was a first baseman and left-handed pitcher for the Birmingham Black Barons and Homestead Grays from 1940 to 1950. The 6-foot-3, 200-pound Perry was a pitcher for much of his Negro League career and went 10-2 in 1948 and 12-4 in 1949. However, Perry primarily played first base in the minor leagues in the Pacific Coast League, International League, Provincial League, and Dominican Summer League until 1954. Perry went on to play in the Mexican League until 1962 and also played winter baseball in Cuba and the Dominican Republic, where he is in that country's Hall of Fame.

Perry, Carlisle

Carlisle Perry was a second baseman, shortstop, and third baseman for the Bacharach Giants, Detroit Stars, Lincoln Giants, Washington Potomacs, Baltimore Black Sox, Cleveland Browns, Hilldale baseball club, Indianapolis ABC's, Richmond Giants, Cleveland Tate Stars, and Norfolk Stars from 1920 to 1926.

Perry, Don

Don Perry was a first baseman for the Washington Braves, Harrisburg Giants, and Madison Stars from 1920 to 1927.

Perry, Hank

Hank Perry was a pitcher for the Hilldale baseball club and Newark Dodgers in 1926 and 1934.

Peters, Frank

Frank Peters was a shortstop for the Peters Union Giants and Chicago Union Giants from 1916 to 1923.

Peters, William S.

William S. Peters was a first baseman and also managed, owned, and operated the Peters Union Giants and Chicago Union Giants from 1887 to 1923.

Peterson, Harvey (Pete)

Harvey Peterson was a pitcher, outfielder, and infielder for the Birmingham Black Barons, Montgomery Grey Sox, Cincinnati Tigers, Memphis Red Sox, and Cleveland Clippers from 1931 to 1937 and again in 1946.

Pettus, William (Zack)

William Thomas was a catcher, infielder, and manager for the Leland Giants, Kansas City Giants, Lincoln Giants, Chicago Giants, St. Louis Giants, Lincoln Stars, Bacharach Giants, Hilldale baseball club, Harrisburg Giants, Richmond Giants, Chicago American Giants, and Brooklyn Royal Giants from 1909 to 1923. In John Holway's book *Blackball Stars,* Judy Johnson recalled the unique glove that Pettus used to play first base: "He filled his mitt with chicken feathers," Johnson said. "Every time he caught the ball, poof, all the feathers would fly out. Like plucking a chicken."

Petway, Bruce
b. 1887, d. 1941

Bruce Petway was a catcher, outfielder, and manager for the Brooklyn Royal Giants, Leland Giants, Chicago American Giants, Philadelphia Giants, Cuban X Giants, and Detroit Stars from 1906 to 1925. According to Robert Peterson's book *Only the Ball Was White,* Petway, born in Nashville, Tennessee, went to Meharry Medical College, but gave up medicine for baseball. In an interview with author John Holway on file at the National Baseball Hall of Fame, Negro League pitcher Bill Drake called the 5-foot-7, 170-pound Petway a great catcher: "Petway in his prime just deliberately let the ball roll, then pounced on it like a cat and threw you out," Drake said. "He'd throw out anybody who could run." One story about Petway is that he threw Ty Cobb out twice trying to steal second base in a winter series in Cuba in 1910. He was also a great base runner himself but not a great hitter, with a .254 career batting average in Negro League baseball. However, he had several outstanding seasons at the plate, batting .349 in 1923 and .341 in 1924.

Petway, Howard

Howard Petway was a pitcher for the Leland Giants in 1906.

Petway, Sherley (Charlie)

Sherley Petway was a catcher and manager for the Chicago Brown Bombers, Detroit Stars, and Cleveland Buckeyes from 1937 to 1944.

Phiffer, Lester (Les)

Lester Phiffer was a shortstop and third baseman for the Kansas City Monarchs from 1951 to 1952.

Philadelphia Alerts

The Philadelphia Alerts were a black baseball team that played in Philadelphia in 1867.

Philadelphia Excelsiors

The Philadelphia Excelsiors were a black baseball team that played in Philadelphia in the 1860s.

Philadelphia Giants

The Philadelphia Giants, a black baseball team that played in Philadelphia, were one of the powerhouse teams of early black baseball. They were started in 1902 by Harry Smith, a sportswriter for the *Philadelphia Tribune*, and Walter Schlichter, a white sports editor for the *Philadelphia Item* newspaper. There were a number of teams in and around the Philadelphia area that were called the Giants, but the Philadelphia Giants stood out because they were such a dominant black baseball team. Declared the Colored World Champions in 1904 and 1906, they had a roster of players that included Sol White (the player-manager who helped assemble the team), John Henry Lloyd, Frank Grant, a boxer named Jack Johnson, who would go on to become heavyweight champion of the world, and a pitcher, Rube Foster, who would go on to have a huge impact on Negro League baseball as an owner. Foster came on in 1904 after beating the Giants in an eight-game series in Philadelphia in 1902 while pitching for the Cuban X Giants. White, also a Negro League historian, particularly praised the 1906 Giants in his book *History of Colored Baseball*, writing that the 1906 championship team faced numerous hurdles because of injuries: "The success of the Philadelphia Giants of 1906 was due no doubt to their gameness,"

White wrote. "A gamer gang of ball players never stepped on a diamond. More or less crippled throughout the season, they played the hardest teams with the same spirit as the weak ones. When the other teams were strengthening by adding stars to their lineup, the Phillies were weakening by accidents and sickness. When the odds against them were the greatest, they seemed the more determined and their nonchalant air bred a personality that told their opponents they would have to play ball or they could not win." One of the minority owners of the Philadelphia Giants was New York promoter Jess McMahon. In 1911, McMahon formed a team in New York called the Lincoln Giants and raided the Philadelphia Giants for many of his ballplayers. Shortly after, the Giants folded. Another version of the Philadelphia Giants—primarily a barnstorming team—was formed in the mid-1930s, owned by Gus Greenlee and Tom Wilson.

Philadelphia Madison Stars

The Philadelphia Madison Stars were a black baseball team that played in Philadelphia in the late 1910s and early 1920s.

Philadelphia Mutuals

The Philadelphia Mutuals were a black baseball team that played in Philadelphia in the 1880s.

Philadelphia Orion Colored Club

The Philadelphia Orion Colored Club was a black baseball team that played in Philadelphia in the 1880s.

Philadelphia Pythians

The Philadelphia Pythians were a black baseball team that played in the 1880s in Philadelphia and in 1887 played in the League of Colored Base Ball Players.

Philadelphia Quaker Giants

The Philadelphia Quaker Giants were a black baseball team formed by white promoter Jess McMahon that played in Philadelphia in the early 1900s.

Philadelphia Royal Giants

The Philadelphia Royal Giants were a black baseball team that played in Philadelphia in the early 1900s.

Philadelphia Stars

When the legendary Hilldale baseball club folded, owner Ed Bolden helped start a new team in 1933 called the Philadelphia Stars. However, the real power behind the club was white promoter Eddie Gottlieb, who was the majority investor, according to Mark Ribowsky's book *A Complete History of the Negro Leagues: 1884–1955*. They had an impressive roster that included manager-pitcher Webster McDonald, Biz Mackey, Chaney White, Jud Wilson, Jake Dunn, and left-handed pitcher Slim Jones. The Stars beat the Chicago American Giants in a seven-game series to capture the 1934 NEGRO NATIONAL LEAGUE championship. It would be their only championship, and after two years in the NEGRO AMERICAN LEAGUE in 1949 and 1950, the Stars folded.

Philadelphia Tigers

The Philadelphia Tigers were a black baseball team organized in 1927. They were owned by numbers racketeer Smitty Lucas and joined the Eastern Colored League in 1928. However, they folded before the season ended. Bill Yancey, one of the top shortstops in Negro League baseball, played for the Tigers.

Philadelphia Tribune

The *Philadelphia Tribune* was a black newspaper that covered Negro League baseball.

Phillips, John

John Phillips was a pitcher for the Baltimore Elite Giants from 1939 to 1940.

Phillips, Norris

Norris Phillips was a pitcher for the Memphis Red Sox and Kansas City Monarchs in 1942 and 1943.

Phillips, Richard

Richard Phillips was a pitcher for the Kansas City Monarchs from 1952 to 1955.

Pierce, Herbert

Herbert Pierce was a catcher for the Homestead Grays from 1925 to 1929.

Pierce, Leonard

Leonard Pierce was a pitcher for the Philadelphia Giants and Wilmington Potomacs from 1924 to 1927.

Pierce, Steve

Steve Pierce was an officer with the Detroit Stars from 1925 to 1928.

Pierce, William

Bill Pierce was a catcher, first baseman, and outfielder for the Chicago American Giants, Philadelphia Giants, Lincoln Giants, Lincoln Stars, Bacharach Giants, Pennsylvania Red Caps of New York, Detroit Stars, Norfolk Giants, Mohawk Giants, and Baltimore Black Sox from 1910 to 1932.

Pierre, Joseph

Joseph Pierre was an infielder for the Kansas City Monarchs in 1950 and 1951.

Pierre, Rogers

Rogers Pierre was a pitcher for the Indianapolis-Cincinnati Clowns, Cincinnati Clowns, Cincinnati Tigers, Colored House of David, and Chicago American Giants from 1934 to 1945.

Pigg, Leonard (Len)

Leonard Pigg was a catcher and outfielder for the Cleveland Buckeyes and Indianapolis Clowns from 1947 to 1953.

Pillar, Jose

Jose Pillar was a pitcher for the Havana Cubans in 1917.

Pillot, Guillermo

Guillermo Pillot was a pitcher for the Cincinnati Clowns and New York Black Yankees from 1941 to 1943.

Piloto, Jose

Jose Piloto was a pitcher for the Memphis Red Sox in 1949 and 1950.

Pinder, Eddie

Eddie Pinder was an outfielder for the Hilldale baseball club from 1914 to 1916.

Pinder, Fred

Fred Pinder was a shortstop for the Hilldale baseball club from 1910 to 1917.

Pinder, George

George Pinder was an outfielder for the Hilldale baseball club in 1910.

Pine, Felix

Felix Pine was a pitcher for the Detroit Stars in 1954.

Pinkston, Albert Charles (Al)

b. 1917, d. 1981

Albert Pinkston was a first baseman for the St. Louis Stars in 1936. The 6-foot-5, 230-pound Pinkston, born in Newbern, Alabama, went on to play minor league baseball in the Provincial League, Eastern League, International League, Western League, and South Atlantic League and also played in the Mexican League until 1965.

Pipkin, Robert

Robert Pipkin was a pitcher for the Cleveland Cubs, New Orleans Crescent Stars, and Birmingham Black Barons from 1928 to 1933 and again from 1940 to 1942.

Pirrone, Joe

Joe Pirrone was a white promoter of the California Winter League in the mid-1930s, a white league that allowed black teams to compete.

Pitts, Curtis

Curtis Pitts was a catcher and shortstop for the Chicago American Giants and Cleveland Buckeyes in 1950 and 1951.

Pitts, Ed

Ed Pitts was a catcher for the Philadelphia Stars in 1940.

Pittsburgh Colored Stars

The Pittsburgh Colored Stars were a black baseball team that played in Pittsburgh in the 1910s and 1920s.

Pittsburgh Courier

The *Pittsburgh Courier* was a black newspaper that covered Negro League baseball.

Pittsburgh Crawford Colored Giants

The Pittsburgh Crawford Colored Giants were a black baseball team that played in Pittsburgh in the late 1920s. A young catcher named Josh Gibson was one of the organizers of the team, but he played for another Pittsburgh team, Gus Greenlee's Pittsburgh Crawfords.

Pittsburgh Crawfords

The Pittsburgh Crawfords began as a local amateur black baseball team, like so many that played in and around the Pittsburgh area, made up of workers from the coal mines. But when racketeer and nightclub owner Gus Greenlee took over operation of the team in 1930, he turned them into a black baseball powerhouse, compiling one of the legendary teams in Negro League history. Greenlee raided much of the hometown rival Homestead Grays, bringing in such stars as Josh Gibson, William "Judy" Johnson, and Jud Wilson, joining other Negro baseball stars such as Satchel Paige, Jimmy Crutchfield, and James "Cool Papa" Bell, with the legendary Oscar Charleston as manager. After playing an independent schedule for two seasons, the Crawfords joined the East-West League in 1932. After first playing games at Ammon Field, the owner also built a ballpark, called Greenlee Field, at an estimated cost of $100,000. The Crawfords also traveled to Monroe, Louisiana, for spring training. The following year, Greenlee formed and presided over the NEGRO NATIONAL LEAGUE, with Pittsburgh as the flagship franchise. The 1935 team won the NNL first-half title and then the league championship by defeating the second-half champions, the New York Cubans, in a seven-game playoff. They also won the 1936 league championship as well. In 1937, the Crawfords suffered a huge blow when Dominican Republic dictator Rafael Trujillo persuaded Paige, Gibson, and a host of other players to come to the Dominican to play for his Santo Domingo team. The Crawfords never recovered. Greenlee sold the team in 1939. The Crawfords moved to Toledo in 1939 and Indianapolis the following year. Another Pittsburgh Crawfords team was formed by Greenlee in the mid-1940s but did not last long.

Pittsburgh Giants

The Pittsburgh Giants were a black baseball team in Pittsburgh that played in the early 1920s.

Pittsburgh Keystones

The Pittsburgh Keystones were a black baseball team that played in Pittsburgh in 1887 in the League of Colored Base Ball Players. The Keystones were the first professional team for which Negro League player, manager, and historian Sol White played. Another version of the Keystones resurfaced in 1922 for one season in the NEGRO NATIONAL LEAGUE when Negro League pitching great William "Dizzy" Dismukes brought some coal miners from Birmingham, Alabama, to Pittsburgh and called them the Keystones, according to John Holway in *Blackball Stars.*

Poinciana Hotel

The Poinciana Hotel was a luxurious oceanfront resort in Palm Beach, Florida, that fielded teams in a hotel league composed of black players, primarily from New York, who spent their winters there and worked at the hotel in the early 1900s.

Poindexter, Robert

Robert Poindexter was a pitcher and first baseman for the Chicago American Giants, Birmingham Black Barons, and Memphis Red Sox from 1924 to 1929.

Poinsette, Robert

Robert Poinsette was an outfielder and pitcher for the Toledo Crawfords and New York Black Yankees in 1939.

Pointer, Robert Lee

Robert Lee Pointer was a pitcher for the Kansas City Monarchs in 1950.

Polanco, Rafael

Rafael Polanco was a pitcher for the Philadelphia Stars in 1942.

Poles, Edward

Edward Poles played shortstop and third base for the Harrisburg Giants and Baltimore Black Sox from 1922 to 1928.

Poles, Spottswood (Spot)

b. 1886, d. 1962

Spottswood Poles was an outfielder for the Harrisburg Giants, Lincoln Giants, Philadelphia Giants, Lincoln Stars, Brooklyn Royal Giants, Bacharach Giants, Richmond Giants, and Hilldale baseball club from 1909 to 1923. He also played in the winter hotel league in Florida and the Cuban Winter League, where he batted .319 during four seasons.

The 5-foot-7, 165-pound Poles, born in Winchester, Virginia, was a fast base runner and was known as the "black Ty Cobb" because of his speed—he is credited with stealing 41 bases in 60 games in 1911 with the Lincoln Giants, with a .440 average. He followed that up with a .398 average in 1912 and a remarkable .487 average in 1914. He was a switch hitter and is believed to have batted around .400 for much of his Negro League career. Records also show that against major league ballplayers in exhibition competition, Poles batted .610. In a newspaper interview, Poles said he was still hitting over .300 when he retired to run a taxi service: "The only thing was that I got tired of all the train travel and carrying those bags around all the time," he said. "So I got out of baseball and bought myself five taxicabs. But I always remember my days in the game, and even though I didn't get the privilege of playing in the majors, I feel that my life hasn't been wasted." Poles was a World War I decorated hero, awarded five battle stars and a Purple Heart while fighting in France.

Pollard, Nat

Nat Pollard was a pitcher for the Birmingham Black Barons from 1946 to 1950.

Pollock, Syd

Syd Pollock was one of the best-known and most controversial white promoters in black baseball. He owned a piece of or all of, or promoted a number of, black baseball teams from 1926 to 1950, including the Cuban Stars, Cuban House of David, Havana Red Sox, Ethiopian Clowns, Indianapolis Clowns, and Cincinnati Clowns. One of his partners was Abe Saperstein, owner and operator of the Harlem Globetrotters, and, like Saperstein, Pollock promoted a clowning type of game on the field much of the time instead of competition. One of his teams, the Ethiopian Clowns (whose owner was listed as Hunter Campbell, a black man, who served as a front for Pollock's ownership), had its players paint their faces and wear costumes. In an interview with author John Holway on file at the National Baseball Hall of Fame, pitcher Dave Barnhill talked about his days with the Clowns: "We'd come to the park with paint on our faces like clowns," he said. "Even the batboy had his face painted, too. We wore clowning wigs and the big old clown uniforms with ruffled collars. My clowning name was Impo. During batting practice we'd play 'shadow ball,' pretend to hit and throw without any ball at all. They'd 'hit' the ball to me. I'd run to field it. I'd jump, turn a flip and throw it like I'm throwing the ball to first base. Then when we were supposed to get to business, we pulled the clown suits off and we had regular baseball uniforms underneath. But we didn't change our faces. We played with our clown paint." In the 1950s, Pollock's Indianapolis Clowns had a young outfielder named Henry Aaron, and the promoter also had three women on the team—Toni Stone, Mamie Johnson, and Connie Morgan.

Polo Grounds

The Polo Grounds was a ballpark in the Bronx that was the home of the New York Giants in the major leagues and also hosted a number of Negro League baseball games.

Pompez, Alessandro (Alex)
b. 1890, d. 1974

Alessandro Pompez was a numbers racketeer from Harlem who became an officer, owner, and promoter of a number of black baseball teams, including the New York Cubans and Cuban Stars from 1922 to 1950. He also served as a vice president of the NEGRO NATIONAL LEAGUE. Pompez worked with mobster Dutch Schultz and later became a fugitive from justice, leaving the country to avoid a crackdown on organized crime in Harlem. He was captured in Mexico and brought back to the United States to testify against a corrupt New York politician named James J. Hines, according to Mark Ribowsky's book *A Complete History of the Negro Leagues: 1884–1955*. He was hired as a scout by the New York Giants and signed Orlando Cepeda to a contract for the Giants. He also served on the committee appointed by baseball commissioner Bowie Kuhn in 1971 to determine which ballplayers would be the first ones inducted into the National Baseball Hall of Fame from Negro League baseball.

Poole, Claude
Claude Poole pitched for the New York Black Yankees in 1945 and 1946.

Pope, David
b. 1925

David Pope was an outfielder for the Homestead Grays in 1946. The 5-foot-11, 180-pound Pope, born in Talladega, Alabama, went on to play minor league baseball in the Provincial League, Eastern League, American Association, and Pacific Coast League. Pope played four major league seasons for the Cleveland Indians and Baltimore Orioles in 1952 and from 1954 to 1956, batting .265 in 230 games, with 12 home runs, 73 RBIs, and 75 runs scored. He retired after playing the 1961 season with Toronto in the International League. Pope also played winter baseball in Puerto Rico and Venezuela.

Pope, Edgar
Edgar Pope was an outfielder for the Atlanta Black Crackers in 1938.

Pope, James
James Pope was a pitcher for the Montgomery Grey Sox, Columbus Blue Birds, and Louisville White Sox from 1931 to 1933.

Pope, William (Willie)
b. 1918

William Pope was a left-handed pitcher for the Homestead Grays and Pittsburgh Crawfords from 1945 to 1948.

Records show that the 6-foot-2, 220-pound Pope, born in Birmingham, Alabama, posted a 6-7 mark for Homestead in 1947.

Porter, Andy (Pullman)
b. 1911

Andy Porter was a pitcher for the Nashville Elite Giants, Cleveland Cubs, Washington Elite Giants, Baltimore Elite Giants, Columbus Elite Giants, Indianapolis Clowns, Newark Eagles, Louisville Black Caps, and Louisville White Sox from 1932 to 1950. The 6-foot-4, 200-pound Porter, born in Little Rock, Arkansas, went 8-0 for Baltimore in 1945 and 10-6 for Indianapolis in 1949. Porter also played in the Mexican League and played winter baseball in Cuba.

Porter, Merle
Merle Porter was a first baseman for the Kansas City Monarchs in 1949 and 1950.

Porter, Wallace
Wallace Porter was a pitcher for the Detroit Stars in 1954.

Portier, James
James Portier was a catcher for the Indianapolis Clowns in 1954.

Portsmouth Firefighters
The Portsmouth Firefighters were a black baseball team that played in Portsmouth, Virginia, in the early 1930s.

Portuando, Bartolo
Bartolo Portuando was a first baseman and third baseman for the Cuban Stars, New York Cuban Stars, and Kansas City Monarchs from 1916 to 1927.

Posey, Cumberland (Cum)
b. 1881, d. 1946

Cumberland Posey was one of the legendary Negro League baseball owners who, along with Rube Foster, remains one of the most influential figures in the history of black baseball. From 1911 to 1946, Posey played for, managed, and then owned the Homestead Grays as well as the Detroit Wolves. He also founded the East-West League and served for a period as secretary and treasurer of the NEGRO NATIONAL LEAGUE. The 5-foot-9, 150-pound Posey was a star athlete at Penn State and Holy Ghost College, playing basketball, baseball, and golf. He operated a black semipro basketball team in 1911 called the Monticellos, which would go on to be one of the top basketball teams in the country. Posey joined the Grays as an outfielder in 1911 when they were the Murdock Grays. He would later become the manager in 1918 and owner in 1920. Posey's Grays were the dominant force in black baseball in Pittsburgh. In *Sandlot Seasons—Sport in Black Pittsburgh*, author Rob Ruck wrote about Posey and the Gray's influence: "Posey put up with little interference off the field. . . . By the 1930s he held sway over black baseball in the area," Ruck wrote. "As the Grays evolved from a Homestead club of industrial workers playing in their free time to the toast of the Pittsburgh sandlots, they became an excellent draw, the best and most popular local black team. The Grays were in great demand by white tri-state semi-pro and sandlot clubs, which realized that when the Grays played the fans came in droves."

In 1929, Homestead joined the American Negro League and had a record of 34-29. They went back to independent play for the next two seasons; also they played Negro National League competition and in 1931 fielded what is considered to have been the best Negro League baseball team ever when they posted a record of 136-17 in independent play. It was the second year that the great Josh Gibson was a member of the Grays and, according to some reports, hit 75 home runs that year against various levels of competitive teams. The 1931 team included other greats such as Oscar Charleston, Jud Wilson, Ted Page, George Scales, and Vic Harris. The pitching staff included Smokey Joe Williams, Willie Foster, and Ted "Double Duty" Radcliffe.

In 1932, the Grays joined the new league organized by Posey called the East-West League and compiled a record of 29-19 before the league folded. The Grays wound up being raided by their new rivals, Gus Greenlee's Pittsburgh Crawfords, who signed away a number of Posey's players, including Josh Gibson. In 1937, the Grays began playing home games in both Pittsburgh and Washington, D.C., playing in Griffith Stadium in the district. The 1937 season began a run of nine straight Negro National League championships to 1945, with Gibson, who returned to the Grays after Greenlee's Crawfords collapsed. Wilson, Buck Leonard, and Cool Papa Bell were featured on teams during that period.

Posey, Seward (See)
Seward Posey, the brother of Homestead Grays owner Cum Posey, was an officer and business manager with the Grays from 1911 to 1948.

Powell, Dick
Dick Powell was an owner and officer of the Nashville Elite Giants and Baltimore Elite Giants from 1938 to 1952.

Powell, Edward (Eddie)
Edward Powell was a catcher for the Washington Black Senators, New York Cubans, St. Louis Stars, and New York Black Yankees from 1936 to 1938.

Powell, Elvin
Elvin Powell was a second baseman for the Memphis Red Sox in 1921.

Powell, Melvin
Melvin Powell was an outfielder and pitcher for the Chicago American Giants, Cole's American Giants, Chicago Columbia Giants, Chicago Brown Bombers, and Birmingham Black Barons from 1930 to 1943.

Powell, Russell
Russell Powell was a second baseman and catcher for the Indianapolis ABC's from 1914 to 1921.

Powell, William
b. 1919
William Powell was a pitcher for the Birmingham Black Barons from 1946 to 1952. Records show that he posted an 11-3 record in 1947, 11-11 in 1948, and 15-4 in 1949. The 6-foot-2, 200-pound Powell also played minor league baseball in the Western League, Pacific Coast League, American Association, International League, Texas League, and South Atlantic League. He also played in the Mexican League and played winter baseball in Cuba.

Powell, Willie (Ernest "Piggy" Powell; Wee Willie)
d. 1987
Willie Powell was a pitcher for the Detroit Stars, Cole's American Giants, Chicago American Giants, Akron Tyrites, and Cleveland Red Sox from 1925 to 1935. In an interview with author John Holway on file at the National Baseball Hall of Fame, former American Giants manager Dave Malarcher said that Powell was one of his best pitchers: "Willie Powell was a great little right-hander," Malarcher said. "He had a fast ball that had a real hop on it, and one of those fadeaway curves that would come up like a fast ball and would just flutter away from you like that."

Presswood, Henry
Henry Presswood was a shortstop and third baseman for the Kansas City Monarchs and Cleveland Buckeyes from 1948 to 1952.

Preston, Al
b. 1926, d. 1979

Al Preston was a pitcher for the Chicago American Giants, New York Black Yankees, and Pittsburgh Crawfords from 1943 to 1952. The 6-foot-1, 180-pound Preston, born in New York, also played in the Dominican Summer League and the Colonial League.

Preston, Robert
Robert Preston was a pitcher for the Baltimore Elite Giants in 1950.

Price, Ewell
Ewell Price was a catcher for the New Orleans Eagles in 1951.

Price, Marvin
Marvin Price was a first baseman for the Chicago American Giants, Cleveland Buckeyes, and New Orleans Eagles from 1950 to 1952.

Price, Willie
Willie Price was a pitcher for the Birmingham Black Barons in 1951.

Pride, Charley
Charley Pride, the famous country-western singer, who topped the charts with such hits as "Kiss an Angel Good Morning," played Negro League baseball for the Birmingham Black Barons and Memphis Red Sox in 1953 and 1954 as a pitcher and outfielder. In a 1997 interview with *Sports Collectors Digest*, teammate Otha Bailey said that Pride was a good ballplayer: "He was a good hitting pitcher," Bailey said. "His bat got so big we let him play the outfield. We picked him up in Mississippi and he had a two-string guitar. He'd sit in the back of the bus singing that country music and we'd jive him about it, say, 'Man, don't be playing that kind of junk. You ain't gonna get nowhere on that.' But he did. He was a millionaire." Pride hurt his arm as a 20-year-old pitcher with Memphis, and the injury cut short his baseball career, although he tried for 10 more years to get a shot at major league baseball with various minor league clubs and had an unsuccessful tryout with the California Angels in 1961. He continued to work out for many years in spring training with major league clubs, including the Milwaukee Brewers.

Prim, William
William Prim was a catcher for the St. Louis Giants, Leland Giants, and Indianapolis ABC's from 1905 to 1911.

Primm, Randolph
Randolph Primm was a pitcher for the Kansas City Monarchs in 1926.

Pritchett, Wilbur
Wilbur Pritchett was a pitcher for the Baltimore Black Sox, Harrisburg Giants, Hilldale baseball club, Brooklyn Royal Giants, Brooklyn Cuban Giants, and Bacharach Giants from 1924 to 1932.

Proctor, James (Cub)
James Proctor was a pitcher and catcher for the Baltimore Atlantics and Baltimore Lord Baltimores from 1884 to 1887.

Proctor, James Arthur (Jim)
b. 1935

James Proctor was a pitcher for the Indianapolis Clowns in 1955. Born in Brandywine, Maryland, the 6-foot, 170-pound Proctor went on to play minor league baseball in the Pacific Coast League, American Association, Eastern League, Texas League, Florida State League, and South Atlantic League. He also played one season for the Detroit Tigers, appearing in just two games, posting an 0-1 record.

Prophet, Willie
Willie Prophet was an outfielder for the Bacharach Giants in 1934.

Pryor, Anderson
Anderson Pryor was a shortstop and second baseman for the Detroit Stars, Milwaukee Bears, New Orleans Crescent Stars, and Memphis Red Sox from 1922 to 1933.

Pryor, Bill
Bill Pryor was a pitcher for the Memphis Red Sox and Detroit Stars from 1927 to 1931.

Pryor, Edward
Ed Pryor was a second baseman for the Pennsylvania Red Caps of New York and Lincoln Giants from 1925 to 1934.

Pryor, Wes (Whip)
Wes Pryor was a third baseman for the Chicago American Giants, Leland Giants, Chicago Giants, St. Louis Gi-

ants, Brooklyn Royal Giants, Mohawk Giants, and Louisville White Sox from 1910 to 1914.

Pugh, Johnny

Johnny Pugh was a third baseman, second baseman, and outfielder for the Brooklyn Royal Giants, Mohawk Giants, Bacharach Giants, Philadelphia Giants, Lincoln Giants, Lincoln Stars, and Harrisburg Giants from 1912 to 1922.

Pullen, Neil

Neil Pullen was a catcher for the Kansas City Monarchs, Baltimore Black Sox, Lincoln Giants, and Brooklyn Royal Giants from 1920 to 1927.

Pulliam, Arthur (Chick)

Arthur Pulliam was a catcher for the Kansas City Giants and Kansas City Royal Giants from 1908 to 1915.

Purcell, Harmon

Harmon Purcell was a pitcher and third baseman for the Memphis Red Sox and Cleveland Buckeyes from 1944 to 1947.

Quaker Giants of New York

The Quaker Giants were a black baseball team in New York that played in the late 1800s and early 1900s and were part of the International League of Independent Base Ball Clubs in 1906.

Quinones, Tomas

Tomas Quinones was a pitcher for the Indianapolis Clowns in 1946 and 1947.

Quintana, Busta

Busta Quintana was an infielder for the Cuban Stars and Newark Dodgers from 1928 to 1934.

Quintana, Pedro

Pedro Quintana was an infielder for the Indianapolis Clowns in 1954.

Radcliffe, Alexander

b. 1905

Alex Radcliffe was a shortstop and third baseman for the Chicago American Giants, Cole's American Giants, Chicago Giants, Cincinnati-Indianapolis Clowns, Kansas City Monarchs, New York Cubans, Birmingham Black Barons, and Memphis Red Sox from 1927 to 1946. The 6-foot, 200-pound Radcliffe, the brother of Ted "Double Duty" Radcliffe, played in the first Negro League All-Star Game, the EAST-WEST GAME, in 1933 and went on to play in 11 other East-West games, with a .341 batting average. Records indicated that Radcliffe, born in Mobile, Alabama, had a .355 career batting average and batted .401 in 1933 and .403 in 1934.

Radcliffe, Everett (Red)

Everett Radcliffe was a shortstop for the Chicago American Giants and Dayton Marcos in 1926 and again from 1934 to 1937.

Radcliffe, Ted (Double Duty)

b. 1902

Ted Radcliffe was a catcher, pitcher, and manager for the St. Louis Stars, Detroit Stars, Homestead Grays, Pittsburgh Crawfords, New York Black Yankees, Columbus Blue Birds, Homestead Grays, Indianapolis ABC's, Brooklyn Eagles, St. Paul Gophers, Gilk-erson's Union Giants, Cincinnati Tigers, Brooklyn Eagles, Birmingham Black Barons, Memphis Red Sox, Louisville Buckeyes, Chicago American Giants, Kansas City Monarchs, Detroit Wolves, Nashville Elite Giants, and Harlem Globetrotters (baseball team) from 1928 to 1950. Born in Mobile, Alabama, Radcliffe left the Crawfords in the middle of the 1934 season to play with a white team in North Dakota in an integrated league with other Negro Leagues and would convince Satchel Paige to join him. Radcliffe was nicknamed Double Duty by newspaper columnist Damon Runyon, who saw Radcliffe catch Satchel Paige in the first game of a 1932 doubleheader at Yankee Stadium and then pitch a 4-0 shutout in the second game.

In a 1992 interview with *Sports Collectors Digest*, Negro Leaguer Jimmy Crutchfield talked about Radcliffe's skills on the mound and behind the plate: "Double Duty could do a credible job pitching as well as catching," Crutchfield said. "He had good control, could throw hard, and had a pretty decent curveball. Plus, on top of that, he had guts. Duty was a very good catcher with a good strong arm. He wasn't a great hitter, but he had a lot of confidence, and that helped. You really had to be careful with him in the clutch."

In a 1991 *Boston Globe* story, Radcliffe, whose brother Alex also played in the Negro Leagues, talked about the responsibilities he had while playing Negro League baseball: "Some years I had to be the

Ted Radcliffe, shown here trying to put the tag on Homestead's Josh Gibson, was nicknamed "Double Duty" by newspaper columnist Damon Runyon after he saw Radcliffe catch Satchel Paige in the first game of a 1932 doubleheader at Yankee Stadium and then pitch a 4-0 shutout in the second game. He was outstanding on the mound, behind the plate, and at the plate, having batted .343 through his career with more than 200 victories. (NATIONAL BASEBALL HALL OF FAME LIBRARY, COOPERSTOWN, N.Y.)

top pitcher, catcher, manager and secretary," he said. "That's four positions. Then I helped drive the bus because the damn driver kept getting drunk all the time." Radcliffe was the NEGRO AMERICAN LEAGUE Most Valuable Player in 1943 and is believed to have hit .343 through his career, with more than 200 wins as a pitcher. In an article in *Midwest Magazine* in 1971, Radcliffe talked about one of his fondest memories in Negro League baseball: "My greatest thrill in baseball was in the East-West game of 1944 before 56,000 people in Comiskey Park. Barnie Morrie, a knuckle baller for the New York Cubans, had beat us 3-1. We put a man on base, my brother Alex doubled into right center, then I came up and hit a homer into centerfield and won the game. You know what the people gave me that day? They gave me $700 for that home run."

Ragland, Hurland Earl

Earl Ragland was a pitcher for the Kansas City Monarchs, Columbus Buckeyes, Dayton Marcos, and Indianapolis ABC's from 1920 to 1921.

Raines, Lawrence
b. 1930, d. 1978

Lawrence Raines was a shortstop for the Chicago American Giants in 1951 and 1952. Born in St. Albans, West Virginia, Raines would go on to play minor league baseball in Indianapolis, Reading, San Diego, and Syracuse and also spend two seasons in the major leagues with the Cleveland Indians in 1957 and 1958, appearing in 103 games, batting .253, with 64 hits and 39 runs scored. The 5-foot-11, 165-pound Raines also played in Japan in

1953, 1954, and 1962 and played winter baseball in Cuba and Puerto Rico.

Raleigh Tigers

The Raleigh Tigers were a black baseball team based in Raleigh, North Carolina, that played in the NEGRO AMERICAN LEAGUE in the 1950s and was one of the final four teams in the league when it folded after the 1960 season.

Ramirez, Ramiro

Ramiro Ramirez was an outfielder and manager for the Havana Stars, Cuban Stars, Bacharach Giants, All Cubans, Havana Red Sox, Baltimore Black Sox, Indianapolis Clowns, Cuban House of David, New York Cuban Stars, Brooklyn Royal Giants, Richmond Giants, Cuban Stars, and Cuban Stars of Havana from 1916 to 1948.

Ramos, Jose

Jose Ramos was an outfielder for the Cuban Stars and All Cubans in 1921 and 1929.

Ramsay, William

William Ramsay was an outfielder for the Chicago Unions in 1889.

Ramsey, Laymon

Laymon Ramsey was a pitcher for the Chicago American Giants in 1951.

Ramsey, Mack

Mack Ramsey was an outfielder for the Chicago Union Giants from 1911 to 1916.

Randolph, Andrew

Andrew Randolph was a first baseman and outfielder for the Argyle Hotel in Babylon, New York, Trenton Cuban Giants, Actives of Philadelphia, and Boston Resolutes. An 1886 *Trenton Times* article about the Cuban Giants described Randolph as "an exceptional good baseman and fair batsman."

Rankin, Bill

Bill Rankin was a pitcher and catcher for the Richmond Giants, Philadelphia Giants, and Washington Potomacs from 1923 to 1927.

Ransom, Joe

Joe Ransom was a catcher for the Cleveland Elites in 1926.

Rasberry, Ted

b. 1913, d. 2001

Ted Rasberry was the owner, operator, and manager of the Detroit Stars and Kansas City Monarchs from 1954 to 1965. He also started and played for the Grand Rapids (Michigan) Black Sox in 1946. In a newspaper interview, Rasberry talked about buying the Monarchs: "Mr. Baird [Tom Baird, who had owned the Monarchs] said he would sell the team, but only to me, because he thought I'd keep them first-class, well-dressed and flashy, which the Monarchs always were," Rasberry said. "So he and I got together and I bought the Monarchs. Then I had to buy the bus. But he had sold all the players [to the major leagues], and all I ended up with was the bus driver and all the uniforms. The purchasing of the Monarchs name was enough," Rasberry said. "There was no getting around it. They were the greatest." When he owned the Detroit Stars, Rasberry had one ballplayer who would go on to become famous in another line of work: "I bought Charlie [sic] Pride his first guitar," Rasberry said. "Charlie [sic] played baseball with me in Detroit." Along with Goose Tatum, Rasberry, born in West Point, Mississippi, also organized a traveling basketball team called the Harlem Satellite Basketball Show Team.

Ray, John

John Ray was an outfielder for the Birmingham Black Barons, Montgomery Grey Sox, Jacksonville Red Caps, Cleveland Bears, Pittsburgh Crawfords, Kansas City Monarchs, and Cincinnati-Indianapolis Clowns from 1932 to 1945.

Ray, Otto

Otto Ray was a pitcher and catcher for the Chicago Giants, Kansas City Monarchs, Cleveland Tate Stars, St. Louis Stars, Toledo Tigers, and Cleveland Browns from 1920 to 1924.

Ray, Richard

Richard Ray was an infielder and outfielder for the Chicago Brown Bombers in 1943.

Rector, Connie

Connie Rector was a pitcher for the Brooklyn Royal Giants, Hilldale baseball club, New York Black Yankees, New York Cubans, and Lincoln Giants from 1920 to 1944.

Redd, Eugene

Eugene Redd was a third baseman for the New Orleans Crescent Stars, Milwaukee Bears, Pittsburgh Keystones, Cleveland Tate Stars, and Kansas City Monarchs in 1922 and 1923.

Redd, Ulysses

Ulysses Redd was a shortstop for the Chicago American Giants and Birmingham Black Barons in 1940 and 1941 and again from 1950 to 1952.

Redding, Dick (Cannonball)

b. 1891, d. 1938

Dick Redding was a pitcher, outfielder, and manager for the Philadelphia Giants, Lincoln Stars, Lincoln Giants, Chicago American Giants, Indianapolis ABC's, Bacharach Giants, Pittsburgh Crawfords, and Brooklyn

Cannonball Dick Redding, shown here on the right with fellow Negro League pitcher Smokey Joe Williams, was an overpowering pitcher who won 29 straight games in his rookie year in 1911, including five no-hitters. He won 20 games in 1915, including an exhibition win over the Philadelphia Athletics, and pitched, played the outfield, and managed in the Negro Leagues from 1911 to 1938. (NATIONAL BASEBALL HALL OF FAME LIBRARY, COOPERSTOWN, N.Y.)

Royal Giants from 1911 to 1938. The 6-foot-4, 210-pound Redding also played winter baseball in Cuba. One story claims that Redding, born in Atlanta, won 29 straight games in his rookie year in 1911, including five no-hitters. He is believed to have won 20 games in 1915, including an exhibition win over the Philadelphia Athletics. In an interview with author John Holway on file at the National Baseball Hall of Fame, Crush Holloway talked about Redding's pitching skills: "Redding had good control, and he'd overpower you, too, like Satchel," he said. In another Holway interview, Negro Leaguer Frank Forbes compared Redding to the great Walter Johnson: "Dick Redding was like Walter Johnson," Forbes said. "Nothing but speed. That's the reason they called him Cannonball. He just blew the ball by you. I've seen Redding knock a bat out of a man's hand."

Reddon, Bob

Bob Reddon was a pitcher for the Cleveland Tate Stars in 1919.

Red Stockings of Norfolk

The Red Stockings were a black baseball team based in Norfolk, Virginia, that played in the late 1800s and early 1900s.

Redus, Wilson (Frog)

Wilson Redus was an outfielder, manager, and coach for the Cleveland Stars, St. Louis Stars, Cleveland Giants, Columbus Blue Birds, Cleveland Red Sox, Kansas City Monarchs, Cleveland Browns, Indianapolis ABC's, and Chicago American Giants from 1924 to 1940. Records show that the 5-foot-6, 155-pound Redus, born in Tulahasse, Oklahoma, batted .355 in 1927, .287 in 1929, .333 in 1934, and .327 in 1936. In documents on file at the National Baseball Hall of Fame, Redus said his greatest thrill was being part of the 1929 Chicago American Giants championship team.

Reed, Ambrose

Ambrose Reed was an infielder and outfielder for the Atlanta Black Crackers, Pittsburgh Crawfords, Hilldale baseball club, Bacharach Giants, and Homestead Grays from 1922 to 1932.

Reed, Andrew

Andrew Reed was an outfielder and third baseman for the Detroit Stars, Chicago Giants, and Chicago Union Giants from 1917 to 1921.

Reed, Curtis

Curtis Reed was an outfielder for the St. Louis Stars in 1937.

Reed, John

John Reed was a pitcher for the Indianapolis ABC's, Cole's American Giants, Chicago Brown Bombers, Chicago American Giants, St. Louis Stars, Indianapolis Athletics, and Atlanta Black Crackers from 1934 to 1942.

Reedy, Buddy
b. 1929

Buddy Reedy was a third baseman, second baseman, and outfielder for the Baltimore Elite Giants in 1950 and 1951. Reedy batted .299 for Baltimore in 1950 and .343 in 1951. The 5-foot-11, 170-pound Reedy went on to play minor league baseball in the South Atlantic League, Piedmont League, Eastern League, International League, and Florida State League until 1962.

Reel, James

James Reel was an outfielder for the Toledo Tigers in 1923.

Reese, Charles

Charles Reese was a pitcher and outfielder for the Chicago Union Giants, New York Stars, Brooklyn All-Stars, and Cuban Giants from 1910 to 1914.

Reese, James

James Reese was a pitcher for the Brooklyn Eagles, Atlanta Black Crackers, Baltimore Elite Giants, and Cleveland Red Sox from 1934 to 1940.

Reese, John

John Reese was an outfielder for the St. Louis Stars, Bacharach Giants, Toledo Tigers, Hilldale baseball club, Detroit Stars, and Chicago American Giants from 1918 to 1931.

Reeves, Donald

Don Reeves was an outfielder and first baseman for the Indianapolis ABC's, Atlanta Black Crackers, and Chicago American Giants from 1937 to 1941.

Reeves, John

John Reeves was a pitcher, outfielder, and third baseman for the Lincoln, Nebraska, Giants from 1890 to 1902.

Reid, Porter

Porter Reid was an outfielder for the Houston Eagles in 1949.

Renfroe, Othello (Chico)
b. 1923, d. 1991

Othello Renfroe was a catcher, outfielder, and shortstop for the Cleveland Buckeyes, Kansas City Monarchs, Atlanta Black Crackers, and Indianapolis Clowns from 1945 to 1953. In an interview with author John Holway on file at the National Baseball Hall of Fame, Renfroe talked about how he got involved in Negro League baseball as a youth: "I was always a nut for baseball," Renfroe said. "I was 13 years old in 1936 down in Jacksonville, Florida, when the Newark Eagles, New York Cubans, Baltimore Elites and Chicago American Giants all trained there, and I was the batboy for all of them. . . . After going to high school and being a bat boy for all those guys, I tell you what I did. I ran away from home in 1938 to be a batboy for the Chicago American Giants. I was 15. . . . When we got to Nashville, the manager, Candy Jim Taylor, said this was about as far as he could carry me, because the owners of the team were getting on him for spending too much money. One guy in particular was kind to me. I talked to Alex Radcliffe, Double Duty's brother, and told him that I was going to hitchhike, do anything, to get to Chicago. So he told me when I got there to see an old-timer named Bingo DeMoss. So I hoboed my way and when the team got there, I was already there ahead of them. Bingo DeMoss took me in just like his son all during the baseball season. His son had gotten killed riding on the back of a truck. You know how Chicago is, he used to run with a gang. Well, DeMoss kind of took me as his boy. . . . I bet he kept me up until two or three in the morning talking baseball."

Renfroe went on to play baseball in Venezuela, Puerto Rico, and Mexico, as well as use what DeMoss, the former Negro League great infielder and manager, taught him to carve out his own Negro League career and wound up being a teammate on the 1945 Monarchs team that included a young shortstop named Jackie Robinson. Renfroe later became a sports broadcaster at WIGO in Atlanta and sports editor of The *Atlanta Daily World.*

Reynold, Jimmy

Jimmy Reynolds was a third baseman for the Indianapolis Crawfords and Cleveland Buckeyes in 1940 and 1946.

Reynolds, Joseph

Joseph Reynolds was a pitcher for the Philadelphia Stars in 1935.

Reynolds, Lou

Lou Reynolds was a first baseman and outfielder for the Chicago Unions and Chicago Columbia Giants from 1897 to 1899.

Reynolds, William

William Reynolds was a shortstop and second baseman for the Louisville Buckeyes and Cleveland Buckeyes from 1948 to 1950.

Rhoades, Cornelius

Cornelius Rhoades was a catcher and outfielder for the Hilldale baseball club and Bowser's ABC's from 1910 to 1918.

Rhodes, Claude (Dusty)

Claude Rhodes was a pitcher for the Columbus Blue Birds, Louisville Black Caps, and Chattanooga Black Lookouts from 1931 to 1933.

Rhodes, Harry

Harry Rhodes was a left-handed pitcher and first baseman for the Chicago American Giants from 1942 to 1950.

Rice, Miller

Miller Rice was an outfielder for the Cincinnati Tigers from 1934 to 1937.

Richardson, Dewey

Dewey Richardson was a catcher for the Hilldale baseball club in 1922.

Richardson, Earl

Earl Richardson was a shortstop for the Newark Eagles in 1943.

Richardson, George

George Richardson was a shortstop for the Algona Brownies and Chicago Union Giants from 1901 to 1903.

Richardson, Glenn

Glenn Richardson was a second baseman for the New York Black Yankees from 1946 to 1949.

Richardson, Henry

Henry Richardson was a pitcher and outfielder for the Washington Pilots, Baltimore Black Sox, Washington Black Senators, Bacharach Giants, Richmond Giants, Cuban Stars, and Pittsburgh Crawfords from 1921 to 1938.

Richardson, James

James Richardson was a pitcher for the New York Black Yankees and Philadelphia Stars in 1934 and 1939.

Richardson, John

John Richardson was a pitcher for the Birmingham Black Barons in 1924 and 1925.

Richardson, Johnny

Johnny Richardson was a shortstop for the Homestead Grays in 1949 and 1950.

Richardson, Norval (Gene)

d. 1998

Norval Richardson was a pitcher for the Baltimore Elite Giants, Kansas City Monarchs, and Birmingham Black Barons from 1947 to 1953.

Richardson, Ted

Ted Richardson was a left-handed pitcher for the Birmingham Black Barons, Indianapolis Clowns, Louisville Black Colonels, and Memphis Red Sox from 1951 to 1955.

Richardson, Vicial

Vicial Richardson was a shortstop for the Cleveland Buckeyes in 1946.

Rickey, Wesley Branch

b. 1881, d. 1965

Wesley Branch Rickey was a major league ballplayer. He was a catcher, outfielder, and first baseman for the St. Louis Browns and New York Yankees from 1905 to 1907 and came back to play two games for the Browns in 1914 while managing the team. In 119 major league games, Rickey batted .239, drove in 39 runs, and scored 38 runs and managed the Browns and the St. Louis Cardinals until 1925. However, it was his work in the front office that made the 5-foot-9, 175-pound Rickey, born in Lucasville, Ohio, a baseball legend. He was the general manager of the Brooklyn Dodgers and the man who engineered the signing of Jackie Robinson to break baseball's color line in 1947. He began the process by starting a new Negro League called the UNITED STATES LEAGUE in 1945. Rickey had been an outspoken critic of the existing Negro Leagues, calling them "rackets" and suggesting they were not run on the up and up. However, many observers believed Rickey started the United States League to scout the talent available in black baseball. The league did not last very long, though, barely making it through the season. Rickey looked elsewhere for the players he wanted, picking Robinson from the Kansas City Monarchs and, following that, with catcher Roy Campanella from Baltimore, pitcher Don Newcombe from Newark, and a number of other players he brought into the Dodgers' minor league system. Rickey was criticized for failing to compensate Negro League team owners properly for signing their players and was despised by black baseball owners, even though he was breaking down the barrier that had held back black players from the major leagues.

In Jules Tygiel's book *Jackie Robinson and His Legacy*, Newark owner Effa Manley talked about the Negro Leagues' inability to get what they felt was proper compensation from Rickey when he began signing players away from Newark, and how they had little recourse to fight it: "We were in no position to protest and he [Rickey] knew it," she said. "He had us over a barrel in a way. The fans would have never forgiven us [for holding players back from major league opportunities], plus it would have been wrong to have prevented the players from going to the major leagues."

Why Rickey made his move—for a noble cause or for purely mercenary reasons—remains in question. In a 1975 interview with the *Memphis Commercial Appeal*, Negro Leaguer Verdell Mathis gave his version of how he believed major league baseball finally integrated: "We used to play in all the big white parks when they [major league teams] were out of town," he said. "We used to play in all but one—Ebbets Field in Brooklyn. But we used the Polo Grounds and Yankee Stadium and didn't need Ebbets. Branch Rickey soon discovered we, the blacks, were filling the stadiums every time we played. He saw Clark Griffith [Washington Senators owner] and asked him about it. Mr. Rickey asked Griffith why the major leagues couldn't buy up all the black franchises and gain the best players off those teams. I'm told that Mr. Griffith just leaned back in his chair and said, 'Naw, we won't do that.' Rickey asked him why not. He said, 'Branch, my friend, I can sit home with my legs crossed and those black players draw 150,000 a year. They support my park, if you want to know the truth. Naw, we won't do that.' Well, Rickey wasn't getting any of that money so he decided to hurt the others where it hurt the most—in their pocketbooks. He went after a black. Took a year researching the black leagues and finally came up with Robinson, a college man, a man he felt could handle the pressure. Oh, Lordy, there must have been 30 guys playing then who were better than

Robinson. But he was the right man for handling what was to come."

Robinson credited Rickey for his willingness to sign a black player, whatever the reason, calling him "courageous." Rickey also was a pioneer in the field of player development, building up a talented and deep minor league farm system that would keep the Dodgers competitive for years to come. He left the Dodgers to run the Pittsburgh Pirates in 1951, where one of the players he had signed was Roberto Clemente. Rickey was inducted into the National Baseball Hall of Fame in 1967.

Ricks, Curtiss

Curtiss Ricks was a pitcher, first baseman, and outfielder for the Cleveland Tate Stars, Dayton Marcos, Chicago American Giants, Cleveland Browns, and Indianapolis ABC's.

Ricks, Pender

Pender Ricks was a first baseman for the Harrisburg Giants and Philadelphia Giants from 1924 to 1928.

Ricks, William

William Ricks was a pitcher for the Philadelphia Stars from 1944 to 1950.

Rickwood Park

Rickwood Park was a baseball field in Birmingham, Alabama, where the Birmingham Black Barons played from 1923 to 1950. It was named for the minor league Birmingham Barons' owner Rick Woodward and had a seating capacity of 9,312.

Riddick, Vernon

Vernon Riddick was a shortstop for the Newark Eagles from 1939 to 1941.

Riddle, Marshall

Marshall Riddle was a second baseman and shortstop for the St. Louis Stars, Indianapolis ABC's, Cleveland Buckeyes, New Orleans–St. Louis Stars, and Jacksonville Red Caps from 1936 to 1943.

Ridgely, Buck

Buck Ridgely was a shortstop for the Baltimore Black Sox, Lincoln Giants, Washington Potomacs, and Harrisburg Giants from 1916 to 1923.

Ridley, Jack

Jack Ridley was a first baseman and outfielder for the Cleveland Cubs, Nashville Elite Giants, and Louisville Red Caps from 1927 to 1934.

Riggins, Orville (Bo)

Orville Riggins was an infielder and manager for the Cleveland Hornets, Homestead Grays, Detroit Stars, Lincoln Giants, Miami Giants, Chicago American Giants, Brooklyn Royal Giants, and New York Black Yankees from 1920 to 1936.

Rigney, Hank

Hank Rigney was an officer with the Indianapolis Crawfords, Toledo Cubs, and Toledo Crawfords from 1939 to 1945.

Rile, Edward

Edward Rile was a first baseman and pitcher for the Dayton Marcos, Homestead Grays, Kansas City Monarchs, Brooklyn Royal Giants, Cole's American Giants, Detroit Stars, Columbus Buckeyes, Lincoln Giants, Chicago American Giants, and Indianapolis ABC's from 1919 to 1926.

Riley, Jack

Jack Riley was a second baseman for the Birmingham Black Barons in 1945.

Rios, Herman

Herman Rios was a shortstop and third baseman for the Cuban Stars, Havana Stars, and Cincinnati Cubans from 1915 to 1924.

Ritchey, John

b. 1923

John Ritchey was a catcher for the Chicago American Giants in 1947, batting .381 that year. The 5-foot-9, 180-pound Ritchey went on to play minor league baseball in the Pacific Coast League and the International League until 1956 and also played winter baseball in Venezuela.

Rivera, Nenene

Nenene Rivera was a pitcher and infielder for the Cuban Stars in 1933.

Rivero, Carlos

Carlos Rivero was a third baseman and shortstop for the New York Black Yankees, Cuban Stars, and Baltimore Elite Giants in 1933 and from 1939 to 1944.

Rivers, Bill

Bill Rivers was an outfielder for the Kansas City Monarchs in 1944.

Rivers, Dewey

Dewey Rivers was an outfielder for the Hilldale baseball club and Baltimore Black Sox in 1926 and 1933.

Robelson, Bing

Bing Robelson was a pitcher for the Bacharach Giants in 1934.

Roberson, Charley

Charley Roberson was a shortstop for the Nashville Elite Giants in 1934.

Roberts, Charley

Charley Roberts was a pitcher for the Washington Black Senators in 1938.

Roberts, Curtis Benjamin, Sr.

b. 1929, d. 1969

Curtis Roberts was a second baseman and third baseman for the Kansas City Monarchs from 1947 to 1950. Born in Pineland, Texas, Roberts played minor league baseball in the Pacific Coast League, American Association, International League, Western League, and South Atlantic League until 1963. The 5-foot-8, 165-pound Roberts also played three major league seasons with the Pittsburgh Pirates, batting .223 with 54 runs scored and 40 RBIs in 171 games from 1954 to 1956. He also played winter baseball in Cuba, the Dominican Republic, Panama, and Nicaragua.

Roberts, Elihu

Elihu Roberts was an outfielder for the Hilldale baseball club and Bacharach Giants from 1916 to 1920.

Roberts, Fred

Fred Roberts was a second baseman for the Chicago Union Giants in 1903.

Roberts, Harry

Harry Roberts was an outfielder and catcher for the Baltimore Black Sox, Norfolk Giants, Norfolk Stars, Homestead Grays, Harrisburg Giants, Pittsburgh Crawfords, and Chicago Columbia Giants from 1920 to 1932.

Roberts, J. D.

J. D. Roberts was an infielder for the Bacharach Giants, Hilldale baseball club, Pennsylvania Giants, Chicago Giants, and Richmond Giants from 1918 to 1924.

Roberts, Leroy

Leroy Roberts was a pitcher for the Columbus Buckeyes, Brooklyn Royal Giants, Lincoln Giants, Hilldale baseball club, Cleveland Giants, Cleveland Red Sox, Madison Stars, and Bacharach Giants from 1916 to 1935.

Roberts, Mutt

Mutt Roberts was a pitcher for the Nashville Elite Giants, Baltimore Elite Giants, Bacharach Giants, and Philadelphia Stars from 1936 to 1939.

Roberts, Ric

Ric Roberts was a sportswriter who covered black baseball for the *Afro-American* and the *Pittsburgh Courier*.

Roberts, Tom

Tom Roberts was a pitcher for the New York Black Yankees, Homestead Grays, Newark Eagles, Philadelphia Stars, and Washington Black Senators from 1937 to 1945.

Robertson, Charles

Charles Robertson was a pitcher for the St. Louis Stars, Birmingham Black Barons, and New Orleans Caufield Ads from 1921 to 1925.

Robinson, Al

Al Robinson was a first baseman and pitcher for the New York Black Yankees and Brooklyn Royal Giants from 1905 to 1912.

Robinson, Arzell (Ace)

Arzell Robinson was a pitcher for the Memphis Red Sox in 1954 and 1955.

Robinson, Babe

Babe Robinson was a pitcher in 1933, 1934, and 1942 for the Cleveland Red Sox, Bacharach Giants, and Boston Royal Giants.

Robinson, Bill (Bojangles)

b. 1878, d. 1949

Bill Robinson was one of a number of black entertainers who were involved in Negro League baseball. The great dancer was the owner and operator of the New York Black Yankees team that began play in 1931. In John Holway's book *Blackball Stars*, Negro League pitcher Chet Brewer said that Bojangles also made a lot of money betting on teams with black players that came to play in the winter league in California in 1935: "Those fellows never heard of Negro players," Brewer said. "Bojangles just got rich beating those big-league players."

Robinson, Bob

Bob Robinson was a catcher for the Leland Giants in 1905.

Robinson, Charles

Charles Robinson was an outfielder for the Chicago American Giants in 1939.

Robinson, Cornelius

Cornelius Robinson was a shortstop and outfielder for the Homestead Grays, Cincinnati Tigers, and Memphis Red Sox from 1935 to 1952.

Robinson, Edward

Edward Robinson was an outfielder for the Louisville White Sox in 1931.

Robinson, Edward (Robbie)

Edward Robinson was an infielder for the Homestead Grays in 1945.

Robinson, George

George Robinson was a pitcher for the Bacharach Giants from 1918 to 1923.

Robinson, Henry

Henry Robinson was a catcher for the Baltimore Elite Giants, Baltimore Grays, and Kansas City Monarchs from 1942 to 1950.

Robinson, Jack

Jack Robinson was a pitcher for the Detroit Stars in 1954.

Robinson, Jacob (Red)

Jacob Robinson was a third baseman for the Chicago American Giants in 1946 and 1947.

Robinson, James

James Robinson was a pitcher for the Brooklyn Royal Giants, Philadelphia Giants, Cuban X Giants, and Cuban Giants from 1893 to 1907.

Robinson, Johnny

Johnny Robinson was an infielder and outfielder for the St. Louis Stars, Memphis Red Sox, and Indianapolis ABC's in 1930 and again from 1938 to 1942.

Robinson, John Roosevelt (Jackie)

b. 1919, d. 1972

John "Jackie" Robinson is one of the preeminent sports figures of the 20th century. When he broke major league baseball's color line in 1947 with the Brooklyn Dodgers, his place in history went far beyond the baseball field. He represented an important change in the social fabric of America. But he also represented the beginning of the end of Negro League baseball. With Robinson's success in Brooklyn, other clubs began signing black ballplayers, and by 1950 many of the talented players who were part of the Negro League system were now with major league organizations.

Born in Stamford, Connecticut, Robinson's family moved to California, where he grew up. He was a star athlete at UCLA, a standout running back and track star as well as a basketball and baseball player. He joined the service and become a lieutenant in the U.S. Army, and found himself facing a court martial in 1944 resulting from an incident when he refused a bus driver's order to go to the back of the bus "where the colored people belong." He won his case and after leaving the army went on to play one season in the Negro Leagues for the Kansas City Monarchs in 1945. The 5-foot-11, 195-pound Robinson batted .387 playing shortstop in 47 games with the Monarchs that season. In an interview with author John Holway on file at the National Baseball Hall of Fame, Newt Allen, Robinson's manager in Kansas City, talked about what a smart ballplayer Robinson was:

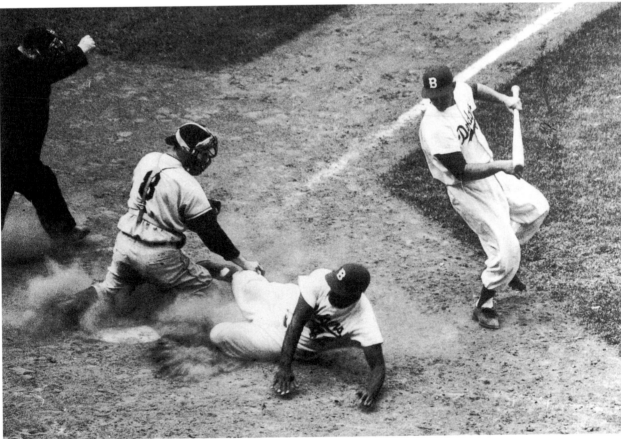

He only played one season of Negro League baseball with the Kansas City Monarchs, batting .387 in 47 games, but Jackie Robinson turned out to be one of the most influential figures in the history of the Negro Leagues. His success in breaking the major league baseball color line with the Brooklyn Dodgers in 1947 brought about the demise of the Negro Leagues, as black players shortly after began signing contracts with major league organizations. The enormous burden of breaking the barrier did not stop Robinson from being a Hall of Famer and a great all-around player, a standout fielder and baserunner as well as a great hitter. In 10 major league seasons, Robinson batted .311, with 947 runs scored, 137 home runs, 734 runs scored, and 197 stolen bases. (NATIONAL BASEBALL HALL OF FAME LIBRARY, COOPERSTOWN, N.Y.)

"He was awfully smart," Allen said. "He didn't have the ability at first, but he had the brains. Jackie was one-third ability and two-thirds brains, and that made him a great ballplayer."

After being signed to a contract by Dodgers general manager Branch Rickey, Robinson played the 1946 season with their minor league club in Montreal, the Royals. His performance on the field, along with his ability to handle the racial hatred that he faced from both opponents and teammates, made his debut a success and paved the way for other black ballplayers.

Robinson was National League Rookie of the Year in 1947, stealing 29 bases and batting .297, with 125 runs scored. He would go on to play 10 major league seasons, compile a career batting average of .311, with 947 runs scored, 137 home runs, 734 runs scored, and 197 stolen bases. He played in six World Series for the Dodgers—all against the New York Yankees. He did all this while facing a barrage of racial attacks from ballplayers and fans, even racism on his own team, all the time forced to control his temper in his rookie season. Rickey had told Robinson that he would have to suppress his reaction to strike back when attacked, at least initially, and he was able to do so, allowing him to slowly gain the respect of even his foes with his performance on the field. In his biography, *My Life in the Negro Leagues*, pitcher Wilmer Fields said that he believed Robinson was the "greatest black baseball player in the world, not so much for his play, but for his outstanding play in the face of the harassment and racial discrimination he took on. Not that Jackie was the only black baseball player who ever encountered racism, but it was the never-ending amount that he took is mind-boggling."

It was difficult for Robinson to endure the abuse because his nature was not to take it. Buck O'Neil, in his autobiography, *I Was Right on Time*, wrote about Robinson's attitude toward discrimination while he was playing for the Monarchs: "Growing up as he did in California, Jackie went to integrated schools and played on integrated teams," O'Neil wrote. "So when he got to the all-black Monarchs and he saw the things they had to put up with—the Jim Crow laws, the separate drinking fountains and restrooms—he became furious. Othello Chico Renfroe, who played left field on that club, later told me that Jackie stormed out of so many places that he left behind a fortune in change. There was an incident in Muskogee, Oklahoma, that year that Hilton [Smith], who was Jackie's roommate, told me about. We had been buying gas for years at a service station there that had just one restroom—and we weren't allowed to use it. We thought nothing of it, and we gave the owner a lot of business anyway. Well, when the bus pulled into Muskogee and stopped at this station, Jackie got out and headed toward the restroom. The owner, who was filling the tank, called after him.

'Hey boy! You know you can't go in there.' Jackie asked him why. 'Because we don't allow colored people in that restroom.' The guys knew about Jackie's hair-triggered temper, so they just stood around, wondering what he was going to do. Jackie turned to the man very calmly and said, 'Take the hose out of the tank.' The owner stopped the pump and looked at him. 'Take the hose out of the tank,' Jackie repeated. Then he turned to his teammates and said, 'Let's go. We don't want his gas.' Well, the Monarchs had two 50-gallon tanks on the bus. That gas station wasn't going to sell 100 gallons of gas to one customer until the bus came back through a few weeks later. The owner shoved the hose back into the tank and said, 'All right, you boys can use the restroom. But don't stay long.' From then on, the Monarchs could use the restroom whenever they passed through. But more importantly, they decided never to patronize any gas station or restaurant where they couldn't use the facilities."

Robinson's time in the Negro Leagues was not easy. According to Jules Tygiel's book *Jackie Robinson and His Legacy*, Robinson "a non-drinker and non-smoker," never quite fit into the boisterous life of the Negro Leagues. Accustomed to the discipline and structure of intercollegiate athletics, Robinson found the loose scheduling and erratic play appalling. Nor did he hide his distaste for being relegated to a Jim Crow league. Though most black ballplayers resigned themselves to their segregated status. Robinson often spoke of impending integration. Teammate Othello Renfroe recalls, "We'd ride miles and miles on the bus and his whole talk was, 'Well you guys better get ready because pretty soon baseball's going to sign one of us.'"

In his own words, Robinson, in his autobiography, *I Never Had It Made*, spoke about the difficult lifestyle he encountered in Negro League baseball: "Blacks who wanted to play baseball could sign up on black teams only," Robinson said. "These teams were poorly financed, and their management and promotion left much to be desired. Travel schedules were unbelievably hectic. Our team played in Kansas City, moved throughout the entire Midwest and sometimes went south and east. On one occasion, we left Kansas City on a bus on a Sunday night, traveled to Philadelphia, reaching there Tuesday morning. We played a doubleheader that night and the next day we were on the road again. This fatiguing travel wouldn't have been so bad if we could have had decent meals. Finding satisfactory or even passable eating places was almost a daily problem. There was no hotel in many of the places we played. Sometimes there was a hotel for blacks which had no eating facilities. No one even thought of trying to get accommodations in white hotels. Some of the crummy eating joints would not serve us at all. You could never sit down to a relaxed hot meal. You were lucky if they magnanimously permitted you to carry out some greasy hamburgers in a paper bag with a container of coffee. You were really living when you were able to get a plate of cold cuts. You ate on board the team bus or on the road." Robinson said he felt trapped in Negro League baseball, but "the solution to my problem was only days away in the hands of a tough, shrewd, courageous man called Branch Rickey, the president of the Brooklyn Dodgers." In 1962, Robinson became the first black player to be inducted into the National Baseball Hall of Fame.

Robinson, Joshua

Joshua Robinson was an outfielder for the New York Black Yankees in 1939.

Robinson, Kenneth (Ken)

Kenneth Robinson was an outfielder, second baseman, and third baseman for the Newark Browns, Brooklyn Royal Giants, Cleveland Bears, Bacharach Giants, and New York Black Yankees from 1931 to 1943.

Robinson, Norman Wayne

Norman Robinson was a shortstop, third baseman, and outfielder for the Birmingham Black Barons and Baltimore Elite Giants from 1939 to 1952.

Robinson, Ray

Ray Robinson was a pitcher for the Cincinnati Buckeyes, Newark Eagles, Cleveland Buckeyes, and Philadelphia Stars from 1941 to 1947.

Robinson, Richmond

Richmond Robinson was an outfielder for the Trenton, New Jersey, Cuban Giants, New York Gorhams, and St. Louis Black Stockings from 1883 to 1886. A May 1886 article in the *Trenton Times* described Robinson, who was born in Washington, D.C., in 1856, as "a general player, good base runner and heavy batter."

Robinson, Robert

Robert Robinson was an outfielder for the Detroit Stars in 1954.

Robinson, Sammy

Sammy Robinson was a pitcher for the Detroit Stars in 1954.

Robinson, Walter

Walter Robinson was a shortstop for the Lincoln Giants, Hilldale baseball club, New York Black Yankees, Harrisburg Giants, and Bacharach Giants from 1925 to 1932.

Robinson, William (Bobby)

b. 1904, d. 2002

William Robinson was a shortstop and third baseman for the Memphis Red Sox, Cleveland Elites, Indianapolis ABC's, Cleveland Red Sox, Cleveland Stars, Detroit Stars, St. Louis Stars, Chicago American Giants, Birmingham Black Barons, and New Orleans–St. Louis Stars from 1925 to 1942.

Rochelle, Clarence

Clarence Rochelle was a pitcher for the Kansas City Monarchs in 1944.

Rodgers, Silvester (Speedie)

Silvester Rodgers was a pitcher for the Baltimore Elite Giants in 1949 and 1950.

Rodriguez, Antonio

Antonio Rodriguez was a pitcher for the Cuban Stars in 1939.

Rodriguez, Benny

Benny Rodriguez was a catcher and outfielder for the Chicago American Giants from 1946 to 1948.

Rodriguez, Conrado

Conrado Rodriguez was a pitcher and outfielder for the Cuban Stars in 1922 and again from 1927 to 1934.

Rodriguez, Hector

b. 1920

Hector Rodriguez was a third baseman for the New York Cubans in 1944. Born in Cuba, Rodriguez batted .238 for New York that season in 34 games. The 5-foot-8, 165-pound Rodriguez went on to play minor league baseball in the International League and Pacific Coast League. He also played in the Mexican League until 1964 and played winter baseball in Cuba until 1960.

Rodriguez, Jose

Jose Rodriguez was a catcher for the Cuban Stars, Detroit Stars, All Cubans, Cuban Stars of Havana, and Kansas City Monarchs from 1913 to 1929.

Roesink, John

John Roesink was an officer and owner of the Detroit Stars from 1925 to 1930.

Rogan, Wilber (Bullet Joe)
b. 1889, d 1967

Wilber Rogan was one of the standout pitchers of all time in Negro League baseball. He pitched for the Pullman Colts, Kansas City Colored Giants, ALL NATIONS team, Los Angeles White Sox, and Kansas City Monarchs. He was also an infielder, outfielder, and manager during his Negro League career, from 1917 to 1946, and also worked as an umpire in the NEGRO AMERICAN LEAGUE. Rogan was also the captain of the legendary black team in the 26th Infantry in the Philippines in 1912 and also played on the talented U.S. Army 25th Infantry team in Fort Huachuca, Arizona, in 1919. Besides being a great pitcher, with a 113-34 record against Negro League competition, Rogan, born in Oklahoma City, was also a standout hitter, batting .343 over his Negro League career, with a .411 average in 1924 when he led the Monarchs to the Negro League World Series against Hilldale. Rogan won two games, lost one, and tied another, batting .325 as the Monarchs won the series. In an interview conducted by author John Holway on file at the National Baseball Hall of Fame, Negro League player Newt Allen said the 5-foot-9, 160-pound Rogan was the "greatest pitcher of all. I'd say Rogan was a better pitcher than Satchel. Rogan was better than Satchel, because Rogan was smarter. He weighed only about 154 pounds, and never wound up. Even with nobody on base, he'd just throw from his shoulder and it was gone. He threw hard, and had everything—fork balls, spit balls, any kind of ball—and he had a master curveball. He was an awfully good hitter, hit anything you threw. For about four straight years he and I played in Cuba together for Adolfo Luque, who used to be a great pitcher for the Cincinnati Reds. They used Rogan in the outfield a lot of times, and he almost won the batting championship down there. You get $100 if you're the leading hitter, and he was way up there in average, but the only thing that kept him from it was that he hadn't play [sic] in enough games. He could hit, and he could run, too. He was a 10-second man [100-yard dash] in the Army."

In another Holway interview, Crush Holloway described Rogan's pitching style: "He had three curveballs, all with the same motion," Holloway said. "He was a great pitcher." Even Paige admitted that Rogan was perhaps the greatest pitcher in Negro League history. "I pitched against Bullet Joe," Paige said. "Rogan was one of the world's greatest pitchers. I never did see him in his prime, if you want me to tell you the truth. I came up

Bullet Joe Rogan was aptly nicknamed for his hard-throwing pitching style that dominated Negro League hitters, with a career 113-34 record against Negro League competition. Rogan, who played and managed from 1917 to 1946 for the Pullman Colts, Kansas City Colored Giants, All Nations team, Los Angeles White Sox, and Kansas City Monarchs, was also a standout hitter, batting .343 over his Negro League career, with a .411 average in 1924. (NATIONAL BASEBALL HALL OF FAME LIBRARY, COOPERSTOWN, N.Y.)

from Birmingham to Kansas City. He beat me 1-0 in the 11th inning. He was the onliest pitcher I ever knew, I ever heard of in my life, was pitching and hitting in the cleanup place. He was a chunky little guy, but he could throw hard. He could throw as hard as Smokey Joe Williams. Oh, yes, he was a number one pitcher, wasn't any maybe so." Rogan was inducted into the National Baseball Hall of Fame in 1998.

Rogers, William (Nat)

William Rogers was a first baseman, third baseman, outfielder, catcher, and manager for the Brooklyn Royal Giants, Harrisburg Giants, Chicago Columbia Giants, Memphis Red Sox, Chicago American Giants, Cole's American Giants, Kansas City Monarchs, Birmingham Black Barons, Brooklyn Eagles, and Knoxville Giants from 1923 to 1946. In a January 1975 article in *Black Sports,* the 5-foot-11, 160-pound Rogers, born in Spartansburg, South Carolina, talked about his hitting in the Negro Leagues: "I was a first-ball hitter and I could hit to left field," Rogers said. "That was my power, in left field. I did so much of that around the league, they said, 'Well, we can't get him out because he hits everything we throw.' I didn't wait for no strikes, anything close I would hit. I never had an argument with an umpire about a ball or a strike. Never argued with him. Because I never let him call me out. Anything close enough to call is close enough to hit. I'd hit anything close. So they started to throw me off-balls [outside pitches]. They'd get that first ball off. Now I'm smarter than they are. I know they are going to throw me a curveball after that first off-pitch, so I was ready for it. One fella got it too close to the plate and I hit a home run."

Records show that Rogers batted between .340 and .380 during his peak years and once had a 31-game hitting streak. He also reportedly hit consistently well against Satchel Paige. In the *Black Sports* article, Rogers talked about one memorable at bat against Paige in a playoff game against Birmingham when Rogers was playing with the Chicago American Giants: 'The first time up I hit the scoreboard and knocked the scores off the board," Rogers said. "Satchel was humming that ball and all you had to do was just meet it. Time him."

Rojo, Julio

Julio Rojo was a third baseman and catcher for the New York Cubans, New York Cuban Stars, Cuban Stars, Havana Stars, Lincoln Giants, Cuban Stars of Havana, Baltimore Black Sox, and Bacharach Giants from 1916 to 1938.

Roman Cities

Roman Cities were a black baseball team out of Jacksonville, Florida, that played in the Southern League of Colored Baseballists in 1886.

Romanach, Tomas

Tomas Romanach was a shortstop for the Cuban Stars and Long Branch, New Jersey, Cubans from 1916 to 1920.

Romby, Robert

Robert Romby was a pitcher for the Baltimore Elite Giants from 1946 to 1950.

Roque, Jacinto (Battling Siki)

Jacinto Roque was an outfielder for the Cuban Stars from 1928 to 1932.

Rosado, Ralph

Ralph Rosado was a catcher for the Detroit Stars in 1955.

Rose, Cecil

Cecil Rose was a pitcher for the St. Louis Stars in 1924.

Rose, Haywood

Haywood Rose was a catcher for the Leland Giants in 1907 and 1908.

Roselle, Basilio

Basilio Roselle was a pitcher for the Cuban Stars and New York Cubans from 1926 to 1935.

Ross, Arthur

Arthur Ross was a pitcher for the Leland Giants and Chicago Union Giants from 1903 to 1905.

Ross, Dick

Dick Ross was an outfielder for the St. Louis Stars in 1925.

Ross, Frank

Frank Ross was a pitcher for the Memphis Red Sox in 1939.

Ross, Gary

Gary Ross was an outfielder for the Indianapolis Clowns in 1952.

Ross, Harold

Harold Ross was a pitcher for the Indianapolis ABC's, Cleveland Browns, and Chicago American Giants from 1922 to 1925.

Ross, Jerry

Jerry Ross was a pitcher for the Cleveland Elites in 1926.

Ross, Sam

Sam Ross was a pitcher for the Hilldale baseball club, Washington Potomacs, and Harrisburg Giants in 1923.

Ross, William

William Ross was a pitcher for the Cleveland Hornets, St. Louis Stars, Homestead Grays, Chicago American Giants, Detroit Stars, and Cleveland Tigers from 1924 to 1930.

Rossiter, George

George Rossiter, a white tavern owner in Baltimore, was the owner of the Baltimore Black Sox from 1922 to 1931.

Roth, Herman

Herman Roth was a catcher for the Chicago American Giants, New Orleans Crescent Stars, Detroit Stars, Milwaukee Bears, and Birmingham Black Barons from 1921 to 1925.

Rouse, Howard

Howard Rouse was an outfielder for the Philadelphia Stars in 1951.

Rovira, Jamie

Jamie Rovira was a third baseman for the All Cubans in 1911.

Rowan, Bill

Bill Rowan was an outfielder for the Kansas City Monarchs in 1951 and 1952.

Rowe, William (Schoolboy)

William Rowe was a pitcher for the Pittsburgh Crawfords, Cleveland Buckeyes, and Chicago Brown Bombers from 1943 to 1945.

Roy, Ormby

Ormby Roy was a shortstop for the Pittsburgh Crawfords in 1930 and 1931.

Royall, Joseph

Joseph Royall was a pitcher, outfielder, and catcher for the Jacksonville Red Caps, New York Black Yankees, Cleveland Bears, and Indianapolis Athletics from 1937 to 1944.

Royal Palm Hotel

The Royal Palm Hotel was a hotel in Miami, Florida, that fielded a team of black ballplayers in the Florida hotel league in the early 1900s.

Royal Poinciana Hotel

The Royal Poinciana Hotel was a hotel in Palm Beach, Florida, that fielded a team of black ballplayers in the Florida hotel league in the early 1900s.

Rue, Joe

Joe Rue was an umpire in the NEGRO NATIONAL LEAGUE in the early 1920s and went on to umpire in the major leagues.

Ruffin, Charles

Charles Ruffin was a catcher and manager for the Pittsburgh Crawfords, Newark Eagles, Houston Eagles, Philadelphia Stars, Toledo Crawfords, and Brooklyn Eagles from 1935 to 1950.

Ruiz, Antonio

Antonio Ruiz was a pitcher for the Cincinnati-Indianapolis Clowns in 1944.

Ruiz, Silvino

Silvino Ruiz was a pitcher for the New York Cubans and Cuban Stars from 1928 to 1942.

Ruppert Park

Ruppert Park was a baseball field in Kansas City, Missouri, where the Kansas City Monarchs played in the 1940s.

Ruppert Stadium

Ruppert Stadium was a baseball field in Newark, New Jersey, where the Newark Eagles played from 1936 to 1948. The New York Cubans also played at Ruppert Stadium, as did several other black baseball teams.

Rush, Joe

Joe Rush was owner of the Birmingham Black Barons from 1923 to 1926 and also served as president and secretary of the Negro Southern League.

Russ, Pythias

Pythias Russ was a shortstop and catcher for the Memphis Red Sox and Chicago American Giants from 1925 to 1929.

Russell, Aaron

Aaron Russell was a third baseman for the Homestead Grays from 1913 to 1920.

Russell, Branch

Branch Russell was an outfielder and third baseman for the St. Louis Stars, Kansas City Monarchs, Cleveland Cubs, and Cleveland Stars from 1922 to 1933.

Russell, Ewing

Ewing Russell was a catcher for the Cincinnati Tigers from 1935 to 1936.

Russell, Frank

Frank Russell was an outfielder, pitcher, and catcher for the Memphis Red Sox, Baltimore Elite Giants, and Birmingham Black Barons from 1943 to 1954.

Russell, John

John Russell was a second baseman and third baseman for the St. Louis Stars, Memphis Red Sox, Pittsburgh Crawfords, Indianapolis ABC's, Homestead Grays, Cleveland Red Sox, and Detroit Wolves from 1923 to 1934.

Russell, Thomas

Thomas Russell was a pitcher for the Cleveland Buckeyes in 1950.

Ryan, Merven (Red)

Merven Ryan was a pitcher for the New York Black Yankees, Pennsylvania Red Caps of New York, Homestead Grays, Pittsburgh Stars of Buffalo, Brooklyn Royal Giants, Hilldale baseball club, Bacharach Giants, Harrisburg Giants, Baltimore Black Sox, Lincoln Stars, Lincoln Giants, and Newark Browns from 1915 to 1934. His best pitch was the fork ball.

Sadler, William
d. 1987

William Sadler was a shortstop for the Washington Black Senators, Bacharach Giants, and Brooklyn Eagles from 1934 to 1939.

St. Louis Black Stockings

The St. Louis Black Stockings were a black baseball team that played in St. Louis, Missouri, in the 1880s.

St. Louis Giants

The St. Louis Giants were a black baseball team that played in St. Louis, Missouri, and featured players such as the great Oscar Charleston. They began play in the early 1900s and were owned by Charles Mills. The Giants were one of the original teams in Rube Foster's NEGRO NATIONAL LEAGUE, formed in 1920 under the ownership of Lorenzo Cobb, but the franchise folded after the 1921 season. During its heyday, the Giants were one of the best teams in Negro League baseball and, according to the white press, perhaps one of the best teams anywhere. In a 1912 article in the *St. Louis Post-Dispatch*, cited in Robert Peterson's book *Only the Ball Was White*, the newspaper called out their white teams in town: "The St. Louis Giants, a black baseball team, have easily beaten everything in town but the Browns and the Cardinals, and neither of these latter will play them." The *Post-Dispatch* wrote, "It requires some courage to predict that colored baseball, like colored pugilism, is to supersede the white brand, but someone has to think ahead and indicate whither we drift, and we therefore wish to go on record as having said that it will. If the Browns and Cardinals will admit the St. Louis Giants to a three-cornered series for the local championship this fall it will begin in St. Louis right away."

St. Louis Pullmans

The St. Louis Pullmans were a black baseball team in St. Louis, Missouri, in the 1920s and 1930s.

St. Louis Stars

The St. Louis Stars were a black baseball team that played in St. Louis, Missouri. The Stars replaced the St. Louis Giants in the NEGRO NATIONAL LEAGUE in 1922. Richard Kent was the owner of the team, and one of their managers was Candy Jim Taylor. Some of the players they had included Cool Papa Bell, Mule Suttles, and Willie Wells. They won the NNL first-half title in 1928 and 1930 and in 1930 faced the Detroit Stars in the postseason, winning the championship in a seven-game series. They disbanded after the 1931 season but were revived in 1937 in the NEGRO AMERICAN LEAGUE, lasting two seasons. In 1941, they were called the New Orleans–St. Louis Stars, playing some games in each city, and though they were called the Harrisburg–St. Louis Stars in 1943, they played all their home games in Harrisburg, Pennsylvania, that year.

St. Paul Gophers

The St. Paul Gophers were a black baseball team that played in St. Paul, Minnesota, in the early 1900s. The Gophers won the Negro Western championship in 1909 and were led by Candy Jim Taylor.

St. Thomas, Larry

Larry St. Thomas was a catcher for the New York Black Yankees and Newark Eagles in 1943 and 1947.

Salas, Wilfredo

Wilfredo Salas was a pitcher for the New York Cubans in 1948.

Salazar, Lazaro

Lazaro Salazar was an outfielder, first baseman, and pitcher for the Cuban Stars and New York Cubans from 1924 to 1936.

Salmon, Harry

Harry Salmon was a pitcher for the Memphis Red Sox, Homestead Grays, Birmingham Black Barons, and Detroit Wolves from 1923 to 1935.

Salters, Edward

Edward Salters was an outfielder for the Detroit Stars in 1937.

Salverson, Henry

Henry Salverson was a second baseman for the Detroit Stars from 1954 to 1955.

Sama, Pablo

Pablo Sama was a third baseman for the Indianapolis Clowns in 1950.

Sampson, Emanual (Leo)

Emanual Sampson was an outfielder for the Birmingham Black Barons from 1941 to 1946.

Sampson, John

John Sampson was an outfielder for the New York Cubans in 1942.

Sampson, Ormond

Ormond Sampson was a shortstop for the Brooklyn Royal Giants, Newark Dodgers, and Atlanta Black Crackers from 1932 to 1938.

Sampson, Sam

Sam Sampson was a second baseman and outfielder for the Jacksonville Red Caps and Cleveland Bears in 1940 and 1941.

Sampson, Thomas (Toots)

Thomas Sampson was a first baseman, second baseman, and manager for the Birmingham Black Barons, New York Cubans, and Chicago American Giants from 1938 to 1949.

San Antonio Black Aces

The San Antonio Black Aces were a black baseball team that had began as the Waco Black Navigators in Waco, Texas, in 1919 before being sold and becoming the San Antonio Black Aces. In an interview with author John Holway on file at the National Baseball Hall of Fame, Negro League great Crush Holloway, a member of the Navigators and then the Black Aces, talked about some of his teammates on the San Antonio club, such as Biz Mackey: "The Aces had High Pockets Hudspeth on first base," Holloway said. "I was second, Laymon Washington in short, Henry Blackman on third. Blackman was a great third baseman. The Aces played in the white Texas League and Southern League parks—Dallas, Fort Worth, Houston, Beaumont, Wichita Falls. That's why those boys from Texas could play so good, they had good grounds. Not like out East, where they had to play on those little old lots. In the Texas League they had a turtle-back diamond, the mound was high, and it kind of rolled down from the pitcher's box to the infield. The ball could hop off there and come down at you. . . . Mackey and about six other guys went up to Indianapolis in 1920. Old man Bellinger . . . Charlie Bellinger, he was a rich millionaire and a politician in San Antonio. He was a friend of C. I. Taylor of the Indianapolis ABC's, and he'd look out for ballplayers for him. Mackey, Blackman, Hudspeth, Washington and two other players—Morris Williams and Bob McClure—went to Indianapolis that year. It broke our club all to pieces."

San Antonio Black Indians

The San Antonio Black Indians were a black baseball team out of San Antonio, Texas, that played in the Texas Negro League in the 1920s.

San Antonio Black Sheepherders

The San Antonio Black Sheepherders were a black baseball team out of San Antonio, Texas, that played in the late 1940s. One of its young players was a shortstop named Ernie Banks.

San Antonio Broncos

The San Antonio Broncos were a black baseball team out of San Antonio, Texas, that played in the early 1900s. One of the players on the Broncos' roster was Negro League pitching great Smokey Joe Williams.

Sanchez, Amando

Amando Sanchez was a pitcher for the Memphis Red Sox in 1948.

Sanchez, Gonzalo

Gonzalo Sanchez was a catcher for the All Cubans in 1904 and 1905.

Sanders, James

James Sanders was an outfielder for the Kansas City Monarchs in 1955.

Sanders, Willie

Willie Sanders was a pitcher for the Memphis Red Sox in 1936.

Sanderson, Johnny

Johnny Sanderson was a shortstop for the Kansas City Monarchs in 1947.

Sands, Sam

Sam Sands was a shortstop and catcher for the Kansas City Monarchs and Indianapolis Clowns from 1950 to 1954.

Santaella, Anastacio (Juan)

Anastacio Santaella was a second baseman and shortstop for the New York Cubans from 1935 to 1946.

Santiago, Carlos

b. 1928

Carlos Santiago was a second baseman for the New York Cubans in 1946.

Santiago, Jose

Jose Santiago was a shortstop and pitcher for the New York Cubans in 1945 and 1946. He went on to play minor league baseball for Stamford and Poughkeepsie in the Colonial League, Farnham in the Provincial League, St. Petersburg and Tallahassee in the Florida International League, and Lincoln in the Western League. The 5-foot-11, 170-pound Santiago also played in the Mexican League, retiring in 1955. He also played winter baseball in Puerto Rico.

Santop, Louis (Tex)

b. 1890, d. 1942

Louis Santop was a catcher, outfielder, and manager for the Oklahoma Monarchs, Fort Worth Wonders, New York Lincoln Giants, Philadelphia Giants, Lincoln Stars, Chicago American Giants, Hilldale baseball club, and Brooklyn Royal Giants from 1909 to 1926. He later managed his own semipro team, the Santop Broncos, and he played winter baseball in the Florida hotel league, as well as winter baseball in Cuba. Santop, born in Tyler, Texas, was one of the top hitters in Negro League baseball, batting .470 in 1911 for the Lincoln Giants. He followed that up with a .422 average in 1912 and .455 in 1914. Near the end of his career, with Hilldale in 1923, Santop batted .333, and .376 in 1924.

In John Holway's book *Blackball Stars*, teammate Frank Forbes said Santop, who was about 6-feet-4 and 240 pounds, was the hardest hitter he had ever seen: "Tex hit a ball 999 miles," Forbes said. "He hit a ball off Doc Scanlan down in Elizabethport, New Jersey, in 1912, and it went over the fence, and it was 500 some feet away. They put a sign on the fence where he hit it." As great a hitter as he was, he committed a costly error that led to the end of his career in the 1924 Negro League World Series when Hilldale faced the Kansas City Monarchs, according to Holway's book. Playing behind the plate, Santop failed to catch a key foul pop fly off the bat of Frank Duncan, who then hit the next pitch down the third base line, driving in two runs and leading the Monarchs to a 3-2 win. Kansas City would go on to win the series, and Santop was out of Negro League baseball within two years.

Saperstein, Abe

Abe Saperstein was a sports promoter who was best known for starting the barnstorming, clowning, basketball team known as the Harlem Globetrotters in 1926. But Saperstein was also involved with Negro League baseball as a promoter, officer, and owner of the Cincinnati Clowns and other versions of the "Clowns" that were the baseball version of his clowning Harlem basketball team. Saperstein also owned pieces of the Cleveland Cubs and the Chicago American Giants from 1932 to 1950 and served as a booking agent and as a promoter for a host of Negro League games and events. Saperstein was president of the Negro Midwestern League and the West Coast Negro Baseball Association.

Saperstein was often accused of exploiting black athletes for profit. Rob Ruck, in his book, *Sandlot Seasons*, wrote that Saperstein was one of several white businessmen who were heavily involved in the controversial promotion of black baseball: "If Nat Strong and Eddie Gottlieb stood accused of the economic exploitation of black baseball, Syd Pollock and Abe Saperstein drew the additional charge of making it out to be little more than a minstrel show," Ruck wrote. "Saperstein made as much, if not more, money out of black sport during the first half of the 20th century as anybody in America. World-renowned for his Harlem Globetrotters basketball team, his introduction to black sports was through baseball. He was a force to be ignored only at great peril."

Sarvis, Andrew

Andrew Sarvis was a pitcher for the Jacksonville Red Caps and Cleveland Bears from 1939 to 1942.

Saunders, Bob

Bob Saunders was a shortstop, second baseman, and pitcher for the Detroit Stars, Bacharach Giants, Monroe Monarchs, Louisville Red Caps, Cleveland Hornets, Memphis Red Sox, and Kansas City Monarchs from 1926 to 1937.

Saunders, Leo

Leo Saunders was a shortstop and pitcher for the Chicago American Giants and Birmingham Black Barons in 1940.

Saunders, William

William Saunders was an outfielder for the Pittsburgh Keystones in 1887.

Saunders, William

William Saunders was a catcher for the Baltimore Elite Giants in 1950.

Savage, Art

Art Savage was an officer with the Cleveland Stars in 1932.

Savage, Bill

Bill Savage was a pitcher for the Memphis Red Sox in 1940.

Savannah Broads

The Savannah Broads were a black baseball team based in Savannah, Georgia, that played in the Southern League of Colored Baseballists in 1886.

Savannah Jerseys

The Savannah Jerseys were a black baseball team based in Savannah, Georgia, that played in the Southern League of Colored Baseballists in 1886.

Savannah Lafayettes

The Savannah Lafayettes were a black baseball team based in Savannah, Georgia, that played in the Southern League of Colored Baseballists in 1886.

Sawyer, Carl

Carl Sawyer was a second baseman for the Detroit Stars in 1924.

Saxon, Thomas

Thomas Saxon was a pitcher for the New York Cubans in 1942.

Saylor, Alfred (Greyhound)

Alfred Saylor was a pitcher, catcher, and first baseman for the Cincinnati Buckeyes, Cincinnati Clowns, and Birmingham Black Barons from 1940 to 1945.

Scales, George
b. 1900, d. 1976

George Scales was an infielder, outfielder, and manager for the Pittsburgh Keystones, St. Louis Stars, St. Louis Giants, Newark Stars, Lincoln Giants, New York Black Yankees, Homestead Grays, Baltimore Elite Giants, Philadelphia Stars, Birmingham Black Barons, and Pittsburgh Keystones from 1920 to 1952. Records show that Scales, born in Talladega, Alabama, had a career batting average of .338, including a .387 average in 1929. In an interview with author John Holway on file at the

National Baseball Hall of Fame, Negro Leaguer Pee Wee Butts said that Scales, who was one of the best curveball hitters in the Negro Leagues, was a good teacher and had particular skills with a bat: "Scales was one of the best fungo men I've seen," Butts said. "He could hit that ball just out of your reach and make you travel for it. I used to have trouble coming in on slow balls. I'd have to come up to throw. He said, 'No, Pee Wee, that's not the way a good shortstop plays.' He drilled me hard until I finally caught on. . . . Scales was a little hard on you, but if you'd listen you could learn a lot." Butts said that Scales helped develop Junior Gilliam as a hitter: "Gilliam was a right-handed batter, but Scales turned him over to be a switch hitter. That's when he started hitting." Scales also had a volatile temper, and, according to Holway *Blackball Stars*, pulled a knife on a teammate on the Homestead Grays in 1931 while in a fight. Scales and Ted Page got into a fight in the shower and had to be broken up several times by teammates, and at one point during the brawl, Scales pulled a knife, but he was stopped from using it by teammates. Scales was one of a group of Negro League players who went to the Dominican Republic in 1937 to play in the the baseball war being waged there between dictator Rafael Trujillo and his political opponents. Scales played for Santiago, one of the teams owned by an opponent of Trujillo.

Scantlebury, Patricio (Pat)

b. 1917, d. 1991

Patricio Scantlebury was a left-handed pitcher for the New York Cubans from 1944 to 1950. Partial records show that he posted a 29-21 career record in Negro League baseball. The 6-foot-1, 190-pound Scantlebury, born in Gatun, Panama, had a brief stint with the Cincinnati Reds in 1956, posting a 0-1 record in six appearances with a 6.63 ERA. He also played for Havana and Toronto in the International League, Seattle in the Pacific Coast League, Dallas in the Texas League, and Texarkana in the Big State League. Scantlebury also played in the Mexican League in 1951, and in Cuba and Puerto Rico for winter baseball. He was the last black player who went directly from a Negro League team to a major league club, according to Robert Peterson's book *Only the Ball Was White*.

Schlichter, H. Walter (Slick)

H. Walter Schlichter was the sports editor of the *Philadelphia Item*, a white newspaper. He founded and operated the Philadelphia Stars from 1902 to 1910, establishing the Stars as one of the premier black baseball teams of that era, battling Frank Leland and other owners on the field and the business offices for control of black baseball. He was also president of the National Association of Col-

ored Base Ball Clubs of the United States and Cuba. In a 1927 article in the *Pittsburgh Courier*, Negro League player, manager, and historian Sol White, who managed Schlichter's Philadelphia team, listed Schlichter was one of the greatest figures in the history of Negro League baseball.

Schorling, John

John Schorling was an officer with the Chicago American Giants from 1911 to 1927. A bartender, Schorling was the brother-in-law of Chicago White Sox owner Charles Comiskey, and his team played in what was originally known as South Side Park, the former home of the White Sox before Comiskey Park was built in 1910, and later known as Schorling Park.

Scotland, Joe

Joe Scotland was an outfielder for the Indianapolis ABC's, Bowser's ABC's, and Chicago Union Giants from 1914 to 1919.

Scott, Bob

Bob Scott was a pitcher and first baseman for the New York Black Yankees and Boston Blues from 1946 to 1950.

Scott, Charles

Charles Scott was an outfielder for the St. Louis Giants in 1919 and 1920.

Scott, Ed

Ed Scott was an officer with the Indianapolis Clowns from 1952 to 1955.

Scott, Elisha

Elisha Scott was an attorney from Topeka, Kansas, who helped write the constitution for the National Association of Colored Professional Base Ball Clubs and the NEGRO NATIONAL LEAGUE in 1920, according to Robert Peterson's book *Only the Ball Was White*.

Scott, Frank

Frank Scott was a second baseman and shortstop for the Chicago Unions from 1887 to 1894.

Scott, Jim

Jim Scott was a pitcher for the Memphis Red Sox in 1950.

Scott, Joe B.

Joe Scott was an outfielder for the New York Black Yankees, Chicago American Giants, Memphis Red Sox, and Pittsburgh Crawfords from 1944 to 1949. He was the first black player to play at Wrigley Field in Chicago and also noted another milestone in an interview with *Sports Collectors Digest* in 1993: "I was one of the first blacks to play against a major league club," he said. "This, remember, was before Jackie Robinson broke the color barrier [in 1947]. During the war years, in 1945, to be exact, I played against the Pittsburgh Pirates in Muncie, Indiana. I was playing for the Right [sic] Field Kittyhawks of Dayton, Ohio, an Air Force team, and was the only black on the field. That game against Pittsburgh definitely was the highlight of my career. I got a chance to face Pittsburgh's great pitchers, including Rip Sewell. The first time up, I heard someone yell, 'Knock him down.' I responded by tripling."

Scott, John

John Scott was a first baseman and outfielder for the Kansas City Monarchs, Birmingham Black Barons, Chicago American Giants, Louisville Buckeyes, and Philadelphia Stars from 1944 to 1950.

Scott, Joseph

b. 1918

Joseph Scott was a first baseman for the Birmingham Black Barons and Chicago American Giants from 1947 to 1950. Records show that the 5-foot-11, 175-pound Scott, who was born in Shreveport, Lousiana, batted .196 for Birmingham in 1948, .238 in 1949, and .226 with Chicago in 1950. In an interview with *Sports Collectors Digest* in 1993, Scott talked about how much he enjoyed his playing baseball for a living: "I really enjoyed my baseball career," Scott said. "We didn't play for the money because there wasn't a lot of money, but it was fun. I really enjoyed the game. Plus, it was better than actually working. . . . I think I was a good player. I was a decent hitter. My average was about .270 to .300 every year, and I was one of the best fielders in the Negro Leagues."

Scott, Robert

Robert Scott was an outfielder for the Lincoln Giants, Hilldale baseball club, and Brooklyn Royal Giants from 1920 to 1927.

Scott, Ted

Ted Scott was a catcher for the Washington Pilots in 1932.

Scott, William

William Scott was an officer with the Louisville Black Caps in 1932.

Scott, William, Jr.

William Scott, Jr., was an outfielder for the Birmingham Black Barons and Philadelphia Stars from 1950 to 1953.

Scott, Willie Lee

Willie Lee Scott was a first baseman for the Indianapolis ABC's, Louisville White Sox, Memphis Red Sox, Chicago American Giants, Homestead Grays, and Columbus Blue Birds from 1927 to 1938.

Scragg, Jesse

Jesse Scragg was a pitcher for the Philadelphia Giants in 1915.

Scroggins, John

John Scroggins was a pitcher for the Kansas City Monarchs in 1947.

Scruggs, Robert

Robert Scruggs was a pitcher for the Cleveland Buckeyes in 1950.

Scruggs, Willie

Willie Scruggs was a pitcher for the Cleveland Buckeyes, Louisville Buckeyes, Houston Eagles, Louisville Black Colonels, Birmingham Black Barons, and New Orleans Eagles from 1949 to 1954.

Seagraves, Sam

Sam Seagraves was a catcher for the Chicago American Giants in 1946.

Searcy, Kelly

Kelly Searcy was a pitcher for the Birmingham Black Barons and Baltimore Elite Giants from 1950 to 1955.

Seay, Richard William (Dick)

b 1904, d. 1981

Richard Seay was a shortstop and second baseman for the New York Black Yankees, Newark Browns, Pittsburgh Crawfords, Newark Eagles, Brooklyn Royal Giants, Philadelphia Stars, Newark Stars, Baltimore Black

Sox, and Pennsylvania Red Caps of New York from 1925 to 1947. He was on the East team that took the field in 1935 in the first EAST-WEST GAME, the Negro League All-Star contest. Seay, born in West New York, New Jersey, was also part of the "Million Dollar Infield" of the Newark Eagles, along with Ray Dandridge, Willie Wells, and Mule Suttles. In an interview with author John Holway on file at the National Baseball Hall of Fame, Seay recalled how he got his start in the Negro Leagues: "I was playing on a little sandlot team in West New York and the Pennsylvania Red Caps saw me and asked me to play with them," Seay said. "We weren't really Red Caps, we just played ball. The only time we'd work was maybe was the day before a holiday. We'd probably make $15 to $20 for that day. Mostly the players were college kids going through school." He is believed to have batted .340 in exhibition games against white major league players.

Segula, Percy

Percy Segula was a pitcher for the Milwaukee Bears, Kansas City Monarchs, and New Orleans Caufield Ads from 1921 to 1923.

Seldon, Alexander

Alexander Seldon was the manager of the Boston Resolutes in 1887.

Seldon, William H.

William Seldon was a pitcher and outfielder for the Cuban Giants, New York Gorhams, Boston Resolutes, Trenton Cuban Giants, York Cuban Giants, York Colored Monarchs, and Cuban X Giants from 1886 to 1899. Records show that in 1891 Seldon batted .326.

Semler, James (Soldier Boy)

James Semler, a numbers runner from Harlem, was an officer with the New York Black Yankees from 1932 to 1948.

Serrell, William (Bonnie)

b. 1922
William Serrell was a second baseman and third baseman for the Chicago American Giants and Kansas City Monarchs from 1941 to 1945 and again from 1949 to 1951. Records show that Serrell batted .376 with Kansas City in 1942, .321 in 1944, and .317 in 1951. The 5-foot-11, 160-pound Serrell, born in Dallas, Texas, also played in the Mexican League from 1945 to 1948 and again from 1952 to 1957. He also played for San Francisco in the Pacific Coast League in 1951. Serrell played winter baseball in Cuba and Puerto Rico. In a 1973 *Black Sports* article, Frank Duncan, Serrell's manager with the Monarchs, said that Serrell was an outstanding player—better than his more famous teammate in 1945, Jackie Robinson: "Jackie wasn't the best player on the club," Duncan said. "No, he wasn't. I knew I had a little kid named Bonnie Serrell at second—slender and hit, oh man he could hit that ball downtown and he wasn't bigger than a midget."

Shackleford, John G.

John Shackleford was a second baseman, third baseman, and manager for the Chicago American Giants, Cleveland Browns, Harrisburg Giants, Birmingham Black Barons, and Cleveland Clippers from 1924 to 1946. He also served as president of Branch Rickey's United States League in 1945.

Shanks, Hank

Hank Shanks was a first baseman for the Birmingham Black Barons in 1927.

Sharpe, Robert (Pepper)

Robert Sharpe was a pitcher and outfielder for the Chicago American Giants, Memphis Red Sox, and Chicago Brown Bombers from 1940 to 1949.

Shaw, Ted

Ted Shaw was a pitcher for the Detroit Stars, Memphis Red Sox, and Chicago American Giants from 1927 to 1931.

Sheelor, James

James Sheelor was a shortstop and second baseman for the Memphis Red Sox, and Chicago American Giants from 1952 to 1955.

Sheffey, Doug

Doug Sheffey was a pitcher for the Hilldale baseball club in 1910.

Shelby, Hiawatha

Hiawatha Shelby was an outfielder for the Philadelphia Stars and Indianapolis Clowns from 1941 to 1946.

Shepard, Freddie

Freddie Shepard was a pitcher and outfielder for the Chicago American Giants and Birmingham Black Barons from 1945 to 1948.

Shepard, Sam

Sam Shepard was an officer with the St. Louis Giants in the 1920s.

Shepard, Tommy

Tommy Shepard was a second baseman for the Birmingham Black Barons in 1945.

Sheppard, Ray

Ray Sheppard was a shortstop and third baseman for the Detroit Wolves, Homestead Grays, Birmingham Black Barons, Indianapolis ABC's, Detroit Stars, Kansas City Monarchs, and Monroe Monarchs from 1924 to 1932.

Sheppard, William

William Sheppard was a pitcher for the Memphis Red Sox and Kansas City Monarchs from 1922 to 1925.

Sherber, Jack

Jack Sherber was an infielder for the New Orleans Eagles in 1951.

Sherkliff, Roy

Roy Sherkliff was a pitcher for the Washington Pilots and Hilldale baseball club from 1931 to 1934.

Sherman, Art

Art Sherman was an outfielder for the New Orleans Eagles in 1951.

Shibe Park

Shibe Park was the Philadelphia Phillies' ballpark in Philadelphia that also hosted Negro League games, including the Hilldale baseball club and other teams. The ballpark was the site of the first black World Series in 1924 between the Hilldale club and the Kansas City Monarchs.

Shields, Charlie

Charlie Shields was a pitcher for the Homestead Grays, New York Cubans, and Chicago American Giants from 1941 to 1945.

Shields, Jimmy

Jimmy Shields was a pitcher for the Bacharach Giants in 1928 and 1929.

Shinn, William

William Shinn was a second baseman for the Louisville Black Caps and New York Black Yankees from 1941 to 1943.

Shipp, Jesse

Jesse Shipp was a pitcher for the New York Colored Giants and Brooklyn Royal Giants from 1908 to 1912.

Shively, George (Rabbit)

George Shively was an outfielder for the Bacharach Giants, Indianapolis ABC's, Bowser's ABC's, Washington Potomacs, Brooklyn Royal Giants, and West Baden Sprudels from 1911 to 1925.

Shorter, Jack

Jack Shorter was a third baseman for the New Orleans Eagles in 1951.

Shreveport Acme Giants

The Shreveport Acme Giants were a black baseball team out of Shreveport, Louisiana, that played in the 1930s and 1940s. One of their managers was Winfield Welch. They were a travel team for the most part and served as a feeder system for the Kansas City Monarchs.

Shreveport Black Sports

The Shreveport Black Sports were a black baseball team out of Shreveport, Louisiana, that played in the Texas Negro League in the 1920s.

Sierra, Felipe

Felipe Sierra was an infielder and outfielder for the Cuban Stars and All Cubans from 1921 to 1932.

Silva, Pedro

Pedro Silva was a pitcher and outfielder for the Cuban Stars and All Cubans in 1921 and 1922.

Silvers, Lindsay

Lindsay Silvers was an infielder for the Philadelphia Stars in 1933.

Simmons, Hubert
Hubert Simmons was a pitcher for the Baltimore Elite Giants in 1950.

Simms, Pete
Pete Simms was a catcher, third baseman, and outfielder for the Philadelphia Stars and Memphis Red Sox from 1952 to 1954.

Simms, Willie
Willie Simms was an outfielder for the Cincinnati Tigers, Monroe Monarchs, Kansas City Monarchs, and Chicago American Giants from 1934 to 1943.

Simpson, Harry Leon (Suitcase)
b. 1925, d. 1979

Harry Simpson was an outfielder for the Philadelphia Stars from 1946 to 1948, batting .242 in 1946 and .244 in 1947. Born in Atlanta, Georgia, the 6-foot-1, 180-pound Simpson went on to play eight major league seasons with the Cleveland Indians, Pittsburgh Pirates, New York Yankees, and Kansas City Athletics. He appeared in 888 games and batted .266, with 752 hits, 73 home runs, 343 runs scored, and 381 RBIs. He also played in the 1957 World Series for the Yankees, getting one hit and driving in one run in 12 at bats. Simpson also played for San Diego in the Pacific Coast League and Indianapolis in the American Association until 1963. He played in the Mexican League in 1963 and 1964. He played winter baseball in Puerto Rico and Cuba.

Simpson, Herbert
Herbert Simpson was a pitcher and outfielder for the Chicago American Giants, Birmingham Black Barons, and Homestead Grays from 1942 to 1951.

Simpson, James
James Simpson was an outfielder for the Trenton Cuban Giants and Philadelphia Pythians in 1886 and 1887.

Simpson, Lawrence
Lawrence Simpson was a pitcher and outfielder for the Chicago Giants, Chicago American Giants, Mohawk Giants, Bowser's ABC's, West Baden Sprudels, and Indianapolis ABC's from 1910 to 1920.

Sims, Harry
Harry Sims was a catcher, outfielder, and first baseman for the Philadelphia Stars in 1951 and 1952.

Sims, Leo
Leo Sims was a shortstop for the Atlanta Black Crackers in 1938.

Singer, Orville (Red)
Orville Singer was an infielder and outfielder for the Cleveland Browns, Cleveland Tigers, Cleveland Cubs, Cleveland Stars, and Lincoln Giants from 1921 to 1932.

Skinner, Floyd
Floyd Skinner was a catcher for the Kansas City Colored Giants in 1917.

Sloan, Robert
Robert Sloan was an outfielder for the Brooklyn Royal Giants from 1919 to 1921.

Smallwood, Dewitt
Dewitt Smallwood was an outfielder for the Philadelphia Stars, Indianapolis Clowns, Birmingham Black Barons, and New York Black Yankees from 1951 to 1954.

Smallwood, Louis
Louis Smallwood was a second baseman for the Chicago Giants and Milwaukee Bears from 1923 to 1929.

Smaulding, Owen
Owen Smaulding was a pitcher for the Cleveland Tigers, Kansas City Monarchs, Birmingham Black Barons, and Chicago American Giants in 1927 and 1928.

Smith, Alphonse (Al)
b. 1928

Alphonse Smith was an outfielder, third baseman, and shortstop for the Cleveland Buckeyes from 1946 to 1948, batting .285 in 1946, .300 in 1947, and .316 in 1948. The 6-foot-1, 190-pound Smith, born in Kirkwood, Missouri, went on to play 12 seasons in the major leagues for the Cleveland Indians, Chicago White Sox, Baltimore Orioles, and Boston Red Sox, retiring after the 1964 season. Smith batted .272 with 164 home runs, 843 runs scored, and 676 RBIs in 1,517 games. He also played winter baseball in the Puerto Rico Winter League.

Smith, Bob
Bob Smith was a catcher for the Detroit Stars in 1954.

Smith, Buster

Buster Smith was a pitcher and first baseman for the Birmingham Black Barons in 1932 and 1933.

Smith, Carl

Carl Smith was a catcher and third baseman for the Homestead Grays, Birmingham Black Barons, and Pittsburgh Crawfords from 1933 to 1938.

Smith, Charles (Chino)

b. 1903, d. 1932

Charles Smith was an outfielder and second baseman for the Brooklyn Royal Giants, Lincoln Giants, and Philadelphia Giants from 1924 to 1932, not playing in 1926. In an interview with author John Holway on file at the National Baseball Hall of Fame, Negro Leaguer Larry Brown spoke of Smith's batting skills: "He was one of the greatest hitters you ever saw," Brown said. "He'd hit them between them, over them, to the opposite field, in the trees, anywhere. And you know what he'd do? Spit at 'em, spit at the second strike and hit the third one."

In another Holway interview, pitcher Willie "Sug" Cornelius called Smith the best hitter he ever faced: "The best hitter I think I faced in my life was a boy named Chino Smith, who played for the Philadelphia Giants. That was the best man I ever faced. I know I had a good curveball and I had a good fast ball, and he hit me just like he knew what I was going to throw. . . . Smith would spit at the first two balls, then tell me, 'Young man, you've got yourself in trouble.' He was a good hitter."

Negro Leaguer Bill Holland, in another Holway interview, said he believed that Smith was better than good: "The greatest hitter I ever saw was a guy named Charlie 'Chino' Smith, who played right field for us on the Lincoln Giants," Holland said. "We called him 'Chino' because he had Chinese-looking eyes. Oscar Charleston was a good hitter, too, but Smith was better because he could hit all kinds of pitching—left-handers, right-handers—didn't mean a thing to him, he hit them all. He had great timing, good eyes. Some hitters are strictly inside ball hitters, everything inside they hit it. If you keep the ball outside, you got them. But if you pitched outside to Smitty, he'd hit the all to left field, a line drive over third base or something. If you pitched it inside, he'd hit it over the fence. That's where his power was, to right field. I think he hit the first colored home run in Yankee Stadium [Smith hit two home runs in the first Negro League baseball game at Yankee Stadium]. And this guy could do more with the fans down on him. He'd get up to bat and the pitcher would throw one in there and he'd spit at it. The fans would boo, and he's come out of the batter's box, turn around and make out like he was going to move towards them, and they'd shout, 'Come on.' He'd get back there and hit the ball out of the ballpark and go around the bases waving his arms at the stands."

Records show that Smith had a career batting average of .375, and batted .422 in 1927, .461 in 1929, when he also led the NEGRO AMERICAN LEAGUE with 23 home runs, and .429 in 1930. He also hit .405 in exhibition games against major league ballplayers.

Born in Greenwood, South Carolina, Smith was small but had a reputation as a tough fighter. The 5-foot-6, 170-pound Smith died at age 29 after contracting yellow fever during a season of winter baseball in Cuba.

Smith, Charlie

Charlie Smith was an infielder for the Washington Black Senators and Newark Eagles in 1938.

Smith, Clarence

Clarence Smith was an outfielder and manager for the Detroit Stars, Columbus Buckeyes, Baltimore Black Sox, Birmingham Black Barons, Bacharach Giants, Cleveland Cubs, and Chicago American Giants from 1921 to 1933.

Smith, Cleveland

Cleveland Smith was an infielder for the Lincoln Giants, Homestead Grays, Philadelphia Tigers, Homestead Grays, Newark Stars, and Harrisburgh Giants from 1922 to 1928.

Smith, Dode

Dode Smith was a pitcher for the Cincinnati–Cleveland Buckeyes in 1942.

Smith, Douglas

Douglas Smith was an officer with the Baltimore Elite Giants in 1943.

Smith, Ernest

Ernest Smith was a catcher for the Chicago American Giants and Monroe Monarchs from 1934 to 1940.

Smith, Eugene

Eugene Smith was a pitcher for the St. Louis Stars, New Orleans–St. Louis Stars, New York Black Yankees, Cleveland Buckeyes, Homestead Grays, Chicago American Giants, Kansas City Monarchs, and Louisville Buckeyes from 1939 to 1951.

Smith, Fred
Fred Smith was a catcher for the St. Louis Stars and Kansas City Monarchs in 1936 and 1946.

Smith, Gene
Gene Smith was a third baseman for the Cincinnati Buckeyes, Jacksonville Red Caps, Indianapolis Clowns, and Cleveland Buckeyes from 1942 to 1946.

Smith, George
b. 1937, d. 1987

George Smith was a second baseman and shortstop for the Indianapolis Clowns and Chicago American Giants in 1952, 1956, and 1957. The 5-foot-10, 180-pound Smith, born in St. Petersburg, Florida, went on to play minor league ball for Knoxville in the South Atlantic League, Denver in the American Association, Syracuse, Buffalo in the International League, and Phoenix and

Eugene Smith was a big right-handed pitcher who, like many Negro League players, moved around from team to team during his career. From 1939 to 1951, Smith pitched for the St. Louis Stars, New Orleans–St. Louis Stars, New York Black Yankees, Cleveland Buckeyes, Homestead Grays, Chicago American Giants, Kansas City Monarchs, and Louisville Buckeyes.
(NATIONAL BASEBALL HALL OF FAME LIBRARY, COOPERSTOWN, N.Y.)

Oklahoma City in the Pacific Coast League. Smith also played four major league seasons, from 1963 to 1966 for the Detroit Tigers and Boston Red Sox, batting .205 with 321 hits, 143 runs scored, and 158 RBIs in 438 games.

Smith, Harry
Harry Smith was an outfielder and first baseman for the Brooklyn Royal Giants, Genuine Cuban Giants, and Philadelphia Giants from 1902 to 1910.

Smith, Harry
Harry Smith was a white sportswriter with the *Philadelphia Tribune* who, along with Walter Schlichter, sports editor of the *Philadelphia Item*, started the Philadelphia Giants in 1902.

Smith, Harvey
Harvey Smith was a pitcher for the Washington Elite Giants and Pittsburgh Crawfords in 1937 and 1938.

Smith, Henry
Henry Smith was a shortstop and second baseman for the Cincinnati Clowns, Chicago American Giants, Jacksonville Red Caps, Cincinnati-Indianapolis Clowns, Indianapolis Clowns, and New York Black Yankees from 1942 to 1947.

Smith, Herb
Herb Smith was a pitcher for the Hilldale baseball club and Philadelphia Stars from 1930 to 1933.

Smith, Hilton Lee
b. 1912, d. 1983

Hilton Smith was a pitcher for the Monroe Monarchs, New Orleans Black Creoles, and Kansas City Monarchs from 1933 to 1948. In an interview with author John Holway on file at the National Baseball Hall of Fame, Negro Leaguer Newt Allen compared Smith to Satchel Paige: "Smith was a lot like Satchel when Satchel first came up," Allen said. "He had his stuff on the ball—curveball, fast ball. His fast ball had a bop on it, his curveball broke, fast and quick, up and down. He'd throw overhand and the ball would come up and break down. He pitched a no-hit ball game against Chicago. It was one of those days where they say you have a field day, everything we did was right. Balls that should have gone for base hits, our boys were standing right there, and we made some spectacular plays behind him. He beat them 3-0."

In another Holway interview, Kansas City catcher Joe Greene said Smith was the anchor of the Monarchs staff, despite the presence of Satchel Paige, and was a good hitter as well: "Hilton Smith was another pitcher who was really good," Greene said. "When anybody speaks about the pitchers on the Monarchs staff, they mention Satchel. But he'd only pitch three innings most of the time, and Smith would relieve him. Smith was a curveball pitcher. He had a real fast curveball. It wasn't a big one, but he had good control. The manager would call him in sometimes to make just one pitch. And he did a lot of the pinch-hitting too. He was a long ball hitter. He couldn't run, but he could really hit. The people knew Smith before they knew Satchel, because he was on the team before Satchel came to the Monarchs. But Satchel got the publicity. Satchel overshadowed him."

Another Negro Leaguer, James LaMarque, agreed: "There was a pitcher named Hilton Smith who was a very good pitcher who got no recognition, no publicity," LaMarque said in a July 1999 interview with *Sports Collectors Digest*: "He didn't do nothing but pitch. He kind of felt bad over the years because he didn't get any recognition. One of the reasons was because Satchel Paige was the drawing card. But he was as good as Satchel, and way back then he was throwing that forkball they talk about now, and he had a knuckler and everything. And he was a good hitter. I have seen him pinch-hit and he could hit the ball a long way, and you could hardly strike him out. He was just an outstanding ballplayer who got no recognition whatsoever."

Smith, Hy

Hy Smith was an outfielder for the Brooklyn Remsens in 1885.

Smith, James

James Smith was an infielder for the Leland Giants, Cuban X Giants, and Chicago Union Giants from 1903 to 1906.

Smith, James

James Smith was a shortstop for the Detroit Stars in 1925 to 1930.

Smith, John

John Smith was an outfielder and catcher for the Birmingham Black Barons in 1942.

Smith, John Ford
b. 1919, d. 1983
John Ford Smith was a pitcher and outfielder for the Chicago American Giants, Indianapolis Crawfords,

Kansas City Monarchs, Indianapolis ABC's, and New York Black Yankees from 1939 to 1950. The 6-foot-1, 200-pound Smith, born in Phoenix, Arizona, batted .378 for Chicago in 1944 and .303 in 1945, and hit .288 for Kansas City and New York in 1948.

Smith, Marshall

Marshall Smith was a pitcher for the Homestead Grays, Baltimore Black Sox, Madison Stars, and Richmond Giants from 1920 to 1924.

Smith, Milton
b. 1929
Milton Smith was an infielder for the Philadelphia Stars from 1949 to 1951. The 5-foot-10, 165-pound Smith, born in Columbus, Georgia, batted .205 for Philadelphia in 1949 and .224 in 1950. He went on to play minor league baseball with San Diego, Seattle, Hawaii, and Sacramento in the Pacific Coast League, Toronto in the International League, and Omaha in the American Association. Smith played one major league season with the Cincinnati Reds in 1955, appearing in 36 games with three home runs, 15 runs scored, and eight runs batted in. He also played winter baseball in the Cuban Winter League, the Dominican Republic, and Panama.

Smith, Monroe

Monroe Smith was an outfielder for the Kansas City Monarchs in 1944.

Smith, Oliver

Oliver Smith was a pitcher for the Cincinnati-Indianapolis Clowns in 1945.

Smith, Percy

Percy Smith was a pitcher for the Indianapolis Clowns from 1952 to 1954.

Smith, Pete

Pete Smith was an outfielder for the Pittsburgh Crawfords in 1937.

Smith, Quincy
b. 1921
Quincy Smith was an outfielder for the Birmingham Black Barons and Cleveland Buckeyes in 1943 and from 1945 to 1946. The 5-foot-11, 170-pound Smith batted .284 for Birmingham in 1945. Smith went on to play

minor league baseball from 1949 to 1954 in the Mississippi–Ohio Valley League.

Smith, Raymond

Raymond Smith was a pitcher for the Philadelphia Stars in 1945 and 1946.

Smith, Red

Red Smith was a pitcher and outfielder for the Lincoln Stars, Lincoln Giants, Hilldale baseball club, Brooklyn Royal Giants, and Bacharach Giants from 1912 to 1920.

Smith, Robert

Robert Smith was a catcher and third baseman for the Memphis Red Sox, Cincinnati Tigers, St. Louis Stars, New Orleans–St. Louis Stars, Chicago American Giants, Pittsburgh Crawfords, Cleveland Cubs, Nashville Elite Giants, and Birmingham Black Barons from 1930 to 1944.

Smith, Sonny

Sonny Smith was a pitcher for the Chicago American Giants in 1951.

Smith, Taylor

Taylor Smith was a pitcher for the Birmingham Black Barons and Chicago American Giants from 1948 to 1953.

Smith, Theolic

b. 1914

Theolic Smith was a pitcher for the St. Louis Stars, New Orleans–St. Louis Stars, Pittsburgh Crawfords, Kansas City Monarchs, Toledo Crawfords, Chicago American Giants, and Cleveland Buckeyes from 1936 to 1951.

Smith, Tobe

Tobe Smith was the owner of the Kansas City Giants from 1907 to 1914.

Smith, Turkey

Turkey Smith was a catcher for the Cincinnati Tigers in 1936.

Smith, Wardell

Wardell Smith was a pitcher for the Chicago American Giants in 1946.

Smith, Wendell

b. 1914, d. 1972

Wendell Smith was sports editor of the *Pittsburgh Courier*, one of the leading black newspapers in the country. Smith was one of the leading advocates of Negro League baseball and was inducted into the National Baseball Hall of Fame in 1994. Smith went to work for the *Courier* after studying at West Virginia State College, working there from 1937 to 1948, and was instrumental in Jackie Robinson's breaking the color barrier in major league baseball.

"Wendell's major ambition in life was to desegregate sports," Frank Golden, a *Courier* reporter and editor, told the *Pittsburgh Post-Gazette* in 1997: "He was vigilant about it, to the point that even some of us got tired of reading it." He had arranged for Robinson to have a tryout with the Boston Red Sox in 1945, along with Philadelphia Stars second baseman Marvin Williams and Cleveland Buckeyes outfielder Sam Jethroe. Nothing came of the tryout, but Smith met with Brooklyn Dodgers general manager Branch Rickey shortly after and told him about Robinson, suggesting he could be the player Rickey was looking for. "I will forever be indebted to Wendell because, without his even knowing it, his recommendation was in the end partly responsible for my career," Robinson wrote in his book *I Never Had It Made*. Another *Courier* reporter, Edna McKenzie, said the impact of Smith's work went beyond the sports pages: "I believe the NAACP and the *Courier* were the two greatest institutions in the world for the elevation of black people," McKenzie told the *Post-Gazette*. "What Wendell was doing was much more important than sports. He was breaking down racial barriers."

Pushing hard for integration, Smith would later attack owners of black baseball teams for holding up the movement of black players into the major league game. "All they cared about was the perpetuation of the slave trade they had developed," Smith wrote, according to Mark Ribowsky's book *A Complete History of the Negro Leagues: 1884–1955*. He wrote, "They will shout to the high heavens that racial progress comes first and baseball next. But actually the preservation of their shaky, littered, infested, segregated baseball domicile comes first, last and always."

Smith went on to work for the *Chicago Herald American* and later worked as a sports anchor for WGN-TV in Chicago and later to WBBM-TV. He also wrote a weekly column for the *Chicago Sun Times*. When black baseball began its sharp decline as major league baseball began to integrate, Smith wrote its obituary: "Nothing was killing Negro baseball but Democracy. The big league doors suddenly opened one day and when Negro players walked in, Negro baseball walked out," Smith wrote, quoted in Jules Tygiel's book *Jackie Robinson and His Legacy*.

Smith, William

William Smith was a second baseman and shortstop for the Newark Eagles in 1938.

Smith, William T. (Big Bill)

William Smith was an outfielder, catcher, and manager for the Cuban X Giants, Genuine Cuban Giants, Brooklyn Royal Giants, Philadelphia Giants, Mohawk Giants, Chicago Unions, Cuban Giants, Memphis Giants, St. Louis Black Stockings, Brooklyn All Stars, and New York Stars from 1883 to 1916.

Smith, Willie

Willie Smith was a pitcher for the Homestead Grays in 1948.

Smith, Willie (Wonderful Willie)

b. 1939

Willie Smith was a pitcher, first baseman, and outfielder for the Birmingham Black Barons from 1958 to 1959, batting .458 in 24 at bats for Birmingham in 1958. The 6-foot, 180-pound Smith, born in Anniston, Alabama, went on to play minor league baseball for Knoxville in the South Atlantic League, Duluth-Superior in the Northern League, Syracuse in the International League, Portland in the Pacific Coast League, and Indianapolis in the American Association in his first year of organized baseball in 1971. Smith played three major league seasons with the Detroit Tigers, Los Angeles Angels, Cleveland Indians, and Chicago Cubs in 1963, 1964, and 1968, appearing in 29 games and posting a 2-4 record with a 3.10 ERA.

Smith, Wyman

Wyman Smith was an outfielder for the Baltimore Black Sox from 1920 to 1925.

Snaer, Lucian

Lucian Snaer was an umpire in the NEGRO NATIONAL LEAGUE in the 1920s.

Snead, Sylvester

Sylvester Snead was a second baseman, shortstop, and outfielder for the Cincinnati Clowns, New York Black Yankees, and Kansas City Monarchs from 1939 to 1946. He batted .185 with Cincinnati in 1932 and .242 for New York in 1946. Snead went on to play minor league baseball in the Provincial League and the Manitoba-Dakota League.

Sneed, Eddie

Eddie Sneed was a pitcher for the Birmingham Black Barons from 1940 to 1942.

Snow, Felton

b. 1905

Felton Snow was a second baseman, third baseman, and manager for the Louisville Black Caps, Louisville White Sox, Columbus Elite Giants, Nashville Elite Giants, Washington Elite Giants, Baltimore Elite Giants, New Orleans Crescent Stars, Nashville Cubs, Cleveland Red Sox, and Philadelphia Stars from 1931 to 1947. Born in Oxford, Alabama, records show that the 5-foot-10, 155-pound Snow had a career batting average of .289.

Soler, Juan

Juan Soler was an infielder for the Detroit Stars in 1955.

Solis, Miguel

Miguel Solis was a third baseman and second baseman for the New York Cubans and Cuban Stars from 1928 to 1936.

Sosa, Ramon

Ramon Sosa was a catcher for the Homestead Grays in 1948.

Sostre, Francisco

Francisco Sostre was a pitcher for the New York Cubans in 1947.

Soto, Joseph

Joseph Soto was a catcher for the New Orleans Eagles in 1951.

Soto, Toney

Toney Soto was the manager of the Havana Cubans in 1917.

Souell, Herbert

b. 1913

Herbert Souell was an infielder for the Kansas City Monarchs from 1940 to 1951. Souell, born in West Monroe, Louisiana, batted .273 for Kansas City in 1942, .311 in 1943, .244 in 1944, and .277 in 1945. Records show he batted .302 in 1948, .255 in 1949, and .301 in 1950. Souell went on to play minor league baseball in the

Manitoba-Dakota League, the Western International League, and the Arizona-Mexico League until 1953. He also played winter baseball in Puerto Rico.

Southall, John
John Southall was a catcher for the Celeron New York, Acme Colored Giants in 1898.

Southern League of Colored Base Ballists
This was a league of black baseball teams organized in 1886 consisting of 10 teams: the Florida Clippers of Jacksonville, the Unions of New Orleans, the Macedonias of Jacksonville, the Eclipse of Memphis, the Georgia Champions of Atlanta, the Fultons of Charleston, the Eurekas of Memphis, the Broads of Savannah, the Lafayettes of Savannah, and the Athletics of Jacksonville. Some teams folded during the season and other new ones joined up—the Jerseys of Savannah, the Montgomery Blues, and the Roman Cities of Jacksonville—but the league lasted just one year.

Sowell, Clyde
Clyde Sowell was a pitcher for the Baltimore Elite Giants in 1948.

Sparks, Joe
Joe Sparks was a shortstop and second baseman for the Chicago American Giants and St. Louis Stars from 1937 to 1940.

Sparrow, Roy W.
Roy Sparrow was an officer with the Washington Black Senators in 1938.

Spearman, Alvin
Alvin Spearman was a pitcher for the Chicago American Giants in 1950 and 1951.

Spearman, Charles
Charles Spearman was a second baseman, third baseman, and catcher for the Cleveland Elites, Brooklyn Royal Giants, Lincoln Giants, Homestead Grays, and Pennsylvania Red Caps of New York from 1919 to 1931.

Spearman, Clyde
Clyde Spearman was an outfielder for the New York Black Yankees, Pittsburgh Crawfords, Newark Eagles, New York Cubans, Chicago American Giants, Birmingham Black Barons, and Philadelphia Stars from 1932 to 1946. He was one of a group of black players who left the Negro Leagues in 1937 to play in dictator Rafael Trujillo's political baseball war that year. Spearman played for one of Trujillo's opponents, the team in San Pedro de Macoris.

Spearman, Henry
Henry Spearman was a third baseman and first baseman for the Pittsburgh Crawfords, Homestead Grays, New York Black Yankees, Washington Black Senators, Newark Eagles, Philadelphia Stars, and Baltimore Elite Giants from 1932 to 1946. Spearman was part of a trade, along with Pepper Bassett, for Josh Gibson, with Gibson going from the Pittsburgh Crawfords to the Homestead Grays in 1937.

Spearman, Jim
Jim Spearman was a pitcher for the Chicago American Giants in 1951.

Spearman, William
William Spearman was a pitcher for the Cleveland Hornets, Cleveland Elites, Memphis Red Sox, St. Louis Stars, and Nashville Elite Giants from 1923 to 1929.

Spedden, Charles P.
Charles Spedden was a white bartender from Baltimore who was an officer and owner of the Baltimore Black Sox from 1922 to 1931.

Speedy, Walter
Walter Speedy was an infielder for the Chicago American Giants in 1914.

Spencer, Joseph
Joseph Spencer was a second baseman and shortstop for the Homestead Grays, Birmingham Black Barons, New York Cubans, Pittsburgh Crawfords, New York Black Yankees, and Baltimore Elite Giants from 1942 to 1950.

Spencer, William (Pee Wee)
William Spencer was a catcher, third baseman, and manager for the Toledo Crawfords, Indianapolis Crawfords, Chicago American Giants, and Toledo Cubs from 1933 to 1940 and again in 1945.

Spencer, Willie

Willie Spencer was an outfielder for the Birmingham Black Barons in 1941.

Spencer, Zake

Zake Spencer was a pitcher for the Columbus Blue Birds, Chicago Columbia Giants, Cleveland Cubs, and Detroit Stars from 1931 to 1933.

Spotsville, Roy

Roy Spotsville was a pitcher for the Houston Eagles and New Orleans Eagles in 1950 and 1951.

Spring Valley Giants

The Spring Valley Giants were an interracial baseball team operated by Robert P. Gilkerson in Spring Valley, Illinois, in 1918.

Stamps, Hulan

Hulan Stamps was a left-handed pitcher for the Detroit Stars, Memphis Red Sox, and Indianapolis ABC's from 1924 to 1933.

Stankie, Eddie

Eddie Stankie was an outfielder for the Birmingham Black Barons in 1951.

Stanley, John Wesley

John Wesley Stanley was a pitcher for the Lincoln Giants, Quaker Giants, Bacharach Giants, Brooklyn Royal Giants, Hilldale baseball club, Philadelphia Stars, New York Cubans, New York Black Yankees, and Baltimore Black Sox from 1928 to 1949.

Staples, John

John Staples was manager of the Montgomery Grey Sox in 1921.

Starks, James

James Starks was a first baseman for the New York Black Yankees, Harrisburg–St. Louis Stars, and Pittsburgh Crawfords from 1937 to 1946.

Starks, Leslie

Leslie Starks was an outfielder for the Kansas City Monarchs, Newark Eagles, and Memphis Red Sox in 1927 and from 1933 to 1935.

Starks, Otis

Otis Starks was a pitcher for the Chicago American Giants, Brooklyn Royal Giants, Hilldale baseball club, Bacharach Giants, Lincoln Giants, St. Louis Giants, and Newark Stars from 1919 to 1939.

Stars Park

Stars Park was the home of the St. Louis Stars.

Stearman, Tom

Tom Stearman was an outfielder for the Kansas City Giants in 1909 and 1915.

Stearnes, Gerald

Gerald Stearnes was a catcher for the New Orleans Eagles in 1951.

Stearnes, Norman Thomas (Turkey)
b. 1901, d. 1979

Norman Stearnes was an outfielder for the Montgomery Grey Sox, Nashville Giants, Lincoln Giants, Detroit Stars, Chicago American Giants, Cole's American Giants, Kansas City Monarchs, Toledo Cubs, Detroit Stars, and Philadelphia Stars from 1920 to 1942 and again in 1945. Stearnes was the leading vote getter chosen by fans to play in the first Negro League All-Star Game, called the EAST-WEST GAME, in 1933. He was one of the best sluggers in Negro League baseball. In an interview with author John Holway in *Blackball Stars*, Cool Papa Bell said "There was no ball player I know that hit more home runs than Turkey Stearnes. And he was one of our best all- around ball players. Everybody knows he was a great outfielder. He could field, throw, run, hit." In another Holway interview, Stearnes said he never counted his home runs: "I hit so many I never counted them, and I'll tell you why. If they didn't win a ball game, they didn't amount to anything. It didn't make any difference if I hit four or five over the grandstand. It didn't make any difference to me, as long as I hit them to try to win the game. That's what I wanted, to win the game. . . . As long as I was winning, I wouldn't think about it. . . . I remember one year, my first year with Detroit in 1923, I think I hit about 50-some. But after I was up here for about a year, I hit so many that that's the reason I didn't count them." Statistics show that Stearnes hit at least 160 home runs against Negro League competition and far more against lesser teams and other opponents. He also had a career batting average of .352, and he hit .430 in his best season in 1935. He also batted .353 in his rookie season with Detroit in 1923, followed by a .346 average in 1924 and .364 in 1925. Stearnes also batted .313 against major

(Left) Norman "Turkey" Stearnes was up there among the biggest bats in Negro League baseball. An outfielder, Stearnes hit at least 160 home runs against Negro League competition and far more against lesser teams and other opponents. In a 23-year career, Stearnes batted .352 and was a fan favorite, the leading vote-getter in a ballot of fans conducted in the black press to play in the first Negro League All-Star Game, called the East-West Game, in 1933.   (NATIONAL BASEBALL HALL OF FAME LIBRARY, COOPERSTOWN, N.Y.)

(Below) Much of life in the Negro Leagues was spent barnstorming, traveling around the country playing small town teams, sometimes as many as 200 games a year. Pictured here while on the road are three Negro League greats with their teammates—Turkey Stearnes, third from the left; Newt Allen, far left; and Bullet Joe Rogan, far right.
(NATIONAL BASEBALL HALL OF FAME LIBRARY, COOPERSTOWN, N.Y.)

league ballplayers in exhibition games. He was a fanatic about hitting, as evidenced by this story teammate Buck O'Neil wrote in his autobiography, *I Was Right on Time*. "One time after a tough loss the Monarchs were in the hotel eating dinner, and the manager, Frank Duncan, asked me to go check on the Gobbler—that's another thing we called Turkey, you see. So I knocked on the Gobbler's door, and he said, 'Come in,' and there he was, sitting in the middle of his bed dressed in his pajamas talking to his bats. He said to the 34-incher, 'I used you and only hit the ball up against the fence.' Then he turned to the 35-incher and said, 'If I had picked you, I would have hit the ball over the fence and we would have tied the game.'" Stearnes was inducted into the National Baseball Hall of Fame in 2000.

Steel, Harry

Harry Steel was a pitcher for the Indianapolis ABC's in 1938.

Steele, Edward

b. 1915

Edward Steele was an outfielder for the Detroit Stars and Birmingham Black Barons from 1941 to 1955 and again in 1958. Born in Selma, Alabama, the 5-foot-10, 195-pound Steele batted .303 for Birmingham in 1944, .352 in 1945, .300 in 1948, .316 in 1949, .306 in 1950, and .370 in 1951. Steele went on to play minor league baseball in the Western League, Texas League, and Pacific Coast League.

Steele, Willie

Willie Steele was an outfielder for the Kansas City Monarchs in 1953.

Stephens, Joseph

Joe Stephens was a pitcher for the New York Black Yankees from 1949 to 1950.

Stephens, Paul (Jake)

Paul Stephens was a shortstop for the Homestead Grays, Philadelphia Giants, Hilldale baseball club, New York Black Yankees, Philadelphia Stars, and Pittsburgh Crawfords from 1921 to 1937. In an interview with author John Holway on file at the National Baseball Hall of Fame, Negro League pitcher Holsey "Scrip" Lee, a teammate of Stephens on the Hilldale club, said that Stephens was one of the best shortstops he had ever seen: "Stephens was the smallest man on the club," Lee said. "And he was the best glove man I know. If the ball hopped bad, he hopped with

it. Yes sir, he'd round those balls up and set himself and throw and be in position where another man would be out of position to throw. How he could jump in position like that I don't know. And he was a pretty good bunter. He could fool the opposition. He'd go back with his bat like he was going to swing, and then just turn it like that and tap the ball. And he was fast, too."

In another Holway interview on file at the Hall of Fame, Stephens said it was his glove that made him a ballplayer: "I had long range in the field, but I was a poor hitter," he said. "I never could hit that curveball. They learned how to hug me with it, and I'd back away, turn my head and fall away." But he would eventually learn to bunt and use his bat and wound up with a career batting average of .258, with a .350 average in 1935 for Philadelphia. He was a standout infielder, and when Stephens played for the Philadelphia in 1934, he teamed up with second baseman Dick Seay to form an outstanding double-play combination that helped the Stars win the NEGRO AMERICAN LEAGUE championship. In the Holway interview, Stephens recounted his experience playing against major league players in barnstorming exhibitions: "I played against Lefty Grove, Rube Walberg, Grover Alexander. . . . We played against Alexander eight or nine times. . . . He was one of the greatest. He played with the House of David then. He'd only pitch three innings. We toured with them two or three weeks at a time twice a year. But I'll tell you the fellow who gave me the most trouble was Dizzy Dean, because he would knock you down. I was the lead-off man and he'd throw at the back of my head, trying to deprive me of my living." He also said that when he first began playing Negro League baseball, it was against his family's wishes: "My father didn't want me to play, so in order to play baseball, you know what I had to do? A train left for Philadelphia at 11 that night, so I yawned and said, 'Well, I think I'll go upstairs and go to bed.' I went upstairs and climbed down the back balcony and hopped the train."

Stevens, Frank

Frank Stevens was an outfielder, pitcher, and first baseman for the Indianapolis ABC's, Chicago American Giants, Toledo Tigers, Cleveland Hornets, Cleveland Tigers, Cuban Stars, and St. Louis Stars from 1921 to 1931.

Stevens, Jim

Jim Stevens was a second baseman for the Philadelphia Stars in 1933.

Stevenson, Lefty

Lefty Stevenson was a pitcher and outfielder for the Indianapolis ABC's, Cleveland Tigers, and Birmingham Black Barons from 1925 to 1928.

Stevenson, Willie

Willie Stevenson was a pitcher for the Homestead Grays in 1940 and 1943.

Stewart, Artis

Artis Stewart was a pitcher for the Cleveland Buckeyes in 1950.

Stewart, Charles

b. 1928, d. 1992

Charles Stewart was an outfielder for the Chicago American Giants in 1951.

Stewart, Frank

Frank Stewart was a pitcher for the Indianapolis ABC's, Washington Elite Giants, and Memphis Red Sox from 1936 to 1940.

Stewart, Leon

Leon Stewart was a pitcher and outfielder for the Newark Eagles and Birmingham Black Barons from 1940 to 1942.

Stewart, Leslie

Leslie Stewart was a catcher for the Philadelphia Giants in 1922.

Stewart, Manuel

Manuel Stewart was a third baseman and pitcher for the Baltimore Elite Giants from 1943 to 1947.

Stewart, Riley

Riley Stewart was a pitcher for the New York Cubans, Memphis Red Sox, and Chicago American Giants from 1946 to 1950.

Stiles, Norris

Norris Stiles was a pitcher for the Cleveland Buckeyes in 1950.

Stills, Jimmy

Jimmy Stills was an outfielder for the Pittsburgh Crawfords from 1928 to 1931.

Stockard, Theodore

Theodore Stockard was a shortstop and third baseman for the Cleveland Tigers, Cleveland Hornets, and Kansas City Monarchs from 1927 to 1928 and again in 1937.

Stockley, Lawrence

Lawrence Stockley was an outfielder for the New York Black Yankees in 1950.

Stone, Ed

Ed Stone was an outfielder for the Brooklyn Eagles, Bacharach Giants, Philadelphia Stars, Newark Eagles, New York Black Yankees, and Pittsburgh Crawfords from 1931 to 1950.

Stone, Toni

b. 1921, d. 1996

Marcenia Lyle, otherwise known as Toni "Tomboy" Stone, made her mark in baseball history as the first woman ever to play professional baseball in the United States. Her opportunity came when Negro baseball was coming to an end, as she played for the San Francisco Sea Lions, New Orleans Black Pelicans, New Orleans Creoles, Indianapolis Clowns, and Kansas City Monarchs from 1949 to 1954.

Stone was born in St. Paul, Minnesota, one of four children. She was an outstanding athlete as a young girl and caught the attention of Gabby Street, a former major league catcher and the manager of a minor league team in St. Paul, and Street invited Stone to come to his camp. With integration in major league baseball draining the talent from the Negro Leagues, remaining teams turned to gimmicks. No team used more box office tricks than the Indianapolis Clowns, often referred to as the Harlem Globetrotters of baseball. One gimmick they used was signing Stone to a contract in 1953. She was brought in to draw fans, but she was a respectable athlete who could play with most of the players in Negro baseball. She batted .243 in 50 games with the Clowns that season and played a solid second base.

The highlight of her career came during a 1953 exhibition game, when Satchel Paige pitched against the Clowns. A large crowd turned out to see Stone bat against Paige, who had told Clowns owner Ed Hammond that he was not going to go easy on Stone. During these games, Paige, ever the showman, asked batters where they wanted the pitch, and they still rarely got a hit. When Stone came to the plate, the story goes that Paige yelled, "How do you like it?" Stone said she yelled back, "It doesn't matter. Just don't hurt me." After looking at two strikes, Stone connected on a single to center. "It was the happiest moment of my life," she said.

Stone played for the Kansas City Monarchs the following season. But her life was difficult on the Monarchs. Her teammates resented her presence, and she left the game after the 1954 season. "I suffered on that team," she said. She reportedly continued to play in men's amateur baseball leagues until she was 60 years old. A pioneer in women's sports, Stone married a pioneer as well—Aurelious Alberga—in 1950, a World War I hero who was credited with being the first black officer in the U.S. Army. In 1997, one year after her death at the age of 75, Stone posthumously was awarded the Wilma Rudolph Award on National Girls and Women in Sports Day.

Stoval, Fred

Fred Stoval was a Southern businessman who owned the Monroe (Louisiana) Monarchs in the 1930s and also financed the Negro Southern League. In an interview with *Black Ball News* in 1993, former Negro Leaguer Marlin Carter talked about how Stoval operated as an owner: "Fred Stoval was a very wealthy man," Carter said. "On his plantation he built a ballpark for his team. He also built a recreation center where the players relaxed when we weren't playing. Stoval spent a lot of money on his ball team. The players lived in houses on Stoval's plantation, and our meals were prepared by a cook that Stoval employed. In 1932, he bought three brand-new Fords for the team to travel in. But, most importantly, we always got paid. All the way around, the Monarchs were a pretty classy operation."

Stovey, George Washington

George Washington Stovey was a pitcher and outfielder who was one of a group of black players who also played for white International League teams near the turn of the 20th century until they were run out of the league by Cap Anson, player-manager of the Chicago White Stockings, who in particular once barred Stovey from taking the field in Newark before a game. Stovey played for the Cuban Giants, Cuban X Giants, York Cuban Giants, Trenton Cuban Giants, Ansonia Cuban Giants, and New York Gorhams, in addition to Newark in the International League, Jersey City in the Eastern League, Worchester in the Northeastern League, and Troy in the New York State League from 1886 to 1896. Stovey was considered one of the greatest pitchers in early black baseball, and Mark Ribowsky in his book *A Complete History of the Negro Leagues: 1884–1955* found this colorful account in the *Binghamton Leader* newspaper of a Stovey appearance: "Well, they put Stovey in the box again yesterday. You recollect Stovey, of course—the brunette fellow with the sinister fin and demonic delivery. Well, he pitched again yesterday, and . . . he teased the [Bridegrooms]. He has such a knack of tossing up balls that appear as large as an alderman's opinion of himself, but you cannot hit 'em with a cellar door. . . . What's the use of bucking against a fellow that can throw at the flagstaff and make it curve into the water bucket?" He was one of a group of black players that

played in the white International League in 1887 and won 35 games for Newark. He had a minor league career record of 60-40 with a 2.17 ERA.

Stratton, Felton

Felton Stratton was a catcher for the Hilldale baseball club in 1930.

Stratton, Leroy

Leroy Stratton was an infielder and manager for the Milwaukee Bears, Nashville Giants, Chicago American Giants, Nashville Elite Giants, and Birmingham Black Barons from 1920 to 1933.

Streeter, Sam (Lefty)

b. 1900

Sam Streeter was a left-handed pitcher for the Atlanta Black Crackers, Chicago American Giants, Montgomery Grey Sox, Birmingham Black Barons, Lincoln Giants, Bacharach Giants, Baltimore Black Sox, Pittsburgh Crawfords, Cleveland Cubs, and Homestead Grays from 1920 to 1936. Streeter, whose best pitch was a spitball, led the Montgomery Grey Sox to the Negro Southern League's first championship in 1920. He played in the first Negro League All-Star Game in 1933, the EAST-WEST GAME. Born in New Market, Alabama, the 5-foot-8, 170-pound Streeter would go on to pitch a half-dozen no-hit games. Records show that he posted an 11-2 mark in 1932 and a 9-1 record for Pittsburgh in 1934.

Streets, Albert

Albert Streets was an infielder for the Chicago American Giants in 1925.

Strong, Fulton

Fulton Strong was a pitcher for the Chicago American Giants, Cleveland Tate Stars, Milwaukee Bears, and New Orleans Crescent Stars from 1922 to 1923.

Strong, Henry

Henry Strong was a shortstop for the Chicago American Giants in 1936.

Strong, Joseph

Joseph Strong was a pitcher for the St. Louis Stars, Hilldale baseball club, Baltimore Black Sox, and Homestead Grays from 1922 to 1937.

Strong, Nat

b. 1874, d. 1935

Nat Strong was an owner, officer, and booking agent for the New York Black Yankees, Cuban Stars, and Brooklyn Royal Giants from 1908 to 1934. A white businessman, Strong got involved in the business of baseball after he graduated from City College in New York when he began investing in local semipro teams and also began purchasing such playing fields as Dexter Park and Brighton Oval. Strong collected fees from teams using these fields, such as the Cuban Giants and Cuban X-Giants. Strong became partners with Walter Schlichter, owner of the Philadelphia Giants. Strong would later take over operation of the Brooklyn Royal Giants and became the most powerful force in New York baseball in the early 1900s. "A black club wanting to do business with Strong did so on his terms. . . . Strong could virtually make or break a club in the lucrative New York market," wrote Rob Ruck in *Sandlot Seasons*. In a 1927 article in the *Pittsburgh Courier*, Negro League player, manager, and historian Sol White named Strong as one of the greatest figures in the history of Negro League baseball. However, Strong would lose his grip on black baseball in battles with Rube Foster, owner of the Chicago American Giants and founder of the NEGRO NATIONAL LEAGUE, and Ed Bolden, owner of the Hilldale baseball club, though Strong would later become partners with Bolden in the EASTERN COLORED LEAGUE. Strong was also the owner of the Brooklyn Bushwicks, a white semipro team in Brooklyn that featured a number of future major league players, and he also formed a booking partnership with another white businessman who would make his mark in black baseball, Eddie Gottlieb of Philadelphia. Strong died of a heart attack in 1935.

Strong, Othello

Othello Strong was a pitcher for the Chicago American Giants from 1949 to 1952.

Strong, Ted

Ted Strong was an outfielder, infielder, and manager for the Indianapolis ABC's, Indianapolis Athletics, Indianapolis Clowns, Chicago American Giants, and Kansas City Monarchs from 1937 to 1951. Strong also played basketball for the Harlem Globetrotters. In his autobiography, *I Was Right on Time*, Negro Leaguer Buck O'Neil wrote that Strong was the tallest shortstop he had ever seen: "Ted Strong, who moved to the outfield a little later on, was our shortstop, maybe the tallest shortstop ever to play the game. He was darn near seven feet tall, a switch-hitter with tremendous power. I saw him hit mammoth home runs from both sides of the plate in one game. Ted was like Cal Ripken, only bigger. They put him at shortstop because he had great hands and a rifle arm. In fact, he was one of the first real tall guys who could do a lot of things."

Strothers, C. W. (Colonel)

C. W. Strothers was an owner and officer with the Harrisburg Giants from 1924 to 1927.

Strothers, Sam

Sam Strothers was a catcher, second baseman, and first baseman for the Chicago American Giants, Leland Giants, Chicago Union Giants, Chicago Giants, and West Baden Sprudels from 1907 to 1918.

Stuart, Joseph

Joseph Stuart was a catcher and pitcher for the Brooklyn Atlantics in 1884 and 1885.

Stubblefield, Mickey

Mickey Stubblefield was a pitcher for the Kansas City Monarchs in 1948.

Sulphur Dell

Sulphur Dell, in Nashville, Tennessee, was the home of the Nashville Elite Giants in 1933 and 1934. It had a seating capacity of about 7,000 and had been built in the 1870s.

Summerall, William (Big Red)

William Summerall was a pitcher for the Memphis Red Sox and St. Louis Stars from 1936 to 1940.

Summers, Lonnie

b. 1915

Lonnie Summers was a catcher and outfielder for the Chicago American Giants and Baltimore Elite Giants from 1938 to 1951. The 6-foot, 210-pound Summers, born in Davis, Oklahoma, played minor league baseball for San Diego in the Pacific Coast League, Lincoln in the Western League, Oklahoma City in the Texas League, and Yakima in the Western International League. Summers also played several years in the Mexican League. He also played winter baseball in Puerto Rico.

Summers, Smith

Smith Summers was an outfielder for the Toledo Tigers, Baltimore Elite Giants, Cleveland Browns, Cleveland Tigers, Cleveland Hornets, and Chicago American Giants from 1923 to 1929.

Sunkatt, Pete

Pete Sunkatt was a pitcher for the Philadelphia Stars from 1943 to 1945.

Surratt, Alfred (Slick)

Alfred Surratt was an outfielder for the Kansas City Monarchs from 1949 to 1951.

Susini, Antonio

Antonio Susini was a second baseman and shortstop for the All Cubans in 1921.

Suttles, Earl

Earl Suttles was a first baseman for the Cleveland Buckeyes in 1950.

Suttles, George (Mule)

b. 1901, d. 1968

George Suttles was a first baseman, outfielder, and manager for the Baltimore Black Sox, St. Louis Stars, Detroit Wolves, Birmingham Black Barons, Cole's American Giants, Chicago American Giants, Washington Pilots, New York Black Yankees, Newark Eagles, Bacharach Giants, and Lincoln Giants from 1918 to 1948. Suttles, born in Brockton, Alabama, was a big man, at 6-feet-6 and weighing as much as 270 pounds and was described in a 1934 article in the *Chicago Defender* as "as big as a mountain and that weight is solid bone and muscle. Mule isn't fat, he's just big. . . . What a ballplayer the big fellow is. He is the greatest hitter this side of Babe Ruth." Suttles played in the first Negro League All-Star Game, the EAST-WEST GAME, in 1933 and was the hero of the 1935 East-West Game, which went down in history as one of the greatest games in Negro League history. Suttle's performance in that game was written up the next day in a glowing report in the *Pittsburgh Courier* by William Nunn: "Suttles threw his mighty body into motion. His foot moved forward. His huge shoulder muscles bunched. Came a swish through the air, a crack as of a rifle, and like a projectile hurled from a cannon, the ball started its meteoric flight. On a line it went. It was headed towards right center. Bell and Gibson were away with the crack of the bat. But so was [Paul] Arnold, center fielder of the East team, and [Alejandro] Oms, dependable and dangerous Cuban star, who patrolled the right garden. No one thought the ball could carry into the stands. . . . The ball continued on its course and the packed stands rose to their feet. Was it going to be caught? Was it going to hit the stands? No, folks! That ball, ticketed by Mule Suttles, CLEARED the distant fence in far away right center, landing 475 feet from home plate. It was a Herculean swat. One of the greatest in baseball. As cheering momentarily hushed in the greatest tribute an athlete can ever receive, we in the press box heard it strike the back of a seat with a resounding thud, and then go bounding merrily on its way. And then . . . pandemonium broke loose. Suttles completed his trip home, the third base line filled with playmates anxious to draw him to their breasts. Over the stands came a surging mass of humanity."

Suttles played in five East-West All-Star games. Suttles was also part of the Newark Eagles "Million Dollar Infield" of 1937. He is believed to have hit 150 home runs during his career against Negro League competition. One game in Memphis, Suttles hit three home runs in one inning. His best season was 1926, when he led the NEGRO NATIONAL LEAGUE with 26 home runs, a .418 batting average, 19 triples, and an astounding .830 slugging average. He hit 11 home runs in 79 at bats against white major league players over his career. Suttles was known for hitting the ball as hard and as far as anyone in Negro League baseball, using a bat that some reports said was 50 ounces. He hit one in Tropical Park in Havana, Cuba, that reportedly traveled nearly 600 feet. It was such a blow that a plaque was put up where the ball landed. He finished his career with a .351 average.

Sutton, Leroy

Leroy Sutton was a pitcher for the Boston Blues, New Orleans–St. Louis Stars, Cincinnati-Indianapolis Clowns, and Chicago American Giants from 1940 to 1946.

Sweatt, George (Never)

George Sweatt was a second baseman, third baseman, and outfielder for the Kansas City Monarchs, Chicago American Giants, and Chicago Giants from 1921 to 1928.

Sykes, Franklin (Doc)

d. 1987

Franklin Sykes was a pitcher for the Hilldale baseball club, Lincoln Stars, Philadelphia Giants, Brooklyn Royal Giants, and Baltimore Black Sox from 1913 to 1926. His best pitch was the spitball.

Sykes, Joe

Joe Sykes was an outfielder for the Cincinnati Clowns in 1942.

Sykes, Melvin

Melvin Sykes was an outfielder for the Hilldale baseball club and Lincoln Giants in 1926.

T

Taborn, Earl

Earl Taborn was a catcher for the Kansas City Monarchs from 1946 to 1951. He was also sold to the New York Yankees organization and played for the Yankees Class AAA team in Newark in 1949.

Talbert, Dangerfield

Dangerfield Talbert was a third baseman for the Chicago Union Giants, Leland Giants, Cuban X Giants, Chicago Unions, and Algona Brownies from 1900 to 1911.

Talbert, James

James Talbert was a catcher for the Chicago American Giants in 1947 and 1948.

Tampa Black Smokers

The Tampa Black Smokers were a black baseball team that played in Tampa, Florida, in the 1930s.

Tapley, John

John Tapley was a third baseman for the Akron Tyrites in 1933.

Tapley, Townsend

Townsend Tapley was a shortstop for the Akron Tyrites in 1933.

Tate, George

George Tate was an officer with the Cleveland Tate Stars from 1918 to 1923 and also served as vice president of the NEGRO NATIONAL LEAGUE.

Tate, Roosevelt (Speed)

Roosevelt Tate was an outfielder for the Nashville Elite Giants, Memphis Red Sox, Birmingham Black Barons, Knoxville Giants, Cincinnati Tigers, Chicago American Giants, Louisville Black Caps, and Louisville White Sox from 1931 to 1937.

Tatum, Reece (Goose)

Reece Tatum was an outfielder and first baseman for the Minneapolis–St. Paul Gophers, Cincinnati Clowns, Birmingham Black Barons, Cincinnati-Indianapolis Clowns, Indianapolis Clowns, and Zulu Cannibal Giants from 1941 to 1949. Tatum was better known as a star with the Harlem Globetrotters basketball team rather than as a baseball player. In an interview with author John Holway on file at the National Baseball Hall of Fame, Negro Leaguer Othello Renfroe said that Tatum "was a showman all the way. Played first base for the Indianapolis Clowns. Tatum was a fair player, not major league timber, but he got the job done. Tremendous fielder around first base. . . . He was very moody, though. Very moody. Did Hilton Smith ever tell you about

Goose Tatum? Goose Tatum stabbed him one time with a screwdriver."

Taylor, Alfred

Alfred Taylor was a first baseman for the Akron Tyrites and Cincinnati Tigers in 1933 and 1936.

Taylor, Benjamin

Benjamin Taylor was a pitcher for the New York Black Yankees in 1947.

Taylor, Benjamin H.

b. 1888, d. 1953

Ben Taylor was a first baseman and manager for the Indianapolis ABC's, Chicago American Giants, Bacharach Giants, St. Louis Giants, Harrisburg Giants, Washington Potomacs, Baltimore Stars, Baltimore Black Sox, Washington Black Senators, New York Cubans, and Brooklyn Eagles from 1913 to 1940. Records show that he batted .354 during his Negro League career and batted .421 in 1921, followed by a .362 mark in 1922. Taylor, born in Anderson, South Carolina, was part of a family affair in the Negro Leagues, along with his brothers Candy Jim, C. I., and Johnny. He was also an umpire in the East-West League in 1932.

Taylor, Charles (C. I.)

b. 1872, d. 1922

C. I. Taylor was a second baseman and manager for the West Baden Sprudels, Birmingham Giants, and Indianapolis ABC's from 1904 to 1922. He also served as vice president of the NEGRO NATIONAL LEAGUE. Taylor was one of the greatest managers in the history of Negro League baseball. Negro League player, manager, and historian Sol White, in a 1927 article in the *Pittsburgh Courier*, named Taylor one of the greatest figures in Negro League baseball history. Taylor managed the Birmingham Giants and moved that team to West Baden, Indiana, where they were called the Sprudels. In 1914, Taylor purchased a half interest in the Indianapolis ABC's and stocked the team with many of his players from the Sprudels and Giants. Taylor later brought up a group of players from the San Antonio Black Aces, such as Crush Holloway, who, in an interview with author John Holway on file at the National Baseball Hall of Fame, praised Taylor's managerial skills: "C. I. was a great manager, a builder, a perfect gentleman," Holloway said. "He knew how to handle men. He made a ballplayer out of me. He instilled that great thing in me—'Be a ballplayer, but be a gentleman.' He was a strict man. I

thought he was a preacher." Taylor was part of a family affair in the Negro Leagues, along with his brothers Candy Jim, Ben, and Johnny.

Taylor, Cyrus

Cyrus Taylor was an outfielder for the Harrisburg Giants, Lincoln Giants, and Baltimore Black Sox from 1923 to 1925.

Taylor, George

George Taylor was a first baseman, catcher, infielder, and outfielder for the Page Fence Giants, Chicago Union Giants, Leland Giants, Lincoln, Nebraska, Giants, and teams in Aspen and Denver in the Colorado State League and Beatrice in the Nebraska State League from 1889 to 1906.

Taylor, James (Candy Jim)

b. 1884, d. 1948

James Taylor was a third baseman, second baseman, and manager for the St. Paul Gophers, Birmingham Giants, Indianapolis ABC's, St. Louis Giants, Cleveland Tate Stars, Dayton Marcos, Cleveland Elite Giants, St. Louis Stars, Chicago American Giants, Washington Elite Giants, Baltimore Elite Giants, Homestead Grays, and Leland Giants from 1904 to 1948. He managed three Negro National League teams to titles—the 1928 St. Louis Stars and the 1943 and 1944 Homestead Grays, winning the black World Series for Homestead in each of those years. Taylor, born in Anderson, South Carolina, was part of a family affair in the Negro Leagues, along with his brothers C.I., Ben, and Johnny. In a 1930 interview, Taylor talked about the problems in Negro League baseball, many of which sound similar to today's problems in Major League Baseball: "We have club owners who have made their mark in life in all sorts of businesses, and only one man who is a real baseball man," Taylor said. "Baseball is a business in itself and cannot be run as any other business." Taylor also lamented the attitude of players who he believed cared more for money than for the game. "We do not have enough players who care enough for the game to stay in condition and always be ready to give their best. The most they care for is the 1st and the 15th [paydays for the month]. They haven't the spirit of the old ballplayer to win ball games and stay in condition as well as look for their pay day."

Taylor, Jim

Jim Taylor was an outfielder for the Cuban Giants in 1896.

Taylor, Joe
Joe Taylor was a catcher and outfielder for the Chicago American Giants from 1949 to 1951.

Taylor, Jonathan
Jonathan Taylor was a pitcher for the Leland Giants, St. Paul Gophers, St. Louis Giants, Chicago Giants, Bowser's ABC's, Indianapolis ABC's, Birmingham Giants, West Baden Sprudels, Hilldale baseball club, Bacharach Giants, Chicago Giants, and Louisville Sox from 1903 to 1921.

Taylor, John (Big Red)
John Taylor was a pitcher for the Kansas City Monarchs, Chicago Giants, Lincoln Giants, Pennsylvania Red Caps of New York, and Chicago American Giants from 1920 to 1928.

Taylor, Johnny
Johnny Taylor was a pitcher for the New York Cubans, Toledo Crawfords, Pittsburgh Crawfords, Bacharach Giants, and Homestead Grays from 1935 to 1945.

Taylor, Johnny
Johnny Taylor was an outfielder for the Birmingham Black Barons from 1943 to 1945.

Taylor, Leroy R.
Leroy Taylor was an outfielder for the Indianapolis ABC's, Chicago American Giants, Detroit Wolves, Kansas City Monarchs, Cleveland Red Sox, Detroit Stars, and Homestead Grays from 1925 to 1936.

Taylor, Olan (Jelly)
Olan Taylor was a first baseman and catcher for the Memphis Red Sox, Cincinnati Tigers, Pittsburgh Crawfords, and Birmingham Black Barons from 1934 to 1946. In 1941, Taylor was voted to the West team in the EAST-WEST NEGRO LEAGUE ALL-STAR GAME.

Taylor, Raymond
Raymond Taylor was a catcher for the Cincinnati Buckeyes, Columbus Buckeyes, Memphis Red Sox, Kansas City Monarchs, Cleveland Clippers, Cleveland Buckeyes, and New York Black Yankees from 1931 to 1946.

Taylor, Rip
Rip Taylor was an outfielder for the Hilldale baseball club in 1931.

Taylor, Robert R. (Lightning)
b. 1917, d. 1999
Robert Taylor was a catcher for the St. Louis Stars and New York Black Yankees, Indianapolis ABC's, and New Orleans–St. Louis Stars from 1938 to 1942.

Taylor, Rolla
Rolla Taylor was a white businessman from Adrian, Michigan, who, along with L. W. Hoch, owned the Page Fence Giants, a black baseball team named after the Page Wire and Fence Co., in the 1890s.

Taylor, Sam
Sam Taylor was a catcher for the Kansas City Monarchs and Indianapolis ABC's in 1953 and 1954.

Taylor, Zach
Zach Taylor was a pitcher for the Memphis Red Sox in 1937.

Teasley, Ronald
Ronald Teasley was an outfielder and first baseman for the Toledo Cubs in 1945.

Tenney, William
William Tenney was a catcher for the Kansas City Giants in 1910.

Tennessee Rats
The Tennessee Rats were a black barnstorming baseball team in the 1910s and 1920s. They are believed to have been the model for the book and film about Negro League baseball, *Bingo Long and His Traveling All-Stars*. Negro League pitcher Chet Brewer, who played for the Rats, said they would "come into town in our Model-T Ford and go up and down the street with a megaphone. We slept in tents, played and clowned. It was the only way we knew to make money."

Teran, Recurvon (Julio)
Recurvon Teran was a second baseman and third baseman for the Cuban Stars, the Cuban Stars of Havana, and New York Cuban Stars from 1916 to 1924.

Terrell, Lawrence
Lawrence Terrell was a pitcher for the Detroit Stars in 1924 and 1925.

Terrill, Windsor

Windsor Terrell was an infielder for the Cuban X Giants, York Cuban Giants, Boston Resolutes, and Ansonia Cuban Giants from 1887 to 1896.

Terry, Ernest

Ernest Terry was the manager of the Pittsburgh Crawfords in 1931.

Terry, John

John Terry was a second baseman and third baseman for the Homestead Grays, Cincinnati Tigers, Newark Dodgers, and Indianapolis ABC's from 1931 to 1936.

Texas Giants

The Texas Giants were a performing black baseball team organized by a player named Jack Marshall in 1929 as part of a traveling baseball road show that played against the New York All Stars.

Texas Negro League

The Texas Negro League was a league of black baseball teams in Texas in the 1920s.

Thomas, Alfred

Alfred Thomas was a pitcher for the Chicago American Giants from 1944 to 1949.

Thomas, Arthur
b. 1864

Arthur Thomas was a catcher, infielder, and outfielder for the Manhattans of Washington, D.C., West End club of Long Branch, New Jersey, Trenton Cuban Giants, Cuban Giants, New York Gorhams, and York Colored Monarchs from 1886 to 1891. Negro League player, manager, and historian Sol White, in his book *History of Colored Base Ball*, wrote that Thomas, born in Washington, D.C., was one of the black ballplayers of his time who could have played in the major leagues. In a May 1886 article in the *Trenton Times*, Thomas was described as "a good general player, a good batsman, fair baserunner and excellent throws to bases." White also wrote that Thomas, who was 6 foot 4, "had a moaning voice and actually would cry when his team lost a game. His facial expressions were paradoxical; when he laughed you would have to look twice to see if he was crying. An extremely hard worker, he ruled the roost, including the captain. With his long arms he would reach out and grab wild pitches and when the ball left his hand for second base it looked like a long snake." Thomas was one of a handful of black ballplayers who played in the white minor leagues, and in 120 games over two seasons, batted .344.

Thomas, Charles

Charles Thomas was a first baseman, outfielder, pitcher, and third baseman for the Philadelphia Giants from 1904 to 1916.

Thomas, Charley

Charley Thomas was a catcher for the Baltimore Black Sox from 1916 to 1922.

Thomas, Clint (The Hawk)
b. 1896, d. 1990

Clint Thomas was an outfielder and second baseman for the Columbus Buckeyes, Darby Daisies, Brooklyn Royal Giants, Hilldale baseball club, Detroit Stars, New York Lincoln Giants, Bacharach Giants, Newark Eagles, New York Cubans, Philadelphia Stars, and New York Black Yankees from 1920 to 1937. Records show that Thomas, born in Greenup, Kentucky, batted .374 with 14 home runs and 21 stolen bases in his first season. He went on to hit .310 for Hilldale in 1923, .342 for the Bacharach Giants in 1929, and is believed to have batted .329 over 1,796 Negro League games in his career. In a 1979 interview with *Golden Seal* magazine, Thomas talked about how he got his nickname while playing for Detroit: "We were playing a doubleheader and Jess [Barbour, the Stars center fielder] got sick," said Thomas, who had been playing second base up to that point but wanted to play center field. "After the first game, when we went back to the clubhouse to change sweatshirts and uniforms, our manager, Bruce Petway, pointed to me and said, 'Well, we're gonna put him in right field and put somebody else on second base.' So I played right field, but kept running over into center to catch balls there. So after the second game was over and we went back to the clubhouse, he [Petway] says, 'That's gonna be my center fielder, right there. You play center field next game, because you're gonna run over and kill the guy playing there now. And we're gonna give him a nickname—the Hawk.' That's how I got my nickname." Thomas also recalled one troubling time while barnstorming in Pennsylvania: "Once when we were playing in Shamokin, they were going to lynch us there. We had to get the state police to take us out of town. The umpires were cheating, and some of our players got angry, and got into a fight with the umpires. They were big boys there, and came after us. We had a hell of a time getting out of there. We left our bats, gloves, everything. The state police took us 12 or 15 miles out of town, but some of them followed, so they

Clint "The Hawk" Thomas was named by the Pittsburgh Couriers to their second team of greatest Negro League players of all time in a 1952 poll and with good reason. As an outfielder and second baseman for the Columbus Buckeyes, Darby Daisies, Brooklyn Royal Giants, Hilldale baseball club, Detroit Stars, New York Lincoln Giants, Bacharach Giants, Newark Eagles, New York Cubans, Philadelphia Stars, and New York Black Yankees from 1920 to 1937, Thomas batted .329.
(NATIONAL BASEBALL HALL OF FAME LIBRARY, COOPERSTOWN, N.Y.)

took us even further." In the *Pittsburgh Courier*'s 1952 poll of the greatest Negro League players of all time, Thomas was selected to the second unit.

Thomas, Dan

Dan Thomas was a second baseman for the St. Louis Stars, Indianapolis ABC's, Cleveland Hornets, Kansas City Monarchs, and Memphis Red Sox from 1921 to 1932.

Thomas, Dan

Dan Thomas was an outfielder, third baseman, and pitcher for the Chicago American Giants, Jacksonville Red Caps, Cincinnati Tigers, and Birmingham Black Barons from 1936 to 1940.

Thomas, David (Showboat)

David Thomas was a first baseman, outfielder, and manager for the Birmingham Black Barons, Montgomery Grey Sox, New York Black Yankees, Baltimore Black Sox, Washington Black Senators, New York Cubans, Lincoln Giants, and Brooklyn Royal Giants from 1923 to 1946. In an interview with author John Holway on file at the National Baseball Hall of Fame, Negro League pitcher Dave Barnhill said that Thomas was one of the best first basemen he had ever seen. "How did he play first?" Barnhill said. "As good as he wanted to. As good as he wanted to." Buck O'Neil, in his autobiography, *I Was Right on Time*, said that Thomas was "the flashiest first baseman I have ever seen." Thomas was one of a group of Negro League ballplayers who went to the Dominican Republic in 1937 to play in dictator Rafael Trujillo's political baseball war. Thomas played for San Pedro, owned by one of Trujillo's opponents. He was also one of the ballplayers that Joe Bostic, editor of the New York black newspaper *People's Voice*, brought to see Branch Rickey in 1945 at the Brooklyn Dodgers training camp in Bear Mountain, New York, for a workout and purported tryout. In Jules Tygiel's book *Jackie Robinson and His Legacy*, Bostic said he picked Thomas because he "was the best fielding first baseman I knew in America at that time, bar none."

Thomas, Frank

Frank Thomas was a pitcher for the Birmingham Black Barons in 1945.

Thomas, Hazel

Hazel Thomas was a pitcher for the Chicago American Giants in 1935.

Thomas, Henry

Henry Thomas was an outfielder for the New York Black Yankees in 1931.

Thomas, Herb

Herb Thomas was a left-handed pitcher for the Hilldale baseball club and the Lincoln Giants in 1929 and 1930.

Thomas, Jack

Jack Thomas was an outfielder and pitcher for the Lincoln Giants, Brooklyn Royal Giants, St. Louis Giants, Pennsylvania Red Caps of New York, Hilldale baseball club, and Bacharach Giants from 1909 to 1931.

Thomas, John

John Thomas was a pitcher for the Birmingham Black Barons and Cleveland Buckeyes from 1950 to 1953.

Thomas, Lacey

Lacey Thomas was an outfielder and pitcher for the Cleveland Bears, Jacksonville Red Caps, and Chicago American Giants from 1934 to 1939.

Thomas, Nelson

Nelson Thomas was a pitcher for the Newark Eagles in 1947.

Thomas, Orel

Orel Thomas was a pitcher for the Detroit Stars in 1937.

Thomas, Walter

Walter Thomas was a pitcher and outfielder for the Kansas City Monarchs, Detroit Stars, Memphis Red Sox, and Birmingham Black Barons from 1936 to 1947.

Thomas, William

William Thomas was an outfielder for the Chicago Brown Bombers in 1943.

Thomason, Charlie

Charlie Thomason was an outfielder for the Newark Eagles from 1941 to 1944.

Thompkins, Allie

Allie Thompkins was an outfielder for the Pittsburgh Crawfords in 1928 and 1929.

Thompson, Buddy

Buddy Thompson was a catcher for the Chicago Brown Bombers in 1942.

Thompson, Frank

Frank Thompson was a pitcher for the Homestead Grays, Memphis Red Sox, and Birmingham Black Barons from 1945 to 1954.

Thompson, Frank Andrew, Jr. (Hoss)

Frank Thompson, Jr., was a pitcher for the Birmingham Black Barons and Baltimore Elite Giants from 1951 to 1954.

Thompson, Frank P.

Frank P. Thompson was the founder of what is believed to have been the first professional black baseball team in 1885, sponsored by the Argyle Hotel, located in Babylon, New York. Thompson had formed a black baseball team called the Keystone Athletics in Philadelphia, and the hotel hired the team to entertain the guests and also work as waiters. They later joined up with the Manhattans of Washington and the Orions of Philadelphia and were called the New York Cuban Giants.

Thompson, Gene

Gene Thompson was a pitcher for the Philadelphia Stars in 1949 and 1950.

Thompson, Gunboat

Gunboat Thompson was a pitcher, first baseman, and outfielder for the Pittsburgh Stars of Buffalo, Lincoln Stars, Lincoln Giants, Detroit Stars, Bacharach Giants, Pennsylvania Red Caps of New York, and Birmingham Black Barons from 1914 to 1920.

Thompson, Harold

Harold Thompson was a pitcher for the Kansas City Monarchs and Cleveland Buckeyes in 1948 and 1949.

Thompson, Henry (Hank)

b. 1925, d. 1969

Henry Thompson was an outfielder, second baseman, and shortstop for the Kansas City Monarchs from 1943 to 1948. He went on to be the first black to play for two major league teams and the first black to play in the American and National Leagues. Thompson, born in Oklahoma City, Oklahoma, was an extremely volatile personality who suffered from alcoholism. He had done time as a youth in reform school and shot and killed a man in 1948 in a bar in Dallas who reportedly was trying to force his attentions on Thompson's sister. He was found not guilty on grounds of self-defense. But he continued to carry a gun throughout his career. "Hank was a little bit off center," Negro Leaguer Stanley Glenn said in a 1997 newspaper interview: "He had a drinking problem and a woman problem. He was like a time bomb. But he was all baseball on the field. He had all kinds of ability." His problems off the field would worsen after he left baseball. "He started to drink a lot," said Negro Leaguer Sammy Haynes: "He wasn't a star anymore, and he wasn't making the kind of money he was used to. He was a good guy, but he just couldn't handle it."

The 5-foot-9, 180-pound Thompson played nine years in the major leagues, briefly with the St. Louis

Browns in 1947—27 games—and then with the New York Giants for the remainder of his career. Over nine years, Thompson batted .267 with 129 home runs, 482 runs batted in, and 492 runs scored in 933 major league games. Thompson was arrested in 1958 for car theft in New York and again in 1961 for holding up a bar. He moved to Texas and was arrested for armed robbery in 1963 and sentenced to 10 years. He served four years and was paroled. He moved to Fresno, California, and worked as a playground director until his death.

Thompson, James

James Thompson was an outfielder, catcher, and first baseman for the Milwaukee Bears, Dayton Marcos, Chicago American Giants, Birmingham Black Barons, Cole's American Giants, Chicago Columbia Giants, and Cuban Stars from 1920 to 1923.

Thompson, Jimmy

Jimmy Thompson was an umpire in the NEGRO AMERICAN LEAGUE in the 1940s.

Thompson, Lloyd
d. 1987
Lloyd Thompson was an outfielder, shortstop, and later a club officer with the Hilldale baseball club from 1910 to 1916 and from 1922 to 1932.

Thompson, Marshall

Marshall Thompson was the manager of the Boston Resolutes in 1887.

Thompson, Richard

Richard Thompson was an outfielder for the Kansas City Monarchs in 1954.

Thompson, Sammy

Sammy Thompson was a second baseman for the Little Rock Black Travelers, Memphis Red Sox, Atlanta Black Crackers, and Cleveland Bears from 1931 to 1938.

Thompson, Samuel

Samuel Thompson was a pitcher for the Indianapolis ABC's, Kansas City Monarchs, Columbus Elite Giants, Detroit Stars, Chicago American Giants, Philadelphia Stars, Baltimore Elite Giants, Nashville Elite Giants, and Monroe Monarchs from 1931 to 1942.

Thompson, Wade

Wade Thompson was a pitcher for the Richmond Giants, Baltimore Black Sox, and Harrisburg Giants from 1922 to 1926.

Thompson, William

William Thompson was a catcher for the Genuine Cuban Giants and Louisville Falls City club from 1887 to 1900.

Thorn, John

John Thorn was an outfielder for the Philadelphia Stars in 1946.

Thornton, Charles

Charles Thornton was a pitcher for the Pittsburgh Keystones in 1887.

Thornton, Jack

Jack Thornton was a second baseman, first baseman, and pitcher for the Atlanta Black Crackers from 1932 to 1937.

Thornton, Jesse

Jesse Thornton was an officer with the Indianapolis Athletics in 1937.

Thorpe, Clarence

Clarence Thorpe was a pitcher for the Bacharach Giants and Hilldale baseball club in 1928 and 1934.

Thurman, Jim

Jim Thurman was a pitcher and outfielder for the Columbus Blue Birds and Louisville Black Caps from 1932 to 1933.

Thurman, Robert
b. 1917, d. 1998
Robert Thurman was a pitcher and outfielder for the Kansas City Monarchs and Homestead Grays from 1946 to 1949. In 632 games, Thurman had a career batting average of .351. Born in Wichita, Kansas, Thurman signed a contract with the New York Yankees and played several years in their organization. He later played for the Cincinnati Reds from 1955 through 1959, batting .246 with 35 home runs and 106 RBIs in 334 games. The 6-foot-1, 205-pound Thurman also played winter baseball in Puerto Rico, where he had a career mark of .323 and was elected to the

Puerto Rican Baseball Hall of Fame in 1991. He later worked as a scout for the Kansas City Royals.

Thurston, Bobby
Bobby Thurston was an outfielder for the Chicago Giants in 1911.

Tiant, Luis, Sr.
Luis Tiant, Sr., was a left-handed pitcher for the Cuban Stars, Cuban House of David, and New York Cubans from 1930 to 1947. In an interview with author John Holway on file at National Baseball Hall of Fame, Negro League pitcher Dave Barnhill talked about playing with Tiant: "This guy had such a good move to first base, a beautiful move," Barnhill said. "He was left-handed. He was pitching for the Cubans in Philadelphia. Goose Curry is at bat. Tiant just tossed the ball to home plate. Then with the same move, next pitch he threw to first. He came with the same move next time, and threw to first—and Goose swung at it." Tiant's son, Luis, used to hang around his father in Cuba when he played with Negro Leaguers down there, Barnhill said. Luis, Jr., would go on to have a great major league career, winning 224 games for the Cleveland Indians, Minnesota Twins, Boston Red Sox, and New York Yankees.

Tiddle, Milton
Milton Tiddle was a catcher for the Kansas City Monarchs in 1955.

Tindle, Levy
Levy Tindle was an officer with the Detroit Stars in 1933.

Tinker, Harold (Hooks)
Harold Tinker was an outfielder for the Pittsburgh Crawfords from 1928 to 1931.

Titus, James
James Titus was an officer for the Detroit Stars in 1937.

Todd, Elzie
Elzie Todd was a pitcher for the Indianapolis Clowns from 1951 to 1952.

Tolbert, Andrew
Andrew Tolbert was a second baseman for the Detroit Stars in 1954.

Tolbert, Jake
Jake Tolbert was a pitcher, catcher, and outfielder for the Detroit Stars and New York Black Yankees in 1946 and 1954.

Toledo Cubs
The Toledo Cubs, also called the Toledo Rays, were a black baseball team based in Toledo, Ohio, that was part of the UNITED STATES LEAGUE in 1945.

Toledo-Indianapolis Crawfords
The Toledo-Indianapolis Crawfords were a black baseball team that split time between Toledo, Ohio, and Indianapolis, Indiana, in 1939 and 1940 in the NEGRO AMERICAN LEAGUE.

Toledo, Julio
Julio Toledo was a first baseman for the Indianapolis Clowns in 1952 and 1953.

Toledo Tigers
The Toledo Tigers were a black baseball team based in Toledo, Ohio, that played in the Negro National League in 1923.

Toles, Ted
Ted Toles was a pitcher for the Pittsburgh Crawfords in 1946.

Toney, Albert
Albert Toney was a second baseman, shortstop, and outfielder for the Leland Giants, Chicago Union Giants, Chicago Giants, Chicago American Giants, Philadelphia Giants, and Algona Brownies from 1901 to 1916.

Topeka Giants
The Topeka Giants were a black baseball team that played in Topeka, Kansas, in the early 1900s organized by Topeka Jack Johnson, a boxer and promoter who used the name of the famous heavyweight champion, Jack Johnson. In an interview with historian Robert Peterson, Arthur Hardy, one of the Topeka Giants' players, described their barnstorming tours: "We always liked to get into town at least by the middle of the morning for advertising purposes," he said. "As a rule, when we went into a town, we would placard it and uniform up and go out and practice so the people could get it noised around that we were in town. Sometimes they set up a parade.

Both teams paraded. That was in Smith Center and Blue Rapids and Frankfort, Kansas. That was the regular program. They had very good bands. Most of those little towns had a municipal band, you know—the band concert once a week was a big event then—and they would lead the parade and we'd march out to the baseball park. In those little towns, we would average $15, $20 a man for a game. The admission charge was 50 cents or 75 cents, kids a quarter . . . and expenses were at a minimum. In those days you could get a good meal for 25 cents and you could get lodging for 50 cents. We did some clowning on the field. But it was done like this: as you know, some people might resent what they might consider you making fun of them. . . . Johnson always insisted that we didn't want to humiliate anybody . . . after all, we were pros and the other teams were fellows who were playing once a weekend . . . and so Topeka Jack would always talk to the local people. He'd say, 'Now what about you folks here? Do you want us to put on some funny kind of acts? Or do you think they would resent it.'"

Torres, Armando
Armando Torres was a pitcher for the Cuban Stars in 1939.

Torres, Ricardo
Ricardo Torres was a catcher for the Long Branch Cubans in 1916.

Torrienti, Cristobal
b. 1895, d. 1938

Cristobal Torrienti was an outfielder and pitcher for the Chicago American Giants, Cuban Stars, Detroit Stars, Gilkerson Giants, and Kansas City Monarchs from 1914 to 1932. Torrienti was one of the greatest Cuban players to have played Negro League baseball. He had a career batting mark of .352 in Cuba and was elected to the Cuban Hall of Fame in 1939. He led the Chicago American Giants to championships from 1920 to 1922, and batted .396 in 1920, .337 in 1921, and .350 in 1922. Records show that the 5-foot-10, 190-pound Torrienti batted .339 over his Negro League career, with 57 home runs, 158 doubles, 169 stolen bases, and also posted a 15-5 record as a pitcher.

Negro League manager C. I. Taylor once said of Torrienti that, "If I should see Torrienti walking up the other side of the street, I would say, 'There walks a ballclub.'" In an interview with author John Holway on file at the National Baseball Hall of Fame, Negro League pitcher Bill Drake said that Torrienti was one of the best he ever faced: "He was one of the best outfielders you

would find, a good hitter and fast as lighting." Drake said. Teammate Jelly Gardner, in another Holway interview on file at the National Baseball Hall of Fame, said he believed that Torrienti was almost signed by the New York Giants: "The Giants had a scout following us—Kansas City, St. Louis and Indianapolis," Gardner said. "He [Torrienti] hit a line drive in Indianapolis that hit the top of the right field wall, and the right fielder threw him out at first. That's how much power he had. . . . The Giant scout was looking at him and he would have went up there, but he had real bad hair. He was a little lighter than I am but he had real rough hair. He was light brown and he would have been all right if his hair had been better." Torrienti was named by the *Pittsburgh Courier* to its all-time black baseball team in 1952. The *Courier* wrote that Torrienti "was one of the best bad-ball hitters in baseball and could hit equally well to all fields." However, he suffered from alcoholism and died at an early age.

Trammel, Nat
Nat Trammel was a first baseman for the Brooklyn Royal Giants and Birmingham Black Barons from 1930 to 1932.

Trawick, Joe
Joe Trawick was a second baseman for the Cleveland Buckeyes in 1950.

Treadway, Elbert
Elbert Treadway was a pitcher for the Kansas City Monarchs and Toledo Crawfords in 1939 and 1940.

Treadwell, Harold
Harold Treadwell was a pitcher for the Bacharach Giants, Brooklyn Royal Giants, Chicago American Giants, Harrisburg Giants, Dayton Marcos, Indianapolis ABC's, Cleveland Browns, Lincoln Giants, and Detroit Stars from 1919 to 1928.

Trealkill, Clarence
Clarence Trealkill was a shortstop and outfielder for the Nashville Elite Giants from 1929 to 1931.

Trent, Ted
b. 1905, d. 1944

Ted Trent was a pitcher for the West Palm Giants, Detroit Wolves, St. Louis Stars, Cole's American Giants, Homestead Grays, Washington Pilots, and Chicago American Giants from 1927 to 1939. He had an outstanding curveball and had a career record of 64-33 against Negro League competition, including a 17-4 mark in 1928 and 29-5 in 1936, with a .308 batting average. He pitched in four straight EAST-WEST ALL-STAR GAMES, from 1934 to 1937. In 1930, Trent defeated a white All-Star team that included players like Bill Terry, Paul Waner, Lefty O'Doul, and Billy Herman in a 5-0 game and struck out Terry three times in that game.

Trice, Robert Lee (Bob)
b. 1926, d. 1988
Robert Trice was a pitcher and outfielder for the Homestead Grays from 1948 to 1950. Born in Newton, Georgia, Trice was the first black player on the Philadelphia Athletics and the first black major league ballplayer for a team in Philadelphia. In three major league seasons, from 1953 to 1955, the 6-foot-2, 190-pound Trice went 9-9 for Philadelphia and Kansas City, with a 5.80 ERA in 26 appearances.

Trimble, William E.
William E. Trimble, a white businessman, was the owner of the Chicago American Giants from 1927 to 1932.

Trouppe, Quincy
b. 1912, d. 1993
Quincy Trouppe was a catcher, outfielder, and manager for the Detroit Wolves, Homestead Grays, Kansas City Monarchs, St. Louis Stars, Indianapolis ABC's, Chicago American Giants, New York Cubans, and Cleveland Buckeyes from 1930 to 1949. He batted .352 for Chicago in 1948 and was a five-time All-Star in the Negro League EAST-WEST GAME. He also managed the Cleveland Buckeyes to two NEGRO AMERICAN LEAGUE titles in 1945 and 1947. Trouppe also played in the Mexican League. Born in Dublin, Georgia, the 6-foot-2, 225-pound Trouppe played six games for the Cleveland Indians in 1952, scoring one run and getting one hit in 10 at bats. He went on to become a major league scout for the St. Louis Cardinals and for Mexican League teams as well.

Troy, Donald
Donald Troy was a pitcher for the Baltimore Elite Giants in 1944 and 1945.

Trujillo All-Stars
The Trujillo All-Stars were a barnstorming black baseball team in the fall of 1937 consisting of players who had left the Negro Leagues during the 1937 season to play in the Dominican Republic in dictator Rafael Trujillo's

baseball political war. They were also known as the Satchel Paige All-Stars.

Trusty, Job
Job Trusty was a third baseman for the Cuban Giants in 1896.

Trusty, Shep
b. 1863
Shep Trusty was an outfielder and pitcher for the Argyle Hotel team, Cuban Giants, Trenton Cuban Giants, Philadelphia Giants, and Philadelphia Orions from 1885 to 1889 and again in 1902. A May 1886 article in the *Trenton Times* said that Trusty, born in Philadelphia,

Quincy Trouppe was an outstanding catcher and manager, a five-time Negro League All-Star, and a championship manager, leading the Cleveland Buckeyes to two Negro American League titles. He played from 1930 to 1949 for the Detroit Wolves, Homestead Grays, Kansas City Monarchs, St. Louis Stars, Indianapolis ABC's, Chicago American Giants, New York Cubans, and Buckeyes. Trouppe played six games for the Cleveland Indians in 1952, scoring one run and getting one hit in 10 at bats. He went on to become a major league scout for the St. Louis Cardinals. (NATIONAL BASEBALL HALL OF FAME LIBRARY, COOPERSTOWN, N.Y.)

was "unquestionably the finest colored pitcher in the country."

Tucker, Henry
Henry Tucker was a politician in Atlantic City, New Jersey, who got the Jacksonville Duval Giants to move to Atlantic City in 1916. Tucker was an officer with the club until 1922.

Tucker, Orval
Orval Tucker was a second baseman for the Boston Royal Giants, Hilldale baseball club, and Baltimore Black Sox in 1930 and 1942.

Tugerson, James
James Tugerson was a pitcher for the Indianapolis Clowns and Kansas City Monarchs from 1951 to 1953. His brother, Leander, also pitched for the Clowns during the same time. The brothers became involved in a dispute in the Cotton States minor league in 1953, according to Jules Tygiel, in his book *Jackie Robinson and His Legacy*. They pitched for the Hot Springs (Arkansas) Bathers, but the attorney general in Mississippi, where a number of league teams were located, ordered that integrated games were a violation of public policy. The club agreed to leave the brothers out of games in Mississippi, but league officials would not allow that policy, Tygiel wrote. However, the National Association of Professional Baseball Leagues determined the Cotton States League could not ban the Hot Springs team for its policies on use of players. Before the season began, the brothers were sent to the Knoxville club in a lower league, the Mountain States League. James Tugerson was recalled to Hot Springs a month later as a result of roster problems from injuries. But when Tugerson was set to take the mound for his first start, an umpire, on orders from the league president, called the game a forfeit in favor of the opposing team. Tugerson filed a $50,000 law suit against the president and the owners of the Cotton States League. A federal judge ruled against Tugerson, and though he appealed the ruling, he dropped the lawsuit in 1954 when he went to play in the Texas League.

Tugerson, Leander (Schoolboy)
Leander Tugerson was a pitcher for the Indianapolis Clowns from 1950 to 1952. His brother, James, also pitched for the Clowns during the same time.

Turner, Aggie
Aggie Turner was a first baseman, second baseman, and outfielder for the Chicago Giants, Chicago Union Giants, Indianapolis ABC's, and ALL NATIONS team from 1911 to 1917.

Turner, Bob
Bob Turner was a catcher for the Houston Eagles and Kansas City Monarchs in 1946 and 1950.

Turner, Clarence
Clarence Turner was a pitcher for the Indianapolis Clowns in 1952 and 1953.

Turner, E. C.
E. C. Turner was a third baseman and shortstop for the Homestead Grays, Brooklyn Royal Giants, Cleveland Cubs, Birmingham Black Barons, New York Black Yankees, and Cole's American Giants from 1925 to 1937. He was also an umpire in the NEGRO NATIONAL LEAGUE.

Turner, Etwood
Etwood Turner was an outfielder for the Toledo Tigers in 1923.

Turner, Henry
Henry Turner was a catcher, outfielder, first baseman, and second baseman for the Cleveland Bears, Jacksonville Red Caps, Harrisburg–St. Louis Stars, Cleveland Buckeyes, and Newark Eagles from 1938 to 1944.

Turner, Lefty
Lefty Turner was a first baseman for the Baltimore Elite Giants and Indianapolis Crawfords from 1940 to 1942.

Turner, Oliver
Oliver Turner was a pitcher for the Chicago Brown Bombers in 1943.

Turner, Thomas
Thomas Turner was a first baseman for the Chicago American Giants in 1947.

Turner, Tuck
Tuck Turner was a pitcher for the Chicago American Giants and St. Louis Stars in 1919, 1923, and 1928.

Turner, Wright
Wright Turner was a catcher for the Pittsburgh Crawfords from 1930 to 1931.

Turnstall, Willie

Willie Turnstall was a pitcher for the Cleveland Buckeyes in 1950.

Tut, Richard (King)

Richard Tut was a first baseman for the Indianapolis Clowns, Cincinnati Clowns, and Bacharach Giants in 1931 and from 1943 to 1950.

Twyman, Oscar

Oscar Twyman was an outfielder for the Lincoln Stars in 1916.

Tye, Dan

Dan Tye was a shortstop, third baseman, and pitcher for the Memphis Red Sox and Cincinnati Tigers from 1930 to 1936.

Tyler, Charles

Charles Tyler was an owner and officer with the Newark, New Jersey, Dodgers in 1934 and 1935.

Tyler, Edward

Edward Tyler was a pitcher for the Hilldale baseball club, St. Louis Stars, and Brooklyn Cuban Giants from 1925 to 1928.

Tyler, Eugene

Eugene Tyler was a catcher and infielder for the Kansas City Monarchs and Chicago Brown Bombers in 1942 and 1943.

Tyler, Roy

Roy Tyler was a pitcher and outfielder for the Cleveland Elites, Columbus Blue Birds, and Chicago American Giants from 1925 to 1933.

Tyler, William (Steel Arm)

William Tyler was a pitcher for the Detroit Stars, Memphis Red Sox, Cole's American Giants, and Kansas City Monarchs from 1925 to 1932.

Tyree, Ruby

Ruby Tyree was a pitcher for the Chicago American Giants, Cleveland Browns, and the ALL NATIONS TEAM from 1916 to 1924.

Tyson, Armand (Cap)

Armand Tyson was a catcher for the Birmingham Black Barons from 1936 to 1940.

Tyus, Julius

Julius Tyus was a pitcher for the Philadelphia Stars in 1947.

Underhill, Bob
Bob Underhill was a pitcher for the Hilldale baseball club in 1924.

Underwood, Ely
Ely Underwood was an outfielder for the Pittsburgh Crawfords and Detroit Stars in 1932 and 1937.

Underwood, Jim
Jim Underwood was a shortstop for the Louisville Black Colonels and Detroit Stars in 1954.

Underwood, Ray
Ray Underwood was a pitcher for the Detroit Stars in 1937.

Union Giants
There were several versions of Union Giants teams, including one operated by William S. Peters in 1915 and 1916 and another by Robert T. Gilkerson later that decade.

United States League
The United States League was started in 1945 by Brooklyn Dodgers general manager Branch Rickey, who had been an outspoken critic of the existing Negro Leagues, calling them "rackets" and suggested they were not run on the up and up. As a result, he said he was starting a new Negro League. Many observers believed that Rickey, who would bring Jackie Robinson to the Brooklyn Dodgers in 1947 to break major league baseball's color barrier, started the United States League, with the help of the former owner of the Pittsburgh Crawfords, Gus Greenlee, to scout the talent available in black baseball. Teams in the league included the Brooklyn Brown Dodgers (also known as the Bombers), Toledo Rays, Chicago Brown Bombers, and teams in Pittsburgh, Chicago, Boston, Detroit, Philadelphia and Cleveland. The league did not last very long, though, barely making it through the season.

V

Vactor, John

John Vactor was a pitcher for the Gorhams of New York, the Pythians of Philadelphia, and the Trenton Cuban Giants from 1886 to 1888.

Valdes, Fermin

Fermin Valdes was a second baseman for the Cincinnati-Indianapolis Clowns in 1944.

Valdes, Rogelio

Rogelio Valdes was a second baseman and outfielder for the Cuban X Giants and All Cubans team from 1905 to 1911.

Valdez, Felix

Felix Valdez was a pitcher for the Memphis Red Sox in 1951 and 1952.

Valdez, Pablo

Pablo Valdez was an outfielder and pitcher for the Cuban Stars, Havana Cubans, and Stars of Cuba from 1910 to 1920.

Valdez, Strico

Strico Valdez was a second baseman and shortstop for the Atlanta Black Crackers, New York Cubans, and Cuban Stars from 1931 to 1939.

Valentine, Jimmy

Jimmy Valentine was a second baseman and third baseman for the Detroit Stars, Louisville Black Colonels, and Memphis Red Sox in 1954 and 1955.

Van Buren, Bill

Bill Van Buren was an outfielder for the Memphis Red Sox in 1931.

Vance, Luke

Luke Vance was a pitcher for the Homestead Grays, Birmingham Black Barons, Detroit Stars, Detroit Wolves, and Indianapolis ABC's from 1927 to 1934.

Van Dyke, Fred

Fred Van Dyke was a pitcher and outfielder for the Adrian, Michigan, Page Fence Giants from 1895 to 1897.

Vanever, Bobby

Bobby Vanever was an infielder for the Kansas City Monarchs in 1944.

Vargas, Guillermo
b. 1919

Guillermo Vargas was an outfielder for the New York Cubans in 1949 and batted .276.

Vargas, Juan
Juan Vargas was an outfielder and shortstop for the Cuban Stars and New York Cubans from 1929 to 1944.

Vargas, Roberto
b. 1929
Roberto Vargas was a pitcher for the Chicago American Giants in 1948, posting a 6-8 record. Born in Santurce, Puerto Rico, the 5-foot-11, 170-pound Vargas was a standout pitcher in the Puerto Rican Winter League, with a mark of 51-24 over 13 seasons. He pitched one season in the major leagues, in 1955 with the Milwaukee Braves, appearing in 25 games, with no won-loss record and an 8.76 ERA.

Varona, Gilberto
b. 1919
Gilberto Varona, born in Cuba, was a first baseman for the Memphis Red Sox from 1950 to 1955 and batted .268 with 35 RBIs in 74 games in 1954.

Varona, Orlando
b. 1926
Orlando Varona, born in Havana, Cuba, was a shortstop for the Memphis Red Sox from 1948 to 1955.

Vasquez, Armando
b. 1922
Armando Vasquez was an infielder and outfielder for the Cincinnati-Indianapolis Clowns, Indianapolis Clowns, and New York Cubans from 1944 to 1952. The 5-foot-8, 160-pound Vasquez, born in Guines, Cuba, batted .239 in 1944 and .246 in 1945. In a 1991 interview with *Sports Collectors Digest*, Vasquez recounted his personal tale of the prejudice Negro Leaguers often faced while traveling: "I remember one time we played in Nashville, and after the game we went downtown to a restaurant to get something to eat. I went into the restaurant first and they threw me out. They told me, 'You gotta go to the back door to buy what you want. You can't come in here.' I got so mad when they told me that. . . . This was my second year, now, and I was just a kid . . . that when I saw a little guy with a small truck filled with watermelon, I went over and bought one watermelon from him. I ate the whole thing. I was so hungry. But I got sick after that and couldn't sleep that night. I remember it because it happened so early in my career." He also talked about some of his more joyful moments: "When I first played at Yankee Stadium in 1944, and later in the Polo Grounds, that was like a dream to me," Vasquez said. "They were places I'd only heard about when I first came to the United States."

Vaughn, Don
Don Vaughn was a pitcher for the Kansas City Monarchs in 1955.

Vaughn, Harold
Harold Vaughn was an outfielder for the Kansas City Monarchs in 1926 and 1927.

Vaughn, Joe
Joe Vaughn was the secretary of the Negro Southern League in 1931.

Vaughn, Oscar
Oscar Vaughn was an outfielder for the New Orleans Eagles in 1951.

Vaughn, Ray
Ray Vaughn was a pitcher for the Newark Browns and Newark Dodgers from 1931 to 1934.

Veadez, Henry
Henry Veadez was an infielder for the Kansas City Monarchs in 1952.

Velasquez, Jose
Jose Velasquez was a pitcher for the Indianapolis Clowns from 1948 to 1950.

Veney, Jerome
Jerome Veney was an outfielder and manager for the Homestead Grays from 1908 to 1917.

Vernal, Sleepy
Sleepy Vernal was a pitcher for the New York Cubans in 1941.

Victory, George M.
George Victory was an officer with the Pennsylvania Giants in 1919 and 1920.

Vierira, Chris
Chris Vierira was an outfielder for the New York Black Yankees in 1949.

Villa, Bobby

Bobby Villa was an outfielder and second baseman for the Cuban Stars of Havana, the All Cubans, the Cuban Stars, and the Stars of Cuba from 1910 to 1922.

Villafane, Vicente

Vicente Villafane was an infielder and outfielder for the Indianapolis Clowns in 1947.

Villodas, Luis

Luis Villodas was a catcher for the Baltimore Elite Giants in 1946 and 1947. The 6-foot-2, 200-pound Villodas, born in Ponce, Puerto Rico, also played in the Dominican Summer League in 1951 and 1952 and the West Texas–New Mexico League in 1954 and 1955. Villodas also played winter baseball in Puerto Rico.

Vines, Eddie

Eddie Vines was a pitcher and third baseman for the Birmingham Black Barons and Chicago American Giants in 1940.

Waco Black Navigators

The Waco Black Navigators were a black team from Waco, Texas, that included future Negro League great Crush Holloway. The team played briefly in 1919 before the club was sold and became the San Antonio Black Aces.

Waco Yellow Jackets

The Waco Yellow Jackets were a black baseball team from Waco, Texas, that played in the 1890s. One of their players in 1896 was a 17-year-old pitcher named Andrew "Rube" Foster, who would go on to become one of the most influential figures in black baseball, both as a star pitcher, owner of the Chicago American Giants, and founder of the NEGRO NATIONAL LEAGUE.

Waddy, Irving (Lefty)

Irving Waddy was a pitcher for the Detroit Stars and Indianapolis ABC's from 1932 to 1933.

Wade, Lee

Lee Wade was a pitcher, outfielder, and first baseman for the Philadelphia Giants, Cuban Giants, Lincoln Giants, St. Louis Giants, Chicago American Giants, Brooklyn Royal Giants, Lincoln Stars, and Pennsylvania Red Caps of New York from 1909 to 1919.

Wagner, Bill

Bill Wagner was a second baseman, shortstop, and manager for the New York Black Yankees, Brooklyn Royal Giants, and Lincoln Giants from 1921 to 1931.

Waite, Arnold

Arnold Waite was a pitcher for the Washington Elite Giants and Homestead Grays in 1936 and 1937.

Wakefield, Bert

Bert Wakefield was a first baseman and second baseman for the Kansas City Giants, Algona Brownies, Chicago Unions, and Chicago Union Giants from 1895 to 1902 and again in 1915.

Waldon, Ollie

Ollie Waldon was an outfielder for the Chicago American Giants and Kansas City Monarchs in 1944.

Walker, A. M.

A. M. Walker was manager of the Birmingham Black Barons in 1937.

Walker, Casey

Casey Walker was a catcher for the Indianapolis Athletics and Newark Dodgers from 1935 to 1937.

Walker, Charles

Charles Walker was an owner of the Homestead Grays from 1915 to 1920. He had started his career with the Grays as a batboy and stayed with the club in a front office capacity until 1934.

Walker, Edsall (Big)

Edsall Walker was a pitcher for the Philadelphia Stars, Baltimore Elite Giants, and Homestead Grays from 1936 to 1945.

Walker, George

b. 1915, d. 1967

George Walker was a pitcher for the Kansas City Monarchs and Homestead Grays from 1937 to 1952. The 6-foot, 180-pound Walker, born in Waco, Texas, had a 12-3 record for Kansas City in 18 games in 1950.

Walker, Jack

Jack Walker was a pitcher for the Newark Eagles, New York Black Yankees, Harrisburg–St. Louis Stars, and Philadelphia Stars from 1940 to 1943.

Walker, Jesse (Hoss)

Jesse Walker was a shortstop, third baseman, manager, and officer for the Cleveland Cubs, Bacharach Giants, Washington Elite Giants, Nashville Elite Giants, Baltimore Elite Giants, Birmingham Black Barons, New York Black Yankees, Cincinnati Clowns, Cincinnati-Indianapolis Clowns, Indianapolis Clowns, Nashville Cubs, Detroit Stars, and Columbus Elite Giants from 1929 to 1955.

Walker, Moses Fleetwood (Fleet)

b. 1857, d. 1924

Moses Walker was a historic figure in black baseball—the first black to integrate white major league baseball, long before Jackie Robinson joined the Brooklyn Dodgers in 1947. A catcher, first baseman, and outfielder, Walker was born in Mt. Pleasant, Ohio, and played college baseball at Oberlin College. He went on to play for Toledo in the white Northwestern League and American Association, Cleveland in the Western League, Waterbury in the Southern New England and Eastern Leagues, and Newark and Syracuse in the International League from 1883 to 1889. He is believed to have batted .251 for Toledo in 60 games in 1883 and hit for the same average in 46 games in 1884. Walker hit .263 with 36 stolen bases for Newark in 1887. The next year Walker hit just .170 for Syracuse in 77 games. His brother, Weldy, also played baseball and was on the Toledo roster with Moses. After Walker was driven out of organized baseball, he ran into some personal problems, got into a fight outside a bar in Syracuse, and stabbed a man to death. Walker was charged with second-degree murder but was acquitted in a trial.

Walker, Pete

Pete Walker was a pitcher, outfielder, and second baseman for the Homestead Grays from 1923 to 1926.

Walker, Robert

Robert Walker was a pitcher for the Homestead Grays and Boston Blues from 1945 to 1949.

Walker, Tom

Tom Walker was a pitcher for the Baltimore Elite Giants in 1945.

Walker, Weldy

b. 1860, d. 1937

Weldy Walker was a catcher, outfielder, and second baseman for Toledo in the American Association, Akron in the Ohio State League, Cleveland in the Western League, and the Pittsburgh Keystones from 1884 to 1887. He was the brother of Moses "Fleet" Walker, played with his brother at Oberlin College, and followed him into major league baseball as the only black players to break the color line at the time. He also played in white minor league organized baseball and fought efforts to bar blacks from playing in those leagues. The Tri-State League, formerly known as the Ohio League, had passed a law in 1888 barring black players. Weldy Walker wrote a letter to the league president protesting the law, and the letter was widely circulated in the press: "The law is a disgrace to the present age, and reflects very much upon the intelligence of your last meeting, and casts derision at the laws of Ohio—the voice of the people—that says all men are equal," Weldy Walker wrote. "I would suggest that your honorable body, in case that black law is not repealed, pass one making it criminal for a colored man or woman to be found in a ball ground. There is now the same accommodations made for the colored patron of the game as the white, and the same provision and dispensation is made for the money of them both that finds its way into the coffers of the various clubs. There should be some broader cause—such as a lack of ability, behavior and intelligence—for barring a player, rather than his color. It is for these reasons and because I think ability and intelligence should be recognized first and last—at all times and by everyone—I ask the question again why was the 'law permitting colored men to sign repealed?'" The law that prohibited black players from playing in the league was repealed a few weeks later.

Walker, William

William Walker was an outfielder for the St. Louis Stars in 1937.

Wallace, Felix

Felix Wallace was an infielder and manager for the Leland Giants, St. Paul Gophers, St. Louis Giants, Bacharach Giants, Famous Cuban Giants, Lincoln Giants, and Hilldale baseball club from 1906 to 1927.

Wallace, Howard

Howard Wallace was a second baseman for the Cincinnati Buckeyes in 1940.

Wallace, Jack

Jack Wallace was a third baseman and second baseman for the Cleveland Cubs, Bacharach Giants, Pennsylvania Red Caps of New York, and Philadelphia Giants from 1926 to 1931.

Wallace, James

James Wallace was a catcher for the Houston Eagles in 1949.

Waller, George

George Waller was an infielder for the Chicago Brown Bombers in 1943.

Walls, Eddie

Eddie Walls was a pitcher for the Cleveland Hornets, St. Louis Stars, and Cleveland Elites in 1925 and 1926.

Walls, James

James Walls was an outfielder for the Kansas City Monarchs in 1954.

Walls, Mickey

Mickey Walls was a pitcher for the Indianapolis Clowns in 1951.

Walton, Fuzzy

Fuzzy Walton was an outfielder for the Pittsburgh Crawfords and Baltimore Black Sox in 1930 and 1938.

Wannamaker, George

George Wannamaker was a third baseman for the Indianapolis Clowns in 1954 and 1955.

Ward, Britt

Britt Ward was a catcher for the Kansas City Monarchs in 1944.

Ward, Ira

Ira Ward was a shortstop and first baseman for the Chicago Giants from 1922 to 1927.

Ward, Pinky

Pinky Ward was an outfielder for the Chicago Columbia Giants, Memphis Red Sox, Cincinnati Tigers, Louisville Black Caps, Brooklyn Eagles, Birmingham Black Barons, Bacharach Giants, Washington Potomacs, and Indianapolis ABC's from 1923 to 1935.

Ware, Archie
b. 1918

Archie Ware was a first baseman for the Kansas City Monarchs, Chicago American Giants, Louisville Buckeyes, Cleveland Buckeyes, Cincinnati Buckeyes, and Indianapolis Clowns from 1940 to 1951. The 5-foot-9, 160-pound Ware had a career-high .349 average for two straight seasons for Cleveland in 1947 and 1948.

Ware, Joe (Showboat)

Joe Ware was an outfielder for the Cleveland Stars, Nashville Giants, Cleveland Giants, Memphis Red Sox, Pittsburgh Crawfords, Akron Tyrites, and Newark Dodgers in 1920 and from 1932 to 1936.

Ware, William

William Ware was a first baseman for the Chicago American Giants from 1924 to 1926.

Warfield, Frank
b. 1895, d. 1932

Frank Warfield was an infielder and manager for the Indianapolis ABC's, St. Louis Giants, Bowser's ABC's, Dayton Marcos, Detroit Stars, Kansas City Monarchs, Baltimore Black Sox, the Hilldale baseball club, and Washington Pilots from 1916 to 1932. Warfield batted .342 for Detroit in 1922. He once got into a fight during winter ball in Cuba with Oliver Marcelle and reportedly bit a piece of Marcelle's nose off. Warfield died of a heart attack when he was the player-manager of the Washington Pilots in 1932.

Warmack, Sam
Sam Warmack was an outfielder for the Hilldale baseball club, Bacharach Giants, Richmond Giants, Columbus Blue Birds, Washington Pilots, and Louisville Black Colonels from 1922 to 1938.

Warren, Cicero
Cicero Warren was a pitcher for the Homestead Grays in 1946 and 1947.

Warren, Jesse
Jesse Warren was a second baseman, third baseman, and pitcher for the New Orleans–St. Louis Stars, Memphis Red Sox, Birmingham Black Barons, Boston Blues, Chicago American Giants, and Boston Royal Giants from 1940 to 1947.

Washington, Bill
Bill Washington was a shortstop and third baseman for the Memphis Red Sox and Philadelphia Stars from 1951 to 1955.

Washington, Edgar
Edgar Washington was a pitcher and first baseman for the Kansas City Monarchs and Chicago American Giants from 1915 to 1920.

Washington, Isaac
Isaac Washington was an officer with the Bacharach Giants in 1928.

Washington, Jasper (Jap)
Jasper Washington was a first baseman, third baseman, and outfielder for the Pittsburgh Keystones, Homestead Grays, Pittsburgh Crawfords, and Newark Browns from 1922 to 1927 and was also an umpire in the NEGRO NATIONAL LEAGUE.

Washington, John
John Washington was a first baseman and third baseman for the Birmingham Black Barons, Montgomery Grey Sox, New York Black Yankees, Pittsburgh Crawfords, Houston Eagles, New Orleans Eagles, and Baltimore Elite Giants from 1933 to 1951.

Washington, Lafayette (Fay)
Lafayette Washington was a pitcher for the Chicago American Giants, Birmingham Black Barons, Cincinnati-Indianapolis Clowns, Kansas City Monarchs, St. Louis Stars, and New Orleans–St. Louis Stars from 1940 to 1945.

Washington, Lawrence
Lawrence Washington was a first baseman for the New York Black Yankees in 1945.

Washington, Namon (Cy)
Namon Washington was an outfielder, shortstop, and catcher for the Brooklyn Cuban Giants, Hilldale baseball club, Indianapolis ABC's, Lincoln Giants, Philadelphia Tigers, Baltimore Black Sox, and Brooklyn Royal Giants from 1920 to 1931.

Washington, Peter
Peter Washington was an outfielder for the Wilmington Potomacs, Washington Potomacs, Philadelphia Stars, Lincoln Giants, and Baltimore Black Sox from 1923 to 1926.

Washington, Ted
Ted Washington was a shortstop for the Philadelphia Stars in 1952.

Washington, Tom
Tom Washington was a catcher and outfielder for the Chicago Giants, Philadelphia Giants, Cuban X Giants, Pittsburgh Giants, and Leland Giants from 1904 to 1911.

Washington Black Senators
The Washington Black Senators were a black baseball team that played in Washington, D.C., in the 1930s.

Washington Browns
The Washington Browns were a black baseball team based in Yakima, Washington, in the 1930s.

Washington Capital Citys
The Washington Capital Citys were a black baseball team in Washington, D.C., in the League of Colored Base Ball Players in 1887. One of the players on the Capital Citys' roster was Frank Leland, who would go on to be a force in Negro League baseball in Chicago,

forming the Chicago Union Giants and later the Leland Giants.

Washington Elite Giants

The Washington Elite Giants existed briefly in 1936 when owner Thomas Wilson moved the team from Nashville, Tennessee, to Columbus, Ohio, and then to Washington that same year. In 1937, the team moved to Baltimore and was known as the Baltimore Elite Giants.

Washington Pilots

The Washington Pilots were a black baseball team in Washington, D.C., that played in the 1920s and 1930s.

Washington Potomacs

The Washington Potomacs were a black baseball team in Washington, D.C., in the 1920s and 1930s.

Waters, Dick

Dick Waters was the manager of the St. Louis Giants in 1916.

Waters, Ted

Ted Waters was a pitcher and outfielder for the Chicago Giants, Hilldale baseball club, Philadelphia Tigers, and Bacharach Giants from 1916 to 1928.

Watkins, John (Pop)

John Watkins was a catcher, first baseman, and manager for the Genuine Cuban Giants, Cuban Giants, Havana Red Sox, and Famous Cuban Giants from 1899 to 1922. Watkins was also considered a clown on the field, a player who entertained the crowds with comedy as well as his play.

Watkins, Murray

Murray Watkins was a third baseman for the Newark Eagles and Philadelphia Stars from 1943 to 1950.

Watrous, Sherman

Sherman Watrous was an outfielder for the Memphis Red Sox in 1952.

Watson, Amos

b. 1926, d. 1997

Amos Watson was a pitcher for the Indianapolis Clowns, Cincinnati-Indianapolis Clowns, Kansas City Monarchs, and Baltimore Elite Giants from 1945 to 1950.

Watson, David

David Watson was a pitcher for the Birmingham Black Barons in 1923.

Watson, Everett

Everett Watson was an officer with the Detroit Stars in 1931.

Watson, George

George Watson was an outfielder for the Detroit Stars from 1922 to 1926.

Watson, Jimmy

Jimmy Watson was a pitcher for the New York Cubans in 1950.

Watson, Robert

Robert Watson was a pitcher for the New York Cubans in 1950.

Watson, William

William Watson was an outfielder for the Bacharach Giants, Pennsylvania Red Caps of New York, and Brooklyn Royal Giants from 1924 to 1926 and again in 1931.

Watts, Andrew (Sonny)

Andrew Watts was an infielder for the Birmingham Black Barons, Cleveland Buckeyes, and Indianapolis Clowns from 1946 to 1952.

Watts, Eddie

Eddie Watts was a first baseman and second baseman for the Cleveland Hornets, Cleveland Elites, and St. Louis Stars from 1924 to 1927.

Watts, Herman (Lefty)

Herman Watts was a pitcher for the Cincinnati–Cleveland Buckeyes, Jacksonville Red Caps, and New York Black Yankees in 1941 and 1942.

Watts, Jack

Jack Watts was a catcher for the Louisville Cubs, Chicago American Giants, Indianapolis ABC's, Dayton Marcos, Bowser's ABC's, West Baden Sprudels, and Louisville White Sox from 1911 to 1919.

Watts, Richard

Richard Watts was a pitcher for the Birmingham Black Barons in 1949 and 1950.

Webb, James

James Webb was a catcher for the Leland Giants in 1910.

Webb, Norman (Tweed)

Norman Webb was an infielder for the St. Louis Pullmans and Ft. Wayne Pirates in 1926 and 1931.

Webster, Charles

Charles Webster was an outfielder for the Birmingham Black Barons in 1950.

Webster, Daniel

d. 1988

Daniel Webster was a catcher and pitcher for the Kansas City Monarchs, Detroit Stars, and Louisville Black Colonels from 1933 to 1938.

Webster, Ernest

Ernest Webster was a pitcher for the Kansas City Monarchs in 1954.

Webster, Pearl (Specs)

Pearl Webster was a catcher and outfielder for the Brooklyn Royal Giants and Hilldale baseball club from 1912 to 1918. Webster died of pneumonia in France while serving in World War I.

Webster, William

William Webster was a catcher, first baseman, and outfielder for the Chicago Giants, Mohawk Giants, St. Louis Giants, Detroit Stars, Dayton Marcos, Lincoln Giants, Brooklyn Cuban Giants, Bacharach Giants, Chicago American Giants, Indianapolis ABC's, and Chicago Leland Giants from 1911 to 1928.

Weeks, William

William Weeks was an officer with the Bacharach Giants in 1922.

Welch, Issac

Issac Welch was an outfielder for the Indianapolis Clowns in 1952.

Welch, Winfield (Gus)

Winfield Welch was an infielder, outfielder, and manager for the New Orleans Black Pelicans, Monroe Monarchs, Shreveport Giants, Cincinnati Buckeyes, Chicago American Giants, New York Cubans, Cincinnati Crescents, and Birmingham Black Barons from 1918 to 1951.

Wells, Willie

b. 1908, d. 1989

Willie Wells was a shortstop, second baseman, and manager for the Detroit Wolves, St. Louis Stars, Kansas City Monarchs, Homestead Grays, Newark Eagles, Chicago American Giants, New York Black Yankees, Baltimore Elite Giants, Memphis Red Sox, and Indianapolis Clowns from 1924 to 1950.

Wells, born in Austin, Texas, was outstanding hitter, with a .328 career batting average against Negro League competition, including a .368 mark in 1929 and .403 in 1930. The 5-foot-8, 160-pound Wells is also believed to have hit 27 home runs in 88 games for St. Louis in 1929. He played in eight Negro League All-Star games, the East-West contest, batting .281 in those games. Wells also batted .410 against major league ballplayers in exhibition games.

In an interview with author John Holway on file at the National Baseball Hall of Fame, Negro Leaguer Newt Allen said that Wells was one of the best shortstops he ever saw: "It was a toss-up between him and Moore, but Wells was a smarter ballplayer than Moore. Willie Wells was an awfully smart player, a good hitter and good baserunner. He played shallow shortstop, but he was fast and could get to the ball. If it hit his glove, he had it. He knew how to play hitters." In another Holway interview, Negro League catcher Larry Brown has no doubt who was the best shortstop he ever saw: "Willie Wells was the greatest that ever played shortstop," Brown said. "I mean that, bar none. I'd put him in front of anybody I know, regardless of race or creed. He could throw, he could hit and he could run. We were in Mexico once, and Willie Wells is managing and playing short. Ray Dandridge is playing second. A guy came up and hit a scorcher. Willie Wells caught the ball right in his face, whipped it to Dandridge, who stepped on second and whipped it back to Willie, who threw the man out going to first. You don't see that today, do you?"

In a 1999 interview with *Sports Collectors Digest*, Negro Leaguer Nap Gulley said that Wells "was the best shortstop we ever had. Nobody ever seen anybody like Willie Wells." In another Holway interview, Negro Leaguer and shortstop Pee Wee Butts talked about Wells's unique glove: "He didn't want padding in his glove," Butts said. "He took the padding out and put some kind of sand or something in the fingers. I don't see how he caught the ball, but I never did see him miss any. . . . He played for Baltimore, even caught for us. He even pitched a couple of games. He didn't have a good arm, but he was pretty smart, studied the hitters. He was like a knuckle ball pitcher, and won two or three games."

Wells was a popular player in Mexico, where he played for four years and was nicknamed "El Diablo" (the Devil) for his style of play. "Intense, that's what I was," Wells said in a newspaper interview. "I just wanted to be the best." Wells was part of the million-dollar infield of the Newark Eagles in 1937. He played winter baseball in Cuba and minor league baseball in Canada at the end of his career. Wells was inducted into the National Baseball Hall of Fame in 1997.

Wells, Willie Brooks

Willie Brooks Wells was a shortstop for the New Orleans Eagles and Memphis Red Sox from 1944 to 1951.

Welmaker, Roy

b. 1916, d. 1998

Roy Welmaker was a pitcher for the Macon Black Peaches, Atlanta Black Crackers, Homestead Grays, and Philadelphia Stars from 1932 to 1945, with a stint in between in the armed services during World War II, where he reportedly once struck out 49 batters in 23 innings in a 24-hour period and then 39 hitters in back-to-back games in service competition, pitching for the black Reception Center team at Fort Benning, Georgia. The 6-foot, 200-pound Welmaker posted a 12-4 record for Homestead in 1945. Welmaker went on to play minor league baseball in the Eastern League and Pacific Coast League.

Wesley, Charles (Two Sides)

Charles Wesley was an outfielder, second baseman, and manager for the Pittsburgh Keystones, Columbus Buckeyes, Memphis Red Sox, Indianapolis ABC's, St. Louis Stars, Birmingham Black Barons, Louisville Red Caps, and Louisville White Sox from 1921 to 1930.

Wesley, Edgar

Edgar Wesley was a first baseman for the Cleveland Hornets, Detroit Stars, Chicago American Giants, Bacharach Giants, and Harrisburg Giants from 1918 to 1931. He was a home run hitter and tied Turkey Stearnes for the league lead in home runs in 1925 with 18.

Wesson, Les

Les Wesson was a pitcher for the New York Black Yankees in 1948 and 1949.

West, Charlie

Charlie West was an outfielder for the Birmingham Black Barons in 1942.

West, James

James West was a first baseman for the Cleveland Cubs, Birmingham Black Barons, Nashville Elite Giants, Memphis Red Sox, Columbus Elite Giants, Washington Elite Giants, Baltimore Elite Giants, New York Black Yankees, and Philadelphia Stars from 1930 to 1947.

West, Ollie

Ollie West was a pitcher for the Pittsburgh Crawfords, Chicago American Giants, Homestead Grays, and Birmingham Black Barons from 1942 to 1946.

West Baden Sprudels

The West Baden Sprudels were a black baseball team in West Baden, Indiana, that were formed as a result of the move by C. I. Taylor of the Birmingham Giants in 1910 to West Baden.

West Coast Negro Baseball Association

The West Coast Negro Baseball Association was a league of black baseball teams that played in the 1930s.

Western League of Colored Baseball Clubs

The Western League of Colored Baseball Clubs was a league of black teams in the western United States in the 1920s.

Weston, Issac (Deacon)

Issac Weston was a pitcher for the Louisville Buckeyes in 1949.

Westport Stadium

Westport Stadium was a ballpark in Baltimore that hosted the Baltimore Black Sox and other black baseball teams, including the 1926 Negro League World Series between the Atlantic City Bacharachs and Chicago American Giants.

Whatley, David (Speed)

David Whatley was an outfielder for the Homestead Grays, Birmingham Black Barons, Cleveland Bears, Pittsburgh Crawfords, Memphis Red Sox, New York Black Yankees, and Jacksonville Red Caps from 1936 to 1946.

Wheeler, Joe

Joe Wheeler was a pitcher for the Baltimore Black Sox, Bacharach Giants, Wilmington Potomacs, and Brooklyn Cuban Giants from 1921 to 1928.

Wheeler, Leon

Leon Wheeler was a pitcher for the Chicago American Giants in 1951.

Wheeler, Sam

Sam Wheeler was an outfielder for the New York Cubans in 1948.

White, Art

Art White was a pitcher for the Indianapolis Clowns in 1948.

White, Arthur

Arthur White was a pitcher for the Newark Dodgers in 1934.

White, Burlin

Burlin White was a catcher and manager for the West Baden Sprudels, Lincoln Giants, Bacharach Giants, Harrisburg Giants, Philadelphia Royal Stars, Quaker Giants, Philadelphia Giants, Boston Royal Giants, Bowser's ABC's, Madison Stars, Hilldale baseball club, and Cuban Stars from 1915 to 1942.

White, Butler

Butler White was a first baseman for the Chicago Giants from 1920 to 1923.

White, Chaney

d. 1965

Chaney White was an outfielder for the Bacharach Giants, Hilldale baseball club, Wilmington Potomacs, Homestead Grays, Quaker Giants, Darby Daisies, Philadelphia Stars, New York Cubans, Baltimore Black Sox, Washington Potomacs, and Brooklyn Royal Giants from 1920 to 1936. According to John Holway in his book *Blackball Stars*, White was a slashing leadoff-type hitter. He was also known as a base runner who would slide with his spikes up high, according to Buck Leonard in Robert Peterson's book, *Only the Ball Was White*.

White, Charles (Hoss)

b. 1920, d. 1998

Charles White was a third baseman and catcher for the Philadelphia Stars in 1950. The 5-foot-11, 200-pound White, born in Kingston, North Carolina, went on to play minor league baseball in the International League and Pacific Coast League and also played two seasons for the Milwaukee Braves in the major leagues, batting .237 in 1954 and .233 in 1955.

White, Clarence

Clarence White was a pitcher for the Nashville Elite Giants, Memphis Red Sox, Louisville White Sox, Monroe Monarchs, and Montgomery Grey Sox from 1928 to 1933.

White, Dewitt

Dewitt White was a catcher for the Detroit Stars in 1954.

White, Edward

Edward White was a pitcher for the Homestead Grays in 1944.

White, Eugene

Eugene White was a third baseman for the Brooklyn Eagles and Newark Eagles in 1935 and 1936.

White, Eugene (Stink)

Eugene White was a second baseman for the Chicago American Giants in 1950 and 1951.

White, Henry

Henry White was a pitcher for the Cleveland Bears in 1940.

White, Lawrence

Lawrence White was a pitcher for the Memphis Red Sox in 1947 and 1948.

White, Robert

Robert White was a second baseman and third baseman for the Pittsburgh Keystones, Toledo Tigers, and St. Louis Stars from 1922 to 1923.

White, Solomon

b. 1868, d. 1955

Sol White was a second baseman, third baseman, outfielder, first baseman, and manager for Toledo in the

American Association, the Wheeling minor league club, York Monarchs Fort Wayne, Indiana, club, Washington Capital Citys, Pittsburgh Keystones, Philadelphia Giants, Quaker Giants, New York Lincoln Giants, Newark Stars, and Cleveland Browns from 1887 to 1912 and again managing from 1924 to 1926. At the age of 60, in 1921, White played in 12 games as a player-coach for the Columbus Buckeyes, batting .167.

The 5-foot-6, 170-pound White was one of the original stars in black baseball and one of a handful of black players who played for white minor league baseball teams. Born in Bellaire, Ohio, White was 16 when he played for Toledo in the American Association. He is believed to have batted .381 for Wheeling in 1887 and .358 for York in 1891. He batted .356 in 683 minor league games, scoring 174 runs and stealing 54 bases.

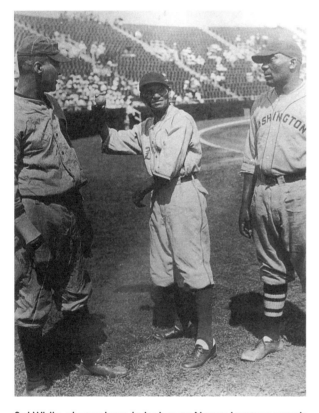

Sol White, shown here in between Negro League greats Smokey Joe Williams and Dick Redding, was one of the pioneers of black baseball, in a number of roles—player, manager, and historian. He played the infield, outfield, and first base, managed from 1887 to 1912, and returned to managing from 1924 to 1926. White helped form the Philadelphia Giants, one of the greatest teams in early Negro League baseball history, in 1902, and the Giants were declared the Colored World Champions in 1904 and 1906. White also authored "Sol White's Official Base Ball Guide," first published in 1907, the definitive work on early Negro League baseball. (NATIONAL BASEBALL HALL OF FAME LIBRARY, COOPERSTOWN, N.Y.)

According to John Holway in his book *Blackball Stars,* winning followed White throughout his career in black baseball, and he was often in demand. Holway wrote that nearly every team that White played on won what was considered the black world championship, and upon losing, the losing team would steal White and then win the championship the following season. He helped form the Philadelphia Giants, one of the most powerful teams in early Negro League baseball history, in 1902.

White was also a Negro League historian, and his book *Sol White's Official Base Ball Guide,* published in 1907, is the definitive work on early Negro League baseball. White's Philadelphia Giants were declared the Colored World Champions in 1904 and 1906, with a roster of players that included John Henry Lloyd, Frank Grant, a boxer named Jack Johnson, who went on to become heavyweight champion of the world, and a pitcher who would have a huge impact on Negro League baseball as an owner, Rube Foster. Foster came on in 1904 after beating the Giants in an eight-game series in Philadelphia in 1902 while pitching for the Cuban X Giants. White particularly praised the 1906 Giants in his book, writing that the 1906 championship team faced numerous hurdles because of injuries: "The success of the Philadelphia Giants of 1906 was due no doubt to their gameness," White wrote. "A gamer gang of ball players never stepped on a diamond. More or less crippled throughout the season, they played the hardest teams with the same spirit as the weak ones. When the other teams were strengthening by adding stars to their lineup, the Phillies were weakening by accidents and sickness. When the odds against them were the greatest, they seemed the more determined and their nonchalant air bred a personality that told their opponents they would have to play ball or they could not win."

One of the minority owners of the Philadelphia Giants was New York promoter Jess McMahon. In 1911, McMahon formed a team in New York called the Lincoln Giants and raided the Philadelphia Giants for many of his ballplayers. White would manage that team as well.

White went on to write about Negro League baseball, work for other black teams in the front office and on the field, and was considered an expert often quoted about the history of the game. White also wrote a column for the New York *Amsterdam News,* and in one 1930 column, he lamented the commercialism that had changed the game: "From a sport baseball has changed to a commercialized activity," White wrote. "To my mind the shift was rather premature for the good of colored baseball. As a business proposition it fell into the hands of men who had lost all the love they ever had for the game. They grabbed the reins and rode into power before the game had developed sufficiently to endure their corrupt methods of commercialized baseball, consequently the game today is far below the standard hoped for by the hard-working men of the past who gave their time and energy to its advancement."

White, Willie
Willie White was a pitcher for the Kansas City Monarchs in 1952.

White, Zarlie
Zarlie White was an outfielder for the Monroe Monarchs in 1934.

Whitley, David
David Whitley was an outfielder for the Kansas City Monarchs in 1955.

Whitney, Carl
Carl Whitney was a pitcher and outfielder for the New York Black Yankees in 1942.

Whittington, Don
Don Whittington was a second baseman and third baseman for the Memphis Red Sox and Philadelphia Stars from 1952 to 1954.

Whitworth, Richard
Richard Whitworth was a pitcher for the Chicago Giants, Chicago American Giants, Bacharach Giants, and Hilldale baseball club from 1915 to 1924.

Whyte, William
b. 1860
William Whyte was a pitcher and outfielder for the Cuban Giants, York Cuban Giants, Trenton Cuban Giants, Boston Resolutes, and St. Louis Black Stockings from 1883 to 1894. Born in Providence, Rhode Island, he is believed to have posted a 26-5 record for Trenton in 1889. He also batted .291 in 1890 for the Cuban Giants.

Wickware, Frank
b. 1888
Frank Wickware was a pitcher for the Philadelphia Giants, St. Louis Giants, Lincoln Stars, Mohawk Giants, Leland Giants, Brooklyn Royal Giants, Chicago American Giants, Norfork Stars, Detroit Stars, and New York Lincoln Giants from 1910 to 1925. He also pitched win-ter baseball in Cuba. Wickware, born in Coffeyville, Kansas, is supposed to have posted an 18-1 record for the Chicago American Giants. He is also believed to have gone 2-2 for the Chicago American Giants in the 1915 Negro League World Series.

Wiggins, Bob
Bob Wiggins was a shortstop for the Chicago Brown Bombers in 1942.

Wiggins, Joe
Joe Wiggins was a third baseman for the Bacharach Giants, Nashville Elite Giants, New York Black Yankees, Baltimore Black Sox, Pittsburgh Crawfords, Cleveland Cubs, and Hilldale baseball club from 1930 to 1934.

Wiggins, Maurice
Maurice Wiggins was a shortstop for the Chicago American Giants in 1920.

Wilbert, Art
Art Wilbert was an outfielder for the Minneapolis–St. Paul Gophers and Cincinnati Clowns in 1942.

Wiley, Joe
Joe Wiley was a third baseman and second baseman for the Baltimore Elite Giants and Memphis Red Sox from 1947 to 1950.

Wiley, Wabishaw Spencer (Doc)
Wabishaw Wiley was a catcher, first baseman, and outfielder for the Lincoln Giants, Brooklyn Royal Giants, Philadelphia Giants, Bacharach Giants, Mohawk Giants, and West Baden Sprudels from 1910 to 1923.

Wilkes, Jimmy
b. 1925
Jimmy Wilkes was an outfielder for the Philadelphia Stars, Indianapolis Clowns, Houston Eagles, and Newark Eagles from 1945 to 1952. The 5-foot-6, 150-pound Wilkes, born in Philadelphia, batted .317 for Newark in 1945, .272 in 1946, .234 in 1947, and .254 in 1948 for Houston. Wilkes went on to play minor league baseball in the Eastern League, Interstate League, and Pioneer League. In his final season, with Indianapolis in 1952, Wilkes batted .325 with 34 RBIs and 45 stolen bases in 292 at bats.

Wilkins, Barron

Barron Wilkins, an underworld figure in Harlem, was a partner with John Connors in the New York Bacharach Giants from 1919 to 1927.

Wilkins, Walter

Walter Wilkins was a pitcher for the Detroit Stars and Louisville Black Colonels in 1954.

Wilkins, Wesley

Wesley Wilkins was an outfielder and pitcher for the Kansas City Giants and ALL NATIONS team from 1908 to 1916.

Wilkinson, James Leslie (J. L.)
b. 1874, d. 1964

James Wilkinson was the owner of the Kansas City Monarchs and one of the most influential figures in Negro League baseball history. Born in Perry, Iowa, Wilkinson grew up in Des Moines, Iowa, and played semipro and professional baseball under the name of Joe Green, according to John Holway in his book *Blackball Stars*. Wilkinson managed a team sponsored by a Des Moines sporting goods store and later, in 1912, formed what was called the ALL NATIONS team, which consisted of black, Cuban, Mexican, and Asian players as well as one girl advertised as "Carrie Nation." Some of the outstanding Negro League players on that team included pitchers Jose Mendez and John Donaldson. In 1920, Wilkinson formed a new version of the Kansas City Monarchs, a powerful club that included Mendez and Donaldson from his All Nations team and several players for the U.S. Army black 25th Infantry team, such as Dobie Moore and Andy Cooper. His brother, Lee Wilkinson, was the booking agent for the Monarchs. The Monarchs went on to be the one of the most stable and successful teams in Negro League baseball history. They played at Muehlebach Field and Municipal Stadium in Kansas City and won a total of 10 Negro League pennants, which tied them with the Homestead Grays for the most among Negro League teams. The Monarchs won three straight NEGRO NATIONAL LEAGUE championships from 1923, when they went 57-33, to 1925, when they posted a 62-23 mark. In 1924, the Monarchs, who had a record of 55-22 that year, defeated the Eastern Colored League champion Hilldale baseball club five games to four, with one tie, in what was recognized as the first Negro League World Series. The following season the Monarchs defeated the St. Louis Stars in a seven-game playoff series to win the league title but lost to Hilldale five games to one in the series. Those Monarch teams, managed by Jose Mendez, included such great Negro

League players as pitcher Bullet Joe Rogan and infielders Newt Allen and Dobie Moore. In 1926, they posted a record of 57-21, winning the Negro National League first-half title, but lost to the Chicago American Giants, the second-half champions, in the championship game. In 1929, with Joe Rogan managing the team, Kansas City won another Negro National League pennant with a record of 62-17, led by a strong pitching staff that included Andy and Army Cooper and Chet Brewer.

In a Holway interview on file at the National Baseball Hall of Fame, former Monarchs player and manager Newt Allen talked about the parks the Monarchs played in and how popular the team was: "They used the park of the old Western League white club at 20th and Olive. . . . In right field they had a 25-foot to 30-foot screen up there, like you have in Boston," Allen said. "But in left field the bleachers went all around from the railroad tracks clear around to 21st Street, from left field to center field. At that time, the capacity was around 25,000. It was single deck, all-wood, nothing was concrete. We used to draw 14,000 to 15,000 people during those times, 18,000 to 19,000 on a Sunday, and ladies night, my goodness, we'd have lots of people."

In 1931, the Monarchs left the Negro National League and began extensive barnstorming tours, with an occasional return to league play, until 1937. Kansas City joined the new NEGRO AMERICAN LEAGUE in 1937 and won five out of six league titles, with Newt Allen as manager and the great Satchel Paige (joining the club in 1940) on the mound, drawing record crowds. Also, a young player named Jackie Robinson joined the Monarchs for one season in 1945.

Wilkinson was the man behind all of this success, and in a Holway interview on file at the National Baseball Hall of Fame, Allen called Wilkinson "one of the finest men I've ever known. He was one white man who was a prince of a fellow. He loved baseball and he loved his ball players. He traveled right along with us every day and stayed at the same hotels we stayed at. We always ate together. He was never a drinking man, never drank anything but milk. He was the swellest guy in the world. You could go to him in the winter and get half of next summer's salary. He was very generous, one of the greatest owners I've ever known."

Allen talked about Wilkinson's experiment with night baseball: "Wilkinson had the All Nations team, and he tried to set up a lighting system in a ball park in Kansas City but wasn't successful with it. When he started the Monarchs he went up to the Giant Light Company of Omaha, and they sold him the idea. He paid $50,000 for a lighting system with a big dynamo engine. He would set it up in center field, have a light on the third base line, one at first base, and two in the outfield. It was a curiosity. People would come out to see if we could really play ball under lights. It was hard at first, but when you began to play under them regularly, the only hard part was when a fly ball was hit. You'd have to wait for it to come out of the dark to catch it. Sometimes a fellow would hit it clear out of sight of the lights, then you had to try to find it. But we got used to it later and developed pretty good judgment of where the ball was."

Wilkinson was also secretary of the Negro National League and treasurer of the Negro American League.

Wilkinson, Lee

Lee Wilkinson was the brother of J. L. Wilkinson, owner of the Kansas City Monarchs, and served as the booking agent for the Monarchs.

Willet, Pete

Pete Willet was a shortstop and outfielder for the Lincoln Giants, Cleveland Browns, Cleveland Tigers, and Homestead Grays from 1923 to 1928.

Willford, Clarence

Clarence Willford was an outfielder for the Philadelphia Stars in 1952.

Williams, Albert

Albert Williams was a pitcher for the Newark Eagles from 1943 to 1945.

Williams, Andrew (Stringbean)

Andrew Williams was a pitcher and manager for the Pennsylvania Red Caps of New York and St. Louis Giants from 1914 to 1925.

Williams, Bert

Bert Williams was an officer with the Philadelphia Giants in 1923.

Williams, Bilbo (Biggie)

Bilbo Williams was an outfielder for the Chicago Brown Bombers and Baltimore Elite Giants from 1942 to 1943.

Williams, Bill

Bill Williams was a pitcher for the Cuban X Giants and Genuine Cuban Giants from 1894 to 1900.

Williams, Bucky

Bucky Williams was a pitcher and infielder for the Pittsburgh Crawfords in 1930 and 1931.

Williams, Charles

Charles Williams was an umpire in the League of Colored Base Ball Players in 1887.

Williams, Charles

Charles Williams was an infielder for the Boston Resolutes in 1887.

Williams, Charles

Charles Williams was the manager of the Brooklyn Remsens in 1885.

Williams, Charles Arthur

Charles Arthur Williams was a shortstop and second baseman for the Memphis Red Sox, Chicago American Giants, Indianapolis ABC's, and Chicago Columbia Giants from 1924 to 1931.

Williams, Charles Henry (Lefty)

Charles Williams was a left-handed pitcher for the Homestead Grays and Detroit Wolves from 1915 to 1934. Williams was an unheralded pitcher, posting a remarkable 29-1 mark, including 26 straight wins, for Homestead in 1930.

Williams, Charley

Charley Williams was a pitcher for the Toledo Cubs in 1945.

Williams, Chester Arthur

b. 1896, d. 1952

Chester Williams was a shortstop and second baseman for the Pittsburgh Crawfords, Memphis Red Sox, Philadelphia Stars, Homestead Grays, Toledo Crawfords, and Chicago American Giants from 1930 to 1943. Born in Tanners, Virginia, the 5-foot-6, 165-pound Williams played for the West team in the EAST-WEST NEGRO LEAGUE ALL STAR GAME.

Williams, Clarence

b. 1866

Clarence Williams was a catcher, third baseman, shortstop, outfielder, and manager for the New York Gorhams, Cuban Giants, Cuban X Giants, Philadelphia Giants, Ansonia Cuban Giants, Smart Set, and Trenton Cuban Giants from 1886 to 1912. Born in Harrisburg, Pennsylvania, Williams also played for Harrisburg in the Atlantic Association in 1890 and batted .256. Over three years, in 102 minor league games, Williams batted .300 with 98 runs scored and 41 stolen bases. Williams was also called the king of baseball coaches in the black press. An 1886 *Trenton Times* article described Williams as a "heavy batsman, fine base runner and good catcher."

Williams, Clarence

Clarence Williams was a pitcher and outfielder for the Washington Black Senators and Baltimore Elite Giants from 1938 to 1940.

Williams, Clarence

Clarence Williams was an infielder for the Chicago American Giants in 1952.

Williams, Clyde

Clyde Williams was a pitcher for the Cleveland Buckeyes from 1947 to 1950.

Williams, Craig

Craig Williams was a pitcher for the Brooklyn Cuban Giants in 1928.

Williams, Elbert

Elbert Williams was a pitcher for the Monroe Monarchs, Louisville White Sox, Detroit Stars, and Brooklyn Eagles from 1931 to 1935.

Williams, Eli

Eli Williams was an outfielder for the Harrisburg–St. Louis Stars, Newark Eagles, Kansas City Monarchs, and Cleveland Clippers from 1943 to 1946.

Williams, Ennis

Ennis Williams was a second baseman for the Baltimore Elite Giants in 1951.

Williams, Felix

Felix Williams was a second baseman, third baseman, and outfielder for the Houston Eagles and Kansas City Monarchs from 1949 to 1954.

Williams, Frank

Frank Williams was an outfielder for the Homestead Grays from 1942 to 1946.

Williams, Fred

Fred Williams was a catcher for the Harrisburg Giants, Washington Potomacs, Indianapolis ABC's, and Brooklyn Royal Giants from 1922 to 1925.

Williams, George

George Williams was an infielder for the Philadelphia Orions, the Argyle Hotel team, Cuban X Giants, New York Gorhams, York (Pennsylvania) Cuban Giants, Trenton Cuban Giants, York (Pennsylvania) Colored Monarchs, and Philadelphia Giants from 1885 to 1902. Williams was the captain of the original Cuban Giants, and, according to Negro League player, manager, and historian Sol White, Williams "was a great player and would have been one of the chosen number for a big league berth." He batted .368 in 108 games for the Trenton Cuban Giants, with 124 runs scored and 69 stolen bases.

Williams, George

George Williams was a shortstop and third baseman for the Cleveland Tigers in 1928.

Williams, George

George Williams was a catcher for the Chicago American Giants in 1952.

Williams, Gerard

Gerard Williams was a shortstop for the Homestead Grays, Lincoln Giants, and Indianapolis ABC's from 1921 to 1926.

Williams, Graham

Graham Williams was a pitcher for the Monroe Monarchs, Homestead Grays, and New Orleans Crescent Stars from 1929 to 1934.

Williams, Guy

Guy Williams was a third baseman for the Cleveland Red Sox in 1934.

Williams, Hank

Hank Williams was an infielder for the Brooklyn Royal Giants, Mohawk Giants, Cuban Giants, Brooklyn All-Stars, and New York Stars from 1911 to 1914.

Williams, Harry

Harry Williams was a third baseman for the Baltimore Black Sox from 1917 to 1923.

Williams, Harry

Harry Williams was an infielder and manager for the Pittsburgh Crawfords, Toledo Crawfords, Baltimore Black Sox, Homestead Grays, New Orleans Creoles, New York Cubans, Baltimore Elite Giants, Harrisburg–St. Louis Stars, New York Black Yankees, Newark Eagles, and Brooklyn Eagles from 1930 to 1950.

Williams, Henry

Henry Williams was a catcher for the St. Louis Stars, Kansas City Monarchs, and Indianapolis ABC's from 1922 to 1931.

Williams, James

James Williams was a catcher for the Brooklyn Remsens in 1885.

Williams, James (Big Jim)

James Williams was an outfielder and manager for the Toledo Crawfords, Homestead Grays, New York Black Yankees, Cleveland Bears, New York Cubans, Birmingham Black Barons, Durham Eagles, and Atlanta Black Crackers from 1934 to 1948.

Williams, James (Nature Boy)

James Williams was a first baseman for the Indianapolis Clowns from 1952 to 1966.

Williams, Jesse

Jesse Williams was a catcher, infielder, and outfielder for the Cleveland Buckeyes and Cleveland Clippers from 1942 to 1947.

Williams, Jesse

b. 1913, d. 1990

Jesse Williams was a shortstop and third baseman for the Indianapolis Clowns and Kansas City Monarchs from 1939 to 1951. Born in Henderson, Texas, Williams had his best season with Kansas City, batting .287 in 1943. Williams also played in the Mexican League, Dominican Summer League, and Pacific Coast League and played winter baseball in Cuba and Puerto Rico. Negro Leaguer Buck O'Neil in his autobiography, *I Was Right on Time*, wrote that Williams "had tremendous range."

Williams, Jim

Jim Williams was a pitcher for the Nashville Elite Giants, Detroit Wolves, and Cleveland Cubs from 1929 to 1932.

Williams, Jim

Jim Williams was an outfielder and first baseman for the New York Black Yankees, Philadelphia Stars, and Newark Dodgers from 1934 to 1937.

Williams, Jimmy

Jimmy Williams was a pitcher for the Chicago American Giants in 1952.

Williams, Joe

Joe Williams was an outfielder for the New York Black Yankees in 1946.

Williams, Joe (Smokey)

b. 1885, d. 1946

Joe Williams was a pitcher and manager for the Leland Giants, San Antonio Broncos, New York Lincoln Giants, Chicago Giants, Chicago American Giants, Bacharach Giants, Detroit Wolves, Mohawk Giants, Hilldale baseball club, and Brooklyn Royal Giants from 1905 to 1934. The 6-foot-5, 205-pound Williams, born in Seguin, Texas, is believed to have posted a record of 28-5 for San Antonio in his first season in 1905 and followed that with a 15-9 record in 1906, 20-8 in 1907, winning 20 again in 1908 and losing only two, and then turning in a remarkable 32-8 record in 1909 against all levels of competition. In 1914, Williams went 41-3 overall and was 12-2 against Negro League competition. Remarkably, at the age of 44 in 1930, Williams had a 7-1 record. In 1924, pitching for the Brooklyn Royal Giants, Williams faced the Brooklyn Bushwicks, a strong white semipro team that was home to many future major league players, and struck out 25 batters in a 12-inning game that he ended up losing 4-3. Williams is believed to have thrown 40 no-hitters against various levels of competition, and major league great Ty Cobb once said that Williams was a "sure 30-game winner." Against major league ballplayers, Williams went 22-7-1.

In an interview with author John Holway on file at the National Baseball Hall of Fame, Negro League pitcher Bill Holland talked about Williams's game on the mound: "He didn't have a lot of different stuff, but he had a terrific fast ball and perfect control," Holland said. "If he caught you swinging at that ball down here at the knees, he'd raise it up to the belt, then up to the letters, pitch you outside, things like that. He didn't have much of a curve or change of pace, but he had terrific speed." In the Holway book *Blackball Stars*, fellow Negro League pitcher Sam Streeter also marveled at the speed of Williams's pitching: "If I was going to pick a man to throw hard, I'd have to pick Joe Williams," Streeter said. "I'd pick him over all of them. They talk about Satchel

Smokey Joe Williams is believed to be the greatest pitcher to ever take the mound in the early days of Negro League baseball and may have been the best ever, perhaps even better than Satchel Paige. One year, in 1914, he posted a 41-3 record against all levels of competition and is believed to have thrown 40 no-hitters against all sorts of teams. Against major league players in exhibition games, the 6-foot-5, 205-pound Williams went 22-7-2. From 1905 to 1934 Williams pitched and managed for the Leland Giants, San Antonio Broncos, New York Lincoln Giants, Chicago Giants, Chicago American Giants, Bacharach Giants, Detroit Wolves, Mohawk Giants, Hilldale baseball club, and Brooklyn Royal Giants. (NATIONAL BASEBALL HALL OF FAME LIBRARY, COOPERSTOWN, N.Y.)

and them throwing hard, but I think Joe threw harder. It used to take two catchers to hold him. By the time the fifth inning was over, that catcher's hand would be all swollen. He'd have to have another catcher back there the rest of the game." There was a report that at the age of 54, Williams pitched a one-hitter against the Kansas City Monarchs.

Williams, John
John Williams was a first baseman and outfielder for the Chicago American Giants, Birmingham Black Barons, and Indianapolis Clowns from 1948 to 1955.

Williams, John (Big Boy)
John Williams was an outfielder, pitcher, and first baseman for the Indianapolis ABC's, St. Louis Stars, Detroit Stars, Homestead Grays, Dayton Marcos, Columbus Elite Giants, and Jacksonville Red Caps from 1926 to 1938.

Williams, John Henry
John Henry Williams was an infielder and outfielder for the Louisville Black Colonels and Birmingham Black Barons from 1951 to 1954.

Williams, Johnny
b. 1916
Johnny Williams was a pitcher and outfielder for the Indianapolis Clowns, Cincinnati-Indianapolis Clowns, Chicago Brown Bombers, Chicago American Giants, and Birmingham Black Barons from 1942 to 1958. The 6-foot-2, 210-pound Williams posted a 6-4 record in 1944 and was 5-6 in 1945. He batted .300 for the Clowns in 1945 and .357 for Birmingham in 1958. Williams also played minor league baseball in the Eastern League and the Pony League and played winter baseball in Cuba and Puerto Rico.

Williams, Larry
Larry Williams was an outfielder for the Kansas City Monarchs in 1955.

Williams, Lem
Lem Williams was an outfielder for the Cuban Giants and Brooklyn All-Stars from 1905 to 1914 and also was umpire in the NEGRO NATIONAL LEAGUE in 1923 and an officer with the Cleveland Stars in 1931.

Williams, Lemuel
Lemuel Williams was a pitcher for the St. Louis Stars and Chicago American Giants from 1937 to 1939.

Williams, Len
b. 1928
Len Williams was an infielder and outfielder for the Indianapolis Clowns in 1950 and 1951. The 5-foot-10, 180-pound Williams went on to play minor league baseball

in the Eastern League, Pioneer League, South Atlantic League, Western League, and Three I League.

Williams, Leroy
b. 1928

Leroy Williams was a shortstop and second baseman for the Newark Eagles and Kansas City Monarchs in 1945 and from 1947 to 1951. The 5-foot-9, 170-pound Williams batted .308 for Kansas City in 1950 and also played for Springfield in the Mississippi–Ohio Valley League that same season.

Williams, Marvin
b. 1923

Marvin Williams was a second baseman for the Philadelphia Stars from 1943 to 1950. The 6-foot, 200-pound Williams batted .338 for Philadelphia in 1944 and .393 in 1945. Williams went on to play minor league baseball in the Pacific Coast League, South Atlantic League, and Texas League and also played in the Mexican League. He played winter baseball in Cuba, Puerto Rico, Venezuela, and Mexico. Williams joined Jackie Robinson and Sam Jethroe in a tryout for the Boston Red Sox in 1944 arranged by *Pittsburgh Courier* Sports Editor Wendell Smith, but nothing came of it.

Williams, Mathis

Mathis Williams was a shortstop and third baseman for the Pittsburgh Keystones and Cleveland Tate Stars from 1921 to 1923.

Williams, Morris

Morris Williams was a pitcher for the Indianapolis ABC's in 1920 and 1921.

Williams, Nelson

Nelson Williams was manager of the Washington Capital Citys in 1887.

Williams, Nish

Nish Williams was a catcher, outfielder, first baseman, and third baseman for the Cleveland Cubs, Nashville Elite Giants, Washington Elite Giants, Columbus Elite Giants, Indianapolis ABC's, Atlanta Black Crackers, and Birmingham Black Barons from 1927 to 1939.

Williams, Norm

Norm Williams was an outfielder for the Nashville Elite Giants in 1930.

Williams, Phil

Phil Williams was a second baseman for the Toledo Crawfords, Baltimore Black Sox, and Jacksonville Red Caps from 1931 to 1939.

Williams, Poindexter

Poindexter Williams was a catcher and manager for the Detroit Stars, Chicago American Giants, Birmingham Black Barons, Kansas City Monarchs, Homestead Grays, Nashville Elite Giants, and Louisville White Sox from 1920 to 1933.

Williams, Ray

Ray Williams was a pitcher for the New York Black Yankees from 1933 to 1941.

Williams, Raymond

Raymond Williams was a pitcher and outfielder for the New York Black Yankees in 1950.

Williams, Red

Red Williams was a shortstop for the Indianapolis ABC's and Cleveland Tigers from 1926 to 1928.

Williams, Rube

Rube Williams was a shortstop for the Chicago American Giants and Indianapolis Clowns in 1952 and 1953.

Williams, Robert

Robert Williams was an infielder and manager for the Indianapolis ABC's, Chicago American Giants, Pittsburgh Crawfords, Homestead Grays, Cleveland Tigers, Cleveland Red Sox, Akron Tyrites, Cleveland Giants, and Columbus Blue Birds from 1918 to 1945.

Williams, Robert (Cotton)

Robert Williams was a pitcher and infielder for the Philadelphia Stars, New Orleans Eagles, Houston Eagles, and Newark Eagles from 1943 to 1951.

Williams, Roy

Roy Williams was a pitcher for the Baltimore Black Sox, Columbus Blue Birds, Pittsburgh Crawfords, New York Black Yankees, Philadelphia Stars, Brooklyn Eagles, Brooklyn Royal Giants, Homestead Grays, and Baltimore Elite Giants from 1929 to 1941.

Williams, Roy

Roy Williams was an outfielder and third baseman for the Chicago American Giants and Birmingham Black Barons from 1952 to 1955.

Williams, Sam
b. 1923

Sam Williams was a pitcher for the Birmingham Black Barons from 1947 to 1952. The 6-foot-1, 160-pound Williams went 28-16 for Birmingham, including a 13-7 mark in 1950. He went on to play minor league baseball in the Texas League, West Texas–New Mexico League, and California League and also played in the Dominican Summer League and the Mexican League.

Williams, Sidney

Sidney Williams was a pitcher for the New York Black Yankees and Newark Eagles from 1943 to 1945.

Williams, Solomon

Solomon Williams was an outfielder for the Baltimore Atlantics in 1884 and 1885.

Williams, Stanley

Stanley Williams was an outfielder for the Birmingham Black Barons in 1955.

Williams, Stuart

Stuart Williams was a second baseman for the Cleveland Buckeyes in 1950.

Williams, Tom

Tom Williams was a pitcher for the Chicago American Giants, Lincoln Giants, Brooklyn Royal Giants, Hilldale baseball club, Chicago Giants, Detroit Stars, and Bacharach Giants from 1916 to 1925.

Williams, Vern

Vern Williams was a pitcher for the Indianapolis Clowns in 1953.

Williams, Walter

Walter Williams was a pitcher for the Celeron, New York, Acme Colored Giants in 1898.

Williams, Walter

Walter Williams was a pitcher for the Philadelphia Stars, Newark Eagles, and Washington Black Senators from 1937 to 1939.

Williams, Willie

Willie Williams was a second baseman and shortstop for the Bacharach Giants and Brooklyn Royal Giants from 1929 to 1933.

Williams, Willie

Willie Williams was a pitcher for the Baltimore Elite Giants, Washington Elite Giants, and Birmingham Black Barons from 1937 to 1941.

Williams, Willie C. (Curley)
b. 1925

Willie C. Williams was a third baseman and shortstop for the Newark Eagles, Houston Eagles, New Orleans Eagles, and Birmingham Black Barons from 1945 to 1954. The 6-foot, 175-pound Williams, born in Holy Hill, South Carolina, batted .333 for Newark in 1945 and .351 for New Orleans in 1951. Williams also played minor league baseball in the Manitoba-Dakota League, Western League, Eastern League, and American Association, and also played in the Dominican Summer League. Williams played winter baseball in Cuba and Puerto Rico. In a 1997 interview with the *Sarasota Herald-Tribune*, Williams said the game they played was popular with baseball fans: "Sometimes we outdrew the major leagues," Williams said. "We'd play the House of David team in Brooklyn and we'd draw 20,000 people, and the [Brooklyn] Dodgers would draw 15,000."

Williams, Wilmore

Wilmore Williams was an outfielder for the Newark Eagles in 1943.

Williams, Woodrow

Woodrow Williams was a pitcher for the Akron Tyrites in 1933.

Willis, Jim (Cannonball)

Jim Willis was a pitcher for the Nashville Elite Giants, Birmingham Black Barons, Philadelphia Stars, Cleveland Cubs, Washington Elite Giants, Baltimore Elite Giants, and Columbus Elite Giants from 1927 to 1939.

Wilmington Giants

The Wilmington Giants were a black baseball team in Wilmington, Delaware, in the early 1900s.

Wilmington Potomacs

The Wilmington Potomacs were a black baseball team in Wilmington, Delaware, in the 1920s.

Wilmore, Alfred (Apples)

b. 1924

Alfred Wilmore was a pitcher for the Baltimore Elite Giants and Philadelphia Stars from 1946 to 1950. The 6-foot-1, 180-pound Wilmore, born in Philadelphia, went 16-11 for Baltimore from 1949 to 1950. He also played winter baseball in Cuba. In a 1992 interview with *Sports Collectors Digest,* Wilmore described how good the 1949 Baltimore Elite Giants team was that won the Negro League championship that season: "We had one of the best teams in Negro ball at that time, and we never lost a game in Baltimore that year," Wilmore said. "We were playing a doubleheader and I remember, because a guy named Joe Black was on the same team. I used to pitch the first game and Joe used to pitch the second game, almost every Sunday, and we'd win." Wilmore said he was discovered by Philadelphia Stars manager Goose Curry while pitching on the playgrounds south of Philadelphia: "He nagged me a couple of times, so I finally met the team bus and we went to Yankee Stadium," Wilmore said. "When we got there he told me to warm up and that's when my big league career started." Wilmore signed a contract with the Philadelphia Athletics in 1952, but he said he hurt his arm shortly after, and his career was over.

Wilson, Alec

Alec Wilson was an outfielder for the New York Yankees in 1939.

Wilson, Andrew

Andrew Wilson was an outfielder and pitcher for the Milwaukee Bears, New Orleans Crescent Stars, and Chicago Giants from 1922 to 1927.

Wilson, Arthur Lee (Artie)

b. 1920

Arthur Wilson was a shortstop for the Birmingham Black Barons from 1940 to 1948. The 5-foot-11, 160-pound Wilson batted .376 from 1944 to 1947 and won the NEGRO AMERICAN LEAGUE batting title with a .402 average in 1948. Born in Springfield, Alabama, Wilson would serve as a mentor for Willie Mays when Mays played for Birmingham. In an interview with writer Eric Enders, Wilson described his own batting style: "I was strictly a line drive hitter," Wilson said. "Most of my home runs I hit between the outfielders and had to run. I wasn't able to hit it out of the park, so I let all the big guys behind me do it. I always batted leadoff, and I was there to get on base." Wilson went on to play minor league baseball in the Pacific Coast League, the American Association, and the International League and eventually made the major leagues briefly with the New York Giants

Arthur Wilson was a line-drive hitting shortstop for the Birmingham Black Barons from 1944 to 1948 and won the Negro American League batting title with a .402 average in 1948. Wilson also served as a mentor for a young outfielder by the name of Willie Mays. After several years in minor league baseball, Wilson played in only 22 games for the New York Giants in 1951, batting just .182, and went on to work as a scout for the Brooklyn Dodgers. (NATIONAL BASEBALL HALL OF FAME LIBRARY, COOPERSTOWN, N.Y.)

in 1951, appearing in just 22 games with a .182 average. Wilson also played winter baseball in Cuba and Puerto Rico and worked as a part-time scout for the Brooklyn Dodgers.

Wilson, Benny

Benny Wilson was an outfielder for the Bacharach Giants, Lincoln Giants, and Pennsylvania Red Caps of New York from 1923 to 1928.

Wilson, Bill

Bill Wilson was a third baseman for the Newark Eagles in 1948.

Wilson, Carter

Carter Wilson was an outfielder for the Chicago Giants, Gilkerson's Union Giants, and Peters' Union Giants from 1920 to 1923. In Robert Peterson's book *Only the Ball Was White*, Wilson talked about his barnstorming days with Gilkerson's Union Giants: "[Robert] Gilkerson would make a skeleton booking for the whole season, covering Sundays and holidays, before the club started out in the spring," Wilson said. "As he went along, he would fill in the other days. He had a letterhead and an ad which said, 'Coming your way soon!,' and he would write the managers of teams and tell them when we would be in their area. And, of course, because Gilkerson's Union Giants were an attraction he could easily fill in those other days. There were very few days when he didn't have a game."

Wilson, Charles

Charles Wilson was a pitcher and outfielder for the Dayton Marcos, Dayton Giants, Detroit Stars, and Columbus Buckeyes from 1917 to 1922.

Wilson, Charles

Charles Wilson was an outfielder and third baseman for the Indianapolis Clowns in 1948 and 1949.

Wilson, Dan

b. 1914, d. 1987

Dan Wilson was an infielder for the St. Louis Stars, New Orleans–St. Louis Stars, Harrisburg–St. Louis Stars, Pittsburgh Crawfords, Philadelphia Stars, Homestead Grays, and New York Black Yankees from 1937 to 1947. Cool Papa Bell said that Wilson was "a good hitter, just as good as some of those in the Hall of Fame and some of those who will go into the Hall of Fame." Wilson's brother Emmett also played Negro League baseball.

Wilson, Ed

Ed Wilson was an outfielder and first baseman for the Cuban X Giants, Colored Capital All-Americans, and Page Fence Giants from 1896 to 1905.

Wilson, Edward

Edward Wilson was a pitcher for the Celeron, New York, Acme Colored Giants in 1898.

Wilson, Elmer

Elmer Wilson was a second baseman and third baseman for the Detroit Stars, Dayton Marcos, and St. Louis Stars from 1921 to 1926.

Wilson, Emmett

Emmett Wilson was an outfielder for the Cleveland Buckeyes, Cincinnati Buckeyes, Cincinnati Clowns, Pittsburgh Crawfords, and Boston Blues from 1936 to 1946. Wilson's brother Dan also played Negro League baseball.

Wilson, Felton

Felton Wilson was a catcher for the Detroit Stars in 1937.

Wilson, Fietman

Fietman Wilson was a pitcher and catcher for the Cleveland Stars and Akron Tyrites from 1932 to 1933.

Wilson, Fred

Fred Wilson was an outfielder, pitcher, and manager for the Newark Eagles, New York Black Yankees, Cincinnati Clowns, and Cincinnati-Indianapolis Clowns from 1938 to 1945.

Wilson, George

George Wilson was an outfielder for the New Orleans Crescent Stars in 1922.

Wilson, George H.

George H. Wilson was a pitcher and outfielder for the Page Fence Giants, Chicago Union Giants, and Columbia Giants from 1895 to 1905. In *History of Colored Base Ball*, Negro Leaguer and historian Sol White wrote that Wilson was "one of the most difficult men to hit among the colored pitchers."

Wilson, Harvey

Harvey Wilson was an infielder for the Toledo Crawfords in 1939.

Wilson, Herb

Herb Wilson was a pitcher for the Kansas City Monarchs in 1928 and 1929.

Wilson, James

James Wilson was an outfielder and second baseman for the Indianapolis Crawfords, Birmingham Black Barons, and Chicago American Giants from 1936 to 1940.

Wilson, James

James Wilson was a pitcher for the Memphis Red Sox in 1947.

Wilson, James (Chubby)

James Wilson was an outfielder for the Newark Dodgers and Bacharach Giants from 1929 to 1933.

Wilson, Jay

Jay Wilson was a shortstop for the Birmingham Black Barons from 1945 to 1948.

Wilson, John

John Wilson was an outfielder for the Chicago American Giants in 1948 and 1949.

Wilson, Jud (Boojum)

b. 1899, d. 1963

Jud Wilson was a third baseman, first baseman, and manager for the Homestead Grays, Pittsburgh Crawfords, Philadelphia Stars, and Baltimore Black Sox from 1922 to 1945. Wilson was a powerful hitter, batting .408 in 1927, .372 in 1930, and .412 in 1934. Wilson is believed to have batted .370 over his Negro League career. He had also batted .356 against white major league players in exhibition games. Wilson's nickname "Boojum" is supposed to have resulted from the sound of the line drives coming off his bat. In an interview with author John Holway on file at the National Baseball Hall of Fame, catcher Larry Brown, a teammate of Wilson's, talked about Wilson's place in history: "He was among some of the greatest third baseman we had," Brown said. "He was a powerful hitter, with a good throwing arm, and a pretty good fast man. . . . In Cuba they called him "Joracon" Wilson— "Big Bull"—and that's what he was." In another Holway interview, Pee Wee Butts talked about the way Wilson played third base: "If he didn't catch the ball, he let it hit in the chest and throw you out," Butts said. "If the ball was hit hard, he wanted it to hit him somewhere so he could pick it up and throw the man out. He never did smile. He was a pretty rough joker, I'll tell you that." Crush Holloway, in another Holway interview, confirmed that Wilson was a tough character: "He was a great hitter, but very radical," Holloway said. "I mean, he was temperamental. He was a hard loser, used to kick up dust. He was hard to get along with on the field, but he was a great ballplayer." He punched out an umpire in a playoff game in 1934. In another Holway interview, former Philadelphia manager Web-ster McDonald talked about how he dealt with Wilson's temper: "Jud Wilson was my captain," McDonald said. "He was temperamental. He'd bang you in the jaw in a minute—anybody. One of our greatest ballplayers. But when I turned my back, he'd go into battle. I didn't want that. I wanted somebody who would talk in the right sense and advocate the rights of all the players on the club. People didn't understand how I handled him as well as I did. I made him captain to calm him, to curb him, give him responsibility. It helped, and he appreciated it."

Jud Wilson's nickname was "Boojum," which is supposed to have come from the sound of the line drives coming off his bat. That's how hard the hot-tempered Wilson hit the ball, and he hit it often, batting .408 in 1927, .412 in 1934, and .370 over his Negro League career as a third baseman, first baseman, and manager for the Homestead Grays, Pittsburgh Crawfords, Philadelphia Stars, and Baltimore Black Sox from 1922 to 1945. (NATIONAL BASEBALL HALL OF FAME LIBRARY, COOPERSTOWN, N.Y.)

Wilson, Percy

Percy Wilson was a first baseman and outfielder for the New Orleans Crescent Stars and Milwaukee Bears from 1922 to 1924 and again in 1933.

Wilson, Pete

Pete Wilson was a first baseman for the Baltimore Black Sox in 1924.

Wilson, Ray

Ray Wilson was a first baseman and pitcher for the Philadelphia Giants and Cuban X Giants from 1902 to 1910. Wilson was captain of the Cuban X Giants.

Wilson, Robert
b. 1925, d. 1985

Robert Wilson was a third baseman and outfielder for the Newark Eagles and Houston Eagles from 1947 to 1950. The 5-foot-11, 200-pound Wilson, born in Dallas, Texas, batted .276 for Newark in 1947 and .352 for Houston in 1949. Wilson went on to play minor league baseball the Eastern League, American Association, Pacific Coast League, and International League. He also played three games for the Los Angeles Dodgers in 1957, with one hit. Wilson played winter baseball in Cuba, Puerto Rico, the Dominican Republic, and Venezuela.

Wilson, Rollo

Rollo Wilson was a newspaperman who served as commissioner of the NEGRO NATIONAL LEAGUE and secretary of the American Negro League from 1929 to 1934. In addition to writing for the *Philadelphia Tribune*, Wilson also wrote for the *Pittsburgh Courier*.

Wilson, Thomas T.
b. 1890, d. 1947

Thomas Wilson was the owner of the Nashville Standards, Nashville Elite Giants, Cleveland Cubs, and Baltimore Elite Giants from 1918 to 1947 and also served as president, vice chairman, and treasurer of the NEGRO NATIONAL LEAGUE and president and secretary of the Negro Southern League. Born in Atlanta, Georgia, Wilson, who, like so many others who became Negro League baseball owners, was a numbers operator and got his start in baseball organizing a semipro team called the Nashville Standards in 1918 and changed the name to the Nashville Elite Giants in 1921. He would also build Wilson Park, the first black-owned ballpark in the South,

completing the stadium in 1929. Wilson moved the team from Nashville to Cleveland in 1931, calling them the Cleveland Cubs, and then back to Nashville soon after. Wilson kept the team there until 1926 when he moved the team to Columbus and again to Washington the same season. In 1937, he moved the club to Baltimore, where the Baltimore Elite Giants played for many years and included such future major leaguers as Roy Campanella and Junior Gilliam.

Wilson, William

William Wilson was a shortstop for the Pittsburgh Keystones in 1887.

Wilson, Woodrow

Woodrow Wilson was a pitcher for the Memphis Red Sox, Kansas City Monarchs, Cuban Stars, and Baltimore Elite Giants in 1931 and from 1936 to 1940.

Wilson Park

Tom Wilson, a former numbers runner in Nashville, Tennessee, built Wilson Park, a new home for his black baseball team, the Nashville Elite Giants, in 1929 in the Trimble Bottom section of Nashville.

Wingo, Doc

Doc Wingo was a catcher for the Kansas City Monarchs in 1944.

Winston, Clarence

Clarence Winston was an outfielder for the Leland Giants, Philadelphia Giants, Cuban X Giants, and Chicago Giants from 1905 to 1923.

Winston, James

James Winston was a pitcher and outfielder for the Chicago Columbia Giants, Chicago Giants, Atlanta Black Crackers, and Detroit Stars from 1929 to 1932.

Winston, John

John Winston was a pitcher for the Detroit Stars in 1955.

Winston-Salem Giants

The Winston-Salem Giants were a black baseball team that played in Winston-Salem, North Carolina, in the late 1930s and early 1940s.

Winters, Jesse (Nip)

b. 1899, d. 1971

Jesse Winters was a left-handed pitcher for the Bacharach Giants, Norfolk Stars, Philadelphia Stars, Hilldale baseball club, Darby Daisies, Harrisburg Giants, New York Lincoln Giants, Newark Dodgers, and Washington Pilots from 1919 to 1933. Born in Washington, D.C., Winters led the Eastern Colored League with a record of 26-4 in 1924, 21-10 in 1925, and 18-6 in 1926. His career Negro League record was 95-54. In the 1924 Negro League World Series, Winters was the winning pitcher in all three of the Hilldale victories, though Hilldale would wind up losing the series, with Winters taking the loss in the deciding game. In an interview conducted by author John Holway on file at the National Baseball Hall of Fame, Negro Leaguer Newt Allen talked about how tough Winters was: "He was a tall left-hander [6-foot-5, 225 pounds], and oh, he was a tough man," Allen said. In another Holway interview at the Hall of Fame, Jake Stephens fondly remember playing behind Winters: "Nip Winters was one of my favorites," Stephens said. "Nip was always crying, 'Give me one more run.' Why, if you got 10 runs, he'd cry, 'Give me one more run.' But I mean, you just didn't beat Nip. He was one of the best left-handers I knew." In another Holway interview, Winters talked about playing against major league players in exhibition competition: "[Lefty] Grove was great, really great," Winters said. "I pitched against him twice, when we barnstormed against Babe Ruth's All-Stars. We'd play 10 to 15 games a year in the New York–New Jersey–Philadelphia area after the regular season. At that time [baseball commissioner] Judge Landis wouldn't let us play a big league team intact. We had to play all-star teams. And what a club Ruth had. Gehrig was on first, Jimmy Dykes on third, Ruth, Al Simmons and Bing Miller in the outfield, Mickey Cochrane catching and Howard Ehmke, Rube Walberg and Lefty Grove pitching. Grove beat me the first game we pitched, 3-1. Miller and Cochrane doubled for one run, another came in on a sacrifice play, and the third scored on an infield out. In the second game, in Philadelphia, I struck Ruth out on a curve away from him, and he grounded out twice. But Gehrig tripled and scored on a fly for one run. We tied it when George Johnson doubled and Biz Mackey singled him home. Then Judy Johnson singled, and Otto Briggs, our center fielder, drove him home to win it, 2-1. Ruth was a fine man to get along with, very friendly. He got a homer off me before the series was over. He hit it over the center field fence in Darby. When he hit one, it was gone. I had a tougher time with Gehrig. I thought he was the tougher man to get out. I always tried to keep the ball on top of him, on his wrists, so he couldn't get his full power on me, but he was still a rough man and could really hit it."

Jesse "Nip" Winters was one of the most outstanding pitchers in Negro League baseball in the 1920s. The tall left-hander led the Eastern Colored League with a record of 26-4 in 1924, 21-10 in 1925, and 18-6 in 1926. From 1919 to 1933 he pitched for the Bacharach Giants, Norfolk Stars, Philadelphia Stars, Hilldale baseball club, Darby Daisies, Harrisburg Giants, New York Lincoln Giants, Newark Dodgers, and Washington Pilots. (NATIONAL BASEBALL HALL OF FAME LIBRARY, COOPERSTOWN, N.Y.)

Wise, Russell

Russell Wise was a first baseman for the Indianapolis Crawfords in 1940.

Witherspoon, Lester

b. 1927

Lester Witherspoon was a pitcher and outfielder for the Homestead Grays and Indianapolis Clowns in 1948 and 1949. The 6-foot-1, 190-pound Witherspoon also played in the Pacific Coast League, Florida State League, Western International League, Southwest International League, and Big State League.

Wolfolk, Lewis

Lewis Wolfolk was a pitcher for the Chicago American Giants in 1923 and 1924.

Womack, James

James Womack was a first baseman and third baseman for the Indianapolis ABC's, Cleveland Tigers, Columbus Blue Birds, Columbus Turfs, Bacharach Giants, Richmond Giants, Baltimore Black Sox, and Cuban Stars from 1923 to 1933.

Womack, Ollie

Ollie Womack was a reporter who wrote about black baseball for the *Kansas City Call*, a black newspaper in Kansas City, Missouri.

Wood, Francis

Francis Wood was a cricket player who helped form the Philadelphia Pythians, a black baseball team in the 1860s.

Woods, Ed

Ed Woods was a pitcher, first baseman, and outfielder for the Chicago Unions, Page Fence Giants, and Ansonia Cuban Giants from 1891 to 1898.

Woods, Milton

Milton Woods was an outfielder for the Kansas City Monarchs in 1952.

Woods, Parnell

b. 1912, d. 1977

Parnell Woods was a third baseman and manager for the Cleveland Bears, Birmingham Black Barons, Cincinnati Buckeyes, Jacksonville Red Caps, and Louisville Buckeyes from 1933 to 1949. He batted .335 to lead the Cleveland Buckeyes to the championship in 1945. He went on to play for Oakland in the Pacific Coast League. Woods, born in Birmingham, Alabama, was the business manager for the Harlem Globetrotters basketball team for 27 years. He also played winter baseball in Venezuela.

Woods, Sam

b. 1922

Sam Woods was a pitcher for the Kansas City Monarchs, Memphis Red Sox, and Cleveland Buckeyes from 1946 to

1954. The 6-foot-2, 200-pound Woods posted a 10-6 mark for Memphis in 1950. He went on to play minor league baseball in the West Texas–New Mexico League, Northwest League, Arizona-Mexico League, and Southwestern League. Woods also played in the Dominican Summer League.

Woods, Tom

Tom Woods was a first baseman for the Philadelphia Stars in 1945.

Woods, Virgil

Virgil Woods was a pitcher for the Detroit Stars in 1955.

Woods, William

William Woods was a shortstop for the Philadelphia Pythians in 1887.

Woods, William J.

William Woods was an outfielder for the Columbus Buckeyes, Indianapolis ABC's, Brooklyn Royal Giants, St. Louis Giants, Chicago American Giants, Bacharach Giants, Washington Potomacs, and St. Louis Stars from 1919 to 1926.

Woolridge, Charles

Charles Woolridge was an outfielder, first baseman, and shortstop for the Cleveland Tigers and Cleveland Elites from 1926 to 1928.

Wooten, Nate

Nate Wooten was a pitcher for the Louisville Black Colonels in 1954.

Wright, Bill

Bill Wright was an outfielder for the Kansas City Monarchs in 1948.

Wright, Bruce

Bruce Wright was a third baseman for the New York Cubans in 1946.

Wright, Burnis (Wild Bill)

b. 1914, d. 1996

Burnis Wright was an infielder and outfielder for the Columbus Elite Giants, Nashville Elite Giants, Washington Elite Giants, Baltimore Elite Giants, and Philadelphia Stars from 1932 to 1945. In a 1999 interview with *Sports Collectors Digest*, former Negro Leaguer Nap Gulley said, "Wild Bill, he had no one else in his category. He was a big man, could run like a deer, and he could do everything. Switch hitter, played the outfield and the infield." Roy Campanella, who played with Wright in Baltimore, said that Wright was "the biggest and strongest and fastest man that I've ever seen. He could run as fast as anyone, and has a strong throwing arm like Stan Musial. Runners were never able to take any liberties on Wright."

The 6-foot-4, 225-pound Wright, born in Milan, Tennessee, batted .300 for Nashville in 1932 and .365 and .410 for Washington in 1936 and 1937. Wright also batted .402 for Baltimore in 1939. He played in eight Negro League All-Star games, the EAST-WEST GAME, batted .333 in 27 at bats, and hit .371 in exhibition competitions against major league players.

Wright also played in the Mexican League, batting .336 over his career there, and was elected to the Mexican Baseball Hall of Fame in 1982. He was called the black Joe Dimaggio, and, in a 1996 interview with *Sports Collector's Digest*, Wright said he could "outrun DiMaggio easy. I could run rings around him. . . . I could drag bunt and I was fast. Really fast. So that's what kept me up in the batting average all the time. When I hit, the first baseman had to play in, he couldn't play too far back, and I could pull the ball. I was strictly a pull hitter, so I'd hit the ball by him."

Wright, Charley
Charley Wright was a pitcher for the Birmingham Black Barons in 1931.

Wright, Clarence
Clarence Wright was a first baseman for the Celeron, New York, Acme Colored Giants in 1898.

Wright, Danny
Danny Wright was a pitcher for the Chicago American Giants, Birmingham Black Barons, and Detroit Stars from 1951 to 1955.

Wright, Ernie
Ernie Wright was the owner and club officer of the Cleveland White Sox, Cincinnati Buckeyes, and Cleveland Buckeyes from 1941 to 1949 and also served as vice president of the NEGRO AMERICAN LEAGUE. Wright had

been a numbers operator in Cleveland when he became involved in black baseball.

Wright, George
George Wright was a shortstop and second baseman for the Brooklyn Royal Giants, Quaker Giants, Chicago Giants, Leland Giants, and Lincoln Giants from 1905 to 1913.

Wright, Henry
Henry Wright was a pitcher for the Cleveland Cubs, Nashville Elite Giants, Birmingham Black Barons, and Columbus Elite Giants from 1928 to 1935.

Wright, Howard
Howard Wright was a pitcher for the Nashville Elite Giants and Bacharach Giants from 1931 to 1933.

Wright, John
b. 1916, d. 1990
John Wright was a pitcher for the Indianapolis Crawfords, Newark Eagles, Pittsburgh Crawfords, Indianapolis Clowns, Toledo Crawfords, and Homestead Grays from 1937 to 1954. Born in New Orleans, the 5-foot-11, 170-pound Wright posted a 25-4 record for Homestead in 1943. He also played in the International League, Mexican League, Venezuela League, and Dominican Summer League. Wright was signed by Brooklyn Dodgers owner Branch Rickey and played with Jackie Robinson on the 1946 Montreal club. He lasted just two games and was back with Homestead the following season. In Robert Peterson's book *Only the Ball Was White*, Robinson recalled Wright's experience in Montreal: "John had all the ability in the world as far as physical abilities were concerned," Robinson said. "But John couldn't stand the pressure of going up into this new league and being one of the first. The things that went on up there were too much for him, and John was not able to perform up to his capabilities. In a number of cities, we had very little pressure. But there was always that little bit coming out. It's wasn't so much based on race—I think most of the Negro players could have gone it as far as race. But because John was the first Negro pitcher, every time he stepped out there he seemed to lose that fineness, and he tried a little bit harder than he was capable of playing. He tried to do more than he was able to do and it caused him to be a lot less of a pitcher than he actually was. If he had come in two or three years later when the pressure was off, John could have made it in the major leagues."

John Wright did not get the acclaim of a Satchel Paige or Leon Day, but he was an outstanding Negro League pitcher, hurling for the Indianapolis Crawfords, Toledo Crawfords, Pittsburgh Crawfords, Newark Eagles, and Homestead Grays from 1937 to 1954. He had one of his most outstanding seasons for Homestead in 1943 when he posted a 25-4 record. (NATIONAL BASEBALL HALL OF FAME LIBRARY, COOPERSTOWN, N.Y.)

Wright, Red
Red Wright was a catcher for the Baltimore Elite Giants in 1948.

Wright, Richard
Richard Wright was a catcher for the Birmingham Black Barons in 1954.

Wright, Robert
Robert Wright was a catcher for the Chicago American Giants in 1915.

Wright, Zollie
Zollie Wright was an outfielder for the New Orleans Crescent Stars, Monroe Monarchs, Memphis Red Sox, Columbus Elite Giants, Washington Elite Giants, Washington Black Senators, New York Black Yankees, Philadelphia Stars, Nashville Elite Giants, and Baltimore Elite Giants from 1931 to 1943.

Wyatt, Dave
Dave Wyatt was an outfielder, second baseman, and shortstop for the Chicago Unions and Chicago Union Giants from 1896 to 1920.

Wyatt, John
b. 1935, d. 1998
John Wyatt was a pitcher for the Indianapolis Clowns from 1953 to 1955. The 6-foot, 200-pound Wyatt, born in Chicago, Illinois, went on to play minor league baseball in the American Association, Southwestern League, South Atlantic League, Pioneer League, Eastern League, Three I League, and Mississippi–Ohio Valley League. He reached the major leagues for the Kansas City Athletics in 1961 and posted a 42-44 record in nine seasons with the Athletics and Boston Red Sox. Wyatt appeared in two games for the Red Sox in the 1967 World Series, with a 1-0 record and a 4.91 ERA.

Wyatt, Ralph (Pepper)
Ralph Wyatt was a shortstop for the Cleveland Buckeyes, Homestead Grays, and Chicago American Giants from 1941 to 1946.

Wylie, Steve
Steve Wylie was a pitcher for the Kansas City Monarchs and Memphis Red Sox from 1944 to 1947.

Wynder, Clarence
Clarence Wynder was a catcher for the Cleveland Buckeyes in 1950.

Wynn, Calvin
Calvin Wynn was an outfielder for the Louisville Buckeyes in 1949.

Wynn, William
William Wynn was a catcher for the New York Cubans and Newark Eagles from 1944 to 1950.

Yancey, Bill
b. 1904, d. 1971

Bill Yancey was a shortstop and manager for the New York Black Yankees, Hilldale baseball club, Atlanta Black Crackers, New York Lincoln Giants, New York Cubans, Brooklyn Eagles, Philadelphia Tigers, Darby Daisies, and Philadelphia Giants from 1923 to 1936 and again in 1945. He later became a scout for the Philadelphia Phillies and New York Yankees and signed a young pitcher named Al Downing for the Yankees. The 5-foot-8, 165-pound Yancey, born in Philadelphia, was also a star basketball player and a member of the Renaissance Five basketball team in 1932, a team that was inducted into the National Basketball Hall of Fame in 1963.

Yankee Stadium

Yankee Stadium, the home of the New York Yankees, also hosted a number of Negro League baseball games, including a 1930 series between the Homestead Grays and the Lincoln Giants. The latter played the first black baseball game earlier that season at Yankee Stadium, which was also the home of the New York Black Yankees. Negro League slugger Josh Gibson is believed to have hit one of the longest home runs in Yankee Stadium history.

Yokeley, Laymon
b. 1906, d. 1976

Laymon Yokeley was a pitcher for the Bacharach Giants, Baltimore Black Sox, Philadelphia Stars, Washington Black Senators, Baltimore Elite Giants, and Brooklyn Eagles from 1926 to 1944. Reports are that Yokeley, born in Winston-Salem, North Carolina, pitched six no-hitters for the Black Sox and won 42 games for the Stars in 1939. The 6-foot-1, 190-pound Yokeley also won eight straight games against white major leaguers in exhibition competition and is believed to have struck out Hack Wilson four times in one game. In a 1952 newspaper interview, Yokeley said the Black Sox were the best team he had ever played for. "We had everything," Yokeley said. "I would put that team up against any big league team."

York, Jim

Jim York was a catcher and outfielder for the Norfolk Stars, Hilldale baseball club, and Bacharach Giants from 1919 to 1923.

Young, Adam

Adam Young was a pitcher for the Philadelphia Stars in 1951.

Young, Berdell

Berdell Young was an outfielder for the Lincoln Giants and Bacharach Giants from 1922 to 1928.

Young, Bob

Bob Young was an infielder for the Cleveland Buckeyes in 1950.

Young, Edward (Pep)

Edward Young was a catcher, first baseman, and third baseman for the Kansas City Monarchs, Chicago American Giants, and Homestead Grays from 1936 to 1947.

Young, Fay

Fay Young was sports editor of the *Chicago Defender*, a black newspaper, and was also secretary of the NEGRO AMERICAN LEAGUE from 1939 to 1948.

Young, John

John Young was a pitcher for the Memphis Red Sox and St. Louis Stars in 1923 and 1924.

Young, Leandy

Leandy Young was an outfielder for the Kansas City Monarchs, Birmingham Black Barons, and Memphis Red Sox from 1940 to 1945.

Young, Maurice

Maurice Young was a pitcher for the Kansas City Monarchs in 1927.

Young, Norman

Norman Young was a shortstop for the Cleveland Buckeyes, New York Black Yankees, and Baltimore Elite Giants from 1941 to 1944.

Young, Roy

Roy Young was an umpire in the NEGRO AMERICAN LEAGUE from 1942 to 1945.

Young, Thomas

Thomas Young was a catcher for the St. Louis Stars, Kansas City Monarchs, New York Cubans, Detroit Wolves, Newark Eagles, Homestead Grays, and Pittsburgh Crawfords from 1925 to 1941.

Young, Wilbur

Wilbur Young was a pitcher for the Birmingham Black Barons in 1945.

Young, William

William Young was an umpire in the East-West League in the 1920s.

Young, William (Pep)

William Young was a pitcher for the Kansas City Monarchs in 1927.

Young, Willie C., Jr.

Willie Young was a pitcher for the Birmingham Black Barons in 1945.

Yvanes, Armando

Armando Yvanes was a shortstop for the New York Cubans in 1949 and 1950.

Z

Zapp, James (Zipper)
b. 1924

James Zapp was an outfielder for the Birmingham Black Barons and Baltimore Elite Giants from 1948 to 1954 and batted .240 for Birmingham in 1948. The 6-foot-3, 230-pound Zapp, born in Nashville, Tennessee, went on to play minor league baseball in the Western League, Mississippi–Ohio Valley League, Longhorn League, and Big State League. In a 1996 interview with *Sports Collectors Digest,* Zapp recalled the finest moment of his Negro League career, in game five of a championship series against Kansas City—Zapp, playing for Birmingham, hit a home run in the bottom of the ninth off James LaMarque to tie the game, which the Barons went on to win 4-3: "I was guessing curveball, but LaMarque threw me two consecutive fast balls. I half swung at each and just fouled them off. The next pitch, I wasn't looking for any specific pitch. He threw a fast ball and I was able to hit it over the left-center field fence. Buck [O'Neil] always says I never should have come to bat that inning. And he's right." With two outs, the hitter before Zapp had grounded to second baseman Curtis Roberts, who failed to handle the routine ground ball.

Zapp, Stephen

Stephen Zapp was an infielder for the Baltimore Elite Giants in 1946.

Ziegler, William (Doc)

William Ziegler was an outfielder for the Chicago Giants and Detroit Stars in 1921 and from 1927 to 1929.

Zimmerman, George

George Zimmerman was a catcher for the Pittsburgh Keystones in 1887.

Zomphier, Charles
b. 1906, d. 1973

Charles Zomphier was an infielder for the Cleveland Hornets, Cleveland Elites, Cleveland Tigers, Cleveland Cubs, Memphis Red Sox, Birmingham Black Barons, St. Louis Stars, and Cuban Stars from 1926 to 1931. He was also an umpire in the NEGRO NATIONAL LEAGUE.

Zulu Cannibal Giants

The Zulu Cannibal Giants were a clowning black baseball team operated by Charlie Henry, a former player for the Harrisburg Giants. In his autobiography, *I Was Right on Time,* Negro Leaguer Buck O'Neil said the Zulu Cannibal Giants "painted their faces, put rings in their noses and played in straw dresses. They looked like extras in a Tarzan movie, and Charlie gave them phony African names, like Bebop and

Sheba and Limpopo. . . . Looking back on it, the idea of playing with the Cannibal Giants was very demeaning." But O'Neil did it for the money, he said. "Just like that, I was playing in a grass skirt," he said. "I hardly gave it a thought at the time, since this was show business as much as baseball. . . . Later on, we wanted our game to stand on its professionalism. The world changed and black people didn't want to be thought of as Zulus or clowns and wouldn't stand for it. But we understood that to draw fans, we were entertainers as well as baseball players, and the game was only part of putting on an exhibition."

Bibliography

BOOKS

Campanella, Roy. *It's Good to Be Alive*. New York: Dell, 1959.

Chambers, Ted. *The History of Athletics and Physical Education at Howard University*. New York: Vantage Press, 1986.

Clark, Dick, and Larry Lester, eds. *The Negro Leagues Book*. Cleveland, Ohio: The Society of American Baseball Research, 1994.

Daniel, Clifton, ed. *Chronicle of America*. Upper Saddle River, N.J.: Prentice Hall, 1989.

————. *Chronicle of the 20th Century*. San Francisco: Chronicle Publications, 1987.

Durocher, Leo, with Ed Linn. *Nice Guys Finish Last*. New York: Simon & Schuster, 1975.

Fields, Wilmer. *My Life in the Negro Leagues—An Autobiography*. Westport, Conn.: Meckler Books, 1992.

Grun, Bernard. *The Timetables of History*. New York: Simon & Schuster, 1975.

Holway, John. *Blackball Stars: Negro Leagues Pioneers*. New York: Carroll & Graf, 1988.

Lester, Larry, Sammy J. Miller, and Dick Clark. *Black Baseball in Detroit*. Charleston, S.C.: Arcadia Publishing, 2000.

Manley, Effa, and Leon Hardwick. *Negro Baseball Before Integration*. Chicago: Adams Press, 1976.

Marden, Charles F., and Gladys Meyer. *Minorities in American Society*. New York: D. Van Nostrand, 1973.

McNeil, William F. *Baseball's Other All-Stars*. Jefferson, N.C.: McFarland, 2000.

Minoso, Orestes (Minnie), with Fernando Fernandez and Bob Kleinfelder. *Extra Innings: My Life in Baseball*. Washington, D.C.: Regnery Gateway, 1983.

O'Neil, Buck, with Steve Wulf and David Conrads. *I Was Right on Time*. New York: Simon & Schuster, 1996.

Paige, Satchel, with David Lipman. *Maybe I'll Pitch Forever*. Garden City, N.Y.: Doubleday, 1961.

Peterson, Robert. *Only the Ball Was White*. New York: Oxford University Press, 1970.

Reichler, Joseph, ed. *The Baseball Encyclopedia*, 7th ed. New York: Macmillan, 1988.

Ribowsky, Mark. *A Complete History of the Negro Leagues: 1884–1955*. New York: Birch Lane Press, 1995.

Robinson, Jackie, as told to Alfred Duckett. *I Never Had It Made*. New York: Fawcett Crest, 1972.

Rogosin, Donn. *Invisible Men*. New York: Atheneum, 1983.

Bibliography

Ruck, Rob. *Sandlot Seasons: Sport in Black Pittsburgh*. Champaign: University of Illinois Press, 1993.

Sowell, Thomas. *Ethnic America: A History*. New York: Basic Books, 1981.

Trouppe, Quincy. *Twenty Years Too Soon*. Los Angeles: S&S Enterprises, 1977.

Tygiel, Jules. *Baseball's Great Experiment: Jackie Robinson and His Legacy*. New York: Vintage, 1984.

White, Sol. *Official Base Ball Guide*. Ed. H. Walter Schlichter. Columbia, S.C.: Camden House, 1984. (Reprint of 1907 original.)

———. *Sol White's History of Colored Base Ball*. Ed. Jerry Malloy. Lincoln: University of Nebraska Press, 1995.

WEBSITES

BaseballLibary.com

BlackBaseball.com

NegroLeagueBaseball.com

OTHER SOURCES

The Ashland Collection at the National Baseball Hall of Fame

The Robert Peterson papers at the National Baseball Hall of Fame

Interviews with former Negro League ballplayers

About the Author

Thom Loverro is a sports columnist for the *Washington Times*. The winner of numerous writing awards, Loverro joined the *Baltimore Sun* in 1984 as a reporter and editor. In 1992, he moved to the *Times*, where he has covered the Washington Redskins, Baltimore Orioles, and a host of other sports, including several Olympics. He also teaches journalism at American University in Washington, D.C. Loverro lives in Columbia, Maryland, with his wife, Liz, and two sons, Rocco and Nick.

Index

Boldface page numbers denote main entries. *Italic* page numbers denote photographs.